D1063728

THE SEAFOOD INDUSTRY

THE SEAFOOD INDUSTRY

Edited by

Roy E. Martin
NATIONAL FISHERIES INSTITUTE

George J. Flick
VIRGINIA POLYTECHNIC INSTITUTE
AND STATE UNIVERSITY

An Osprey Book
Published by Van Nostrand Reinhold
New York

An Osprey Book
(Osprey is an imprint of Van Nostrand Reinhold)

Library of Congress Catalog Number 89-78442
ISBN 0-442-23915-7

Printed in the United States of America

Van Nostrand Reinhold
115 Fifth Avenue
New York, New York 10003

Van Nostrand Reinhold International Company Limited
11 New Fetter Lane
London EC4P 4EE, England

Van Nostrand Reinhold
480 La Trobe Street
Melbourne, Victoria 3000, Australia

Nelson Canada
1120 Birchmount Road
Scarborough, Ontario M1K 5G4, Canada

16 15 14 13 12 11 10 9 8 7 6 5 4 3 2 1

Library of Congress Cataloging-in-Publication Data

Martin, Roy E.
The seafood industry / Roy Martin and George Flick.
p. cm.
Includes bibliographical references.
ISBN 0-442-23915-7
1. Fish trade. 2. Shellfish trade. 3. Aquaculture industry.
I. Flick, George. II. Title.
HD7450.5'M37 1990
338.3'727—dc20 89-78442
CIP

Contents

Preface

Although there are excellent books on specific aspects of the seafood industry, few, if any, offer both the breadth and depth of information that the editors and authors of *The Seafood Industry* provide here.

The Seafood Industry is designed to cover the spectrum of seafood topics, taking the products from the water to the dinner plate and every stop in between. Information and insights into commercially important species of finfish and shellfish and their handling and processing are furnished. Chapters are included on such wide-ranging topics as retail merchandising of seafood, plant cleaning and sanitation, transportation, and product packaging. Emerging issues and interests, such as aquaculture, waste treatment, and government regulations, also are covered.

The information is written so that the processor, wholesale buyer, retailer, or consumer can understand it and put it to practical application. Yet the student and the scientist can find much valuable information within the various chapters. The material included here has proven its practicality, as it is adapted from a self-study course that has been used by hundreds of people in roughly forty states and fifteen foreign countries.

The editors and authors have made every effort to furnish the most up-to-date information and technologies available. However, as with any dynamic industry, change is constant. Fishery stocks ebb and flow; consumption patterns shift; new technologies are devised and implemented; and government rules and regulations are rewritten and enacted.

In seeking the best information available, chapter authors were selected from among the most knowledgeable seafood experts from around the United States, including individuals from private industry, universities, and seafood specialists from Sea Grant Marine Advisory Service and the Cooperative Extension Service.

Although this book is intended to encompass the vast topic of seafood and the industry built around this resource, certain limitations had to be imposed. The materials focus primarily on the industry in the United States, although where innovations or activities in other countries have an impact on the U.S. industry, those are covered. Each chapter in *The Seafood Industry* could receive—and in many cases has received—booklength treatments. However, for this text the editors decided to provide information on as wide an array of topics as possible and then to give each topic as much detail as space permitted.

We have drawn together what we feel is the broadest spectrum of information currently available on this dynamic industry. It is our sincere hope that this information will serve the seafood industry, those interested in this important industry, and the consuming public.

ACKNOWLEDGMENTS

As with any undertaking of this size and scope there are many people who need to be thanked and whose efforts need to be recognized. First, a tremendous debt of gratitude is owed the various authors who have readily given of their valuable time and expertise to make this book what it is.

In addition, three individuals at Virginia Polytechnic Institute & State University should be singled out. Geoffrey Knobl provided most of the computer-generated graphics scattered throughout the book. Charles Stott edited the manuscript and pulled the text and illustrations together into their final form.

Lastly, and most importantly, Mrs. Maria Chase patiently and with great good humor typed each chapter and, without complaint, made change after change as the manuscript was revised and pared from its original format, which she also had typed. Her patience and persistence made this book possible.

Contributors

Genaro C. Arganosa, Department of Food Science and Technology, Virginia Polytechnic Institute & State University, Blacksburg, Virginia

Mala A. Barua, Department of Food Science and Technology, Virginia Polytechnic Institute & State University, Blacksburg, Virginia

Anthony P. Bimbo, Zapata Haynie Corporation, Reedville, Virginia

Brian G. Bosworth, Department of Fisheries and Wildlife Sciences, Virginia Polytechnic Institute & State University, Blacksburg, Virginia

Michael Castagna, Eastern Shore Laboratory, Virginia Institute of Marine Science, College of William & Mary, Wachapreague, Virginia

Charles W. Coale, Jr., Department of Agricultural Economics, Virginia Polytechnic Institute & State University, Blacksburg, Virginia

Robert L. Collette, Division of Science and Technology, National Fisheries Institute, Arlington, Virginia

Laurie M. Dean, Nutritionist, Private Industry, Norfolk, Virginia

Leopoldo G. Enriquez, Department of Food Science and Technology, Virginia Polytechnic Institute & State University, Blacksburg, Virginia

George J. Flick, Department of Food Science and Technology, Virginia Polytechnic Institute & State University, Blacksburg, Virginia

Michael G. Haby, Texas Agricultural Extension Service, Texas A&M University, Port Arkansas, Texas

Cameron R. Hackney, Department of Food Science and Technology, Virginia Polytechnic Institute & State University, Blacksburg, Virginia

Gi-Pyo Hong, Department of Food Science and Technology, Virginia Polytechnic Institute & State University, Blacksburg, Virginia

Jhung Won Hwang, Department of Food Science and Technology, Virginia Polytechnic Institute & State University, Blacksburg, Virginia

John D. Kaylor (retired), National Marine Fisheries Service, Northeast Fisheries Center, Gloucester, Massachusetts

Tyre C. Lanier, Department of Food Science and Technology, North Carolina State University, Raleigh, North Carolina

Robert J. Learson, National Marine Fisheries Service, Northeast Fisheries Center, Gloucester, Massachusetts

George S. Libey, Department of Fisheries and Wildlife Sciences, Virginia Polytechnic Institute and State University, Blacksburg, Virginia

Joseph J. Licciardello, National Marine Fisheries Service, Northeast Fisheries Center, Gloucester, Massachusetts

Roy E. Martin, National Fisheries Institute, Arlington, Virginia

Michael W. Moody, Cooperative Extension Service, Louisiana State University, Baton Rouge, Louisiana

Michael J. Oesterling, Virginia Institute of Marine Science, College of William & Mary, Gloucester Point, Virginia

W. Steven Otwell, Food Science and Human Nutrition, University of Florida, Gainesville, Florida

Michael Paparella, Salisbury, Maryland. Retired from the Horn Point Environmental Laboratory, Cambridge, Maryland

Jon Porter, Chemical Services Division, Henkel Corporation, Plymouth Meeting, Pennsylvania

Thomas E. Rippen, Virginia Polytechnic Institute & State University, Seafood Experiment Station, Hampton, Virginia

Donn R. Ward, Department of Food Sciences and Technology, North Carolina State University, Raleigh, North Carolina

THE SEAFOOD INDUSTRY

CHAPTER 1

A History of the Seafood Industry

Roy E. Martin

Humans fished before the dawn of written history using birds' beaks for hooks and plant stalks for line. Early cave pictures show drawings of fish and fishing. Mounds of cast-off shells from prerecorded times have been found in China, Denmark, Brazil, and the United States. Although fishing was difficult because of a lack of efficient gear, it was easy to walk out at low tide and pick up shellfish, or spear fish in shallow water.

As populations grew, people tended to settle near the sea or large river systems where fish and shellfish were readily abundant as food, and sea lanes became important for commerce, trade, communication, and transport. The need for more food and bigger fish encouraged fishermen to develop new gear design and more efficient methods of fishing and to travel even farther from shore. As a result of larger catches, the fishing enterprise expanded from a small boat, local village business to one that permitted additional onshore people to enter the business of the fishery.

Fishing was often the reason, accidentally or not, for discovering new lands, finding new travel routes using trade as an excuse for expansion, and sometimes going to war. As nations organized large fishing fleets, they became sea powers.

The enormous fishing grounds of the North Atlantic lured European fisherman westward even before 1500. In fact, commercial fishing was the first industry of the New World; cod was the draw of the Grand Banks of Newfoundland. So numerous were these fish that in the early 1600s the Englishman Bartholomew Gosnold named a nearby peninsula Cape Cod. Fish were salted and packed in barrels, and shipped back to England. The state seal of Massachusetts has a codfish on its crest and shield.

The fishing industry is diverse and many segments developed independently.

THE FISH-CURING INDUSTRY

The fish-curing industry of the North Atlantic coast of North America dates back to the year 1500, at least, and legends of activities go back even earlier. An extensive fish-curing industry was carried on for more than one hundred years before there was a permanent settlement. As early as 1580 more than three hundred ships from Europe were salting cod in this area. Newfoundland was colonized because of the fish-curing industry, which remains a factor in the province's economic life.

Early colonists in New England and the Maritime Provinces could not have survived without the salt cod and smoked herring they prepared. Although fish meant food to these colonists, cured fish soon became their capital resource and their stock-in-trade for purchasing supplies. Cod, their most abundant fish, could be manufactured into a durable protein food product, withstand the primitive shipping and storage conditions of the day, and was comparatively low in price. Other cured fish such as smoked halibut and herring, pickled sturgeon, and salt salmon were soon being shipped abroad. Out of this grew the so-called triangular trade: salt fish to Europe; manufactured goods from Europe to the West Indies; and sugar, rum, and molasses to New England.

The trade in salt fish stimulated other industries, and capital was gradually accumulated so that the colonists could go into the shipping business. Before the end of the sixteenth century, more efficient, faster vessels were developed to meet the needs of an expanding fishery.

The fish-curing industry continued to grow and prosper, dominating the economic life of the New England colonies in the late seventeenth and early eighteenth centuries. The large amount of money to be made led to disputes between the British and the French over fishing grounds and fish-curing locations. Both groups wanted to secure this trade for themselves. Attempts were made to establish fishing boundaries, but they were poorly defined, and fishing rights over a wide area were the cause of frequent bickering, sometimes flaring up into undeclared warfare. The fishermen and curers of New England and Nova Scotia played an important part in England's conquest of Canada, because for them the fishing rights meant life or death.

The disputes did not end with the ousting of France, but continued between the New England colonists and the English. The English Parliament in 1775 prohibited the New England colonies from trading directly with foreign countries and prevented New England vessels from fishing on the banks off Newfoundland, in the Gulf of St. Lawrence, and on the coasts of Labrador and Nova Scotia where they had been accustomed to fishing. This restriction meant ruin to the New England fish-curing industry, and the edict was one cause of the Revolutionary War.

The treaty of peace negotiated in 1783 was delayed because the American delegates insisted on securing favorable fishery rights. They regarded these rights as so important that they refused to sign a general treaty of peace that left the fishing rights for later adjudication. Finally, the American delegation obtained a treaty article on fisheries which granted favorable conditions to the United States.

The New England fish-curing industry generally prospered under the new republic and was able to secure salt-cod markets in southern Europe and the Mediterranean. Disputes again arose with Great Britain over trade, the interpretation of fishery rights, and the impressment of American fisherman and seamen into the Royal Navy. Restrictions and embargoes were imposed by both Great Britain and the United States, resulting in a decline in the salt-fish industry after 1807. The War of 1812 almost ruined the industry; the war was so unpopular among shipping, commercial, and fish-curing groups that there was a move toward secession in some New England states.

At the end of the War of 1812, the British claimed that the war abrogated the treaty of 1783; the United States claimed that the treaty was still valid. The British seized some American fishing vessels, and it seemed for a time that a new war might break out. Tension was eased by the signing of a new fishery convention in 1818. It was followed, however, by a whole series of disputes about interpretation, at times resulting in severe diplomatic tension for the United States with Great Britain and with Canada.

Trouble occurred less frequently during the last decades of the nineteenth century as refrigeration developed and wider markets were created in the United States for fresh fish, making salting and drying of fish on the northeastern coast less important.

FISH CANNING

An overview of the U.S. fish-preserving industry during the past half century shows a decline in production of cured fish but an almost continuous growth in the canning industry.

The first record of canning seafood in the United States was in 1815 when Ezra Daggert and Thomas Kensett canned salmon, lobsters, and oysters on a site near what is now Battery Park in New York City. In 1825 Kensett applied for U.S. patents for the "preserving of animal, vegetable, and other perishable foods," but these patents were not granted until some ten years later, presumably because patent officials doubted the idea's practicality. For years following these early canning operations there was no significant development in seafood canning.

Increased production was gradual over a twenty-year period beginning in 1844. The first large increase in demand came during the Civil War when preserved foods were needed for the troops. This increased demand also created additional consumers for canned seafoods. Men who became acquainted with these products in the army demanded canned foods on their return home and introduced them to their neighbors.

Kensett was the first to break away from home kitchen methods and deserves credit for developing the first canned product, oysters, to receive wide distribution. The pioneer development of the industry in the Chesapeake Bay area, the first important canning center, is due to his efforts. Others are said to have engaged in the industry in the Baltimore area before Kensett, and it is believed that oysters were canned as early as 1819. The first systematic effort at large-scale development, however, was made by Kensett in 1844, when he began packing oysters in Baltimore. Oysters were the first canned product that became popular. Large inland cities could get fresh Baltimore oysters packed in ice through the winter, but people in smaller communities seldom enjoyed such a luxury. The countryman's greatest treat when he went to town was an oyster stew. Baltimore and Boston firms canned oysters so they would keep for months and could be bought at any country grocery store by people who had never eaten a fresh oyster.

Tin containers for packaging processed foods were first used in the 1840s. Sardines were first canned in Maine about 1850; a turtle cannery was established in Florida in 1866; a cannery for menhaden was established on Long Island in 1872; and it is known that mackerel, clams, lobsters, and crabs were being canned by 1880. It is probable that tuna, alewives, and shad were not canned until early in the twentieth century. The production of canned products in the United States and Alaska in 1880 had an estimated value of $15 million.

Canning Salmon

Salmon, one of the most important canning industries, had its beginnings during the Civil War period. Although it is claimed that the first salmon canned on the American continent was Atlantic salmon packed in St. Johns, New Brunswick, in 1839, the salmon fishery was never of economic importance on the Atlantic Coast. The industry really began in California, where George and William Hume with A. S. Hapgood started the Pacific salmon canning industry. The Hume Brothers, who had worked as fishermen at their home in Maine, went to California as Forty-niners. They noticed that salmon were plentiful in the Sacramento River and believed that money might be made canning the fish. They went back to Maine on a visit, persuaded Hapgood, a lobster canner, to return west with them, and the first Pacific salmon pack was made in Sacramento in 1864.

Using these primitive methods, two thousand cases of salmon were canned that first year and sold at five dollars per dozen cans to a San Francisco merchant. Reacting to reports of extremely favorable conditions on the Columbia River, the Humes moved to Eagle Cliff, Washington, and made the first pack of Columbia River salmon in 1866.

As a result, the rush to pack salmon was on, and within a few years hundreds of operations were set up on the Columbia River and in Alaska. Having to make cans by hand hampered operations, but because of the great demand, the pack by 1876 was 450,000 cases.

As the sale of canned salmon increased steadily, the industry sought new and profitable locations, first at New Westminster on the Fraser River in British Columbia in 1867; then at Mukilteo, on Puget Sound, Washington Territory, in 1877; and, although Alaska is today the most important salmon canning area, its first cannery was not built until 1878 at Klawak, on Prince of Wales Islands.

Today consumers have more than fifty canned fish and seafood products available, thanks to the ingenuity of the fishery industry. Canned fishery products total more than 1.3 billion pounds (590 million kg) and are worth some $1.5 billion.

THE SHRIMP FISHERY

The shrimp industry, as it is known today, began off the coasts of Georgia, North Carolina, and South Carolina. Around 1915, the first shrimp trawl was employed from open skiffs converted from the bluefish hook-and-line fishery. Gasoline engines became the major source of power during the 1920s. A small single otter trawl was manually operated from the vessel. Flat nets of a very simple design were utilized during the early days. Interestingly, this trawl proved so efficient that it is still used today.

During the 1930s, diesel engines were first utilized aboard shrimp boats, eventually making it possible to use larger and more powerful vessels. The use of larger trawls coincided with this important evolutionary process in the shrimping industry. The large offshore vessels used today were not necessary then because the fishery was confined to inshore waters.

Expansion of the fishery occurred significantly after World War II aided by the availability of large war surplus diesel engines. Numerous fishermen entered the fishery during the postwar boom.

The offshore white shrimp grounds were fished on a significant scale. Fishermen regularly ventured into water more than 60 feet (18.3 m) deep in pursuit of shrimp. White shrimp became such a highly exploited resource that production declined.

During the late 1940s, several changes contributed to the evolution of shrimping vessels and gear. Declining stocks of white shrimp led fishermen to direct their efforts toward catching brown shrimp, a deep water fishery, that when established changed the requirements of vessels and shrimping methods. The establishment of a brown shrimp fishery also generated interest in the pink shrimp that stocks Florida's Torugas grounds.

The increased interest in shrimp led to improvements in gear technology. First, the two-seam balloon trawl was introduced (1947) in the Gulf. This net, with its redesigned jib, was an improvement over the earlier flat net, producing a better overhand and more even mesh strain than the flat net. Greater horsepower meant larger trawl capabilities and increased harvesting capacities. Numerous fishermen increased their trawl sizes—vessels of 50 to 55 feet (15.2 m to 16.8 m) in length were being built with an occasional vessel of 60 feet (18.3 m) beginning to appear at the close of the 1940s. During this period some electrical devices, including fathometers and automatic pilots, also came into common use.

Perhaps more advancements were introduced into the shrimp industry in the 1950s than during any other period. This decade saw further increases in horsepower, electronics, and gear improvements. The four-seam balloon (semiballoon) trawl was introduced in 1950. It spread more effectively than the flat and two-seam balloons and maintained a better shape in the water.

Spec Harris of Freeport, Louisiana, designed the western jib, which is essentially a flat net with modification to the corner pieces. It is still the most commonly used trawl in the Texas Gulf shrimp fishery.

The shift to deep water brown and pink shrimp grounds necessitated larger vessels, a need compounded by the discovery and development of the fishing grounds off Mexico. A distant water fleet required larger vessels that could remain away from port for an extended period of time. Increased power, often surpassing 200 horsepower, coincided with larger vessel development.

The most important gear modification during the 1950s was the conversion to double-rigged vessels. Two smaller trawls actually caught more shrimp than an equal size single trawl. This concept created a more efficient onboard handling operation and enhanced safety at sea. Also during this period synthetic twines began being used, increasing strength and durability of trawls.

Advancements in marine electronics continued. Virtually all vessels began using depth sounders. Radio capability was the most significant electronic change during the decade. With radios becoming common, a communications link was established which significantly enhanced harvesting efficiency. The ability to communicate with other vessels aided extensively in the location of shrimp, and greater safety at sea was ensured. Radio direction finders were installed on a number of vessels.

During the 1960s, increasing horsepower and a corresponding tendency to use larger vessels were the most significant changes to occur. Expansion of fisheries into South America greatly influenced vessel length; shrimp trawlers 73 feet (22.2 m) in length were regularly constructed.

Some larger Texas trawlers began towing a third rig from the stern of their vessels, using an A-frame to accommodate this modification, but fishermen had mixed results with the technique. The primary difficulty was that of a "robbing" effect from the trawls being towed too close together. Vessels with longer than usual outriggers were able to overcome this problem.

Further implementation of electronics continued. Radar came into use, and depth sounders and related equipment were improved. Some fishermen began experimenting with military surplus Loran equipment and rapidly identified the benefits of the navigational devices.

During the early 1970s, length of vessels increased more than the amount of engine horsepower. Although several types of engines with larger horsepower were installed on some boats, most new engines remained in the 365 horsepower range. A remarkable increase in the number of steel hull vessels occurred, although wooden vessels continued to be added to the industry at a significant rate, and the first fiberglass and aluminum trawlers entered the fisheries.

In roughly the same period, Gulf fishermen perfected a trawling technique utilizing two small nets, twin trawls, on the single cable. Again, the theory was that two smaller nets are more efficient than a single larger one. This gear modification significantly increased trawl efficiency, and the majority of Gulf shrimp trawlers soon adopted this technique, utilizing four trawls per vessel instead of two.

Another gear modification was tried although not generally accepted, but recent technological advancements may present new opportunities for it. The former Bureau of Commercial Fisheries gear unit developed an electric shrimp trawl designed to shock burrowing shrimp from the seabed. Experiments proved that brown shrimp could be harvested during the daytime utilizing this gear. This innovation could have been an excellent opportunity for expanding potential shrimping efforts because presently brown shrimp can only be harvested at night. Several trawlers experimenting with this gear achieved significant daytime catches. A few inherent problems with the system resulted in a profound inconsistency of catch, however. Because of its expense and inconsistencies, the electronic trawl was ultimately abandoned. Recent modifications have been introduced into the United Kingdom where several vessels have adopted its use.

Improvements in electronics increased shrimping productivity. In addition to radar and depth recorders, the navigational equipment Loran A became a universal tool in the shrimping fleet, providing locations of productive fishing grounds and helping fishermen avoid numerous hazards to trawl gear.

More recently, several other gear changes have been introduced to the shrimping industry but have not yet been widely accepted. The National Marine Fisheries Service (NMFS) has been working on a Trawl Efficiency Device, an apparatus to exclude by-catch (any species other than the targeted species) from shrimp trawls, and tests have provided encouraging results. The TED consists of a frame which is installed between the body and cod end (closed saclike part) of the trawl. Shrimp are allowed to pass through the apparatus while larger fish and debris are rerouted through an exit. If perfected, the TED could provide additional improvements in trawl efficiency by decreasing drag in the cod end.

Rapid improvement of marine electronics occurred in the early 1980s. The Loran C Navigational System's increased accuracy has aided shrimping operations. Track plotters associated with Loran C have proven effective in defining concentrations of shrimp and trawlable bottom areas. Another electronic device, the depth recorder, has been greatly improved. Recent production of chromascopes, machines that record in color, assist in defining bottom types and fish compositions of the seabed. These recorders have increased shrimp harvesting.

On the processing end of the business, the freezing of shrimp probably was the most important single factor governing the progress of the shrimp industry. The adaptability of shrimp to the freezing process allowed more time for marketing and distribution and eased the urgency that previously dictated sales policies and prices for the producer. The growth of the entire frozen food industry resulted in wider distribution for shrimp. Facilities for handling frozen vegetables and fruits were likewise suited for handling frozen seafoods.

CANNING OYSTERS, CLAMS, AND CRABS

Although Baltimore was the center of the osyter canning industry for many years, oysters are packed there only occasionally today. The catch in the Chesapeake Bay region has decreased greatly, and it is now more profitable to market these oysters fresh. The greater portion of the oyster pack is now prepared on the Gulf Coast. The most recent development in the oyster industry is the establishment of oyster canning on the Pacific Coast. The introduction of the Japanese or "Pacific" oyster created a surplus, which was unmarketable in the raw condition. After several years of experimental work, this oyster was canned commercially in 1931. The pack in that year was 7,930 cases, increasing to 118,853 cases in 1936.

The first clam cannery in the United States was started in 1878 at Pine Point, Maine. The pack of canned clam products was small for some years because of considerable difficulty with discoloration, but production slowly increased when this problem was overcome. P. F. Halferty developed a method for canning minced razor clams about 1900, building up a commercial clam canning industry in Oregon, Washington, and Alaska. The inclusion of minced clams, broth, and clam chowder in the list of products increased the value of canned clam products until they are now fifth in order of importance of canned fishery products, thereby displacing oysters.

Crab was first canned in the United States by James McMenamin of Norfolk, Virginia, in 1878. The greatest difficulty was with discoloration. In 1936 a method to overcome discoloration was developed, and in 1938 the Harris Company packed the common or blue crab of the Atlantic Coast commercially. Although the crab canning process is said to have been developed in 1892, the Japanese industry was not established on a commercial scale until 1908. Japanese canned crab began to enter U.S. markets in appreciable quantities during World War I. In 1931 imports amounted to almost double the domestic production of fresh and canned crabmeat. A domestic crab canning industry has been developed in Alaska, Oregon, and Washington; processing and other technical difficulties have been overcome and a market has been developed in the Pacific Coast states.

THE FISH CANNING INDUSTRY

Because of the large supply of groundfish in the North Atlantic, numerous attempts have been made to develop a canning industry, but they have not been particularly successful because of competition with other canned fishery products or insufficient advertising. Cod and haddock products such as fish flakes, fish cakes or balls, and finnan haddie (smoked haddock) have not found a wide market outside the New England area and are packed on a limited scale. Fish cakes were first packed in Boston in 1878, and finnan haddie was first packed about 1890. Fish flakes, or "salad fish," the flaked meat of cod and haddock, are believed to have been developed by the Burnham and Morrill Company of Portland, Maine, in 1898.

At the turn of the century, the industry was experimenting with a variety of products—pickled sturgeon, carp, shark meat, and menhaden—that are not found on the market today. Some of these packs did not make good products; others were not in sufficient demand; in other instances, the cost of raw material became too great for profitable operation.

About 1900 the annual pack of canned fishery products was less than half of what is produced today, and it was thought that production could not be increased greatly or even maintained. At the same time these gloomy predictions were being made, the canning of fishery products was actually at the threshold of its greatest development.

Canned tuna is one of the more recently developed canned fishery products, first packed commercially in 1909. The packing of tuna began at the Southern California Fish Company, which began experiments in 1905. The raw material was albacore, which when cooked resembled chicken in taste and flavor. This characteristic flavor added impetus to the experiments, but it was not until 1907 that the efforts were rewarded. The first successful pack was produced in 1909 when 2,000 cases were packed and marketed.

Mackerel was canned in small quantities in New England as early as 1843, but its introduction into the general canned food market did not occur until 1927 when George Ogawa put up a pack of 10,725 cases of California mackerel "salmon style," priced to compete with cheaper varieties of salmon. Production of Pacific mackerel increased to 388,500 cases in 1928 and reached a peak of 1,795,700 cases of 48 one-pound (454 g) cans in 1935.

Sardines were first packed in France, in 1834, and by 1860 a substantial market had been created for French sardines in the United States. Efforts were made to establish an American industry in 1871 utilizing young menhaden as raw material. In 1877 Julius Wolff began canning small herring at Eastport, Maine, and is credited with starting the first really successful American sardine cannery. By 1906 a large number of sardine canners were operating in northern Maine and nearby Canada. Several efforts were made during the 1890s to establish sardine canning on Puget Sound or in Alaska where large quantities of herring were available, but all of these operations were short-lived.

The famed California sardine industry began in 1900 when Frank E. Booth moved to Monterey, California. Booth and his father were already involved in the canning of salmon in their Pittsburg (California) plant. It was his background in the canning and packing of fish that prompted Booth to consider the possibility of canning the abundant Monterey Bay sardine. Upon his move to the bayside community, Booth founded the F. E. Booth Company in a plant near the aged and historic Monterey Customs House.

Not long after Booth launched his California sardines, a second man, also destined to become an important figure in Monterey's multimillion-dollar sardine industry, arrived. Knute Hovden, a recent immigrant from Norway, a graduate of the Norwegian National Fisheries College, and a skillfully trained professional in the fish packing field, teamed with Booth. Between them the highly competitive and extremely profitable Monterey Bay sardine canning industry continued to develop and expand.

With Booth and Hovden perfecting the canning phase, the biggest problem became getting a steady supply of fish. Able to handle 5 tons (4.5×10^3 kg) of sardines per day, but with an inconsistent daily catch, Booth and Hovden sought ways to increase and ensure the size of the catch.

In 1904 Pietro Ferrante arrived in Monterey with many years of fishing experience, and quickly gained a reputation as both a man of vision and of considerable fishing talent. It was only natural that Ferrante soon joined forces with Booth and Hovden. Ferrante was convinced that a new approach to catching sardines was needed if they were to reap the bounty of the bay. Remembering the lampara boat and net method of fishing he had been familiar with in the Mediterranean, Ferrante redesigned the lampara net and adapted it for Monterey's deep water bay. The lampara net is designed to encircle an entire school of fish. The word lampara was derived from the Italian word *lampo*—meaning lightning—because the net was designed for a fast cast and haul. Ferrante also urged other Italian fishermen in California to come to Monterey and join him in the hunt for sardines.

With the aid of the lampara net and with the knowledge and skill of the newly arrived fishermen, the sleepy bay community experienced a gradual but significant change. By 1913 the canning industry had "come of age," and was no longer looked upon as being in the crude and experimental stage. In keeping up with the canners, the fishing crews were catching as many as 25 tons (2.3×10^4 kg) of sardines in a single night. (The ideal fishing conditions were on dark moonless nights when the fishermen could best spot the phosphorescent glow of a school of sardines and, in turn, know where to place their nets.)

With the supply of fish no longer a problem, Hovden branched out and opened his own cannery in 1914 on what was then an uncluttered stretch of Monterey beach. Others followed, and it was not long before the shoreline was lined with the noises and smells of several canneries. By 1918 Monterey boasted a total of nine canning plants and packed a total of 1.4 million cases of sardines as compared to a mere 75,000 cases three years before.

The early 1920s were the peak years of the lampara boat and net method of fishing. With the introduction of the half-ring net in 1925, the half-ring boat also appeared. This boat differed only slightly from the lampara boat, boasting a winch, a mast, and a boom. With the use of the rings more fish could be caught per haul as the net rings pursed (or pocketed) the net, thus trapping the fish and making it difficult for them to escape.

In time the lampara boats and the half-ring boats became outmoded with the introduction of the popular purse seiner, whose net, when full of trapped fish, formed a purse. With the word *seine* describing the type of net commonly used by the sardine fishermen, the vessel became known as a purse seiner. Varying in size, the largest of the purse seiners approached 100 feet (30.5 m) and carried nets capable of encircling the width of a football field and dropping to a depth equaling the height of a ten-story building. This new class of boat was capable of fishing hundreds of miles at sea and carrying 100 to 150 tons (9.07×10^4 kg to 1.36×10^5 kg) of fish. With the purse seiner, the sardine fishing in and around the Monterey Bay area took on an added dimension.

Through the 1930s and into the 1940s, the Monterey fishing fleet and its supporting cast of canneries continued to grow and prosper. In 1930 the catch was 159,000 tons (1.44×10^8 kg); by 1935 it had jumped to 230,000 tons (2.09×10^8 kg), and during the early 1940s there were years when the catch approached the almost unbelievable figure of a quarter of a million tons (2.27×10^8 kg).

With the constant and abundant supply of fish, cannery operators learned that not only was there money to be made in canning fish but in the processing of fish by-products as well. With fish meal becoming widely used for poultry and livestock feed, as well as being in demand as fertilizer, the oil from the fish (which at one time was considered waste) was sought for use in the manufacture of soap, paint mixer, vitamins, glycerine (for ammunition), shortening, salad oil, and the tanning of leather. By 1945 Monterey boasted nineteen canneries and twenty reduction plants for the development of fish by-products, and a fishing fleet of over a hundred vessels. During this period Monterey was known as the sardine capital of the world, and in total tonnage ranked third among the world's major fishing ports (second only to Stavanger, Norway, and Hull, England).

During 1939 the catch was 215,000 tons or 430 million pounds (195×10^6 kg) of sardines, which with an average of approximately three fish to the pound represent a staggering 1.2 billion individual sardines. If the total number of sardines caught were placed end to end, the row would stretch 203,600 miles (327,592 km)—a distance nearly equal to that from the earth to the moon. The same row of fish if placed end to end around the equator would circle the earth eight times with over 3,600 miles (5,792 km) of fish left over.

Although 1945 was the high point of Monterey's sardine industry, 1946 marked the beginning of its decline. Fish continued to be caught and canneries continued to work, but the handwriting was on the wall. The 1946 catch was nearly 100,000 tons (9.1×10^7 kg) under the 1945 mark, with the 1947 catch being over 100,000 tons (9.1×10^7 kg) less than that. The 1948 catch plummeted to a disastrous 14,000 tons (1.3×10^7 kg). Much of that amount was trucked to the Monterey canneries from more abundant fishing grounds to the south.

In 1949 the industry, for reasons unknown, received a most welcome shot in the arm as the catch jumped to 41,000 tons (37.2×10^6 kg). During the 1950 season the fleet recorded a catch of 132,000 tons (119×10^6 kg). Even though the 1950 catch was over 100,000 tons (9.1×10^7 kg) less than the catch of 1945, the industry's dollar turnover was the greatest in its history. As the 1950 season came to a close, for all intents and purposes, so did Monterey's sardine industry. The 1951 catch was embarrassingly small, and by 1952 canneries were closing at such a rapid rate that only a brief mention of their closing made the local papers.

As the canneries closed, many of the purse seiners found their way to various southern ports where sardines were still to be caught. With the harbor relatively empty of purse seiners and much of Cannery Row on the auction block, Monterey's sardine industry became little more than a memory. The industry had gone from boom to bust in less than fifty years because of polluted water, warmer climates, changes in currents, recurring cycles and, of course, the distinct possibility that the once-abundant sardines were simply fished out.

THE HADDOCK FISHERY

Compared with the cod fishery, which was centuries old, a substantial commercial haddock fishery was late in developing in New England. Cod were considered best for salting (haddock were unsuitable for that purpose), but use of ice made trade in fresh fish possible and haddock came into its own, growing quickly in public esteem. Haddock fillets cut and frozen at dockside soon found acceptance far inland.

On the haddock grounds, dory fishing with hook and line yielded slowly to trawling after the turn of the century. Beam trawls were supplanted by otter trawls, improved versions of which are now the main commercial gear. However, hook-and-line fishermen persisted alongside trawlermen for a long time. In the late 1920s, roughly half the catch was still taken by longlines, and a small fraction still is.

Between 1891 and 1901, U.S. haddock landings averaged nearly 27,500 tons (2.5×10^7 kg) annually. Catches grew in size with increasing numbers of trawlers through the 1920s until a peak of 132,000 tons (119×10^6 kg) was reached in 1929. Operating under the mistaken notion that fish resources were infinite, there was an all-out effort to harvest as much as possible to meet the demands of the marketplace. After 1929, haddock resources showed signs of stress. Fishermen and fishery scientists worried as catches dropped sharply, and many fishermen were forced to switch to other species. In the 1930s the U.S. Bureau of Fisheries initiated biological studies of haddock and a new system of statistical reporting.

When fishermen stopped overfishing haddock, average U.S. catches settled to about 70,000 tons (6.35×10^7 kg) annually, 52,000 (4.7×10^7 kg) of these from Georges Bank and the Gulf of Maine. These levels, close to the estimated long-term sustainable catch, prevailed from the mid-1930s to 1960.

In 1949 it was agreed by all countries concerned that scientific management of the fish resources in this region be carried out cooperatively, and a treaty that year founded the International Commission for the Northwest Atlantic Fisheries (ICNAF). Haddock off the U.S. coast were not a target of European fishermen in ICNAF's early years; nevertheless, haddock stocks soon benefited from ICNAF research and regulation. Investigations of the effects of trawl mesh size on catches showed that enlarged mesh openings would reduce waste of undersized groundfish. When new mesh regulations were issued in 1953, harvesting became more efficient and discards of small haddock were fewer.

During the 1960s unprecedented numbers of foreign vessels, many from the Soviet Union, appeared on the principal haddock grounds off Georges Bank. At first, the Soviets mainly sought Atlantic herring and silver hake, but in the mid-1960s, their attention was drawn to large numbers of young haddock spawned in 1962 and 1963. At the same time, U.S. and Canadian fishermen intensified their own efforts to catch haddock. The result was an all-time peak catch in 1965 of 165,000 tons—three times the estimated annual sustainable yield for Georges Bank. The collapse of the resource followed soon after.

ICNAF moved to reverse the disaster, making major spawning grounds off-limits to trawlers in the spring and cutting the allowable catch for 1970 and 1971 to 12,000 tons (1.1×10^7 kg) from Georges Bank and the the Gulf of Maine. This number was halved during four of the five succeeding years; in 1974 it was set at zero, with a by-catch allowance of 6,000 tons (5.4×10^6 kg). Recovery of haddock stocks began, but too slowly for New England fishermen. They joined in support of a new law providing more direct control over exploitation of traditional resources. In this way, collapse of the Georges Bank haddock resource played a significant part in enactment of the present "200-mile-limit (322 km) law," the Magnuson Fishery Conservation and Management Act of 1976 (MFCMA).

Under MFCMA, the United States took unilateral control of most fish and shellfish within a 200-mile (322 km) zone off the coast, and management was required to be based on "optimum yield" (maximum sustainable yield modified by certain economic, social, and ecological considerations). Eight Regional Fishery Management Councils came into being. Management of the haddock stock fell to the New England Council, which gave it top priority. Optimum yield, in the council's judgment, would be the yield that would most effectively speed recovery of the stocks. So they set this limit at 6,200 tons (5,636 metric tons) to be taken only incidentally when fishing for other species. Of this total, 6,000 tons (5,454.5 metric tons) were designated for commercial harvest, and 200 tons (181.8 metric tons) for recreational fishermen.

The 200-mile (322 km) declaration gave the United States control over the destiny of its industry. With management authority over its coastal zone and the decision-making authority over the fish resources within it, the United States could take the steps necessary to ensure future resource supply through effective conservation measures.

As the new council took over, the haddock 1975 year class was the first good one in years. Assessments in 1977 showed it to be much stronger than the long-term average, and many times stronger than those produced during the years of collapse. Haddock were so plentiful that fishermen on some grounds could avoid them only by keeping their nets out of the water. Catch limits had suddenly become quite impractical, but they were cumbersome to change under MFCMA. Massive discarding at sea was one result; misreporting of catches was another. Council managers could not change limits until November 1977, and by that time much damage had been done. Thousands of tons of haddock had been wasted and masses of data vital for management planning lost.

Thereafter, constraints on the fishery were progressively eased. By the 1979–80 fishing year, optimum yield for Georges Bank and the Gulf of Maine had been raised to 32,500 tons (2.95×10^7 kg) on the strength of the 1975 year class, and 1979 survey results revealed that still another good year class, from 1978, would recruit to the Georges Bank fishery in 1980. With two such year classes in the water, there was reason to hope for recovery of New England's haddock fishery. Unfortunately, recruitment did not continue to improve; subsequent year classes have been weak, adding little to the resource. Evidence shows stocks sinking again toward levels seen a decade ago. Recovery may require the kind of circumstances for recruitment success which rarely occurs.

EARLY PACIFIC FISHERIES

Early fisheries on the Pacific did not affect U.S. international relations to the same extent as the Atlantic fisheries, because the development was much more recent and different in character. The difference, possibly, is because development occurred at a period when canning and refrigeration were replacing curing as the principal methods of preservation, and also when more of the fishing took place in clearly defined territorial waters.

Although there have been numerous disputes between Canada and the United States over Pacific fisheries, they have been minor compared with those in the Atlantic. In the 1930s Japan moved into fishing grounds off the coast of Alaska and interfered with U.S. vessels which were catching and salting cod. The cod fishermen threatened to shoot any Japanese obstructing their operations. Japanese fishing was a matter of great concern to the Pacific coast fishermen, but little notice was taken nationally until it was shown that the Japanese were catching salmon despite an understanding to the contrary. The controversy was still unsettled when Japan and the United States went to war in 1941.

Cured fish were the first manufactured products prepared on the Pacific coast, where Indians had an extensive dried-salmon industry on the Columbia River long before the coming of white people. The fish were traded to the plains tribes of the interior. The Indians still dry small amounts of salmon for their own use. The Russians operated a commercial salted-salmon industry in Alaska at the beginning of the nineteenth century, shipping products as far as St. Petersburg. Soon afterward the Northwest Fur Company started a salmon-salting business on the Columbia River. The Northwest Company merged with the Hudson Bay Company which shipped salt salmon to Hawaii, Australia, China, Japan, and the eastern United States. American fishermen salted salmon in Alaska while it was still a Russian possession. A number of the large salmon canneries of today began as salmon salteries.

The presence of cod off the coast of Alaska was discovered in the 1860s, and the possibility of building a prosperous salt-cod industry was one argument for the purchase of Alaska. Recent, but still incomplete, studies have established that the Pacific banks are larger and of greater potential production than the Grand Banks off the coast of Newfoundland. Yet, utilization today is less than it was thirty years ago.

During World War II the Pacific coast fish-curing industry was much more adversely affected than its counterpart on the Atlantic coast. With the Alaskan area considered a combat zone, almost all fishing and fish-curing activities were stopped, and all but one of the cod-salting vessels was requisitioned by the government. The loss of foreign markets and the effect of pricing regulations were other unfavorable factors.

THE MENHADEN FISHERY

Menhaden are herring-like fish that inhabit the coastal waters of the western Atlantic Ocean and Gulf of Mexico. The menhaden fishery is the largest of all fisheries in the United States and the basis of one of the leading fishing industries in the world. More than twenty-five reduction plants receive and process the fish into meal, oil, and condensed solubles. Landings in 1981 amounted to 2.6 billion pounds (1.2×10^9 kg), valued in excess of $100 million, and produced 271,000 tons (2.4×10^8 kg) of meal, 291,000 tons (2.6×10^8 kg) of oil, and 100,000 tons (9.1×10^7 kg) of solubles, with an estimated value of $167 million. Most of the meal is used as poultry feed; the oil is exported to Europe for use in the production of margarine. As of this writing, the U.S. Food and Drug Administration has not approved fish oil for human use although a petition to request such use is being developed.

Fishing for menhaden is one of the oldest industries in the United States. North American Indians taught early settlers to place a fish in each hill of Indian corn. Although menhaden probably were never widely used this way, the practice led to their use for enriching soils when crops along the New England coast and on Long Island began to fail in the late 1700s. By 1820 a fishery was organized for the purpose of supplying menhaden for fertilizer.

During the War of 1812 the use of fish oils in paints led to the utilization of menhaden for this purpose. The early menhaden oil industry was centered in New England where the large, oily fish were encountered in abundance along the coast during the summer. Despite the highly profitable market for menhaden oil, the industry grew rather slowly until about 1860 when the introduction of the mechanical screw press and the use of steam power made practical the oil-recovery process by a factory operation. During the following decade, many new factories were built and improvements in the methods of catching and processing the fish followed. Development of suitable methods of preserving the fish press cake, accumulated from the oil extraction process, also provided the basis of another phase of the menhaden oil industry that was to continue for the next fifty years—the production of fish fertilizer. By 1870 more than ninety menhaden reduction plants had been established from Maine to North Carolina.

Prior to 1875 the New England states accounted for the greatest part of the annual menhaden production. In 1876 the catch amounted to approximately 170,000 tons (1.5×10^8 kg) from which nearly 3 million gallons (11×10^6 l) of oil and over 50,000 tons (45.4×10^3 kg) of fertilizer were produced. Maine accounted for nearly half the total fish production in that year. Several years later the fish failed to appear in the waters north of Cape Cod, and except for certain seasons, the fish have not been abundant in the coastal waters in that area since.

Following the collapse of the New England fishery, the industry expanded southward and by 1900 was centered in New Jersey and Virginia. Although menhaden were known to be in the Gulf of Mexico during the early years of the oil industry on the Atlantic coast, it was apparently the collapse of the New England fishery that motivated development of the Gulf fishery. Records show that menhaden were landed on the west coast of Florida and in Texas waters prior to 1902, but there are no records of further landings in those states until 1918. The first landings of menhaden in Mississippi waters were reported in 1939 and in Louisiana in 1948.

Records of menhaden landings in the first decade of the twentieth century are lacking, but in 1912 the catch amounted to 356,000 tons (3.2×10^8 kg), the largest reported to that time, with Virginia accounting for more than half the total production in that year. Although incomplete, records show that, except for two or three years, the total annual menhaden catch from 1912 to the beginning of World War II remained relatively stable, fluctuating between 118,000 tons (1.1×10^8 kg) and 406,000 tons (3.7×10^8 kg) and averaging 243,000 tons (2.2×10^8 kg). The discovery of vitamin B_{12} as an important constituent of the animal protein factor found in fish meal made menhaden even more valuable, and following World War II the catch increased markedly. Growth of the fishery catch during the 1950s more than doubled and remains at about that level today.

THE WHALING INDUSTRY

Whaling, too, has its place in history. This industry was well established in Europe before the American colonists took up the work. There is evidence that the Indians practiced offshore whaling before the arrival of white people. Whaling to some meant food, but more important was the use of whale oil for lamps and candles. These by-products stimulated the industry's growth.

Early in colonial history, Boston was the center of the whaling industry, then Nantucket, and finally New Bedford. Bigger, stronger ships were built, becoming factory, home, and storehouse, all in one. Expeditions for the sperm whale often lasted as long as three or four years.

The need for whale oil declined sharply after oil was discovered in Pennsylvania in 1859, and the East Coast industry suffered further decline when the New

England whaling fleet was destroyed during the Civil War. The opening of the West shifted the focal point of the industry there. Bowhead whaling from California to Alaska replaced most of the East Coast fishery. By the end of the 1800s, whales in the Northern Hemisphere were becoming scarce. Therefore, world whalers turned their sights to the Antarctic. In 1931 there were forty-one whaling factory ships operating with an annual catch of about 40,000 whales. With sailing restrictions during World War II, the industry declined again.

In 1946 the International Whaling Commission was established to place restrictions and quotas on the taking of certain species of whales that were becoming rare and were in danger of extinction.

In 1971 the U.S. government, in support of the commission and yielding to public pressure, ordered an end to whaling by U.S. fishermen; the only exception was that Alaskan Eskimos could maintain a small catch for sustenance purposes only. To further discourage worldwide whaling, the United States forbids the sale of whale products.

AN OVERVIEW OF OUR HERITAGE

Ports such as Gloucester, New Bedford, Boston, San Franciso, Monterey, San Pedro, San Diego, and Seattle were home to some of our earliest commercial companies.

Let your imagination wander back to the sights, sounds, and activities of such famous places as the Boston Fish Pier, New York's Fulton Market, Monterey's Cannery Row, or San Francisco's Fisherman's Wharf: two- and three-masted schooners pulling up to the wharf with sails down and holds open; baskets of fish being lifted ashore; carts filled to overflowing with fresh fish being pushed across the wharf to waiting fish skinners in old, oak-timbered market stands; teamsters whistling and cracking their whips over horse-drawn wagons piled high with barrels and wooden boxes of dried and salted fish.

Out of this profusion of activity grew many familiar seafood companies. The following names and dates are not all-inclusive but serve as examples of certain periods of early industry growth.

Booth	1848
Smith Brothers	1848
Gorton-Pew Fisheries	1849
Calib Haley & Company	1859
New England Fish Company	1868
Paladini Inc.	1868
R. W. Claxton	1881
Isaac Fass	1883
Salasnek Fish House	1891
Crocker & Windsor	1895
Standard Fish Company	1895
Tilghman Packing Company	1897
San Juan Fishing & Packing Co.	1903
Mid-Central Fish	1905
Bumble Bee	1906
Marshall Smoked Fish	1908

Vita Food Products	1910
Los Angeles Smoking & Curing	1912
Lynch Foods	1912
Eacho Fish Company	1914
Farmers Seafood	1918
Burhops	1926
Slade Gorton	1929
Certi-Fresh	1932
Morley Sales	1933
J. J. Camillo	1934
J. W. Ferguson	1938

These names represent some of the many pioneers of our seafood heritage. Today's industry numbers more than 2,500 companies engaged in the many facets of processing, selling, and distribution of some 350 varieties of fish and shellfish.

Consider the expressions borrowed from our sea heritage: a fish story, windfall, blubber, taut ship, salty tale, flounder around, he's a little shrimp, that's a whale of a story, and so on.

As the country expanded and developed so did the industry. Gone are the days of running down to the wharf at dawn to choose dinnertime delicacies. Gone are days of the fishermonger calling, "Fresh fish! I got fre-e-e-esh fish!" Gone are those fish markets with sawdust on the floor. Gone are those early model trucks carting fish and seafood to hotels and hospitals.

Refrigeration. Jet planes. Modern processing methods. Supermarkets. These are the symbols of our age which finds people eating fresh fish and seafood in inland cities far from the seven seas. Yet just as today's processors, producers, or distributors take pride in the advancement of their industry, so did yesterday's peddlers take pride in their trade. There is no business like the fish business . . . now or then.

REFERENCES

Ackerman, E. A. 1941. *New England Fishery Industry*. Chicago: University of Chicago Press.

Andreeu, N. N. 1966. *Handbook of Fishery Gear and Its Rigging*. Jerusalem, Israel: Wiener Bindery Ltd.

Anon. *National Fisheries Institute Yearbooks, 1946–53*. Washington, DC.

Anon. 1970. *Twenty-Fifth Anniversary of the National Fisheries Institute Commemorative Issue*. Washington, DC.

Blake, W. H. 1922. *In a Fishery Country*. Toronto: Macmillan of Canada.

Cooke, M. C. 1889. *Toiler in the Sea*. New York: E. & J. B. Young.

Frye, J. 1978. *All the Men Singing*. Virginia Beach: Donning.

Hennessey, T. M. 1983. *The U.S. Fishery Industry & Regulatory Reform*. Wakefield, RI: Times Press.

Innis, N. A. 1940. *The Cod Fisheries*. New Haven, CT: Yale University Press

Knight, H. G. 1977. *Managing the Seas Living Resources*. Lexington, MA: D. C. Heath.

Smith, F. G., & Chapin, H. 1954. *The Sun, the Sea, & Tomorrow*. New York: Scribner & Sons.

Traung, J. O. 1955. *Fishery Boats of the World*. London: Fishery News Books.

CHAPTER

2

Harvesting Techniques

Robert L. Collette

Fishing, born from the need to gather whatever food nature provided, was one of the earliest methods of obtaining food. Little is known about how the early fishing tools developed. It is known that ancient man fashioned hand spears for the animals he hunted, and it is likely that these weapons also served as the first devices for capturing fish. Indeed, these simple spears served as a prototype for more advanced wounding gear.

A tool called the gorge is known to have been used in the Paleolithic era some half a million years ago. It was a short, straight, or curved piece of wood, bone, or other material sharpened at both ends that we speculate was baited and attached to the end of a fiber line. When struck by a fish, the gorge would wedge in its mouth. Although not documented, it is suspected that during this same period our ancestors also learned to entrap fish in small rivers, bays, and inlets.

Historically much of the basic gear used by modern fishermen was developed in Neolithic times, roughly 10,000 B.C. Barbed hooks, nets, gaffs, sinkers, and fiber lines were used by the Egyptians, Greeks, and Romans during this period. The Mayan and Aztec tribes of Central and South America reportedly used the hook-and-line, net, harpoon, and trap, and as early as 1500 B.C. The Chinese fisherman of the period were known to use spun-silk fishing lines.

The pace at which we moved from ancient fishing methods and primitive gear to today's modern techniques has varied considerably. Two factors influencing this evolution were the need to catch fish in bulk rather than singularly, and the need to expand fisheries from shallow waters to greater depths. Today, many variations of the net, trap, and hook-and-line have evolved for specialized fisheries. The greatest changes have come in the materials and design of these nets and traps, in the methods of detecting fish, and in the boats rigged for fishing.

CLASSIFICATION OF HARVESTING TECHNIQUES

Techniques for harvesting fish involve both (1) fishing methods, the ways in which fish may be captured, and (2) fishing gear, the implements or tools used for that capture.

With the hundreds of fish and shellfish species of commercial importance, each with its own characteristic habits and environment, modern fishermen have to use a variety of fishing gear and methods. One common way to classify harvesting techniques is to group them by the gear employed. Fishing gear used today may be grouped into the following categories:

1. Encircling or encompassing gear (seines)
2. Entrapment gear (pound nets, traps, and pots)
3. Lines (troll and longline)
4. Scooping gear (reef net and fish wheel)
5. Impaling gear (harpoon, spear)
6. Shellfish gear (dredges, rakes, tongs, etc.)
7. Entanglement gear (gillnet or trammel net)
8. Miscellaneous and experimental gear

Certain gear such as the harpoon, fish wheel, and some experimental devices are of little commercial significance in world fisheries so we do not discuss them in detail. Nets of all types (some of which were previously listed under separate gear categories) are grouped together and discussed first, since fish nets collectively take most of the world's commercial fisheries catch.

NETS

There are two main types of nets: nets that are used in motion that are drawn, hauled, or towed, and nets that remain stationary or static. Nets are designed for the habits and environment of the fish they are intended to catch. Therefore, some are designed to work at the bottom, others at mid-water or at the surface.

Nets in Motion

The purse seine is a motion net designed for and especially effective in the capture of schooling fish such as mackerel, tuna, sardines, salmon, herring, and menhaden. All purse seines work on the same principle: a wall of net is used to encircle a school of fish. The top of the net is fitted with numerous corks or floats for support, and the bottom of the net is weighted to keep the wall of webbing in an upright position. A pursing cable (purse line) is threaded through rings sewn onto the bottom of the net to allow the fisherman to close off or purse the bottom of the net, thus trapping the fish in an inverted umbrella-shaped enclosure. The basic operation of the purse seine is similar to closing off the drawstrings of an old-fashioned purse.

There are essentially two techniques used to set and haul purse seines. The two-boat system (Fig. 2-1) is commonly used on the East and Gulf coasts of the United States in the menhaden fishery. This system utilizes two small seine boats that are lashed side by side and towed behind a larger carrier or mother ship when on the fishing grounds.

The seine boats are shallow-draft, open boats usually constructed of aluminum and varying in length from 32 to 36 feet (9.7 to 10.9 m). They are hung from the carrier vessel, one on each side. Half of the seine net is carried in each seine boat. The menhaden purse seines used in the two-boat system average 200 fathoms (1,200 feet/365.8 m) in length and 10 fathoms (60 feet/18.3 m) in depth.

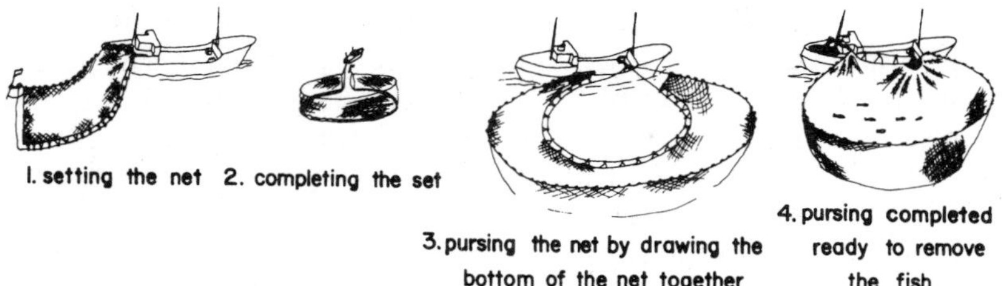
I. setting the net
2. completing the set
3. pursing the net by drawing the bottom of the net together
4. pursing completed ready to remove the fish

Figure 2-1. The Operations Are Basically the Same in Both One-Boat (above) and in Two-Boat Purse Seining. The net is set (far left); the set is completed in a one-boat operation (second from left); the net is pursed by drawing the bottom of the net together; and the pursing is completed in preparation for removing the fish (far right).

Spotler aircraft accompany the seine boats in the search for schools of menhaden. When a school is spotted, the two seine boats begin setting their respective ends of the net. This operation is directed from the spotter aircraft. The seine boats deploy in almost opposite directions, eventually forming a circle around the school. When the two boats meet to form the circle, the ends of the purse line are run through pulleys on either side of the seine, which are attached to a heavy lead weight called a tom. The tom is sent overboard and the ends of the purse line are then hauled together with the aid of a hydraulic power block.

After pushing the seine, the tom is retrieved and the wings of the seine are hauled into the seine boats using power blocks in each boat. The fish are gradually concentrated in the bunt, a section of the net made of heavy twine, positioned between the two seine boats. Once the carrier vessel is alongside, the cork line is secured to its side to form a tight pocket from which the fish cannot escape. A flexible suction hose, attached to a centrifugal pump, is then lowered from the carrier into the net, and the fish are pumped into the hold.

One-boat seining is generally practiced on the Pacific Coast of the United States in the salmon, anchovy, mackerel, and tuna fisheries. The size and design of the West Coast seines differ depending on the species being harvested and local regulations. Seines carried on tuna boats are typically the largest, up to 3,600 feet (10973 m) long and 300 feet (91 m) in depth.

In one-boat seining, the net is carried aboard the carrier vessel (seiner), with an auxiliary boat assisting in setting and hauling it. When a school is sighted, the seiner is maneuvered into position to head off the school. The skiff is put down, and one end of the net, including the purse line, is put into the water and held in position by the skiff. To surround the school of fish, the skiff begins towing away from the seiner as the larger vessel encircles the fish. At the close of the set, the skiff and the seiner turn toward each other. After the skiff comes alongside, the seine is pursed from the seiner and then hauled aboard using a power block. Fish are then brailed (captured with dip nets) or pumped into the hold.

Drum seining is a version of purse seining used exclusively in the Pacific Northwest. The operation of drum seining is similar to the one-boat operation we just described. It differs only in that a large drum, usually hydraulically powered, is mounted at the stern of the seiner, and the entire net is spooled during hauling.

The lampara net is an encircling type net, which is considered the forerunner of the purse seine. The lampara was introduced by Italian fishermen in California late in the last century (Browning, 1974). It is shorter and shallower than the purse seine and can be set and hauled in less time and with less power. It also lacks rings but has a relatively large, simple bunt area and comparatively short wings. The mesh in the wings is generally large; in the bunt it is very small. The gear is set in a circular fashion, similar to the purse seine, and hauled by pulling both wings simultaneously. Lampara nets were used in the defunct California sardine fishery, along the West Coast to take bait for the tuna fishery, and throughout the West Coast mackerel and squid fishery.

Haul or beach seines are the simplest type of seining net. The haul seine, a long strip of netting with the head line (cork line) buoyed and the ground line weighted, is operated from shore. One end of the net is retained on land and the other is drawn through the water encircling the school of fish, and brough back to land. Smelts, shad, striped bass, croaker, bluefish, and weakfish can be caught with haul seines.

Trawling is the most important fishing method used to harvest demersal (bottomfish) species such as cod, haddock, rockfish, flat fish, shrimp, and so on which normally inhabit waters near the seabed. The trawl is a conical-shaped net with a wide mouth and tapers to a socklike or cod end in which the fish collect. Trawl nets consist of the upper and lower nets, joined together at the sides with the upper net extending over the lower net like a roof.

Trawls are subdivided into several categories depending on the method used to spread the net mouth open. In the United States two trawling techniques are used, the beam trawl and the otter trawl (Fig. 2-2), which is by far the more important. These nets range up to 100 feet (30.5 m) across the mouth with a depth of 20 feet (6.1 m) and length of 150 feet (45.7 m). The otter trawl uses two otter boards (or doors) attached by bridles to the wings of the trawl. The boards spread the trawl mouth horizontally. Towing warps (cables) are attached to the opposite side of the boards.

Floats give the headrope buoyancy, which together with a weighted line at the footrope or groundrope, keeps the mouth of the trawl open. On rough fishing grounds the groundrope may be fitted with wooden or steel rollers to assist the net in getting over rocks and debris.

On traditional East Coast or Atlantic otter trawlers, large trawl winches are placed just forward of the house. The trawl nets are shot (set) and hauled from blocks secured to two heavy A-frame gallows mounted on one side of the vessel, usually starboard. In operation the cod end goes overboard first, followed by the midsection, wings, and doors. When the doors are properly set and spaced, the warps are paid out rapidly and the vessel gains speed slightly. When the net sets

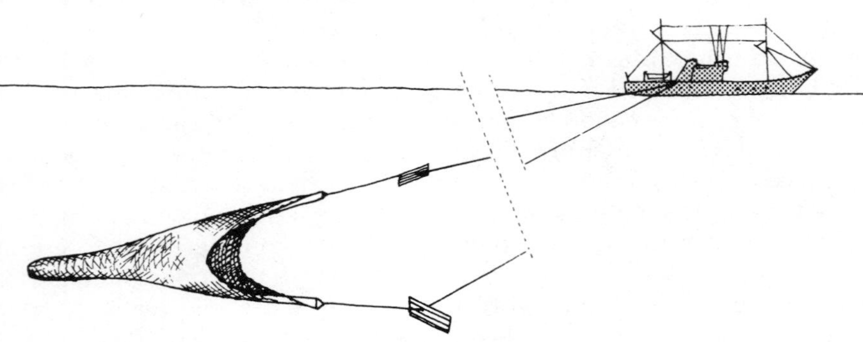

Figure 2-2. Otter Trawl Net.

on the bottom, the warps are drawn together near the stern. Trawling speed is usually between 2 and 5 knots (3.7 to 9.3 km/hr) depending on which fish species is being targeted. Trawling time ranges from thirty minutes to three hours. The process is reversed in hauling back. When the net is alongside the vessel, the doors are hooked to the gallows frames and the bulk of the net is hauled in with the help of quarter ropes. When enough of the trawl is aboard, the cod end is hoisted over the rail by a haul line. Once the cod end is aboard, the fish are released on deck by loosening its puckering strap.

On the West Coast a somewhat different technique is used in operating otter trawl gear. With the possible exception of some halibut schooner vessels, which by design may still use the side trawl method, a large majority of the Pacific trawls are shot over the stern (Fig. 2-3). Typically trawling is carried out by Pacific combination vessels that operate both in the seining and trolling fisheries. When trawling, a pair of gallows frames are secured on each side of the stern with the winch mounted aft of the pilothouse. The combination boats may also use hydraulic drums to assist in setting and hauling the trawl, which is spooled onto the drum from the stern with only the cod end strapped over the side. On some modern vessels stern ramps have been constructed so that the entire trawl can be hauled from the stern.

In bottomfishing, otter trawls are sometimes fished using a two-boat system. Each vessel has one of the towing warps attached to one wing of the trawl. This method is used only for very large nets and is rarely seen in the U.S. fisheries today.

In the early 1900s the shrimping industry switched from haul seines to trawls. Shrimp trawls are much like the East and West Coast otter trawl used for bottomfish, except they generally are smaller and lighter. Shrimp trawlers use double towing booms or outriggers secured to both the main mast and to a larger lifting boom. The towing booms can be rigged to pull one or two nets. In operation, the net(s) is towed from warps, which pass from a winch just behind the pilothouse through a block at the tip of the towing boom. In single-rig towing (one net) the two warps pass through blocks on the same boom, and in double-rig towing (two nets) a single warp for each net passes to blocks at the end of each boom.

Over the last few decades the beam trawl, from which the otter trawl evolved, has been largely replaced by otter trawl, which is more efficient in handling and fishing. In beam trawling, a tapered wooden beam is used instead of otter boards to spread the mouth of the net. To the ends of the beam U- or D-shaped runners are attached. The trawl, about 25 feet (7.6 m) long and tapering to a narrow pocket, is secured directly to the beam and runners. Beam trawls are operated similarly to other trawls, except they are always set from the ship's stern.

Figure 2-3. Side-Trawling (Left) and Stern-Trawling (Right).

Stationary Nets

The gillnet is one of the oldest types of stationary net. Browning (1974) observed that gillnets apparently are a logical, evolutionary development of the simple haul seine. As the name suggests, gillnets are designed to catch fish by the gills as they swim into it. The fish are held or become entangled in the net by their gills as they struggle to escape. The gillnet hangs vertically in the water, although some slack is built into the net to allow it to bulge. It is designed in this manner so fish swimming into a taut section of webbing do not bounce away from it but will entangle themselves.

Like seines, gillnets are vertical walls of webbing and are secured to a cork line and weighted lead line, which keep the net upright in the water column. The length, depth, and mesh size of gillnets vary with federal and state regulations as well as with the fish species being targeted. Two basic forms of the gillnet are commercially important in the United States: the drift net in its several forms and the set or anchor net. Drift nets are used typically on the high seas; set nets are used most often in inshore fisheries. The drift gillnet, designed for pelagic (surface or mid-water) fish such as mackerel, salmon, and saithe, are rectangular and are usually fished in a straight line. Drift nets are commonly set at the surface but can also be fished at intermediate depths or near the bottom. Different sets are made by varying the float and weight rigging.

Since gillnets typically are hung and float from the surface, they are visible to the fish, and therefore are usually fished at night. Once set, drift nets are allowed to drift anchored. Fishermen use marker buoys, or sometimes lanterns attached to floats to follow the drift of the net.

Set gillnets are put out along the seafloor to catch bottom-living fish, such as mullet cod and flatfish. These nets can be held in place by anchors or stakes when the set nets are fished from shore or shallow water. Some gillnets are set so that they fish the middle-water column. These nets are anchored to the bottom and supported by buoys (Fig. 2-4).

Trammel nets, sometimes called tangle nets, are derived from the gillnet (Fig. 2-5). They have three sheets of netting suspended from a common cork line and attached to a lead line at the bottom. The middle net is of fine mesh, loosely hung; the mesh of the two outer sheets is usually three times larger than the center-net mesh. Fish swimming against the trammel net draw the smaller inner mesh

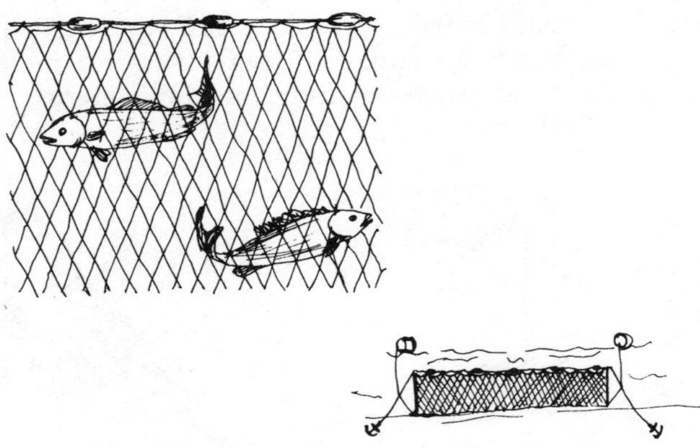

Figure 2-4. Gillnets.

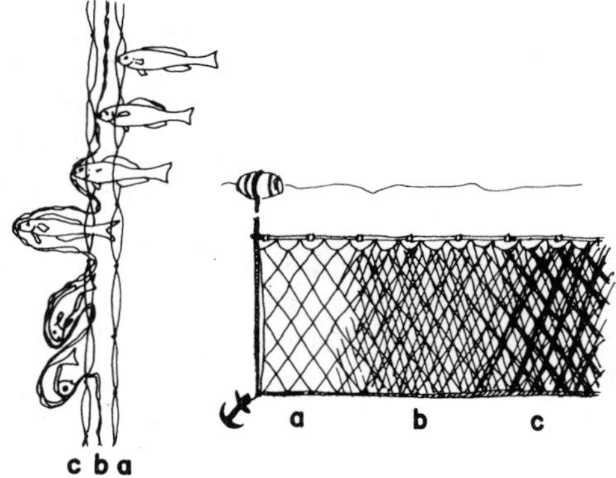

Figure 2-5. Trammel Nets.

through one of the outer meshes and become trapped in the pocket which forms in the net. These nets are typically set in strings by one boat.

Gill and trammel nets usually remain set for twelve to twenty-four hours. They are hauled with the aid of a power roller, although the fisherman must manually assist to get a smooth winding of the net onto the reel. Most gillnet boats are rigged to work their nets from the stern. A noticeable exception exists in the Columbia River salmon gillnet fishery where small boats called bow-pickers are rigged to haul their nets from the bow.

TRAP AND POT GEAR

A wide variety of traps and pots are used to capture fish and shellfish. Capture by trap gear generally depends on attracting fish or shellfish to pots by means of bait or by leading fish into an enclosure, which is the case with pound nets, trap nets, and weirs. Numerous variations in the form and construction of the trap nets are used in American fisheries, but we describe only a few of the more common. First we cover weirs, as they are the primitive prototype of modern trap gears.

Weirs are usually set at a point of land that extends into the water for some distance or in channels, where the tide is strongest, to take advantage of the tendency of fish to stay in a strong current. The weir's main body is a large circular or heart-shaped enclosure, constructed by driving long, heavy posts into the bottom, with smaller posts set closely between. In the traditional weir, fine brush is then interwoven between these smaller posts, horizontally on the lower portion and vertically in the upper part, which is visible at high tide. A lead of brush extends from the shore to the mouth of the trap. These leaders may be as much as 500 feet (152.4 m) long and extend inside the mouth 5 feet (1.5 m) or more. The openings at the mouth are made wide enough for a dory to enter and work the trap.

In most applications, netting has replaced the brush formerly used in the heart of the weirs. During harvesting, a dory enters the weir and the mouth is closed by dropping a net. In some weirs, seines are used to capture the fish; in others, the trap bottom is raised by means of pulleys, and fish are herded into one section where they can be brailed or pumped on board.

Pound nets, which still see limited use in the harvesting of sardine, salmon, and other fish, are slightly more complex than the fish weir. In its simplest form a pound net (Fig. 2-6) consists of three parts: (1) the leader, extending from the shore or shallow water; (2) the heart or wings, a heart-shaped enclosure that deflects the fish; and (3) the pot. The fish are captured and removed from the pot, sometimes called the crib, pound, or pocket. Some pound nets are designed with two or more heart pockets.

Leaders used to guide fish through the series of progressively smaller compartments are up to 800 feet (244 m) long. The lead extends into the entrance of the heart, and fish move from the heart into the pot through an opening called a gate, situated directly in the center. The pound net's pot, which varies in size, is composed of small mesh netting supported by large, anchored poles. This section, like its equivalent in the weir, often has a net bottom secured to the sides. When harvested the bottom is raised, and the fish are brailed or pumped from the pot. In larger pound nets the fish are seined from the inner pocket.

Trap nets are similar in construction to pound nets except the former are supported by floats instead of by poles or stakes. The lead, heart, and pot of a trap net may extend 40 feet (12.2 m) up from the bottom but are completely submerged with only marker buoys visible at the surface.

Fish and shellfish pots or basket traps are one of the primary pieces of harvesting gear used for several commercially important species of crab and lobster. Other species commonly captured by this type gear are shrimp, eel, crawfish, sea bass, and octopus. Dozens of variations in pot design exist, but only the more common pots used in the U.S. fisheries are discussed here.

Crab Pots

On the West Coast, an important type of pot is used in the dungeness crab fishery (Fig. 2–7). The dungeness crab is harvested in estuaries, bays, and along coastal shorelines, usually where smooth, sandy bottoms are found.

The pot is a circular, stainless steel frame, covered with soft stainless steel wire. It ranges in size from 36 to 48 inches (0.91 to 1.22 m) cross and weighs 75 to 160 pounds (34.1 to 72.6 kg). Usually two cone-shaped tunnels are placed at opposite sides of the pot's rounded surface. The tunnels are ramplike structures leading

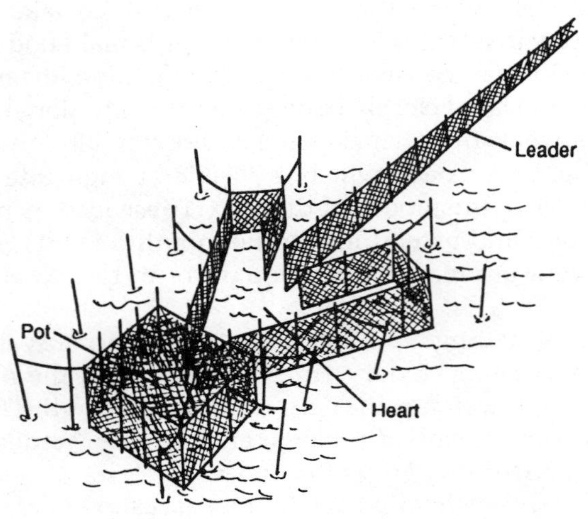

Figure 2-6. Pound Net.

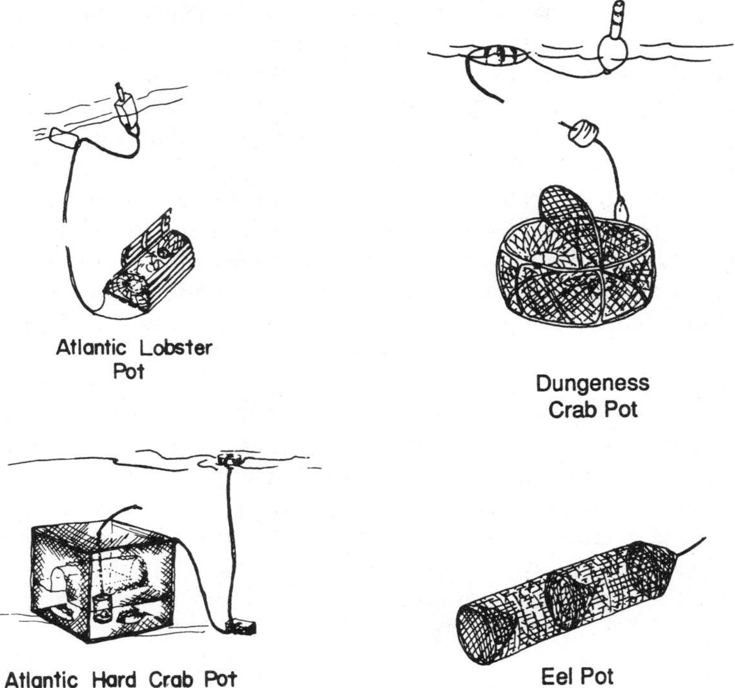

Figure 2-7. Various Pots and Traps Used in Harvesting Seafood.

crabs to the opening (eye) and into the pot. The opening is constructed of small-diameter stainless steel rods equipped with single or double triggers, which are free-swinging, gatelike devices extending from the top of the opening downward across the bottom.

As the crab enters the pot, the trigger closes, preventing escape. The lower flat portion of the pot is weighted so that the pot will sink to the bottom. The lid, one-half the top portion of the pot, is hinged and when closed is held in place with steel hooks attached to rubber bands. A small ring opening on the top or side gives undersized crabs an escape route.

Methods of fishing the pots are generally the same, with only the baits, time of the season, and vessel size differing. Pots are typically baited with herring, squid, or shad and are set in rows, with varying lengths and number of pots. A single line and cylindrical plastic buoy attached to each pot marks the position.

When hauling, the crab vessel usually travels against the current, allowing time to gather in the buoys and start hauling the pot by the time the vessel is over it. Using a crab power block, the pots are taken abroad, emptied, and rebaited before the next pot is hauled. An average boat can haul and reset about 300 pots a day.

Dungeness crab pots served, more or less, as the basis for the development of the Alaskan king crab pot. The king crab pot is similar in construction but much larger and often rectangular rather than circular. The pots are 7 to 9 feet (2.1 to 2.7 m) square, 34 to 36 inches (76.2 to 91.4 cm) deep, and weigh 300 to 400 pounds (136.4 to 181.8 kg) each. Like the dungeness crab pots, king crab pots are fished singularly from a buoy line.

Another important type of pot gear is used in the blue crab fishery, based on the East and Gulf Coasts of the United States. The blue crabs are smaller than dungeness or king crabs so the pot size and design are substantially different. Blue crab pots, introduced to the Chesapeake Bay blue crab fishery in the 1930s, usually are cubical in shape, 2 feet (61 cm) square, and constructed of wire mesh or a rigid metal frame. The pots are divided into a lower chamber, which contains a bait holder and funnels or passageways from the outside, and an upper or trap chamber. Crabs enter the bait chamber through funnels located at the pot's lower edges and then after taking the bait, swim upward through an opening into the trap chamber. Crabs are removed by spreading an opening in one seam at the top and shaking the crabs from the pot. Set singularly on buoy lines along the flat, sandy, or muddy edges of bays and channels in depths from 1 to 10 fathoms (1.8 to 18.3 m), the pots are usually lifted every day and are hauled by hand.

Lobster Pots

Three basic types of lobster pots used throughout the U.S. fishery are recognized by their geometric shapes: the half-round pot, the rectangular pot, and the square pot. These pots are usually constructed of wooden laths or wire. Nearly all modern lobster pots consist of one or two funnels (heads) of coarse netting that slope upward toward the center of the net. The lobster enters through the funnels into the chamber compartment, or kitchen, in search of bait. After grabbing the bait, the lobster moves through a second funnel into another compartment, sometimes called a parlor, where it becomes trapped. It is removed through a door on top of the pot.

In the northern lobster fishery, pots are baited with fish like salted herring, menhaden, skate, and scup. The pots are either set on a single buoy or several may be attached to a longline called a trawl line and weighted so they rest flat on the bottom. Offshore lobster pots are set in trawl lines and are generally larger, heavier, and sturdier than those used in inshore waters.

Pots are hauled after soaking (fishing) one, two, or sometimes three nights, depending on the rate of deterioration of the bait and on the number of pots being fished. As with crabbers, lobster boats are rigged to store the catch live in seawater barrels or tanks.

HOOK-AND-LINE FISHING

Hook-and-line fishing has been used throughout the world for centuries. The objective of modern hook-and-line fishing, comments Alverson (1963), is to orient fishing lines to obtain maximum geographic coverage by the hooks while minimizing the effort needed to handle the gear.

Hook-and-line fishing can be divided into four categories: (1) hand lines, (2) pole and lines, (3) troll lines, and (4) longlines or set lines.

Hand lines are important in the Gulf of Mexico snapper fishery and in some small inshore fisheries. In red snapper fishing, lines about 60 fathoms (360 feet/110 m) long, with two hooks at the end and a lead sinker placed about 1 fathom (6 feet/2 m) above, are set from the deck of the vessel when fish are located. The lines are forked at the end, providing room for two hooks, and are held apart by wire spreaders. Artificial spoons, or sometimes herring, are used as bait and the lines are retrieved using hand reels.

In major commercial fisheries, the pole-and-line method is most prominent in catching tuna and mackerel-like fishes. The poles function to hold lines above deck level. A common rig has two or more poles set in sockets on each side of the boat, and two more lines are set from the stern. In the California tuna fishery, the ends of the poles are laced with a linen or nylon loop to which a 30–48-inch (76–112-cm) length of heavy cotton line is attached. From the cotton line a wire leader is added, with a barbless hook baited with herring or a feather jig (two or more hooks embedded in a small metal fishlike lure) attached to the edge of the leader. Vessels involved in pole and line fishing vary in size and construction from small motorized boats to larger diesel-powered vessels. In the Unites States, yellowfin, skipjack, and albacore tuna are the principal species harvested by this method.

Trolling adds motion to the bait or lure being used. Simple trolling may be conducted by one line, although the modern troll fisheries, such as that for Pacific salmon, use as many lines as possible. Large outriggers or spreader poles are used to space the lines, which are rigged with numerous lures or baited hooks. At the end of the trolling line "cannonballs," 10–50-pound (4.5–22.7-kg) weights, carry the lines to the desired depth and help prevent fouling. Several lines can be fished from each outrigger, and as many as fifteen lures or baited hooks are attached to each line. The number of lines and lures trolled varies with the species sought and is sometimes governed by conservation laws.

Depending on the target species, lures or baited hooks can be fished from the surface down to 80 fathoms (240 feet/146 mm). During fishing, the troller moves forward at the desired speed giving action to the lures. In the salmon fishery, lines are hauled by reels or spools known as gurdies. These gurdy assemblies can be worked by hand but are more often powered by motor or hydraulics.

Longline or set line fishing uses a main or groundline that has a number of short branch lines (droppers, gangens, or offshoots) where baited hooks are attached. Longlines (Fig. 2–8), which may be fished on the bottom, at intermediate depths, or near the surface, have the advantage of needing fewer people to handle the large number of hooks that are fished over a wide area. The halibut fishery of the Pacific Northwest is one of the world's principal longline fisheries. Here the groundline consists of a single string of ten skates (the primary unit of the longline) of 300 fathoms (1800 feet/549 m) each. Hooks are attached to gangens spaced along the groundline. Each skate, with 80 to 120 evenly spaced hooks, is coiled and baited prior to fishing.

When setting the gear, a flag marker—a bamboo pole with a light attached at the top—buoy keg, and anchor are put over as the vessel runs ahead. As the vessel continues on course, the longline is played out through a chute on the stern.

A line vessel may set any number of skates to form a string of gear. When the complete string has been set, another anchor line and float marker are dropped.

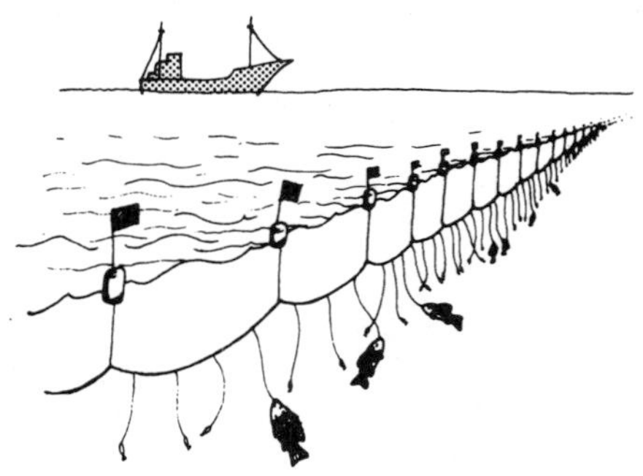

Figure 2-8. Longline sets.

After the gear has been adequately fished, one end of the longline is picked up and the gear retrieved using a power gurdy. As fish are brought to the surface they are gaffed and lifted aboard. During the process the lines are recoiled, baited with herring, octopus, or other baits and readied for the next set. Pelagic species can be fished by longline by rigging the groundline with floats.

Schooners and West Coast combination vessels are the most often used vessels in the halibut longline fishery. However, longline gear can be fished from almost any properly equipped vessel.

SHELLFISH DREDGING AND SCOOPING GEAR

Shellfish such as oysters, clams, mussels, and scallops are sessile (not free-moving) marine animals and hence are harvested by different means than other marine species. Some simple devices popularly used for taking these shellfish include shovels, tongs, and rakes. A somewhat more sophisticated technique, which uses gear known as a dredge, is found in oyster, clam, and scallop fisheries.

Tongs consist of two rakes fixed to the ends of long wooden poles and hinged together with rakelike teeth facing each other. A basketlike frame is attached to each rake to collect the oysters. Oyster tongers typically fish oyster beds or reefs from small wooden, shallow-draft boats usually powered by outboard motors.

The fisherman stands on the deck of the boat, lowers the tongs to the bottom, and by opening and closing the handles, scoops up a quantity of oysters between the heads (Fig. 2–9). The tongs are lifted and the oysters piled on deck. Although slow and laborious, this method is still practiced in many areas because of the limited investment in gear. In some areas tonging is the only method available, as dredges are often considered destructive to natural reefs and are therefore prohibited on public reefs (Fig. 2-10).

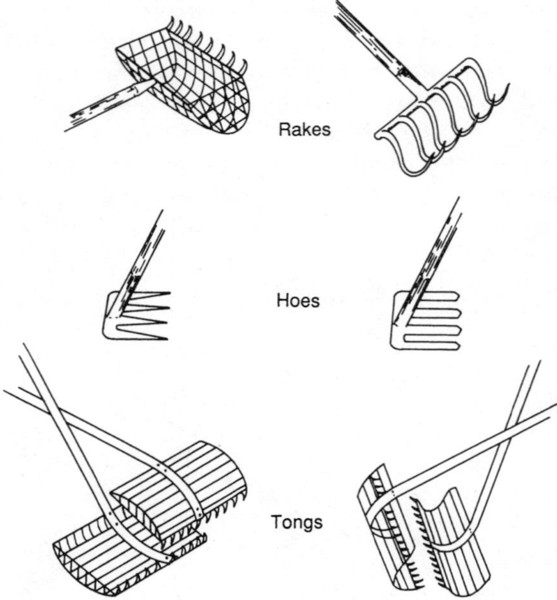

Figure 2-9. Hand-operated Tongs and Rakes Used in Seafood Harvesting.

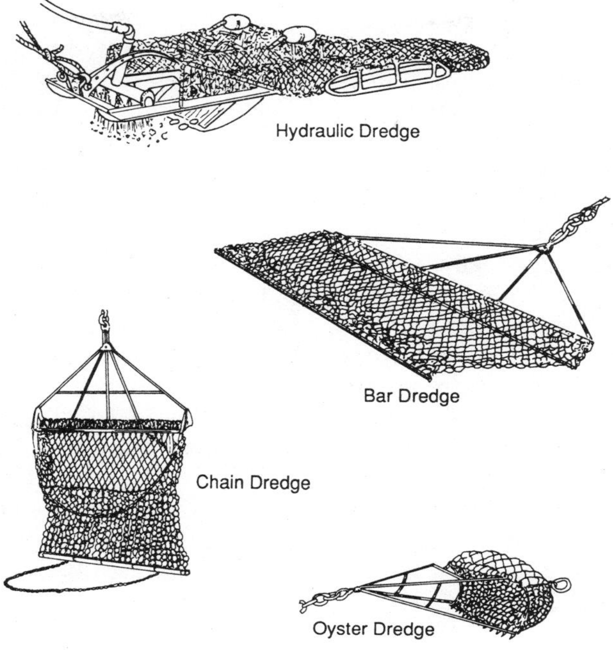

Figure 2-10. Dredges.

Oyster dredging boats tow a dredge or drag consisting of a metal frame that has a toothed "raking" bar across the front, which in turn is attached to a bag-shaped net made of metal rings. The frame is connected to a towing cable by a triangular A-frame. As the dredge is towed across the reef, the rake bar dislodges the oysters, and they roll back across the drag bag into the metal mesh bag. When the bag is full the dredge is lifted and the contents dumped onto the deck.

Specialized suction and scoop dredges are also used in this fishery. A suction dredge creates suction at the head of the dredge. Oysters and water are suctioned up to a continuous conveyor located on the deck. The scoop-type harvester consists of a rakelike dredge with steel teeth. The dredge, which rests on runners to prevent excessive digging, is attached to a chain conveyor. In operation, oysters raked by the dredge are scooped by conveyor's loops and carried to the deck.

Clams and mussels are taken by various types of rakes or by dredge. A regular clam rake is similar to a common steel garden rake except it is heavier and has longer, sharper teeth that are spaced about an inch apart and are curved distinctly upward. Clam rakes varying in widths and handle lengths are designed for shallow water digging. A basket rake is one adapted for digging clams in deep water with a handle that may be 35 feet (11 m) long, much longer than the regular clam rake. The end of the basket-rake handle is fitted with a crosspiece to aid in dragging it across the clam bed, and a basket of wire or netting is attached to the back of the rake to hold the clams. A third rake used in harvesting clams, the bull rake, has a long handle like the basket rake but does not have a mesh basket attached. The bull rake is designed much like the regular clam rake only it is wider and has more teeth. All clam rakes can be operated from small boats, but the regular clam rake can also be handled from shore. In either case, the teeth are worked into the sand or mud of the bottom, and the rake is then pulled in and lifted out of the water.

As in the oyster fishery, the majority of clams are taken by dredge. Clam dredges are operated with or without hydraulic equipment. The hydraulic or jet dredge is most often used for surf clams and ocean quahogs because of its effectiveness in extracting these mud-burrowing clams. During operation, pressurized water supplied by a hydraulic pump on board the vessel is pumped through jets located in front of the toothed bar. The jets of water loosen the bottom, allowing the clam to be scooped more efficiently. The hydraulic dredge may collect the clams in a metal ring bag or deposit them directly on deck via a conveyor.

Essentially all commercially harvested scallops are taken by dredge. The scallop dredge consists of an iron framework about 3 by 1½ feet (91 by 46 cm), with an attached netting bag, which will hold one to two bushels of scallops. A single scallop boat often pulls several dredges across the scallop grounds.

Among the many scallop dredge styles, the scraper is one of most popular. It has a rigid, triangular iron frame; a raised crossbar connecting the two arms; and a lower strip of iron, about 2 inches (5 cm) wide and set at an angle, for digging in the sand.

Abalone, sponges, and sometimes oysters are harvested by hand by fishermen who use various hand tools to gather the shellfish. The catch is stored in a net bag until it is full, then it is raised to the surface and emptied by a second fisherman tending the vessel. Although tedious, this method is extremely selective.

MISCELLANEOUS AND EXPERIMENTAL GEAR

Here we briefly describe some additional fishing methods, which either have a limited impact on commercial fisheries or are still in the experimental stage of development.

Jigging is a hook-and-line technique used most notably to harvest squid, although it is not used to any significant extent in U.S. fisheries. Jigging involves setting a line with baited hooks or lures; then a jigging machine provides a constant jerking motion on the line to induce fish to take the hook.

Harpooning is of great historical but declining importance. It is still the major method for taking whales, but whaling has been banned by most nations including the United States. Swordfish, shark, and tuna are still taken by harpoon, although longline methods have all but replaced it in those fisheries. In practice, harpoons can be thrown by hand or shot from a gun.

Cast nets, circular-shaped nets popular along the gulf of Mexico and on the Pacific Coast, were once important gear in the shrimp fishery but today are more often used by sport fishermen. A cast net is draped over one arm and thrown so it spreads out in a flat circle; the weight of the lead line carries it to the bottom.

Gigging is another method used primarily by sport fishermen. The fisherman, using a spearlike instrument called a gig, wades through shallow waters and spears or gigs the fish when it has been spotted. Flounder are often caught by this method.

A number of fishing techniques rely on physical or chemical stimuli such as light, electricity, and odors. Most of these methods are experimental, although lights already have practical application and are used in a variety of fisheries to attract fish into traps or to aggregate them so they may be netted. Lights are used to capture bait fish and are used extensively in the eel fishery. Although electricity for shocking or guiding fish has been used experimentally since World War II, it has not yet been employed extensively in marine fisheries.

REFERENCES

Alverson, Dayton L. 1963. "Fishing Gear and Methods." In *Industrial Fishery Technology,* edited by Maurice E. Stansby. Huntington, NY: Krieger.

Browning, Robert J. 1974. *Fisheries of the North Pacific.* Anchorage, AK: Alaska Northwest.

Schmidt, Peter G. 1960. "Purse Seining: Deck Design and Equipment." In *Fishing Boats of the World,* edited by Jan-Olof Traung. London: Fishing News (Books) Ltd.

Tressler, Donald K., and Lemon, James. McW. 1951. *Marine Products of Commerce.* New York: Reinhold.

CHAPTER

3

Groundfish

George J. Flick, Gi-Pyo Hong, Jhung Won Hwang, and Genaro C. Arganosa

In commercial fishing, groundfish (or bottomfish) are defined as those species that feed on the bottom, sometimes referred to as demersal organisms because they live close to the bottom of a body of water that is limited by the continental shelf. On the East Coast of the United States, this range extends out in places over 200 miles (322 km); the West Coast has a much narrower shelf extending only about 10 miles (16 km). During the last twenty years, populations of many bottomfish species have decreased greatly. However, groundfish as a whole still represent about 12 percent of the weight of all finfish landed by U.S. fishermen and about 20 percent of the value. Table 3-1 lists the major fish species caught on both the East and West coasts.

Table 3-1. ***West and East Coast Common Groundfish Species***

	Occurrence	
Species	West Coast	East Coast
Butterfish		X
Cod	X	X
Flounder		X
Grouper		X
Hakes	X	X
Haddock		X
Halibut	X	
Ling cod	X	
Mackerel	X	X
Perch	X	X
Plaice		X
Pollock (whiting)	X	X
Rockfish	X	
Sablefish	X	
Sea Bass		X
Scup		X
Sole		
Yellow fin	X	
Other	X	
Turbot		X
Witch flounder		X
Yellow tail		X

THE COD FAMILY

Spanish explorers came to the New World to find gold and precious stones, but the French and Portuguese, followed by the English, crossed the Atlantic to catch fish, especially the Atlantic cod. In the sixteenth century, French and Portuguese vessels fished the Grand Bank off Newfoundland. By the early seventeeth century, the New England colonists were fishing for cod in the local waters. In 1748 the first catch of cod from Georges Bank was landed.

Cod probably has influenced the course of American history more than any other marine fish. Its white flaky flesh was the foundation of power and wealth in colonial America. Cod was the first product shipped out of colonial Massachusetts. A large wooden codfish carving was hung in the Massachusetts State House in 1784 and still occupies an honored position there.

As a commercial fish, cod had no peer. It was abundant all year, and when split, salted, and dried, it kept almost indefinitely in any climate. Many long sea voyages would not have been possible without dried cod, as ships could carry no perishable food as staples.

The cod family, from an economic point of view, is the most important of all the fish families, and members of the cod family are second only to the herring family in volume of commercial landings (Table 3-2). In 1987 30.2 billion pounds (13.7×10^9 kg) of the cod family were landed worldwide compared with 49 billion pounds (22×10^9 kg) of the herring family. In contrast to the herring family, which is often used for industrial purposes, almost all of the cod, haddock, hakes, and whitings are used for human food.

Classification

Twenty-five species of fishes in the cod family, *Gadidae,* are listed by the American Fisheries Society. They include (1) toothed cod, *Arctogadus borisovi;* (2) polar cod, *Arctogadus glacialis;* (3) Arctic cod, *Boreogadus saida;* (4) saffron cod, *Eleginus gracilis;* (5) Pacific cod, *Gadus macrocephalus;* (6) Atlantic cod, *Gadus morhua morhua;* (7) Greenland cod, *Gadus ogac;* (8) cusk, *Brosme brosme;* (9) fourbeard rockling, *Enchelyopus cimbrius;* (10) burbot, *Lota lota;* (11) haddock, *Melanogrammus aeglefinus;* (12) silver hake (whiting), *Merluccius bilinearis;* (13) Pacific hake, *Merluccius productus;* (14) longfin hake, *Phycis chesteri;* (15) luminous hake, *Steindachneria argentea;* (16) red hake, *Urophycis chuss;* (17) Gulf hake, *Urophycis cirratus;* (18) Carolina hake, *Urophycis earlli;* (19) southernhake, *Urophycis floridanus;* (20) spotted hake, *Urophycis regius;* (21) white hake, *Urophycis tenuis;* (22) Pacific tomcod, *Microgadus proximus;* (23) Atlantic tomcod, *Microgadus tomcod;* (24) Atlantic pollock, *Pollachius virens;* and (25) walleye (Alaska) pollock, *Teragra chalcogramma.*

Table 3-2. ***World Commercial Catch of Fish by Species Groups, 1984–87 (1,000 metric tons, live weight)***

Species Group	1984	1985	1986	1987
Herring, sardines, anchovies, etc.	19,619	21,101	23,968	22,227
Cods, hakes, haddock, etc.	12,258	12,451	13,535	13,703
Freshwater fishes	8,024	8,746	9,481	10,142
Miscellaneous marine and diadromous fish	8,426	8,773	9,510	9,622
Jacks, mullets, sauries, etc.	8,562	8,013	7,182	7,866
Redfishes, basses, congers, etc.	5,448	5,208	5,994	5,732

Although European ichthyologists separate hakes and cods because of differences in the structure of the skull and ribs, some American experts group them into a single family, and they are so listed by the American Fisheries Society.

The Cods

Cods are soft-finned fish lacking true spines, although in the whiting, the dorsal and anal fin rays are so stiff they feel like spines. The cod family is distinguished from other soft-rayed fish by their large pelvic fins situated under or in front of the pectorals (not behind as in salmon and herring). Generally fishes of cold water, most cods live close to the bottom. Table 3-3 lists the changes in various cod species landings over a thirteen-year period from 1974 to 1987.

Codfish are found on both sides of the Atlantic Ocean, in the north Pacific Ocean, and in the Arctic Ocean down to about 1,500 feet (457 m). The best cod fishing grounds are offshore banks including Georges Bank, 150 miles (241 km) off Boston, Massachusetts and Grand Bank off Newfoundland where modern trawlers may take 35 tons (32 metric tons) of cod in a few hours of fishing.

The most important of the cods is the Atlantic cod, which includes several geographical subspecies. These are the Baltic cod *(Gadus morhua callarias)* found in the Baltic Sea and parts of the North Sea; the Kildin Island cod *(Gadus morhua kildinensis)*, which lives in a salt pond, Lake Mogilno, on an island in the Baltic Sea; and the White Sea cod *(Gadus morhua marisalbi)*, found in the Arctic Sea. The Greenland cod, *Gadus ogac*, often considered a separate species, is found mostly in inlets and in the shallow water of the Arctic Ocean from west Greenland to Point Barrow, Alaska. Additionally, the Pacific cod *(Gadus macrocephalus)* is considered by most taxonomists as a separate species.

Atlantic Cod

In a side view, the Atlantic cod (Fig. 3-1) is oval with three distinct dorsal fins, two anal fins, and a nearly square tail. Its color varies from olive green to reddish brown

Table 3-3. ***World Commercial Catch of Cod Family, Excluding Hakes (1,000 metric tons, live weight)***

Species	1974	1987
Atlantic cod	2,811,495	2,054,721
Pacific cod	161,533	441,107
Greenland cod	3,391	4,017
Polar cod	125,188	11,713
Haddock	581,488	398,522
Pollock	716,411	17,868
Alaska pollock	4,907,362	6,703,868
Ling	67,328	58,124
Blue ling	9,782	27,365
Norway pout	895,499	321,082
Bib	25,067	24,496
Blue whiting	45,863	707,955
Atlantic tomcod	271	10
Grenadier	14,100	30,380

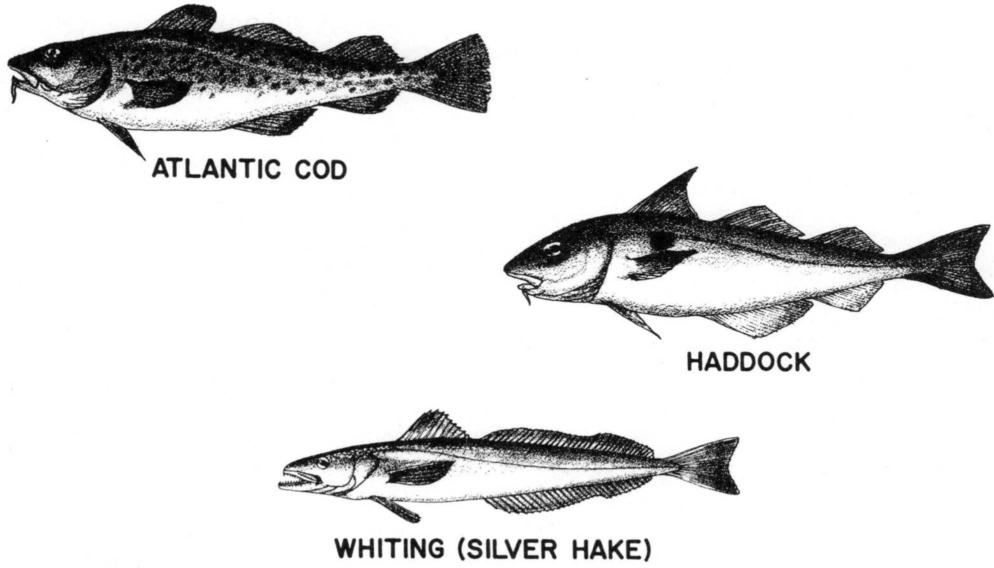

Figure 3-1. Atlantic Cod, Haddock, and Whiting (Silver Hake) Are Three of the More Common Groundfish.

depending on its habitat. The lateral line is white, and the skin has many small scales. Most cod average about 3 feet (91.4 cm) long and weigh 10 to 25 (4.5 to 11.3 kg) pounds. A giant cod caught by commercial fishermen off the Massachusetts coast in 1895 measured over 6 feet (1.8 m) in length and weighed 211¼ pounds (95.8 kg). It was obviously an old fish, but no one knows how old.

Although the cod is a demersal (bottom-living) fish, when in search of food it may be found near the surface. It prefers rocky, pebbly, or sandy bottoms, and water temperatures from 32 to 50°F (0 to 10°C). An adult cod feeds mostly on smaller fish such as sand eels, herrings, other small cod, and on shellfish such as shrimp, mussels, clams, crabs, and squid. When hungry, it will eat almost anything, even false teeth, old boots, and pieces of wood. At times, it eats small floating mollusks, which can cause it to give off a strong odor of iodine when cooked. Cod migrate principally because of changes in the temperature of the water, better availability of food, and the search for suitable spawning locations.

Growth rates differ from ground to ground, but the cod is relatively fast growing and can theoretically live to 50 years of age. A one-year-old cod is usually about 7 inches (18 cm) long; a two-year-old will be about 14 inches (35.6 cm); and by the end of the third year, the cod is about 22 inches (55.9 cm) long, though growth is slower in colder waters. Cod in Arctic waters reach maturity in six to eight years at 6 to 8 inches (15.2 to 20.3 cm) in length.

The cod is one of the more prolific fishes. It has been calculated that if all the eggs spawned by all female cod in one season were to survive, the oceans would be one mass of cod. One female cod may release 3 to 7 million eggs at a time. Spawning takes place in shallow waters (30 to 150 feet or 9.1 to 45.7 m) usually in the early spring. At 43°F (6.2°C), hatching may be expected in fourteen or fifteen days, and then the newly hatched larvae feed mainly on plankton and drift with surface currents. When the larvae have grown to about 3 inches (7.6 cm), they move to the ocean bottom where they feed on worms and small shrimps. Only a few out of the millions of eggs spawned will survive to become mature fish.

Pacific Cod

The Pacific cod is also known as cod, true cod, and gray cod. In appearance and habits, it resembles its cousin, the Atlantic cod. In 1987 close to 170 million pounds (77.2×10^6 kg) of Pacific cod were landed in the United States with a value of $31.4 million. The five-year average (1982 to 1986) was 104.0 million pounds (47.2×10^6 kg) compared with 91.5 million pounds (41.3×10^6 kg) of Atlantic cod. The Pacific cod has a large head, three dorsal fins, and two anal fins. Its color is brown to gray on the upper surfaces and white on the anal and caudal fins with many brown spots on the back and sides. It grows fast, reaching an average length of 3 feet-3-inches (99 cm) and a weight of 35 pounds (15.9 kg) in two to three years.

Pacific cod are found in the North Pacific Ocean from California to northern Alaska and in a great arc to Korea. Spawning takes place in winter or early spring, although the spawning grounds are relatively unknown. As many as half a million eggs may be produced by each female and they hatch in eight or nine days at 52°F (11°C). The young fish usually migrate northward to the colder waters of Washington, Oregon, or Alaska. They mature within two to three years with an eight- to nine-year life span.

The Pacific cod's white flesh has a mild flavor and flakes easily. It is marketed as fresh and frozen fillets with some of the catch sold as whole fresh fish.

Polar Cod

The polar cod (Fig. 3-2) normally grows only 6 to 8 inches (15 to 20 cm) long but may grow to 15 inches (38 cm). It resembles the pollock and is found in the Arctic Ocean from Greenland to Siberia. It is circumpolar, traveling the White Sea to Iceland, Greenland, Canada, Alaska, and so on. It may be distinguished from related species by a forked tail and slender body. The polar cod is generally not considered important for human food.

A cousin, the Arctic cod, is being fished by the Norwegians for meal and oil but is also of little importance as a food.

Greenland Cod

The Greenland cod is very similar to the Atlantic cod in form but lacks the distinguishing round spots of the Atlantic cod, and its lateral line is not accompanied by a light longitudinal stripe on the tail like the Atlantic cod. It grows to 28 inches (71 cm) long and ranges from west Greenland, west to Point Barrow, Alaska, and then along the Arctic coast east and south to the Miramichi estuary, Gulf of St. Lawrence, and Cape Breton Island. Its commercial importance is indicated by a catch of 4,017 tons (3,643 metric tons) in 1987 (Table 3-3).

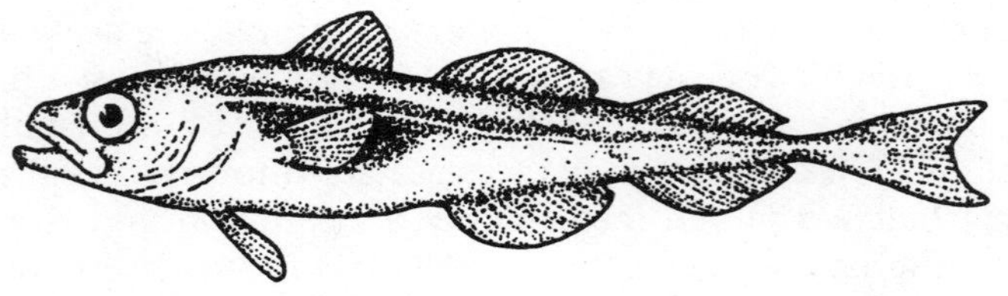

Figure 3-2. Polar Cod

Haddock

The most valuable member of the cod family in the United States is the haddock (Fig. 3-1), which has as distinguishing marks a black lateral line; a sooty black shoulder blotch called the "Devil's thumb print" or "St. Peter's mark"; and a pointed first dorsal fin.

Haddock are found in the North Atlantic Ocean along the coasts of Newfoundland, Nova Scotia, and the Gulf of Maine, and on Georges Bank. In the northeast Atlantic, it is found off the coast of northern Europe, the British Isles, and Iceland. Haddock are bottom-dwelling fish in areas where water temperatures range from 35 to 48°F (1.7 to 8.9°C). They are usually caught on an ocean bottom that is of hard, smooth sand, gravel, or broken shell. They like smooth areas between rocky patches.

Haddock in the Gulf of Maine spawn from late February until May with a peak in March and April. A prolific fish for its size, a single haddock may produce from 150,000 to 1 million eggs. A 19½-inch (49.5 cm) female produces 169,000 eggs; a 24-inch (61 cm) one, 634,000 eggs; and a 28¼-inch (71.8 cm) one, 1.84 million eggs. Spawning occurs near the seabed but the eggs are buoyant and are found near the sea's surface. Haddock eggs hatch in thirteen to twenty-four days at 41°F (5°C) and the larvae, about 3/16 inch (0.5 cm) long, drift with the current. The tiny haddock are nourished at first by the egg yolk and later feed on zooplankton. At about four to five months, the young haddock start to descend to the ocean floor where they live the rest of their lives, eating shrimp, crabs, worms, squid and, at times, small fish.

During its first three years, a haddock grows fast. A one-year-old haddock averages 7½ inches (19.1 cm) long; a two-year-old haddock, 12¼ inches (32 cm); and a three-year-old haddock, 17 inches (43.2 cm). The haddock seldom grows longer than 36 inches (91.4 cm) or weighs over 25 pounds (11.3 kg).

Most of the U.S. haddock catch is taken with otter trawls, funnel-shaped nets that are towed over the seafloor behind a fishing vessel. Some haddock are also caught with longlines, fish traps, and gillnets.

From 1924 to 1966, the haddock fishery never yielded less than 100 million pounds (45.4×10^6 kg), but by 1976 the catch was only 12.8 million pounds (5.8×10^6 kg). In 1986 the catch was reduced to 10.9 million pounds (4.9×10^6 kg); in 1987 to 6.7 million pounds (3×10^6 kg).

Caught, handled, and processed much the same as Atlantic cod, haddock is used to make a number of smoked fish products, like finnan haddie and other cold-smoked products such as the golden cutlet and the smoked single fillet. The chemical composition of haddock flesh is similar to that of cod.

Atlantic Pollock

The Atlantic pollock (Fig. 3-3), also known as pollock, is another cod relative. It is dark greenish in color and usually olive or greenish gray with silver tints on the

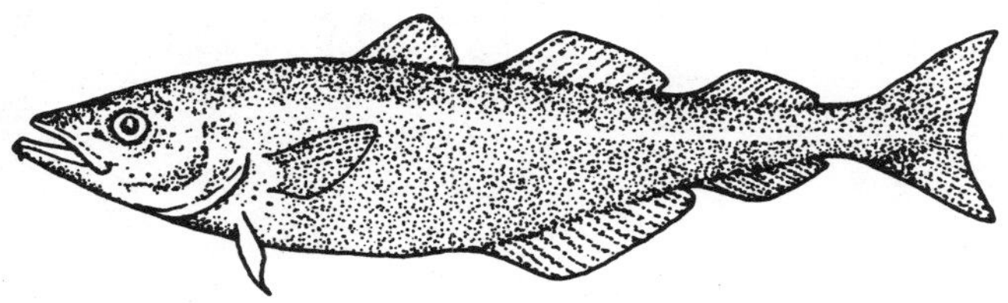

Figure 3-3. Atlantic Pollock.

lower side. A light lateral line extends the length of the body and is in contrast to the dark sides. It has a spindle-shaped streamlined body with a forked tail. Atlantic pollock average 2 to 3 feet (6 to 9 m) long and weigh 4 to 12 pounds (1.8 to 5.4 kg). Large pollock feed on other fish; smaller ones feed on crustaceans.

The pollock is seldom taken at temperatures above 50°F (10°C), and most are caught in mid-water using high opening trawls. One of the most active members of the cod family, it occurs in large schools that may be found at any level between the surface and the bottom.

Spawning in late fall and early winter, large pollock may produce over 4 million eggs, although the average number is about 22,000. The buoyant eggs hatch in six days at 50°F (10°C) water temperature. The fish will be 5 to 7 inches (13 to 18 cm) long by the end of the first year and usually reach 18 inches (45.7 cm) after three years.

Small pollock migrate into coastal waters in the spring, remain all summer, then move to deeper water in the winter. Pollock often school at this time with 80 percent of the landings taken during October, November, and December.

The pollock is similar in flavor, odor, and texture to cod and haddock and is usually marketed in fillet form. It makes a good, dry salt fish and some are smoked.

Alaska Pollock

The Alaska or walleye pollock (Fig. 3-4) is an important food fish, with pollock blocks accounting for 25 percent of all block imports in 1976. The Republic of Korea is a principal supplier of pollock blocks, followed by Japan.

The Alaska pollock, low in the marine food chain, feeds on planktonic crustaceans such as copepods, amphipods, and shrimplike eupahusiids. These are concentrated in the nutrient-rich, shallow waters of the continental shelf and slope. The pollock usually matures at three to four years when it is about 15 inches (38 cm) long.

HAKE

The origins of the word *hake* are not clear. According to the Oxford English Dictionary the first usage was in the fourteenth or fifteenth century, and the word as presently understood refers in general to the genus *Merluccius* and several other genera of gadoid (codlike) fishes.

Fish species classified in the genus *Merluccius* as well as several other genera are often considered to be members of a family Merluciidae, which, although related, are distinct from the Gadidae or cod family. The various named species of *Merluccius* are rather similar in appearance, and there is not at this time any good way to assign correct scientific names to *Merluccius* from many regions of the world. There

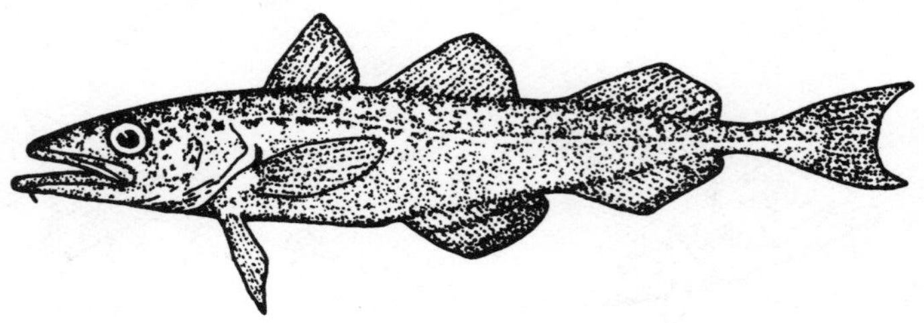

Figure 3-4. Alaska (or Walleye) Pollock.

may be as few as four or as many as fifteen or more different biological species. Whatever the number and correct scientific names of *Merluccius* species, all are known in English-speaking countries as hake.

Other English language names, chiefly whiting, also are used for *Merluccius*. The U.S. Food and Drug Administration has approved the designation as whiting of five nominal species of *Merluccius bilinearis* from the East Coast of North America; *productus* from the West Coast of North America; *capensis* from South Africa; *gayi* from Chile; and *hubbsi* from Argentina. In South Africa, stockfish is another name for *Merluccius*.

Hake is used as a common name for a number of kinds of fish other than *Merluccius*. Among the Gadidae are six species of Urophycis from the western Atlantic: *chuss*, red or squirrel hake (Fig. 3-5); *cirratus*, Gulf hake; *earlii*, Carolina hake; *floridanus*, southern hake; *regius*, spotted hake (Fig. 3-6); and *tenuis*, white, black, mud, or Boston hake. Several other species of Urophycis live along the East Coast of South America but do not have English language common names. The related gadid genus Phycis has one western Atlantic species, *P. chesteri* (Fig. 3-7), called the long-finned hake and two eastern Atlantic species known as forkbeards. Two members of the gadoid family Moridae must be listed, the nearly cosmopolitan deep-sea *Antimora rostrata*, known as blue hake, and the New Zealand *Lotella rhacina*, called southern hake or rock cod. Finally, *Rexea solandri*, a member of the Gempylidae or snake mackerel family, and not related to the cods, has hake as an alternative name in both New Zealand and Australia.

As noted earlier, the name whiting is used interchangeably with hake for *Merluccius;* however, it is used also for fishes that are not called hakes. Among them are three species of European Gadidae: *Merlangius merlangus*, whiting; *Trisopterus luscus*, whiting pout, an alternate name for bib; and *Micromesistius poutassou*, blue whiting (caught rarely off the U.S. East Coast where it has no common name). Whiting is also an alternate name for the eastern North Pacific gadid *Theragra chalcogramma*, often called walleye pollock. Members of the genus *Menticirrhus* of the croaker family Sciaenidae, not at all closely related to gadoids and with three Atlantic and one Pacific U.S. species, are known collectively as whitings, although each also has other common names. Species belonging to several other families of fishes unrelated to gadids are known as whitings; among them are the spiny-rayed *Sillaginidae* of the Indian Ocean and western Pacific, and the *Odaciidae*, called rock whitings, wrasse-like (spiny-finned) fishes of Australia and New Zealand. Finally sand whiting is listed as an alternate for the bothid flatfish, *Scopthalmus aquosus*, most commonly known as windowpane.

Obviously, the nomenclature of hakes and whitings is complex. Positive iden-

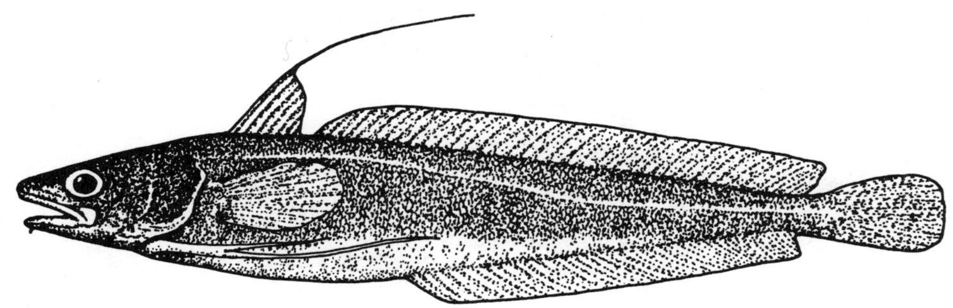

Figure 3-5. Red Hake.

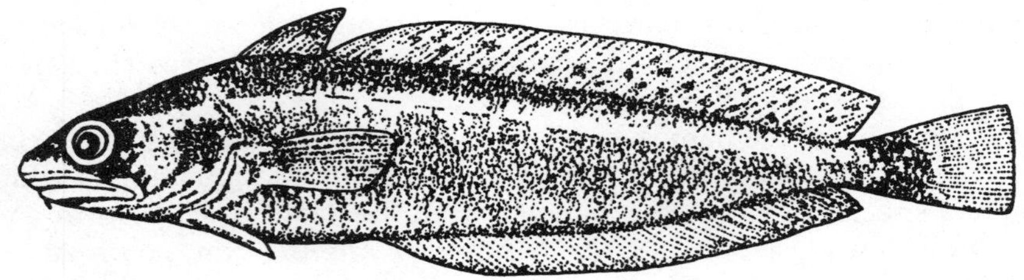

Figure 3-6. Spotted Hake.

tification of a species referred to under these names may require reference to a Latinized scientific name, although even some of these are subject to question. Yet hakes are found worldwide.

Whiting or silver hake (Fig. 3-1) are found on the continental shelf from Newfoundland to South Carolina. In winter, they move into deeper water and go further south. Whiting are silvery over the whole body with brown or dark gray tints on the upper surface of the body. They have two dorsal fins and one anal fin with no barbel on the lower jaw. They reach a length of about 2½ feet (76.2 cm) and a weight of 5 pounds (2.3 kg).

Whiting are lean, firm-textured, flaky fish and are very tasty. The two major U.S. market forms are either headed and eviscerated fish or filleted. A small amount of the headed and eviscerated whiting is smoked.

Pacific hake (Fig. 3-8) are found from the Gulf of California to the Gulf of Alaska and from the surface to almost 3000 feet (915 m). Most Pacific hake are long, with a record length of about 3 feet (91 cm). Their color ranges from gray to dusty brown with a brassy overtone. Because of certain deficiencies of texture of the flesh, the Pacific hake has not commanded a very large market, although recent attempts to popularize this fish may result in more widespread acceptance.

White hake, also called Boston hake, is muddy colored or purplish brown on the back. The sides may be bronze, and the belly is grayish white or yellowish white, peppered with tiny black dots. The maximum length is about 4 feet (1.2 m), the weight 40 pounds (18 kg), but most average no more than 5 to 8 pounds (2.3 to 3.6 kg). There are only two dorsal fins (the second is much longer than the first), one anal fin, and the ventral fins are long and narrow. Found in deep water from Newfoundland to Cape Hatteras, the white hake is usually found on soft, muddy bottoms, where it feeds on small crustaceans, squid, and small fish. Larger fish are usually marketed as fresh or frozen fillets; smaller ones are used for animal feed.

The *red hake* (Fig. 3-5) usually weighs 1 to 3 pounds (454 to 1361 g) and seldom measures over 30 inches (76 cm) long. It is reddish in color on the back and sides

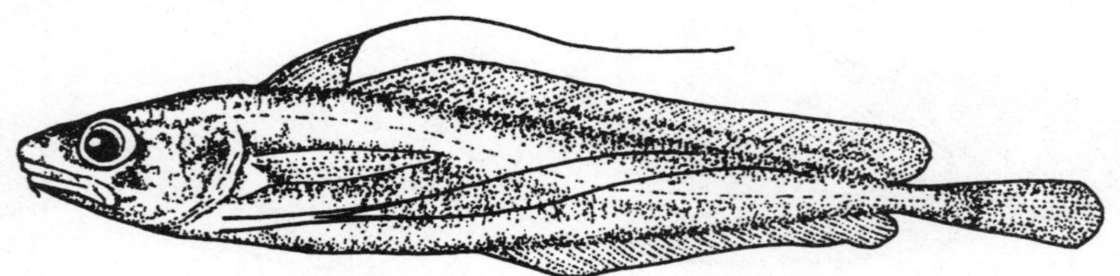

Figure 3-7. Long-finned Hake.

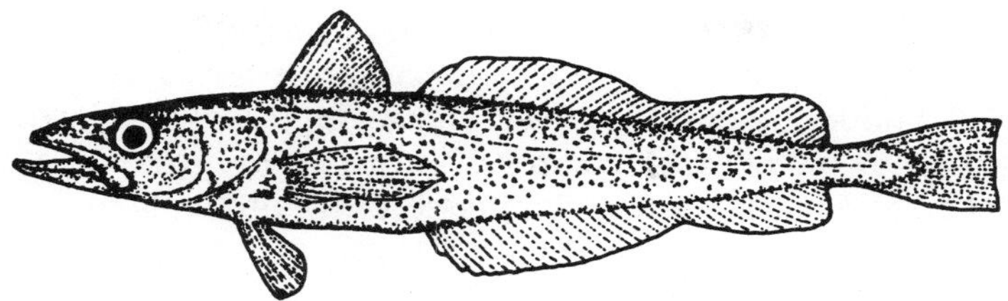

Figure 3-8. Pacific Hake.

and white to yellowish on the belly. Red hake is abundant off the U.S. East Coast and could be used to produce fish protein concentrate. A 5-year average landing (1982 to 1986) of red hake was 4.66 million pounds (2.1×10^6 kg) with 4.43 (2.01×10^6 kg) million pounds landed in 1987.

Sluggish swimmers, red hake are usually found over soft bottoms. The young hakes are abundant and usually remain close to shore in eel grass beds, where they feed on small crustaceans, squid, and small fish. Spawning usually occurs from July through September in shoal waters. Red hake grows to 8 inches (20 cm) by the end of the first year and from 16 to 19 inches (41 to 48 cm) at 3 years of age. Dense schools of red hake migrate in early spring into shoal waters. Hakes move around less than cod and haddock and tolerate a greater temperature range. Red hake is usually marketed as fresh or frozen fillets with smaller fish used for mink, cat, and poultry feed.

The *South African hake,* called stockfish by the South Africans, is a fairly large fish, growing up to 4 feet (1.2 m) long. It is silvery gray with a spot of black on the inside of its lower front fins. A bottom dweller, it is usually caught by trawlers in huge nets pulled along the sea bottom in depths of 1,800 feet (549 m). Large amounts of the South African hake are made into fish blocks, which are used for producing fish sticks and portions.

Argentine hake is usually found off the coast of Uruguay during winter (May and June). The schools then concentrate in the southern Argentina region. It has been estimated that a possible annual yield of 1.2 million pounds (545×10^3 kg) could be exported. Most of the production goes into fillet blocks, but consideration is being given to boil-in-the-bag frozen products to take advantage of superior packaging.

The *blue whiting,* a gadoid fish, can be recognized by its bluish color, long slender shape, and lack of barbel. It is usually found in waters about 600 feet (183 m) deep, at or beyond the edge of the continental shelf. It is distributed from the Mediterranean to Norway and Iceland, with some found in the Barents Sea. Large amounts have been located west of Britain and in the Norwegian Sea.

A stock of at least several million tons of blue whiting is thought to exist in the northeast Atlantic west of the British Isles. At present, it appears most likely that this species could sustain an annual yield of over 1 million metric tons (1.1 million tons), which could be used in the manufacture of a wide range of fishery products. Considerable research is being carried out by Great Britain to market this fish in the form of fish blocks.

Utilization of Hake

In recent years hake has become an increasingly important world fishery. In the 1960s hake was used mainly for fish meal production, especially in South America. At the same time, active interest developed for certain Atlantic hake stocks for human consumption. During the last few years, with growing pressure on cod supplies, hake has emerged as one of the more promising substitutes for white-fleshed fish such as cod, haddock, flounders, soles, and so on. In 1984 the catch decreased to 1.1 million tons (0.997 metric tons), but in 1987 increased to 1.6 tons (1.45 metric tons). This is a substantial reduction when compared to the 1976 volume.

World Catch

World production of hake increased at a rate of nearly 8 percent per year from 1971 to 1976. The catch in the thirty-six major producing countries rose from 1.5 million metric tons (1.7 million tons) in 1971 to 2.1 million metric tons (2.3 million tons) in 1976. The Soviet Union is by far the largest producer of hake. The Russian catch has declined in recent years and its catch may decline even further with the advent of extended fishery jurisdictions around the world.

The second largest producer and market is Spain. Its catch has risen by the use of long distance freezer trawlers but, like the Soviet Union, Spain's catch of hake may decline somewhat in the future.

African production is dominated by South Africa, which regularly accounts for about 90 percent of that area's production and has been stable in recent years.

The area where production is growing the fastest is North and South America. Here production increased by 13 percent per year from 1971 to 1976. Argentina and Peru account for nearly two-thirds of the catch in the Americas at present.

Potential Catches

World attention has turned to the potential increases in hake production in Latin America. About half of the relatively untapped potential is found on the Patagonian Shelf off Argentina and Uruguay. Additional potential is in the eastern Pacific, from Washington to Chile. (See Table 3-4.)

Europe and North America are experiencing increasing difficulty in obtaining supplies of traditional white-fleshed species at prices the consumer is prepared to pay. Catches of the most popular white-fleshed species for the North American and European markets declined in the 1970s. The catch of Atlantic cod, haddock, and various flatfish peaked (see Table 3-5) at 5.6 million tons (5.1×10^6 metric tons) in 1969, and since then the combined catches have dropped nearly 30 percent or 1.5 million tons (1.36×10^6 metric tons) during the past eighteen years. The 1.5 to 2 million tons [$(1.4–1.8) \times 10^6$ kg] of hake produced annually help supply the demand caused by the shortfall in traditional species.

Hake Products

A listing of hake products produced in Uruguay indicates that a wide variety of processes and styles are available in the world markets: headed and gutted; headed

Table 3-4. *Estimated Hake Potentials in North and South America*

Country	Potential (metric tons)
Chile	100,000
Peru	200–250,000
Argentina-Uruguay	750,000
Mexico	300–400,000
United States (Washington and Oregon)	90–150,000
Total	1,440–1,650,000

Table 3-5. *World Production of Atlantic Cod, Haddock, and Selected Flatfish (1,000 metric tons, live weight)*

Year	Atlantic Cod	Haddock	Flounders, Plaice, Soles, etc.	Total	Short fall
1965	2,726	748	724	4,198	
1968	3,867	487	969	5,323	
1969	3,577	902	1,077	5,556	
1970	3,076	913	1,044	5,033	523
1971	2,851	506	1,154	4,511	1,045
1975	2,430	529	1,091	4,050	1,506
1976	2,385	520	1,074	3,979	1,577
1987	2,054	398	1,279	3,731	—

and gutted, without tail or fins, scaled and dressed; individual quick frozen (IQF) fillets; IQF fillets with and without skin, boned; layer pack interleaved fillets; shatter pack interleaved fillets; and frozen blocks.

The most important single market for hake products is for fillet blocks in the United States and is based on the consumption of fish sticks and portions. Other markets for hake blocks are in Europe and Australia. Although the markets for dressed hake in the United States and Europe are limited, compared with those of fish blocks and frozen fillets, they are expanding.

Production of salted hake is limited at present; however, there is a large world market for salted products. There has been a recent increase in the production of dried-salted hake—a product that resembles salted-dried cod but costs less. Great prospects for salted products exist in Latin America.

Peru is a good example of the evolution of hake products being produced in South America. Fish meal accounted for 90 percent of the hake used in Peru from 1967 to 1970, but by 1976 about 90 percent of the hake catch there was used to process products for human consumption.

Hake is generally not used in canned products. However, different whitefish preparations, including hake, could be canned in forms such as fish patties, fish balls, and so on. Hake also can be prepared as paste and sausages. A preliminary investigation showed that all species, examined from South American waters except one, had good gel-forming capacity and were thus suitable for kamaboko. Kamaboko and fish sausage make up 26 percent of Japanese fish consumption.

Foreign Trade

The major hake markets are the United States and Europe, and to a lesser extent, Australia, Brazil, and some African countries. The United States consumes all the hake it produces and imports considerable quantities, and the same is generally true for Europe, although Spain does export some hake. With European fish catches leveling off and consumption growing, we can expect larger imports of hake by Europe. Hake is being supplied to these markets from South America and South Africa. The amount of hake exported from Russia, which catches a large share of the world's hake, remains unknown.

In most producing countries, domestic demand may continue to rise. However, all countries attach great importance to foreign trade to get the most from their resources and investments.

Out of a technically accessible market of 455,000 tons (413 × 10^5 metric tons), Latin American trade accounts for 23 percent or 105,000 tons (95.3 × 10^5 metric tons) despite the fact that stocks and production capacity vastly exceed this figure. The remaining 77 percent is supplied by, in order of importance, the Soviet Union, Spain, Japan, South Africa, and Poland.

The spread of extended fisheries zones could drastically reduce the catches of German and Spanish long distance fleets, which catch about 150,000 tons (136.1 × 10^5 metric tons) of hake off West Africa. The same restrictions could affect the Soviet, Japanese, and Polish factory ships. Thus world trade could increase by as much as 300,000 tons (272 × 10^5 metric tons) to meet these demands.

United States

The U.S. fishing industry participates in commercial fisheries for four hake species. Three of these, silver hake (whiting), red hake, and white hake, are harvested off the coasts of New England and the mid-Atlantic states, and the fourth, Pacific whiting, is found off the coasts of Washington, Oregon, and California. Hake is also imported in sizeable quantities by the United States, usually from South America, South Africa, and New Zealand.

Like other members of the Gadidae family found in the U.S. Fisheries Conservation Zone—such as Atlantic cod, cusk, and walleye (Alaska) pollock—hakes are white-flesh, mild-flavor, low-fat demersal fish. Although in a broad sense there is some substitutability among the various white-fleshed fishes, each species has its own unique characteristics which are taken into account by processors and consumers and influence product form, price, market demand, and consumption patterns. In the following sections, markets for each of the four hakes are described individually and in the context of the general market for all bottomfish products.

Silver hake, whiting, has been an established food fishery since the 1920s. Whiting is generally sold either round or dressed in fresh fish markets from New England south to Virginia, or frozen headed and gutted (H&G) and distributed throughout the nation with the majority of sales in the Northeast, mid-Atlantic, and Midwest states.

Fresh whiting is sold in the round to local fresh markets, primarily in ethnic communities existing in fishing ports and large cities of the Northeast and mid-Atlantic states. These ethnic communities are largely populated by blacks and people of Mediterranean heritage. Most New England landings not sold locally are trucked to the Fulton Fish Market in New York. When supply exceeds demand in the Fulton market, the surplus whiting are sold to markets in Delaware, Pennsylvania, Maryland, and Virginia. There is currently no market for fresh whiting south of Virginia. Indications are that existing markets for fresh whiting are saturated, and new fresh markets would take time and expense to develop.

For headed and gutted (H&G) preparations, a 6- to 8-ounce (170- to 227-g) headless fish is desired, packed in cardboard cartons holding 1½, 3, 5, or 10 pounds (0.7, 1.4, 2.3, or 4.5 kg). Retailers often prefer 1½- or 3-pound (0.7- or 1.4-kg) cartons so they do not have to thaw and repackage prior to sale. Frozen H&G is an inexpensive product and is especially popular in black and Spanish-speaking areas of the East and Midwest. At least one processor of H&G has recipes and labeling in both Spanish and English on the box.

At present, domestic H&G production does not fill the U.S. demand. In 1978 approximately 6 million pounds (2.7 × 10^6 kg) of H&G were imported, primarily from Argentina, Peru, and South Africa. South American whiting often has a few cents per pound price advantage over domestic and South African whiting, but poor quality product, especially from Peru, has tended to limit the U.S. demand. Although some buyers still import Peruvian whiting for price considerations, many no longer do so, believing the low price does not justify the sacrifice in quality.

It appears that there is at least modest potential for expansion of domestic H&G markets, as a minimum to substitute for some of the 6 million pounds (2.7×10^6 kg) of imported product and possibly to service new markets that would open in response to a good quality, moderately priced product with steady supply.

Fillets and Fillet Blocks

The United States imported approximately 20 million pounds (9.1×10^6 kg) of whiting fillets in 1978, far more than the 1 million pounds (454×10^3 kg) of domestic production. Domestic fillets were hand cut, mostly from larger whiting. Most whiting landed domestically are under 1 pound (454 g) round weight and yield fillets of less than 3 ounces (85 g) in weight. There appears only limited potential for expanding the fillet market because most users prefer a 4-ounce (113-g) minimum fillet size. The small fillets can be used in fillet blocks, which appears to have a greater chance for market expansion. In recent years increasing amounts of whiting fillet blocks have been imported for secondary processing into breaded and battered sticks and portions.

Cod is still the preferred species for battered portions, especially for restaurant use, but demand for whiting is growing, both as a cod substitute and to service new demand for whiting as a unique product in itself. Increasing numbers of buyers are reportedly asking for whiting by name rather than settling for whiting only when cod is not available.

It is estimated that almost one-half of 1978 whiting block imports were defatted whiting *(Merluccius hubbsi)* from Argentina. Many buyers prefer defatted whiting because removing the layer of fatty tissue leaves a pure white fillet comparable in appearance to cod and reduces the incidence of rancidity. Defatted whiting is significantly lower-priced than cod although more expensive than regular whiting and pollock blocks.

Industrial

In general, a large catch of whiting over several days causes an oversupply on the fresh fish market, with a resulting decline in the ex-vessel (off the boat) price. There is little motivation to expand the whiting industrial fishery. When food fish ex-vessel prices are low, fishermen generally will land whiting for industrial use in an attempt to salvage a day's fishing effort. Increased markets and processing capacity for food fish would be much preferred by fishermen.

U.S. Export Markets

At present, export markets for U.S. whiting do not exist. There has been increased interest in the United States to export whole fish to Nigeria and other African nations, but it appears likely that the offered price will not be sufficient to attract industry to produce a whole-frozen product from whiting.

In southern Europe, especially Italy, there are markets for whiting estimated at over 100,000 metric tons (110, 230 tons) per year. Demand is highest, however, for larger H&G whiting [over 9 ounces (255 g), finished weight]. Most U.S. whiting are not large enough to produce this size of product. Demand exists in southern Italy for a 5- to 9-ounce (142- to 255-kg) fish with only the tail and fins removed, but tariffs, taxes, and shipping and handling charges do not make export of these smaller fish profitable.

Red Hake

U.S. red hake landings in 1978 were only 4.8 million pounds (2.2×10^6 kg). By 1987 the landings were slightly reduced to 4.7 million pounds (2.1×10^6 kg). Only 10,000 pounds (4540 kg) were reported as processed into fresh fillets in 1976; the remaining fish were sold whole to fresh fish markets.

Most red hake is white-fleshed although occasionally ruptured blood vessels can cause a pink hue. It is often prepared in the traditional New England method of corned hake with pork scraps and is also used for chowder and fish salad.

Several problems tend to limit red hake's marketability. It has softer flesh than whiting or cod, and the name "hake" is not as familiar to consumers as the "whiting" nomenclature used for silver hake. Filet blocks prepared from red hake generally have been of unsatisfactory quality because the flesh develops a rubbery texture. Research is currently underway to produce an acceptable red hake block.

Red hake is also a component of the mixed industrial fishery described for silver hake. As is the case for silver hake, use of red hake for food fish is economically preferable to increased industrial use.

White Hake

Even though white hake is white-fleshed and mild-tasting, its market potential is limited at present. As with red hake, white hake is softer fleshed than whiting, and again consumers are often unfamiliar with the product name.

Pacific Whiting

Like whiting (silver hake) and other *Merluccius* species, Pacific whiting is a white-fleshed, mild-tasting fish. Historically, Pacific whiting was landed by U.S. fishermen primarily for the industrial meal fishery with only small amounts being headed and gutted or filleted for human consumption. As the fishery develops, ex-vessel prices may be expected to rise but the addition of large-scale, mechanical processing should be more efficient than current smaller-scale, hand-processing operations, and wholesale prices should remain about constant.

The West Coast fishing industry has shown interest in developing large-scale markets for Pacific whiting. Optimum yields for the stock have been set at 175,000 metric tons (192,901 tons), most of which has been allocated to foreign fisheries.

Filets, fillet blocks, and H&G forms are produced from Pacific whiting. Several impediments to market development do exist, however, and need to be dealt with before development of the fisheries can proceed. The skin of Pacific whiting tends to be thinner than other commercially harvested species and the flesh is tenderer. Pacific whiting also exhibits a substantial incidence of a myxosporidian parasite in the flesh, which releases an enzyme upon death of the fish that breaks down the muscle tissue and causes the flesh to become mushy and thus unacceptable to consumers.

Laboratory research has chemically neutralized the parasitic action in minced

Pacific whiting but until a method is commercially available, competitive, and approved by the U.S. Food and Drug Administration, marketing efforts will need to work with this problem.

Apparently the parasitic action can be curtailed if Pacific whiting is deep-fried quickly at high temperatures. Institutional users generally cook breaded and battered fish this way but retail consumers often do not. Processing Pacific whiting into fillet blocks and targeting the institutional market for sticks and portions may be a way to enter the market with a quality product.

Concerns also have been voiced by buyers about the fragility of Pacific whiting fillets, which often break apart in handling before cooking. Processing fillet blocks rather than individual fillets could solve this problem.

Size is another problem for large-scale development of H&G Pacific whiting. Many consumers are used to buying New England and imported H&G which measure 6 to 8 inches (15.2 to 20.3 cm) and are packaged in 10-inch (25.4-cm) cartons. Pacific whiting, generally about 14 inches (36 cm) H&G, do not fit readily into the traditional size cartons.

The presence of parasites eliminated major European markets for Pacific whiting, but other possibilities exist for export. Product developmental work perhaps could establish export markets for dried Pacific whiting (stockfish) and cured, salted Pacific whiting. Africa, the Caribbean, and South America currently consume substantial quantities of these products. Although cod is the traditional stockfish species, hake is increasingly utilized as a low-priced substitute.

Other nations, primarily the Soviet Union, Poland, Bulgaria, and the German Democratic Republic, harvest substantial quantities of Pacific whiting. These nations engage in limited trade and information exchange with the United States, so it is not known how or whether they neutralize the parasite problem. Although some arrangements are already in effect between the United States and the Soviet Union for transfer at sea of U.S. landed Pacific whiting, more work would be necessary by the Pacific whiting industry to fully evaluate the potential of exporting Pacific whiting to those nations currently harvesting it.

Conclusions

As U.S. usage of bottomfish fillet blocks increases, there are opportunities for U.S. processed hake blocks to substitute for imported blocks and supply new demands. Although all U.S. hakes are white-fleshed and mild-tasting, only silver hake has a consistently firm flesh texture which makes it comparable with most imported whitings and cod. More technological research in improving flesh consistency is necessary before Pacific whiting, red hake, and white hake blocks can become fully developed markets.

There is also potential to substitute for imported products and develop new markets in the United States and abroad for H&G, filleted, cured, minced, and chowder products. However, impediments caused by variations in species size, texture, and nomenclature will need to be counteracted by innovative marketing techniques.

POLLOCK

A close relative of the cod and haddock, pollock is found in the cool coastal waters from Cape Hatteras northward to Newfoundland, Greenland, and Iceland, and in

European waters from the coast of France to the northern coast of Norway. This species, called saithe or coalfish in Europe, has been fished heavily in northern European waters for more than fifty years. Landings from the entire North Atlantic, for all countries, reached a high of 1 billion pounds (4.54×10^8 kg) in 1966 but have been declining since. Judging from the comparative landings, pollock is not nearly as abundant off the North American coast as on the eastern side of the North Atlantic.

On the North American side, the pollock is abundant only over a short part of its range. Being a cool-water fish, rather than a cold-water species, it is most abundant off western Nova Scotia and in the Gulf of Maine. It is comparatively scarce south of Georges Bank or north of southern Newfoundland. The bulk of the catch is taken with bottom otter trawls in depths less than 600 feet (183 m) with the greatest quantities apparently along the steep slopes between 240 and 600 feet (73 and 183 m).

Most of the pollock from this side of the Atlantic are taken in the Nova Scotia banks, with fishing effort centered around western Nova Scotia and eastern Georges Bank. In recent years, Canada has landed the greatest portion of this catch, with the U.S. landings a distant second. There has been a drop in pollock landings from the Northwest Atlantic since 1964. Canadian landings in particular have declined because of the drop in catch from the Nova Scotia banks. It seems likely that fishermen would fish harder for pollock on the Nova Scotia banks if large quantities were available.

The U.S. catch of pollock generally has been taken by boats fishing for other species, such as haddock. There has been little opportunity, therefore, to measure the fishing effort directed specifically toward pollock. Without a measure of this fishing effort and its effect on pollock abundance, it is difficult to estimate the pollock population. The comparatively small landings of pollock from the Gulf of Maine, however, suggest that increasing the fishing there would raise the catch. Pollock congregate in the southern Gulf of Maine to spawn during the late fall and winter. It is likely that greater quantities of these spawners could be taken if more boats fished there.

With the U.S. pollock catch largely incidental to fishing efforts for other species, there are few favorite grounds. Some of the best fishing is on the spawning concentrations located over the area from Stellwagen Bank to Jeffrey's Ledge. In addition, good catches are made at times on the northern edge of Georges Bank, on Grand Manan Banks, and on the Nova Scotian shelf in the general vicinity of Browns Bank. Pollock landings at New England ports are, as expected, highest in the fall and early winter—the spawning time.

The fish spawn for the first time at ages 4 to 7, and growth slows after age 6. Pollock feed largely on small fishes, such as herring, whiting, and sand eels, and on the kinds of shrimp found in the upper layers of water. These feeding habits bring them far above the bottom at times, and bottom trawls are sometimes ineffective for catching them. As cool-water fish, they are unlikely to be found in upper waters when the water temperature is above 52°F (11°C). And even the harbor pollock are not abundant in water over about 60°F (15°C).

The otter trawl is the primary gear used for catching pollock, although lines, gillnets, purse seines, and midwater trawls also have been used with some success.

Shipboard handling of fresh pollock greatly affects landed quality. The shoreside processor cannot improve the quality of what is delivered to him, so the fisherman bears the greatest responsibility for a high quality product.

Fresh U.S. caught pollock usually is marketed whole or as skinned or unskinned fillets. The fillet size from small pollock is similar to that from haddock, and consumer acceptance is good. The long, thick slab fillets from large pollock, however, meet with sales resistance. Studies have shown that these thick fillets can be split into two or more thinner fillets, which then can be cut further into fillet-shaped pieces of acceptable size.

Steaks and chunks are market forms most often used for the large pollock landed by the U.S. fleet. They can be prepared from fresh, iced fish with special power-driven circular knives. It is more common, however, to freeze the fish and then to cut the steaks and chunks with a band saw. Superior flavor comes from the unfrozen fish or from fish frozen at sea.

HALIBUT

In the early days the English thought highly of halibut, serving it on holy days. Since *butte* was the middle English word for flatfish or flounder, "holy butte" eventually became halibut.

Before the mid-1800s, cod was the main species sought by fishermen from the northwest Atlantic region, because the cod could be preserved by salting with subsequent drying. The fish were beheaded, split, and salted after landing in port. On boats that made fishing trips of several days, weeks, or months, the eviscerated fish were beheaded, split, salted, and held in kench (piles of salted fish) aboard the boat. In those days the Atlantic halibut, *Hippoglossus hippoglossus,* was considered a trash fish and a pest since it often ate the cod caught on hooks.

With the advent of ice for preserving fish aboard boats, fishermen began to fish for other species, including halibut that were found to have good eating quality. The fish could then be brought to shore and sold for consumption in the fresh state. By adequate icing, fish could be preserved and sold as fresh fish inland at some distance from the shore. Because halibut is one of the most delectable of species, it soon became popular and was subsequently sought in quantity in the waters off the northeast United States and off Canada.

Physical Characteristics

The halibut, largest of the flatfishes, is a kind of flounder, and like flounders, it maintains a lateral position so that one of its sides is up and the other down. Its large mouth, which extends back to the eyes, is filled with sharp, curved teeth. In proportion, it is about one-third as wide as it is long, but compared with other flounders, it is relatively thick. The tail of the halibut is wide with a slight concave curve. Two small similar ventral fins are located just below the gill covers; the dorsal fin starts above the eye and extends to the narrow part near the tail. The anal fin is similar to the dorsal fin but somewhat shorter, starting behind the pectoral fin. It is preceded by a sharp, spinelike projection of bone which, in young fish, projects exteriorly but in the old fish is hidden by the skin. The pectoral fins are not alike; the one on the upper side is obliquely pointed, and the pectoral fin on the lower side is rounded.

Halibut weighing 600 to 700 pounds (272 to 318 kg) have been caught off the U.S. East Coast but such large fish are rare. Now the large females average between 100 and 150 pounds (45 to 68 kg) and the large males, 150 to 200 pounds (68 to 91 kg). At the same age the female is larger than the male. A 24-inch (61.0 cm) long halibut (head and tail included) weighs about 5.5 pounds (2.5 kg); a 74-inch (188-cm) halibut weighs about 215 pounds (98 kg). Commercial sizes of halibut are "chicken," weighing 5 to 10 pounds (2.3 to 4.5 kg); "medium," weighing in at 10 to 60 pounds (4.5 to 27.2 kg); "large," weighing 60 to 80 pounds (27.2 to 36.3 kg); and "whales," weighing 80 pounds (36.3 kg) or more.

In the western Atlantic, halibut are found from the Gulf of St. Lawrence and the Grand Banks off Newfoundland to Nantucket Shoals, but rarely as far south as New York.

Off the U.S. East Coast, directed halibut fishery no longer exists. All the halibut caught is incidental to efforts directed at other species.

It is reported that during the mid-1880s some 10 million pounds (4.5×10^6 kg) of halibut were harvested from the northwest Atlantic Ocean. Halibut were gradually depleted from this area by overfishing and by taking fish during the spawning season. Eventually this species, which at one time was plentiful inshore, could only be caught in deep-water banks, and it even became comparatively scarce in these areas. From 1965 to 1973, most of the catch was made by Canadian fishermen—about 4 million pounds (1.8×10^6 kg). The U.S. catch was less than 250,000 pounds (113×10^3 kg) annually but remained rather constant throughout that period. As many as fourteen countries fish for halibut, but the combined catch by countries other than Canada and the United States dropped remarkably from 1965 to 1970 when, it appears, only Canada and the United States landed any sizeable quantities.

On the East Coast all of the halibut caught is handled fresh. When brought aboard fishing boats the throat is cut, the belly is split, and the gills and entrails are removed by hand. The surface and belly cavity are then washed with seawater. The belly cavity (sometimes called the poke) may be filled with ice, and the fish are placed in hold pens in layers alternated with layers of ice. Boats may remain at sea for 7 to 10 days, but the halibut keeps well under suitable icing and generally reach port in good condition. At times, some surface yellowing of the white side of the fish has occurred because of the growth of a fresh water bacteria, *Pseudomonas flourescens*. On the West Coast this problem was solved by chlorinating the water used to make the ice used aboard the fishing boats.

Halibut Utilization

Halibut are used mainly as food, although they also are used in the manufacture of other products of commerce. When landed in port, the fish are hoisted from the hold to the dock. They are then beheaded, washed, and placed in boxes in alternating layers with ice. In this condition they are shipped to the retailer or to a commission agent who will reship to retailers.

Halibut are generally consumed as steaks, mainly because of their relatively large size. The steaks are made by cutting the body of the fish into transverse slices about 3/4 inch (1.9 cm) thick. Halibut, at its highest quality, is among the best tasting of meats and is worth the high price it commands—a price comparable to high-priced beef. It has a somewhat meaty, though unique taste that is very tender without being mushy. Unfortunately, halibut that has never been frozen is rarely available, and most of the halibut consumed has been caught off the West Coast of the United States or in other remote areas and arrives on the U.S. East Coast as a frozen product.

The fat in halibut, as in some other fish, is relatively high in the polyunsaturated fraction, and it is therefore readily oxidized, giving rise to rancid off-flavors and off-odors. Without proper handling and care, frozen halibut steaks can become rancid to some degree. In addition, the meat may become tough, and in some cases it may even become dehydrated, which accelerates rancidity and further depreciates the quality of the texture. Thus, although halibut is an excellent food fish, an experience with improperly handled halibut may cause consumers to believe otherwise.

In medium-sized or large halibut, portions of flesh from either side of the head weigh 0.5 pound (0.2 kg) or more, and these halibut cheeks are considered by many to be the most delectable parts of the fish. These are cut out by inserting a pointed knife below the eye and circling the cheek cavity while leaving a narrow strip of intact skin. The flesh is then cut through to the intact skin and then pulled away from the skin. Generally, halibut cheeks are sold as a fresh product although small quantities may be frozen.

The Atlantic halibut, which with suitable fishing regulations might have continued to provide a significant amount of animal protein to the consuming public, has become of little importance as a food for humans due to extreme fishing pressures over an extended period of time.

Halibut heads, with or without the cheeks, are used to manufacture fish meal, a cooked dehydrated product used to supplement feed for cattle, hogs, and chickens. Halibut livers are rich in vitamin A and once brought a good price because the oil could be extracted and used for medicinal purposes. When synthetic vitamin A was developed, halibut livers became less important, although there is still some utilization. The livers are taken and held under refrigeration when the fish are eviscerated aboard the fishing boat. In port, the livers are heated and pressed to obtain an oil-water-protein mixture which is allowed to settle or is centrifuged to obtain the clarified oil. The oil content is in the range of 5 to 19 percent.

Halibut skins have been used to produce fine leathers by the chrome tanning process. Halibut leathers are easily dyed in a variety of colors and have an attractive surface design left when the scales are removed from the follicles.

SABLEFISH

Sablefish range from Baja California north to the Bering Sea and southwest to the coast of Japan, but most are located in the Gulf of Alaska. Sablefish (Fig. 3-9) are most abundant at depths of more than 200 fathoms (366 m) on blue clay and hard mud bottoms in or near submarine canyons and gullies and are less abundant in areas that have sandy and rocky bottoms. In general, sablefish dwell on the sea bottom, but, when young, they are found feeding well off the bottom.

Sablefish live at least twenty years, but most of the fish caught are 3 to 8 years old

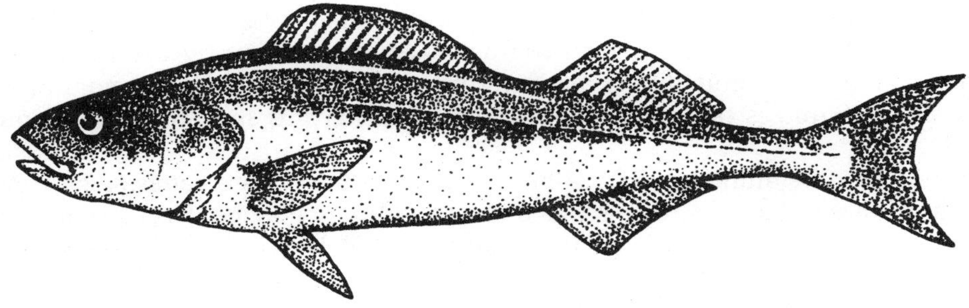

Figure 3-9. Sablefish.

(2.2 to 6.4 pounds/1.0 to 2.9 kg). Sablefish are top carnivores and appear to be opportunistic feeders, with a diet that includes pollock flatfish, saury, rockfish, shrimp, small sablefish, and herring.

For centuries, Indians along the Pacific Coast caught sablefish for food. The commercial fishery began in the middle of the nineteenth century; however, until 1905, most of the sablefish were caught incidentally by fishermen in search of halibut off the coasts of Washington and British Columbia. Until 1958, fishermen from Canada and the United States were responsible for landing nearly all the sablefish. Landings ranged from 4.4 to 21 million pounds (2 to 9.5 $\times$ 10^6 kg), with the largest catches made during World War II. The market demand for fish livers in the 1930s and 1940s helped spur development of the fishery.

During the 1960s, Russia and Japan began fishing for sablefish. The landings peaked at 144.2 million pounds (65.5 $\times$ 10^6 kg) in 1972, with Japan taking 70 to 80 percent. In 1973 and 1974 the Republic of Korea and Taiwan began catching significant numbers of sablefish. However, the passage of the 1976 Fishery Conservation and Management Act greatly reduced the catches of sablefish by foreign vessels within the 200-mile (322-km) fisheries economic zone. The reduction of foreign catches has led to greater development of the fishery by American fishermen.

In the 1970s California became the dominant Pacific Coast state for sablefish landings. This dominance resulted from two new trends in the fishery: an increased use of traps, and the shifting of the fishery southward and into deeper water. Monterey became the main port for sablefish landings. The fishery developed rapidly off southern California south of Point Conception where landings increased from 250,000 pounds (113 $\times$ 10^3 kg) in 1976 to over 5 million pounds (2.3 million kg) in 1978 and 102 million pounds (46.3 $\times$ 10^6 kg) in 1987.

Harvesting Gear

The major types of gear used in the sablefish fishery are trawls, longlines, and traps. In the early years of the fishery, longlines modified from halibut longlines were the principal type of gear used. As trawling moved into deeper water in the 1960s and 1970s, and as the Japanese began to dominate the fishery, bottom trawls became the major type.

In 1969 and 1970, a sablefish trapping system was developed. These rigid, steel-framed, rectangular traps measure approximately 3 feet (0.9 m) by 3 feet (0.9 m) by 8 feet (2.4 m) and are usually fished on longlines. Some traps are designed to be collapsible. Tests of these traps have shown they are quite effective and selective for sablefish in depths greater than 1,200 feet (366 m).

In 1973 Korean vessels started using a different style of trap, which has a truncated cone 28 inches (71 cm) high and shaped like a shallow, inverted flowerpot. American fishermen in southern California currently use the Korean-style trap, but they must obtain a permit from the California Department of Fish and Game. Squid is the preferred bait, although herring and anchovies also are used.

When fish are numerous, a 24-hour soak produces large catches. However, when fish are not as plentiful, soaks of up to 72 hours may be necessary for good results. Under most conditions, little additional catch is realized by soaking the gear longer than 48 hours. For most vessels optimum fishing can best be accomplished by twelve strings of gear working six strings each day.

The United States processes sablefish in five forms: smoked, fillets and steaks, salted, animal food, and pickled. Often a large pecentage of the catch is exported. Sablefish has several market names in its different processed forms. The consumer often sees smoked sablefish as smoked Alaskan cod, and fresh and frozen fillets as butterfish.

Sablefish are usually landed in the round (whole), then are graded by size into small (less than 4¼ or 5 pounds/1.9 or 2.3 kg), medium (4¼ or 5 to 7 pounds/1.9 or 2.3 to 3.2 kg), and large (over 7 pounds/3.2 kg). Higher prices per pound are paid for larger sablefish. The smoked fish market prefers fish over 5 pounds (2.3 kg); small fish are usually processed into fillets and sold as butterfish.

The outstanding characteristic of sablefish flesh is its oiliness. Sablefish has a fat content of about 14 percent as compared with chinok salmon, which contains 11.5 percent fat, and halibut, about 1.1 percent. The oily flesh makes sablefish ideal for smoking, but difficult to freeze for long periods. Sablefish flesh is about 13 percent protein (oysters, 8 percent; salmon, 16 percent) and 71.5 percent moisture (oysters, 85 percent; salmon, 68 percent).

OTHER SPECIES

Burbot

A freshwater relative of the Atlantic cod, the burbot, *Lota lota,* is found in the Great Lakes and in smaller lakes and some rivers of the north central states and Canada. It usually remains in the deeper part of the water. A long and rather slender fish with three whiskerlike barbels, it looks more like cusk than a cod. The average size is about 15 inches (38 cm) long and 1 pound (454 g) in weight.

Burbot's flesh resembles that of cod and haddock. Salt burbot is very much like salt codfish and is very popular in Europe for its white and delicate flesh. Large quantities of burbot are marketed as pet food.

Tomcod

There are two tomcods: (1) the Atlantic tomcod, *Microgadus tomcod,* and (2) the Pacific tomcod, *Microgadus proximum.* The Atlantic tomcod, also called frost fish, looks exactly like Atlantic cod except it is much smaller and has a blotchier color pattern. The maximum length is about 14 inches (36 cm), with most 9 to 12 inches (23 to 31 cm) long. The Pacific tomcod is found from California to Alaska. Both species live in estuaries or shallow water and are often caught by recreational fishermen. Tomcod has limited commercial use as human food because it is not abundant enough.

European Cods

Some members of the cod family which are landed in England and northern Europe are the big or whiting pout, *Trisopterus luscus;* the European whiting, *Merlangius merlangus merlangus;* the poor cod, *Trisopterus minutus minutus;* the Norway pout, *Trisopterus esmarkii;* and the fork beard, *Phycis blennoides.* The European ling, *Molva molva,* is dried as stockfish in Iceland, but it is not common to the Atlantic waters of North America.

Fourbeard Rockling

The fourbeard rockling, *Enchelyopus cimbrius,* occurs on both sides of the North Atlantic. Its back is brown or dark olive and it has a white belly dotted with brown.

On the North American side, it is found from Newfoundland to New York in coastal waters and as far south as North Carolina on the continental shelf. It is small, reaching a length of about 1 foot (30 cm). A bottom-dwelling fish found in depths of water from 2,000 to over 4,000 feet (610 to 1,220 m), it has no economic value.

Cusk

Cusk, *Brosme brosme,* occurs on both sides of the Atlantic. On the North American side, it is found from Newfoundland to Cape Cod and may go as far south as New Jersey in waters from 60 to 1,800 feet (18 to 549 m). It prefers cool water and a rough, rocky, gravelly, or pebbly bottom. Its color varies according to the bottom where it lives: The back ranges from sooty to dull reddish brown with grayish lower sides; white dorsal, anal, and caudal fins have black margins edged narrowly with white. It is easily distinguished from other relatives because it only has one dorsal fin. Its average length is 1½ to 2½ feet, and the ranges vary from 5 to 30 pounds (2.3 to 13.6 kg). Spawning takes place in spring and summer. The cusk is a good food fish marketed largely as fresh and frozen fillets in the commercial fisheries north of Cape Cod. Unlike most other bottomfishes, it does not school but is solitary. It is usually caught incidental to cod fishing. The European cusk (torsk) is found on the European coast, on the north coasts of the British Isles, Denmark, the northern part of the North Sea, and Kattegat to Iceland, and the Murman Coast.

False Cods

Because of the successful marketing of cod, a number of "false cods" have appeared, including the sablefish, also called blackcod, *Anoplopoma fimbria;* the longspine channel (thornyhead) cod, *Sebastolobus alrivelis,* found from Baja California to the Aleutian Islands; the chilipepper, *Sebastes goodei,* from Baja California to Cape Scott; the lingcod or cultus cod, *Ophiodon elongatus,* southern California to northwestern Alaska; and the bull or blue cod, *Scorpaenichthys marmoratus,* actually a sculpin whose common name is cabezon, which is found off the Pacific coast. Most of these species belong to the scorpion fish family, *Scorpaenidae.*

EAST COAST GROUNDFISH

Handling at Sea

About 85 percent of all New England groundfish are caught by otter trawls, although a few small vessels use handlines, longlines, and gillnets. Most of the requirements for general sanitation apply equally to otter trawls and longlines but one special requirement pertains to line-caught fish. When trawl-caught fish are brought aboard the vessel they are all handled the same way, regardless of the form in which they are to be sold. Later, they are handled specially, depending on whether they are to be sold as round fish or as dressed fish. Longline fish should be stunned to stop them from struggling, which, in turn, prevents their blood vessels from rupturing and helps to keep blood out of the fillets.

After the fish are recovered from the trawl net, they are dumped on deck and washed. Those fish that command the highest price usually receive immediate attention. Depending on the laws, the fish may be directly iced, or the fish are eviscerated, washed, sorted into species and size groups, and then iced down in the boat's hold using bulking, shelving, or boxing.

Bulking, where the fish are placed in a large pile with alternating layers of ice and fish, is the poorest method of storing fish because they may be crushed with a loss in moisture and accompanying physical damage. Shelving involves placing the fish in a pen and using shelves so that the combined depth of fish and ice will not exceed 3 feet (0.9 m) without a shelf for support. The third method, boxing, employs either plastic or metal boxes and is considered the optimum storage method, as the fish are usually stacked less than 12 inches (31 m) high. The boxes are capable of being stacked in a way so that meltwater from the upper boxes does not drip into those below, and no additional handling of the fish is necessary on unloading or handling at the plant. Consequently, quality can be more easily maintained. The amount of ice used to keep fish cold varies with every season but usually 2 pounds (910 g) of fish require 1 pound (454 g) of ice. In cold weather, a ratio of 1 part ice to 3 parts fish may be used; in very hot weather, the ratio of ice to fish may approach 1 to 1.

The most important single factor controlling spoilage of fresh fish is storage temperature. Temperature regulates the onset of rigor mortis and also the lag period and growth rate of spoilage microorganisms. Although the flesh of freshly caught fish is sterile, microorganisms are present on the skin and in the slime layer, gills, and gut. Initially, the numbers on the skin average about 10^3 to 10^7 per square centimeter (6.5×10^3 to 6.5×10^7/inch^2), but through mishandling and contamination from the deck and in the pens, the bacterial load can increase rapidly. The types of bacteria that eventually induce spoilage in iced North Atlantic (temperate water) fish are termed psychrophilic or psychrotrophic, which signifies a tolerance for low temperatures. They constitute the natural microflora of newly caught fish and may also be picked up during subsequent handling. These bacteria are capable of growing at temperatures slightly below freezing, but grow most rapidly in the temperature range of 68° to 77°F (20 to 25°C). As the temperature is lowered and approaches 32°F (0°C), the growth rate of fish spoilage bacteria is drastically retarded. A reduction in storage temperature of 3° at just above freezing adds proportionately more to the keeping time of fish than a similar reduction at a higher temperature. Consequently, it behooves the fisherman to rapidly lower and maintain the temperature of the fish to as close to freezing as possible in order to obtain maximum shelf life. This goal can be accomplished by the judicious use of various cooling media.

Refrigerated Seawater

Using refrigerated seawater (RSW) or refrigerated brine for storing fresh fish on the fishing vessel provides (1) greater speed of cooling, (2) less textural damage due to reduced pressure upon the fish, (3) lower holding temperature, (4) greater economy due to time and labor saved, and (5) longer effective storage life of the fish. The real advantage of RSW compared with freshwater ice appears to be that the brine temperature can be maintained at about 30°F (–1°C), which is just above the freezing point of fish.

The rate of bacterial growth on fish is depressed considerably by a slight decrease in temperature in the region of 32°F (0°C). Storage of whiting in RSW at 30°F (−1°C) can extend the storage life about three days compared with ice storage. Where the RSW-held fish did not lose any soluble protein (compared with a slight loss for iced fish), there was a significant increase in sodium chloride content, which would restrict its use in low sodium diets. The frozen storage life at 0°F (–18°C) was comparable for whiting stored for two days in either RSW or ice. Beyond a two-day holding period, the RSW fish had the longer frozen storage life; thus, for trips of short duration, the full potential benefit of RSW storage of whiting may not be realized.

Whole whiting kept on ice for five days were considered unmarketable because of very soft texture whereas fish held in RSW maintained a firm texture after five to six days. Studies confirmed that better frozen storage characteristics are obtained with fillets from RSW fish compared with ice fish.

Although it is now generally regarded that the storage life of whole fish is longer in RSW than in ice, the shelf life is limited by the uptake of water and salt, particularly with lean fish and with some other species, because of the development of oxidative rancidity. The salt concentration of whiting fillets cut from whole fish stored five to six days in RSW was reported to be 0.82 to 0.85 percent. This salt concentration was not considered objectionable but rather was said to enhance the acceptability of the bland-flavored whiting. A problem common with all fish species held in RSW is the eventual growth of spoilage bacteria in the brine, with the resulting foul odors that can be imparted to the fish.

Chilled Seawater

For the small boat fisherman, the benefits of RSW storage can be attained without a mechanical refrigeration system through the use of chilled seawater (CSW) or slush ice. This method entails stowage of fish, ice, and seawater in tanks in the ratio of 3:1:0.5–1. The exact proportions for maintaining temperatures slightly below freezing [32°F (0°C)] depend on temperature of the fish and seawater and duration of the trip. Successful results have been reported with herring and mackerel. With this system it is important that ice and seawater be mixed together just before loading the tanks with fish and that efficient circulation be maintained.

Unloading and Handling at the Wharf

Once the fishing vessel arrives at port, the fish are sold directly to a processor or distributor or are sold at auctions, which are rare except in New England.

If the fish were accurately sorted at sea, they can be repacked into wax-coated cardboard boxes for reshipping or processing. If the catch was not sorted, the fish are deiced on landing at shore, sorted by species and size, then repacked and iced. The normal method of icing is to pack one layer of ice and fish, and a second layer of ice on top. The boxes usually contain 100 pounds (45.4 kg) of fish and about 25 pounds (11 kg) of ice.

Today the usual market forms of cod are dressed fish, steaks, skin-on fillets, and skinless fillets. Dressed and steaked cod are sold freshly iced, and the fillets are sold both fresh and frozen.

Processing

In a typical processing plant, the fish are processed either by machine or by hand. Machines are usually used for cod, haddock, and flounder; hand processing is used for other species. Although machines are available for most species, only a few fish are mechanically processed since the equipment is expensive, species dependent, and a single machine usually cannot process all sizes. Consequently, mechanization is utilized only when a large volume of a particular species is available. In a mechanized plant, the fish scales are removed by a series of rotating serrated disks, a second process removes the fillet, and a third operation may be used to remove the skin. Haddock, however, is usually marketed with the skin on to distingusih it from the lower priced cod.

In hand processing, the scales are removed manually with a hand scaler or mechanically with a rotating cylinder. After scaling, the fish are filleted and in some cases skinned by hand or machine. After processing, the fish are given a final rinse that may contain salt (sodium chloride) or phosphates (sodium tripolyphosphate) to retain moisture within the fillet. This practice is being used less since consumers have become concerned with additives, especially increased salt, in their diets.

Packing

Fresh fillets are usually packed in 10-, 20-, or 30-pound (4.5-, 9.1- or 13.6-kg) rectangular metal or, in recent years, in less costly and slightly smaller plastic containers. The fillets may be either layer-packed or wrapped in a flexible film and then packed. When layer packing is used, absorbent pads are used to absorb moisture that may be released during storage and distribution. The fillet containers are packed with ice in master cartons, usually cardboard, for final shipment. Frozen fish are either layer packed or bulk packed in 5- or 10-pound (2.3- or 4.5-kg) wax-coated boxes. After filling, the cartons may be given an overwrap and placed in trays for freezing in either sharp or plate freezers, or they may be placed in racks for blast freezing. After freezing, the packages are put in master cartons and held in a cold storage room.

Fillet Blocks

Fillet blocks of cod, imported for the production of fish sticks and portions, are prepared by placing the boneless and usually skinless fillets in a fiberboard container. The most popular weights of fish blocks are 13.5 pounds (6.1 kg), 16.5 pounds (7.5 kg), and 18.5 pounds (8.4 kg). For freezing, the blocks are put in a tray and placed into a multiplate compression freezer with spacers slightly smaller in depth. This method causes a slight compression that smooths out the surface and fuses the fillets into a single block.

The fish blocks are further processed by cutting them with a band saw or gang saw (series of circular saw blades on a single axis) or by shearing with a guillotine-type machine into fish sticks or larger fish portions of 1.5 to 5 ounces (43 to 142 g). These sticks or portions are covered with a liquid batter and then dusted with bread crumbs. Recently, a processing technique using a tempura-type batter as the sole covering has been successful. Tempura is a viscous batter which is applied over a flour or dry batter base and then fried. As with the frozen cod fillets, a storage temperature of at least 0°F (–18°C) should be maintained to retain the quality of the sticks and portions.

Salted Cod

Although the amount of salted fish produced in the United States is very small, imported salt-dried cod is still used as such or as fish cakes. Salt-dried fish is normally prepared by heading the eviscerated fish and splitting it open to the tail (see Chapter 22 for more details).

Salt content of cod varies from 4 percent for very lightly salted to 20 percent for a heavily salted product, which is usually dried to about 40 percent moisture content. At low temperatures of 32 to 40°F (0 to 4.4°C) no bacterial spoilage in hard cures may be noticed for years. With lighter cures, storage at chill temperatures is essential. Salt cod, after dying, is often skinned and boned by hand and packaged in small wooden boxes or plastic films in 1-pound (454-g) portions.

Quality Factors

Usually the "last-caught" fish are the most desirable and are used for fresh fish markets in noncoastal areas. The "first-caught" fish are sent to nearby markets or may be placed in the frozen fish trade. Boxed fish and short-shelved fish possess a higher quality than bulked fish and may receive a premium price.

Unless special care is provided, significant quality may be lost on the fishing vessel and during unloading and processing because of the following factors.

Deck Temperature

The temperature on the deck of a fishing vessel can easily exceed 120°F (49°C). Fish that are not quickly placed in the hold and properly iced can quickly decrease in quality.

Sorting Stick or Pitchfork

Sorting sticks, with their sharp protruding spike, and pitchforks used on most fishing vessels cause physical damage and provide a mechanism for microbial invasion. This damage reduces consumer appeal and can lead to a higher deterioration rate.

Vessel Procedures

Once the fishing vessel lands, care should be taken to separate fish species because some fish have storage odors that can be transferred to other fish, thereby reducing acceptability. Any practice that reduces product quality should be avoided. These would include stepping on the fish during sorting and handling, subjecting the fish to excessive impact [dropping fish more than 3 feet (0.9 m)], or placing the fish in contact with bilge water.

Temperature

Temperature is of ultimate importance. If the quantity of ice is insufficient to keep the fish near or at 32°F, (0°C) enzymatic and microbial spoilage can occur at a rapid rate, particularly if the fish were harvested when environmental factors and the physiological state of the fish could result in a more rapid decomposition rate. One of the greatest areas of concern is the processing plant where fish may not be processed quickly enough to maintain the product at a desirable temperature. If the fish are packed at 50°F (10°C) or higher, they may take forty-eight to seventy-two hours or more to properly cool. It is important that distributors, retailers, and restaurateurs do their part to maintain product quality. In many cases, cold rooms are maintained at temperatures near 40°F (4°C) to reduce live shellfish mortality. Although this temperature is ideal for shellfish, finfish will rapidly deteriorate if stored at this temperature for even a few days. Also improper display practices in the retail showcase can be a major cause of product spoilage.

Sanitation

Optimal quality of fish aboard a fishing vessel is obtained in part by maintaining as low a microbial load on the fish as possible through sanitary handling practices and by preventing multiplication of the microorganisms present by means of adequate cooling. Heavy microbial loads imparted to fish through improper handling aboard fishing boats result in shorter shelf life. Equipment, food contact surfaces, utensils, and workers can affect the quality of fish if proper cleaning and sanitation practices are not followed. The large microbial population on the fish can be transferred to equipment or surfaces and back to processed fish. If proper cleaning and sanitation practices are not followed, large quantities of microorganisms will accumulate, providing for rapid product deterioration. Unsanitary practices are a major cause of product deterioration and disease outbreaks. If consumers are assured of safe, high-quality fresh fish products, they are more likely to increase their consumption of seafood.

EAST COAST FISHING INDUSTRY: A HISTORICAL PERSPECTIVE

Groundfish products—flounders, Atlantic cod (hereafter referred to as cod), haddock, pollock, and ocean perch—play a major role in the U.S. fresh fish industry. In 1979 fresh and frozen groundfish fillets accounted for 68 percent of the quantity and 76 percent of the wholesale value for the fresh and frozen fillets from all species.

Most U.S. groundfish processing (more than 70 percent by both quantity and wholesale value of fillets) is done in Massachusetts. In 1979 processing plants there produced 85 million pounds (38.6×10^6 kg) of the 119 million pounds (54×10^6 kg) of U.S. fresh and frozen groundfish fillet and $133 million of the total wholesale value of $186 million. Knowledge of Massachusetts' groundfish industry is therefore important in choosing management alternatives required by the Fishery Conservation and Management Act of 1976 (FCMA).

Fresh groundfish production in Massachusetts is a result of three separate but interconnected industries: fishing, processing and retailing. In 1979 about 450 boats [in excess of 5 tons (4.5 metric tons) gross weight] landed and sold their catch to processing firms and brokers at various Massachusetts ports. Most of these boats are owned by fishing families or are partnerships among the captain and various crew members so the sales of fresh groundfish by boats to processing firms are transactions between independent companies. Ex-vessel prices are determined either through auctions (as in Boston and New Bedford), individual negotiations, or consignment sales. Round or drawn fish arrive at the processing plants and are usually filleted, skinned, and packaged into 10- or 20-pound (4.5 or 9.1 kg) containers. Other products include steaks, frozen fillets, frozen blocks, and frozen and packaged dinners and portions.

The FCMA of 1976 added a political dimension to the financial interdependence among sectors of the groundfish industry. The act established a 200-mile (322-km) offshore conservation zone and created Regional Fishery Management Councils to plan for optimum utilization of traditional commercial species and to encourage commercial development of nontraditional species. The New England Fishery Management Council's conservative program concentrated on quotas for traditional species, and subsidies and gear development programs were introduced to encourage landings of nontraditional species.

When applied, quotas usually have affected the various Massachusetts ports differently, as these ports traditionally have specialized by species: Boston has harvested and processed primarily cod, haddock, and pollock; New Bedford, flounders; and Gloucester, ocean perch. The ports have tended to land the species they process, but there has been considerable movement of fish among ports both within and outside of the Commonwealth. Therefore, the processing industry at each port is more complex than is reflected by local landings.

The early 1970s were characterized as a period of stagnation for the groundfish industry in Massachusetts. Landings declined until 1977, averaging only about half of what they were in the early 1960s. Revitalization of the groundfish industry began with the FCMA in 1976, and by the end of the decade, landings, production, and wholesale value of processed products had increased by 44, 50, and 62 percent, respectively.

After steadily declining throughout the 1960s and early 1970s, the abundance of haddock roughly doubled on Georges Bank and in the Gulf of Maine between 1975 and 1979, matching the increase in cod abundance due to unusually large hatches for both species in 1975.

However, not all species shared in the recovery. Yellowtail flounder, the leading groundfish species, steadily declined in landings and production after 1972. It appears the fleet in Massachusetts, especially in New Bedford, increased concentration on cod and haddock as those stocks increased and the availability of yellowtail decreased.

The sharp drop in ocean perch landings in Massachusetts from 1964 through 1970 does not seem to have been due to declining abundance in the Gulf of Maine. Rather, the aging fleet of large steamers, built in the 1930s and used in Gloucester and Maine, were not being replaced. A 5 million pound increase in Massachusetts ocean perch landings after 1974 was misleading, as landings in Maine dropped by 13 million pounds (5.9×10^6 kg) over the same period. The overall decline in ocean perch landings was due to declining abundance in the Gulf of Maine and the restriction of U.S. vessels from the Canadian grounds since 1978. Between 1970 and 1974 the quantity of ocean perch processed in Massachusetts was about double what was landed there, with the difference made up of Canadian imports and Maine landings. The major products during that period (about 40 percent of the total) were frozen breaded fillets, which could be produced from imported Canadian fresh or frozen fillets. From 1975 through 1979, processed products roughly equaled landings in the Commonwealth as frozen breaded fillets dropped to 20 percent of the total and imported Canadian fresh and frozen fillets dropped from an average of 62 million pounds (28.2×10^6 kg) from 1970 to 1974 to 47 million pounds (21.4×10^6 kg) during the second half of the decade. These figures suggest that as landings of cod, haddock, pollock, and ocean perch increased and transportation facilities for fresh fillets improved, fresh fillets were substituted for frozen breaded ocean perch fillets.

The pattern of landings by species throughout Massachusetts has changed. Groundfish landings decreased in Boston and New Bedford during the 1970s while landings more than doubled in Gloucester and the other ports. However, Boston and New Bedford processing plants continued to dominate the processing sector. Boston processing plants increased their purchases of unprocessed cod, haddock, and pollock from Gloucester, and other ports in Massachusetts, Maine, and Canada, while New Bedford's primary dealers sold less unprocessed cod and haddock to Boston.

The traditional specialization of landings and processing by species among Massachusetts major ports also changed. New Bedford traditionally was very highly specialized, primarily landing and processing flounders. But as the landings of yellowtail flounder dropped from a high of 71 million pounds (32.3 million kg) in 1978, the New Bedford fleet and plants adjusted by landing and processing greater amounts of cod and haddock. Flounder production dropped by 8 million pounds (3.6 million kg) while cod production increased by 23 million pounds (10.4 million kg) and haddock production increased by 11 million pounds (5 million kg) in New Bedford plants during the 1970s when processed products overtook landings for both species.

These results indicate that when a favored traditional species became less available, Massachusetts groundfish industry found it more profitable to turn to other traditional species rather than toward nontraditional species. Wholesale price increases during the 1970s help explain why processing firms were not anxious to turn toward nontraditional species. Also, developing markets for nontraditional species was costly and could not be recouped over a long period, because once the market was established, other processing firms would enter and bid down the high rates of return. The increasing prosperity of the traditional groundfish industry was much more appealing to established processing firms.

The choice of a different traditional species over a nontraditional species is easy to understand once we consider the components of a switch to nontraditional species. Boats must change gear, work procedures, and trip patterns. Skippers must learn the location and habits of the new species. Unloading facilities and methods must be changed. Processing plant equipment and work must be adapted to the new species. And, most importantly, plant owners, managers, and salespeople must make new marketing arrangements with new customers in an initial atmosphere of apprehension between buyer and seller. Furthermore, all these changes require financing and must happen more or less simultaneously among participants who may not have been especially cooperative in the past.

However, the promotion of a nontraditional species succeeded when pollock was introduced in Boston. The Boston Fisheries Association and the U.S. Bureau of Commercial Fisheries (predecessor to the NMFS) promoted pollock through advertising, supermarket displays, and subsidies for pollock landings during the 1960s in a successful campaign to encourage demand for and supply of pollock when haddock was becoming scarce. Boston processing plants were able to initiate and maintain their predominance in the pollock market throughout the 1970s. Anyone planning to utilize nontraditional species should consider the experience of the Boston pollock industry, although pollock may be a special case because it is a close substitute for cod and haddock in fishing, processing, and retailing.

WEST COAST FISHING INDUSTRY: A HISTORICAL PERSPECTIVE

The groundfish resources of the eastern Bering Sea and Aleutian Islands regions are among the world's largest. At the peak of foreign fishing (1971–1974), these regions produced animal catches in the range of 2.2 to 2.5 million tons (2.0 to 2.3 × 10^6 metric tons). With enactment of the 1976 FMCA, the Bering Sea resources within the 200-mile (322-km) limit came under domestic jurisdiction. Provisions of the FCMA mandate that management policies be set up to protect and conserve these resources and promote the development of domestic fisheries. At present, groundfish in the Bering Sea are harvested exclusively by foreign fisheries with the exception of U.S. fisheries for Pacific halibut.

Our intent here is to acquaint you with the Bering Sea groundfish resources by describing domestic and foreign fishing in the region in terms of species taken, magnitude of catches, and fishing areas, and to discuss the current condition and allowable catches of various commercial species.

The Bering Sea's unique geographic, climatic, and oceanographic conditions combine to create an environment favorable for supporting the very large populations of groundfish (in addition to some of the world's largest bird and marine mammal populations). Although the processes responsible for these large populations are not fully understood, they probably originate from the upwelling of nutrient-rich water along the south side of the Aleutian Islands and subsequent mixing of Pacific Ocean and Bering Sea waters, the seasonal extremes in climate with a buildup of nutrients during winter months, and the expansive nature of the continental shelf in the eastern Bering Sea.

The continental shelf and slope are prominent features of the eastern Bering Sea and the location of a majority of demersal resources; most of this shelf area lies within the U.S. 200-mile (322-km) fishery conservation zone.

A second major feature of the region is the Aleutian-Commander Islands arc, a chain of more than 150 islands that forms a partial barrier to the exchange of water between the Pacific Ocean and Bering Sea. Continental shelf areas throughout most of the chain are narrow and frequently discontinuous between islands but broaden in the eastern Aleutians.

The Bering Sea climate is mainly subarctic, except in the southernmost part that lies in the temperate zone. These climatic conditions produce subzero water temperatures and pack ice cover over extensive areas of the continental shelf in the northern and eastern Bering Sea in winter and spring. These conditions cause extensive offshore movement of groundfish to the deeper, warmer waters of the outer shelf and slope in winter. Pack ice begins to form in November, usually reaches maximum coverage in late March, and begins to retreat northward in April or May, making the Bering Sea generally ice free by early summer. The outer shelf between the Pribilof Islands and Unimak Island and the deeper waters of the Bering Sea are generally ice free throughout the year due to the influence of warmer Pacific Ocean waters.

The Bering Sea supports about three hundred species of fish, the majority of which live on or near the bottom. About thirty-one species from the demersal or semidemersal group are presently used as food fish. Because of their abundance or high market value, the following seven species are consistently targeted by foreign and domestic fisheries:

Pollock, *Theragra chalcogramma*
Pacific ocean perch, *Sebastes alutus*
Atka mackerel, *Pleurogrammus monopterygius*
Sablefish, *Anoplopoma fimbria*
Yellowfin sole, *Limanda aspera*
Greenland turbot, *Reinhardtius hippoglossoides*
Pacific halibut, *Hippoglossus stenolepis*

The following five species are occasionally targeted:

Pacific cod, *Gadus macrocephalus*
Rock sole, *Lepidopsetta bulineata*
Flathead sole, *Hippoglossoides elassodon*
Arrowtooth flounder, *Atheresthes stomias*
Rattails, *Corypahenoides* spp.

Abundance of the nineteen remaining species is relatively low and they form only an incidental part of catches[1,2]:

Harlequin rockfish, *Sebastes variegatus*
Rougheye rockfish, *Sebastes aleutianus*
Dusky rockfish, *Sebastes ciliatus*
Northern rockfish, *Sebastes polyspinis*
Shortspine thornyhead, *Sebastolobus alascanus*
Shortraker rockfish, *Sebastes borealis*
Darkblotched rockfish, *Sebastes crameri*
Yelloweye rockfish, *Sebastes ruberrimus*
Blue rockfish, *Sebastes mystinus*
Sharpchin rockfish, *Sebastes zacentrus*
Splitnose rockfish, *Sebastes diploproa*
Yellowmouth rockfish, *Sebastes reedi*
Alaska plaice, *Pieuronectes quadrituberculatus*
Rex sole, *Gluptocephalus zachirus*
Butter sole, *Isopsetta isolepis*
Longhead dab, *Limanda proboscidea*
Dover sole, *Microstomus pacificus*
Starry flounder, *Platichtys stellatus*
Skates, *Raja* spp.

Many other species are taken during fishing operations, and some of these, such as sculpins, may be utilized for reduction to fish meal along with wastes from filleting operations and food fish that are too small for filleting.

North American Fisheries

Although utilization of Bering Sea bottomfish resources by U.S. and Canadian fishermen has been relatively minor, fishing activities date back more than one hundred years. Pacific cod was the first species taken, initially by an exploratory effort in 1864 and then on a regular annual basis starting in 1882. The North American cod fishery reached it peak during World War I when estimated annual catches ranged from 13,228 to 15,432 tons (12,000 to 14,000 metric tons). In comparison, the current large foreign fishery annually takes about 63,933 tons (58,000 metric tons) of Pacific cod from the eastern Bering Sea. Following 1920, numbers of

---

[1]Includes species that may be marketable as food fish but are not targeted because of their low abundance.
[2]Because of problems in identification of rockfish, the species listed may be incomplete or contain species not actually occurring in the Bering Sea–Aleutian Islands regions.

North American vessels and their catches gradually declined until the fishery was terminated in 1950.

Although cod fishermen reported the presence of Pacific halibut in the Bering Sea as early as the 1800s, these fish were not harvested commercially until 1928, and commercial fishing remained sporadic in the 1930s and 1940s. The fishery started on a regular annual basis in 1952 but catches remained low through 1957, ranging from only 26.5 to 174.2 tons (24 to 158 metric tons) per year. Effort by the U.S. and Canadian fisheries increased substantially in subsequent years. Catches reached a high of 5,400 tons (4,900 metric tons) in 1963, declined steadily to 190 tons (173 metric tons in 1973, and since then have been relatively low, ranging from 285 to 495 tons (260 to 450 metric tons) a year. Reduced catches resulted from a decline in abundance of Pacific halibut and resulting restrictions placed on the fishery. Factors possibly contributing to the decline include overfishing by the North American and Japanese setline fisheries in the early 1960s, high incidental catches of juveniles in foreign trawl fisheries, and adverse environmental conditions.

There also has been a minor commercial halibut fishery by U.S. and Canadian vessels in the Aleutian Islands since 1960. Catches from the Aleutian region have ranged up to 198 tons (180 metric tons) annually.

Foreign Fisheries

Five foreign countries (in addition to Canada) have participated in the groundfish fisheries of the eastern Bering Sea and Aleutian Islands. Japan has had the longest history of fishing in the region and has mounted the greatest effort over the years. The first documented fishery for demersal species was by the Japanese in the eastern Bering Sea in 1958, followed by the Soviet Union, which has the second largest removal of groundfish in the region. The Japanese and Soviet fleets were followed by those of the Republic of Korea (ROK) in 1967. The number of vessels and magnitude of the ROK catches has remained much smaller than that of Japan and the Soviet Union. The Taiwanese also have had a fishery in the eastern Bering Sea since 1974 but involving only one or two trawlers. Polish vessels fished briefly in the eastern Bering Sea in 1973. Since then, Poland has agreed to abstain from further fishing in the eastern Bering Sea but has been allowed to fish in certain waters of the Aleutian Islands, a fishery they have not pursued, however.

Magnitude of Foreign Catches

Statistics for the total catches of groundfish in the eastern Bering Sea and Aleutian Islands waters have always been much greater in the eastern Bering Sea than in the Aleutians. Even during the period of the Aleutian area's peak catches (1964 and 1965), which coincided with relatively low catches in the eastern Bering Sea, the Aleutian Islands had only about a third of the catch taken in the eastern Bering Sea. In subsequent years as the fishery for walleye pollock in the eastern Bering Sea developed, the total groundfish catch in the Aleutians fell to 5 percent or less than that of the eastern Bering Sea.

In the eastern Bering Sea, total catches of groundfish have reached two peaks. The first and smaller peak occurred during 1960 to 1962 when Japan and the Soviet Union were intensively targeting yellowfin sole and other species that reached a maximum of 788,140 tons (715×10^3 metric tons) in 1961. Catches declined from 1963 to 1965 because of reduced abundance of yellowfin sole. After the Japanese developed shipboard methods of producing surimi, their fishery for walleye pollock developed rapidly, and the total groundfish catches rose again to reach a second, much higher peak of over 2.2 million tons (2×10^6 metric tons) per year from 1971 to 1973. Since that time, catches have decreased because of restrictions stemming from evidence of declining abundance of pollock and other species. By 1977, catches had declined to about 1.1 million tons (1×10^6 metric tons) but catches were higher in 1978 at about 1.51 million tons (1.37×10^6 metric tons).

Flounders (primarily yellowfin sole) were the major species in eastern Bering Sea catches until 1963, after which walleye pollock predominated. The proportion of pollock in the total foreign catch of groundfish increased from about 44 percent in 1964 to about 72 percent in 1968 and, from 1971 to 1977, represented 81 to 85 percent of the total groundfish catch.

Japan has taken the major share of the groundfish catches in the eastern Bering Sea, accounting for at least 68 percent of the total foreign catches annually and usually between 80 and 90 percent of the catches.

The foreign fisheries in the Aleutian Islands region differ from those in the eastern Bering Sea in a number of respects. Overall catches have been much lower, trends in catches and major species in catches have differed, and the Soviet Union rather than Japan has taken the greatest share of the catches. Total groundfish catches in this area reached a peak of 125,660 tons (1.14×10^5 metric tons) in 1965, a few years after the fishery was initiated in 1962. Since then, total catches have fluctuated at a lower level, ranging from about 39,680 to 88,180 tons (3.6 to 8×10^4 metric tons) annually.

Pacific ocean perch and other rockfish were the primary target species in the Aleutians until recent years. Rockfish catches reached their peak in 1965 at 120,150 tons (1.09×10^5 metric tons) but since then have shown an almost continual decline. Catches of other groundfish have increased since 1971 with walleye pollock and Atka mackerel accounting for most of this increase. Atka mackerel was the most abundant species in catches in the Aleutian area in 1976 and 1977 at 22,045 and 23,700 tons (20 to 21.5×10^4 metric tons), respectively. Flounders have formed only a minor part of catches in the Aleutians with Greenland turbot and arrowtooth flounder the main species taken.

REFERENCES

Bakkala, R., Hirschberger, W., and King, W. 1979. "The Groundfish Resources of the Eastern Bearing Sea and Aleutian Islands Regions." *Marine Fisheries Review*. 41(11):1

Cohen, D. A. 1980. "Names of the Hakes." *Marine Fisheries Review*. 42(1):2.

Cooperative Extension Service. *The Sablefish Fishery*. Berkeley: University of California.

Food and Agriculture Organization of the United Nations. 1987 *Fishery Statistics: Catches and Landings* (Vol. 64). Rome.

Georgianna, D., and Ibara, R. 1983. "Groundfish Processing in Massachusetts During the 1970s." *Marine Fisheries Review*. 45(1):1.

Jensen, A. C. 1965. *Haddock*. Fishery Leaflet 5.8. Washington, DC: U.S. Dept. of the Interior, Bureau of Commercial Fisheries.

Lane, J. P. 1969. "Recommendations for Improving the Quality of Vessel-Caught Groundfish." *Fisheries Industrial Research*. 4:203.

Licciardello, J. J. 1980. "Handling Whiting Aboard Fishing Vessels." *Marine Fisheries Review*. 42(1):21.

National Marine Fisheries Service. Research Report No. 1, Northwest Atlantic Fisheries. *Pollock*. U.S. Department of Commerce.

Nickerson, J. T. R. 1978. "The Atlantic Halibut and Its Utilization." *Marine Fisheries Review*. 40(7):21.

Patashnik, M., Groninger, H. S., Jr., Barnett, H., Kudo, G., and Kourg, B. 1982. "Pacific Whiting, *Merluccius productus:* I. Abnormal Muscle Texture Caused by Myxosporidian-Induced Proteolysis." *Marine Fisheries Review*. 44(5):1.

Ryan, J. 1979. "The Cod Family and Its Utilization." *Marine Fisheries Review*. 41(11):25.

Whitaker, D. R. 1980. "World Utilization of Hake." *Marine Fisheries Review*. 42(1):4.

CHAPTER

4

Pelagic Fish

John D. Kaylor and Robert J. Learson

The term *pelagic* is derived from a Greek word meaning the sea or open ocean. When applied to fish, it generally means those species adapted to living not far from the ocean surface. The pelagic fish of commercial interest may be found from top surface waters to depths as great as 656.2 ft (200 m) or more.

Oddly, pelagic fish of commercial importance are found in just a few families, the most important of which are the herrings, *Clupeidae;* the anchovies, *Engraulidae;* the mackerel-tuna family, *Scombridae,* and the jacks, *Carangidae.* Other pelagic species which are sold in the United States include the swordfish, *Xiphiidae,* and in the last few years, the dolphin fish of the family *Coryphaenidae,* which is marketed under the Hawaiian name of mahi-mahi.

Statistics of the worldwide catch of fish show a ratio of nearly 3 pelagic to about 1 of nonpelagic (groundfish)—remarkable because we harvest far more species (and families) of groundfish than pelagic fish. The one single species of fish caught in the greatest abundance (7.4×10^6 tons, 6.7×10^6 metric tons) worldwide in 1987 was Alaska pollock, a groundfish. But the next four species in total catch in 1987 were all pelagic species: Japanese Pilchard, 5.8 million tons (5.3×10^6 metric tons); South American Pilchard, 5.2 million tons (4.7×10^6 metric tons); Chilean Jack Mackerel, 2.4×10^6 tons (2.68×10^6 metric tons); and Peruvian Anchovy, 2.3×10^6 tons (2.1×10^6 metric tons).

PHYSICAL ADAPTATION

Fish have adapted to living in a dense medium (either fresh or salt water) in many ways. In order to propel themselves in a watery world with the greatest economy of effort, most have streamlined bodies. The mackerel family, which includes the mackerels, bonitos, and tunas, has achieved the greatest degree of streamlining. These pelagic fish are rapid swimmers and have cigar-shaped bodies that are slightly thicker in front to facilitate the streamlining effect. Their fins can be folded back into depressions to reduce drag. They also have small finlets between the tail and the upper dorsal and lower anal fins which act like slotted flaps on the wing of an airplane. These finlets help reduce the flow and reduce turbulence and resulting drag over the tail fin.

The ultrastreamlining of some pelagic fish enables them to attain remarkable speeds. Usually speeds of fish are divided into three categories: cruising speeds are those used for ordinary travel; maximum sustainable speeds can be kept up for a considerable time; top speed is an explosive burst of speed for a short time only.

The top speed performers are all pelagic fish. The maximum speed for mackerels *(Scomber)* is 20.5 miles per hour (33 km/hr) and is topped by the barracuda *(Sphyraena)* with a 27 mile/hr (43 km/hr) limit and the dolphin *(Coryphaena)* at 37 (59.5 km/hr). The dolphins are exceeded by the bonito *(Sarda)* and the tuna *(Thunnus)* at 40 to 50 miles/hr (64 to 80 km/hr). The champion is the swordfish *(Xiphias)* that can hit speeds of about 60 miles per hour (96.5 km/hr).

One point often ignored in fish speeds is the chief propellant—the tail fin. All the piscatorial speed demons have either deeply forked tails like the mackerels, or lunate or crescent-shaped tails like the tunas, bonitos, and swordfish (see Fig. 4-1). These two shapes are well adapted to high cruising speeds and top speeds when necessary.

MUSCULATURE

In nature, some animals are placid and slow-moving like cows, and others are as swift as greyhounds. Among fish, swimming muscles make the fundamental difference between the slow and the fast. Fish muscles are of two types—white and red. Normally, the white muscle fibers make up the mass of muscle segments commonly called flakes. The red muscles are found as a layer on top of the white muscles. Mackerel is a fish with this two-toned musculature (Fig. 4-2). The red muscles have much fat, a rich supply of blood, and contain a red oxygen-carrying protein called myoglobin which accounts for the dark color.

The red muscles of pelagic fish enable them to swim at a constant speed in order to obtain food or to accomplish spawning migrations, which may involve many hundreds or even thousands of miles. They really are the cruisers of the fish world. Their normal speed is higher than that of most fish, and, on average, they can swim for long periods of time at 6 knots (11.1 km/hr). This speed is quite fast when compared with most members of the cod family that cruise at about 2 knots (3.7 km//hr).

Figure 4-1. Forked Tail, Like That of the Mackerel (Left) or Lunate Tail, Like That of the Swordfish (Right) Are One Sign of the Sea's Speed Demons.

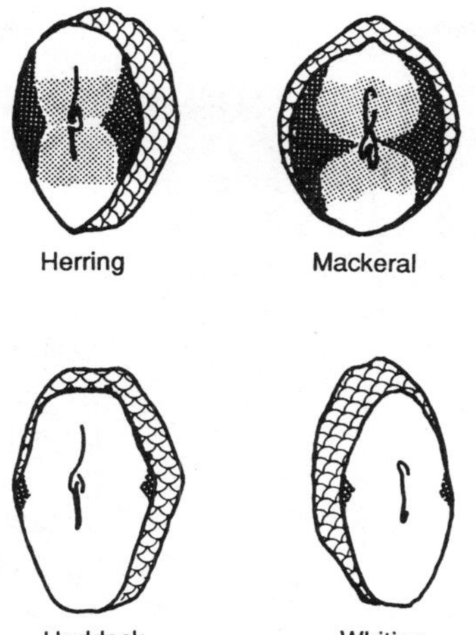

Figure 4-2. Comparison of Dark Muscle Size in Active (Top) and Less Active Fish (Bottom).

When danger threatens, pelagic fish can shift into high gear by calling on the white muscles that instantly go into powerful action. Instead of requiring oxygen, they rely on stored glycogen (called animal sugar) to energize muscles for movement. The only trouble is that once their glycogen supply is exhausted, it takes about a day or so to replenish it. If the danger has passed, the recovery is normal. However, some tunas can become so agitated when caught in nets that they actually die in a frenzied state.

METHODS OF CAPTURE

Most pelagic fish travel in schools of varying sizes, from a few dozen to scores of thousands. The most effective methods of capture vary for different species and are due primarily to the habits of each species. Listed here are the more common pelagic species and their chief methods of capture.

Species	Methods of Catch
Anchovy	Purse seines
Dolphin	Troll lines
Herring (Maine)	Purse seines, weirs
Jack mackerel	Seines, lampara nets
Mackerel (Atlantic)	Purse seines
Florida pompano	Trammel nets, runaround gillnets
Sardine (pilchard)	Purse seines, drift nets
Sprat	Purse seines, haul seines
Swordfish	Longlines, harpoons
Tunas	Purse seines, lampara nets, troll lines, handlines, and harpoons

PRESERVATION

Maine Sardines

Immature herring, *Clupea harengus harengus,* are usually held alive in the net for about a day to purge them of feed. This procedure is necessary because if the fish are full of feed when they are brought to the cannery, enzymes in the gut will become activated, causing rapid deterioration and belly-blown fish. The fish are transferred to the carrier boat by suction pump, and as they are being put in the hold, salt is added for its preservative, firming, and flavoring action. Because of the demands of consumers for less salt in their diets, the practice of salting sardines aboard vessels is now being limited. Refrigerated seawater systems and chilled seawater, a mixture of ice and seawater, are being used to a larger extent in recent years.

The carrier boats discharge the fish by suction pumps at the cannery where the fish are flumed into holding tanks which also serve as brining tanks. At this point the fish are salted to maintain a desired level of salt. The fish are then conveyed to the packing tables where packers using scissors cut the heads and tails from the fish and place them in open cans. Some of the larger canneries have installed automated cutting machinery to perform the trimming process. The cans are then placed on special wire racks on wheeled carts and rolled into a steam box for a preliminary cooking. Afterward, the racks are inverted to drain any water and oil resulting from the cooking process. The cans are then conveyed to a machine that fills each one with oil. Most Maine packs contain soybean oil, although cottonseed, olive, and peanut oils can also be used, or they may be filled with mustard, tomato, or pepper sauce. The oil or sauce is added hot to create a partial vacuum in the can. After filling, the cans are immediately sealed, placed in baskets, and sterilized by steaming at 250°F (121°C) under 15 pounds (6.8 kg) of pressure in retorts (industrial pressure cookers). Upon cooling the cans are washed, inspected for proper seals, and cased for shipping.

In recent years the Maine sardine industry has been packing herring steaks from fish too large to be packed as sardines. For these packs the herring are sliced into approximately ¾-inch (1.9-cm) slices after trimming and packed and processed in the same manner as the sardine packs. The Maine Sardine Council, which is funded by the industry, grades samples from every lot of sardines produced in Maine.

Norway Sardines

The processing of Norway sardines is similar to Maine processing except that two different species of fish are commonly canned in Norway. One is the same species as the Maine herring, *Clupea harengus harengus.* The other is a herringlike fish called *sprat* in English and termed *brisling* in Norwegian *(Sprattus sprattus sprattus).* We make a distinction between the two Norway sardine packs later in this chapter in a section that also explains why these packs require different labels so as not to mislead the consumer.

An additional difference between Norway- and Maine-produced sardines is that a considerable portion of the Norway pack is smoked, and Maine packs are not.

Portuguese Sardines

For the most part, about the only packs of true sardines found in the United States originate in Portugal and contain the fish whose scientific name is *Sardina pilchardus.* This sardine differs from the herring and sprat sardines in one very important respect: The viscera of sardines are much larger and must be removed, whereas with herring and sprats the temporary starving of the fish in nets (twenty-four hours) is sufficient.

An additional difference is that despite the improvement in mechanization of processing equipment, there is still some extra hand labor required to prepare the skinless and boneless fancy packs. Although some variations in processing do occur, in general the steps are the same for all sardines.

Tuna

Tuna arrive at the canning factory having been frozen at sea. Once at the plant, they are thawed and mechanically conveyed to butchers who slit the belly wall and remove the viscera. They are then spray rinsed and placed in special baskets, which are tiered in wheeled racks. The racks of raw tuna are rolled into large cookers for a precooking operation, where steam is introduced to raise the temperature to an average of 216°F (102.2°C). The length of cooking time varies depending on the size of the fish, with large fish requiring a cooking time of eight hours or more.

After the precooking operation, the fish are cooled to make them firm. When cooled sufficiently, the heads are removed and the bodies are skinned and split into lengthwise quarters. The dark meat is separated from the light meat, which is all that is used for human consumption. The light meat quarters or loins are then mechanically cut and packed into cans. Salt is added mechanically to those packs requiring salt, although an increasing amount is now packed without added salt. The final step before sealing the cans is to add a packing medium such as vegetable broth, oil, or water. The cans are then sealed under vacuum and passed through a cleaning operation to remove any surface oil or other packing medium. The final step is to heat the cans in a retort or autoclave to a temperature that will kill all microbial life within the cans.

Mackerel

Unlike tuna, mackerel are delivered fresh to the cannery. They are placed in slots on a conveyor which carries them to circular knives set to cut the fish to fit the can. They then pass to a cleaning or dressing station, where the fish are cut along the belly and the viscera are removed, including the kidney which lies lengthwise along the backbone. The next step is to remove any traces of blood. Then the fish are subjected to a brine soaking to firm the fish, remove any remaining traces of blood, and to lend flavor. Some canneries omit the brining operation and simply add salt to each can before it is filled.

A split and a whole body section of cut mackerel will fill a 1-pound (454-g) tall can solidly. After being filled, the open cans go to an exhaust box where they are subjected to a hot steam treatment to expel any trapped air. Upon leaving the exhaust box, the temperature of the open cans runs about 145°F (62.8°C).

From this point, the cans travel on a conveyor that tilts them to remove any liquid that has accumulated. The liquid is replaced by the desired packing medium, which may be brine, oil, tomato sauce, or other flavoring. Next, the cans go to a seaming machine where the lids are sealed on the cans. From here the cans are rapidly moved through a mechanized washing operation that removes any packing medium, liquids, or particles of fish. The final operation consists of heating the cans in a retort or autoclave to the temperature that kills all microbial life within the can with the least damage to the sensory attributes of the final product.

Anchovies, Mediterranean Style

The only pack of anchovies now commonly found on store shelves is the Mediterranean style because it is canned and has a longer shelf life than Scandinavian anchovies. The processing of Scandinavian anchovies is not described here because they have a limited shelf life and therefore are not generally shipped to the United States.

Genuine cured anchovies are made only from a European fish related to the herring family. Its scientific name is *Engraulis encrasicholus,* and it is the only member of the family Engraulidae in the European-Mediterranean waters. The preparation of this type of anchovy is more of an art than a science as we see in the following description of the process.

Freshly caught anchovies are beheaded by hand in a way that removes the entrails at the same time. The fish are placed in special barrels and then a layer of salt is added. Then a layer of fish is placed at right angles to the preceding layer, and alternate layers of fish and salt are made until the barrel is nearly full. At this point the fish are topped with a layer of salt and a weighted cover to keep the fish pressed down. After a few days, the anchovies will sink somewhat and the cover and top layer of salt are removed. More fish are layered in the barrel, followed by a layer of salt, until the barrel is filled again and the weighted cover is replaced. The purpose of the weighted cover is to force out any air bubbles in the liquid extracted from the fish flesh and to prevent any entrance of air to the fish.

The curing process takes at least six to seven months at a temperature between 60 and 68°F (15.6 and 20°C). The point at which the peak of perfection is reached is determined by an expert who judges by color (red) and flavor and odor. The changes that take place in the curing period are entirely enzymatic and not bacterial in origin. If the cure meets the approval of the expert, the curing process is stopped by chilling the fish.

Once cured, the anchovies undergo a labor intensive operation that accounts for their high price. First, they are given a brine wash and the skin is rubbed off; the tail is snipped and each tiny fish is filleted by hand; the backbone is removed in sections, and each fillet is blotted to remove moisture. The fillets are packed in cans by layering successively, and then the can is filled with olive oil. The cans are then hermetically sealed but not heat processed.

Menhaden

Atlantic and Gulf menhaden (*Brevoortia tyrannus* and *Brevoortia patronis*) support the largest and one of the oldest fisheries in North America. Menhaden belong to the herring family and resemble the alewife and shad in appearance. They have at least thirty common names but are most often called pogies or bunkers. The Atlantic mehaden ranges from Florida to Nova Scotia; the Gulf menhaden, a subtropical species, ranges from southern Florida to the Yucatán Peninsula.

Historically, the abundance of menhaden has fluctuated wildly from year to year. For example, the 1988 U.S. catch of Gulf menhaden was 30 percent less than the 1987 catch, a drop of over half a billion pounds. The average catch of menhaden for both the Atlantic and Gulf species from 1983 to 1987 was 2.7×10^9 pounds (1.2×10^9 kg).

Menhaden are a very fatty species, ranging up to 18 percent fat, and are not consumed as fresh, frozen, or canned products. They do, however, represent the principal species for the fish meal industry of the United States, accounting for almost 80 percent of production (2.18×10^8 pounds/98.9×10^6 kg). Fish meal is used primarily for animal feed, and the oil is mainly an export product. The chief market for crude fish oil is Northern Europe where it is refined and manufactured into margarine. Small amounts of refined fish oils are used in a variety of industrial products because of their special properties. See Chapter 20 for a discussion of fish meal and oil processing.

NUTRITIONAL VALUE

All pelagic species have one thing in common: a high fat content. The unique composition of the fats or lipids in fish, and especially pelagic fish, has a special nutritional value to consumers. In recent years, many studies have shown a correlation with animal fat consumption and cardiovascular diseases (heart disease and stroke). Organizations such as the U.S. Food and Drug Administration, the National Institutes of Health, and the American Heart Association have recommended that people reduce their consumption of saturated fats, which are derived primarily from meat products, and increase their consumption of unsaturated fats, which are derived from fish and vegetable products. Studies on Greenland Eskimos and Japanese consumers have indicated that people with diets high in fish consumption also have lower death rates from coronary heart disease. The implication of these studies is that increasing the consumption of seafoods which have high levels of polyunsaturated fats may reduce the risk of heart disease and stroke.

All pelagic species contain significant levels of polyunsaturated fatty acids (PUFAs) and are the prime source of Omega-3 fatty acids which are those that reportedly have a major effect on reducing blood cholesterol levels. According to scientists from the National Marine Fisheries Service Gloucester Laboratory in Gloucester, Massachusetts, pelagic species can contain almost 3 grams (0.11 ounces) of Omega-3 fatty acids per 100 gram (3.5 ounce) serving. Out of eighteen finfish species analyzed for their Omega-3 fatty acid content, mackerel, herring, tuna, and Maine sardines were the four highest. Just one can of sardines will provide 2.7 grams (0.1 ounce) of Omega-3s. The addition of pelagic species to diets can greatly increase intake of PUFAs and potentially reduce cardiovascular disease.

LABELING

Many pelagic fish are important products in international trade and include such well-known canned foods as sardines, pilchards, anchovies, sprats, mackerel, tuna, and bonito. There is a complexity in national and international identification of both common names and scientific equivalents that is mind-boggling. Following is a conservative listing of products you are likely to encounter.

Sardines and Sardinelike Products

International standards (Codex Alimentarius Commission) state that the name sardines is to be reserved solely for that fish whose scientific name is *Sardina pilchardus*. It is canned almost exclusively in Portugal, Spain, and Morocco and does not occur anywhere in North American waters. It is usually labeled as "Imported Portuguese Skinless and Boneless Sardines."

At present, American sardines are being eclipsed both because of a serious shortage of supply and by aggressive European marketing pressures. Because of the disastrous decline of the California sardine *Sardinops sagax,* no California sardines are allowed to be packed until fish stocks recover. At present, the only canning of sardines in the United States is done in Maine where there are fourteen sardine canneries. By law, this product is permitted to be labeled as sardines but the word "Maine" must qualify the word sardines. The labeling should then list the brand name and "Maine Sardines." The qualifier "Maine" is required because the fish that is canned is an immature herring and not a true sardine. Few people realize that much of the imported Norwegian pack of sardines is comprised of exactly the same herring whose scientific name is *Clupea harengus harengus.*

Norway packs two distinct species of fish, and each is usually labeled differently. The pack containing immature herring (the same as that which Maine packs) is labeled as "Norway Sardines" followed by a declaration of the packing medium, such as sild sardine oil (herring oil), and will often list the number of fish, such as "one layer 6–12 fish" or "two layers 16–24 fish." The term *sild* is both the Norwegian and Danish name for herring.

The second species of fish packed in Norway as a sardine is the sprat whose scientific name is *Sprattus sprattus sprattus.* Again, the labeling requires the designation of "Norway Sardines." Some Norwegian packers have their labels declare "brisling sardines" in very bold type. In Norwegian, brisling means that herring-like fish which is called sprat in English. Not found in waters outside the northern European Atlantic, it is generally considered superior to the herring. The difference in price between packs of sild and brisling sardines is appreciable.

Anchovies

Anchovies are prepared almost exclusively in Europe and in two different styles involving several species of fish. The first is the Mediterranean style, which is descended from the type of cure once used by the ancient Greeks and Romans. Its perfection lies in a special process of salting and fermentation. The only fish permitted in this pack is the true anchovy, *Engraulis encrasicholus.*

The second type of anchovy packed in Europe is produced in the Scandinavian countries of Sweden, Norway, and Denmark, with Sweden in the lead. Like the Mediterranean type, this product relies on a special salting and fermentation process. Unlike the Mediterranean style, it does not use the true anchovy but instead uses the same herring and sprats described under Norwegian sardines. Long usage has dictated that these two species of fish may properly be labeled as anchovies when prepared by salting and fermenting but must revert to the labeling of sild and brisling sardines when hermetically sealed and treated like sardine-type products.

Tunas

Members of the family Scombridae constitute an important source of food worldwide. The customs governing the labeling of tuna are even more involved and complex than those for canned sardines. Biologists recognize thirteen species scattered among four genera to be true tunas.

Tunas recognized as true tunas by scientists are not always recognized as tunas by different governments. For example, U.S. laws prohibit the labeling of bonito as tuna, yet Canada permits it. Japan, on the other hand, considers about five species of what we call tunas to be actually bonitos. However, our main concern here is with labeling requirements in the United States where about a dozen species of the family Scombridae may may properly be labeled as tuna. Only one tuna, the albacore *Thunnus alalunga,* can be labeled "white" tuna. All others are required to be labeled as "light" tuna.

Label declarations may vary as to the form of pack, whether solid pack, chunks, flakes, or grated. The solid pack and chunks of both white and light meat tuna predominate. Prominent label declarations are now evident for those packs with no added salt aimed at consumers who must limit their intake of sodium.

QUALITY FACTORS

Maine Sardines

All other things being equal, the greater the number of fish in the can, the more choice is the pack. When very small fish are packed (sixteen to twenty-four fish) the most attractive way to pack them is to make a double layer and cross pack them, that is, the fish lie parallel to the ends of the can. Normally fish running eleven to twelve to the can (a desired size) are packed with the head end toward the ends of the can. The fish are alternated head and tail to present an even fill. The least number of fish permitted is four.

Head ends should be cut evenly and the fish packed belly side up to present a silvery appearance. All fish in each can should be of the same size. If the packing medium is oil, it should be clear and not turbid or cloudy. The flavor of the fish should be mild and without a strong salt flavor, which would indicate improper brining procedure. If other packing media are used, such as tomato sauce or mustard, they should be homogeneous and not curdled.

Processing is the same for Norway sardines as for Maine sardines except that the number of fish per can is generally greater.

Portuguese Sardines

The true Portuguese sardine grows larger than either the herring or sprat, but despite the difference in size, the ex-vessel price is much greater than that for herring or sprats. Quality factors to look for are six or more skinless and boneless fish with no trace of visceral matter. Maine and Norway sardines do contain entire viscera but little or no food in the gut. Fish should be packed in the can head to tail and arranged to present white and dark portions of flesh evenly. The oil (usually olive) should be clear and not cloudy or turbid. The flavor is milder than the herring sardines and sprat, and the flesh is firmer than either. The abundance of white meat has aptly led some to compare this true sardine to the position held by the white-meated albacore tuna among all the tunas.

Tunas

Standards of identity, definitions, and standards of fill of container for tuna were announced by the Food and Drug Administration in 1959. In 1965 federal specifications for canned tuna were issued by the General Services Administration for the use of all federal agencies.

A primary factor is the color of the meat and whether it accords with the can label declaration as "white" or "light." Two other color designations, "dark" and "blended," are provided for in the definitions, but they are for limited or specialized markets. The label declaration of white applies only to the albacore tuna whose reflectance value exceeds 6.3 Munsell units. Similarly, light meat tuna must have a reflectance value not lower than 5.3 Munsell units.

The oil (when used) should be clear, typical of the kind (soy, cottonseed, etc.)

and not cloudy or turbid. The values for free fatty acids, smoke point, and moisture content should fall in the range established by the manufacturer of the oil.

The more serious defects to look for are honeycombing of the flesh, nonuniformity of color, extraneous foreign material, short weight, and off-flavors caused by rancid oil, sour flesh, or scorched or overcooked cans.

Mackerels

The Atlantic mackerel, *Scomber scombris,* is seldom packed now, but a close relative, the chub or Pacific mackerel, *Scomber japonicus,* enjoys a small annual pack. The jack mackerel, which is a carangid, *Trachurus symmetricus,* and not a true mackerel, is packed extensively.

The chief factor to look for here is broken body meat. If the mackerel are improperly brined before being placed in the cans, they do not attain the firmness that is desired for a good commercial pack. The liquid packing medium is usually a brine, which becomes quite turbid and cloudy after it is heated in a retort. True mackerels usually have a better flavor than jack mackerel.

Anchovies, Mediterranean Style

The Mediterranean-style anchovy is usually in one of two styles. The more common style is that of tiny, thin fillets packed flat in successive layers to fill the can. The other consists of anchovy fillets rolled around a caper, a cured olive, or other suitable small piece of vegetable that has been pickled in vinegar for preservation. Regardless of the type of pack, the anchovies should be red in color (due to fermentation process) and smoothly prepared without ragged edges. Some packs may contain mustard and vinegar as well as the oil, making for a zesty packing medium.

Because of their high salt content, anchovies are never eaten as they come from the can but are freshened in water for about fifteen to twenty minutes and then used with other foods as appetizers in salads, other fish products, quiches, and as anchovy paste, creams, and butters.

CHAPTER

5

Shellfish-Mollusks

Michael Castagna

The harvesting of mollusks is an important industry in the United States, providing a value of more than $40 billion. The fishery is based primarily on the harvest of bivalves (two-shelled mollusks) such as clams or oysters, but gastropods such as abalone or conchs, and cephalopods such as squid or octopus are also harvested. The mollusk harvest takes place along the entire coast of the United States, from coastal bays and estuaries to the edge of the continental shelf.

The earliest settlers harvested shellfish, and midden heaps (piles of shell) found in many areas along the coast show that the American Indians also consumed oysters, clams, and conchs. The Indians also used the shells for tools, decorations, and for barter. The quahog, or hard clam, bears the scientific name of *Mercenaria* in reference to its use as a kind of currency by the American Indians.

NATURAL HISTORY

Most of the mollusks such as clams, oysters, and abalone have a similar life history. As water temperatures warm up in the spring or early summer, the reproductive organs develop sperm or eggs. When water temperatures reach a critical level and development of reproductive products is complete, the mollusks spawn. Most bivalves release eggs and sperm into the water where external fertilization takes place as eggs and sperm meet. The fertilized eggs develop into free-swimming planktonic larvae that drift within the water mass at the whim of wind and tides. This process disperses the larvae to populate areas away from the parents. After two or four weeks the larvae will have changed into seed, or spat, which sink to the bottom, or, in the case of oysters and mussels, attach themselves to the substrate, where they settle and grow.

The gastropods and cephalopods usually practice internal fertilization and lay their eggs inside of capsules, which are attached to the bottom or other suitable substrates. These offspring hatch from the eggs as completely formed juveniles instead of larvae.

Most commercial species of mollusks become sexually mature at about one year of age. Later, perhaps in their second or third year, about half change sex and become female. Some species like oysters can change sexes periodically, but many others change sex only once.

Almost all commercial shellfish are prolific. It is estimated that a clam is capable of spawning up to 60 million eggs per year; an oyster might yield approximately five times that number per year.

FEEDING

Most commercial bivalves are filter feeders, obtaining their food by pumping water through their gills, where by a sophisticated sorting method they select certain food particles which are passed to the mouth and into the stomach. Gastropods often graze along the bottom for food. Some are specialized feeders seeking live prey or are scavengers of dead fish or shellfish. Cephalopods, the squid and octopus, are usually hunters, capturing fish or crabs to eat.

THE MOLLUSK AND PUBLIC HEALTH

Shellfish are sometimes eaten raw or lightly steamed. With this lack of thorough cooking, it is important that shellfish come from unpolluted waters. The Food and Drug Administration, the Public Health Service, and state health departments all monitor shellfish harvesting areas to prevent harvesting from polluted areas.

CONSERVATION REGULATIONS

The mollusk fishery can be divided into the inshore fisheries, which includes bays, lagoons, and estuaries, and the offshore fisheries on the continental shelf. The inshore fisheries are the older, more traditional fisheries and are encumbered with more traditions and regulations on types of harvesting gear, seasonality, size of animals taken, and quotas on size of harvest. The offshore fisheries often have quotas on size of harvest and some areas are closed, but there are seldom regulations on the type of harvesting gear or size of animals.

MAJOR COMMERCIAL SPECIES

Surf Clam

Surf clams *(Spisula solidissima)* (Fig. 5-1), also known as hen clams or skimmer clams, are found along the Atlantic coast from Newfoundland to North Carolina, up to depths of 200 feet (61 m). The clams that make up the commercial catch are four to six years old and range in length from 6 to 9 inches (15.2 to 22.9 cm).

In 1980 37.7 million pounds (17.1×10^6 kg) were landed, valued at $19.1 million. In New England, about 1918, an inshore fishery developed for surf clams, which were harvested from a boat using rakes. Hand tongs were also used in the early days of the industry. As power boats became more common in the 1920s, scraper-type dredges, which would scoop 6 to 9 inches (15.2 to 22.9 cm) into the bottom, came into use. These dredges allowed harvesting in deeper water.

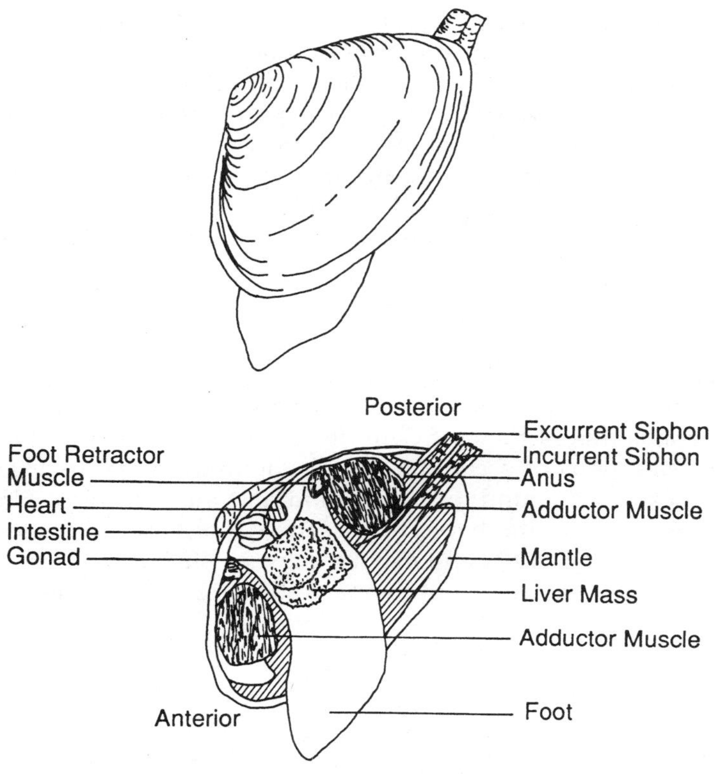

Figure 5-1. Surf Clam.

No significant advancements took place in the surf clam fishery until World War II brought a large increase in the demand for food. A hydraulic jet dredge was developed which pumped a jet of water into the bottom ahead of the cutting bar of the dredge. This method was so much more efficient that abandoned fishing areas, where clams were no longer dense enough to harvest by conventional scrape-type dredges, could be successfully harvested. Hydraulic dredges also resulted in a great reduction in broken clams and it could harvest hard bottom areas that scrape-type dredges could not. The hydraulic dredge, considerably modified, improved, and enlarged from the early models, is now the mainstay of the surf clam industry.

As inshore surf clams were removed, larger boats were necessary to move farther offshore and the fishery moved south to the New Jersey coast, then to the Delmarva Peninsula and the Virginia capes.

It now has been overfished to the extent that there are regulations which restrict entry into the fishery and the number of hours fished per boat per week until an industry-wide monthly quota is reached. In addition, New Jersey has closed some fishing areas to encourage the repopulation of the surf clams. This management strategy appears to be successful, and other states may soon follow suit.

Processing

After the harvest, the clams are placed in metal-mesh cages, which hold 30 bushels (1,057 liters) each. These are mechanically unloaded at the dock and stored, if necessary, in a refrigerated room. They are then dumped onto a conveyor belt which moves the clams through a gas flame to open the shell. Some processors use a steam or hot water bath to open the shells. Then the clams are carried to a table where the meats are extracted from the shell by shuckers, and the viscera, referred to as the sand bag, is removed. These two steps are often still done by hand, but mechanical shakers and eviscerators are also being used. The meats are then washed and cut or diced for packing and freezing. The surf clam meats are frozen in 4-inch (10.2 cm) thick sheets, called blankets, for sale and shipment to food processors and restaurants. Surf clams are usually served in chowders, soups, or fried clam strips.

Ocean Quahog

The ocean quahog *(Arctica islandica),* or mahogany clam (Fig. 5-2), is found from southern Newfoundland to just north of Cape Hatteras, North Carolina. Although its range overlaps that of the surf clam, it is usually found in deeper water. The heaviest concentrations of ocean quahogs are found from 90 to 480 feet (27.4 to 146.3 m) deep and are found buried in sand and mud bottoms. Growth rate is extremely slow. Most of the harvested ocean quahogs are 3½ inches (8.9 cm) to about 5 inches (12.7 cm) long, and may be between 60 and 130 years of age. They do not reach sexual maturity until they are about 12 years of age.

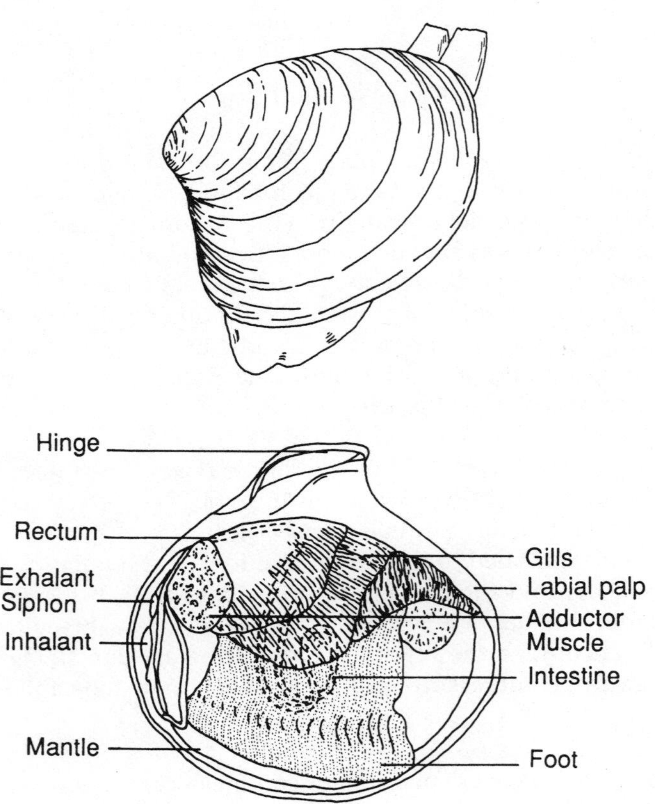

Figure 5-2. Quahog Clam.

Present Status

The commercial fishery for the ocean quahog started in the mid-1940s but did not become an important fishery until the 1960s, following the decline of the surf clam fishery. As surf clam stocks were reduced, the same boats were used to harvest the ocean quahog. In 1980 33.8 million pounds (15×10^6 kg) of ocean quahog were harvested with a value of $10.2 million. Surf clam processors can process quahogs with little or no modification of their equipment. Even though currently there are ample stocks of ocean quahogs, recruitment and growth of young clams may not keep up with the harvest. A management plan may prolong the use of the stocks but may not maintain the fishery.

Processing

The ocean quahog is prepared and marketed in the same manner as surf clams.

Hard Clam

Hard clams *(Mercenaria mercenaria)*, or northern quahogs, are found from the Gulf of St. Lawrence to the Gulf of Mexico and have been introduced to Humboldt Bay, California, and Southampton, England. They inhabit shallow areas where they burrow into sand or mud bottoms.

These clams are sold in the shell by size. They are graded as little neck, cherrystone, and chowder. Little necks and cherrystones bring the highest prices and are almost always in demand. Clams take three to five years to reach little neck size. Cherrystone and chowder sizes take five to ten and eight to twelve years, respectively.

The annual catch of clams has declined since 1950 when 21 million pounds (9.5×10^6 kg) of meats were landed, compared to 13 million pounds (5.9×10^6 kg) in 1980. However, their value increased dramatically from $7.3 million in 1950 to $44.1 million in 1980.

Hard clams are harvested by several hand and mechanical methods: They are raked from the bottom; they are hand tonged; and they also are patent tonged with tongs that are raised and lowered by a power winch. In shallow areas hard clams are collected by wading or treading (feeling for the clams with moccasin-covered feet). In intertidal areas clams are often harvested by clam signing. The harvester looks for the siphon holes, or sign, and then digs up the clams with a clam pick, which resembles an 18-inch (45.7 cm) two-pronged fork with the prongs bent at right angles to the handle. Since the mid-1950s, a more efficient device called a hydraulic dredge has been used for harvesting shallow-water mollusks. The hydraulic dredge, suspended from a vessel, jets water into the bottom ahead of the dredge blade, making a solution of the sand, mud, shells, and clams. The clams are washed back into the dredge by water pressure and onto a chain link conveyor belt that carries them to the surface.

Present Status

The importance and value of the hard clam fishery is increasing. Although production in some traditional harvest areas in the Northeast is decreasing, due to pollution or overfishing, new areas in the Southeast are opening. Clams from polluted areas can be used, but they must first be replanted in unpolluted areas and allowed to cleanse themselves over several weeks before being sold, a process that greatly increases production costs. The demand for large-size clams has decreased due to the commercial and institutional use of surf clams or ocean quahogs, but may increase as surf clam landings decline.

Processing

The smaller hard clams are usually sold live and in the shell and are consumed raw, steamed, or as specialty items such as clams casino. Chowder clams are either sold in the shell or fresh shucked for further processing. Surf clam processors occasionally process chowder clams in the same manner as surf clams.

Soft Shell Clam

The soft shell clam *(Mya arenaria)*, or steamer clam (Fig. 5-3), is an inshore species found from Labrador south to North Carolina and later introduced to the West Coast. They are found in sand-mud bottoms in intertidal to subtidal inshore areas and are tolerant of a wide range of salinities and temperatures.

Like most clams they grow faster in warmer waters. It takes them about six years to reach market size in Maine, four years in Massachusetts, but only eighteen

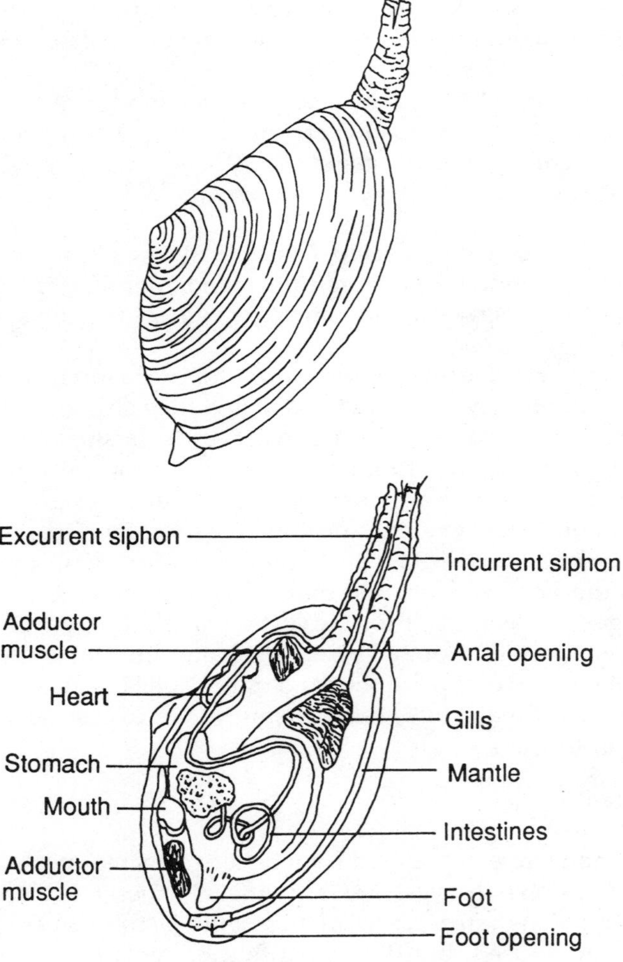

Figure 5-3. Soft Shell Clam.

months in Maryland. Soft clams in the Chesapeake Bay grow rapidly but are subject to heavy predation, and massive die-offs occur due to oxygen deficiencies and periods of low salinity caused by heavy rains.

In 1980 the U.S. catch was almost 9 million pounds (4.1×10^6 kg), valued at $15.4 million. Maine was the leading state in landings with 5.7 million pounds (2.6×10^6 kg) followed by Maryland. This fishery was originally based in Maine and Massachusetts, supplemented by imports from Canada. The clams were dug by hand from extensive intertidal flats using a clam hack. In the 1950s the hydraulic dredge was introduced into the Chesapeake Bay, opening a significant new area for soft clam harvesting. The Chesapeake Bay has a relatively low tidal fluctuation and few intertidal areas for clamming. The newly introduced hydraulic dredge made practical the harvest of deeper subtidal areas.

Processing

Soft clams are sold in the shell for steamed clams or as a shucked and frozen product used in restaurants as breaded and fried clams. They also are sold fresh shucked in cans or frozen.

Scallops

Bay scallops are harvested from all U.S.coasts in shallow bays. Another species, the calico scallop, found in abundance off the Atlantic coast of Florida, is also sold as a bay scallop. Both species grow to market size in about 12 months.

The Atlantic sea scallop is found from Labrador to North Carolina. The most important harvesting areas are Georges Bank shared with Canada and near the Virginia capes. This species takes from three to six years to reach market size. In 1987, 7.3 million pounds (3.31×10^6 kg) of sea scallop meats were valued at $28.1 million.

On the northwest coast of the United States the weather vane scallop and the rock scallop are harvested for a limited market.

The scallops are usually harvested using a wide shallow dredge similar to an oyster dredge except the rock scallop which is harvested by divers.

Processing

Scallops are usually shucked by hand and the adductor muscle, referred to as the heart, is saved and the rest of the viscera discarded. The Atlantic sea scallop is usually shucked and iced aboard ship. The meats are sold fresh or frozen. Recently some bay scallop meats have been sold whole (viscera and adductor together) either fresh or frozen.

Manila Clam

The Manila clam *(Tapes philippinarium)*, or Japanese little neck, is found on the U.S. West Coast. It was introduced with shipments of oyster seed from Japan and has become the most important commercial clam on the West Coast. In the past ten years, an average of more than 850,000 pounds (390×10^3 kg) were harvested, worth about $6 million, by hand digging or raking in intertidal areas. Certain leased areas in Washington state are presently being harvested by hydraulic dredges similar to those used in the soft clam industry. The industry is growing rapidly and has already replaced the native clam harvest.

Processing

The Manila clam is sold and processed like the East Coast hard clam. It seldom reaches chowder size, so most are sold and used like little neck and cherrystone hard clams.

Geoduck

The geoduck *(Panopea generosa)*, a large 7- to 9-inch (18- to 23-cm) clam, is found from Alaska to the Gulf of California from shallow waters to intertidal beaches. It is commonly found burrowed 2 to 3 feet (0.6 to 0.9 m) into mud bottoms on the coast of northwestern states. This clam originally supported only a sport fishery in the intertidal areas, but in recent years it has been harvested commercially by divers, who upon finding its siphon holes, jet the mollusk out of the bottom with a high pressure jet of water.

Fishing areas, catch limits, and open seasons are regulated.

Processing

Generally a specialty item in stores and restaurants, the geoduck is sold shucked and frozen or fresh in the shell.

Oysters

Oysters (Fig. 5-4) are found on all U.S. coasts in shallow waters. Their range often extends into brackish water, such as in tidal creeks and estuaries. Along the Atlantic and Gulf coasts the commercial oyster is the Virginia oyster, *Crassostrea virginica*. The West Coast had a native oyster that is no longer commercially available due to overfishing and other problems. The oystermen started importing juvenile oysters from Japan and the industry is now based on this Japanese oyster, *Crassostrea gigas*. Oysters grow to market size in three to six years depending on their environment.

The oyster fishery involves more than just harvesting wild oysters. Oystermen often lease bay or tidal river bottoms from state or local agencies for the planting and cultivating of oysters. This process involves placing oyster shells onto these bottom areas in the spring of the year, when the oysters have spawned and oyster larvae are in the water, thus furnishing the metamorphosing oyster larvae attractive surfaces for attachment. These shells, called cultch, with their "catch" of oysters, called spat, are often moved during the following fall to other areas where they can grow more rapidly. They are broadcast over the bottom so they are not too

Figure 5-4. Oysters.

crowded and can be harvested easily when they reach market size. This method frees the original area so that more cultch can be placed on the bottom to collect spat the next spring.

After the oysters reach maturity, they are harvested using an oyster dredge. The dredge, a rectangular steel frame with a series of teeth, digs the oysters from the bottom mud as it is towed across the bottom. The dredge, towed by a boat, is usually hauled aboard with a winch and the catch is dumped and sorted by hand.

The oyster fishery is one of the oldest shellfish industries, and since it is inshore with the oyster grounds often spanning more than one municipality or extending over state boundaries, it is encumbered with more regulations than any other fishery. For instance, in many areas, oysters can only be harvested with tongs. In certain areas of the Chesapeake Bay they must be harvested by sail-driven dredge boats—the famous skipjack oyster schooners. Because they are inshore, beds are often subject to closure due to pollution.

Present Status

The oyster industry used to be the most important shell-fishery in the United States but recently has greatly declined. Pollution of inshore waters was probably responsible for much of the decline, but economics, disease, and overfishing were also problems in certain areas. In 1980 49 million pounds (22×10^6 kg) of oysters were harvested in the United States with a value of more than $70 million. The high cost of production has made oysters a luxury item.

Processing

Oysters are processed and sold in several ways. Many smaller sized oysters are steamed open, the meat removed by mechanical shakers, and then canned or frozen for use in chowders, soups, or processed in cakes or sticks. Others are served raw, on the half shell, or packed fresh in cans and sold to retailers.

European or Flat Oysters

In recent years in the clean, clear, cold waters of Maine, the culturing of the European oyster *(Ostrea edulis)* has become a growing industry. The European oyster was introduced to Maine waters in 1949 but never developed into a natural fishery. In the early 1950s, methods had been found for artificially spawning the oysters and rearing the young to market size. In the European oyster, the eggs are fertilized on the gills and brooded there until they reach a certain stage in development. At that time they are expelled into the water in a process known as swarming.

Most of the oysters are grown on rafts and sold in the shell to a limited, fairly local market. Oysters reach a marketable size of about 2½ inches (6.4 cm) in two to four years.

Squid

The squid fishery in the United States is active on both the Atlantic and Pacific coasts, with most of the harvest exported to foreign markets such as Japan and northern Europe. Squid (Fig. 5-5) are harvested by two methods, jigging and trawling.

In 1980 9.8 million pounds (4.4×10^6 kg) of squid were landed from the Atlantic

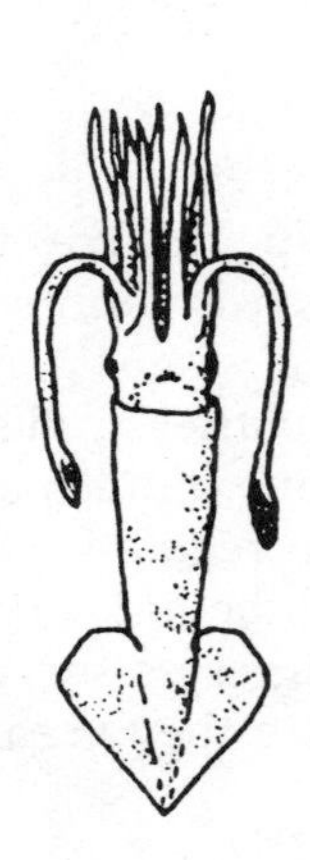

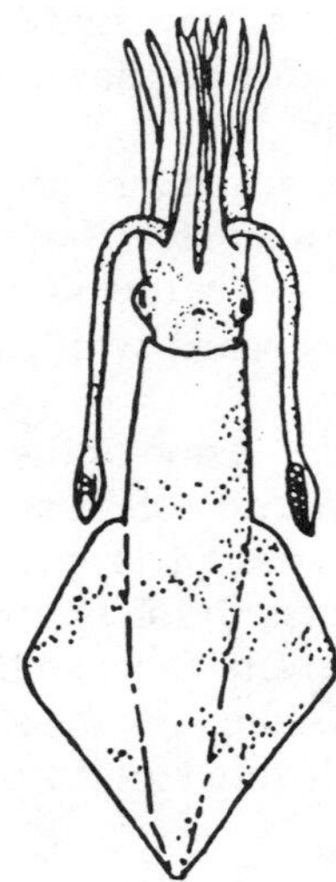

Figure 5-5. Illex (left) and Loligo (right): Two Types of Squid.

and 25 million pounds (11.3×10^6 kg) from the Pacific Ocean, valued at $3.1 million and $2.2 million, respectively.

Jigging squid is carried out by fishermen who lower lights from the vessel to just below the water surface. Elliptical wooden lures, about the size of a spark plug, with a ring of barbless fishhooks fastened to the bottom, are lowered below the lights and then hauled aboard the boat. The squid catches and clings to the jig and is entangled in the circle of barbless hooks. The recent introduction of automated jigging machines has made jigging an attractive fishing method.

Squid are also taken by trawl net fishing. The trawl is hauled through the water at the depth where the squid are congregating and then hauled aboard the vessel. Congregations of squid are found by electronic fish finders carried aboard the ships.

Due to the improved fishing method (automated jigging), expanding markets, and improved demand, this fishery should grow in importance.

Processing

The squid are usually cleaned and packed in ice or salted aboard the vessel. To have room for this type of operation the vessels are usually quite large, often over 200 feet (61 m) in length. Most of the squid are frozen and shipped overseas.

Blue Mussel

The Atlantic Coast blue mussel *(Mytilus edulis)* fishery, which has been small, has grown in importance in recent years. In addition to a small wild harvest usually done by hand raking, tonging, or using an oyster dredge, a mussel culture industry is starting in the Northeast. Natural mussel set is collected on plastic ropes or plastic mesh tubes hanging from rafts. When the mussels reach market size of $2\frac{1}{2}$ inches (6.4 cm) in about eighteen months to two years, they are harvested.

Processing

Most mussels are sold in the shell. However, some are steamed, and the meats that are removed from the shell are canned either plain or in special sauces.

Abalone

The abalone is a gastropod, or snail, although it does not look like most snails. There are a number of species found on rocky outcrops and bottoms, where they graze on the encrusting organisms that grow on the hard surfaces. Abalone are found along the California and Oregon coasts and are harvested almost exclusively by divers. In the early days of the fishery, sufficient numbers could be found in shallow waters so that diving was not required. Divers now seek out the abalone on submerged rocky ledges and pry them loose with a small prying bar. Both the commercial divers and sport divers are licensed, and there are strict regulations governing number and size of the abalone captured.

Processing

Abalone are usually sold fresh at the local market where they command a high price, often as high as $30 per pound (454 g). They are sometimes dried for export to Japan and China, where they are considered medicinal and the price increased accordingly.

CHAPTER

6

Shellfish-Crustaceans

Michael J. Oesterling

Crustaceans are members of the phylum Arthropoda, which also includes insects, spiders, centipedes, and millipedes. Among the 26,000 known species of crustaceans are some of the most popular and valuable seafood products: crabs, shrimp, and lobsters.

Man's interest in crustaceans dates back thousands of years. Drawings of crabs have even been found on Egyptian temple walls. The early Latins placed the crab in the zodiac about 2100 B.C., and the ancient Greeks included the crab constellation and crab in their mythology. One myth explains the origin of the crab constellation: While Hercules was battling the Hydra, a jealous Juno had a crab nip at Hercules's ankles to distract him. When Hercules crushed the crab, Juno raised it to a place among the stars as a reward for its sacrifice.

The name *crustacean* is derived from the Latin word for shell. Indeed, the hard exoskeleton is such a prominent anatomical feature that crustaceans are often referred to as shellfish. Crustaceans have several other characteristic features: They have mandibles as mouth parts, possess two pairs of antennae, and breathe through gills derived from leg appendages. Crustaceans are found in great variety in both freshwater and saltwater habitats.

Among the crustaceans, the animals of the order Decapoda are of primary economic interest. The 8,500-plus species of decapods represent about one-third of all crustaceans. The name *decapod* means ten feet; all decapods have five pairs of thoracic appendages. In many decapods the first pair of legs is modified into claws or pinchers used for prey capture and defense. Many decapods qualify as important food resources; they are abundant, wholesome, and accessible. Of particular interest are the true crabs, the shrimp (penaeid and pandalid), and lobsters (American and spiny).

One feature that all crustaceans have in common is their hard outer shell and the need to shed this shell in order to grow. This shedding process, termed ecdysis, is an important event in the lives of all crustaceans. In many cases a critical phase of reproduction occurs at molting.

The actual process of molting and growth is complex. Prior to shedding, a new shell begins forming underneath the old one. In some species there are visible indications that molting is about to occur. As the time approaches, the crustacean resorbs some carbohydrates, proteins, and calcium from the old shell. These substances are stored within the body and used to help form the new shell. Muscle attachments to the old shell are loosened and reattached to the forming shell. In most instances a portion of the stomach lining is lost; hence all feeding ceases. Finally the old shell splits open along predetermined fracture lines and the animal simply backs out of the old shell. At this time the crustacean is very soft and defenseless. For this reason, molting takes place in hiding. Just before and immediately after molting, large quantities of water may be absorbed to aid in expanding the new shell to a larger size than the old shell. The amount of size increase is probably controlled by both genetics and by environmental conditions. After a period of hours or days, the new shell hardens completely. The interval between molts depends on the size of the individual, with younger individuals molting more frequently than older ones.

CRABS

No other group of decapods is so diverse in terms of habitat and lifestyle as the crabs. They are found in fresh and salt water, in warm and cold temperatures, and range in size from giant to almost microscopic. Some crawl, some swim.

Many regions of the United States have its locally caught crab that finds favor with the residents of the area. Some crab species, such as the blue crab and king crab, have been heavily exploited and are regular items in many seafood restaurants. The figures (Table 6-1) on commercial crab landings for 1988 show the economic importance of crabs in the United States.

The crab is covered by a hard outer shell known as the exoskeleton. The top, or dorsal, side of a crab is covered by a single heavy piece of exoskeleton called the carapace (Fig. 6-1) that covers the crab's head and thorax regions. Stalked eyes are located at the front of the body and the rostrum, an extension of the exoskeleton, is located between the eyes.

The ventral (bottom) side of a crab looks nothing like the carapace. The most striking feature is the turned-under abdomen (Fig. 6-2). The abdomen of the crab corresponds to the "tail" of the shrimp, crayfish, and lobster. Markings on the abdomen reveal the crab's sex: The male has a long pencil-shaped abdomen; the female has a broad, semicircular marking. Under the abdomen are fine legs called pleopods, commonly known as swimmerets. Female crabs use these swimmerets

Table 6-1.

Species	1988 Poundage	1988 Value
Blue crab *(Callinectes sapidus)*	218,700,000	$ 84,400,000
Snow or Tanner crab *(Chionoecetes* spp.)	146,300,000	137,100,000
Dungeness crab *(Cancer magister)*	47,400,000	54,800,000
King crab *(Paralithoides camtschatica)*	21,000,000	84,200,000
Other species	22,200,000	23,100,000
Stone crab *(Menippe mercenaria)*		
Jonah crab *(Cancer borealis)*		
Rock crab *(Cancer irroratus)*		
Total	455,600,000	$383,600,000

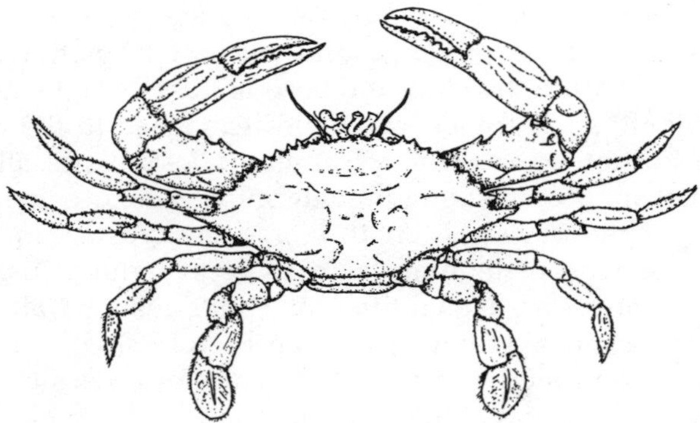

Figure 6-1. Blue Crab.

as attachment for their eggs. Besides the abdomen, the other notable features of the crab's ventral side are the thoracic divisions that appear as sections of the shell.

Crabs have a number of paired appendages, including five pairs of legs, or pereiopods. The first pair is modified to be the chelipeds, ending in the chela, or pinchers. They function in defense and feeding. The remaining pairs of pereiopods are for locomotion and may also be used in food gathering.

Pereiopods are the most obvious of the crab's paired appendages, but there are others just as important. Most of these are centered around the crab's head region. Between the eyes are two pairs of filamentous, hairlike structures, the antennae and the antennules. The antennules are generally smaller than the antennae and are located directly on either side of the rostrum. Between the antennules and eyes are the

Figure 6-2. Ventral Surfaces of Blue Crab. Male (top, left); Immature Female (top, right); Mature Female (bottom).

antennae. Together the antennae and antennules are part of a crab's sense of smell, receiving chemical "odors" from the water. They also are sensitive to touch.

The internal systems of crabs are complex and are not discussed here. However, a brief comment on the most visible of these systems, the respiratory, is appropriate. Along the sides of the body cavity are the gill structures. These appear as eight pairs of frilly, fingerlike projections. The gills, often referred to as "dead man's fingers," are the sites where oxygen is obtained and waste materials such as carbon dioxide are removed. Water enters the gill chamber near the base of the claws, flows upward over the gills, and passes out at the sides of the mouth.

Blue Crab

The blue crab *(Callinectes sapidus)* supports a large commercial fishery along the eastern seaboard of the United States and Gulf of Mexico. Actually there are two blue crab fisheries, one for hard-shelled crabs and one for soft-shelled crabs. Soft-shelled crabs are blue crabs that have recently shed (molted) their hard outer shell. These crabs command a premium price in the marketplace. Because of the blue crab's economic value a great deal of information is available on all aspects of the fishery and biology of the species.

It is found along the Atlantic coast from Nova Scotia to northern Argentina and throughout the Gulf of Mexico. The blue crab is most abundant in the Chesapeake Bay, which annually produces close to 50 percent of the hard crab harvest and 75 percent of the soft crab harvest. Although not native to Europe, individual crabs have been found along the European coast and in the Mediterranean Sea. It is believed that these crabs "hitchhike" in ballast tanks, or cling to ocean-going vessels.

The blue crab typically inhabits coastal areas, from the shoreline to a depth of approximately 300 feet (91 m), but it is most abundant in coves, bays, and estuaries, at depths up to 115 feet (35 m). It has been taken from freshwater environments such as Florida's Salt Springs and St. Johns River, and from hypersaline (supersalty) lagoons, such as Laguna Madre de Tamaulipas in Mexico. The blue crab's normal diet includes fishes, bottom invertebrates (clams, snails, worms, other crabs, etc.), and plant matter. Although it is considered a scavenger, it is more properly classified as an omnivore that prefers fresh to decaying flesh.

The blue crab generally lives two to three years, with the adult stage being reached after twelve to eighteen months. Its life history begins with the mating of a sexually mature male and female. The female blue crab mates only once in her lifetime, just after the molt that marks her transition from juvenile to adult. Unlike the female, the male reaches sexual maturity before he is fully grown. A male may mate with more than one female and at any time during his last three growth stages.

Prior to the female's molt, she moves to lower salinity waters and pairs with a male who will carry or cradle her underneath him. At this time both crabs are called doublers or buck-and-rider. The female completes her final molt in this cradled position and becomes an adult. While she is in the soft intermolt stage, copulation takes place. The male transfers his sperm to the female, which she stores in seminal receptacles within her body. The sperm are able to live for about one year. Following copulation, the male again cradles the female beneath him until her new shell hardens. This cradling serves two purposes. It assures that there will be a male present at the one stage in the female's life when she is able to copulate. It also serves to protect her while she is in the soft stage and extremely vulnerable to predators. Once the female's new shell has hardened, the male releases her.

Spawning (laying of eggs) usually takes place one to nine months after mating, usually in the spring and summer months. It is generally thought to occur in higher salinity waters at the mouths of estuaries and offshore areas. Egg laying is quite rapid and may be completed within two hours. Eggs are passed from the ovaries through the seminal receptacles to be fertilized on their way to the outside of the female. As the eggs pass out of the body, they are attached to the small swimmeret appendages on the female's abdomen. When first laid, the eggs are orange, but as they mature, they turn yellow, then brown, and finally dark brown.

At the time of spawning, the female blue crab lays 700,000 to 2 million eggs, but only about one ten-thousandth of 1 percent of the eggs will survive to become mature crabs. The eggs are carried seven to fourteen days, at which time they hatch into planktonic zoea, which are only about 1/24 inch (1 mm) long. The zoeal phase has seven stages and lasts thirty-one to forty-nine days, depending upon water temperature and salinity. The optimum ranges for development are 66° to 84°F (19° to 29°C) and 23 to 28 parts per thousand salinity. The zoea then metamorphose into the single megalops stage which has both planktonic and benthic (bottom) affinities. After six to twenty days the megalops changes into the first crab stage, at which time the crab form is first seen.

Larval (zoea) development takes place "offshore" in more saline waters than the confines of the estuary. The young crabs, however, spend the majority of their growing life within the nursery grounds of the estuary. During the megalops and first few crab stages, there is a movement shoreward toward the nursery grounds. Figure 6-3 illustrates the movements of the blue crab during its life cycle.

Following the first crab stage, growth is rapid. Adulthood is reached twelve to eighteen months after egg hatching. After reaching the adult stage, blue crabs live about one year longer.

King Crab

The king crab *(Paralithoides camtschatica)* (Fig. 6-4) is the most commercially valuable crab species in the United States. It is the largest crab harvested, with an average weight of 10 pounds (4.55 kg).

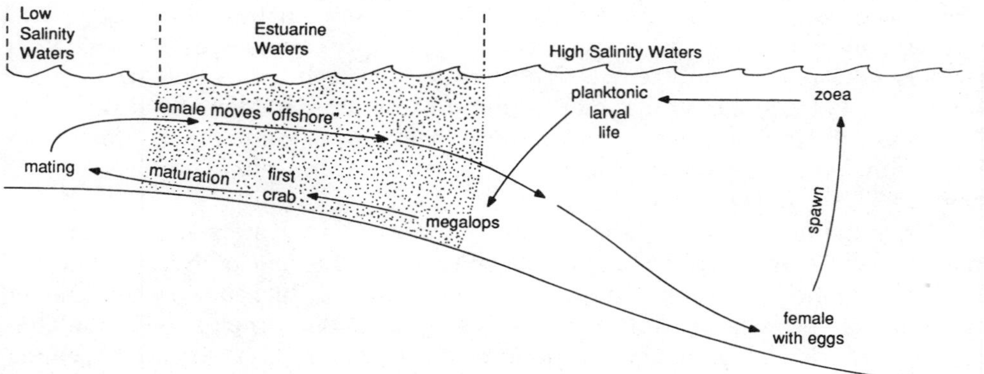

Figure 6-3. Life Cycle of Blue Crab. Mating of sexually mature crabs takes place in lower salinity, inshore waters. Following mating, the female moves to higher salinity waters to spawn and hatch her eggs. Eggs hatch as zoea, spend some time in the plankton, then settle to the bottom as megalops. During the megalop and first few crab stages, the young blue crab moves shoreward to estuaries. There the crab grows until the entire process starts over again.

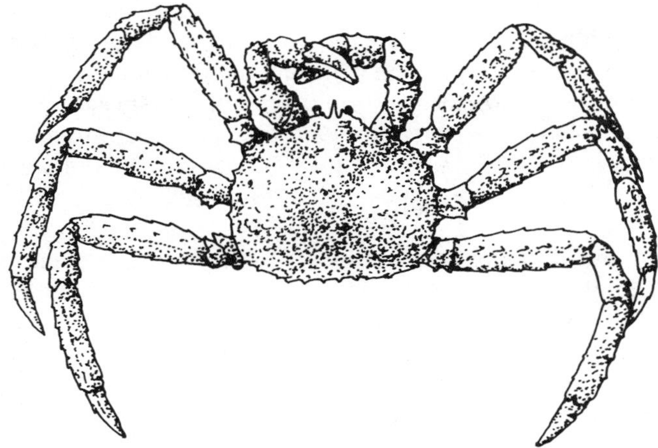

Figure 6-4. King Crab.

The range of the king crab extends from Korea and the Sea of Japan, northeastward to Kamchatka (Russia) and into the Bering Sea, eastward along the Aleutian Islands to Bristol Bay, into the Gulf of Alaska, and southward to Queen Charlotte Sound in southern Alaska. It is most abundant in the eastern Bering Sea and the northwestern Gulf of Alaska. Adult king crabs inhabit the deep waters of the continental shelf, occurring at depths greater than 600 feet (182 m). Male crabs tend to be found at greater depths (900 feet/274 m) than females. The king crab's normal diet consists of brittle stars, sea urchins, and starfish, and to a lesser degree, other crustaceans, polychaetes, and seaweed. King crabs may live twenty to twenty-five years and grow to weigh more than 25 pounds (11.5 kg), with a leg span of over 6 feet (1.8 m).

The life cycle of the king crab (Fig. 6-5) begins in late winter or early spring when

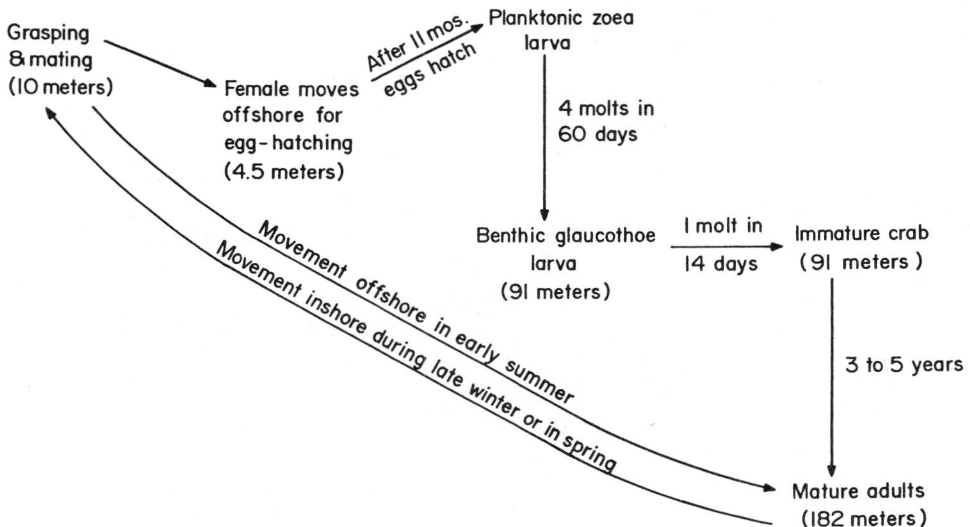

Figure 6-5. Life Cycle of the King Crab. (Numbers in parentheses represent approximate water depth at which events occur.)

sexually mature adults migrate shoreward for mating. Mating takes place in waters shallower than 60 feet (18.2 m) from late March through early May. Prior to actual copulation there is a courtship period during which the male grasps the chela of the female in a face-to-face position. Although grasping may last five to seven days, the act of mating lasts only a few minutes. Mating occurs immediately following a molt by the female. The male king crab may even assist the female in getting out of her old shell. After the female has completed her molt, the male will flip her over and begin mating.

Following mating and the hardening of her shell, the female begins to move offshore for egg hatching, which occurs in approximately 150 feet (46 m) of water. The female carries the eggs for about eleven months, after which they hatch as zoea larvae only 1/32 inch (1.12 mm) long. The immature king crab will molt several times a year until it reaches maturity; the molting period will then lengthen. A king crab becomes sexually mature at the age of five or six years, at a carapace width of 3.5 inches (8.9 to 10.2 cm) and a weight of about 2.2 pounds (1 kg).

One- and two-year-old king crabs exhibit a unique gregarious behavior of grouping together into "pods." The young crabs climb onto each other forming assemblages (pods) that may be 12 feet (3.7 m) long and comprise thousands of individuals. These aggregations move slowly along the bottom and may serve as protection against predators. Occasionally the crabs disband either to feed or to change location. During this time there is a gradual movement toward the deeper waters inhabited by the adults. As they get older, king crabs abandon the habit of podding; three- and four-year-old crabs spend more time grazing and tend not to form pods. Older adult crabs, however, may also form aggregates. In contrast to the juvenile pods that lack any orientation, older adults, in groups of 2,000 to 6,000, pile on top of another, each facing outward from the center of the group. The reasons for this action are unknown.

Cancer Crab

Crabs of the genus *Cancer* (family Cancidae) occur worldwide in temperate regions. In the United States there are East and West Coast species that are harvested either in directed fisheries or as incidental catches. On the Pacific Coast, the Dungeness Crab *(Cancer magister)* (Fig. 6-6), named after a small fishing village, supports a large commercial fishery. Harvested to a lesser degree from the Atlantic Coast are the Jonah crab *(Cancer borealis)* and the rock crab *(Cancer irroratus)*.

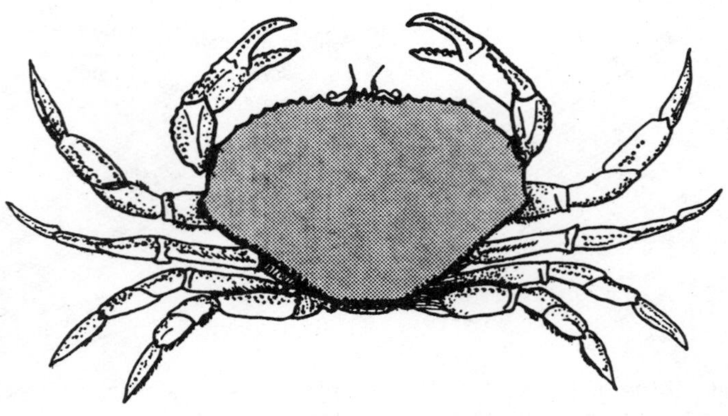

Figure 6-6. Dungeness Crab.

The ranges of these three species occur within the same latitudes on both coasts. The Dungeness crab is found from the Aleutian Islands southward to Magdalena Bay in Baja, California. It occurs from shore to approximately 300 feet (91.5 m). Jonah and rock crabs are found from Nova Scotia to the South Atlantic states. The rock crab is found in shallower waters in the north and deeper (up to 1,887 feet/575 m) in the south of its range. The Jonah crab is generally found in deeper waters than the rock crab (to 2,625 feet/800 m), although their ranges overlap in places and at certain times of the year. All three species are more abundant in the northern portions of their ranges.

The life cycles of the *Cancer* crabs are very similar. We use the Dungeness as a representative for this group (Fig. 6-7). The following description is based on Dungeness crabs living in California waters. The life cycle events of those to the north follow the same general sequence but occur in different months, as a result of lower temperatures.

Mature Dungeness crabs mate annually, completing an entire reproductive cycle each year. Mating between hard-shelled males and soft-shelled females occurs in oceanic waters from March through May. As the time for mating approaches the male Dungeness carries the female in a belly-to-belly embrace. This lasts for approximately seven days; on the eighth day the female struggles to escape. The male releases the female, permitting her to right herself. As the female sheds her shell, the male encircles her with his claws and legs. Immediately after the female has completed her molt, the male turns her over onto her back; the female extends her abdomen and the male inserts his copulatory pleopods into her seminal receptacles. Copulation lasts from 30 to 120 minutes, after which the male again carries the female for several days. Sperm are stored internally until October or November, at which time eggs are extruded and fertilization takes place. From 1 to 2 million eggs are carried on the female's abdomen until late December or mid-January, when they hatch as zoea larvae.

There are five zoeal stages and one megalopal stage, which last for a total of 105 to 125 days. The optimum environmental ranges from zoeal development are 50 to 57°F (10.0 to 13.9°C) and 25 to 30 parts per thousand salinity. Due to the seaward movement of surface waters, the planktonic zoeae are transported offshore. Megalopae are found offshore during March but move shoreward and are found concentrated near shore in April. Following the single megalops stage, the first crab stage occurs.

Young crabs abound in areas where currents are likely to concentrate megalopae until they are ready to settle out. Hence the youngest crabs are patchily distributed on the nursery grounds both in the ocean and in coastal bays. For the next several

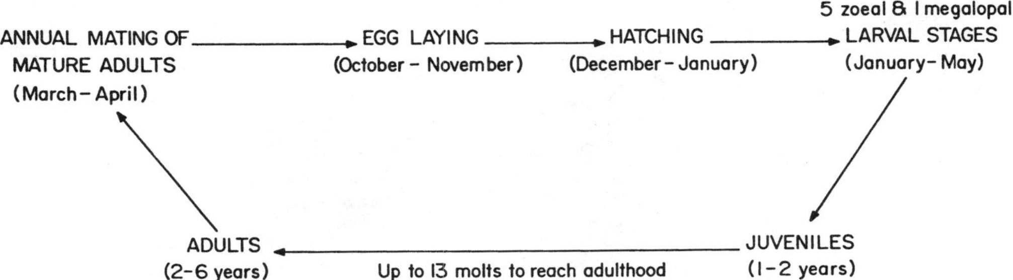

Figure 6-7. Life Cycle of the Dungeness Crab. The months given are for a California population of dungeness crab. In more northern environments, the life cycle events occur later.

years growth and frequency of molting varies with crab size, sex, and location (bay or ocean). Crabs growing within bay systems molt more frequently than their counterparts in the ocean. During the first two years of life both sexes increase in size at the same rate. After this time, however, females shed less frequently and do not grow as large as males. Dungeness crabs become sexually mature after approximately one year and may live to be six years old.

SHRIMP

Every seafood lover is familiar with shrimp. Shrimp constitute the most valuable commercial fishery in the United States; total shrimp landings for 1988 were 330.9 million pounds (1.5×10^8 kg), valued at approximately $506 million. The consumption of shrimp in the United States is so large that an additional 503.9 million pounds (229×10^6 kg), valued at $1.8 billion, were imported in 1988.

Worldwide, there are over eighty different species of shrimp caught for food. Within the United States shrimp are harvested from all the waters surrounding the continental United States, Hawaii, and Alaska. The U.S. shrimp fishery relies on two basic types of saltwater shrimp: penaeids and pandalids. The more familiar is the penaeid shrimp group, which includes such U.S. species as the pink shrimp *(Penaeus duorarum)*, the white shrimp *(Penaeus setiferus)*, and the brown shrimp *(Penaeus aztecus)*. There are many other penaeid species regularly imported to the United States.

The other saltwater shrimp commonly marketed are members of the pandalid group. U.S. representatives are the northern spot prawn *(Pandalus platyceros)* and northern pink shrimp *(Pandalus borealis)*. Generally, pandalids are smaller than the penaeids and are more cold water species; the penaeids are tropical or subtropical.

Not all shrimp found in U.S. markets belong to these two groups. Other U.S. species include rock shrimp (*Sicyonia* spp.), seabobs *(Xiphopenaeus kroyeri)*, and royal red shrimp *(Hymenopenaeus robustus)*. In addition, there are freshwater shrimp, often referred to as prawns. Although some of the largest specimens, prawns are not heavily exploited in the United States. We concentrate here on the more common penaeids and pandalids.

At first glance it would appear that shrimp (Fig. 6-8) bear little anatomical resemblance to crabs. A closer examination, however, will reveal the similarities.

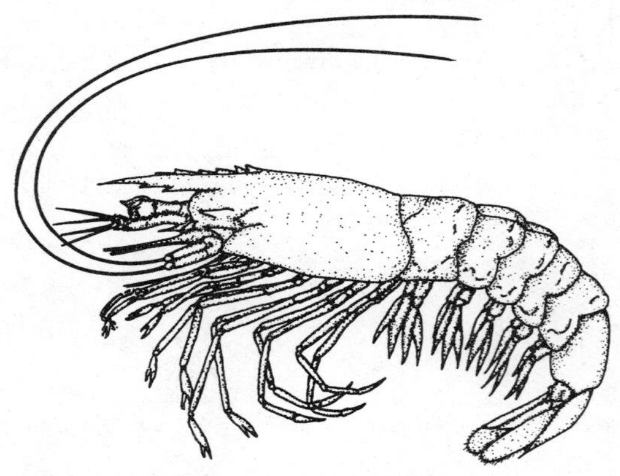

Figure 6-8. Shrimp.

The shrimp's body is divided into two distinct sections: the cephalothorax, covered by the carapace, and the abdomen. In crabs the carapace is flattened dorso-ventrally (top to bottom); in shrimp the carapace is compressed laterally to a more rounded shape. In both cases the carapace houses the important internal organs. The most visible anatomical difference between shrimps and crabs is the abdomen. In shrimp the abdomen extends out from the carapace; in crabs it is tucked under the carapace.

Shrimps and crabs have analogous appendages, although the appendages may differ in appearance. Both have antennae and antennules, one pair of mandibles, two pairs of maxillae, three pairs of maxillipeds, five pairs of pereiopods, and pleopods.

In the shrimp, the antennae may be of considerable size, sometimes longer than the body. Additionally, the inner branches of the antennae are greatly modified, taking the form of a horizontal blade called the scaphocerite, which functions as a stabilizer during swimming.

Pereiopods (walking legs) of shrimp have the same basic parts as those of crabs. In shrimp, however, the third maxilliped is modified into a leglike structure, thus giving the appearance of six pairs of walking legs. Unlike crabs, shrimp have exposed swimmerets (pleopods) on the abdomen. Also unlike crabs, the shrimp use their pleopods in swimming.

Within the family Penaeidae there are unique structures or modifications used during reproduction. Female penaeids have a peculiar copulatory structure between the last pair of walking legs called the thelycum, which serves as the storage location for spermatophores. In the males, the first pair of pleopods is modified to be a copulatory appendage, called a petasma, which functions in spermatophore transfer.

Shrimp can move around in several different ways. Using their pereiopods, they can walk over the bottom. They can use their pleopods to rise up in the water column and swim. From either the walking or swimming position they can move backward quickly by flexing their abdomens.

Penaeid Shrimp

With few exceptions, penaeid shrimp are found in estuaries and near-shore environments, occurring over a variety of bottom types. They may occupy different environments during different stages of their life cycle. Because their environmental requirements and habitat preferences overlap, several species may occur in one area. The bulk of the commercial harvest of penaeids in the United States takes place in the Gulf of Mexico and in the southern Atlantic Ocean, although penaeids do occur as far north on the Atlantic seaboard as Massachusetts.

Because the penaeids are so commercially valuable, their life cycles are very well known. The major U.S. species complete their life cycle within one year, although specific details vary from place to place and from year to year, depending on temperature, salinity, food availability, and other environmental conditions. To illustrate the basic pattern, we use the pink shrimp *(Penaeus duorarum)* as an example.

Pink shrimp are distributed from the shallows to depths of about 295 feet (90 m) from the lower Chesapeake Bay through the Florida Straits, around Mexico to the top of the Yucatán Peninsula. The major centers of abundance are off western Florida and in the southeastern Bay of Campeche, Mexico.

This species is very active at night, feeding and moving about. During the day it usually burrows into the bottom.

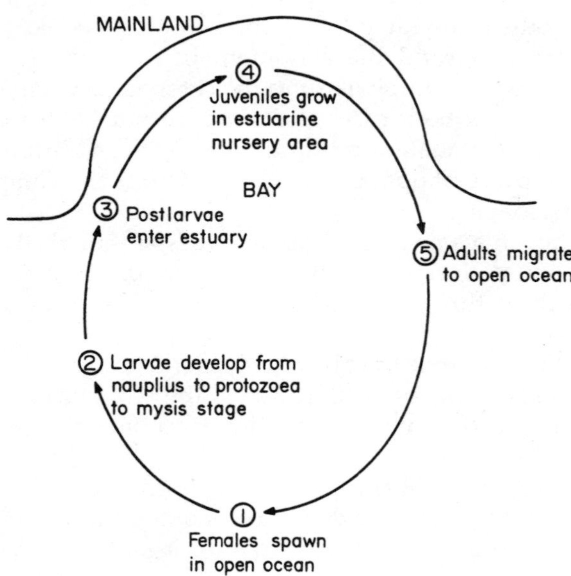

Figure 6-9. Life Cycle of Shrimp. The complete cycle, from spawning to adulthood, takes approximately one year.

During its life, the pink shrimp completes several migrations (Fig. 6-9). The first involves moving offshore for mating and spawning. As in other crustaceans, mating occurs between a hard-shelled male and a female in the soft stage immediately following a molt. Fifteen to twenty days after mating, spawning occurs, with eggs being fertilized as they pass from the female's body. Unlike many other decapod crustaceans, the female pink shrimp does not carry the eggs attached to her body, but broadcasts them into the water column. Here, as plankton, the eggs and developing larvae are at the mercy of the currents and tides. Spawning is most prevalent from April through July. Shrimp weighing between 0.4 and 2.4 ounces (10 and 67 g) may produce 44,000 to 535,000 eggs.

Eggs hatch in approximately fourteen hours in a water temperature of 80.6 to 84.2°F (27 to 29°C). Following egg hatching a progression of larval forms takes place.

During the postlarval stages, the young shrimp move back toward the coast. Catching currents moving landward, they are carried or swim into the protected bays, estuaries, and shallow lagoons that act as nursery grounds for the growing shrimp.

Once on the nursery grounds, growth is rapid. However, the growth rate slows with age and is different for males and females. A shrimp that measures 5.5 inches (140 mm) is approximately one year old. Male shrimp attain maximum lengths of 5 to 5.5 inches (130 to 140 mm) and weights of 1.0 to 1.2 ounces (30 to 35 g). Female pink shrimp grow much larger, reaching lengths of 6.3 to 6.7 inches (160 to 170 mm) and weights of 2.8 to 3.2 ounces (80 to 90 g).

Young shrimp seek shallower, often fresher, portions of the estuaries where they find abundant food supplies, a wide variety of plant and animal matter. With increasing size, the young shrimp move gradually into deeper, saltier water, finally returning to the open sea with approaching maturity. Individuals that survive to maturity may live another year or longer.

Pandalid Shrimp

Pandalid shrimp are found primarily along the southern and western coast of Scandinavia, off western Greenland, in the Gulf of Maine, and along the Pacific coast from Alaska to Oregon. *Pandalus borealis* predominates in the northern shrimp fishery, both in New England and Alaska. *Pandalus platyceros* contributes significantly to the Washington and Oregon shrimp fisheries. The life cycles of all the pandalids are very similar, but differ significantly from those of the penaeids. We describe the spot prawn *(Pandalus platyceros)* as an example of the pandalid life cycle.

Spot prawns and the other pandalids produce eggs and sperm from the same gonads but at different times in their life cycles. At age 1.5 years they mature as males, then pass through a transition or intersexual phase at 2.5 years, finally becoming functional females at 3.5 years. Both male and female spot prawns are capable of multiple spawnings. Unlike the more prolific penaeid, spot prawns produce only 2,000 to 5,000 eggs per female at first spawning; subsequent spawnings result in only 10 to 1,000 eggs per female. Also different is the fact that pandalids carry their eggs attached to their pleopods until hatching.

Following mating in autumn, the female carries the eggs for about five months, and hatching occurs in late March or early April. At 52°F (11°C) spot prawn larvae pass through five larval stages in thirty-five days before metamorphosing to postlarvae. There are four postlarval stages which last an additional forty to fifty days. Larvae of spot prawns are positively phototactic and appear to molt mostly at night. As in other crustaceans with pelagic larvae, the earliest stages are most vulnerable to predation and death by other causes.

By midsummer late larvae and early postlarvae are found in shallower waters, less than 180 feet (55 m), where they remain through autumn and part of the winter before returning to deeper waters. One year after hatching, spot prawns are back on the adult grounds. They average 0.8 inches (20 mm) in length and weigh 0.2 ounces (5.6 g). Relatively few spot prawns live beyond four years, but they can reach a length of 10 inches (254 mm).

LOBSTERS

Lobsters are truly a luxury food item. Two kinds of lobsters are harvested commercially in the United States: the "true" or American lobster *(Homarus americanus)* and the spiny lobster (*Panulirus argus* and *Panulirus interruptus*) (Fig. 6-10). These species are easily distinguished from each other. The true lobster has heavy claws, which the spiny lobster lacks. The spiny lobster has "horns" above the eyes which are not present in the true lobster. True lobsters have marketable meat in the claws, body, and tail; in spiny lobsters only the tail is marketed. Together all species of lobsters accounted for over $120 million in revenue to fishermen in 1988 (American lobsters, $145.2 million; spiny lobsters, $23 million).

The basic body form of the lobster is similar to that of the shrimp. The most obvious difference is the large claws of the American lobster. These, however,

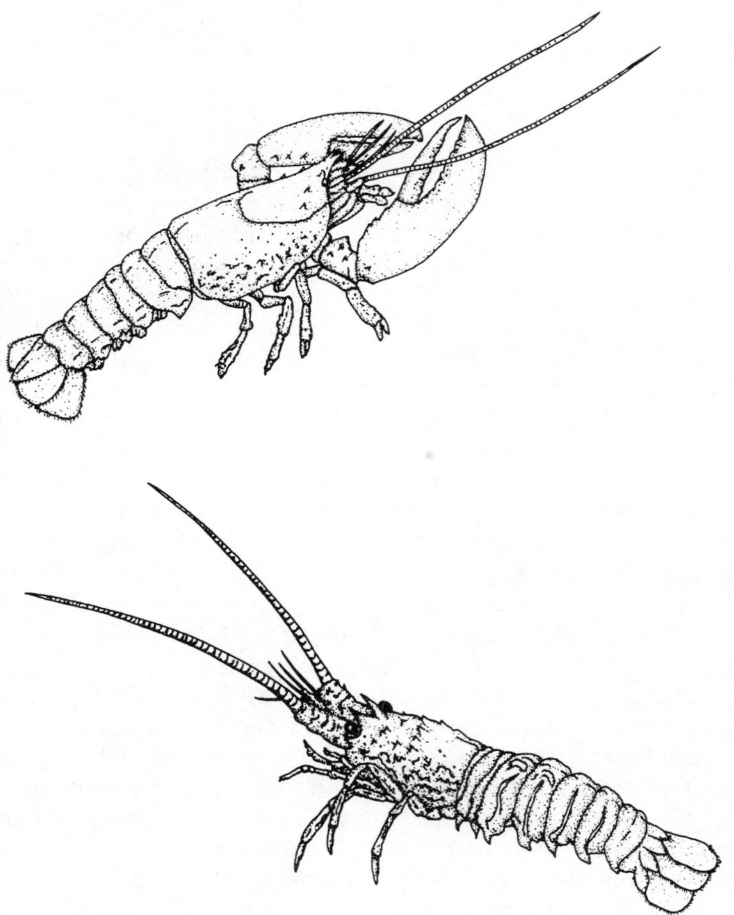

Figure 6-10. American Lobster (top) and Spiny Lobster (bottom).

correspond to the chelipeds of the crabs and are nothing more than modified pereiopods. A difference exhibited by the spiny lobsters is the presence of long stiff antennae, often longer than the animal's body.

Spiny Lobsters

Spiny lobsters, which belong to the family Palinuridae, are principally tropical and subtropical in distribution. In 1988 total U.S. landings of spiny lobster were 7.2 million pounds (3.3×10^6 kg) valued at $23 million. Primarily two species of spiny lobsters are fished commercially: in Florida, *Panulirus argus,* and in California, *P. interruptus.* The Florida landings account for over 75 percent of the total weight and value; hence we use *P. argus* for descriptive purposes.

The Florida spiny lobster is found on reefs or among rocks or other objects which afford protection or places of concealment, from North Carolina southward through the Gulf of Mexico to Brazil and throughout the Caribbean islands. It occurs over a range of water depths from low tide lines to 300 feet (91 m).

The life history of *P. argus* is shown in Figure 6-11. The male passes sperm in a

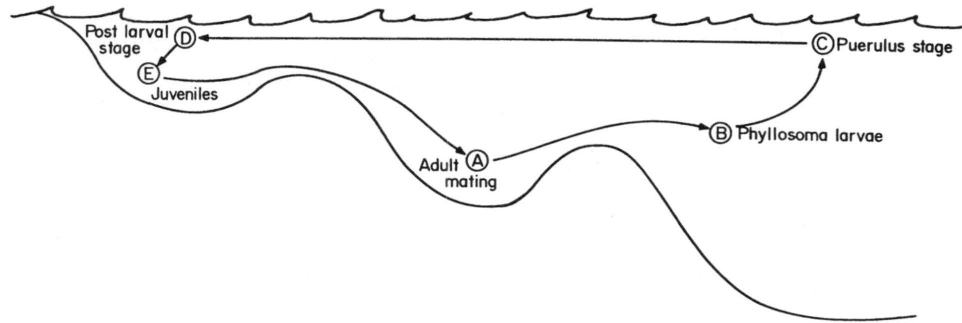

Figure 6-11. Life Cycle of the Spiny Lobster. **A.** Adult spiny lobsters mate in offshore reefs. The female carries the eggs for about a month. **B.** Eggs hatch as planktonic phyllosoma larvae. **C.** Postlarval stage, a transparent replica of the adult. **D.** After moving to shallow nursery areas and becoming benthic, the pueruli undergo as many as eleven postlarval molts over a period of two to three years. **E.** Juvenile spiny lobsters begin to move to offshore reefs.

viscous fluid that becomes attached to the female's abdomen. This fluid hardens to form a sperm sac, also called tar spots. When the female extrudes eggs, she breaks the sperm sac with her legs. As the eggs pass by the sperm sac they are fertilized and then become attached to the swimmerets on the female's abdomen. The number of eggs produced varies with carapace size: A female with a carapace length of 3 inches (7.6 cm) produces about 0.5 million eggs; one of 5-inch (12.7-cm) carapace length about 1.5 million eggs. The eggs hatch after about one month. The larvae of spiny lobster are flattened, leaf-shaped, planktonic organisms known as phyllosomes. After three to six months and six to eleven stages the phyllosoma metamorphoses into a puerulus or first postlarval stage. Pueruli, shaped like miniature adults but colorless and without a soft exoskeleton, move to shallow waters to begin their benthic existence. After up to three years and as many as eleven postlarval stages in this nursery area, juveniles mature and move to offshore reefs. It then takes up to three years for them to attain harvestable size. Adults may grow to approximately 18 inches (45 cm) in length and may live to be fifteen to twenty years old.

American Lobster

When people think of lobster, the American lobster is usually what comes to mind. It is perhaps the most universally recognized crustacean.

American lobsers are confined to the cooler temperate region waters between Newfoundland and North Carolina. Although they can be located from the intertidal zone to 1,575 feet (480 m) on the continental slope, they are usually at depths of 13 to 164 feet (4 to 50 m).

Lobsters are by nature secretive and nocturnal, hiding during the day. Although they will live on nearly any type of bottom, they prefer areas where ledges or boulders provide sheltered hiding places. Lobsters feed on a wide variety of bottom invertebrates including crabs, polychaete worms, mollusks, and starfish.

The life history of American lobsters is similar to that of other crustaceans in most aspects. Prior to mating, a sexually mature female lobster (weighing at least 1.1 pounds/ 500 g) will seek out the shelter of a large male lobster, and mating takes place shortly after the female has molted. The male transfers sperm to the female using modified pleopods; sperm is stored in the seminal receptacles of the female. It will be almost twelve months before egg extrusion and fertilization occurs. The number of eggs laid varies with the size of the female, ranging from a few thousand to almost 100,000. Eggs are carried on the pleopods of the female for another ten to twelve months before they hatch.

Following the extended brooding period, eggs hatch and planktonic zoea larvae emerge. After approximately two weeks, the larvae transform to the fourth stage (first postlarva) at which time they assume the characteristic lobster shape. At this time the tiny lobsters seek suitable bottom habitats to begin their benthic existence.

Growth rates among lobsters vary depending on food availability and water temperature. Hence it is difficult to estimate the time it takes an individual to reach adult status. It is known that between twenty and twenty-five molts will occur from the first stage larva to maturity. Of these, the first ten will occur in the first year of life. During the next four years the young lobster will have two to four molts a year. Molting generally occurs less frequently than once a year after the lobster has reached a carapace size of over 15 inches (38 cm). Sexual maturity is reached in five to seven years. After the onset of reproductive activity, the growth rates for males and females differ, because the female molts and carries eggs in alternate years, while the male continues to molt yearly.

Lobsters can reach weights of more than 40 pounds (18 kg). The American lobster may also be one of the longest lived of all crustaceans. A 35 pound (16 kg) lobster is over fifty years old.

REFERENCES

Bliss, Dorothy E. 1982. *Shrimps, Lobsters and Crabs.* Piscataway, NJ: New Century.

Cobb, Stanley J. 1976. *The American Lobster: The biology of Homarus americanus.* Marine Technical Report No. 49. Kingston, RI: University of Rhode Island.

Huner, Jay V., and Brown, E. Evan. (eds.). 1985. *Crustacean and Mollusk Aquaculture in the United States.* New York: Van Nostrand Reinhold.

Schmitt, Waldo L. 1965. *Crustaceans.* Ann Arbor: University of Michigan Press.

Warner, William W. 1976. *Beautiful Swimmers: Watermen, Crabs and the Chesapeake Bay.* Boston, MA: Little, Brown.

Williams, Austin B. 1984. *Shrimps, Lobsters, and Crabs of the Atlantic Coast of the Eastern United States, Maine to Florida.* Washington, DC: Smithsonian Institution Press.

CHAPTER

7

Miscellaneous and Underutilized Species

Gi-Pyo Hong, Jhung Won Hwang, and Michael Paparella

There are at least 2,200 species of finfish in the coastal and inland waters of the United States and Canada, of which only 25 percent are currently harvested for human food. This tremendous imbalance could be remedied by utilizing species that are not being caught or are being thrown away as "trash fish" in the by-catches for more traditional species. Every year as much as 21 million tons (19×10^6 metric tons) of edible marine fish are thrown away at sea by shrimp trawlers.

NEED FOR EXPLOITATION

In light of ever-increasing costs of harvesting and processing seafood, consumers as well as processors can no longer afford to waste the ocean's resources. Although domestic production remains relatively constant, the American consumer's appetite for seafood has increased. During the past two decades seafood consumption in the United States has exceeded the country's rate of population growth, resulting in increased imports. This increased consumer interest in seafood is seen particularly in the rapidly growing fast-food and restaurant chains.

TRADITION AND CONSUMER ACCEPTANCE

Both the fishing fleets and seafood production facilities are bound by tradition. Fish harvesting and production concentrate on just a few species, such as tuna, shrimp, cod, haddock, and flounder. Today's top five edible species account for about 60 percent of the volume, and 70 percent of the value of the edible fish landed in the United States. The increased American appetite for seafood seemingly yearns for very little variety. Therefore, the key to the seafood industry's future success in the United States could depend on gaining greater consumer acceptance of seafood varieties not familiar to the American palate.

Squid is an example of consumer prejudice in the United States. The squid is considered a true delicacy in nearly every country in the world, but in the United States, it is used mainly as fish bait. Foreign fishing fleets harvest millions of pounds of squid off U.S. shores. Gaining consumer acceptance of squid as an American food may be as simple as using the Italian word *calamare* (ca-la-ma-ray) as a substitute for squid. Many tasters who are delighted with the product may have been reluctant to try it if it had been called squid. Evidently foods are savored with prejudices as well as with taste buds.

MISCELLANEOUS UNDERUTILIZED SPECIES

Black Mullet

The black mullet *(Mugil cephalus)* weighing an average of 1.3 pounds (0.59 kg), is also known as the striped or jumping mullet. Its characteristic name comes from the unique habit of mullets to jump out of the water. The mullet has a blue-gray and green upper body and silvery belly. It has scales with dusky centers forming longitudinal lines along the sides, with a bluish spot at the base of the pectoral fin. This species grows up to 2.5 feet (76 cm) in length.

It travels in schools and is commonly found along the South Atlantic and Gulf Coasts. The best commercial fishing can be found in the geographical range from Texas to North Carolina. The common harvesting methods use runaround gillnet and the common haul seine at the mouth of rivers, in bays, and off beaches from October to January. The U.S. five-year harvest average (1975 to 1979) was 14,740 tons (13,400 metric tons). The estimated potential annual harvest is 55,000 to 110,000 tons (50,000 to 100,000 metric tons) (National Marine Fisheries Service 1981). Mullet is an important species in the commercial fisheries of the southern states.

Chemical composition is 19.4 percent protein and 5.5 percent fat. The flesh is nutty in flavor and high in fat. It can be fried, baked, grilled, or smoked. Mullet is unusual in that it has a gizzard, which can be prepared in similar fashion to chicken gizzards. Another important economical benefit is its prized roe.

Blue Runner

Blue runner *(Caranx crysos)* weighs an average of 4 pounds (1.8 kg) and reaches a length of 2 feet (61 cm). It is commonly referred to as the hardtail. The upper body is greenish bronze and the lower is silvery bronze. There is usually a spot on the rear part of the gill cover. Since the blue runner is a member of the Carangidae family, it is an active swimmer, commonly found in warm seas from Brazil to Cape Cod, and as a stray in Nova Scotia. Like the jack crevalle, only small hardtails, less than 1 foot (30 cm) long, are found north of Cape Hatteras, North Carolina.

In the United States the commercial geographic range is off the Mississippi, Alabama, and Florida coasts. The principal harvesting season is from May to September. The harvesting average in 1975 to 1979 was 66 tons (60 metric tons) but the estimated annual harvest could be 55,000 to 276,000 tons (50,000 to 250,000 metric tons) (National Marine Fisheries Service, 1981). Common harvesting methods include the haul seine and the gillnet.

Blue runner is important commercially in the Atlantic Ocean off the coasts of Africa and America. The meat, which is rich in fat, is valued along the Gulf of Mexico.

Butterfish

Butterfish *(Peprilus triacanthus)* is also known as dollarfish, silver dollar, and harvestfish. There are several genera in the butterfish family but *Peprilus triacanthus* is the most common commercial species. This shiny fish has a bluish back and silvery sides and belly. It has a thin body with small scales that are easily rubbed off. The butterfish is a small fish: An adult ranges from 6 to 10 inches (15 to 25 cm) long and weighs up to 1 pound (454 g), with the larger sizes commanding higher prices.

The butterfish is found from Nova Scotia to North Carolina. It travels in loose schools and is often found throughout the water column. Its meat is 17.7 percent protein, 7.2 percent fat, and 1.3 percent carbohydrate. The fish gets its name from its normally high fat content, and its meat is mostly dark and has an excellent flavor.

Carps

Minnows are another name for carps (Cyprinidae family). They are found in North America (northern Canada to Mexico), Africa, and Eurasia. Carps have pharyngeal teeth in one to three rows but never more than eight teeth in any one row. Some minnows have spinlike rays in the dorsal fin. Many species are less than 2 inches (5.1 cm) long.

There are about 194 genera and 2,070 species of carp, making it the largest family of fishes. Of this figure, some 1,850 species are known from Eurasia and Africa, and about 220 from North America, where the dominant genus is *Notropis,* with about 110 species.

Cutlassfish

Cutlassfish *(Trichiurus lepturus)* is a silvery species distributed in warm seas of the Atlantic, the Gulf of Mexico, and the West Indies. In the western Atlantic it is commonly found around North Carolina. It is a commercial fish only in the Atlantic Ocean along the coasts of Africa and South America.

It is 20.4 to 22.8 percent protein, 1.2 to 9.4 percent fat, and 1.2 to 1.4 percent ash.

Eels

Other names for eels *(Anguilla rostrata)* are the American eel, the silver eel, and the freshwater eel. Despite their snakelike appearance, eels are true fish, possessing gills and very small scales. They have pointed snouts and relatively large mouths. Colors vary from olive green, dark brown, gray to black, but all have yellowish bellies. Their upper body colors can change to conform with the colors of the bottom of the sea. Mature females are 2 to 3.5 feet (61 to 107 cm) long; males are smaller.

American eels are found in coastal streams, rivers, ponds, lakes, and estuaries from Greenland to the Gulf of Mexico. They are bottom-dwelling, nocturnal in habit, and feed on invertebrates and small finfish. This species is plentiful from the Chesapeake Bay north to Long Island, with the Delaware River estuary system serving as the prime fishing area.

This species has a peculiar life history, spending most of its life in fresh or brackish water but returning to the sea to spawn. This living pattern is referred to as catadromous, the opposite of the anadromous lifestyles of the shad and the salmon.

Mature adult females, usually eight to ten years old, will cease feeding. Their eyes become larger to help with navigation; their upper body turns to silvery-black and their bellies to silver. At this stage they are known as silver eels. They leave their inshore habitats in late fall to meet swarms of males at brackish river mouths and then continue their migration to the Saragasso Sea, southeast of Bermuda.

Spawning in midwinter, the females are capable of laying up to 20 million eggs before presumably dying. The hatched larvae, called leptocephali, looking very little like an adult eel, are transparent and ribbonlike. In spring the larvae drift with the currents in a one-year journey which brings them to the North American coastline. By this time they have metamorphosed into adult forms, except they are about 3 inches (8 cm) long and totally transparent; thus they are known as glass eels. As the young eels migrate to freshwater, they acquire the pigmentation of adults and are called elvers. Female elvers travel into freshwater rivers, ponds, and lakes; males prefer to spend their lives in the brackish coastal streams and estuaries.

Currently, a small number of fishermen harvest eels, primarily using baited wire pots. Most of the U.S. commercial catch is exported to Europe or sold to local smokers, with smaller eels marketed locally as bait.

The meat is 18.0 percent protein and 17.3 percent fat. Eel meat has a very firm texture, a high fat content, and a full flavor. It is grayish in the uncooked state but turns white when cooked. Delicatessen specialties made from hot smoked eel meat, such as canned jellied eel, are in great demand.

Angler, Monkfish, or Goosefish

The upper portion of the *Lophius americanus* body is chocolate brown, mottled with pale and dark browns; the belly is a dirty-white color. The general geological distribution is from south of Newfoundland to North Carolina. The American angler is found from shallow waters to depths of more than 2,000 feet (610 m).

Spawning occurs in the spring and early summer. The eggs are laid in a ribbon of mucus to form broad sheets, jellylike in texture, containing a single layer of eggs. These sheets, which are 25 to 35 feet (7.6 to 10.7 m) long and 2 to 3 feet (0.6 to 0.9 m) wide, float near the surface of the water. It is estimated that 1.25 million eggs are contained in a single sheet. The angler grows to 4 feet (1.2 m) long, weighing more than 50 pounds (23 kg).

Although a good fish for consumption few goosefish are marketed. It is sometimes accidentally caught by anglers who are fishing for other species.

Gulf Quahog

Other common names for *Mercenaria campechiensis* are the hard clam and the Southern quahog. Clams are found in commercial quantities in Louisiana with an average weight of 1.3 pounds (0.59 kg). The harvesting season is yearlong, using a clam dredge or harvesting them manually.

Jack Crevalle

Jack Crevalle *(Caranx hippos)*, also known as the common jack, reaches up to 2.5 feet (76 cm) and weighs up to 20 pounds (9 kg). The upper portion of the body is bluish or bronze-green and the lower is silvery, often with golden yellow blotches. There is a distinct spot on the hind edge of the gill flap. The young have five to six vertical dark bars. The jack crevalle is an oily fish closely related to the blue runner and the pompano.

It lives in the tropical and subtropical seas of the Atlantic, Indian, and Pacific oceans. In the United States, the commercial fishery grounds are in Florida, principally during the harvest months of April to November when it is taken by the common haul seine or the runaround gillnet. The Jack crevalle is also a popular sport fish with recreational anglers because of its strong fighting characteristics.

The U.S. harvest from 1975 to 1979 was 882 tons (800 metric tons) (National Marine Fisheries Service, 1981). The meat is 19.9 percent protein, 1.2 percent fat, and 0.6 percent carbohydrate. The jack crevalle is high in oil, making it ideal for broiling, baking, and smoking.

Jonah Crab

The Jonah crab *(Cancer borealis)* is closely related to the rock crab, and the two are not easily differentiated in the marketplace. The Jonah grows larger than the rock crab and has more pronounced claws, thicker legs, and rough shells. In addition, the tooth-edged part of the shell is jagged, not smooth or granulated as in the rock crab. Jonah crabs are brick red to purplish above and yellowish below. Fully grown crabs measure from 6 to 7 inches (15.2 to 17.8 cm) across and average about 1 pound (0.45 kg).

Jonah crabs also extend into deeper waters than the rock crabs. The Jonahs are found from the coastline to the upper continental slope at depths of 100 to 1,300 feet (30 to 400 m), with larger crabs tending to inhabit deeper and colder waters. They range from Nova Scotia to Florida but are most abundant off the coast of New England and the mid-Atlantic states.

Most of the Jonah crab harvest is a by-catch of the offshore lobster fishery. Lobsters are of more value to the fishermen, so Jonah crabs are brought in more often when the lobster catch is down. However, this trend is changing, and a growing fishery with special crab pots now exists.

Despite its excellent flavor, it has never been important commercially because of its limited distribution. Jonah crabs are becoming more attractive to fishermen because the claws are large enough to be sold like stone crab claws, which are very popular in Florida. Thus large Jonah crabs command a higher ex-vessel price than rock crabs or small Jonah crabs.

Little Tuna

The upper portion of the little tuna *(Euthynnus alleteratus)* body is steel blue and the lower sides and belly are silvery white. The upper sides also have distinct irregular oblique bands sloping from the top edge of the back to the head.

The little tuna travels in large schools offshore, feeding on other fish. This species grows up to 2.5 feet (0.76 m) and occurs in the warmer waters of all oceans. It is distributed in the subtropical and tropical waters of the Atlantic Ocean, including the Mediterranean Sea, and as stragglers north of Cape Cod, Massachusetts.

Little tuna is not important commercially. It is caught in small numbers in the east, from St. Helena to Senegal and in the west from the Cape Cod peninsula to the Gulf of Mexico. It is a common catch of offshore anglers.

The meat is not as high in quality as the albacore and yellowfin. The meat is 24.5 percent protein and 2.9 percent fat; the composition in the roe contains similar ratios: 23.5 percent protein and 3.3 percent fat (Bykov, 1984). The color of the meat ranges from buff to light brown, and heat processing causes the meat to become lighter. Frying makes the flavor mildly acidic, with dense and hard consistency, giving the meat a pleasant taste and smell. Tuna is generally used for canning.

Mackerel

Mackerel *(Scomber scombrus)* is also called the Atlantic mackerel, the Boston mackerel, and the tinkers. It is distributed in the northern Atlantic along the European coast from the White Sea (where it enters in warm years) to the Black Sea, along the American coast from Cape Hatteras, North Carolina, in the south to the Labrador peninsula in the north.

The mackerel is distinguished by its brilliant color pattern. The upper half of its body is iridescent blue-green with a vertical black wavy band, and the lower half and belly are silvery white. The iridescence fades soon after death, but the color pattern remains as a distinguishing characteristic. The mackerel has a fusiform shape and deeply forked tail. Its scales are small and smooth, giving a velvety feel to the skin.

Atlantic mackerel average 14 to 18 inches (36 to 46 cm) long and 1 to 2.5 pounds (0.45 to 1.1 kg) in weight. It reaches its prime when it is the fattest, which is at the end of summer and during the fall. It feeds little over the winter but eats greedily after spawning. A 14-inch fish will weigh about 1 pound (0.45 kg) in the spring and 1.25 pounds (0.57 kg) in the fall.

Smaller mackerels, called "tinker" mackerels, are harvested in the early spring. They generally weigh less than a pound (0.45 kg) and measure 6 to 10 inches (15 to 25 cm).

The Atlantic mackerel is an oily fish, high in omega-3 fatty acids that are believed to reduce the serum cholesterol level. The chemical composition of the meat is 19.1 percent protein and 16.3 percent fat.

The meat is soft and tasty; depending upon the fat content, taste properties vary from satisfactory to good. Canned and smoked products can be made from the mackerel.

Menhaden

Other common names of menhaden *(Brevoortia tyrannus)* are mossbunker, bunker, porgy, fatback, bug-mouth, and shad.

Combined annual landings of Atlantic coast and Gulf of Mexico menhaden species collectively comprised the largest commercial fishery by weight (29 percent of total seafood catch and 35 percent of total finfish catch) and eighth largest in dollar value in 1984 in the United States (NMFS, 1985).

Menhaden differ from their herring relatives by the size of their head, which is scaleless and very large. Another distinguishing feature is that their scale margins are nearly vertical and edged with comblike teeth. Their mouth is relatively large and toothless.

Adult menhaden average 12 to 15 inches (30 to 38 cm) long and 10 to 16 ounces (284 to 454 g). They are dark blue, green, blue-gray, or blue-brown above, and their sides and belly are silvery with a strong yellow or brassy luster. A conspicuous dusky spot is found on each side behind the gill cover and is followed by smaller dark spots. The meat is 13 percent fat and 17.9 percent protein.

Menhaden inhabit inner-shelf water from Maine to Florida. They are seasonal migrators and are found in the northern portion of their range only during warmer months. It is exclusively the older and larger fish that make this long journey, only to return south again when the water cools. Menhaden travel in a large, dense school which darken the water's surface like the shadow of a cloud. Because of their dense schooling behavior and near-surface occurrence, aircraft are used to spot menhaden for the commercial fisherman.

Although menhaden is rarely eaten directly as food in the United States, it has many uses. One of the oldest American industries is the processing of menhaden into fertilizer. Today, menhaden are processed into fish meal, oil, and protein solubles (see Chapter 20). To provide improved utilization, menhaden also is being converted into surimi, minced products, and other food analogs. In addition, the U.S. Food and Drug Administration has been petitioned to approve menhaden oil as an ingredient in further-processed foods, such as ice cream, candies, and margarine. In Europe, it is already made into margarine for human consumption. The meal and soluble proteins are excellent supplements in animal feed. Menhaden's value may increase as the demand for protein increases.

Ocean Pout

Ocean pout *(Macrozoarces americanus)*, or American eelpout, is caught from Newfoundland south to Delaware. The average ocean pout is 25 inches (63.5 cm) long and weighs 2.5 pounds (1.1 kg).

The ocean pout is a bottom species, commonly found in depths of 50 to 250 feet (15.3 to 76.3 m) and has been caught at depths of over 600 feet (183 m). The proximate composition of the meat is 18.8 percent protein and 2.6 percent fat.

The ocean pout was marketed in quantities for the first time during World War II, but discovery of a parasite in the flesh, which resulted in the condemnation of large amounts of fish, discouraged the fishery to the extent that commercial landings today are negligible.

Red Hake

Red hake *(Urophycis chuss)* is also known as ling and squirrel hake. The hake is a member of the cod family but its body is more slender, softer, smaller, and has long feelerlike ventral fins, with only two dorsal fins.

Red and white hakes are similar and not easily distinguished when marketed. One indication is the upper jawbone, which extends to the rear edge of the eye in the white hake, but only to the rear edge of the pupil in the red hake. If the filamentous part of the first dorsal fin is undamaged, it is much longer in the red hake, measuring three to five times the length of the fins. The red hake, which ranges from 9 to 30 inches (23 to 76 cm) long and weighs 0.3 to 14.0 pounds (0.14 to 6.4 kg), is generally smaller than the white hake.

The red hake is found along the coast of North America. It is a bottom dweller, usually found from the tidemark to depths of 1,000 feet (305 m). Larger fish leaves the coastline for the summer to seek the cool, deeper water.

The chemical composition of the meat is 81.9 percent moisture, 17.5 percent protein, 0.4 percent fat, and 1.4 percent ash. Hake is sold primarily for food, though some red hake is used for industrial processing and has been found suitable for surimi-based products. The meat of the red hake is rough in consistency and the taste is inferior to cod. The liver can be used for canning. Oil may be extracted although its vitamin content is not very high.

The hake does not keep well so it must be carefully handled and processed soon after being caught. It should be noted that the hake is among the least expensive of the white fish.

Red Crab

The red crab *(Geryon quinquedens)* is bright red when pulled from the deep dark waters along the edge of the continental shelf from Nova Scotia to Cuba at depths of up to 7,000 feet (2,134 m). Until recently, most of the red crab landed in the Northeast were caught by offshore lobstermen laying traps in deep underwater canyons.

Now specially designed crab pots and live tanks, combined with modern processing technology, allow fishermen and processors to maintain a reliable supply. Males weigh up to 2.25 pounds (1.02 kg) and females up to 1.25 pounds (0.57 kg). But the yield is very high at 23 percent. The meat is removed in a manner similar to the blue crab.

The commercial potential of red crab has not been realized, although seafood processors in several states have expressed interest in this resource.

In the mid-Atlantic region it is sold live or fully cooked as the red crab, or the "Big Red" crab. Since the largest red crab processor in the Northeast markets the red crab under the "Cape Cod" brand, numerous wholesalers have now started selling the red crab as the Cape Cod crab. Actually the crabs are neither caught nor processed near Cape Cod.

An unrelated species of the snow crab caught by the Japanese and the Korean fishermen in the North Pacific is frequently marketed as the "red crab." This imported crab is priced well under the true red crab, and its culinary quality is notably inferior to the true red crab.

Red Porgy

Red porgy *(Pagrus sedecim)* is also commonly called white snapper and pink porgy. The name white snapper was coined by red snapper fishermen in the northern Gulf of Mexico, who frequently landed them. This colorful species commonly occurs in many international waters. In the United States, the principal commercial fishing areas are in the South Carolina to Georgia area. This species, weighing on the average 5.5 pounds (2.5 kg), is harvested by trawl nets from January to April.

The red porgy is not well known to American consumers, yet despite its expense, it is in great demand in Mediterranean countries and in the Orient.

Sheepshead

Sheepshead *(Archosargus porbatocephalus)* is a greenish yellow species, also known as the fathead, with seven dark vertical bars on its sides. Although it is commercially harvested all year, the principal harvesting season is from November to March. Spawning occurs during the spring.

It is generally found from Texas to Cape Cod, and as a stray in the Bay of Fundy. The species is common from Virginia to New York. The primary commercial fishing area is in the Gulf of Mexico. United States harvest from 1975 to 1979 averaged 441 tons (400 metric tons) primarily using a runaround gillnet and otter trawl.

The sheepshead is generally considered a valuable food source only in the south Atlantic and Gulf coast states. One to 4 pounds (0.45 to 1.8 kg) is the usual weight; older fish may be up to 20 pounds (9.1 kg). This species grows in length to 2.5 feet (76 cm). It prefers oyster beds and muddy shallow waters, allowing easy access to its diet of oysters, crabs, and barnacles.

Silvery Anchovy

As its name implies, the color of the silvery anchovy *(Anchoa argyrophanus)* is silvery and translucent. A wide silvery band, 1.5 times as wide as the eye, is found on the length of the body. The maximal growth is up to 6 inches (15 cm). This fish is found mostly in the Gulf Stream. Although it is not commonly found inshore it does appear occasionally inshore from the south of Cape Cod.

Skates and Rays

The skates (Rajidae family) and the rays (Dasyatidae family) are fishlike vertebrates with well-developed jaws and bony teeth. The skin is covered with small, toothlike enamel projections. The front edges of the pectoral fins are united with the head. Most of the forms in this group have a flattened, disclike body.

The various species are widely distributed from the subpolar to tropical zones. In the cooler waters of the temperate and the subpolar zones, the skates are most numerous both in number of species and in individuals. In the warm waters of the tropical and the subtropical zones, the rays predominate. In general, members of this group live on or near the bottom and frequently bury themselves partially or completely in the mud or sand. Among the sting rays, their long, whiplike tails are armed with one or more poisonous spines. The spines are also present on the tails of some of the butterfly rays, the cow-nosed rays, and the eagle rays. The spines may be as long as 5 inches (12.7 cm) in some species. The sting rays can be dangerous when accidentally disturbed by a swimmer or when captured.

The chemical composition of the meat of the skates is 20.3 percent protein and 0.2 percent fat. The pectoral fins (wings or saddle) of some of the larger species are marketed for food. Many species are used for bait in crab and lobster traps and, more recently, as a source of fish meal.

Spanish Sardine

Spanish sardine *(Sardinella anchovia)* is a silvery fish growing up to 7 inches (18 cm) long, and is found in the western Atlantic Ocean from Cape Cod to Rio de Janeiro. It is commercially important in the western Central Atlantic. This species is not common close to the shore but is found offshore in midwater and in deep depths.

Chemical composition of the meat is 3.4 percent fat and 21.8 percent protein; the whole fish is 8.5 percent fat and 18.3 percent protein (Bykov, 1984). Cooking makes the meat soft and tasty. The processing applicaton generally used is canning.

Smooth Dogfish

The smooth dogfish *(Mustelus canis),* which is about the same size as the spiny dogfish, is one of the most abundant sharks along the East Coast. In the shallow waters of the Delaware Bay, where it is found in great numbers during the summer, more smooth dogfish are caught than all other sharks combined. Its migration is temperature dependent, so it will seek warmer waters in the fall.

Instead of the ferocious jaw that sharks are generally famous for, the smooth dogfish has many low, flat pavement-like teeth that crush and grind rather than bite or tear. The tasty smooth dogfish is caught and sold together with the spiny dogfish.

Because the smooth dogfish is usually caught close to beaches and around sandbars, it is often erroneously called the "sand shark." But the true sand shark *(Odontaspis taurus)* has much sharper teeth and weighs considerably more. The smooth dogfish is frequently taken in large numbers by the commercial fisheries, but only a limited quantity is marketed. It is a common catch for surf casters and recreational boat fishermen.

Spiny Dogfish

Spiny dogfish *(Squalus acanthias)* is named for its weapon of defense. Along the front of each dorsal fin is a long spine which stands more or less upright when the shark curls its body into a bow. The spiny dogfish is a small, slender-bodied fish, 2 to 3.5 feet (61 to 107 cm) long and weighing 5 to 10 pounds (2.3 to 4.5 kg). It is slate gray above, sometimes tinged with brown, with grayish white sides and a white belly. On each side there is a row of small white spots which fade with age.

The spiny dogfish inhabits temperate and subarctic waters, including both sides of the North Atlantic and North Pacific. It is abundant off the U.S. East Coast in spring, summer, and fall, but spends its winter offshore in deeper waters and/or south. The dogfish travels in large schools, is a bottom feeder, and does not have the sharp teeth found in most other sharks. Yet, many fishermen consider the spiny dogfish a nuisance that can cause considerable damage to their nets.

The chemical composition of the meat is 18.5 percent protein and 10.8 percent fat. The spiny dogfish is traditionally known as "rock salmon" in Great Britain and is used to make the dish fish and chips. Germany and France import just the belly flaps of this shark. The smoked meat is considered a delicacy there.

Most of the dogfish caught in the United States is exported to these countries. The small quantity sold domestically is marketed as "grayfish" or simply as "shark." The use of the spiny dogfish for food in the United States began around 1975. It is primarily marketed as fresh, smoked, or processed meat (Holts, 1988). Since the early 1980s, the dogfish has been promoted in the mid-Atlantic region.

Squid

Other names for the squid are the calamari, the calamare, and the inkfish. The squid is a close relative of the octopus and the cuttlefish and a more distant relative of the clam, the mussel, the scallop, and the oyster. Instead of having a protective external shell, the squid has a compact internal shell called the pen or quill. This singular slender chitinous pen, which runs within the dorsal side of the body cavity or mantle, is all that remains of the shell. Within the mantle is an ink sac, which is used in defense. The sac contains a blackish brown fluid or ink, which can be ejected to the outside through a siphon to form an inky cloud that aids the squid's escape.

The mantle is a hollow cone or cigar-shaped piece of flesh which is open at one end. Popping out of the opening is a head with two large black eyes. Ten appendages arranged in five pairs surround the head. Four pairs are known as arms and are short and heavy, and the remaining pair is lighter, twice as long, and called tentacles. These appendages are equipped with suction cups which are used to seize and hold the prey. For simplicity, in most cookbooks all ten appendages are referred to as tentacles.

Two slightly lobed fins are located near the terminal end of the mantle on the dorsal side. The squid can propel itself by moving these fins, but for quick movement it uses jetlike propulsion, which is accomplished by shooting water out through the siphon with great force, resulting in a quick motion in the opposite direction.

The live squid has typically a milky, translucent color. However, as a defense mechanism it has the ability to change color or blend with its background. The fresh squid has a creamy-colored skin with reddish brown spots. Pinkening of the skin is an initial indication of aging.

These are approximately 350 species of squid worldwide, and this class of shellfish is considered to be one of the world's most underutilized fish resources. Chemical composition of the squid (*Loliginidae* spp.) is 15.3 percent protein, 1.0 percent fat, and 3.0 percent carbohydrate.

In U.S. waters, most of the squid harvest consists of three species.

1. California squid *(Loligo opalescens)*. Other names: Monterey squid, Opal squid, San Pedro squid, calamari grande. It is the smallest squid (10 to 12 inches (25 cm to 30 cm) across) marketed and appears frozen on the East Coast. It is harvested in winter months when it moves inshore to spawn. Traditionally, this species accounts for the bulk of the domestic catch of loligo squid, but stocks have been rapidly disappearing.

2. North Atlantic loligo or long-finned squid *(Loligo pealii)*. Other names: winter squid, Boston squid, bone squid, trap squid. Atlantic long-finned squid ranges from Nova Scotia to Venezuela and occurs commonly from Massachusetts to North Carolina. It has a broad pen and long fins that equal half the mantle length. The long-finned squid is generally smaller and has thinner mantle walls than the short-finned squid. Tender unless overcooked, it is regarded in the East as the superior squid.

3. North Atlantic or short-finned squid *(Illex illecebrosus)*. Other names: summer squid, bait squid. The short-finned or summer squid commonly occurs from the Maritime provinces to New Jersey. It has a slender pen, and its fins are one-third the length of the mantle. The short-finned squid is larger, has a thicker mantle wall, and usually sells for less than the long-finned squid. *Illex* can be quite tough and easily overcooked, making it tougher. Once harvested almost exclusively for use as bait or animal food, it is now marketed as a food item. It has found consumer acceptance equal to the long-finned squid.

Oriental and Mediterranean people have been eating squid for centuries, but it is predominately these ethnic groups which consume most of the squid in the United States. However, this trend is changing as Americans are becoming more aware of squid as a delicious food.

The firm white meat of the squid consists mostly of fine muscle fibers with connective tissues and little fat. Therefore, it has firmer texture than chicken or beef. After cleaning, the yield of the edible meat (mantle, fins, tentacles, and arms) is 60 to 80 percent.

If cooked improperly, the squid will become tough and rubbery. It is best to cook squid quickly (under one minute) or to cook it over thirty minutes using a slow moist cooking method. The meat is mildly flavored, almost to the point of being bland, and takes on the flavors of the ingredients. The ink of the squid can be used in many dishes to add flavor, aroma, and color.

Whiting

Whiting *(Merluccius bilinearis)* is also called Atlantic whiting, silver hake, and winter trout. The hake and the whiting are names often used interchangeably for the many species of this fish. The whiting is a distant relative of the cod family but much smaller, averaging only 14 inches (36 cm) long and less than 2 pounds (0.9 kg). The whiting is also referred to as winter trout, or more properly the silver hake, because of its silvery iridescent color. It is a slender, streamlined fish with soft-rayed fins. The long body has small scales, a relatively small tail, and a lateral line running down the length of the fish. The whiting has a flat-topped head with large eyes and a large mouth with two or more rows of sharp teeth. This species is gray, mottled with brown above and silvery iridescent on its lower sides and belly. The whiting differs from other hake by lacking a chin barbel and having ventral fins which are not altered into long feelers.

It inhabits the continental shelf from Newfoundland to North Carolina but is most important commercially from Maine to New Jersey. It may live in depths up to 3,000 feet (912 m) during the winter months, preferring warmer water than other members of the cod family. This fish is sometimes called the "frostfish" because sudden cold snaps may freeze large quantities and wash it ashore before it migrates into deeper waters. The whiting is a bottom dweller by day, moving toward the surface at night to feed. It does not school often but will swim together at times. Like the sea trout, the whiting is tender and must be packed and handled carefully to avoid crushing.

Chemical composition of the meat is 16.1 percent protein and 1.2 percent fat. It contains a much greater quantity of fat than most members of the cod family. The liver oil contains a little more than 1,000 IU/g of vitamin A and about 80 gamma/g of vitamin E. The whiting, if properly frozen, is close to the white navaga in taste. It makes delicious dishes when fried.

DEVELOPMENT PROJECTS

In attempting to make underutilized species more appealing to consumers, it must be remembered that acceptance of various fish differs by geographic region. Catfish does not enjoy the same acceptance nationally as it does in the southern states. Tuna steaks, highly popular in seacoast states, are uncommon in the inland states. Tilefish, which is said to taste like lobster, is unknown to many lobster lovers. This lack of name recognition or name appeal (unappetizing names like wolf-fish, rat-tail fish, gagfish, etc.) are factors working against the acceptance of many species.

Educating consumers and processors about these underutilized species is one solution. The seven regional Fisheries Development Foundations, financially supported by the National Marine Fisheries Service, have been making headway in both education and promotion.

The seven foundations are the mid-Atlantic Fisheries Development Foundation, the Gulf and the South Atlantic Fisheries Development Foundation, the New England Fisheries Development Foundation, the Great Lakes Fisheries Development Foundation, the West Coast Fisheries Development Foundation, the Alaska Fisheries Development Foundation, and the Pacific Tuna Development Foundation.

Mid-Atlantic Fisheries Development Foundation

The development program for underutilized species in the mid-Atlantic region covers the activities of the area encompassing New York, New Jersey, Pennsylvania, Delaware, Maryland, and Virginia. The activities described in the plan are intended to help remove economic and technological impediments to the development of a strong fishing industry in the mid-Atlantic region.

The foundation reports that the waters of the mid-Atlantic region are abundant, with at least 150 species of seafood harvestable, but the number of species actually caught and utilized by the seafood industry is considerably less than half that number. Probably no more than thirty species, including shellfish, are of commercial importance. The more abundant and commercially important finfish and shellfish species in this region include menhaden, surf clam, whiting, ocean quahog, fluke, sea trout, sea bass, blue crab, sea scallop, porgy, oyster, and tilefish. Other species, both finfish and shellfish, are harvested on a lesser scale, but the current market price makes them valuable. Examples include squid, deep sea red crab, and the Jonah crab.

The foundation classifies underutilized species as the red hake, squid, mackerel, dogfish, butterfish, and herring. Other species having development potential but lower in priority than these six species are the eel, the Jonah crab, the blue mussel, the carp, and the skates. Although not harvested as fully as the resource may allow, any one or more of these species could become a significant portion of the total catch in the foreseeable future, if current unfavorable market conditions change.

Gulf and South Atlantic Fisheries Development Foundation

Waters of the Gulf of Mexico and the South Atlantic support several important fisheries with landings totaling about 2 billion pounds (908×10^6 kg) annually. The area accounts for about 33 percent of all the U.S. landings and about 25 percent of the value of the domestic catch. But estimates show that the potential of the underdeveloped fisheries is even more impressive.

Coastal pelagic species are important underutilized stocks. There are about eleven major species of coastal pelagic fish found in the Southeast. Unlike groundfish, utilization of the coastal pelagic stocks (excluding menhaden) is at a minimum. The species include the scaled sardine, the Spanish sardine, the round herring, the silver anchovy, the chub mackerel, the bumper, the rough scad, the round scad, the thread herring, the cutlassfish, the black mullet, the blue runner, the jack crevalle, the lady fish, the red porgy, the sheepshead, and the little tuna. The potential catch is great, with an estimated standing stock of close to 7.7 million tons (7×10^6 metric tons). If this estimate is valid, the resource is essentially untouched.

New England Fisheries Development Foundation

The New England Fisheries Development Foundation reviewed nontraditional species to determine which would be the most promising from the industry's view. These factors include present and future resource availability, market potential, and the ability to use existing harvesting, holding, and processing techniques.

Development activities have been directed toward the following underutilized species: squid, whiting, red hake, ocean pout, skates, dogfish, goosefish, butterfish, herring, mackerel, deep sea red crab, Jonah crab, rock crab, ocean quahogs, mussels, and conchs.

Great Lakes Fisheries Development Foundation

The Great Lakes, stretching more than 800 miles (1,296 km) from east to west and 500 miles (810 km) from north to south, have many common characteristics. Yet each lake, because of its geographical location, size, and depth, is noted for certain species of fish. Lake Superior, the largest, the deepest, and the most northerly lake, is noted for its trout and whitefish. Lake Erie, the smallest and the shallowest, has the largest number of different species.

The fisheries are being expanded as new and more efficient gear is being developed, and shoreside facilities are being modernized to accommodate the increased harvest. Fisheries for the following species are being developed: the buffalofish, the carp, the freshwater mullet, the freshwater drum, the rainbow smelt, the white bass, the whitefish, and the yellow perch.

West Coast Fisheries Development Foundation

The West Coast Fisheries Development Foundation has focused development activities on squid, mackerel, mussels, whiting, and baitfish.

Alaska Fisheries Development Foundation

The Alaska Fisheries Development Foundation is involved with both at-sea and shore-based pollock processing. It is also engaged in the marketing of the sablefish.

Pacific Tuna Development Foundation

The Pacific Tuna Development Foundation, based in Honolulu, Hawaii, is concerned primarily with the tuna fisheries. However, because of its location it is doing developmental fisheries work in Guam and Samoa. Progress in this area will depend upon the development of techniques to extend the storage life of high quality products.

REFERENCES

Borgstrom, G. 1965. *Fish as Food* (Vol. 4). Orlando, FL: Academic Press.

Bykov, V. P. 1984. *Marine Fishes.* Rotterdam, Holland, and New Delhi, India: A. A. Balkema.

Fontaine, B. V. 1979. *Seafood Adventures from the Gulf and South Atlantic.* Tampa, FL: Gulf and South Atlantic Fisheries Development Foundation, Inc.

Holts, D. B. 1988. "Review of U.S. West Coast Commercial Shark Fisheries." *Marine Fisheries Review.* 50(1):1–8.

Johnson, J. C., Griffith, D. C., and Murray, J. D. 1987. "Encouraging the Use of Underutilized Marine Fishes by Southeastern U.S. Anglers." Part I, "The Research." *Marine Fisheries Review.* 49(2):122–137.

Martin, R. E., Flick, G. J., Hebard, C. E., and Ward, D. R. 1982. *Chemistry and Biochemistry of Marine Food Products.* New York: Van Nostrand Reinhold.

Murray, J. D., Johnson, J. C., and Griffith, D. C. 1987. "Encouraging the Use of Underutilized Marine Fishes by Southeastern U.S. Anglers." Part II, "Educational Objectives and Strategy." *Marine Fisheries Review.* 49(2):138–142.

National Marine Fisheries Service. 1985. *Current Fishery Statistics, 1984.* USDA, NOAA 8360.

National Marine Fisheries Service. 1981. *Gulf and South Atlantic Fishery Products.* Tampa, FL: Gulf and South Atlantic Fisheries Development Foundation, Inc.

Nelson, J. S. 1984. *Fishes of the World* (2nd ed.). New York: Wiley.

Nettleton J. 1985. *Seafood Nutrition: Facts, Issues and Marketing of Nutrition in Fish and Shellfish.* New York: Van Nostrand Reinhold.

Perlmutter, A. 1961. *Guide to Marine Fishes.* New York: New York University Press.

CHAPTER

8

Processing Finfish

George J. Flick, Mala A. Barua, and Leopoldo G. Enriquez

Within the past forty years, consumers have made major changes in their food purchasing habits. For centuries, fresh fish and shellfish were purchased at retail markets and converted into dishes at home. As social patterns changed and disposable income increased, consumers began to purchase partially or fully prepared seafoods. These convenience dishes, although more expensive than the raw product, provided convenience for consumers at a reasonable price. Today, fabricated and further processed seafood products are commonplace items. Most traditional convenience products were coated (battered or breaded); the new items use minced fish (surimi) as the primary ingredient. Coated product sales have not experienced substantial growth in recent years; however, the consumption of surimi products has increased significantly. This chapter discusses both coated and mince-based products and provides you with sufficient information to obtain an in-depth knowledge of further processed seafoods. The first part of the chapter discusses mince, and the second part, the use of mince in kamaboko or analog products. The final section is devoted to seafood coatings.

MINCE

The world's consumption of fish could be more than doubled if its great unused resources were fully exploited. These resources remain unused not through a lack of catching technology, but through an inability to transform the raw materials into stable, acceptable products and to distribute these products at an affordable price. Developments in minced fish technology could make a major contribution to increased exploitation.

Minced fish, which is flesh separated in a comminuted form from the skin, bones, scales, and fins, is a versatile but unstable commodity. To a large extent, its properties are determined by the nature and quality of the raw material. First we review the materials used for mince production, then we discuss mechanical and nonmechanical separation processes that can be used and note the effects that nonflesh contaminants can have on the mince quality. Third, we review the susceptibility of mince to fat, protein, color, and microbial degradation and discuss the means available for stabilizing the mince against such effects. Fourth, we show how these techniques can be used in preparing a wide range of mince-based products. Finally, the current status of mince production is briefly reviewed, and we draw conclusions about areas needing further development.

Most of the information is drawn from the extensive published literature on minced fish but relates almost exclusively to the resources and technologies available. It is dominated by work in the Japanese surimi and kamaboko industry.

We limit our discussion to mince from bony fish, omitting the potential for minces from crustacean, mollusk, and cartilaginous raw materials. Nevertheless, studies on materials such as krill, whose exploitation will depend on mechanical separation and whose mince products require extensive stabilization and transformation, may contribute greatly to the exploitation of minced fish.

Raw Materials and Sources

In principle, bone separation processes can be applied to any species of fish, crustacean or mollusk. In practice, these processes can be best justified for those species where significant added value will accrue. Separation techniques can increase yields obtained from currently utilized commercial species by reclaiming flesh from filleting wastes and other by-products. They can increase the exploitation of underutilized species by transforming them into products that are in greater demand and can upgrade those species that have previously been used for industrial or animal feeding purposes. They can also be used to exploit by-catch materials that otherwise would be discarded at sea.

Different raw materials have different technological properties, and to a large extent, the raw material species or species mix determines both the degradative problems and the potential process and product applications of the mince. Compositional changes due to spawning cycles and seasonal response have a major effect on fat and protein quality. Obviously conditions and handling methods throughout the world generate raw material of widely differing qualities, and most minced fish technologies are more sensitive to raw material qualities than those that use intact flesh.

Commercial Fish

With commercial species, mince technology can obtain a higher yield from whole (headed and gutted) fish and can reclaim additional flesh from filleting wastes. Frozen blocks prepared from both are now major commodities in international commerce.

In developed countries, such trade is based predominantly on the gadoid fish: cods, hakes, haddocks, pollocks, and croakers. Mince yields are generally high and the microbiological quality good. However, the color, texture, and taste of commercial blocks are highly variable. One distinguishing feature of these species is the presence of trimethylamine oxide (TMAO) as the principle osmo-regulatory agent. The enzymic degradation of TMAO to dimethylamine (DMA) and formaldehyde can cause severe textural damage through formaldehyde cross-linking of the flesh proteins, and this degradation is accelerated in the frozen storage of mince made from these species. (This effect is discussed later.) Protein degradation, the major problem in frozen storage, is accelerated by the mincing process and exacerbated by the presence of blood and several organs. Oxidative rancidity can be evident in minces from the higher fat (1 to 3 percent) gadoids; this is greatest when dark muscle and blood are present. Color problems arise from skin, blood, and ultimately protein degradation.

Despite the predominance of gadoid minces on the world market, minces are prepared from other commercial species. In the West these include several flatfish—the soles (*Parophrys* and *Microstomus* spp.) and the flounders (*Bothidae* and *Pleuronectidae*). Odor and flavor problems arise from the high skin contamination levels in flatfish minces, however.

Major fisheries are developing for the South Pacific and South Atlantic hakes (*Merluccius* spp.). A significant proportion of the catch is too small, soft, or parasitized for fillet product, and large amounts of block frozen mince are generated at relatively high yield. Hake minces seem particularly susceptible to TMAO breakdown-induced problems; frozen stability has been studied intensively. Equipment specifically for the heading and gutting of small hake is being developed, which should facilitate mince production.

Another commercial fishery of particular interest in the Americas is the rockfish (*Sebastes* spp.), although markets are limited by the short storage life of frozen fillets. Shelf life quality could be extended through the mincing process by the incorporation of antioxidants that prevent fat rancidity and cryo-protectants that prevent protein degradation during frozen storage.

Much work has been done on the production of stable minces from Alaska pollock, both by the Japanese and other nations. As can be seen, mince production from existing commercial species and their by-products has been confined to the developed world. A similar pattern emerges for the world's underutilized species.

Underutilized Fish

The world's consumption of fish could be greatly increased if presently underutilized or unused resources were brought into the human food chain. There is a major incentive to apply mince technology to many of these species because of the intractable problems in processing and marketing them by other means.

In the developed world, fish resources are underexploited because of difficulties of processing, consumer unfamiliarity, or inherent quality problems. In the early 1970s, studies of the newly discovered Atlantic deep and mid-water resources showed that mincing was the only way of removing the undesirable connotations of species identity from the often grotesque characteristics of the whole fish. Mincing also allowed correction of the high moisture content and soft texture of many species.

Another major resource of great potential includes the lanternfish and bericoid species. The flesh of some deep-water species contains high levels of possibly toxic waxes, but mincing and washing of the mince may reduce the waxes to acceptable levels.

A resource more likely to achieve commercial exploitation through mince production is the blue whiting *(Micromesistius poutassou)*. Extensive studies have been undertaken on the frozen stability of blue whiting mince; stabilization of both protein and the fat fractions is necessary, and mince color is poor. The same considerations probably apply to the large stocks of southern blue whiting *(Micromesistius australis)*.

Much research effort also has been given to the development of mince products from the American mullet *(Mugil cephalus)*. The use of antioxidants has overcome the problems of oxidative rancidity experienced in mullet fillet. Other underutilized species studied by American and Canadian workers include the sea trouts *(Cynoscion)*, croaker *(Micropogon)*, ribbonfish *(Trichiurus)*, argentine *(Argentina)*, cusk *(Brosme)*, turbot *(Atheresthes)*, grey cod *(Gadus)*, thorneyhead *(Sebastolobus)*, red hake *(Urophycis)*, and menhaden *(Brevoortia)*. Other underutilized species used for mince production are predominantly temperate species used to produce frozen mince blocks.

Generating mince from underutilized tropical and subtropical species has received less attention, despite the large tonnage potential in the areas where the need for food protein is greatest. Chemical and sensory tests were performed on minces from six tropical species from the Malaysia Coast: grunt *(Pomadasys argyreus)*, lizardfish *(Saurida tumbil)*, ponyfish *(Leiognathus splendens)*, catfish (*Arius* spp.), threadfin bream *(Nemipterus japonicus)*, and cutlassfish *(Trichiurus lepturus)*, and another project looked at the relative frozen stability of minces from sixteen underutilized Australian species. In India, the preparation of frozen mince from anchovies (*Thrissocles* spp.), croaker *(Johnius dussumieri)*, and other species has been studied. Acceptable products were generated, although some protein and fat degradation was apparent. Indian butterfish *(Lactarius lactarius)*, croakers (*Otolithus* spp.), and ribbonfish *(Trichiurus lepturus)* were used in deboned, partially hydrolyzed products. Mince production from croakers and lizardfish also has been studied in the Philippines, and acceptable sausages and cakes have been manufactured.

By-catch

Several million tons of fish are caught and discarded every year in the world's shrimp fisheries, predominantly in tropical and subtropical waters. Shrimping is generally conducted by small trawlers with limited hold capacity and few crew members. Thus substantial incentives of added value or government control are needed to induce the landing, sorting, and handling of this wasted resource. Although government programs of control and subsidy have had some success in exploitation of by-catch in some countries, full exploitation will only be achieved when the shrimp fisherman can command a higher price for by-catch than is currently realized through industrial applications. By-catch is plentiful, but it should not be regarded as cheap.

Most work on mince production relates to the by-catch from the shrimp fisheries of the Caribbean and the gulfs of Mexico and California. However, the raw material differs from that encountered in the Caribbean, the Arabian Gulf, and elsewhere in that the incidence of fatty pelagic fish is low (relative frequency 0.9), the mean fish length is small (4 inches/10 cm), the proportion of marketable species is low, and consistency is high (eight species constitute 74 percent of the by-catch). These factors combine to make mince production an attractive option for Mexican by-catch utilization. Although the small size eases many aspects of handling, it makes evisceration a major problem, so mince products from whole fish are being studied. The occasional occurrence of toxic pufferfish and possibly scorpion fish will require careful attention to sorting procedures, however.

In Mexico, a major effort has been made in the production of precooked, rapid-salted, dried fish cakes. Consumer acceptance is high, and the technology should be applicable elsewhere. Other applications include frozen, canned, and smoked mince, dried mince flour, and silage from mincing waste. A frozen mince product called Pepepz has been commercialized in Mexico by Productos Pesqueros

Mexicanos. The low levels of fatty pelagics and of DMA/formaldehyde-producing gadoids allow frozen mince of good storage stability to be produced.

In the Gulf of Mexico and the Caribbean, by-catch is of a larger mean size and contains a higher proportion of commercial species. It has led to research into the production of frozen mince blocks from sorted by-catch. Mince has been successfully produced from Caribbean sheepshead *(Archosargus)*, black drum *(Pogonias)*, tilapia *(Tilapia)*, croaker *(Micropogon)*, sand trout *(Cynoscion)*, mullet *(Mugil)*, cutlassfish *(Trichiurus)*, spot *(Leiostomus)*, kingfish *(Menticirrhus)*, robins *(Carangidae)*, flying fish *(Exocoetidae)*, and catfish (*Anarchichas* spp.).

Programs for mince production from by-catch are under way in Guayan, India, Thailand, and Indonesia, and similar programs are planned elsewhere. The major technological problems probably will be in the maintenance of raw material quality under tropical conditions and in producing affordable products, while offering the shrimp fisherman a sufficient price to encourage landing. This example illustrates the challenge for mince technology in the developing world: to generate acceptable value for money products at a minimum of added cost.

Small Pelagics

The world catch of small pelagic species exceeds 20 million tons (18.1×10^6 metric tons) annually, but half the landings are reduced to fish meal. This quantity could be more than doubled, given suitable handling and utilization technology. The inherent instability of these materials and the high catch rates require fast, mechanized systems for optimal utilization. Mince technology may offer the best potential for increased exploitation. Several major drawbacks can be overcome by mincing: fat degradation can be minimized by protective additives; proteolytic degradation can be reduced by washing; protein functionality can be better manipulated; and undesirable connotations of species identity can be removed. However, of all the materials studied for mince production, the small pelagics seem the most difficult. These problems arise mainly from the high (but variable) levels of polyunsaturated fats, the effects of fat-degradation products on taste and texture, and the contamination of minces by the highly proteolytic gut contents.

Major species studied for mince production include the mackerels *(Scomber)*, horse mackerels *(Trachurus)*, herring *(Clupea harengus)*, sardines (*Sardina* and *Sardinops*), sardinella *(Sardinella)*, sprats *(Sprattus)*, anchovies (*Engraulis* and *Thrissocles*), and menhadens (*Brevoortia* spp.). Oily nonpelagic industrial fish also have been studied, including capelin *(Mallotus)*, sand eel *(Ammodyte)*, and Norway pout (*Trisopterus* spp.). Most research has centered on oxidative and enzymic fat degradation and has generally found that in all but canned applications such reactions are accelerated by the mincing process. However, it is also evident that some mince is less susceptible to oxidative rancidity than would be expected, and that proper handling and storage combined with appropriate treatment can produce stable materials. (In some countries a certain degree of rancidity may be acceptable.)

It is apparent that, apart from proteolysis (protein breakdown) by gut enzymes, the protein stability of pelagic minces is generally good. Several studies indicate that mincing does not damage the texture of pelagic flesh as much as it does marine demersal materials. Color problems may prove more limiting in the applications of pelagic minces. These materials can suffer toxicological problems arising from microbial contamination from the gut-in whole fish minces, from histamine formation in scombroid (tuna or tuna-related fish) minces, and from the concentration of pesticides and other toxins in larger pelagic fish taken in polluted waters.

There is much active research into producing minces from the major underutilized pelagic resources of the Northern Hemisphere, including the European horse mackerel, the Baltic herrings and sprats, and the Black Sea sardine. Research in the Southern Hemisphere seems less evident, despite the majority of the underutilized pelagic resources lying in those waters.

Freshwater and Aquaculture

Freshwater species contribute more than 10 million tons (9.1×10^6 metric tons) to the annual world fish catch, yet there is the potential for several million tons more and the potential productivity from aquaculture is limited only by investment and profitability. Commercially significant freshwater species are generally more consistent in their properties than the marine resources. Technology for producing mince from these species should be widely applicable.

The delicate bone structures of most freshwater fish make filleting difficult, and mincing can markedly improve recovery. With the exception of the freshwater pelagics—the shads—fat contents are low and their bland taste allows minces to be used in nonfish products and as meat extenders. However, the highly unsaturated fatty acids require particular attention to storage conditions.

Extensive studies have been undertaken on mince from the mullet or sucker of the Great Lakes *(Catostomus commersoni).* Stable frozen and canned products have achieved good consumer acceptance and are preferred to marine species products. Carp *(Cyprinus carpio)* minces have also been produced in the United States from both cultured and natural sources.

Again, less work has been done on minces from tropical and subtropical species, although acceptable products have been made from the ubiquitous tilapia.

Separation Process

Fish mince quality depends on the raw material and also on the separation process. The process sequence, the equipment used, and the operating conditions can influence the potential usefulness of the final product.

Anatomy and Biochemistry

Mincing is not a simple separation of flesh from bone. Separation processes effectively fractionate the raw material into a range of anatomically and physiologically distinct components which can affect the mince's texture, flavor, and appearance. The criteria for a separation process cannot be established until the desirable and undesirable components are identified.

Most apparent is, of course, the bone fraction, which can be up to 15 percent of whole or gutted fish, or more than 30 percent of filleting wastes. Several problems are associated with bone contamination of minces.

1. Physical injury can result from the consumption of sharp, hard, or pointed bone fragments.
2. The visible presence of even soft or harmless bone is considered aesthetically undesirable in most of the world.
3. Smaller bone particles can cause a gritty texture.

4. Bone contents over 2 to 3 percent can approach threshold toxicity levels for fluoride content.
5. Bone marrow exudate has been implicated in the development of oxidative fat rancidity.

Bone is not, however, a constant material. The skull and vertebrae are more highly calcified than the spine, ribs, and pin bones. Thus the mincing of heads and frames can give a higher proportion of hard, brittle fragments than is obtained in mincing whole fish or fillets. Calcification varies between species—most notably between pelagic and demersal fish—and increases with age. Most commercial and national quality specifications for minced fish define limits for bone content based on weight, number, or size distribution.

A variety of mince contaminants can damage texture or texture stability. Degradation by the cross-linking of proteins with formaldehyde from the breakdown of TMAO has been mentioned. The reaction is enzymic, seems to be limited to certain species, and occurs predominantly in frozen storage. (In other systems, TMAO is degraded to trimethylamine.) The major enzyme source is the kidney. This enzyme is heat labile but is reactivated by an unidentified compound in the muscle. Thus localized heat treatment is *not* sufficient to prevent texture degradation. Other sources of the enzyme include the blood and blood clots; the pyloric caeca; the dark brown lateral muscle, and possibly the skin. Mincing these species, reportedly, can accelerate formaldehyde-mediated denaturation, presumably by the mixing of the source organs with the flesh. Apparently preparing minces from mixed species (e.g., by-catch) that contain these formaldehyde-producing species can cause degradation of the flesh of nonproducing species also.

Significant texture degradation can arise through enzymic proteolysis (protein breakdown) of the minced fish. This process is most apparent when whole fish are used, and gut proteases (protein that breaks down muscle tissue) are dispersed through the muscle tissue. Even low levels of contamination by visceral materials from gutted fish can cause extensive proteolysis of the mince. Other active proteases include the catheptic enzymes of the muscle tissue itself and those generated by microbial spoilage.

Minces from both demersal and pelagic species are susceptible to extensive fat degradation; therefore, separation methods should aim to reduce both the source of the fat and the materials catalyzing the fat decomposition. High levels of unstable, polyunsaturated lipids are found in the skin, in the subcutaneous and dark lateral tissue, in the viscera, and in the brain and nerve tissues. Contaminating minces with these materials may cause flavor and oxidative rancidity. The mincing process can accelerate the degradation by dispersing the fat-degrading enzymes, by accelerating nonenzymic oxidation through increased surface area, and by dispersing organic and inorganic oxidation catalysts. The enzymes are found mainly in contamination by visceral material and in the dark muscle. Nonenzymic degradation is catalyzed mainly by the hemoproteins (hemoglobin, myoglobin, and oxyhemoglobin) in the bone marrow, in blood vessels, and in the flesh itself. Skin also contains pro-oxidant components.

Mincing frequently results in a product that is darker than the raw material, because of the contamination by melanoid skin pigments, by the black belly membrane, by blood, and by head and gut contents. On longer term storage, browning and yellowing reactions of the proteins and lipids also become apparent. (Color standards have been developed for frozen mince blocks.)

Visceral contamination is mainly associated with the aesthetic aspects of taste, texture, and color, but consideration also must be given to possible toxicological and microbiological factors, which can only be assessed by examining the specific raw material. Despite the presence of food poisoning organisms in the guts of several species used for mince production, no instances of disease-causing bacterial spoilage have been reported. Similarly, although many species concentrate pollutant heavy metals and pesticides, no problems have been reported in commercial mince products. Problems may occur, however, with parasite contamination. Many species used for mince production—particularly the underutilized marine resources—can be heavily parasitized. Worms and larvae in the flesh will be transferred to the mince, many surviving intact.

Although, in general, parasites from marine fish are aesthetically unappealing rather than harmful, there are technological problems associated with the rapid proteolysis caused by myxosperidia. On the other hand, there are potential dangers to human health associated with some parasites of freshwater fish. The risk of nitrosamine formation in nitrite-treated DMA-producing species is well known. These reactions are accelerated in mince products by the dispersion of hemoglobin, which acts as a catalyst. Although washing and antioxidant treatment can reduce the effect, DMA-producing species should not be used for nitrite-cured mince products.

Toxins can arise in mince from contamination by certain fat products—notably high levels of sphingomyelins and other complex lipids from nerve tissue and the brain, and the reaction products from advanced oxidative fat degradation. Potent neurotoxins can arise from visceral contamination of mince from certain tropical species; again, raw material sorting is the only effective method of control.

Lastly, consideration should be given to the distribution of nonpoisoning bacteria in the raw material. In whole fish, the highest bacterial counts are found in the viscera and on the skin and gills. However, the mincing of whole (gut-in) fish gives a mince with counts similar to that obtained from degutted fish. More significant are the differences in filleting fractions, where it is generally found that frames give higher counts than minces from fillets, V-cuts, or frame trimmings. The mincing process itself also will increase bacterial counts.

Mechanical Separation

Most separation techniques use a perforated filter to screen the flesh from nonflesh components. Early separation devices were adapted from those used in the fruit and meat processing industries, but now a wide range of machinery specifically designed for fish separation is available (Fig. 8-1). Three operating principles are used. A belt and perforated drum system (a variation of this system has been developed where the belt and drum surface move at different speeds, thus increasing the shear rate and consequent yield); a screw feed and perforated cylinder system; and two concentric cylinders—the inner perforated and rotating. All have their advantages and disadvantages. The belt-and-drum systems benefit from readily adjustable pressure and easy cleaning, although belt wear can be high when using raw materials with large or hard bone particles. Some residual bones from fillets or gutted whole fish are needle-shaped and the mince may consequently exceed some specifications for limits of bone. Some bone particles in mince made from skeletons of whole fish that have had fillets removed but still carry some flesh are blunt and irregular in shape. These products might not meet

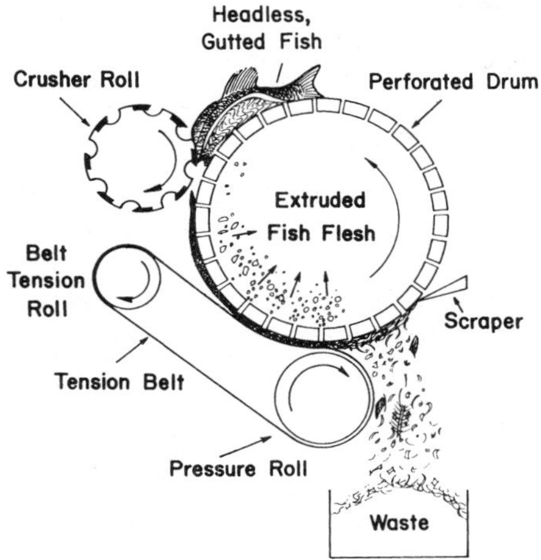

Figure 8-1. Mechanical Flesh Separator.

specifications limiting the permitted weight of bone present. Use of a drum with smaller perforations reduces bone content, but also yields a mince of poorer texture; perforations from 1/25 to 1/4 inches (1 to 7 mm) are available commercially, but a 1/8 inch (3 mm) drum generally offers the most reasonable compromise. Screw cylinder systems do not have the same wear problems, but generate higher shear rates and consequent textural damage. In general these latter systems are more expensive, but all systems give similar yields: 60 to 80 percent for whole fish and 30 to 70 percent for fillet wastes. Despite their apparently simple operating principles, however, the relationships between pressure, perforation size, and perforation area with yield, contaminant levels, and shear damage are complex.

As problems have developed, machine designs have been adjusted. The high spoilage rates of minces have led manufacturers to remove dead spaces from the fish-carrying areas. Recognizing that ferric contamination from machinery can accelerate oxidative fat degradation, stainless steel and nonmetallic materials are being used for components that come in contact with the mince. Oxidation can be further reduced by separation under water or under washing solutions.

Mechanical filters that screen bone from untreated raw material are now the most widely used. However, several alternative methods are evolving. Fine pastes can be obtained by grinding and filtering; bone-free minces can be obtained by tumbling and screening; and precooking can be used to weaken connective tissue. Traditionally such techniques have been used prior to manual picking or deboning, but now mechanical systems have been developed. These methods have the advantages of reducing nonprotein contamination, softening bones, and reducing texture and flavor degradation; however, protein functionality is lost. Mince, of course, can be generated by the comminution of bonefree flesh obtained by traditional filleting methods.

Many operators now use multipass systems, whereby high-quality mince is generated by low pressure and intermediate perforation size. Extra yield is obtained by generating lower quality minces at higher pressure and lower perforation sizes on subsequent separation steps. Machines are also available for the heading, gutting, dressing, and prebreaking of many species that can be used whole for mince production, notably for consistent catches of small pelagics. However, a major need for mechanical heading and gutting systems for mixed material, such as by-catch, remains. Consideration is also being given to mechanization of bone separation systems suitable for some developing countries.

Physical Quality Effects

Mechanical deboning systems obviously have a major effect on mince quality; therefore, understanding these effects is vital for the optimization of the product.

A strong positive correlation is found between screen perforation size and bone content in the mince. Similar relationships are found between both the degree of preprocessing size reduction and separation pressure with final bone content. Increasing perforation size also increases the proportion of thin, sharp bones in the mince. More difficult to establish are the relationships between the shear and pressure conditions of the separator and the damage to texture and storage stability. It is important to distinguish between direct pressure effects and the effects of increased dispersion of degradative enzymes.

There is increasing evidence that high shear rates damage protein functionality. Increasing pressure can lead to a reduction in water-binding capacity and to an actual loss of water content. Conversely, increasing the raw material's water content has been found to correlate with increasing susceptibility to shear damage during mincing. Extremes of pressure can have dramatic effects on mince: Above 4,200 psi (300 kg/cm^2) significant fat separation occurs and rancidity development is accelerated; above 21,000 psi (1,500 kg/cm^2) a large proportion of the protein is solubilized and denatured—although yields are substantially improved. Excessive protein denaturation damages most mince applications.

Increasing pressure and shear may increase mince discoloration and susceptibility to protein degradation in storage. Shear has less effect on immediate lipid degradation, although the effects of pressure on temperature and subcutaneous fat release can damage longer term lipid stability.

For mechanical separators, the effects of pressure, perforation size, and perforation area on bone content, protein functionality, discoloration, and lipid stability can only result in a compromise for optimal machine conditions.

Nonmechanical Separators

In addition to mechanical deboning systems, several chemical and biochemical techniques have been developed. Protein can be recovered from both whole fish and filleting waste by enzymic or acid proteolysis followed by centrifugal or filtration bone separation. Yields are high but protein functionality and integrity are generally low. These materials are best suited as inert extenders in composite products.

Washing

Many mince processes employ postseparation washing to remove inorganic salts, water-soluble proteins, pigments, visceral contamination, bacteria, and decomposition products. In some species, fat content also can be reduced, and the washing of minces from whole fish can provide products of similar quality to those obtained from gutted material. Washing of gadoid mince can eliminate formaldehyde production from TMAO, and washing is essential in applications such as kamaboko production where acceptable products cannot otherwise be produced. It is generally achieved by multiple washes in chilled, preferably chlorinated, water followed by pressing, centrifugation, or rotary sieving. Alkaline washes can inhibit protein hydrolysis by acid proteases, although fish flesh may contain alkaline proteases that will be activated by such treatment. Washing with ascorbic or citric acids may inhibit degradation of flounder minces. Reduction of washwater pH also can reduce color, water uptake, protein loss, and TMAO levels.

Although washing improves the texture of finely minced gel products, it has less effect on coarse-textured minces. Similarly, although washing may be necessary for minces heavily contaminated with pigment or visceral material, it has little effect on the flavor or appearance of minces from higher quality raw materials. Washing has little effect on muscle tissue that is inherently colored, such as the gray flesh of saithe and blue whiting, the dark flesh of pelagic species, and the green flesh of certain tropical by-catch species. Discolored minces may be acceptable for incorporation into meat products, as discussed later.

The need for a washing step should be carefully considered, as it can have many undesirable effects. Gross protein yield loss can be substantial, up to 25 percent, and soluble micronutrients including vitamins, minerals, and free fatty acids are also lost. This method can lead to the secondary problem of effluent disposal. Washing with hard water can damage texture and catalyze fat degradation; washing with seawater or brine can further increase protein loss. Despite the availability of effective dewatering machinery, it is difficult to control the final water content of the washed mince. In many situations, washing of the raw material prior to mincing is more appropriate and is a good manufacturing practice.

Mince Stabilization

As mentioned, mincing can accelerate the degradation of fats, proteins, color, and bacteriological quality. This section reviews work on the stabilization of fish minces, and the next section discusses the product applications of these technologies.

Fat Stability

Fat degradation is a major problem in minces from both fatty and low fat species. It occurs in all product applications except canned systems.

Fish fats in mince are characterized by their high levels of long-chain polyunsaturated fatty acids. Although these may be nutritionally desirable, they are highly susceptible to enzyme hydrolysis and nonenzymic oxidation. Undoubtedly, the mincing process accelerates these reactions—through physical surface effects and through the dispersion of catalytic contaminants. However, measuring fat degradation is extremely difficult, and it is less clear which reactions are increased by mincing and what effects they have on sensory quality.

Fat Stabilization

Several approaches are available for the stabilizing of fats in fish minces. Most widely studied is the use of antioxidants.

Polyphosphates are added to minces mainly to enhance protein functionality and water binding. They have been found to have antioxidative properties, particularly when in combination with other additives.

Several process techniques can inhibit fat degradation. Glazing and oxygen-impermeable packaging inhibit the oxidative deterioration of frozen mince blocks.

Studies have confirmed that oxidation is a surface effect, that impermeable packaging has a greater protective effect than degassing and elimination of occluded air, and that slow frozen glazes are more effective then rapidly frozen glazes. Impermeable packaging is also one of the most effective means of protecting dried mince product.

Rapid heat treatment of minces at temperatures above about 120 to 140°F (49 to 60°C) deactivates lipolytic enzymes, thus protecting the mince against free fatty acid formation. However, cooking tends to enhance oxidative deterioration. An effective way to prevent oxidation is to hydrolyze the fats with added lipase and then wash out the free fatty acids. Washing also can remove other oxidation catalysts from the mince, although careful control of wash-water temperature is needed to prevent acceleration of oxidative degradation.

Much work has been done on understanding and controlling fat degradation in minced fish. However, fat stability remains a major factor limiting the use of many small pelagic and underutilized species for mince production.

Protein Stability

Much recent work has been done on the nature, stability, and enhancement of fish protein functionality. The proteins of deboned mince are both particularly susceptible to degradation and yet of high inherent functionality. Minced fish has particular problems of protein stability; but it is also a versatile material in terms of the wide range of technological properties that can be exploited in process and product development. The functional properties of major interest are heat-setting capacity, gel-forming ability, and water-binding capacity. Maintaining these properties requires that the myofibrillar proteins are preserved in their native, nondenatured form. This process, in turn, requires minimizing a range of degradative reactions.

Color Stability

As with fillet materials, the mince products' color and appearance are vital consumer attributes. In developed countries, whiteness and homogeneity of color are major parameters in products such as mince blocks and kamaboko. In the developing world also, products such as the fish balls of South East Asia must be white or a uniform gray; in other products such as spiced or dried mince, color is less important.

The mincing process generally has the greatest effect on color; however, further degradation can occur during storage. Yellow/brown discoloration occurs in frozen minces, and bacterial and nonenzymic browning occurs in nonfrozen materials. Oxidative discoloration of fats and blood pigments also can be extensive. Color assessment and specification can be by subjective or instrumental methods.

Several techniques are available for improving mince color. Most commonly used is water washing, which can be effective for whole fish, frame, and mixed by-catch minces.

The alternative to whitening is color masking, such as incorporating fish mince into products where we expect to have a darker color. Such products include those where mince is used as a meat extender or in smoked, spiced, or curried minces.

Bacteriological Stability

The major determination of mince's microbiological quality is the quality of the raw material. Thus protracted holding of filleting wastes before mincing or poor storage of whole fish raw materials increase total counts in the minced product and increase the risk of spoilage. "Dustbin" practices of stockpiling prior to mincing should be avoided. Under good hygienic conditions, preprocessing raw materials by scaling, heading, and evisceration has little effect on the mince's final quality. Even mincing gut-in materials leads to only small increases in counts, and no pathogenic species are found in the viscera of most raw materials. Similarly, if temperature and cross contamination are controlled, the mincing process should not lead to more than one log cycle[1] increase in counts. Standards of process hygiene have been defined by two Food and Agriculture Organizations of the United Nations. The bacteriology of commercial frozen mince blocks produced under such conditions has been extensively studied, and the large majority fell within international trading standards.

However, in many countries, potential raw materials for mince production are spoiled or semispoiled. Although most of these materials occur in the tropics and thus contain thermophilic spoilers highly amenable to chill or iced stabilization, many current practices generate raw materials of high initial counts. Under such conditions, mincing will lead to substantial increases in microbial counts by dispersion of high levels of surface contamination throughout the muscle tissue. Minces prepared under even the most controlled conditions are extremely susceptible to postmincing contamination. Thus minces with high levels of initial contamination have an extreme risk of spoilage in handling, storage, and further processing. In wet minces, initial spoilage is predominantly putrefactive, and the product becomes inedible before there is any risk of toxicity. However, poor handling practices can lead to contamination by food poisoning organisms. The presence of scombroids (e.g., tuna and bonito) and certain other species in the raw material can also introduce toxin producers into the mince.

Mince Products

The range of mince products established in the world market is limited and dominated by block frozen materials in the West and surimi in Japan. We discuss these forms briefly here, but more emphasis is given to product technology currently under development.

Frozen Products

The annual production of frozen blocks probably amounts to more than 550,000 tons (500×10^3 metric tons), although the statistics are inadequate. Blocks can be produced solely from minces or from mixtures of mince and fillet in various proportions. Producing mince blocks is generally done in molds in plate freezers, often with the incorporation of salt, phosphate, sugars, and other additives. Manufacturing practices and standards are suggested by the Food and Agricultural Organization/Codex Alimentarius and have been adopted by most producing countries. The primary aim is to produce frozen blocks of uniform shape that can be cut, with little or no waste, into many smaller portions of specific size, shape, and weight.

Requirements for the rectangular blocks are as follows:

1. Skinless, boneless fish flesh
2. Absence of foreign bodies
3. Reproducible weight

---

[1]An increase by a factor of 10; for example, 100 in a log increase over 10 and 100,000 in a log increase over 10,000.

4. No voids or ice pockets
5. Specified dimensions with sharp edges
6. Smooth surfaces
7. Protection from physical damage
8. Protection from dehydration

Headed and gutted fish, fillets, V-cuts, and frames are all used as raw materials in commercial mince block production. These materials mainly come from established white fish sources, but increasingly also from underutilized white fish, pelagic, and mixed by-catch species. Thus blocks of a wide range of composition and sensory properties are produced. It has been common practice to confine the proportion of mince added to fillet blocks to about 15 percent of the total mixture.

Although mince blocks are a major commodity in international trade, they are only intermediates in the manufacture of final retail products, such as battered fingers, sticks, steaks, and cakes. A retail trade is also developing in the United States and Japan for bulk packs of frozen mince for further preparation by the consumer. This concept could be extended to chilled and intermediate moisture products.

Mince should be frozen as soon as it is made or immediately incorporated into products and then frozen within five hours of manufacture; products should be kept chilled while awaiting freezing. The storage life of frozen mince made from good quality cod and haddock flesh is at least six months at –20°F (–29°C) or three months at 0°F (–18°C) without any significant loss of quality, but mince from hake and Alaska pollock apparently have a shorter cold storage life as do minces that include kidney or gut. Minces made from fatty fish require protection against oxidation in cold storage.

Frames and Cartons

In the normal procedure for making a mince block, the appropriate weight of material is hand packed into a waxed cardboard carton fitted into a frame contained in a shallow, light metal tray. The frames, often divided to accommodate two cartons, should be strongly constructed of aluminum or galvanized steel in order to withstand the pressures when the block expands during freezing. Aluminum frames are preferred because they are less likely to damage the plates of the horizontal plate freezer, although deformation can occur more easily during handling and during freezing if the carton is overfilled. The length and width of the frame space should be accurate to 1⁄25 inch (1 mm) to provide a block of precise dimensions.

The carton is formed by a folded, one-piece waxed and scored card of food grade quality with either a smooth or dimpled surface. It helps maintain fish quality by providing protection from dehydration in storage and transportation, from damage in handling, and from dirt and bacteriological contamination. It also allows easy release from the frame and from the frozen block of fish. Some processors believe dimpled surfaces make release easier and give a smoother block surface with few voids. Much of the carton's protection is lost if it is opened (for example, to inspect the block in quality control) because the intimate seal between fish block and carton is broken.

The folded cartons are fitted in the frames on trays, with all the carton tabs overlapped on the outside to prevent them from being embedded in the block. The space formed by the carton can be termed a mold.

Packing

The mold must be filled with the correct amount of fish because underfilling results in voids; overfilling results in some material being squeezed out on the freezer plates, bulging of the surfaces, uneven contact with the freezer plates, and possibly fracture of welded joints on the frame. Allowance must be made for the block to expand during freezing. The weight of fish will vary slightly with species; the amount of mince required for a given volume is less than the amount of fillet. After weighing, the fish should be transferred quickly to the mold because delays can result in drip loss. The balance pan should be kept free of drip and residue. By strict control, the block weight can be kept within 5 percent of the desired value.

Mince added to fillet blocks should be distributed throughout the block to avoid a sandwich effect of a layer of mince in the middle and to avoid concentrations of mince. Usually the mixture of fillets and mince is spread from the center and pressed into the corners to form a block with random packing.

After the mold is filled, the surface is smoothed and the carton closed so that the overlapping cover edge fits between the side of the carton and the frame to prevent the edge from being embedded in the block. Normally the trays and frames containing the filled molds are stacked on a pallet to accumulate a full load for the horizontal plate freezer. In handling the loaded trays, care should be taken to ensure the mold does not slip through the frame and become trapped between the base of the frame and the tray. If frozen in this position, contact with the freezer plate will be poor, and it may be difficult to remove the frozen block from the frame. Long delays in accumulating a freezer load should be avoided. If considerable drip accumulates before freezing and it can be foreseen, some compensation for weight loss should be made when the mold is filled in order to prevent voids. Accumulation of drip also results in ice pockets in the frozen block.

Freezing and Storage

Before loading the freezer, the freezer plates should be clean and free from residues of frozen fish and ice which might cause indentations on the blocks or damage to the cartons. Any drip accumulated in the tray should be poured off. The freezer should be loaded evenly to maintain good contact between blocks and plates and to prevent warping of the plates. Spacers should be inserted where there are no blocks, and frames of different thicknesses must never be stacked on the same plate.

Given good contact and efficient heat transfer with a refrigeration temperature of –40°F (–40°C), blocks up to 2.5 inches (6.4 cm) thick can be frozen to a mean temperature of –20°F (–29°C) in less than two hours. If these practices are followed, one defrost of the freezer in twenty-four hours will be sufficient for cleaning.

When removing frozen blocks from the frames, the block should be pushed evenly from the bottom surface to avoid damage to the carton; the cover or lid tends to be torn if the blocks are pushed out from the top surface. The blocks are packed in corrugated cardboard master cartons for added protection and easier handling during cold storage and distribution. To obtain maximum storage life, the frozen blocks should be transferred immediately to cold storage at –20°F (–29°C).

Reformed, Transformed, and Textured Products

As they come off the separator, fish minces are amorphous granular slurries. Coarse minces may have a perceptible structure of fibers and fiber bundles; fine minces and minces from soft-textured species have a homogeneous pasty consistency. Thus some forming or structuring process is needed to achieve higher levels of textural integrity.

Intact fillets have three levels of texture: fibrosity, flakiness, and gross bulk structure. If fillet simulation is required, forming techniques can achieve some or all of these. Frozen mince blocks achieve fibrosity from the inherent characteristics of the mince and gross structure from compaction in the freezer mold. Mixed mince and fillet blocks also have some degree of flakiness similar to the structure of an intact fillet. Flakiness can be achieved in all mince products by several reforming techniques. Most widely studied has been the use of alginate gels to set the mince into a sheet structure, followed by layering and compaction of the sheets to simulate the myotome flakes. Fibrosity can be enhanced by the incorporation of spun vegetable protein fibers, extrusion-textured vegetable protein, precooked fish muscle, and alkali/acid-precipitated mince protein fibers.

Few of these flake- or fiber-forming processes are practiced commercially. Extensively used, however, are techniques for the forming of individual portions from mince. Regular portions can be cut from frozen mince blocks. Blocks can also be portioned by frozen extrusion forming; this method eliminates yield loss in sawdust but can cause shear damage to the muscle proteins. A wide range of machinery is available for the low pressure extrusion forming of fresh minces. An infinite variety of shapes and sizes can be produced, including fillets, shrimp tails, balls, and regular geometric portions. Additives such as salt, phosphate, soy protein, and gums are used to obtain the optimal characteristics for extrusion and to control the final product texture. Colors, flavors, and seasonings also can be used. A range of high quality products aimed mainly at developed Western markets are manufactured using extrusion-forming techniques. The firm, elastic textures are particularly suited to shellfish and mollusk analogues. The incorporation of shrimp into mince portion can markedly improve acceptability and oxidative stability.

Formed products such as sausages, cakes, patties, balls, loaves, and burgers are well established in many countries. Although their forms vary with cultural preferences, many of these products are ideal vehicles for minced fish. Mince in sausage products is the most extensive, an industry dominated by Japanese kamaboko production. Outside Japan, most mince sausage products are fine-textured, heat-set emulsion products rather than heat-set protein gels.

Mince is used as an extender in meat-based sausages in the United States. The color of frame mince and pelagic mince is effectively masked in products such as frankfurters; usage levels are limited by flavor effects. Mince has also been used as a meat extender in patties and burgers. Other emulsified mince products include highly comminuted, soft-textured pastes—for use as such or as spreads and dips—and coarsely chopped products such as fishburgers and loaves. The formation of oil-in-water emulsions may be effective in reducing contact between the fish fat and ambient oxygen.

Mince can be used as an ingredient in many composite products. The ubiquitous fish cakes, rissoles, and croquettes are generally bonded with cereal flours or starches, seasoned to local preference, and preserved chilled or frozen. Higher levels of mince are used in traditional products such as fish balls (Southeast Asia and Scandinavia) and Gefilte fish (Israel, Europe, and the United States). Such products are being further developed in the United States and elsewhere. In the United States high levels of mince are used in fish patties.

Other formed products studied for mince utilization include fried or extrusion-expanded, starch-based snack products, sliced salmon, or saithe analogues and filled products.

Surimi and Kamaboko

Japan produces more than 1.1 million tons (1×10^6 metric tons) of kneaded mince products annually. The manufacturing technology for kamaboko, chikuwa, and satsumaage and for the intermediate surimi has been unique to Japan for centuries. However, extensive fundamental studies into the properties of mince proteins and the more recent expansion of the industry into foreign markets suggest that the Japanese experience may be of value in the development of mince technologies elsewhere.

Surimi is the semiprocessed intermediate mince material used in the preparation of a wide range of finished products. We discuss this product in depth later in this chapter.

Production and Marketing

A wide range of technologies are available for manufacturing mince products, although information on the degree of commercial exploitation is limited. Here we briefly review the state of development of the mince industry. Japan's surimi industry is well established, with rigorously defined standards for materials, manufacturing practices, and finished product quality. In the West also, trade in frozen mince blocks is well advanced. Canada and Western European countries are major producing and exporting nations; the United States is the largest importer, although its domestic production is increasing. Australia also imports mince blocks. Large tonnages are produced by Eastern block nations for internal consumption.

Extensive work has been undertaken to define standards for mince block production and utilization. The Food and Agriculture Organization and participating countries have contributed to the development of the Codex Alimentarius Draft Standard for minced and mixed blocks, and to the Proposed Draft Code of Practice for Minced Fish. These documents detail the range of minimum product quality standards required for international trade and the associated standards for raw material quality and manufacturing practice. Discussions continue, however, on the problems of product identity, description, and labeling. Agreement will have to be reached on the nature and extent of classification needed for the infinite variety of raw material species, mince-to-fillet ratios, and bone content found in commercial mince blocks and finished products.

Less advanced is the commercial development of minces from underutilized raw materials and their use in novel technologies. The potential supply of mince and minced products greatly exceeds the present demand. Consumption could be increased by the use of mince as an extender in existing products—both fish and meat—but the greatest potential may be in the manufacture of new product forms that exploit the natural advantages of the material. This type of diversification requires careful process and product development, thorough acceptability and market testing, and rigorous quality standards. Every effort should be made to prevent poor quality products from jeopardizing the potential and future of minced fish. Unfortunately, some damage was done in Europe and the United States when insufficient knowledge on the stabilization of minces led to consumer dissatisfaction with poor quality products and when ill-conceived publicity on alternative species caused suspicion with the consumer and within the trade. With a few notable exceptions, there has been insufficient investment in acceptability and market testing of mince products.

In the developed world, a successful example of mince technology has been developed. Some twenty products have been introduced, including frankfurters, balls, chowders, and untreated mince. The intention was to transform a range of unfamiliar or underutilized species and filleting wastes into mince products acceptable as such and with demonstrable market potential. After basic studies into stabilization and structuring of the raw materials, processes and formulations were developed, screened, and market tested in supermarkets, restaurants, and schools. Unprocessed frozen minces seem particularly successful in the United States, Japan, and elsewhere. In the developed world, however, the cost advantage of mince is confounded by the consumer perception of price as an indicator of quality.

In the developing world, a good example is the Mexican by-catch program. A detailed study to characterize the resource was followed by the development of salt-dried, canned, frozen, and smoked product technologies. Most emphasis has been given to the rapid salt-dried cake and to Pepepez's frozen portion reformulated into fish shapes. Extensive market testing indicated the products were highly acceptable and price competitive. An industrial model demonstrated that manufacture would give satisfactory returns to the shrimp fishermen and to the processor, while allowing this wasted resource to contribute to the nutritional needs of developing nations.

Conclusions

Mince separation techniques have been applied to a range of raw materials, including commercial and underutilized species, whole fish and filleting waste, by-catch, and pelagic and freshwater sources. For many of these fish, mincing is the only viable means of utilization. Although the largest tonnages of mince are presently generated from commercial gadoid species, the greatest potential is seen in the by-catch and small pelagic resources of the developing world.

Development of separation processes is now highly advanced, with a wide range of separators available commercially. Current development efforts are aimed at designing whole process lines, in the realization that methods of preparation and handling have a greater effect on final product quality than the actual separation stage. Although mechanical separators are highly effective at removing bone, skin, and connective tissue, they are less efficient in the removal of other contaminants. Combined chemical and physical methods may be preferred for the removal of fat, guts, and pigment from small pelagic and industrial fish. This area merits further development.

All minces are inherently unstable. Fat degradation is a major problem with both fatty and low-fat species. Oxidation and rancidity occur in dried and frozen minces; fat hydrolysis occurs in fresh materials. Canned minces are relatively stable. Several chemical and natural antioxidants have been identified, together with physical methods of limiting oxidation. However, fat stability is still the major factor limiting the use of many small pelagic and other underutilized species in mince production. Further work is needed in the elimination of oxidation catalysis, in the removal of fat by washing or lipolysis, and in the development of inherently stable products such as oil-in-water emulsions and Maillard-reacted[2] intermediate moisture products.

Mince proteins are both highly functional and highly unstable. Frozen denaturation can be minimized by a wide range of cryoprotectants, although they can cause excessive rubberiness and other sensory defects. Less work has been done on protein degradation in nonfrozen systems. Even mild drying processes cause extensive mince denaturation, although this can be advantageous in accelerating drying rates. A large number of functionality-enhancing additives and ingredients are used in mince products, although in many instances more use could be made of the inherent properties of the mince itself.

Mince whiteness is a major consumer attribute in most countries. Color degradation occurs by pigment contamination at the separating stage and during storage. Color can be controlled by pretreatment of the raw material, by washing or bleaching the mince, or by incorporation of whitening.

Commercial mince products already established in the world market are limited and dominated by block frozen materials in the West and by surimi in Japan. Recent developments of mince product technology in the developed countries are mainly frozen and canned. They include extrusion-formed portions, sausages, balls, pastes, and extended meat products. Of particular interest are unprocessed minces for further preparation by the consumer.

Except for a few traditional products such as fish balls and fermented pastes, mince technology in the developing world has yet to be fully exploited. The reasons for this are several and indicate areas where further development is needed.

The major resources of by-catch and small pelagics are well suited to mechanical separation. However, there are often insufficient facilities and incentives to land them with the high quality required for mince production.

Electrically powered mechanical separators are suitable for many situations; however, less costly mechanical separators with a higher quality and output than manual picking are more appropriate elsewhere.

Many products require mince from gutted, dressed fish. There are no machines available for the gutting of mixed materials such as by-catch, and it is unlikely they will be developed. Machines are available for the gutting of small pelagics, but they are expensive and restricted to fish of basically the small size. More appropriate would be nonmechanical techniques for removing the viscera and other contaminants, and the continued development of gut-in products.

Most successful have been dried products from low-fat minces, particularly the rapid salt dried materials. Further investment in acceptability and market testing should be encouraged.

Canning, one of the most effective means of mince stabilization, would be particularly appropriate in those countries with excess canning capacity. However, little work has been reported in these areas.

Although it is likely that the greatest potential is in new product forms that exploit mince's natural advantages, more effort is needed to match the major

---

[2]Maillard reaction is a complex chemical reaction involving amino acids and reducing sugars that determine the color of many processed foods.

advances in mince technology in the developed world to the resources and food preferences of the developing countries.

As little as ten years ago, technology availability was the major factor limiting the enormous potential of minced fish utilization. Many solutions have been found and the requirement now is for energetic investment in their implementation.

SURIMI

Surimi is a refined form of minced fish meat. It is not in itself a foodstuff; rather it is an intermediate raw material from which the traditional Japanese kneaded foods called *kamaboko* are manufactured. Imitation shrimp, scallop, and crab meat products are also made from surimi. The Japanese word *surimi* literally means "minced meat"; however, surimi is more than minced meat. Its two major distinguishing features are its gel-forming capacity, which allows it to assume almost any texture desired, and its long-term stability in frozen storage, imparted by the addition of sugars as cryoprotectants.

When fish muscle is separated from bones, skin, and entrails, and then comminuted, it is called minced meat (Fig. 8-2.). Minced meat becomes raw or unfrozen surimi after it has been washed to remove fat and water-soluble constituents.

Raw surimi is a truly bland material, because its flavor components are removed by the leaching process. More importantly, the washing isolates the fish meat's myofibrillar protein, which is insoluble in fresh water and possesses the essential gel-forming capacity so prized by the kamaboko maker.

When raw surimi is mixed with antidenaturants and frozen, the product is called frozen surimi. The antidenaturant additives, usually sugar compounds such as

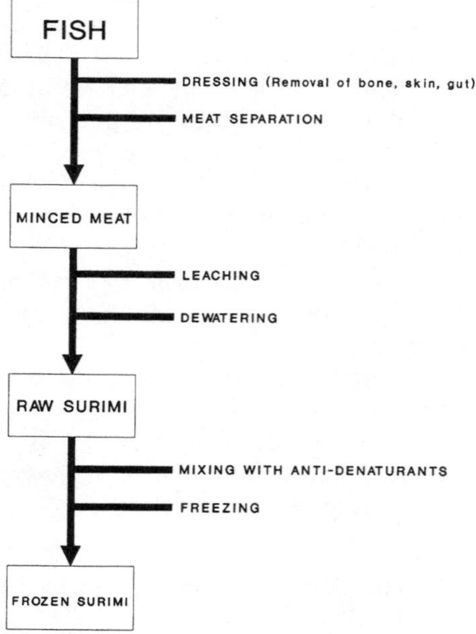

Figure 8-2. Definition of Surimi.

sucrose and sorbitol, give surimi the ability to resist freeze denaturation, which is an irreversible change in the protein resulting in a reduction in gel strength. If these cryoprotectants are not used, the surimi's gel-forming capabilities will be lost due to denaturation of its proteins, which can occur even while the material is frozen. Thus, the term *frozen surimi* has more to do with the use of antidenaturants than with the freezing process itself. Since about 95 percent of all surimi produced today is frozen using cryoprotectants, the term surimi generally denotes frozen surimi.

Just as surimi is more than minced fish meat, a surimi-based product such as imitation crab is more than surimi. To make the imitation crab and other more traditional kamaboko products, surimi is partially thawed, mixed with a small amount of salt to make the protein soluble, blended with other ingredients and flavors, kneaded and formed to create the desired texture and shape, and cooked by steaming, broiling, or frying (Fig. 8-3).

For approximately 1,500 years, the Japanese have made surimi-based products. Traditional methods consisted of processing the fish into raw surimi and then kneading it immediately into a finished product. Since both fish and raw surimi would denature quickly, the entire process had to be performed soon after the fish was landed. The advent of frozen surimi in 1960 revolutionized the traditional methods for making surimi-based products. With year-round availability of frozen surimi, kamaboko manufacturers were no longer dependent on unstable local fish catches and raw surimi. Tremendous expansion of the surimi-based product industry was made possible by this important change in the nature of its raw material. The industry also rapidly modernized its productivity to keep pace with the growing demand.

Thus technological developments, plus the vast resources of hitherto underutilized Alaska pollock in the North Pacific Ocean, helped fuel phenomenal growth of surimi and surimi-based product industries during the 1960s. Within thirteen

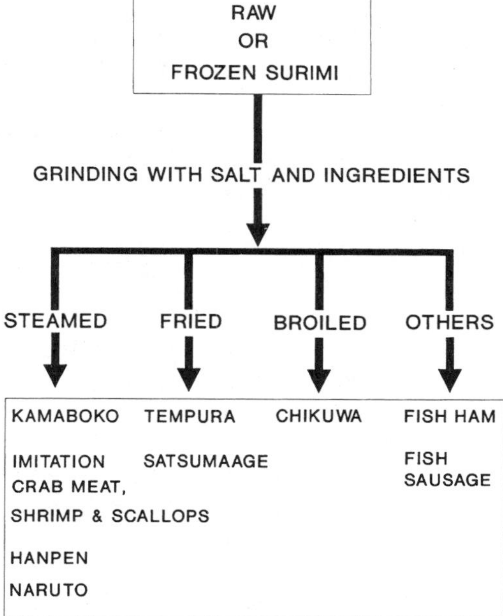

Figure 8-3. Definition of Surimi-Based Products.

years from its introduction of frozen surimi in 1960, the Japanese surimi-based product industry doubled in size, producing 391,300 tons (355 × 10^3 metric tons) annually. By 1984 the surimi industry had grown into a $500 million business in Japan.

Alaska pollock is the staple raw material fish for the Japanese surimi industry. Although almost any fish can be used to make surimi, no other species matches its combination of abundance, economy, and quality.

From 1980 to 1984, an annual average of about 1.7 million tons (1.5 × 10^6 metric tons) of Alaska pollock was used for surimi production by the Japanese, about 87 percent of all the raw material fish used for surimi during that time.

Automation of Surimi Production

New methods for producing a stable frozen surimi from Alaska pollock allowed surimi manufacturing to evolve into an automated mass production system to keep pace with expanding demand. Automation was essentially completed within a decade of the introduction of frozen surimi. The most important machines contributing to this achievement were the screw press and the rotary washing screen or sieve.

The screw press is a highly efficient dewatering machine which reduces the water content of the washed mince, thus maximizing the concentration of protein in the surimi. Before this press was developed the dewatering process was accomplished by a basket-type centrifuge.

Because the centrifuge's efficiency was limited, it became the major bottleneck in surimi production operations. A centrifuge could process only about 1,100 pounds (500 kg) of minced meat a day; a single screw press could handle as much as 22 tons (20 metric tons), and, more importantly, the screw press could be integrated into a continuous operation with the washing procedure.

Surimi production was further streamlined by the rotary screen, which combines the functions of washing and preliminary dewatering. Inserted between the washing tank and screw press, the rotary screen improved the efficiency of both washing and dewatering procedures.

Another machine of special note is the refiner. Previously the straining procedure to remove membranes, bones, and tendons from the washed minced was applied after dewatering. The straining procedure was slow and adversely affected quality because the mechanical pressure applied to the meat generated heat. The refiner is not only more efficient in removing impurities but also is exempt from the heat problem because it works directly on the washed meat, which is temperature-buffered by its high water content.

Surimi-Based Imitation Seafood Products

Adopting the bland-tasting Alaska pollock as the overwhelming staple raw material for surimi meant that kamaboko products were lacking in variety. As early as 1970, some surimi-based product manufacturers began to experiment with new product concepts and with ways of incorporating new flavors into their kamaboko. Initial market success came in 1973 when the first surimi-based crabmeat with imitation flavor was introduced. Another major breakthrough occurred in 1976 when a process was developed that could create a fibrous texture extremely similar to that of a natural crab leg.

The invention of imitation crab legs was called the greatest achievement of the postwar Japanese seafood processing industry. Today, there are imitation scallops and shrimps and many other varieties, manufactured by nearly fifty producers.

Reflecting widespread consumer acceptance, the production of shellfish analogs has risen sharply. Statistics compiled by the Japanese show that the 1984 production of shellfish analogs was 78,620 tons (71,323 metric tons), constituting about 7 percent of all the surimi-based products manufactured that year. The surge of imitation crab production since 1981 coincided with, and is largely responsible for, the recovery of kamaboko production as a whole since 1981.

Surimi from Underutilized Species

For almost twenty years, Japan has extensively tested fish species other than Alaska pollock as raw material for frozen surimi. These experiments included species belonging to the white-fleshed deep-sea cod family, the abundant domestic species such as sardine and Pacific mackerel which feature dark meat, the Antarctic krill, and sharks.

Deep-sea cod (*Mora pacifica* Waite) off New Zealand was studied as early as 1970 for its suitability in surimi-based products. In 1976 a high-grade surimi was successfully produced from hoki *(Macrourus novaezelandiae)* and deep-sea whiptail *(Lepidorhynchus denticulatus)* aboard a factory trawler. Similar tests were performed using forked hake *(Podonema longipes),* a species caught in large quantities along with Alaska pollock, and on blue whiting *(Micromesistius poutassou),* an Atlantic species of the cod family.

Two test products of Antarctic krill surimi have been conducted, but, because of the extreme difficulty of performing a sufficient dehydration on the krill meat, which has a strong tendency to swell when washed, the krill surimi exhibited poor gel strength. Attempts to use shark meat as raw material started in 1982, and a method for producing high-grade surimi from shark meat is believed to have been found. In 1977 the Japanese government launched a five-year program to develop surimi from the dark meat of sardine and Pacific mackerel. If their meat could be converted to surimi, the rapidly growing landings of these species would more than offset the impact of declining Alaska pollock catches.

A new method had to be developed to achieve this objective because the dark fish muscle of sardine and Pacific mackerel loses its freshness very quickly after the death of the fish. Its pH level drops below 6, prompting denaturation of actomyosin. The large amount of fat and pigment in the dark meat cannot be removed with regular washing procedures such as used for Alaska pollock. Unless dark-fleshed fish can be used to produce surimi of analog production quality, the price and product availability will experience substantial changes.

End Products of Surimi

Surimi is the intermediate raw material from which the end products called *neri-seihin* (surimi-based products) are manufactured. About 90 percent of surimi-based products are various types of fish cakes called kamaboko. Less than 10 percent of surimi-based products are represented by fish sausage, fish ham, and fish burgers. Imitation crab and other surimi-based shellfish analogs may be included as kamaboko.

Kamaboko products are divided among three major categories: steamed, broiled, and fried. Typical steamed kamaboko is called itatsuki (board-mounted) kamaboko, but the variety also includes imitation seafood, naruto, and hapen, spongy marshmallow-like products which contain entrapped air. The typical broiled kamaboko is chikuwa, which has the shape of a hollow bamboo stem. Typical fried kamaboko (age-kamaboko) products are satsuma age and tempura. Kamaboko is also given various names depending on product shapes, such as sasa (bamboo-leaf shaped), soba (noodle-shaped), date-maki (whirled or rolled), and so on.

The main ingredient of kamaboko is a homogeneous gel of ground fish muscle, obtained by kneading the thawed frozen surimi or raw surimi into a paste with salt. It also contains other ingredients such as sugar, starch, sweet sake, sodium glutamate, and egg whites. Example formulations for typical kamaboko products are shown in Tables 8-1 and 8-2.

Surimi-based products are prepared by extruding the surimi paste into various shapes resembling such shellfish meat as king or snow crab legs, crab claws, lobster tails, scallops, or shrimp. The closer the analog resembles the natural product, the greater the extrusion sophistication. The product may be divided into four major categories according to their fabrication and structural features: molded, fiberized, composition-molded, and emulsified (Fig. 8-4).

Molded

Molded products are made by molding the chopped surimi into the desired shape and allowing it to set and form an elastic gel. Molding may be accomplishd by either a single extrusion or a coextrusion.

For the former, the paste is extruded through a single opening of the nozzle without concurrent texturization. For the latter, the paste is extruded through a nozzle having many separate openings such that strings of extrudate are laid over one another during forming. Coextrusion therefore gives a meatlike texture, whereas the single extrusion results in a uniform and rather rubbery mouthfeel. Restructured shrimp from broken or odd-shaped shrimp of low value and shrimp-flavored surimi-based products are in this category.

Fiberized

Fiberized products are made by extruding the paste into a thin sheet through a rectangular nozzle (Fig. 8-5) having a narrow opening 1/25 to 1/8 inch (1 to 3 mm high). The extruded sheet is then partially heat set and cut into strips of desired width by a cutter, similar to a noodle cutter, having a clearance which allows only partial cutting (four-fifths of the thickness), so that a sheet of strips results. Surimi used in this process should be of top grade so that the paste remains sufficiently

Table 8-1. *Typical Ingredients in Kamaboko (in Percent)*

Ingredients	Odawara Kamaboko	Toyohashi Chikuwa
Surimi	76–84	80.2
Additives:		
Salt	4.2–5.3	2.6
Sugar	11.9–19.5	6.4
Sodium glutamate	1.2–2.0	1.2
Potato starch	0–6.5	—
Wheat starch	—	5.6
Sweet sake	4.8–6.5	4.0
Egg white	Small amount	Small amount
Total	100	100

Table 8-2. ***Typical Ingredients in Imitation Seafood Products (in Percent)***

Ingredients	Crab	Scallop	Shrimp
Surimi	55.0	60.0	68.0
Egg white	8.0	5.0	4.0
Starch	5.0	4.3	11.0
Sorbitol	0	0	0.2
Salt	1.5	1.0	1.0
Sugar	0.6	0	0
Sweet sake	1.0	0.5	0
Chemical seasoning	2.3	2.7	0.4
Natural coloring	0.1	0	0.08
Water	25.0	25.0	11.32
Crab essence	2.5	0	0
Scallop essence	0	1.5	0
Vegetable oil	0	0	2.5
Seasoning	0	0	1.5

cohesive and elastic while it is stretched, cut, and pulled. The greatest pulling tension occurs between the cutter and wrapper. Fine strips are preferred for the fibrous crab-leg product, whereas wider stips are more suitable for the simulated shellfish in the form of sea flake and chunk.

The resulting sheet of strips is folded into a bundle of fibers by a simple narrowing device called a rope former. The rope is then colored, wrapped, and cut into a desired length. The crab-leg product is produced by a straight cut; the flake and chunk types are formed by an oblique cut, which gives the rope a zigzag pattern when it is unfolded. During the folding process, the finished product's texture can be further altered by manipulating the adhesion between the folded layers.

In recent years, substantial improvement has been made in these fiberized products. As a result, consumer acceptance has greatly increased. Nonetheless, there is still plenty of room for improvement, particularly in texturization techniques, flavor, and color.

Composite-Molded

For composite-molded products, the strings of desired length are mixed with or without surimi paste and extruded into a desired shape. Strings are produced either by the method described earlier or by slicing a block of surimi gel (approximately 1.2 to 1.6/3 to 4 cm thick) into thin rectangular sheet (about $\frac{1}{25}$ inch or 1 to 2 mm thick), followed by stripping into a desired width. This type of product gives a better bite than the strictly molded variety, which tends to be rubbery and uniform in texture. Composite-molded products are found in chunk form and sold mixed with fiberized products. Another type of composite-molded product called "fish ham" is prepared by mixing the dice of cured tuna and pork into the fish paste before extrusion.

Emulsified

To make an emulsified type of product, surimi is treated similarly to meat when it is processed for emulsion products. The level of fat added is usually less than 10

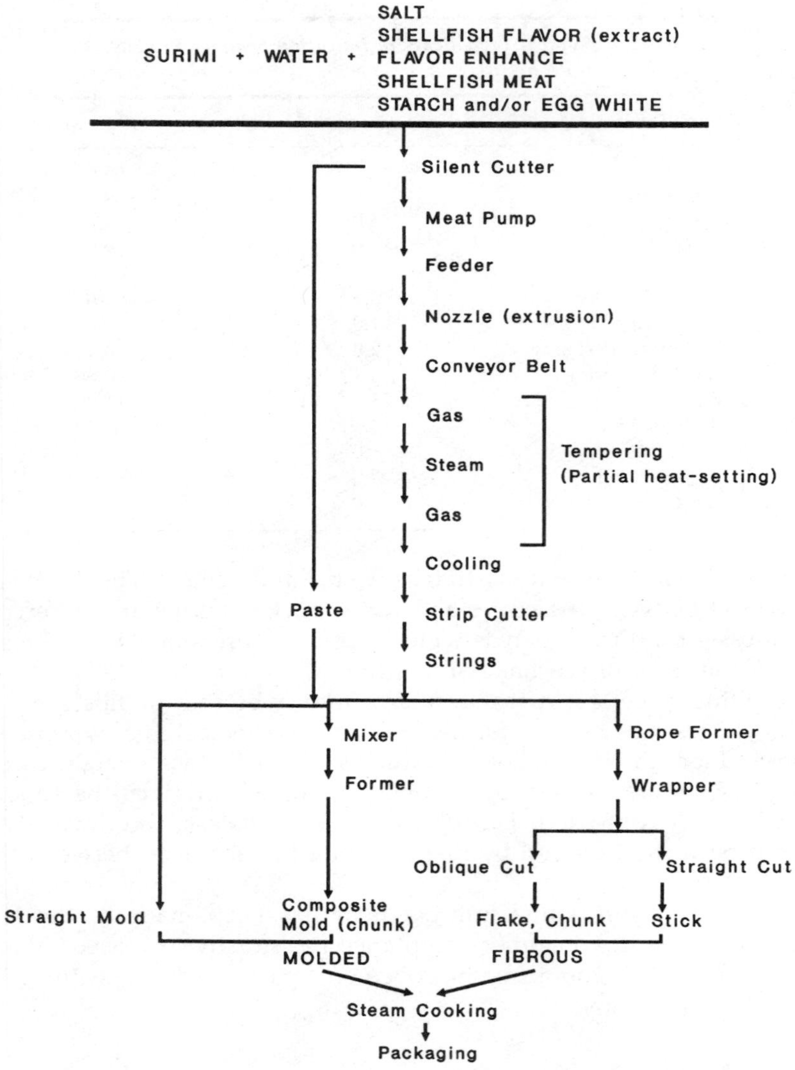

Figure 8-4. Process for Making Fibrous, Flake, Chunk, and Composite-Molded Products.

percent, and the type of fat used is not limited to animal fat. In fact, vegetable oil is often added, because, unlike mammal and bird meat, fish meat readily produces a stable emulsion with oil. For wiener-type products, the resulting paste is stuffed into casings and steam- or smoke-cooked. The sausage-type products are still in an experimental stage in the United States, but a variety of these products have been developed and successfully marketed in Japan for more than twenty years. Sausage-type products can be produced by a method similar to our composite-molded products.

Desirable Properties for Raw Material

Important qualifications for the raw material fish for surimi are

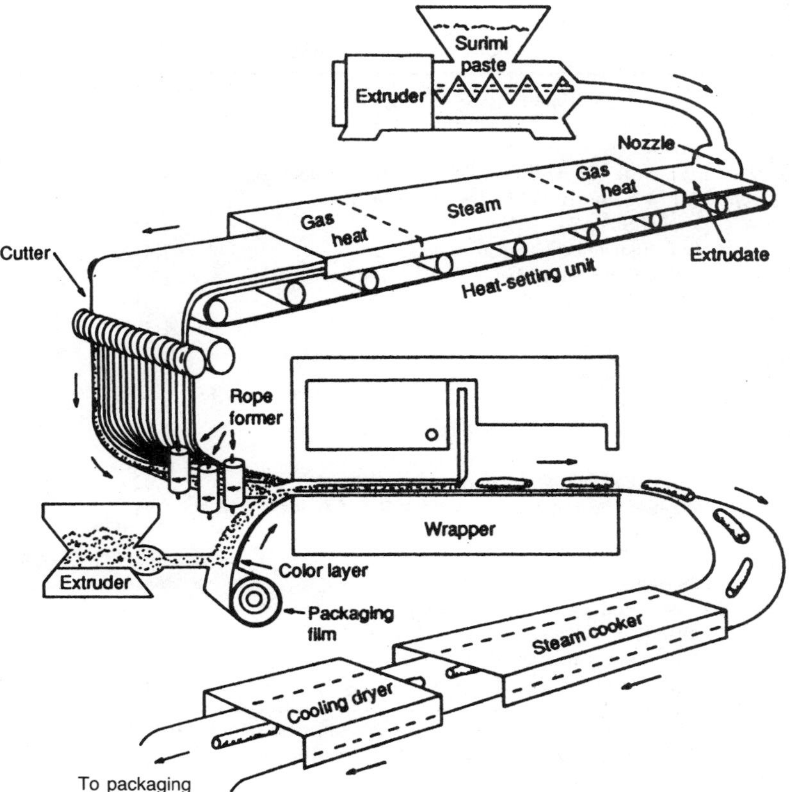

Figure 8-5. Small-Scale "Crab-Leg" Processing Line.

Strong gel-forming capability when processed into surimi-based products
Good organoleptic quality (taste, odor, appearance)
White flesh
Year-round availability
Abundance
Reasonable price

Unfortunately, no fish species meets the full set of these qualifications. As shown in Tables 8-3 and 8-4, the gel-forming capability, traditionally the most important characteristic, varies widely from species to species. In general, gel strength is higher in saltwater fish than in freshwater fish, and greater in white-fleshed fish than in dark-fleshed fish.

If gel strength is deemed the major criterion, croaker ranks very high among the white-fleshed fish. Lizard fish and cutlass fish, two other species favored as raw material for surimi, also exhibit high gel strengths. It is noteworthy that the gel strengths of these species are more than twice that of the most widely used species, Alaska pollock. Croaker, lizard fish, cutlass fish, and sharptoothed eel are still important raw materials for some well-known name-brand surimi-based products in Japan.

The fish species with relatively high gel strengths account for only a small portion of the surimi produced annually in Japan, averaging only 12.8 percent

Table 8-3. *Gel-forming Capacity of White-Fleshed Fish*

White-Fleshed Fish	Gel Strength
Croaker *(Nibea mitsukurii)*	1,560
Barracuda (*Sphyraena schlegeli* Steindachner)	1,560
Yellow-belly threadfin bream (*Nemipterus bathybius* Snyder)	1,536
Lizardfish *(Saurida undosquamis)*	1,430
Cutlassfish (*Trichiurus lepturus* Linne)	1,334[1]
Jarbua therapon *(Therapon jarbua)*	1,317
Striped mullet (*Mugil cephalus* Linne)	1,293
Unicorn leatherjacket *(Aluterus monoceros)*	1,273
Leatherjacket *(Navodon medestus)*	1,164
Red seabream *(Chrysophrys auratus)*	1,158[1]
Frigate mackerel *(Auxis thazard)*	1,110
Brill *(Pseudorhombus cinnamoneus)*	1,083
Puffer *(Labocephalus lunaris spadiceus)*	1,020
Red bigeye (*Priacanthus macracanthus* Cuvier)	918
Sharptoothed eel *(Muraenesox cinerus)*	792[1]
Red gurnard *(Chelidonichthys kumu)*	616
Needlefish *(Ablennes anastomella)*	612
Alaska Pollock *(Theragra chalcogrammus)*	555[2,3]
Cuttlefish *(Sepia esculenta)*	543[1]
Hoki *(Macrourus novaezelandiae)*	477[3]
Angler *(Lophius litulon)*	438

Note: Gel strength is expressed in g/cm^2 after heating fish muscle for 20 minutes at 140°F (60°C), unless otherwise specified as follows:

[1]Heating temperature 122°F (50°C).

[2]Heating temperature 104°F (40°C).

[3]Frozen fish.

between 1980 and 1984. In particular, Japan's catch of croaker decreased sharply from 43,000 tons (39,000 metric tons) in 1976 to 26,500 tons (24,000 metric tons) in 1984.

The predominance of Alaska pollock as the raw material fish indicates that quantity and economy have largely replaced gel strength as the main qualifications for the raw material. Even the Alaska pollock's bland taste is probably no longer a drawback, because it allows imitation flavors to be incorporated readily into the kamaboko, as has been demonstrated by the imitation crabmeat, scallop, and shrimps.

SURIMI MANUFACTURING PROCEDURES FOR WHITE-FLESHED FISH

Surimi technology has evolved largely through the refinement of manufacturing procedures based on trial-and-error experience. Scientific understanding of these procedures has lagged behind practical advancements.

The most important progress has come in three key areas: (1) how to maximize the leaching effect with the least amount of water; (2) how to separate the meat from impurities; and (3) how to mechanize the manufacturing procedures.

Table 8-4. *Gel-forming Capacity of Dark-Fleshed Fish, Shark, and Freshwater Fish*

	Gel Strength
Dark-Fleshed Fish	
Pacific blue marlin *(Makaira mazara)*	2,937
Flying fish *(Prognichthys agoo)*	1,470
Dolphin-fish (*Coryphaena hipprus* Linne)	1,431
Purse-eyed scad *(Selar crumenophthalmus)*	1,078
Horse mackerel (*Trachurus japonicus* Temmink & Schlegel)	1,023
Japanese sardine *(Etrumeus micropus)*	933[1]
Pacific saury *(Colorabis saira)*	624
Yellowfin tuna *(Thunnus albacares)*	561[2,3]
Pacific mackerel (*Scomber japonicus* Houttuyn)	543[1]
Sardine *(Sardinops melanosticta)*	447[2]
Skipjack tuna *(Katsuwonus pelamis)*	321[3]
Wavyback skipjack (*Euthynnus affinis yaito* Kishinoue)	222[1,3]
Sharks	
Dog-shark *(Scoliodon walbeehmi)*	1,143[1]
Smooth dog-fish (*Mustelus manazo* Bleeker)	690
Whiptail-ray *(Dasyatis akajei)*	540[1]
Smooth dogfish (*Mustelus griseus* Pietschmann)	540
Freshwater Fish	
Tilapia (*Tilapia mossambica* Peters)	867
Common carp (*Cyprinus carpio* Linne)	600[1,3]
Snakehead *(Channa argus)*	423[1]

Note: Gel strength is expressed in g/cm^2 after heating fish muscle for 20 minutes at 140°F (60°C), unless otherwise specified as follows:
[1]Heating temperature 122°F (50°C).
[2]Heating temperature 104°F (40°C).
[3]Frozen fish.

Handling of Raw Material Fish

How the raw material fish is handled prior to mincing is crucial to the quality of surimi. The success of the handling methods is judged on whether the fish entering the meat separator are (1) fresh and (2) clean.

Freshness is a principal factor affecting gel-forming capability; a high-grade surimi cannot be manufactured from fish lacking freshness. Table 8-5 shows variations in gel-forming capability in kamaboko associated with different degrees of freshness. Clearly, freshness has a decisive influence on its gel-forming capability, and the deficiency in gel-forming capability resulting from lack of freshness cannot be amended with a leaching process.

A top grade surimi is made aboard factory ships by using very fresh fish, although the manufacturing procedures employ no more than two cycles of washing. Ship-processed surimi generally exhibits a gel-forming capacity higher than that of land-processed surimi which has gone through several cycles of leaching.

The Technical Institute of Japan Surimi Association has the following recommendations on handling raw material fish following delivery to the plant:

Table 8-5. *Gel Strength in Kamaboko Due to Varying Degrees of Freshness in Raw Material Fish*

	Fish Condition			
	Extremely Fresh	Quite Fresh	Fairly Fresh	Not Fresh
Gel strength of kamaboko made from				
Unleached surimi	1,100	600	350	150
Leached surimi	1,200	850	650	400

Note: Units are in gr · cm.

The fish may be stored in the (wooden) fish box surrounded by crushed ice.
The fish may be stored in a tiled circulating tank approximately 1 meter deep, filled with water and floating ice. The fish stored in the tank should not be piled higher than about 20 to 24 inches (51 to 61 cm) from the tank floor.
When stockpiling the fish in the open air, place the fish on a permeable mattress about 4 inches (10 cm) above ground level. The fish may be piled about 20 inches (51 cm) high and covered with crushed ice, and the arrangement may be repeated to create layers of fish.
Care must be taken not to allow the fish to freeze under any cirumstances.

The dressed fish entering the meat separator must be clean and free of any remnants of intestinal tracts, black belly membranes, blood clots, and other impurities which are difficult to remove in the subsequent procedures. To ensure cleanliness, a recommended practice is to wash the fish twice, once immediately after the removal of head and guts and again immediately before the fish is fed into the meat separator. Soft water is recommended for washing fish, instead of a ground water which contains dissolved salts and metals.

Surimi producers try to avoid processing fish that are in rigor and employ systems that handle fish gently at all times. Physical and chemical properties of fish muscle undergo major postmortem changes that significantly affect functional properties. Although surimi attains its maximum gel strength when fish are processed immediately after death, it is impractical to attempt processing all fish before onset of rigor. While in rigor, the fish is difficult to handle and cannot be cleaned readily. In addition, surimi made from fish muscle during rigor mortis tends to have a fishy odor. Therefore common practice is to begin processing just after rigor mortis fades, about five hours after death. Rough handling of fish can bruise the muscle, which leads to softening of the tissues and an inferior quality end product.

Leaching

Washing the minced fish meat in the process of manufacturing kamaboko (surimi-based product) began in Japan about 1910 as a means of removing fats, oils, and fishy odor as well as providing a white tint to the product. The washing also resulted in reinforcing the product's gel strength.

The Japanese word for the washing process, *mizusarashi,* literally means "leaching with water." Several functions are performed by this process.

Mechanical Separation of Impurities

Mechanically stirring the mixture of minced meat and water releases the fat and oil from the muscle tissue and floats them out as the supernatant, which is readily removed by draining. Also separated from the meat are the remnants of digestive organs, which tend to float out along with the fatty substances.

Washing

The washing dilutes blood, pigments, and other impurities in the minced meat which may cause discoloration to the product or catalyze denaturation of protein.

Leaching

Fresh water leaches out water-soluble components of the muscle tissue and inorganic salts believed to contribute to freeze denaturation of surimi. The leaching of water-soluble components in turn isolates the muscle contractile protein, which is responsible for surimi's gel-forming capacity.

Repeated washing reduces residual water-soluble proteins in the meat, which in turn reduces the rate of contractile muscle protein denaturation. Although scientific understanding of why this process occurs is still incomplete, it seems the greater the number of washing cycles, the stronger the gel-forming capability of the surimi.

About 75 percent of the water used in a surimi plant is expended on the washing process. The water is costly by itself and results in additional expenses for wastewater treatment. The current method of washing is designed to minimize water use by combining a washing (or leaching) tank and a rotary sieve in succession. This is called a "continuous washing" system, and the meat travels between the two via a vacuum pump. Surveys have revealed that a plant employing the continuous washing system would normally use water at a rate of about twenty-five times the weight of the surimi it produces.

Properties of Leaching Water

Principal factors determining the effectiveness of the leaching water are the hardness and the acidity or alkalinity. The good surimi-based products in Japan traditionally have been attributed to the superior water quality in the region where they are manufactured. Namely, the water at Odawara, a place well known for its excellent kamaboko, has a medium hardness (calcium content of 20 to 40 mg percent). Water of medium hardness makes a good leaching water, because it replenishes the loss of hardness as washing cycles are repeated, preempting the development of hydrophilic tendency in the meat. Meat swelling is likely to occur more readily in the latter part of the washing process; therefore, it is a good practice to perform the last washing cycle with water containing 0.1 to 0.3 percent sodium chloride. Magnesium chloride or calcium chloride may also be used.

Degrees of Leaching

As much as 50 percent of all water-soluble components in the fish muscle are removed in the first leaching cycle. Additional cycles, while removing diminishing amounts of water-soluble components, serve to extract blood, dark pigments (melanin), black membranes, and other impurities as well as bleaching the product. One additional benefit arising from repeated leaching cycles is the reinforcement of gel strength in the kamaboko. The gel-forming capacity is proportional to the number of leaching cycles to which the fish meat is subjected.

In general, thirty to forty minutes is sufficient to achieve the objectives of leaching. The water used in leaching may be ten times the amount of surimi produced, and this amount may be divided into three cycles. The water requirement may be reduced somewhat, but not below seven times the output. Surimi prepared with the leaching water five times its weight deteriorates rather distinctly while in cold storage. Aboard the factory ship where very fresh fish are processed, the leaching water volume can be as little as three times the amount of surimi produced.

Effects of Salt Concentration

The gel-forming component of fish proteins varies widely in water-holding characteristics as a function of salt concentration. A very low salt content causes the water-holding tendency to rise. Under this condition, frequently caused by the washing cycle that removes water-soluble salts, the meat tends to hydrate and swell. Such meat is difficult to dewater, so it is advisable to add sodium chloride prior to the dewatering process.

Effects of Water Temperature

Warm wash water is more conducive to dewatering than cold water. Although the cold water is desirable to preserve product quality, this benefit may be outweighed by the loss of efficiency in the dewatering procedure when the water temperature is very low. Japan's Surimi Association recommends that the water being used for the last washing cycle be about 50°F (10°C) in order to achieve a reasonable dewatering efficiency.

Straining and Dewatering

The minced, washed, and leached fish meat is a wet slurry containing fragments of bones, ligaments, scales, and water, which must be removed. In the old procedure, the meat slurry was first dewatered before subjecting it to a strainer. As the dewatered meat was strained by being forced through tiny holes in a strainer, heat was generated in the meat being processed, causing harm to the protein. Use of a self-cooling strainer somewhat alleviated but did not eliminate the heat problem. A better solution was the refiner, a straining machine which could work on a wet slurry. The refiner is placed ahead of a dewatering machine, or screw press, so that the wet but drip-free meat emerging from the rotary sieve in the last washing cycle is strained first in a refiner and dewatered later in a screw press (Fig. 8-6).

The introduction of a screw press as the standard dewatering machine was one of the most significant breakthroughs in surimi production. The product could flow continuously through the screw press, hence the name "continuous dewatering machine" used by some manufacturers. It purges water from the meat slurry by squeezing it into a progressively reducing chamber with the aid of a rotating screw, while allowing the pressurized water to escape through tiny drain holes.

Although the screw press is universally used in surimi plants today, the refiner is not as predominant. Many surimi plants still use a self-cooling strainer, and some adhere to the old practice of dewatering first and straining later.

Additives

Minced fish meat's chief ingredient is the muscle contractile protein that provides an elastic property when processed into surimi-based products. Elasticity is closely

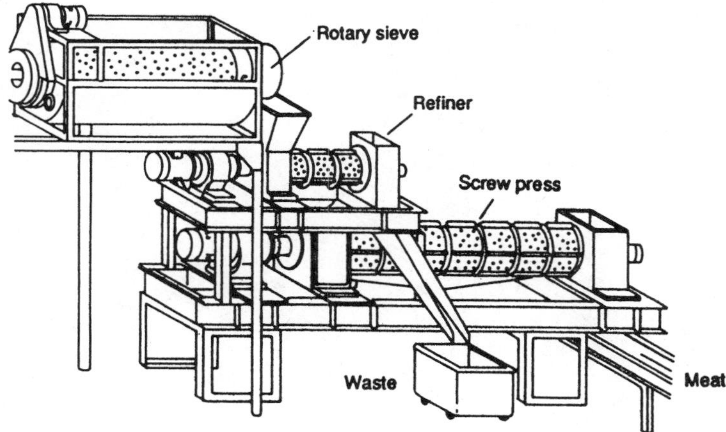

Figure 8-6. Arrangement of a Refiner.

correlated with the sensory (taste and odor) quality of the product and is a highly prized property of kamaboko.

A surimi that can be stored while retaining its gel-forming capability became a reality only with the discovery of additives that can be mixed into the raw surimi to protect the myofibrillar protein from freeze denaturation. Consequently, surimi destined for cold storage is mixed with antidenaturant additives before being frozen. Because the mixing procedure may generate heat, the mixer may be equipped with a self-cooling device. A vacuum mixing chamber may help purge air bubbles from the product. A silent cutter can also be used for mixing the cryoprotectant additives into raw surimi.

The first antidenaturant additives involved only sucrose, glucose, sorbitol, and polyphosphates (pyrophosphate and tripolyphosphate). Since then, a number of other chemicals have come into use. At least nine different varieties of sugar, including galactose and lactose, are known to be effective as antidenaturants for fish protein. Some amino acids and carboxylic acids also have been found to be effective antidenaturants. How these chemicals protect fish protein from freeze denaturation remains unanswered. Accordingly, the prescription of the antidenaturant additives being used today is experimental.

Tables 8-6 and 8-7 summarize the recent standards for surimi additives. The components in the additives are sugar, polyphosphate, salt, and glyceride. Additives for salt-free surimi, which represents virtually all land-processed surimi and most of ship-processed surimi, include all the components except salt. Additives for salt-added surimi do without polyphosphate, but contain salt.

Sugar, the most important component, comprises 8 percent of the salt-free surimi and 10 percent of the salt-added surimi. Half the sugar is provide by sorbitol in order to avoid an excessively sweet taste and a brownish tint in the kamaboko that could result from a high sugar content. The content of polyphosphates ranges between 0.2 and 0.3 percent of frozen surimi. Although a higher content is more effective in preserving water-retaining and gel-forming capabilities of surimi, polyphosphates adversely affect the taste of kamaboko and must be held below 0.3 percent. Glyceride reduces the size of ice crystals in frozen surimi through its emulsifying action and provides a soft, fine texture to kamaboko.

The role of polyphosphates as an antidenaturant has long been questioned,

Table 8-6. *Food Additives for Land-Processed Frozen Surimi (in Percent)*

Raw Material Fish	Grade	Sucrose	Puribesuto[a] TP433	Puribesuto[a] TP423
	Special	4.0	4.6	0
Alaska pollock	1	4.0	4.6	0
	2	4.0	4.6	0
	Off-grade	4.0	4.6	0
Atka mackerel	1	4.0	0	4.5
	2	4.0	0	4.5
Blenny	Special	4.0	4.6	0
	1	4.0	4.6	0

[a]Puribesuto is a prescribed additive developed in 1978. Puribesuto TP433 contains 87 percent D-sorbitol, 6.5 percent polyphosphate, and 6.5 percent glyceride. Puribesuto TP423 contains 89 percent D-sorbitol, 4.4 percent polyphosphate, and 6.6 percent glyceride.

Table 8-7. *Food Additives for Ship-Processed Frozen Surimi (in Percent)*

Fish	Surimi Type	Sucrose	Sorbitol	Polyphosphate	Salt
Alaska pollock	Salt-free	4	4	0.3	0
	Salt-added	5	5	0	2.5

whereas the role of sugars has been well documented. Some studies suggest that polyphosphates enhance the antidenaturant function of sugar when the two are used together. Other studies indicate that polyphosphates play little, if any, role in providing antidenaturant protection to surimi but help reinforce the gel strength. Because the safety of polyphosphates as food additives has not been fully ascertained, some researchers suggest that the Alaska pollock salt-free surimi may be prepared without polyphosphates as an additive.

Freezing and Cold Storage

Surimi which has been dewatered and mixed with antidenaturant additives is ready for freezing. The product is weighed into 22-pound (10-kg) blocks each, put in polyethylene bags, and placed in freezer pans.

The formation of large ice crystals, which occurs in the critical temperature range of 30 to 23°F (−1 to −5°C) should be avoided. This objective is accomplished by freezing the product quickly or minimizing the time the product remains exposed to the critical temperatures. Comparing three commonly used freezers—the contact freezer, semi-air-blast freezer, and air-blast freezer—the contact freezer is reported to be preferable, although other freezers could be made to perform as well by controlling carefully the amount of load relative to the freezing ability. The important conclusion is that the storage temperature should remain below −4°F (−20°C) with minimum fluctuation.

THE SURIMI PRODUCTION PLANT

Figure 8-7 shows a typical flow diagram for manufacturing frozen surimi from white-fleshed fish. The frozen surimi is essentially a minced, water-washed, stabi-

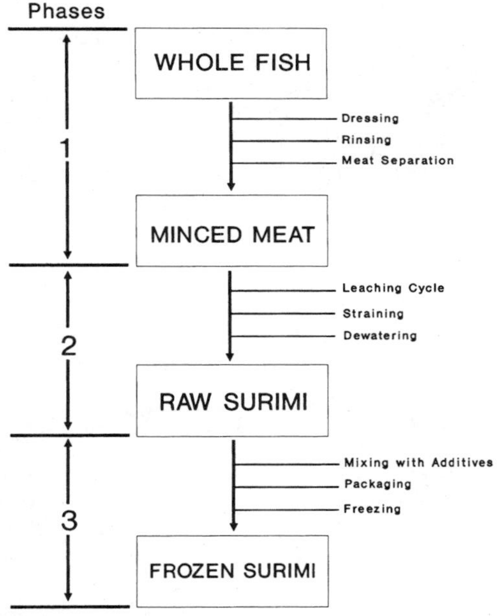

Figure 8-7. Typical Surimi Manufacturing Procedures for White-Fleshed Fish.

lized, frozen fish paste. The manufacturing procedures feature mincing, water washing, and stabilizing steps as essential components. Thus, the process flow diagram may be considered to consist of three phases:

Phase 1: Mincing	The whole round fish is transformed into mincd meat after removal of head, guts, bones, and skin.
Phase 2: Leaching	The minced meat acquires gel-forming capability after being leached with cold water. It has now become a surimi.
Phase 3: Stabilizing	Adding antidenaturants gives the surimi resistance to freeze denaturation.

Procedures at Shore Plants

Figure 8-8 shows an example of an equipment arrangement in a land-based plant. Although this example represents some of the most current technology, some old methods are still practiced by a number of manufacturers. The practice of dewatering the wet mince before applying a strainer is widely followed.

The fish dressing machine is standard equipment aboard a factory ship because it helps minimize the labor requirement, but even the most automated shore plants often depend on manual labor for fish dressing because it maximizes yield and roe extraction.

Maximum fish yield, the conservation of energy, and effluent disposal are major concerns. To reach these objectives a number of plants have incorporated steps designed to recycle the wastes emerging from the meat separator, the leaching cycles, and the straining and dewatering processes in order to recover protein of secondary quality.

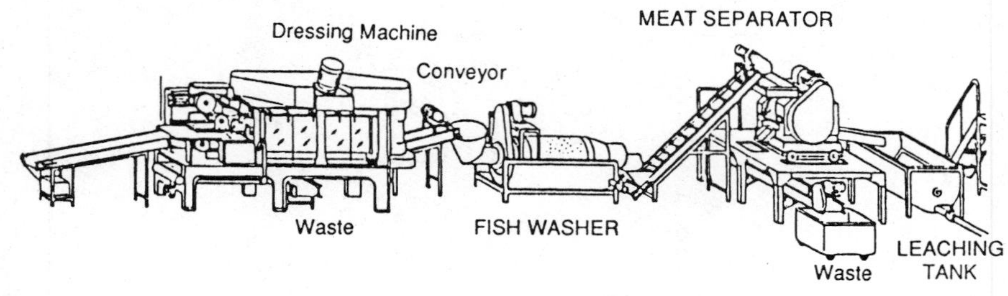

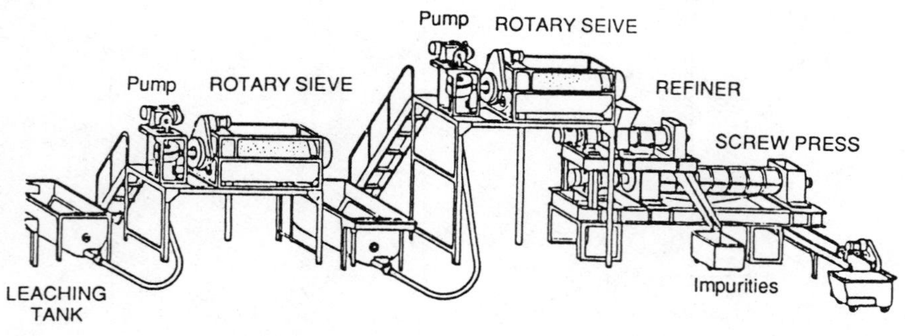

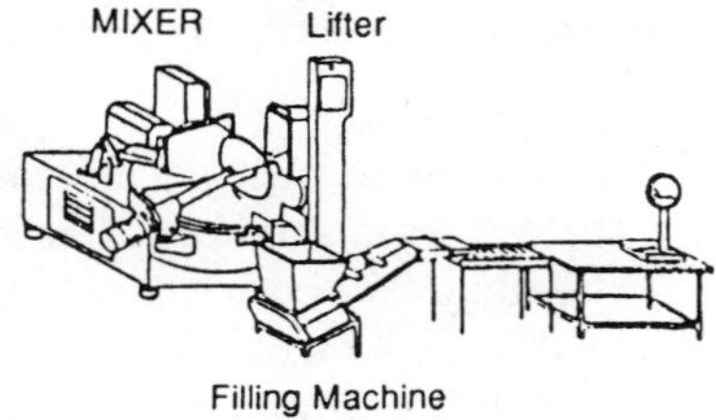

Figure 8-8. An Example of Equipment Arrangement in a Land-Based Surimi Plant.

Plant Layout

Using the system shown in Figure 8-7, our sample plant can process 10 tons (9.1 metric tons) of raw material fish on an eight-hour day basis. Daily use of water includes 60 tons (54.5 metric tons) of chilled water and 20 tons (18.1 metric tons) of tap water.

The Phase 1 operations at this plant follow standard procedures. The Phase 2 operations include innovative recycling procedures to recover secondary grade surimi. In the Phase 2 operations, the washing process takes place in two serial cycles each featuring a leaching tank and rotary sieve. In the first cycle, the minced meat is first washed in the stirring tank with an adjusted pH level and rinsed in a rotary sieve. The meat slurry then proceeds to the second cycle, which essentially repeats the same procedures.

The product emerging from the second washing cycle, a partially dewatered wet

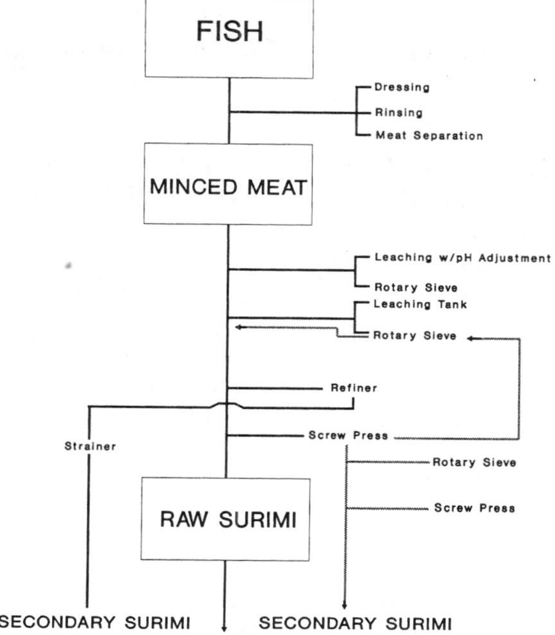

Figure 8-9. One Example of Procedures in a Surimi Manufacturing Plant.

surimi, is passed through a refiner to be strained and subsequently through a screw press to be dewatered. The transfer of the product between the cycles is performed by meat pumps, with the aid of holding tanks.

The waste from the refiner is placed in a stand-by strainer to recover secondary grade surimi. Optionally, waste from the screw press may also be recycled. One such procedure takes the waste back through the rotary sieve of the second washing cycle; an alternative procedure routes the waste to a separate rotary sieve connected to an independent screw press. (A different manufacturing procedure is represented by Fig. 8-9).

SURIMI BASED ON DARK-FLESHED FISH

Sardine and Pacific mackerel have long been used as the raw material for some special surimi-based products, such as kuro-(black) hampen, a product known for its excellent taste. However, surimi-based products based on these dark-fleshed fish have not received a significant level of consumer acceptance because of its weak gel strength and the product's dark color and fishy aroma. Developing an improved fish-cake product from dark-fleshed fish, particularly from sardine and Pacific mackerel, began to receive industry attention in the late 1960s when the bottomfish harvest in the western Japan and the East China seas began to decline sharply. By 1965 a method of leaching the dark fish meat in an alkali salt solution to improve gel strength had been patented.

Efforts to develop the technology for using dark-fleshed fish species began in earnest in 1977 when the Japanese Fisheries Agency launched a five-year program because of the uncertain future of the supply of Alaska pollock, which had already declined considerably. The catches of sardine and Pacific mackerel in Japan's home waters, on the other hand, had shown a dramatic rise, with combined catch of both species of 1.38 million tons (1.25×10^6 metric tons) in 1972 and 3.59 million tons (3.26×10^6 metric tons) by 1978.

Key problems of using dark-fleshed fish as the raw material for surimi were (1) the relatively high content of fat and its strong affinity to the flesh and skin, (2) the dark meat containing blood streaks and strong pigments, (3) the small size of the fish, (4) rapid loss of freshness, (5) rapid reduction in the pH level after death, (6) the rapid rate of protein denaturation, and (7) the brief landing season of the raw material fish. These problems made it difficult to apply the frozen surimi technology that had been developed for white-fleshed fish.

Products based on two methods developed during the Fisheries Agency Program have exhibited an excellent capacity for cold storage as well as a high level of consumer acceptance. Sardine surimi has been reported to have a cold storage capacity for up to two years with little evidence of denaturation. A Pacific mackerel surimi exhibited virtually no deterioration after fourteen months in cold storage.

Technical Problems with Dark-Fleshed Fish

The difficulty of manufacturing frozen surimi equipped with antidenaturant properties is compounded in the case of dark-fleshed fish because of a host of chemical, physical, physiological, and biological characteristics unique to these fish species.

Rapid Protein Deterioration

Migratory fish species such as sardine and Pacific mackerel contain a large amount of glycogen (a type of sugar somewhat similar to starch) in their muscle in order to support their energetic lifestyle. When the fish die, the glycogen degrades into lactic acid, which affects the gel-forming capabilities.

Freshness is extremely short-lived in sardine and Pacific mackerel. The gel strength drops rapidly in surimi products, particularly during the early period of storage. Defining "critical" freshness of the fish as where the surimi made from it is capable of showing a minimum acceptable gel strength of 300 to 400 g · cm, the critical freshness is reached after one day of storage for unfrozen sardine, after two days of storage for unfrozen Pacific mackerel, within one day for frozen sardines, and in less than one day for frozen Pacific mackerel. In both sardines and Pacific mackerels, smaller fish lost freshness more rapidly than large ones.

Other factors affecting gel strength in kamaboko products from dark-fleshed fish include the age, the fish school, and the season of landing. In particular, summer sardines are known to have less gel strength than winter sardines, partly because of the greater fat content in summer fish and because of the greater difficulty in preserving fish in summer.

Large Content of Water-Soluble Protein

The dark flesh of sardine and Pacific mackerel contains a distinctly large amount of water-soluble protein, a component which must be removed through the leaching process because of its suspected role in thwarting acceptable gel forming. The soluble protein, which will wash out in the wastewater, requires additional effort for waste treatment in surimi production from dark-fleshed fish. Soluble protein in the dark flesh dissolves very slowly in normal fresh water; therefore a special leaching method must be used to maintain a resonable speed in the leachng treatment.

Large Content of Dark Muscle Tissue

Dark muscle tissue comprises as much as 10 to 20 percent of the muscle in sardine and Pacific mackerel. By comparison, it constitutes only a few percent in white-fleshed fish. The dark muscle tissue, because of its large content of fat and hemoglobin pigment and a proportionally lower content of gel-forming protein, could cause a reduction in gel strength and an increase in the stain and fish odor if mixed into surimi. Thorough removal of dark muscle tissue during the dressing process is an important step in surimi produced from dark-fleshed fish.

Large Content of Fat

Although dark-fleshed fish generally contain larger amounts of fat than white-fleshed fish, this fat content also undergoes acute seasonal fluctuations. The fat content in sardines is reported to fluctuate between 2.6 and 18.4 percent, and that in Pacific mackerel between 2.1 and 28.7 percent. A particular problem is that the fat which adheres to the underside of the skin in dark-fleshed fish is liable to oxidation after the death of the fish, causing fishy odor and discoloration of the flesh. During surimi production, this fat mixes into the minced meat after the passage through the meat separator, if not removed during the fish dressing process. Consequently, the wastewater from the leaching treatment of dark-fleshed fish can contain a large amount of fat, necessitating added effort for wastewater treatment.

Manufacturing Procedures

Four different surimi manufacturing procedures have been developed in Japan specifically for the dark-fleshed species. Two of them have already been applied to commercial production; the other two are still experimental.

Japan Surimi Association (JSA) Method

The JSA method is intended to allow maximum utilization of the existing surimi production facilities built for Alaska pollock. The resulting product has numerous advantages, including inexpensive production facilities, high productivity, high yields, and good taste. The product is suitable as the material for fried kamaboko, broiled kamaboko, and fish sausage, so commercial-scale production using the JSA method has been launched in some areas. Disadvantages include its dark appearance, weak gel strength, and fishy odor, as the mechanical fish dressing procedure and the subsequent processing procedures are unable to completely remove the dark muscle tissues.

Because sardines are generally small, and only small Pacific mackerel are used for surimi production, a mechanical fish dresser is used instead of manual labor to remove bones as well as head and guts. A single dressing machine can handle as many as 500 sardines or 300 to 400 Pacific mackerel per minute.

The highlight of the JSA method is the leaching process, which, as shown in Fig. 8-10, is performed in three cycles:

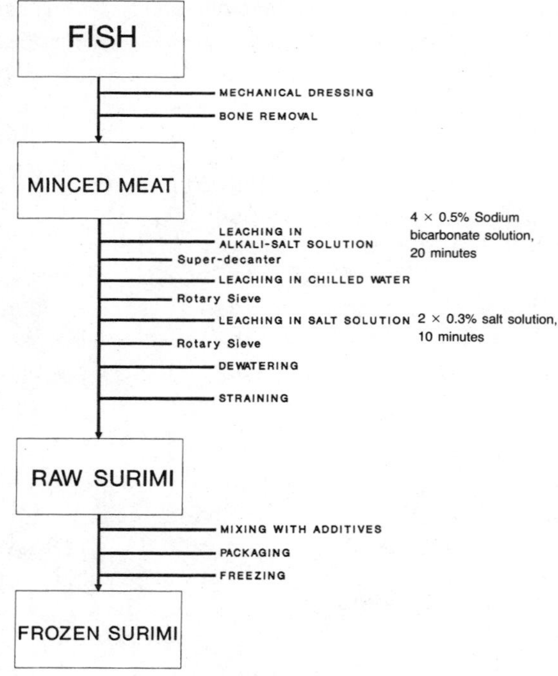

Figure 8-10. Flow Diagram of JSA Method for Manufacturing Surimi from Dark-Fleshed Fish.

First cycle:	In 0.5% sodium bicarbonate solution; amount, four times the weight of the meat; duration, 20 minutes.
Second cycle:	In chilled water; amount, four times the weight of the meat; duration, 15 minutes.
Third cycle:	In 0.3% salt solution; amount, twice the weight of the meat; duration, 10 minutes.

The sodium bicarbonate solution maintains a neutral pH level during the leaching process which enhances the products' gel strength. Salt solution is used in the third leaching cycle to facilitate the dewatering process.

The JSA recommends three leaching cycles for dark-fleshed mince. Additional cycles will give the product a whiter appearance and a higher gel strength but will reduce the yield.

The leached meat is dewatered in the screw press. Use of a refiner on a wet slurry is not recommended for dark-fleshed meat, as the mixture of fat, water, and protein can cause the formation of an emulsion that is extremely difficult to dewater.

Jet Method

The jet method features a special meat separation procedure in which light muscle tissue is separated from the rest of the fillet with the aid of a high-pressure jet, which also provides some degree of leaching. The method almost completely removes the dark-muscle tissue and fat, giving the product a white appearance and high gel strength with an almost complete lack of fishy odor. Disadvantages are expensive facilities, low yield, and relatively low productivity. See Figure 8-11 for an illustration of this method.

The filleted fish is placed on a net conveyor with the open side up, so that the exposed meat will directly face the overhead jet. The jet is applied to a slowly passing file of fillets, with a pressure of about 140 to 280 psi (10 to 20 kg/cm^2). Pressure may be varied depending on the speed of the conveyor, freshness of the fish, and the desired yield and gel strength. Light muscle tissue is fragmented by the jet and separates from the fillet, leaving behind the skin with its attached fat and dark muscle tissue. The fragmented meat is collected in a rotary sieve where it is rinsed continuously by a shower.

The separated meat, which receives some leaching in the meat separation process, is dewatered in a screw press before passing through the leaching cycles. The first cycle is performed in 0.05 to 0.1 percent sodium bicarbonate solution about five times the weight of the meat for twenty minutes, and the second cycle in chilled water five times the weight of the meat for fifteen minutes. A super-decanter is used following the first leaching cycle to ensure thorough removal of suspended fat.

Other Methods

Two other methods were introduced during the Japanese national progam between 1977 and 1981. Both methods aimed to reduce water requirements in the production process and could cut water use by half as compared with the previous two methods described. One method micronized the minced meat before leaching,

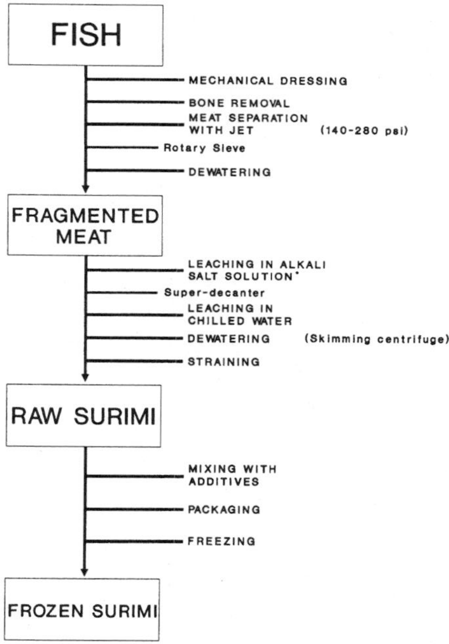

Figure 8-11. Flow Diagram of Jet Method for Manufacturing Surimi from Dark-Fleshed Fish. Leaching in alkali salt solution: (5 × 0.05–0.1% sodium bicarbonate solution, 20 minutes).

and the second method recycled the wastewater between successive leaching cycles. Figures 8-12 and 8-13 illustrate the flow diagrams of these methods.

In the micronization method, minced meat is brought to a neutral pH level by soaking in an equal amount of 0.8 percent sodium bicarbonate solution. The minced meat is then micronized and passed through a leaching device: three serially connected drums containing agitated water. A small test plant program showed a yield from this method of about 17 percent, but it varies depending on the meat recovery procedures used following the leaching process. The product exhibited a white appearance and a markedly low fat content. The expensive facilities required and the low yield were the main drawbacks.

Surimi Quality

Methods for defining the quality of land-processed frozen surimi have been revised numerous times since standards were introduced in 1964. Unlike ship-processed surimi, for which quality is relatively uniform and consistent, quality of land-processed surimi varies widely largely due to the freshness of the raw material fish.

Although the Japan Surimi Association (JSA) quality standards for surimi were revised in 1978, in practice the 1974 standards continue to be influential among most of the country's surimi manufacturers. In 1974 the old grade rankings of "special," A, B, and C were renamed as "special," first, second, and "off-grade." A new requirement for acceptable gel strength was incorporated in the 1974 revision. As shown in Tables 8-8 and 8-9 the current grade standards incorporate four major criteria: water content, additives, the folding test for elasticity, and gel strength.

The 1978 revision (Table 8-10) was intended to enhance the sugar content allowance from 5 percent to about 8 percent for salt-free frozen surimi, while

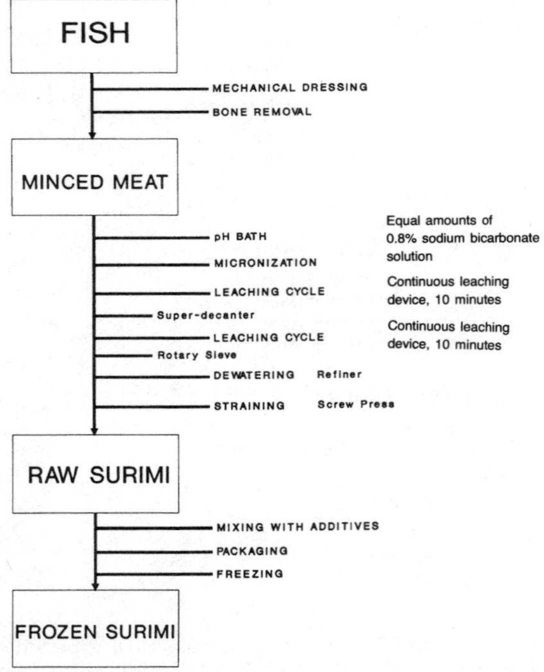

Figure 8-12. Flow Diagram of Micronizing Method for Manufacturing Surimi from Dark-Fleshed Fish.

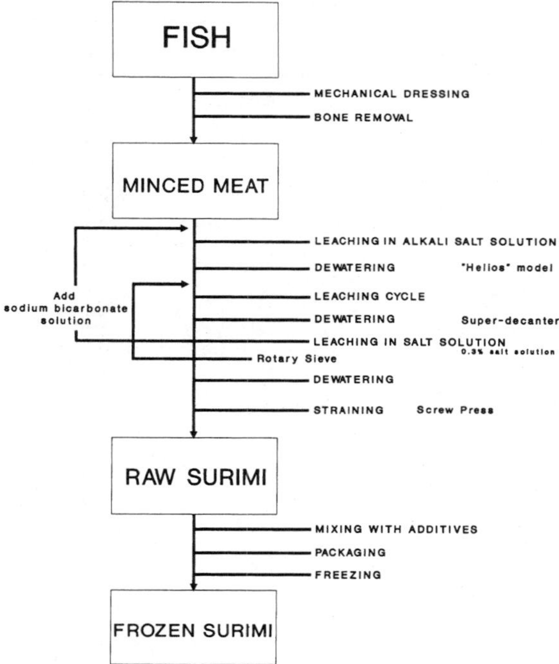

Figure 8-13. Flow Diagram of Wastewater Recycling Method for Manufacturing Surimi from Dark-Fleshed Fish.

introducing quality standards for products using Puribesuto as an additive. The revision also tightened the allowable water content while upgrading the quality.

As much as 90 percent of Japan's land-processed surimi is classified as grade 2, although a wide variability exists among these products. This situation has resulted

Table 8-8. *1974 JSA*[a] Quality Standards for Salt-Free Land-Processed Frozen Surimi

Fish	Grade	Water Content (%)	Additives (%)		Folding Test[c]	Yield Stress (g)
			Sugar[b]	Phosphate		
Alaska pollock	Special	79	5	0.2	AA (0%)	350
	1	80	5	0.2	AA (3%)	330
	2	81.5	5	0.2	AA (5%)	280
	Off-grade	82.5	5	0.2	AA (10%)	
Atka mackerel	1	79	5	0.1–0.2	AA (3%)	350
	2	80	5	0.1–0.2	AA (5%)	300
Blenny	Special	79	5	0.2	AA (0%)	350
	1	80	5	0.2	AA (3%)	350
Flatfish	Special	79	5	0.2	AA (0%)	350
	1	80	5	0.2	AA (3%)	350
Wachna cod	2	81.5	5	0.2	AA (5%)	300

[a]JSA = Japan Surimi Association
[b]Sugar = Sucrose or sorbitol
[c]( ) = Potato starch content

Table 8-9. *1974 JSA*[a] Quality Standards for Salt-Added Land-Processed Frozen Surimi

Fish	Grade	Water Content (%)	Additives (%)			Folding Test[c]	Yield Stress (g)
			Sugar[b]	Salt	Phosphate		
Alaska pollock	Special	75	10	1–1.5	0–0.2	AA (0%)	350
	1	76	10	1–1.5	0–0.2	AA (3%)	330
	2	77	10	1–1.5	0–0.2	AA (5%)	280
	Off-grade	78	10	1–1.5	0–0.2	AA (10%)	
Atka mackerel	1	75	10	1–1.5	0–0.2	AA (3%)	350
	2	76	10	1–1.5	0–0.2	AA (5%)	300
Blenny	Special	75	10	1–1.5	0–0.2	AA (0%)	350
	1	76	10	1–1.5	0–0.2	AA (3%)	350
Flatfish	Special	75	10	1–1.5	0–0.2	AA (0%)	350
	1	76	10	1–1.5	0–0.2	AA (3%)	350
Wachna cod	2	77	10	1–1.5	0–0.2	AA (5%)	300

[a]JSA = Japan Surimi Association
[b]Sugar = Sucrose or sorbitol
[c]( ) = Potato starch content

partly from the insufficiency of the existing quality standards and partly from a lack of compliance with the quality standards, which are essentially voluntary. Inconsistent quality in grade 2 products has caused a considerable number of claims from users. The Japanese Fisheries Agency announced a plan for a feasibility study aimed at government-regulated quality standards for land-processed surimi in place of the existing industry-regulated standards.

In factory ship operations in which the fish is processed into surimi as soon as it is caught, freshness is not an issue. Table 8-11 shows the composition standards for

Table 8-10. *1978 JSA*[a] Quality Standards for Salt-Free Land-Processed Frozen Surimi

Fish	Grade	Water Content (%)	Additives (%)[b]			Folding Test[c]	Yield Stress (g)
			Sucrose	Puribesuto TP433	Puribesuto TP432		
Alaska pollock	Special	77	4.0	4.6	0	AA (0%)	350
	1	78	4.0	4.6	0	AA (3%)	330
	2	79.5	4.0	4.6	0	AA (5%)	300
	Off-grade	80	4.0	4.6	0	AA (10%)	300
Atka mackerel	1	77	4.0	4.6	4.5	AA (3%)	330
	2	78	4.0	4.6	4.5	AA (5%)	300
Blenny	Special	77	4.0	4.6	0	AA (0%)	350
	1	78	4.0	4.6	0	AA (3%)	350

[a]JSA = Japan Surimi Association
[b]Puribesuto TP433 consists of D-sorbitol 87%, glyceride 6.5%, and polyphosphate 6.5%.
Puribesuto TP432 consists of D-sorbitol 88.9%, glyceride 6.7%, and polyphosphate 4.4%.
[c]( ) = Potato starch content

Table 8-11. ***Industry Quality Standards for Ship-Processed Frozen Surimi (in Percent)***

Fish	Surimi Type	Sucrose	Sorbitol	Polyphosphate	Salt
Alaska pollock	Salt-free	4	4	0.3	0
	Salt-added	5	5	0	2.5

ship-processed surimi. Factors other than freshness, such as the size of the fish, location of catch, season of catch, method of catch, and handling of the fish after the catch also contribute to surimi quality.

BATTERS AND BREADING

Ingredients used in batter and breading formulations fall into two groups: those that comprise the bulk of the formula and those that are present in relatively small quantities. The first group would include flour, eggs, milk; the second would contain greens, spices, whey, leavening agents, starch, salt, and sugar. These ingredients, from a quantitative perspective, determine the physical differences in batters and breadings.

Consumer appeal and texture of a coating vary among the types of products such as red and white meat, fish and shellfish, and vegetables. Even within a group, such as fish and shellfish, the physical characteristics may vary depending on consumer preference within a market area. For example, corn breading might be preferred in the South; flour coating would be used in the Northeast.

Flour in a dry batter mix constitutes approximately 80 to 90 percent of the total weight; in a breading mixture, it normally ranges between 70 and 80 percent. Major flour sources include corn, rice, soy, and barley. Wheat flour differs from the others because it has the ability to form a cohesive mass when hydrated and subjected to mixing. There are also differences in the wheat flour depending on whether soft or hard wheat is used.

Several major characteristics or functional properties can be used to distinguish between breadings. These are as follows:

Mesh

Breadings can range from ½-inch (1.3-cm) cubes to fine particles that will pass through a 80-mesh standard sieve. Typical breadings, however, will pass between a No. 5 U.S. and a No. 80 U.S. sieve. Particle size is the major factor affecting the appearance and texture of the coated food. If fine mesh is used, the batter's ability to absorb liquid is increased. A coarse coating can result in a loosely adhering product that will fall off during handling or transportation. Consequently, breadings are chosen that usually range between a U.S. No. 20 and 60 screen.

Browning Rate

The amount of sugars in the coating largely determines browning rate. A fast browning rate provides for high processing rates, which could permit either the use of a shorter frying time and/or lower temperature. Using shorter frying time and lower temperatures reduces shrink, while faster processing increases efficiency and reduces labor and capital equipment expenditures. In some applications, reducing the sugar content and retarding the browning rate is desirable, particularly with large or thick foods which require long frying times. Consequently the ability to vary browning rates permits the balancing of color, texture, and cooking time.

Moisture and Oil Absorption

The rate at which a particular breading absorbs moisture and oil depends on several factors, including particle size and porosity. A coating with a porous structure will absorb and release moisture and frying oil faster than a more dense product. There are various types of prepared breadings which are applied to battered foods to enhance their appearance or sensory qualities (Table 8-12).

Battered and Breaded Seafoods

Seafood accounts for approximately 50 percent of all frozen battered and breaded products in the United States. Precooked and raw fish portions are the most frequently coated products followed in order by specialty products such as shrimp, fish sticks, and scallops. Breadings have been long used in the seafood industry, but the application of batters did not come into prominence until the 1960s. In the mid-1960s, a relatively new concept called batter frying became prevalent within the seafood industry. In this process, the food is usually given a predust with flour or dry battermix, coated with a batter, and prefried to set the batter and impart the desired frying oil content for enhanced texture and quality. Table 8-12 shows basic types of coating systems that duplicate traditional methods of preparing products manually. The batters can be either tempura (leavened) or nonleavened (Table 8-13). Production rates for batter fried products are half that for

Table 8-12. ***Basic Machining Characteristics of Breadings***

Breading Type	General Characteristics	Machine Handling
Free-flowing breading	Fine, uniform granulation, not fragile	Easy to handle, flow without problems in machinery
Coarse breading (Japanese, Pandora, Panko, Oriental)	Nonuniform granulation, fine and coarse particles, fragile	Extremely difficult to handle, presents two challenges to the processor: Breading must be prevented from grinding up Product must be uniformly coated on top and bottom with the same ratio of fine and coarse crumbs
Flour-type breading	Usually raw flour; can be a dry batter mix, for example.	Difficult to handle, material packs and bridges easily. This type of breading must be driven (pushed) through the machine.

Source: Stein Associates, Inc.

Table 8-13. *Basic Machining Characteristics of Batters*

Batter type	Mixing	Temperature	Viscosity control
Non-leavened (conventional)	Can be pumped. Batters are mixed continuously to keep batter solids in solution. Viscometer cup reading to 25 seconds.	Preferably under 10°C (40–50°F)	It is possible to obtain a continuous viscosity control. Units automatically mix dry batter mix with water to a preset thickness (viscosity) and maintains that thickness continuously. It also controls the batter temperature.
Leavened (tempura)	Cannot be pumped. Mixing must be done quickly and then stopped. Mixing is not done continuously after that. Batter should be transferred quickly to the applicator.	"Cold batter" 4–7°C (40–45°F) "Warm batter" 18–24°C (65–75°F)	There is no continuous viscosity control. Identical batches only.

Source: Stein Associates, Inc.

a breaded product due to the space between products on the conveyor belt and additional time required for coating and draining. One of the biggest challenges limiting the expanded consumption of battered products is the inability to produce a microwavable product that retains crispiness.

A problem associated with battered products has been the uneven distribution of coating on the product. In some instances the batter fails to coat the entire product leaving large void areas. Also, the coating can be too heavy or so thin that it loses flakes or chips off.

An effective quality assurance program should be initiated to ensure the production of high quality battered and breaded food products. The program should include all incoming fish blocks and other frozen seafood products. Quality control examinations are important to ensure that the block adheres to purchase specifications such as block dimensions and weight, microbial counts, foreign matter, water content, additives, evidence of decomposition, or quality determination (freeze-thaw cycling), and species. Quality assurance is important because seemingly minor compositional properties, such as water, can have a direct effect on batter adhesion or cooking time. All quality assurance programs should include an examination of batter mixes, breading, and batter ingredients. The quality program also should extend to storage conditions because experience has shown that products stored in a dry, cool environment produce higher quality batter coatings.

An important step in monitoring quality is proper batter mixing. Cold water increases batter adhesions; consequently most processors maintain water temperature at 50°F (10°C) or lower. The batter mix is hydrated by adding water either in a mixing bowl with a large whip or an automatic batter mixing machine. The batter should be mixed past the point where no unwanted lumps remain. In most cases, a batter will perform better if mixed for a longer, rather than shorter, period. Too little mixing results in a partially hydrated batter with poor preparation characteristics, lumps, and gummy textures.

Batter viscosity should be monitored and closely regulated during production. There are several methods of measuring viscosity, and it is recommended that measurements be taken on the production line and the laboratory. All adjustments to the batter should be made as soon as possible.

Prior to battering, seafood products are generally given a predusting to create a product surface that will increase batter adhension. Salt has been used as an additive to increase adhesion because it melts the ice on the product surface and the resulting liquid can hydrate the product, thereby improving adhesion. It is sometimes appropriate to include taste and odor ingredients in the predusting. Their inclusion in the batter can affect product characteristics such as browning.

After predusting, the product is moved through the batter applicator on a conveyor belt. Batter applicators are usually of two types: (1) the product being coated is completely submerged in batter and (2) the batter is poured on in a continuous cascade. The amount of batter pickup is affected by several factors including line speed or degree of bacteria hydration. Incomplete coverage can be caused by line speed, product shape, faulty or lack of predusting material, and the degree of glazing on the product surface.

The final operation, the prefrying, sets the batter coating and facilitates further processing. Prefrying produces a desirable color, provides a crunchy texture, and improves sensory characteristics. Proper prefrying depends on maintaining frying oil temperatures at the desired temperature, ensuring that the oil is replaced or filtered as necessary, and that frying time is properly maintained. Prefrying times of thirty seconds are usual.

After cooking the product is usually frozen. Care should be exercised to ensure that the products do not cover each other or touch during frying, as this can cause the batter coating to be removed when the product is separated at packaging. All products should be frozen as quickly as possible to ensure the coating adheres to the product.

REFERENCES

Hutcheson, J. 1988. Personal Communication. Sandusky, OH: Stein Associates, Inc.

Lee, Chong M. 1984. "Surimi Process Technology." *Food Technology*. 38(11):69–80.

Sonu, Sunee C. 1986. *Surimi*. NOAA Technical Memorandum NMFS. NOAA-TM-NMFS-SWR-013. U.S. Department of Commerce. Washington, DC: U.S. Government Printing Office.

Suderman, Darrel S., and Cunningham, Frank E. 1983. *Batter and Breading Technology*. New York: Van Nostrand Reinhold.

CHAPTER

9

Processing Mollusks

Cameron R. Hackney

Nearly all mollusks are processed prior to use. Processing may vary from boxing bivalves for the live market to further processing including frozen, canned, and pickled products.

The industry depends on natural stocks which fluctuate from year to year. The varying supply often causes processors to be reluctant to expand their operations, to adopt new technology, or to make major investments in new product development. The processing of mollusks tends to be labor intensive with relatively little mechanization. Processing of mollusks is done for several reasons: to convert the raw material to a more desirable form, to preserve the products, to maintain quality, to more fully utilize the raw product, and to assure safety. Mollusks such as clams and oysters are shucked to provide a usable market form. Molluscan shellfish are smoked, frozen, or canned to prolong shelf life and stabilize the quality.

PROCESSING FOR THE LIVE MARKET

Bivalve mollusks, including oysters, mussels, and clams, often are presented to the consumer in the live state; however, they are often processed for the live market. Bivalves can survive out of the water for extended periods, which allows them to go through the processing chain.

Temperature control is the most critical factor for providing a good product, yet few harvesting boats provide refrigerated storage. Soft shell clams are harvested primarily during the warm summer months, and although oysters and clams are mostly harvested during the winter and spring, some are harvested in the summer. On-deck temperatures in the summer often exceed 86°F (30°C), which can reduce product quality. For optimum quality and shelf life, bivalves should be cooled and stored at temperatures less than 50°F (10°C).

Processing shellfish for the live market is usually limitd to washing, sorting, and packing. Oysters are often received as clusters or clumps covered with mud. Because single oysters are desired for the half-shell market, the clusters are broken into singles manually and the shell debris is discarded. Once the oysters are broken apart, they are often sorted by size; a medium size oyster is preferred for the half-shell market. Some restaurants prefer the outside shell to be relatively free of mud, although the mud serves to keep the oyster moist and tends to keep the oyster alive longer. A variety of washing methods, from hand scrubbing to mechanical pressurized washing, can be used to clean the shellstock. Simply hosing down a pile of oysters rarely provides effective cleaning. Once the oysters are sorted and washed they are boxed and shipped to market.

Hard clams *(Mercenaria mercenaria)* often are sold in the shell by size, with smaller clams being higher priced. The clams are sorted either manually or mechanically, and then washed and boxed for shipment. The Manila clam *(Tapes philippinarium)* is handled in a manner similar to the Mercenaria clam. The soft shell clam *(Mya arenaria)* also is washed and boxed before sale. The clams are often placed in clean water for a short time to remove grit and sand from the intestinal area.

Mussels destined to be sold live are processed by removing the beard. Live mussels sell very well along the eastern seaboard and to a lesser extent along the Pacific coast. Mussels represent one of the best current opportunities for seafood market development, as the product is cheap and plentiful thanks to aquaculture techniques.

Wet storage of bivalves is limited but may be practiced more in the future. Requirements for wet storage are similar to those for depuration and are covered under Part II of the National Shellfish Sanitation Program Manual of Operations. Wet storage can be used to prolong shelf life and improve taste. For example, "salty" oysters are preferred for the half-shell market, but much of the available shellstock is harvested from low salinity waters. Oysters are osmoconformers (their internal salt content reflects that of the surrounding water), so when shellstock is placed into higher salinity water, their salt content quickly changes to match that of the environment.

PROCESSING FOR THE FRESH MARKET

Mollusks are processed for the fresh market in a variety of ways, from shucking of bivalves to cleaning of squid. Most processing is done manually. Mechanical means of shucking bivalves are used, but products of mechanical shucking most often are further processed.

Bivalves

Shucking is the process of separating the meat of bivalves from their shell. Those destined for the fresh market are usually shucked by hand, a labor intensive job requiring considerable skill. Each bivalve requires a slightly different method of shucking, and methods can vary from one region to another. For example, the most common way to shuck oysters is to insert the shucking knife through the lip or bill of the oyster, cut the abductor muscle, and remove the body from the shell. In some areas, however, oysters are opened by "popping the hinge," in which the knife is inserted between the hinge of the oyster and twisted to break it apart. In general, the first method gives the better product, and a number of variations of this method are used commercially.

As oysters are removed from the shell they are sorted by size. Eastern oysters *(Crassostrea virginica)* are normally packed according to the number of meats per gallon: Very small has over 500 meats; small or standard has 301 to 500; select or medium, 211 to 300; extra select or large, 160 to 210; and counts of extra large less than 160. Price normally increases with size.

After shucking, the meats are washed and packed. Washing is often done by blowing, a process in which air is pumped into the bottom of a tank to agitate the oyster meats. Grit and shell particles settle to the bottom. After ten to fifteen minutes the air is shut off and water is added and allowed to overflow the tank. When the water is clear, the oysters are removed and packaged. Oysters have a standard of identity which requires that they not be exposed to water for more than thirty minutes or be blown for more than fifteen minutes, and the oysters must be packed dry. After packing, they tend to lose liquid, which is called free liquor. The amount of free liquor depends on the season of harvest, the condition of the oyster, and geographic location of harvest. Oysters may lose 30 percent of their weight as free liquor, although losses of 5 to 15 percent are more the norm.

Until the mid-1980s, the eastern oyster dominated the fresh oyster market; however, in recent years *C. gigas* has increased its market share significantly, even in the East and Gulf Coast areas. *C. gigas* tend to be large. Their appearance is somewhat different than that of the eastern oyster. They tend to be larger, whiter, and often have a dark area around the gills. Also, the liquor in the containers is often cloudy, which is considered a defect in packs of *C. virginica* but is normal for packs of *C. gigas*.

More than twenty-two species of clams are listed by the U.S. Food and Drug Administration as being harvested commercially or recreationally. Only five of these species are of commercial importance: the hard clam *(M. mercenaria)*, the surf clam *(Spisula solidissima)*, the ocean quahog *(Arctica islandica)*, the soft shell clam *(M. arenaria)*, and the geoduck *(Panope generose)*. These five species account for 99 percent of the commercial catch.

Most clams are shucked by hand. The hard clam is held in the palm of the hand with the shell hinge against the palm. A strong, slender knife is inserted between the halves and the shell is pried open, the abductor muscles cut, and the meat removed from the shell. Other clams are also shucked by hand. Clams are washed—sometimes by blowing as described for oysters—packaged, and sold. Most hard clams that are shucked are chowder clams, which are large and destined to be minced for clam chowder.

Geoduck clams are often very large, averaging 3 pounds (1.36 kg), but can go up to 15 pounds (6.8 kg). The geoduck is mostly neck, and the meat yield is about half the original weight.

Surf clams, ocean quahogs, and occasionally large hard clams are shucked mechanically. The clams are either placed on a flat conveyor belt and passed through an open gas flame or are steamed at high temperature in pressure vessels. The heating, which often partially cooks the meat, greatly weakens the muscle-shell bond, and the meat is removed from the shell by tumbling. The meat and shells are separated in a brine tank.

Currently in the United States, there are four commercially important species of scallops: the sea scallop *(Placupecten megellanicas)*, the bay scallop *(Aequipecten irradienas)*, the calico scallop *(Argopecten gibbus)*, and the Pacific sea or weathervane scallop *(Patinopecten caurinus)*. In the United States only the abductor muscle is consumed, but Europeans consume the entire scallop. There also is demand for the abductor muscle with the roe attached.

Sea scallops usually are processed on board ship, and the hand shucking process is similar to that for oysters. The soft body parts are removed leaving only the eye or abductor muscle. In some cases, sea scallops destined for export to European markets are processed so that the roe (gonads) remain attached to the eye. In Europe, the roe are esteemed as a delicacy and are even more desirable than the eye. The meat's color may range from white to gray or bluish, and even a slight yellowish or pinkish coloration is not uncommon. The meat is packed into bags and stored in ice. The scallops must be at least 3.5 inches (8.9 cm) in shell diameter and average no more than thirty per pound with a 10 percent variance. (A 20 percent variance is allowed during the winter months.)

Bay and calico scallops usually are shucked on land. Their small size makes them uneconomical to shuck by hand on ships, although they are often shucked by hand on shore.

Scallops also are shucked mechanically. Machines that use a shock-heat-shock method have been used on ships, although currently most are used ashore. In this process, the scallops are passed through a sorter to remove trash and then are fed into a tank of hot water 176 to 212°F (80 to 100°C) or through a steam tunnel by rollers that grip the shells and sling them against a steel baffle. They are removed by conveyor and undergo a second shock-heat-shock treatment. Then they are dropped onto a vibrating screen that separates the meat and viscera from the shells. The animal then goes to an eviscerator that grips and pulls the viscera from the meat. The meat is then washed or it may be placed in a brine tank to remove shell fragments. The meats are then inspected and washed. There are, of course, many variations on these procedures.

Gastropods

Two species of abalone (*Haliotitis rufescens* and *H. corrusala*) are harvsted and processed commercially. Most often they are sold fresh. The foot of the abalone is the only part consumed by humans. The muscle is very tough and usually must be tenderized.

The Queen conch *(Strombus gigas)*, generally harvested from Central American waters, is usually cut from the shell on board and then taken to a processing facility. Conch is processed by knocking an elongated hole in the spire; a razor-sharp blade is used to cut the animal free from its shell.

The viscera and other soft parts are removed from the foot and the tough dark skin is removed. The marketable meat yield is about half the total in-shell weight. Ocean conch imported in the United States is frozen. Most conch processed in the United States is actually welk, a distant relative. Two species are important: the knobbed welk *(Busycon carica)* and the channeled welk *(B. canaliculatum)*. Most are steamed in retorts and sold as precooked meats, although some are available raw. Another species, the waved welk *(Buccinum undatum)*, is found from New England to northern Europe, achieving most of its commercial importance in the United Kingdom.

Cephalopods are often sold as is for the fresh market or with minimal processing. The popularity of cephalopods is increasing in the United States but are far more popular in Europe and Asia. Squid is the most common cephalopod in U.S. markets. The yield is very high, with 80 percent of the animal potentially consumable.

Squid are cleaned by first removing the intestines, which come out when the head is pulled free. The pen (a remnant of a shell) is removed next, the mantle is then skinned, and the tentacles cut from the head. This process is done completely by hand and is labor intensive.

Cuttlefish are cleaned in a manner similar to squid. Octopus are processed for the fresh or frozen market by simply inverting the head and removing the intestines.

FURTHER PROCESSING

Batter and *Breading Operations*

Many molluscan products are sold battered and breaded. Coating seafood with batter and/or breading before cooking is a common practice of homemakers, food processors, and commercial food service establishments. Commercial batter and breading of seafood, including mollusks, followed by freezing offers a widely valued convenience to consumers. The United States is the world's largest consumer of breaded seafood products. Breaded mollusks such as oysters and scallops tend to cater mostly to luxury consumer markets or to the restaurant trade.

Batters and breading enhance product appearance and taste characteristics, including a more desired texture, color, and flavor. They also act as a moisture barrier, holding in the natural juices, thus often making the product tenderer.

In general, a batter refers to a liquid mixture of water, flour, starch, and seasoning into which seafood products are dipped. Breading is defined as a dry mixture of flour, starch, and coarse seasoning that is applied to moistened and battered products before cooking.

Examples of batter and breaded products, which are usually sold frozen, are scallops, oysters, clam strips, clam cakes, and squid rings. The mollusks are prepared as described for fresh seafood. Refer to Chapter 8 for a more detailed discussion of batter and breading operations.

FREEZING

Frozen molluscan products available commercially include most of the types described for the fresh market as well as battered and/or breaded products. In many cases, freezing is a normal part of processing; nearly all commercial battered and breaded products, for example, are frozen, and welk and conch are primarily available as a frozen product. However, some mollusks freeze better than others, and the frozen storage life will vary with species. Other important considerations include packaging, rate of freezing, and storage temperature. In general, oxygen-impermeable packing is best. Also, the faster the freezing rate and the lower the storage temperature, the better the product. It is important that the product to be frozen is of good quality. Quality deteriorates during frozen storage, thus freezing should *never be* used as a means of salvaging product near the end of its fresh shelf life.

Oysters

Most shucked oysters are sold fresh, but many food service establishments prefer frozen oysters because they provide ease of storage and a constant supply. Oysters change composition, especially after spawning in the summer, which affects yields. Also demand patterns are such that shortages often occur during Thanksgiving and Christmas holidays. Although it affects oyster appearance and quality, freezing can provide an adequate supply of good quality oysters year round.

The free liquor content of previously frozen oysters may be as high as 20 to 30 percent; therefore, the yield is less. Freezing also may cause the oyster to darken. The amount of darkening depends on freezing rate: Slow freezing greatly increases both darkening and free liquor content. Oysters should not be frozen in 1 gallon (3.78-l) metal cans because the freezing rate is slow and metal ions may accelerate darkening. It is better to freeze them in oxygen-impermeable bags, which are laid flat to increase surface area. Both Eastern oysters and Western oysters may be frozen for at least ten months and maintain acceptable quality.

Clams

Only a small part of the total clam harvest, mostly clams going to the chowder market and for further processing, is frozen, and frozen storage is limited to four to six months at 0°F (−18°C) because of rancidity and toughening. As with oysters, the packaging, freezing rate, and storage temperature affect quality.

Surf clams, ocean quahog, and large hard clams are often frozen after mechanical shucking. After the clams are removed from the shell, the viscera is removed. The meats are then washed and cut or diced for packaging and freezing. Previously, this industry used mostly surf clams, but species management practices have caused many plants to also process ocean quahogs and, more rarely, the hard clam.

Scallops

Scallops, especially breaded scallops, are often sold frozen. In 1978 almost 62 million pounds (28×10^6 kg) of scallop meats were breaded and frozen, but by 1980 the amount of breaded and frozen decreased to 50 million pounds (22.7×10^6 kg), largely because of a decrease in the availability of scallops. Scallops, which also are frozen without breading, have a frozen shelf life of about twelve months at 0°F (−18°C).

Conch and *Welk*

Almost all the conch and welk meat is frozen, especially the Queen Conch. Once processed, it is frozen in 5- to 10-pound bags (2.3- to 4.5-kg).

Abalone

As mentioned earlier, only the foot of the abalone is consumed. In preparation for freezing, the muscle is sliced across the grain into half-inch (1.27-cm) steaks. The critical part in the process is the tenderizing step. The steak slices are put on a table and allowed to relax, then hit just once with a wooden mallet. Most of the abalone meat is consumed in California, where state regulations prohibit it from being shipped beyond state boundaries. Abalone is found in other countries, including Korea and South Africa, and products from these nations occasionally find their way to American markets.

CANNING

Many species of molluscan shellfish are canned throughout the world. In the United States, clams and oysters are the most important canned molluscan shellfish. Other canned species include mussels, cockles, squid, scallops, snails, and abalone.

Oysters

Various standards for canned oysters are covered by the U.S. Food and Drug Administration; the standards of identity, which includes standards of fill container, require a drain weight of at least 59 percent of capacity. Currently, oysters are canned primarily in three areas of the United States: the East Coast from Maryland to Florida; the state of Washington on the West Coast; and the Gulf Coast, which produces the most canned oysters. The volume of oysters canned is small compared to the quantity sold fresh, but they are still a popular item and can be found in most supermarkets.

Oysters for canning may be shucked either mechanically or by hand. For mechanical shucking, the oysters are first washed, often with high pressure, to remove mud and debris. After washing they enter a steam tunnel or retort. The best results are obtained by using a preheated stage followed by a short cooking at high temperatures and pressure in special retorts. This process causes the hinge material to degrade, thus causing the shell to gap wider. Once the oysters are steamed, they are conveyed to shucking units where the meats are separated from the shells. Mechanical shucking has the advantage that all oysters are shucked. The oysters are cooked slightly, which makes them unsuitable for the fresh market, although they are excellent for canned products.

The oysters are packed by hand into "C" enameled cans, with Number 2 and Number 95 the most popular sizes. Fill-in weights depend on the oysters' condition and composition, which change with season, water salinity, and other environmental factors. If the oysters are mechanically shucked, the amount of cooking incurred during steaming affects the fill-in weight, as the oysters may lose considerable weight during heating.

After the oysters are put in the cans, a weak brine solution, heated to near boiling, is added. The cans are then closed and retorted.

Four different styles of canned oysters are on the market: whole, stew oysters, oyster stew base, and smoked oysters. Canned stew oysters are prepared by chilling the oyster meat to firm the flesh, then slicing the meats in a mechanical slicer. Fifty grams of meat are allowed to a 10-ounce (280-g) can, and just prior to sealing, a mixture of milk, salt, monosodium glutamate, and disodium phosphates is added. Some packers also add oyster nectar, which is prepared by boiling whole oysters. Finally, a small amount of butter is added and the cans are vacuum-closed and retorted. Canned oyster stew base consists of sliced oysters and nectar. The user then makes a stew as desired. This product is mostly canned for the institutional market in large cans.

Smoked oysters are made from precooked whole small oysters or from sliced large oysters. The meats are placed into a 20° S (salinometer) brine for three to four minutes, then drained, spread onto racks, and smoked two to three hours. Sugar can be added to the brine for flavor. The meats develop a dark golden color and smoked taste. The smoked meats are packed into 301×10^6 (3.9-ounce/110-g) cans or glass jars to which salad oil is added. The containers are vacuum-sealed and processed. Many smoked oyster products are from Korea where *C. gigas* is used. Smoked oysters canned on the East and Gulf coasts of the United States are *C. virginica*.

Clams

At least fourteen species of clams are canned in various countries. In the United States, six species are canned, with hard clams, soft shell clams, and razor clams *(Silliqua patula)* accounting for most of the production.

On the U.S. East Coast, where Maine, Maryland, Massachusetts, and Florida account for most of the processing, the hard shell and soft shell clams are the principal species canned. The clams are washed and retorted under pressure. They are removed from the steamer and sorted by size, small or large, and by color, light or dark. Hand shucked clams also are used.

The clams are packed into "C" enameled cans, including sizes 211 × 400, 307 × 409, and 300 × 404, with the first two being preferred. Clams shrink considerably during processing, so "fill weights" are greater than "drain weights." Dark discoloration is a problem sometimes encountered with canned clams.

On the West Coast, particularly Oregon, Washington, and Alaska, the razor clam is the principal clam canned, usually as minced clams. The clams are washed and scalded. The meats are shaken out of the shells and split along one side to remove sand and mud. They are washed a second time and the siphon, body side walls, and stomach are removed. The remainder is chopped and packed into cans. Brine or clam juice is added, then the cans are closed and processed.

Other Mollusks

Although clams and oysters account for most canned mollusk production in the United States, other species, including mussels, scallops, abalone, cockles, donax, snails, and squid are also canned. The canning of mussels *(Mytilus edulis)* is a small but growing industry on the U.S. East Coast. They are first steamed five to ten minutes, then shucked and packed into cans. Juice from the steaming process and salt are added.

Canning of scallops is done almost exclusively in Japan. The scallop meat is packed with a 2 percent brine and processed. Abalone of the family Haliotidae are sometimes canned in other countries and have been canned in the United States, where the foot muscle is minced and canned. In other countries, such as Japan, the processing is different. After the animal is removed from the shell, the visceral mass and mantle fringe are trimmed. The meat is then washed, dry salted for twenty-four to forty-eight hours, rubbed to remove mucous substances, and canned.

Cockles (*Cardium* spp.) canning is a minor industry in the northwestern United States but an important industry of Western Europe. In Spain, they are washed, steamed, shucked by agitation, and canned. In France, they are pickled prior to canning. They are then drained, packed into jars, covered with a spiced vinegar, and processed. Donax (*Donax laevigata)*, which is found on the Florida and Southern California coasts, is used primarily in soups prepared by boilng the entire mollusk. Land snails, escargots, are also canned with and without shells. Finally, squid is canned in the United States and several other countries. In the United States, squid is canned in oil; in Japan, it is canned after boiling and seasoning. For canning, the squid is cleaned as described for fresh marketing. It is washed, blanched at 104 to 122°F (40 to 50°C) in salt water, and the skin is removed. The squid may be minced (in Japan) or canned as mantles in oil.

PICKLED MOLLUSKS

Pickling seafood with vinegar and spices is an ancient form of food preservation. It is more often used with fish, but some mollusks are also processed this way.

In the 1800s, pickled molluscan products, especially oysters, were prepared commercially over most of the U.S. Atlantic Coast. They are not nearly as popular now but are prepared in some areas, especially in Virginia and Louisiana, for local consumption.

Pickled mussels are becoming a popular seafood. Mussels are plentiful and cheap because of aquaculture techniques, and the acceptance of pickled mussels is increasing. Clams are also pickled but to a lesser extent than mussels and oysters. Pickled cockles are common in France. The meat is dipped in 3 percent salt brine, drained, and covered for three days with a 3 percent vinegar solution containing 3 percent salt. The cockles are then drained, packed, and covered with spiced vinegar.

REFERENCES

Borgstrom, G. 1965. *Fish as Food* (Vol. 4). Orlando, FL: Academic Press.

Brownell, W., and Stevely, J. 1981. "The Biology, Fisheries and Management of the Queen Conch *Strombus gigas.*" *Marine Fish. Rev.* 43(7):1–12.

Desrosier, N., and Tressler, D. 1977. *Fundamentals of Food Freezing.* New York: Van Nostrand Reinhold/AVI Publishing Co.

Lopez, A. 1987. *A Complete Course in Canning.* Book III, *Processing Procedures for Canned Food Products.* Baltimore: The Canning Trade, Inc.

Peters, J. 1978. "Scallops and Their Utilization." *Marine Fish. Rev.* 40(11):1–9.

Suderman, D., and Cunningham, 1983. *Batter and Breading.* New York: Van Nostrand Reinhold.

Wheaton, F., and Lawson, T. 1985. *Processing Aquatic Food Products.* New York: Wiley.

Wheelen, J., and Hebard, C. 1981. *Seafood Product Resource Guide.* Annapolis, MD: Mid-Atlantic Fisheries Development Foundation.

CHAPTER 10

Processing Crustaceans

Donn R. Ward

Crustaceans make up a relatively small proportion of the marine food products marketed. However, the diversity of the species and the high prices they command make them especially important.

BLUE CRAB

The scientific name of the blue crab, *Callinectes sapidus*, suggests two notable attributes of the species. "Calli" is the Latin word for beautiful, "nectes" and "sapidus" the Latin words for swimmer and savory, respectively. The blue crab is a swimming crab and therefore has a well-developed set of swimming muscles. The meat from the blue crab is quite flavorful.

Processing

Barrels of crabs arrive at processing plants either directly from the boats or in trucks, which have transported crabs from other landing sites. The crabs are weighed, then dumped into large stainless steel baskets. During the winter dredging season, the crabs are run through a tumble spray washer prior to being dumped into the baskets. This washing step is essential for dredged crabs because they are covered with sand and grit from being buried in the sandy bottom.

Although subsequent handling and cooking methods vary depending on regional customs and state laws, the processing of blue crabs has changed little since fresh crabmeat was first marketed in the late 1800s. It is a very labor-intensive industry, with most of the picking still done by hand. (See the end of this chapter for the steps involved in removing the meat from the crab.)

Currently, the industry processes live crabs either under steam pressure or in boiling water. Some states, such as Maryland, North Carolina, and Florida, have regulations which stipulate that "crabs shall be cooked only under steam pressure." Some regulations go so far as to stipulate cold point temperature minimums; for example, the rules governing crabmeat operations in North Carolina state "Crustacea shall be cooked under steam pressure until such time that the internal temperature of the center-most crustacean reaches 235°F" (112.8°C). The regulations for processing crabs in Texas simply state "Crabs shall be cooked so as to provide a sterile crab."

Cooking live crabs in a steam retort is the most common processing method. However, a major problem is the lack of uniformity among processors with respect to the times and temperatures used in the steam cook process. Investigators have reported cooking times ranging from three to twenty-three minutes as well as steam temperatures ranging from 240° (115.5°C) to 250°F (121°C). Health departments prefer long cook times at high temperatures because microorganisms found as part of the natural microflora of the crab are more apt to be destroyed with increased cooking temperature and time of exposure.

From the processor's perspective the issue is economics The higher the temperature and/or the longer the cook time, the lower the yeild of picked meat. The yield loss is the result of moisture loss from the edible tissues. Short cook times cause less drying of the meat and therefore produce greater yields. Since the average yield of picked meat from a blue crab is approximately 10 percent, this is a problem to which crab processors are acutely sensitive.

After cooking, the crabs are moved to a cooling room and air-cooled to ambient temperatures within thirty minutes. The cooling room is usually a screened area with fans blowing across the crabs. Before the crabs are moved to the cooked cooler (33 to 40°F/0.6 to 4.4°C) they must be cool enough that steam is no longer rising from them. If cooked crabs were moved immediately to the cooler, without a precooling period, steam rising from the crabs would condense on the ceiling of the cooler and drip back down on the crabs. This could potentially contaminate the cooked crabs and result in what is termed a "sour crab."

In some states the practice is to deback (remove the top shell), eviscerate (remove internal organs), and wash the crabs after cooling to ambient temperature before placing the crab cores in refrigerated coolers (33 to 40°F/0.6 to 4.4°C). [After overnight cooling, whole debacked crabs (or crab cores) are taken to the picking room where pickers hand-pick the meat from the crabs.]

Blue crab meat is available in several different forms:

1. *Lump (back fin):* includes all meat from the body portion adjacent to the back fin appendage. Since the meat can be picked in relatively large lumps and generally contains fewer shell pieces, it commands a premium price.
2. *Flake (regular or white):* all meat from the body portion except lump.
3. *Claw:* all meat from the claw appendages.
4. *Special:* originally intended to consist of all meat from the body part of the crab in normal proportions (i.e., all lump meat and all flake meat). In recent years, however, it has come to mean the same as flake (regular).
5. *Deluxe:* term has no specific meaning and therefore can be whatever the wholesaler or retailer desires it to mean. The term is usually used to describe various mixtures of lump and flake.

The technology used in processing blue crabs has changed little in the past century. Most of the picking is still done by hand. In recent years, however, increasing efforts have been made to perfect various machines for picking meat from the blue crab. Cockey (1980) noted that the different design principles for extracting meat from the crab include vacuuming, squeezing the meat from the leg and bodies with rollers, throwing the meat from the cores by centrifugal force, shaking meat from the core by vibration, or crushing in a hammer mill and separating the meat from the shell by brine flotation. These machines and methods have met with varying degrees of success.

One major disadvantage of the machines mentioned is that none allows removal of the back fin portion as one large lump. Inasmuch as consumers desire to purchase crabmeat in lump form and are willing to pay a premium price, it is doubtful that hand picking will give way totally to machine picking in the near future.

The possibility exists, however, that "imitation lump" could be developed by binding the smaller flake meat pieces into larger pieces. Some preliminary work has been done in this area by the National Marine Fisheries Service in Gloucester, Massachusetts.

Pasteurization

Most muscle protein foods, particularly seafoods, are quite perishable. Under normal refrigeration, fresh crabmeat has a shelf life of approximately seven to ten days. This relatively short shelf life places severe restrictions on the processor, who must process and market the product quickly. It limits the marketing radius, and the potential for economic growth. One alternative to the shelf-life problem is freezing. Although blue crab meat can be frozen, it does not freeze as well as most seafood products. Another approach has been pasteurization.

In the blue crab industry, pasteurization *used to be* defined as the process of heating every particle of crabmeat in an approved hermetically sealed container to a temperature of at least 185°F (85°C) and holding it at that temperature for at least one minute. This definition worked fine as long as the industry pasteurized meat in 1-pound (454 g) 401×301 cans [4 1/16 inches (10.3 cm) in diameter by 3 1/16 inches (7.8 cm) in height]. In recent years the industry has begun pasteurizing products in 8 oz. and 12 oz. cans, as well as 16 oz. cans of different shapes. This change made it necessary to redefine the pasteurization process requirements. You can obtain additional information on pasteurization standards from the Shellfish Institute of North America, 1525 Wilson Blvd., Suite 500, Arlington, VA 22209.

Pasteurization extends the shelf life of blue crab meat by destroying the bacteria that would cause spoilage of the fresh product under normal refrigeration conditions. Pasteurized crabmeat, like pasteurized milk, *must* be kept refrigerated. However, since the normal spoilage microorganisms have been destroyed, pasteurized crabmeat has a shelf life of at least six months. Once the can has been opened, the crabmeat should be used within five to seven days.

Pasteurization allows processors to stock up during periods of crab abundance. Furthermore, it allows consumers, particularly those in inland markets, to purchase crabmeat year round. And just as importantly, the pasteurized product is almost indistinguishable in taste and texture from the fresh product.

SHRIMP

The commercial shrimp industry is one of the largest seafood industries in the United States in both value and quantity of product caught. There are two commercially important shrimp fisheries: the North Pacific and Alaska area, and the southern fishery located in the South Atlantic and Gulf of Mexico.

In the southern fishery, there are three major commercial species: the white shrimp *(Penaeus setiferus)*, the brown shrimp *(Penaeus aztecus)*, and the pink shrimp *(Penaeus duorarum)*. In some areas vessels return to port daily, whereas boats equipped with freezers or adequate ice storage may remain on the fishing grounds for two to three weeks.

Handling of shrimp on board the vessel is vitally important. On completion of a tow, the contents of the net are dumped on the deck of the vessel, and the shrimp are separated from the "trash" (i.e. anything that is not shrimp). The latter is usually discarded overboard. Crew members quickly remove the heads of the shrimp by hand, and the "headed" shrimp are then shoveled into baskets and washed with a stream of water.

It is important to head and wash the shrimp before storage. Although the procedure is referred to as heading, in fact crew members remove not just the head but the entire cephalothorax section, which contains the gills and many of the organs associated with the digestive tract. Studies have shown that removal of this section removes a significant source of bacteria as well as active enzymes that can hasten deterioration of the shrimp. Thorough washing is important since this further reduces bacteria and enzymes.

Once headed and washed, two different methods can be used to preserve the catch: icing or brine freezing. Boats using ice usually immerse a basket of shrimp in a "dip" solution prior to placing the shrimp on ice in the vessel's hold. The dip retards the formation of black spot (see later discussion).

Another method of preserving shrimp at sea is the use of brine freezing. According to an article written by Bruce Cox of Texas A&M University, the use of freezers aboard shrimp vessels has been both cursed and applauded by boat owners. The process can produce very favorable results, but attention to detail is important. The following information on brine freezing was adapted from Cox's article.

The proper use of freezer brines is very important. An efficient brine should rapidly freeze shrimp or bring them close to freezing, so that they can be completely frozen in the boat's hold. Proper brine freezing helps prevent black spot and dehydration. Correct mixtures of salt, corn syrup, and dip powder effectively retard dehydration and black spot formation.

Salt in the proper concentration (23 percent) reduces the freezing point of a brine tank to −6°F (−21.1°C) whereas only slightly less salt significantly affects the freezing capabilities of the brine tank. Corn syrup in the brine mixture coats the shrimp with an elastic coating and helps prevent black spot and dehydration. Regulator table sugar becomes brittle and will flake off during the trip. Corn syrup acts as a chemical reducing agent, robbing the black spot enzymes of oxygen which is required to complete the black spot reaction. The syrup coating also holds moisture inside the shrimp, preventing dehydration. Sodium bisulfite (dip powder), like corn syrup, is a chemical reducing agent that effectively binds oxygen so that it is unavailable to the enzymes responsible for black spot formation.

Approximately 50 pounds (22.7 kg) of headed shrimp are placed in open mesh sacks and then submerged in the brine tanks. Shrimp should not be allowed to soak for more than fifteen or twenty minutes; otherwise the shrimp will become too salty and eventually toughen. Once brine freezing is complete, the bags are placed in the freezer hold.

At the dock, boats that stored shrimp on ice will flood the hold to melt the ice. The shrimp are then removed by vacuum pumps to wash tanks in the processing plant. Bags of brine frozen shrimp are off-loaded from the boats and emptied nto thaw tanks. Shrimp remain in these tanks for five to ten minutes to allow the frozen shrimp to separate.

From this point on, whether the shrimp were iced or frozen, the process is much the same. The shrimp are graded according to size. Size grades of shrimp are expressed as "count," meaning the average number of shrimp to the pound. Following are the common commercial size categories:

Less than 10
10–15
16–20
21–25
26–30
31–35
36–40
41–45
46–50
51–60
61–70
more than 70

After grading, the shrimp are packed in 5-pound (2.3-kg) boxes and frozen in a blast freezer or plate freezer. After the product is thoroughly frozen, it is removed from the freezer, the top of the box is opened, and about 8 ounces (237 ml) of water is sprayed on the shrimp. The lid is closed and the box inverted. This method allows a solid block of ice and shrimp to form, protecting the shrimp from freezer burn.

Black Spot

Black spot, also called box ring, ice burn, and ringer shrimp, is a dark discoloration that may form on stored shrimp (Fig. 10–1). Black spot is caused by a biochemical reaction, called melanosis, that is produced from naturally occurring compounds in the shrimp shell and is similar to the reaction that takes place when a person gets a suntan.

Black spot is not caused by excessive levels of spoilage bacteria. In fact, large numbers of actively growing bacteria may reduce the formation of black pigment, by using up oxygen that the black spot reaction also requires.

Since the reaction is similar to suntanning, exposure to sunlight speeds up the process. For example, after eleven days of storage in ice, shrimp that had been

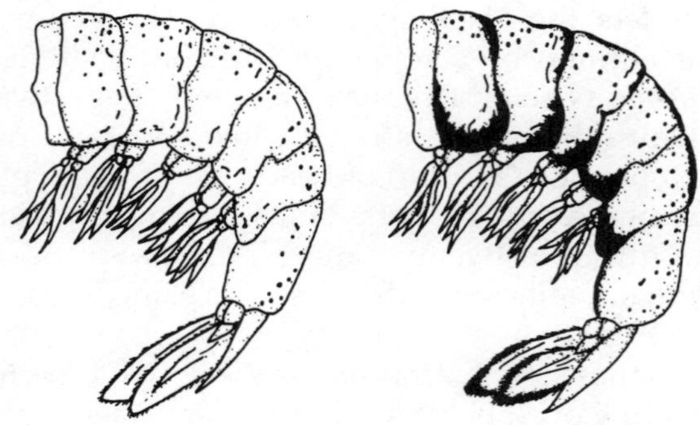

Figure 10-1. The Appearance of a Normal Shrimp (left) and One with Black Spotting (right).

placed immediately in the hold had 14 percent black spot; shrimp exposed to the sun for two hours before storage had 55 percent. Six hours of exposure resulted in 98 percent black spot. Interestingly, holds that are overinsulated or overiced can also increase the occurrence of black spot. In order to reduce black spot development the ice must melt. Melting ice washes away some of the compounds associated with the reaction and decreases the oxygen contact with the shrimp.

Shrimp molting cycles also influence susceptibility to black spot. As shrimp prepare to molt they build up materials needed for a new shell. One of these materials is an amino acid called tyrosine, an essential compound in black spot production. As a result, shrimp are more susceptible to black spot development just prior to molting and least susceptible just after molting.

Prevention of Black Spot

Efficient handling on deck, immediate, thorough washing, and storage on good quality melting ice are the most natural and effective means of controlling black spot. Rapid handling on deck reduces exposure to sunlight and elevated temperatures which speed up the chemical reaction leading to black spot.

Chemicals have also been used to control black spot development. The chemicals evaluated include sodium sulfite, sodium bisulfite, sodium metabisulfite, ascorbic acid, ethylenediaminetetraacetic acid (EDTA), baking soda, and others. The most commonly used is sodium bisulfite, often referred to as "dip." Sodium bisulfite is a strong reducing agent which competes with tyrosine for molecular oxygen, thus preventing the oxygen from entering the reaction which leads to black spot.

Any shrimper or processor using sodium bisulfite must exercise care and caution. There is a small percentage of the population which exhibits an allergic response to sulfites, and in some instances these reactions can be quite severe. As a result, there is controversy regarding the use of sulfiting agents in foods. Although it is still legal to add sulfiting agents to shrimp to retard the formation of black spot (up to 100 ppm, measured as SO_2 on the edible meat), there is active research to find an acceptable alternative. Also, if a sulfiting agent is used in excess of 10 ppm, the current limit of detection, it must be listed on the product label.

KING CRAB

The king crab *(Paralithudes camschatica)* is an extremely large crab, weighing as much as 24 pounds (11 kg). Fishing areas extend in a large crescent from Southeastern Alaska to the Bering Sea side of the Aleutian Peninsula and island chain.

Only healthy male king crabs are kept because conservation regulations prohibit the taking of females. The crabs are held live on board the boats in tanks containing either circulating seawater or refrigerated seawater. Occasionally in-shore day boats will bring in the crabs as a deck load.

At the processing plant, crabs from the fishing vessels are processed immediately or placed in holding tanks of circulating seawater similar to those found on the boats. Only live crabs are processed. During the butchering operation, the back shell is pulled off, the crab cut in half, and the viscera and gills removed. The butchered sections are then thoroughly washed to remove blood and viscera.

Two methods of precooking the crab sections are commonly used depending on whether the crabmeat is to be canned or frozen. The first method, the two-stage cook, is most commonly used by canners. After the first wash, the crab sections are placed on a wire mesh conveyor that transports them through a tank of water heated to 155 to 159°F (68.3 to 70.6°C). The conveyor speed is controlled so that the sections remain in the heated water for ten to twelve minutes. After emerging from the first cook tank, the crab sections are thoroughly washed with cold water to reduce product temperature and remove uncoagulated blood. The removal of the blood is an extremely important step, particularly for crabmeat that is to be canned. Should blood remain, the copper in the blood can produce a blue or black discoloration, often referred to as "blueing", in the canned product.

After the first cook and wash, but while the sections are still warm, meat is removed by passing the sections between rollers. The squeezing action breaks the shell just enough to force the meat out while the shell proceeds on through the rollers. The meat is then thoroughly washed again to remove traces of blood, shell particles, and traces of viscera.

After the second wash, the meat is cooked again to fully coagulate the protein and shrink the meat so that proper fills may be obtained in the cans. A continuous cooker is normally used, with the meat passing in approximately four minutes through a water tank or steam tunnel maintained at 210 to 212°F (98.9 to 100°C). The meat is then spray-washed, inspected, and passed to the packing table, where cans are filled by hand. Packers cut the large leg sections to fit the can and fill most packs with one layer of leg meat, followed by smaller sections and shoulder meat. Parchment paper ends are commonly used to minimize possible tin-plate discoloration and to prevent meat from sticking to the can lid.

Cans of packed meat are thermally processed to render the product commercially sterile. The time and temperature used will vary, depending on the can size and shape. Canned king crabmeat should be stored at a relatively cool temperature to minimize color and flavor changes. It should be marketed within one to two years for best quality.

The second method is the single-stage cook, which is primarily used by processors who freeze the final product, although some canners also use this method. In the single stage process the crabs are only cooked once. Following butchering and washing, the crabs are cooked at 210 to 212°F (98.9 to 100°C) for twenty to twenty-two minutes. The sections are spray-washed to cool the product, and the meat is removed from the shell by techniques similar to those described for the two-stage process.

Once the meat has been removed, it is thoroughly washed. However, because of the more rigorous initial heat treatment the blood is coagulated and therefore very difficult to remove. Most canners do not use this method of processing since the likelihood of blueing is greatly increased. Meat from this processing method is, however, quite suitable for freezing.

In general, king crab meat is much more suitable for freezing than other crab species. It can be stored up to a year at 0°F (−18°C) with good acceptability. King crab meat is usually frozen as a large block, incorporating 250 ounces (7.1 kg) of crabmeat and 24 ounces (0.68 kg) of water to fill the voids. The blocks are inspected and packaged in a suitable film and wax-board carton, then frozen and glazed. Institutional products are made from these large blocks by sawing the frozen blocks into 1- or 1.5-pound (454- or 681-g) units.

Frozen king crab sections (meat in the shell) have become very popular with retail and institutional buyers. To provide this product, the butchered sections are chilled, thoroughly washed, trimmed, and divided into uniform 10-pound (4.5-kg) lots. The sections are then frozen and glazed. Extra glazing is necessary at the shoulder end, where the meat is exposed, to prevent dehydration. Signs of dehydration are yellowing and then honeycombing (spongy appearance) of the meat. The shoulder of the crab is enclosed by a yellowish membrane so it is important to distinguish between the natural yellow of the membrane and yellowing of the meat due to dehydration and rancidity.

REFERENCES

Cockey, R. R. 1980. "Bacteriological Assessment of Machine-Picked Meat of the Blue Crab." *J. Food Protect.* 43:172.

Cox, B. Undated. *Freezing Shrimp at Sea.* College Station, TX: Texas A&M University.

Phillips, S. A., and Peeler, J. T. 1972. "Bacteriologica Survey of the Blue Crab Industry." *Applied Microbiol.* 24:958.

Ulmer, D. H. B., Jr. 1964. "Preparation of Chilled Meat from Atlantic Blue Crab." *Fishery Industrial Research.* 2:12.

Van Engel, W. A. 1962. "The Blue Crab and Its Fishery in Chesapeake Bay." *Commercial Fisheries Review.* 24:9.

CHAPTER

11

Freshwater Fish

Thomas E. Rippen

Freshwater fish make up less than 5 percent of the commercial harvest of wild fishery stocks in the United States, yet several species find traditional markets, primarily in the Midwest, where they are highly prized. Consequently, seafood firms wishing to serve inland customers should evaluate local consumption patterns prior to introducing unfamiliar products.

Most freshwater fishing in the United States remains centered in the Great Lakes area, despite a dramatic decline of food species in recent years. Great Lakes is the collective name for lakes Superior, Michigan, Huron, Erie, and Ontario, which all drain to the Atlantic via the St. Lawrence River. Combined with the large lakes of central and western Canada, they contain approximately 40 percent of the world's fresh surface water. This chapter emphasizes these traditional North American fisheries with occasional reference to less important lakes and river systems. The bias toward North American fisheries should not be misinterpreted as suggesting that other freshwater systems are insignificant. Subsistence fishing on Lake Titicaca and the greater Amazon drainage of South America and on the large rivers of China, for example, has had a major economic and historic impact on the people of those regions. Likewise, important targeted fisheries exist for pike and whitefish in scattered locations in Europe and Asia, as they do for nile perch in Lake Victoria, Africa. The U.S. experience is highlighted as a study of commercial freshwater fishing, reflecting dynamic social values and market demand.

This chapter also is confined to selected wild freshwater species. Most freshwater trout, catfish, and crayfish are produced under controlled conditions, which will be discussed in Chapter 18. Some species or populations of sturgeon, salmon, eels, shad, and other fish inhabit fresh waters during a portion of their life to spawn or feed, but they are generally considered marine species and as such are discussed in detail elsewhere.

During storage and preparation, fish performance varies according to their physiological and biochemical makeup, which in turn is dictated by their environment. This chapter addresses factors that distinguish freshwater species from their saltwater relatives. We also discuss processing methods, products, and distribution channels.

CURRENT STATUS

The overall effect of the activites of humans and alien fish has been a shift in market products from large, high valued species to small fish of low value. The successful stocking of salmonids, including coho and chinook salmon, may help control populations of nuisance fish but has little direct impact on regional fishing fleets. Most bordering states are committed to recreational rather than commercial fisheries. Species of trout, salmon, walleye, blue pike, smallmouth bass, and several others are generally not permitted or are limited in the U.S. commercial catch. Access to the commercial fishery is controlled by gear and license restrictions. Wisconsin issues about 200 licenses per year, Michigan and Ohio about 100 each, with another 100 issued by the combined states of Minnesota, Pennsylvania, Indiana, and Illinois. These states plus New York contain 4,678 miles (7,527 km) of shoreline, equaling Ontario's waterfront.

By contrast, Canada regulates the commercial harvest of most traditional and introduced species including lake trout, walleye, northern pike, sturgeon, splake, and Pacific salmon. Ontario issues about 1,000 licenses each year written for a wide variety of gear types including over 13 million yards (11,887 km) of gillnet, a net which has been severely restricted by most states in the United States. Whitefish, yellow perch, and chubs are the most valuable species in the U.S. catch; yellow perch and walleye account for the high value of the Ontario harvest. For example, in 1981 we saw a total catch average of $.32 per pound ($.70 per kg) for 47 million pounds (21×10^6 kg) for the U.S. fishermen and $.51 per pound ($1.12 per kg) for 61 million pounds (27.7×10^6 kg) for Canadian fishermen.

Most U.S. fishing occurs in the western Great Lakes with only a minor fishery in lakes Erie and Ontario. Canadian fleets account for nearly all the increased catch in the eastern lakes. Sales of smelt, yellow perch, and walleye have elevated the value of landings from Canadian waters of Lake Erie from $6 million in the middle 1970s to $20 million in the early 1980s.

The discovery of DDT, PCBs, dieldrin, mercury, and other contaminants in Great Lakes fish hampered the fishing industry as certain species were banned. Several contaminants monitored by state and federal agencies have generally fallen below tolerance levels, permitting the sale of some formerly banned products. Unfortunately recent research has renewed concerns about contaminants and has led to heightened regulatory activity.

OTHER FISHERIES

Traditional fisheries exist in the Mississippi River and its tributaries, certain inland U.S. lakes, notably the Red Lakes and Boundary Lakes of Minnesota, and the large Canadian lakes of the prairie provinces and Northwest Territories. Historically, the Mississippi River system produced landings rivaling the Great Lakes, but now much of the catch has a lower market value. Carp, buffalo, sheepshead, and various catfish still predominate.

The Boundary Lakes (Lake of the Woods and Rainy Lake) have annually produced large yields of walleye, northern pike, and lake herring, but Minnesota is currently buying out the last of the commercial licenses in these waters. An Indian gillnet fishery on the Red Lakes is highly productive, producing up to 700,000 pounds (318,000 kg) of walleye a year, 1 million pounds (4.54×10^5 kg) of yellow perch, 80,000 pounds (36,400 kg) of whitefish, 50,000 pounds (22,700 kg) of northern pike, and 1 million pounds (454,000 kg) of suckers and sheepshead.

Canada's inland fisheries include eleven commercially important lakes in Manitoba, Saskatchewan, Alberta, and the Northwest Territories. Walleye, whitefish, northern pike, lake trout, sauger, lake herring, and arctic char are the most valuable species. They are harvested primarily with gillnets fished in either open water or under the ice and with poundnets, trapnets, and seines.

MARKETS/PROCESSING

The freshwater industry remains based on traditional products and markets. Most fish are wholesaled fresh, usually whole but also dressed, filleted, or chunked. Typically family-owned or cooperative fishing operations on the Great Lakes include a simple shoreline facility for cutting, icing, boxing, and storing the catch. The fish are sold locally or shipped (usually contracted with trucking firms) to wholesale distributors in major cities, most notably Chicago.

Many of these small businesses operate a smokehouse for hotsmoking (kippering) drawn, dressed, or chunked fish. Chubs, lake whitefish, lake herring, and imported whiting are species commonly selected for smoking. Smoked products are mostly consumed locally although the Great Lakes Fish Producer's Cooperative and a few large volume processors and distributors ship finished products to distant metropolitan centers, including New York and Miami. Some of the most modern processing and distribution plants are located in Canada. They are generally very competitive with U.S. firms, offering buyers attractive prices and relatively stable supplies, although seasonal gluts contribute to periodically suppressed prices.

The historically important salt-cured lake herring trade has virtually disappeared. Years of poor catches and changing consumer attitudes are probably responsible. Efforts by processors to diversify their product lines have met with encouraging but generally modest results. Some whitefish roe is screened, washed, and brined for further processing into caviar; certain underutilized species, including suckers, lake herring, and round whitefish, are mechanically deboned to make mince.

Freshwater fish are the primary ingredient in processed products destined for the Jewish trade, notably gefilte fish, which is made by cooking seasoned fish dumplings in a vegetable/fish stock. Important species include whitefish, carp, and walleye.

COMPOSITION AND QUALITY

Shelf Life

In general, spoilage patterns are similar for freshwater and saltwater fish. Bacterial composition may be somewhat different during certain stages of decomposition but proteolytic (protein-consuming) microorganisms lend familiar putrifactive flavors and odors to both groups. As with saltwater fish, enzymatic activity varies with species and season.

Despite similarities, freshwater products, on average, maintain quality longer than do their marine counterparts. This fact is generally attributed to the presence of light weight compounds known as osmoregulators in saltwater fish. Although important for balancing flesh "salt" content with the marine environment, bacteria readily break down these compounds as a food source. Deterioration of osmoregulators is associated with ammoniacal odors and with undesirable texture changes during frozen storage of susceptible seafoods.

Freshwater fish must deal with a harsh environment relatively free of electrolytes. As a result, water invades their tissues under osmotic pressure and must be excreted as copious dilute urine. They do not drink. Chemical osmoregulators would be counterproductive. Consequently, related shelf-life problems are notably absent.

Red Versus White Muscle

As with saltwater species, freshwater fish have muscle ranging from white to well-defined regions of white meat and dark meat to mostly dark meat. However, few species of freshwater fish contain flesh as highly pigmented as some migratory saltwater fish. The red blood pigment, hemoglobin, and muscle pigment, myoglobin, bind oxygen for transport and storage. These pigments can release oxygen for desirable chemical reactions in the tissues while making it unavailable for detrimental reactions.

Saltwater species that require great quantities of energy for swimming rely primarily on metabolism of tissue oils, an oxygen-consuming process. Consequently, most free swimming species are both dark-fleshed and oily. Freshwater species are less likely to expend large quantities of energy for movement. Even species that do, such as migratory freshwater trout, function with little red muscle probably because they frequent well-oxygenated water. A few freshwater fish that are highly pigmented may have adapted to low oxygen environments. Carp and bullhead catfish are examples.

Edibility

Marketing strategies often emphasize oil content, color, texture, and flavor intensity as a basis for classification of fish species. Lake trout, lake whitefish, and similar freshwater species may prove helpful for supplementing light-mild-oily categories not always available from marine fisheries. Other lake fish can be substituted for traditional lean, mild marine fish without compromise. Walleye and yellow perch are highly regarded among higher priced lean species; freshwater smelt, suckers, sheepshead, and several other inexpensive fish are also fine eating and serve to round out product lines at lower cost than many comparable saltwater products.

Off-Flavors

When comparing flavor of fresh products, few distinctions can be made between freshwater and saltwater species. However, earthy, musty, or weedy off-flavors, when they occur, are encountered primarily in freshwater fish. These flavors occur more by season and location than by species.

Regional consumer bias against certain fish may be related to poor experiences with local supplies. Even fish normally in high demand such as walleye may accumulate a "muddy" flavor at times, while the same species caught in another location may be unaffected.

The organic compounds geosmins and 2-methylisoborned are produced by certain microorganisms and algae and are readily absorbed by fish, lending disagreeable flavors and odors to their flesh. Fish need not ingest the plants to become tainted but probably pick up the compounds from the water via the gills and epithelial tissues. Other off-flavors can be traced to decayed organic matter or, rarely, chemical contamination.

Objectionable flavors appear most commonly in fish taken from shallow, weedy lakes and slow-flowing streams. Large bodies of water typical of most commercial fisheries are less affected.

Parasites

Parasites may be found in nearly all saltwater and freshwater fish, often appearing as cysts or worms in the flesh or viscera. They are characterized by complex life histories typically requiring one or more intermediate host. Only parasites that need both cold-blooded and warm-blooded animals during their life cycles are capable of infecting humans who consume them in fish.

Saltwater seafoods may contain roundworms (nematodes) capable of causing severe but temporary digestive upset in humans. The Food and Drug Administration has expressed concern that pathogenic nematodes may become a problem because of the increased popularity of raw or lightly marinated fish.

Perhaps due to the proximity of freshwater environments to many warm-blooded animals, freshwater fish may represent a greater health concern than do saltwater fish. Also, nonpathogenic but unsightly infestations can be especially troublesome to firms marketing affected products. Tapeworms and flukes occasionally infect consumers of raw freshwater fish.

Northern pike, walleye, and burbot from the northern midwest United States have the highest incidence of tapeworms. Complete coagulation of fish muscle by cooking, pickling, or salting kills harmful parasites and accounts for the scarcity of clinical cases in the United States. In most cases, frozen storage also destroys parasites. To prevent the migration of roundworms from the viscera to surrounding meat, the fish should be thoroughly iced and problem species marketed in eviscerated forms.

Contaminants

Pesticides, heavy metals, and other contaminants in fish flesh have adversely affected regional fisheries around the world. The U.S. freshwater industry has been affected by regulatory action and by consumer response to a list of chemicals and trade names, including DDT, PCB, PBB, dieldrin, and Mirex.

An estimated 5,000 to 10,000 new chemicals are produced each year, of which 1,000 are introduced into commerce. To protect consumers from possible harmful effects, the Toxic Substance Control Act of 1976 requires that certain classes of chemicals be screened for toxicity before they are cleared for use. In addition, it allows for federal regulation of the production and application of these chemicals. More recent legislation has strengthened enforcement capabilities. Once chemicals are in use, the Food and Drug Administration establishes and enforces limits on the amounts of certain substances that may appear in foods. State departments of commerce, health, and natural resources also commonly enforce measures to reduce public exposure to contaminants.

Although new contaminants in fish are identified periodically, monitoring programs have documented reduced concentrations of several of these substances in recent years. As mentioned, few products are currently banned from the marketplace by legislation. Concerned consumers should know that commercially sold fish are routinely evaluated for major contaminants. Sport fishermen, who may eat considerable quantities of problem fish without the benefit of such sampling, are at greater risk.

SELECTED SPECIES

Whitefish

Whitefish, which account for a significant portion of the trade in inland markets, is a collective name for certain members of the Salmonidae family including true trout and salmon. They are characterized by an adipose fin (a small rayless projection behind the dorsal fin), a small delicate mouth, white flesh, and mild flavor.

Lake Whitefish

Virtually all the whitefish sold under the name are lake whitefish *(Coregonus clupeaformis)* (Fig. 11-1). A large, relatively oily whitefish, they grow to more than 12 pounds (5.5 kg) but average 2 to 5 pounds (0.91 to 2.27 kg). They are found from New England to Minnesota and north to the arctic and Alaska. In recent years, Canada has increased its percentage of the catch as fishermen work the deep cold lakes of the north-central provinces and Northwest Territories. They produce about 20 million pounds (9.1×10^6 kg) each year by fishing gillnets even under thick ice.

Lake whitefish are marketed whole, dressed, chunked, and filleted. The roe is fine in texture and remains tender when cooked. Market demand is strong for eggs processed as "golden" caviar or whitefish caviar. Although commonly sold fresh, large quantities of frozen, smoked, and canned lake whitefish (combined with other species as gefilte fish) are also distributed.

Chubs (Lake Herring)

Several species of small whitefish are marketed in the United States as chub, especially when drawn and smoked. Among biologists, "cisco" is the more universally accepted name for this group. Fish sold as "lake herring," "tullibee," or "cisco" are usually *Coregonus artedii.* Other chubs include deepwater cisco *(Coregonus johannae),* longjaw cisco *(Coregonus alpenae),* shortjaw cisco *(Coregonus zenithicus),* shortnose cisco *(Coregonus reighardi),* and blackfin cisco *(Coregonus nigripinnis).* Additional market names include bloater and grayback. Sometimes the term chub implies a smoked product because it is the most common market form. Seafood suppliers and buyers should communicate clearly, due to confusing whitefish nomenclature.

Other Whitefish

Round whitefish or menominee *(Prosopeum cylindriceum)* is a common resident to cold lakes of northern New England, the Great Lakes, and Canada. Compared to

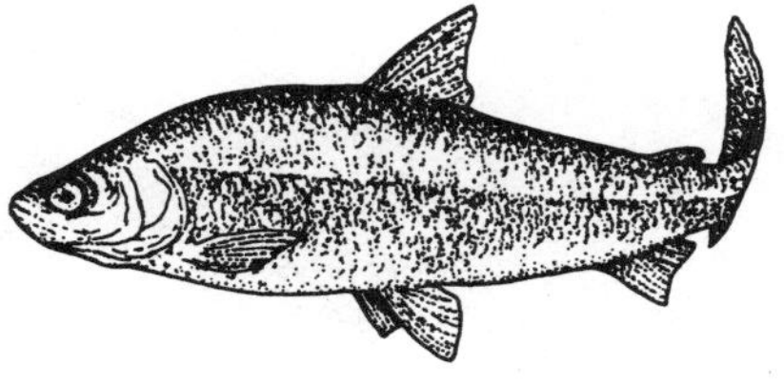

Figure 11-1. Lake Whitefish, the Primary Species Sold as Whitefish.

some members of the whitefish family, round whitefish is lower in oil content and, as the name implies, round in cross section. It is smaller than lake whitefish and finds only limited, usually local, markets despite desirable eating qualities.

Inconnu or sheepfish is a very large whitefish of northwestern Canada and Alaska. They are found in large lakes and streams where they migrate to sea. Anadramous (migratory) individuals may reach 50 pounds (22.7 kg); landlocked specimens are somewhat smaller. Inconnu (French for unknown) possess white, oily, mild flesh but find few buyers in the United States, possibly due to limited experience with the species. Perhaps 50,000 pounds (2.27×10^4 kg) are shipped to the lower regions of the United States.

Yellow Perch

Yellow perch *(Perca flavescens)* (Fig. 11-2) is among the most valuable species in the freshwater industry, remaining a mainstay of many United States and Canadian fishing ports. In recent years imports from Canada have dominated the market. The high value of Ontario landings is largely attributed to perch. Recent Ohio legislation banning small-mesh gillnets may virtually eliminate that state as a source of supply from Lake Erie, a historically important fishery.

Yellow perch are true perch (family Percidae) closely related to walleye and sauger. They have little in common, either taxonomically or gastronomically, with white perch, ocean perch, or a dozen other species commonly referred to as "perch." The term lake perch may refer to either yellow or white perch. Yellow perch are widely distributed from South Carolina north to Nova Scotia and west to the Great Lakes and west-central Canada.

Although yellow perch average under 1 pound (0.454 kg), their simple skeletal structure and small visceral cavity lend them to commercial filleting, sold fresh or frozen. Other forms include whole and, less commonly, breaded and frozen. Yellow perch are recognized by the presence of two spiny dorsal fins, a greenish to yellow body with dark vertical bands, and yellow to orange pelvic fins. The flesh is firm, white, lean and mild but distinctive. Well-handled fresh or frozen perch generally retain quality longer than many species. Gillnetters find they hold up well in their nets and are slow to develop signs of enzymatic softening.

Walleye

Another member of the perch family, walleye *(Stizostidion vitreum)*, is similar to yellow perch both in general appearance and in eating quality. They are larger however, reaching 10 pounds (4.5 kg) or more although averaging 2 to 4 pounds (0.9 to 1.8 kg). Their back is dusky, grading to bronze-gold on the sides. Long recognized for their culinary quality, walleye were known as salmon to early settlers. The meat is fine-textured, firm, white, lean, and mild.

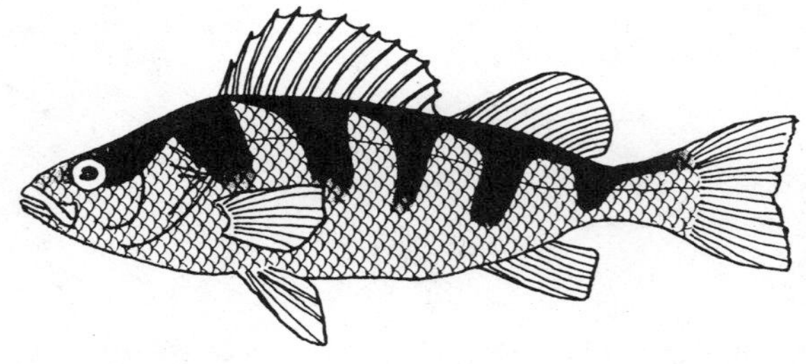

Figure 11-2. Yellow (Freshwater) Perch.

Its natural range extends from North Carolina to New England, west to the Rocky Mountains and north to the Hudson Bay. Largely protected as a gamefish in the United States, most of the 12 million pounds (5.45×10^6 kg) available are imported from Canada. Small quantities are available from New York, Pennsylvania, and American Indian fisheries. They are available fresh or frozen, whole, dressed, filleted (skin off or on), and as breaded fillets. They also appear as an ingredient of gefilte fish. Shelf-life characteristics and fillet yield are similar to yellow perch.

Walleye are usually marketed under that name or walleye pike in the United States but are recognized as yellow pickerel by the Canadian government. Suppliers may list them as yellow pickerel or yellow pike, although as a percid, walleye are unrelated to pike or pickerel. As an adaption to low light levels, their eyes are naturally opalescent, which negates cloudiness as an indicator of quality.

Sauger *(Stizostidion canadense)* is a close relative and, though somewhat smaller, nearly identical to walleye in appearance. Look for the absence of a white tip on the lower lobe of the tail fin, characteristic of walleye. Sauger enter markets mostly as an incidental catch of the walleye fisheries. Eating quality is similar to walleye and blue pike but is considered by some to be slightly less desirable.

Blue pike *(Stizostidion v. glaucum)* is a subspecies of walleye found in deepwater areas of Lake Erie and Ontario not frequented by walleye. They are distinguished from walleye by their larger eyes and gray body and lack the walleyes' golden hue. Taxonomic opinion varies on whether so-called blue pike from other lakes or even Lake Ontario are the subspecies or simply color variant populations of walleye.

Lake Trout

Lake trout, these largest of North American trout (technically called char), are found in cool, deep lakes across northern America (Fig. 11-3). They are available from Canadian, Wisconsin, and Minnesota sources and certain midwest American Indian companies fishing under treaty. Lake trout (Salvelinus *namaycush)* are also known as mackinaw, togue, namaycush, forktail, and Great Lakes trout. They average about 4 to 5 pounds (1.8 to 2.3 kg) in the commercial catch but may reach 50 pounds (22.7 kg) or more. Like whitefish and other salmonids they possess a small fleshy adipose fin on their back behind a spineless dorsal fin. They have large mouths and sharp teeth. Coloration is dull but distinctly marked with light spots on a darker background.

Lake trout are among the most oily of commercial fish ranging up to 22 percent fat for the common species. The closely related siscowet, or fat trout, may contain more than 50 percent fat. These deep water trout are only occasionally available on the market, usually in a smoked form. Lake trout populations were decimated by the lamprey invasion of the 1940s and 1950s. Current Great Lakes stocks are maintained by ongoing stocking programs because current cultured varieties cannot naturally reproduce. There is some hope that wild western brood stock will

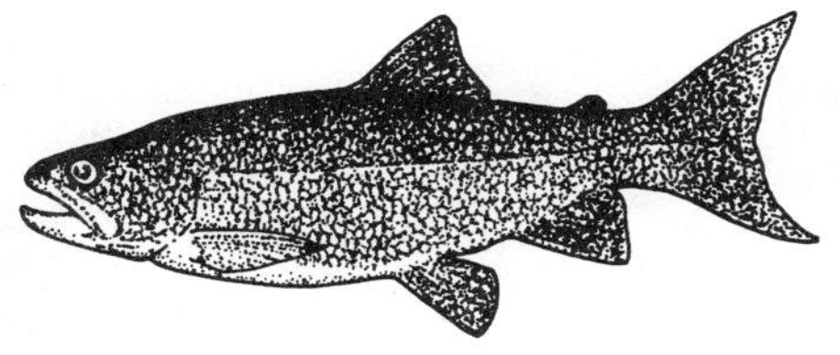

Figure 11-3. Lake Trout, the Largest of North American Trout.

help reestablish a self-sustaining population in the future. A lake trout/brook trout hybrid known as splake has been introduced and is harvested by Ontario fishermen.

Smelt

Several small, slender species of fish may be called smelt but the one most important commercially is rainbow smelt or lake smelt *(Osmerus mordax).* It is a silvery to greenish fish usually under 8 inches (20.3 cm) long with a rather large mouth for its size and characteristically sharp teeth, even on its tongue. Its small silvery scales are easily rubbed off. An anadramous fish by nature, living in saltwater and entering freshwater streams to spawn, it has adapted so well to freshwater habitats that it is often considered a freshwater fish. Smelt are widely distributed in the Great Lakes region and in the Northeast where they are taken by a variety of gear including small-mesh gillnets, pound nets, and trawls. Some states manage smelt as forage for game fish and do not issue commercial fishing permits. Much of the supply comes from Canada.

Often labeled as fatty fish, smelt are actually quite lean, about 2 percent fat, although a much more oily cousin, the eulachon or Columbia River smelt, is locally popular in the Northwest. Some buyers consider lake smelt better eating than Atlantic or Pacific species. Smelt are available nearly year round either fresh or frozen, headed-and-gutted, or whole. They are nearly always breaded and fried, and eaten bones and all. Although shelf-life properties are generally good, the delicate flavor and texture that smelt are noted for are quickly lost when mishandled.

Other Species

Small but regionally significant quantities of other wild harvest freshwater fish are also caught in North America, most finding local or ethnic markets. *Catfish* are mostly cultured but fisheries remain in the Great Lakes, Mississippi drainage, and some coastal tributaries of the East and Gulf coasts. Channel catfish (Fig. 11-4) are the primary target although the highly regarded blue catfish and, to a lesser extent, white catfish and bullheads are also available. Catfish tolerate low oxygen levels and are one of the few fish sometimes marketed alive. They may be held in drums or tubs on fishing vessels, then transferred to aerated tanks at shoreside facilities. They are also marketed dressed (headed-and-gutted, skinned) and, to a lesser extent, filleted or steaked.

Pike are large, toothy fish that frequent northern lakes and streams from New England to the Midwest and most of Canada. The northern pike *(Esox lucious)* (Fig. 11-5), the only species supporting a commercial fishery, grow to 25 pounds (11.4 kg) but 4 to 7 pounds (1.8 to 3.2 kg) is more common. They are recognized by their

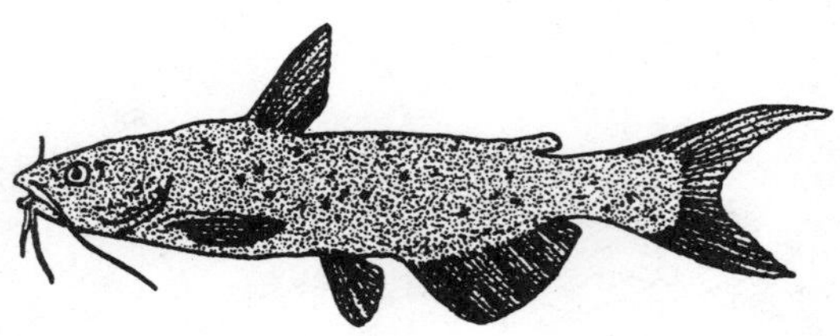

Figure 11-4. Channel (or Spotted) Catfish.

Figure 11-5. Northern Pike.

long, slender shape and greenish skin covered with yellow or cream-colored oval spots. Supplies come primarily from Canada since they are protected in the United States. Much of the catch is exported to Europe where the same species is also native but exists in numbers too low to satisfy the strong demand. The name, pike, is occasionally confused with market terms for walleye, yellow pike, blue pike, and yellow pickerel. In fact walleye are sometimes called walleye pike. Such confusing nomenclature is unfortunate because the two species are unrelated and dissimilar in appearance and eating quality. Northern pike are a lean (1 to 2 percent fat), very firm and mild fish containing numerous Y bones (forked intermuscular bones). They are sold whole or cut into most market forms, fresh or frozen.

Carp (Cyprinus carpio) (Fig. 11-6) is popular in many ethnic centers. Nearly 30 million pounds (13.6×10^6 kg) are harvested commercially in the United States each year, mostly from the Mississippi River system, the Great Lakes, and from states issuing permits as part of fish control programs. Because of a propensity for concentrating geosmin compounds, they are best when harvested in winter or from bodies of water where algae are not a problem. The flesh is often oily, ranging from 2 to 25 percent fat, and has a distinctive but pleasant flavor. Carp are usually marketed whole or in finished products, such as gefilte fish.

White perch (Morone americana) (Fig. 11-7) is both a freshwater and saltwater species. It is not a perch at all but a small relative of the striped bass and sea basses. Lake Erie's white perch populations have increased in recent years as large numbers have migrated from the Atlantic by way of the Welland Canal. The harvest has also increased somewhat in the mid-Atlantic marine fisheries since 1985. Fillets are sometimes sold as lake perch, a name also used for the higher valued yellow perch. To add to the confusion, white perch is also a market name for freshwater drum, otherwise known as sheepshead or freshwater croaker.

A closely related species, the *white bass (Morone chrysops)* (Fig. 11.8), is an important fish in the Lake Erie fisheries both in Canada and the United States. It resembles a silvery, panfish-sized striped bass, having narrow dark stripes that run the length of the body. The average size is about 1 pound (454 g) although some individuals approach 4 pounds (1.8 kg) especially in southern and southwestern

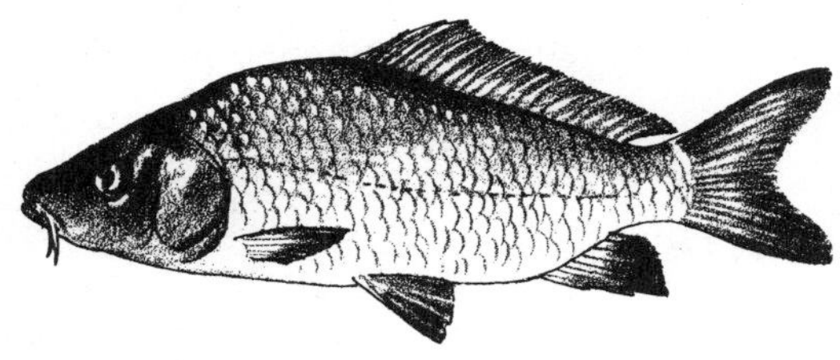

Figure 11-6. Carp.

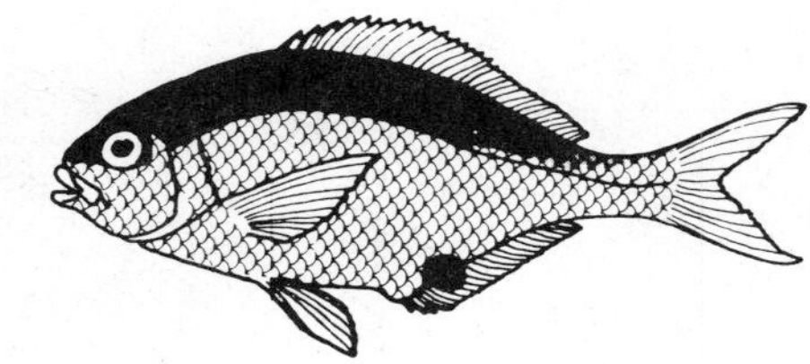

Figure 11-7. White Perch.

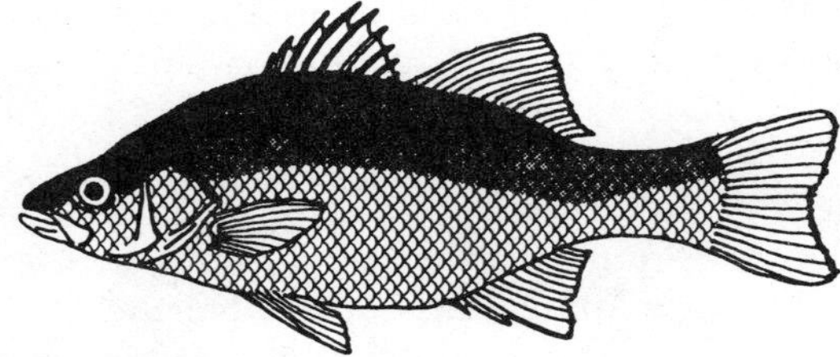

Figure 11-8. White (Freshwater) Bass

reservoirs where they have been stocked for recreational fishing. White bass produce boneless fillets of good eating quality.

Suckers make up another family of freshwater fish of some importance. The white sucker or freshwater mullet *(Catostomus commersoni)* is probably the most significant commercial species. Although harvested primarily in the Great Lakes, it is widely distributed east of the Rocky Mountains. As with some of the other suckers, it is well known for its numerous fine bones which limit market potential. The fish are sometimes split and scored to reduce bone size, which then soften during cooking. Several processing plants have used this species to produce boneless minces. It is a drab green to nearly brassy-colored fish of about 2 to 3 pounds (1 to 1.4 kg). Other suckers include three species of *buffalo* (large fish resembling carp harvested in the Mississippi valley south of the Great Lakes); the *longnose sucker;* ten species of *redhorse;* two species of *quillback* or carpsucker; the *spotted sucker;* and the *blue sucker.*

Other North American freshwater fish occasionally seen in the markets include *crappie,* various *sunfish, freshwater drum, rock bass, burbot, lake sturgeon* from Canadian sources, *eel, bowfish, gar, paddlefish,* and *alewives* (smoked or cured). The American paddlefish *(Polyodon spathula),* also known as spoonbill cat or spoonbill sturgeon, provides the roe for much of the "American sturgeon" caviar on the market. It is not related to either sturgeon or catfish. Most alewives, *gizzard shad,* and *goldfish* are sold for commercial bait or industrial applications.

As mentioned previously, *Pacific salmon* species stocked in the Great Lakes are tightly managed for recreational purposes; however significant quantities are marketed. The State of Michigan awards a contract for sale of adult salmon taken at weirs where eggs and milt (the male's sperm) are collected for culture, and Canada permits limited fishing.

ACKNOWLEDGMENTS

Information contained in this chapter was provided by the following individuals: Ronald E. Kinnunen, District Extension Sea Grant Agent, Michigan Sea Grant

College Program, Michigan State University; Mark Malchoff, Regional Extension Specialist, New York Sea Grant Extension Program, Cornell University; Jeff Gunderson, Fisheries Agent, Minnesota Sea Grant Extension Program, University of Minnesota; Fred Snyder and David Kelch, Ohio Sea Grant Program, Ohio State University.

REFERENCES

Anon. Variously dated. *Food Fish Facts.* A series by the National Consumer Educational Services Office, National Marine Fisheries Services, U.S. Dept. of Commerce.

Dore, I. 1982. *Frozen Seafood—The Buyer's Handbook.* Huntington, NY: Osprey Books.

Harris, L., Kevern, N., and Kinnunen, R. 1984. *Commercial Fishing in the Great Lakes.* Michigan Sea Grant College Program report.

Higashi, G. 1985. "Foodborne Parasites Transmitted to Man from Fish and Other Aquatic Foods." *J. Food Technology.* 39(3):694.

McClane, A., and deZanger, A. 1977. *The Encyclopedia of Fish Cookery.* New York: Holt.

Nettleton, J. 1985. *Seafood Nutrition: Facts, Issues and Marketing of Nutrition in Fish and Shellfish.* Huntington, NY: Osprey Books.

Seagran, H., Smith, S., and Buettner, H. 1976. "Lake and River Fisheries." From *Industrial Fisheries Technology,* edited by M. Stansby. Huntington NY: Krieger.

Tainter, S. and White, R. 1977. *Seines to Salmon Charters.* Extension bulletin E-1000, Michigan State University.

CHAPTER

12

Packaging

Tyre C. Lanier

Packaging innovation has been slow to come in the fishing industry. Today a large quantity of seafood is still moved to market essentially unpackaged. Whole or gutted fish are iced in fish holds, deiced, and sorted upon landing, and then reiced in bulk containers to be hauled to local fish markets. At the market, whole, dressed, or filleted fish are displayed and offered for sale (still unpackaged) on a bed of ice. A switch from wooden to waxed or plastic-coated corrugated boxes as the bulk shipping container has been the sole packaging improvement in this marketing scheme, and a folded newspaper remains the most common form of final product protection. Meanwhile, prepackaged meats and poultry have come to dominate the largely fishless self-service meat counters of America's supermarkets.

Frozen seafood products have fared somewhat better, judging from the large selection of attractively packaged raw and processed fish products available in supermarket frozen food sections. Unfortunately, the appearance of some packages is better than their ability to protect product quality. Thus consumers complain about off-flavors and rubbery, watery texture of otherwise attractively packaged products.

WHY PACKAGE

Obviously, the seafood industry continues to grow despite a lack of adequate packaging. However, future expansion of seafood sales will mean moving products through longer distribution chains to reach inland markets. Thus packaging will play a key role in the shift from shop to supermarket merchandising of seafoods, and to ensure high quality, good sales appeal, and consumer satisfaction.

Adequate packaging should

1. *Protect* the product.
2. *Sell* the product.
3. Aid in *convenient use* of the product

Before discussing the many types of packaging materials available for use with seafood, it is important to consider how each of these important functions pertains to the packaging of fishery products.

Protecting the Product

Chilled Product

Even when chilled, fishery products are among the most perishable food products known. Three factors contributing to this rapid loss of quality are *bacterial growth:* fishery products are an excellent source of nutrients for bacteria, which convert these nutrients into foul-smelling compounds; *fat oxidation:* the fats and oils of fishery products are unsaturated and tend to break down easily into rancid compounds; and *enzyme attack:* several digestive and muscle enzymes of fish and shellfish actively break down muscle proteins, which may result in soft, mushy textures.

The action of enzymes can be controlled only by maintaining the product at temperatures as low as possible. Packaging cannot be expected to help much in this respect, except as an insulator during shipment. Low temperature is also essential to minimizing bacterial growth. Packaging can play a key role in the inhibition of bacteria by controlling the environment to which the product is exposed.

Vacuum packaging removes most of the available oxygen needed by spoilage bacteria. Removing oxygen also inhibits fat oxidation and rancidity. An inert gas such as nitrogen can be back-flushed into the package to achieve the same effect. For such packaging to be effective in inhibiting spoilage, a high-barrier packaging film is necessary to prevent the leakage of oxygen into the package. The gas permeability of a particular film is determined by its chemical composition. Materials such as polyethylene, polyvinyl chloride (PVC), and polypropylene allow a relatively high rate of exchange of gases between the inside and outside of a package, whereas materials such as nylon and polyvinylidene chloride (Saran) are excellent barriers to gas transmission. Films may be laminates or coextruded to consist of two or more layers of materials which differ in composition (Fig. 12-1). In this way, several properties such as gas permeability, heat sealing ability, and flexibility at cold temperatures may be built into the same film to meet packaging needs.

Unfortunately, removing oxygen from a package may favor the growth of the bacteria which can produce botulinal toxin. This eventuality is likely to occur when the product is temperature abused such that it is allowed to warm to a fairly high temperature for an extended period. In such cases, it is highly unlikely the product would be edible. However, even the slim possibility of botulinal toxin developing

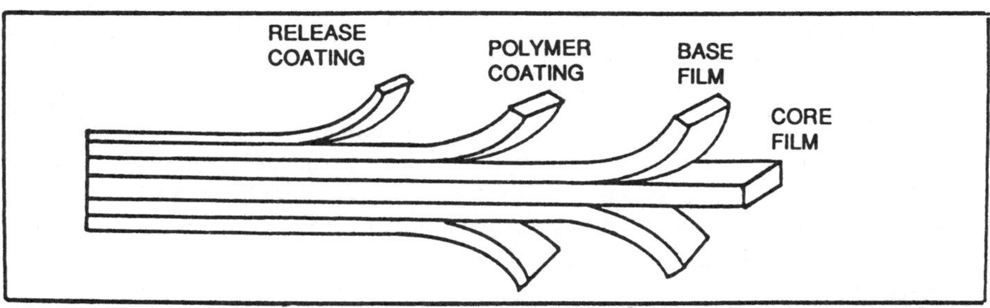

Figure 12-1. An Example of a Laminated Film.

is enough to deter most packers from currently considering vacuum packaging of chilled fish in a barrier-type film.

Vacuum packaging in permeable films that allow gas exchange with the air does not seem to offer any increased safety risk over conventional meat wraps. Such a package would not by itself, however, increase the shelf life of the product, except by preventing further contamination of the product (from hands, air, dust, etc.). Vacuum packaging of frozen fish in oxygen-impermeable (high barrier) films is highly recommended, provided the package is removed or opened prior to thawing.

The concept of modified or controlled atmosphere packaging also has been applied to chilled fish in recent years. In most cases, a gas mixture containing air (or oxygen) and carbon dioxide (CO_2) is injected into a package or shipping container either on a one-shot (modified atmosphere) or continuous (controlled atmosphere) basis. Although reports vary, they indicate that at levels of 30 to 50 percent CO_2 or more, a maximum inhibition of spoilage bacteria is achieved. Extremely high levels of CO_2 do not seem to result in significantly more shelf life and may acidify the product, resulting in flavor or color changes.

As with vacuum packaging, a barrier-type film must be used to prevent loss of CO_2 from the package if the modified atmosphere is to be effective. Many manufacturers claim merely exposing the product to CO_2 will result in increased shelf life, but controlled studies have disproved this claim. The use of a barrier film with this type package again led some researchers to question its safety, even when air or oxygen is incorporated into the gas mixture. Those bacteria which survive the inhibiting effect of the CO_2 may use up the remaining oxygen in the package, thus again possibly favoring toxin formation if the product is temperature abused. For these reasons, it may be advisable to use modified atmosphere packaging only with bulk containers for shipping and storage in which the temperature can be rigidly controlled.

Frozen Product

Although frozen fish are not subject to spoilage by bacterial attack, fat oxidation, enzyme activity, and moisture migration do contribute to quality loss in many cases. Maintenance of a low storage temperature with few temperature fluctuations (such as may be caused by cycling of refrigeration equipment) helps control these factors. The enzyme effect, which in this case produces a rubbery texture rather than the mushiness caused by protein breakdown, would not be significantly affected by the type of package used. Packaging can, however, control fat oxidation and moisture migration very effectively.

Glazing fish "packages" in a protective coating of ice prevents moisture from leaving the meat causing so-called freezer burn. In addition, it slows the movement of oxygen into the meat thus preventing oxidation of the fats.

A skintight vacuum package (obtained by using a shrink film, which we discuss later) of high barrier film performs the same function as a glaze. However, it is generally preferable to a glaze because it is more durable in rough handling, offers better protection against fat oxidation, is more attractive, and can function as the final consumer package when printed with appropriate label information. The film should be skintight to avoid the creation of voids in the package to which moisture could migrate from the fish causing product damage, and frost accumulation under the film that detracts from product attractiveness. Tightly sealed wax or plastic-impregnated cartons may provide some protection against fat oxidation, but do little to protect the product from freezer burn.

Selling the Product

Many processors understand that a package needs to protect the product but do not realize the important role which packaging plays in selling the product.

At Retail

A bulk package can provide retailers with certain conveniences of storage and handling, which may sell them on the product or program. The retail consumer package may also offer the convenience of having the product prepackaged, weighed, priced, and dated.

Institutional

Institutional users of seafoods prefer packaging that fits their particular type and size operation. Ovenable trays, single portion packaging, or a wide variety of other specialized packages may be used to meet their needs. Proper packaging eliminates the need to handle fish, with the drip or odor problems which have come to be associated with fishery products.

Consumer

The consumer is more interested in the product than the package, therefore a primary function of the package is to provide information about the product. Some consumers, accustomed to evaluating fish quality by smell as much as by sight, may sniff a package in an effort to detect off-odors. To allow for this inspection, packaging film of intermediate gas permeability (more permeable than barrier films but less permeable than conventional meat wraps) may be the best choice for many seafood products. It allows the normal odors of good quality seafood to escape the product at such a slow rate that sniffing the sealed package would reveal little odor. Its limited permeability, however, allows odors to escape sufficiently to prevent accumulation of odors that might be objectionable when the package is first opened, regardless of the freshness.

For a chilled product, visibility is important. Clear films with no fogging and dry, fresh-looking product make the best first impression. Consumers like to inspect as much of the product as possible to determine quality. When packaging many fish species, lay fillets with both skin side up and meat side up so the buyer can make a rapid species identification and an adequate quality inspection.

Transparent films also may be used with frozen fish to heighten the visual impact and quality image. The film should be skintight with no frost accumulation within the package.

Product information may be printed on a separate label or directly on the film and should contain such points as

1. *Brand Name and Logo:* To assure the purchaser that the product can be easily identified and, depending upon its quality, either repurchased or avoided in the future.
2. *Product Description:* The product should be clearly described, with common species names used to avoid confusion. Any special attributes of the

product (coating, sauces, etc.) should be brought to the consumer's attention.

3. *Open Dating:* An open date is a "use by" or "good until" date used by many consumers to judge quality shelf life of packaged, perishable products. Open dating has become almost mandatory for chilled products, but may be coded for frozen products to avoid consumer discrimination against products which are high in quality but which have less remaining shelf life than products recently stocked.
4. *Price:* As seafood prices increase, it is often advisable to package smaller quantities to avoid the shock of a high price on individual packages.
5. *Product Usage Information:* Many consumers are afraid of preparing fishery products. They have enjoyed seafood in restaurants but doubt their own ability to prepare it at home. Easy directions for preparation can enhance sales of many seafood products. Printed pictures of "serving suggestions" can add eye appeal and suggest new recipes, which also can be included in the package information.
6. *Nutrition Information:* Consumers are often concerned with good nutrition. Although not necessarily expected or required, including nutrition information is a good idea, particularly on packages of frozen, specially prepared seafood. Packages making nutritional claims for the product are required by law to give a full nutritional label stating serving size, calories, and U.S. Recommended Daily Allowance (RDA) of several major nutrients supplied by each serving.
7. *Inspection Labeling:* Federal inspection is highly regarded by most consumers and, if used by the packer, the inspection and Grade A labeling should be prominently displayed. Regional or private inspections should also be featured when performed in order to bolster consumer confidence in product quality.
8. *Convenience:* Aspects of the package or product should be brought to the consumer's attention.

Product Usage and Convenience

Convenience is not just a function of how the product is prepared prior to sale (whole, fillet, breaded portion, etc.), but also of the package construction and function. Packages which are easy to open, resealable, or which have portions individually wrapped can make using the product a more pleasant experience. Packages can protect, help the product sell, and contribute to easy handling and preparation as well.

A final note of caution concerning packaging and merchandising: Consumers have developed clear ideas about which types of packages "go with" which product forms. To illustrate this point, consider one manufacturer's attempt to market peanut butter in squeeze tubes. The product was a complete failure because consumers had come to associate this type package with toothpaste, not food. In a similar manner, it has been found that retail packages for chilled seafood should mimic closely the appearance of the conventional foam tray-film overwrap meat package to which customers have become accustomed. Such variations as blue trays instead of white, or vacuum film bags instead of film overwrap are acceptable, but substantial variations from this theme have met with consistent consumer resistance. Through long experience, consumers have come to associate wax board cartons, plastic bags, and cello-wrappers with frozen foods; semirigid vacuum pouches and window cartons with processed and cured meats; and foam-tray overwraps with fresh meats. Introducing new package design usually requires strong promotion and clear labeling to overcome consumer resistance to change.

PACKAGE SELECTION

Consumer/Retail Packaging

Chilled Products

Most chilled seafoods are raw, with the exception of some smoked seafoods and the newer category of simulated shellfish. These simulated products may be packaged similarly to cured or processed meats, such as country ham and hot dogs, in vacuum-type (tight fill) pouches. Certainly, rigid temperature controls are necessary to assure a safe product when such packages are constructed of oxygen-impermeable film. Such packages can be made several ways. For draw-down mold packages, for instance, a bottom layer of semirigid film is heated and drawn down into a mold the size of the package base to form the cavity in which the product is placed. Alternatively, the heated film may be drawn down over the product itself, with the product serving as the "mold." After filling, a cover sheet of film is stretched tightly across the open side, usually under vacuum, and heat-sealed to the molded film's edges. The sealed package may then be passed through a "shrink tunnel" where it is heated to allow the specially treated film to shrink and form a skintight package around the product.

Other skintight vacuum packages may be made by enclosing the product either between sheets or flexible film or in a preformed flexible film bag, followed by heat sealing under vacuum and passage through a shrink tunnel. When bags are used, either a vacuum chamber heat-sealing machine or nozzle-type vacuum-draw sealer may be used. Sealing between sheets of flexible film is accomplished on equipment similar to that described for the draw-down mold packages.

Most chilled fish and other raw fishery products are commonly prepackaged on shallow clear or foam plastic trays overwrapped with a transparent plastic film. An absorbent paper pad, covered with plastic to avoid sticking to the product, is sandwiched between the product and the tray to absorb moisture. A film overwrap, a single sheet of transparent film, encases the tray and the product. Usually the film used for this application is polyethylene or polyvinyl chloride of the same type used for wrapping red meat cuts. These films have a high oxygen permeability to maintain the bright red color of meats, which is stabilized by oxygen. The films pose no problem with fishery products, although the product can be smelled through the film. Conversely, some fatty fish may absorb off-odors through such films. Vacuumized bags of a less permeable (but not barrier) film are being evaluated for fresh fish in trays. The overall appearance of the product in trays is reported not to be noticeably different from the traditional overwrap package. Care should be taken, however, to avoid overheating the film in the shrink tunnel which may cause the foam trays to warp or break.

Recent attempts to incorporate modified (CO_2-containing) atmospheres into consumer chill packages have used both the tray-bag package just mentioned and a rigid container. These rectangular containers, normally of clear plastic, may be preformed or formed on a draw mold machine. The package is filled and then sealed with a flexible, transparent top sheet heat-sealed to the flanges of the rigid container. The CO_2-containing gas is purged into the container just prior to sealing the top film. Such a package is currently being marketed, although there has been some consumer resistance to this new package design for chilled fish.

With almost any package of chilled seafood a dry appearance improves the quality image. Product weepage is best controlled by constantly maintaining the product near 32°F (0°C) or below and using an absorbent pad. "Fog" accumulation, which hides the product from view, can be controlled by coating the underside of the package film with a wetting agent to prevent water droplets from forming.

Wet packs of such seafoods as oysters and scallops commonly consist of round containers of either metal, plastic, or coated paperboard, with snap-on or crimped lids. The product should be visible through the lid or a side window made of a clear plastic. The rectangular, rigid, heat-sealed containers previously mentioned also make an attractive wet pack. These may be clear or opaque with the product clearly visible through the top film.

Frozen Products

Retail packages of frozen fishery products may be of the raw types (shrimp, fillets, etc.) or processed/convenience foods (breaded portions, stuffed clams, etc.). Packaging for the raw seafoods is generally simpler in design and more functional (protecting the product) than eye appealing. Raw products traditionally have been packed by smaller production-oriented seafood firms; the larger marketing-oriented food processing companies have marketed most processed and prepared seafoods.

Probably the most popular type of package used today for frozen seafoods is the wax- or plastic-coated paperboard carton. When properly sealed, these cartons can provide both a good oxygen and moisture barrier. A protective overwrap of plastic, coated cellophane, or coated paper may be used, and the product may be encased in an inner bag for additional protection. The greatest disadvantage of these packages is the presence of voids when the package is loose-filled. In such cases, frost accumulation occurs from moisture migration within the package, and freezer burn can result. In addition, these cartons do not always provide a good oxygen barrier and rancid flavors may develop. For solid blocks of frozen fillets or other block-frozen seafoods, however, such a package can provide good protection and stacks neatly and compactly both in the store and home freezer. For added convenience, fillets are often layer-packed with sheets of plastic film sandwiched between fillets to ease removal of separate fillets and to facilitate rapid thawing.

Many frozen seafoods are also packaged in plain coated cellophane or plastic bags or wrappers. These are some of the least costly packages available and can provide a good moisture vapor-oxygen barrier with the correct film selection and proper sealing. Again, frost accumulation is a problem and is especially troublesome when less flexible films such as cellophane, which cannot adhere tightly to other than rectangular-shaped products, are used. However, cellophane films are known to handle well on automatic packaging machinery, having fewer machinery problems than many films.

High barrier, shrink-film vacuum packaging certainly offers the most protection to frozen seafoods. Whereas a glaze may reduce the likelihood of freezer burn (moisture loss) in loose-filled carton- or wrapper-packaged seafoods, rough handling of the package can result in shattering or flaking of the glaze and a lack of protection. High barrier vacuum shrink films provide a tougher protective coat.

Rupture of the film at any point may cause only a small surface area of product being exposed to oxidation or freezer burn, as the remainder of the package will cling tightly to the product. These films are not cheap, however, and some packers are concerned about the safety of such packaging in cases of severe temperature abuse. On consumer package labels it is wise to include a statement such as "open wrapper before thawing" to ensure proper handling.

Foil laminates (metal foil bonded to a plastic or other flexible film) provide excellent barrier/protective properties also. These packaging materials are again more costly, and do not allow a view of the packaged product, but for frozen items they may provide a higher quality image. Additionally, they may be useful in some "cook-in-the-package" applications. The ultimate in convenience packaging for frozen seafoods are those packages which may be used directly as containers for cooking the product. One such package is the so-called boil-in-bag pouch, which may be of nylon or a similar transparent, flexible film or a foil laminate. They are excellent for such heat-and-eat products as sauces, stews, bisques, and chowders, as well as some chunky-type dishes. For processed seafoods of a less fluid form, such as fillets in sauce, stuffed items, and so on, aluminum or the newer ovenable paperboard trays are popular. The selection of ovenable paperboard as opposed to aluminum allows easier preparation in either microwave or conventional ovens. Convenience of preparation is becoming an increasingly desirable factor with today's busier lifestyles. It may be a particularly important factor in marketing seafoods, which traditionally have been viewed as difficult or distasteful to prepare at home.

Freeze-Thaw Products

"Slacking out" of frozen products for sale as chilled products has been a widely used, though seldom advertised, practice in the seafood trade. Recent research and commercial experience have shown that such a practice, properly controlled, can produce a product of high quality and similar salable life as most so-called fresh fish. Additionally, marketing studies indicate that consistent high quality is more important in consumer purchasing decisions of chilled fish than is the handling method employed. Freeze-thaw handling can help alleviate seasonable market gluts and the associated variable pricing and availability which can hamper successful supermarket retailing of chilled fish. Two methods may be employed successfully to merchandise freeze-thaw handled fish. First, the fish may be glazed or, preferably, vacuum packaged for bulk frozen storage until markets are available. Fish are then rapid thawed and packaged for retail in a manner identical to fresh fish. In the second method, the fish are frozen in the retail consumer package, thawed, and sold chilled in the same package. This method requires special packaging to achieve good quality maintenance in both the frozen and thawed-chilled product. One solution has been to glaze the fish, prior to packaging, in an air-permeable film of the fresh meat type. The glaze provides protection to the product while frozen. A specially designed foam tray with grooves and an extra-absorbent pad removes all traces of the glaze from the package upon thawing, leaving a dry, fresh appearance to the chilled, packaged product. Such techniques are equally adaptable to many shellfish and could help fishery product sale.

Bulk Packaging Techniques

The master carton (Fig. 12-2) is an important part of the bulk shipping container. These cartons are normally of wax- or plastic-coated corrugated paperboard, and

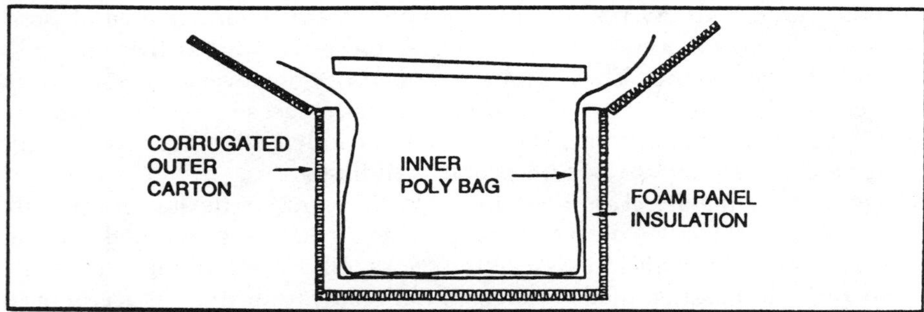

Figure 12-2. Insulated Master Shipping Carton.

may be strapped shut for added protection. If the product is frozen or an internal refrigerant (ice, CO_2 snow, etc.) is to be contained in the package, an inner wall consisting of a rigid foam box or panels may be used to insulate the container. If ice is to be used in the container, a plastic inner lining may be necessary to prevent leaking. Variations on this general design may include the following:

1. Corrugated dividers in the package interior to protect individual retail packages from shock and stacking pressure.
2. Use of a barrier-type inner bag for modified atmosphere packaging of the retail packages within.
3. Use of a long, low-profile master carton to eliminate crushing of the inner packages caused by their being stacked too high.
4. Coating the outside of the master carton with shiny metallic foil to shield the package from rising temperatures when in direct contact with the sun's rays.

The remaining components of a bulk shipping container are the inner (bulk or retail) containers and an optimal refrigerant such as ice or dry ice when mechanical refrigeration is either not used or is used as supplement for added safety. With frozen foods, the outer master carton is often omitted when the inner containers hold 10 pounds (4.5 kg) or more of product. Chilled product also may be packaged either in bulk (10 to 20 pound/4.5 to 9.1 kg), or retail-sized (1 to 3 pound/0.45 to 1.36 kg) inner containers within the master carton.

Chilled Products

As mentioned, large quantities of chilled seafoods are still shipped loose, packed in ice, in wooden or wax/plastic-coated corrugated boxes. The seafood is usually in direct contact with the ice; however, some delicate products such as fillets may be contained in metal trays or plastic bags immersed in the ice. Although packaging with ice maintains product quality reasonably well, it has several drawbacks:

1. *Product Temperature:* Melting ice maintains the product temperature at 32°F (0°C). A more ideal temperature to prolong shelf life would be near 29°F (1.7°C), just below the freezing point.
2. *Leakage, Leaching:* Ice packs are leaky and normally must be isolated from other food shipments. Although melting ice may have benefits in terms of

"washing" bacteria off the product, leaching of the tissues can also result in significant product weight shrinkage.

3. *Weight of Ice:* Shipping products on ice increases the shipping weight by 30 to 50 percent and is thus more expensive.

Bulk shipping containers which rely on mechanical refrigeration or non-ice refrigerants avoid these problems. The simplest of these may consist of the same types of inner packs as are used for isolating the product from the ice in iced packs, but they are contained in a master package with no ice. Besides the metal trays and plastic bags mentioned earlier, one well-known system recently introduced is a high density polyethylene deep tray with a flexible film heat-sealed on the top lid. This package is leak and odor free and quite strong. The containers are normally made to hold either 10 or 20 pounds (4.5 to 9.1 kg) of seafood and are sized to fit inside a master corrugated carton. They are actually larger versions of the rigid plastic trays previously described for retail packaging. The seafood from such containers must be repackaged in smaller quantities for supermarket sale or may be simply displayed on ice in fish retail outlets.

Some refrigerants other than ice which may be used in master cartons of chilled fish include CO_2 snow (dry ice) and the reusable "blue ice" refrigerant packs. CO_2 snow has been widely used to top-coat master cartons of chilled poultry. It may be conveniently generated by expanding liquid CO_2 through special nozzles. This "snow" is very cold (-78.9°C) and the crust freezes the product which is in direct contact with it. As the snow "melts" (sublimates) it forms CO_2 vapor, which inhibits bacterial growth when the master carton or shipping container is sealed. Care must be exercised, however, to exhaust CO_2 from the packing and storage areas to prevent suffocation of the workers.

Reusable refrigerants may be constructed to melt at temperatures below 32°F (0°C), thereby maintaining a lower temperature than ice. These products must be reused to be economical, however.

A unique freeze-thaw approach to handling chilled fish, developed by National Marine Fishery Service scientists, involved freezing fish and allowing them to thaw slowly in transit. Such a system might require an absorbent foam or similar material to take care of the thaw-dip associated with such a handling method.

Frozen Product

Master cartons for frozen seafoods which are glazed or packaged in smaller bulk or retail-sized containers may often have many openings to allow free exchange of cold air with the packaged product. Within the inner bags or cartons, the product may be individually quick frozen (IQF) and loose-filled, or tightly frozen together in either blocks or layer packs. Layer packs separate the seafood layers by pliofilm, parchment, or waxed paper. A satisfactory layer pack would ensure easy removal of each product yet be less expensive than producing IQF products.

HANDLING CHARACTERISTICS OF PACKAGING MATERIALS

Handling characteristics include the performance characteristics of the packaging materials during the actual packaging process (often called machinability characteristics of the material) as well as the strength and durability of the material when it is in contact with irregular product surfaces and/or when it is subjected to physical abuse in normal distribution.

Machinability characteristics which may be important, depending on the type of packaging equipment used, could include tear strength, stretchability, shrinkability, slippage, and heat-sealing or closure-sealing capacities.

If the material is to bear printed information, its inking characteristics would be important, although the type of printing process is often more important than the material being printed upon. Tack strength is often important with flexible films which must bond easily to each other or to another material. Machinability is influenced by both machine design and package material characteristics; both should be well matched for satisfactory performance in high-speed packaging operations.

The toughness of the packaging material is usually a function of cost for a given category of packaging materials, whether clear film, paperboard, metal foils, or rigid plastics. For cost effectiveness, the materials selected should only be durable enough to provide the level of package protection needed at a particular stage of distribution. For example, master cartons of corrugated paperboard, possibly with dividers to compartmentalize the retail packages, can be much cheaper protection during shipping than the highly durable clear packaging films for the retail package. Keep in mind, however, that products in self-service counters are often roughly handled by both store personnel and consumers. Frozen products receive especially rough treatment, so packaging materials for frozen products must remain pliable and be able to withstand shock at low temperatures. Packaging films used to overwrap or bag chilled seafoods with sharp fins or bones must also be especially tough unless the package is designed to avoid contact between the film and the product.

CHAPTER

13

Freezing

Joseph J. Licciardello

When fish is frozen and stored at subfreezing temperatures, bacterial growth is arrested, and both enzyme and chemical actions are slowed to a rate that is commensurate with the temperature. Thus the fish is preserved, and the shelf life is extended until the retarded chemical/enzymatic reactions eventually produce undesirable quality changes in either flavor, texture, or appearance.

Bacteria, like all other living cellular forms, require free water for growth and multiplication. The reason that their growth is suppressed in frozen foods is that most of the water has been frozen into ice and is not available as free water. Dehydration, another method of food preservation, is similar to freezing in that there is insufficient free water available to permit the bacteria to grow and multiply.

Freezing may destroy from 50 to 90 percent of the bacteria on fish. During frozen storage there is a continued slow steady die-off of the bacteria, with the rate of decrease depending on the temperature and bacterial species. Results of a study showing the effect of freezing and frozen storage on bacterial content of haddock are presented in Table 13-1.

That portion of the original microbial population that does survive freezing and storage will remain viable during frozen storage, but in a dormant state. Upon defrosting, these surviving microorganisms will begin to grow and reproduce. If the fish are held for a sufficiently long period at temperatures above freezing, these bacteria will ultimately cause spoilage. However, thawed fish does not spoil faster than never-frozen fish. In a study with cod, frozen-thawed portions were found to have as long or a slightly longer iced-storage life compared with nonfrozen portions.

FACTORS AFFECTING FROZEN SHELF LIFE

The most important factor governing the storage life of frozen fish is storage temperature—the lower the temperature, the longer the shelf life. As a general rule, the rate of chemical reactions doubles for every 10° increase in temperature. Quality deterioration in frozen foods is a result of chemical reactions, so the

Table 13-1. ***Effect of Freezing and Storage on Total Bacterial Counts of Haddock***

Time at Which Counts Were Made	Total Bacterial Count Per Gram: Fresh Sample	Slightly Stale Sample	Stale Sample
Just before freezing	25,000	500,000	12,000,000
Immediately after freezing	1,500	28,000	950,000
After 1 month at 0°F (–18°C)	900	16,000	430,000
After 6 months at 0°F (–18°C)	00	14,000	300,000
After 12 months at 0°F (–18°C)	600	11,000	270,000

importance of decreasing the storage temperature to as low as is economically feasible is apparent. For many chemical reactions to take place free water is required, and although most of the water in fish has been frozen at a temperature of 18°F (–7.8°C), a small amount of unfrozen water remains even at temperatures below 0°F (–18°C). Table 13-2 shows the reported proportion of water frozen in fish at various temperatures.

Composition

The proximate composition (moisture, fat, protein, ash) of fish is species-related. The attribute more closely associated with frozen storage life is probably the fat content because of its susceptibility to oxidation and concomitant rancid odors/ flavors. Although there is no official definition for lean or fatty fish, an arbitrary definition would classify fish with less than 2 percent fat as "lean," between 2 and 5 percent fat as "moderately fat," and greater than 5 percent as "fatty." Table 13-3 provides a list of the average fat content of various seafoods and their classification based on average fat content. Rancidity is not usually a major problem with lean fish such as cod and haddock, and quality loss during frozen storage is generally associated with a textural toughening. However, rancidity is more of a problem with fatty species such as mackerel, herring, and salmon. It should be noted that with some species, particularly the pelagic fish, fat content varies seasonally. For example, mackerel can have a fat content of 20 to 25 percent prior to spawning, and about 5 percent immediately following spawning. Fatty fish do not undergo serious textural changes during frozen storage.

Condition of the Fish

Fish to be frozen should be as fresh as possible because freezing and frozen storage cannot improve quality. At best, frozen storage will only maintain fish in about the

Table 13-2. ***Percentage of Water Frozen in Fish as a Function of Temperature***

Temperature (°F/°C)	Percentage of Water Frozen
30.3 (–0.9°C)	0
30 (–1.1°C)	32
28 (–2.2°C)	61
26 (–3.3°C)	76
24 (–4.4°C)	83
22 (–5.5°C)	86
18 (–7.8°C)	89

Table 13-3. *Average Percentage of Fat Content and Range for Various Types of Seafood*

Lean		Moderately Fat		Fatty	
Clam, soft shell	2.0 (1.4–2.5)	Barracudas	3.2 ± 0.4 (0.2–10)	Albacore	5.4 ± 0.9 (0.7–18)
Cod	0.5 ± 0.2	Bluefish	3.8 ± 0.8 (2–5)	Butterfish	7.2 ± 1.9 (1–24)
Crab, blue	1.0 ± 0.1 (0.4–1.5)	Halibut (Atlantic)	2.4 ± 0.9 (0.7–5.2)	Dogfish	14.5 ± 2.2
Crab, king	0.7 ± 0.2 (0.2–1.4)	Scup	3.7 ± 0.8 (1.2–5.9)	Eel	17.3 ± 2.6 (13–22)
Flounder	1.0 ± 0.2 (0.1–2.9)	Smelt	3.9 ± 0.7 (2.3–6.7)	Herring (Atlantic)	15.7 ± 1.9 (2.4–29)
Grouper	0.8 ± 0.2 (0.2–2.3)	Swordfish	4.1 ± 0.7 (2.0–6.4)	Mackerel (Atlantic)	16.3 ± 2.1 (1–24)
Haddock	0.5 ± 0.2 (0.1–1.2)	Tuna (yellowfin)	2.2 ± 0.5 (0.1–9.5)	Salmon (Chinook)	11.5 ± 2.4 (2.2–19)
Hakes (Urophycis)	0.7	Turbot	2.9	Salmon (Coho)	5.7 ± 0.5 (3.1–9)
Halibut (Pacific)	1.1 ± 0.2 (0.6–3.6)	Weakfish	3.2 ± 0.4 (1.4–4.3)	Shad	8.3 ± 1.7 (1.7–15)
Ocean perch	1.3 ± 0.2 (0.6–2.2)	Whiting (Atlantic)	2.4 (0.7–5.0)	Trout (rainbow)	11.7
Oysters	1.5 ± 0.1 (0.7–2.6)				
Pollock (Atlantic)	0.5 ± 0.1 (0.2–1)				
Scallop	0.7 ± 0.2 (0.3–1.6)				
Squid	1.0 ± 0.2 (0.5–1.4)				

same condition as it was just prior to freezing, and the frozen storage life of poor quality fish will not be as long as that of good initial quality fish. For example, silver hake stored two days postmortem in ice prior to freezing were found to have a storage life of twelve months at 0°F (–18°C) whereas fish held four days in ice only had a frozen storage life of six months. In addition, poor initial quality frozen fish will drip more upon defrosting, which will affect the texture of the cooked fish.

Season of Year

During spawning and immediately thereafter, the energy reserves (stored fat) of the fish are at their lowest. To compensate for this depletion of fat, the flesh contains more water than normal and is relatively soft. Fish which have been frozen in this condition will have a less desirable texture after freezing, because of excessive water drip upon thawing.

Rigor Mortis

Immediately after death, fish muscles are limp and pliable, but soon afterward they contract, become rigid, at which time the fish is said to be in rigor. After a period of time, depending on the temperature, the muscles relax, once again become soft, and rigor is said to be resolved. Fish muscle contains a carbohydrate (glycogen) which serves as an energy source of muscular activity. The more glycogen present at the time of death, the longer the fish remain in rigor. This characteristic is desirable in that bacterial growth is retarded while fish are in rigor. Fish which are in poor physical condition, such as after spawning, or fish which have struggled hard during capture will have depleted most of their glycogen and will consequently undergo a short period of rigor. The state of rigor has an important bearing on the quality of frozen fish in that it can cause gaping, excess thaw drip, and toughness. Gaping is a condition when individual muscle flakes have become separated and the fillet appears ragged. This condition can result when the fish muscle undergoes rigor at a high temperature, particularly if the glycogen content is high. In this situation the muscle contraction is so great that the bonds of connective tissue holding the muscle flakes together are broken. The drastic muscle contraction that occurs at a high rigor temperature will also be responsible for a greater drip loss and toughness after thawing and cooking. Gaping can also result when an attempt is made to straighten out bent fish in rigor in order to facilitate filleting. This action forces muscle fibers to break and separate.

If a fish has been filleted prerigor, the fillet will shrink when rigor does develop, more noticeably if the temperature is high, due to muscular contraction, and the texture will probably be tough. In addition, the frozen fillet may show a gray discoloration, which is a physical effect resulting from cutting across prerigor muscle fibers. When whole fish undergo rigor, shrinkage is at a minimum because the muscles are anchored to the skeletal frame. Nevertheless, if a fish is frozen before the onset of rigor, the process of rigor will take place slowly during frozen storage, and resolution will eventually occur. But if the frozen flesh is cooked before rigor has been resolved, the muscle will contract during cooking, lose cellular fluid, and be tough. This phenomenon is known as thaw rigor and it can be a problem with high quality fillets frozen aboard freezer trawlers within a few hours after capture before the fish have passed through rigor. Even fish sticks made from prerigor fish can undergo distortion during cooking. To avoid thaw rigor, it is recommended that the fish be conditioned prior to thawing or cutting into sticks by holding for a period of time at a relatively high temperature in the freezer, thus inducing rigor.

Throughout this discussion we have stressed the adverse effect of excess thaw drip on the texture of cooked fish. Thaw drip can be mitigated somewhat by a brief dip in a salt solution prior to freezing. This treatment solubilizes the surface protein, forming a skin on the cut surface and thus helping seal in the moisture. A ten- to twenty-second dip in 3 to 6 percent brine should suffice. Brine dips should not be applied to fatty fish because of the possibility that this treatment may promote rancidity. This danger can be averted by using one of the phosphates, such as sodium tripolyphosphate or hexametaphosphate in the dip solution in lieu of the salt. However, either of these treatments increases the sodium content of the fish flesh, which may be undesirable in this age of dietary salt consciousness. In employing dips for fish fillets, the processor should be ever aware of the potential hazards of increased bacterial buildup in the brine solution unless proper temperature control is maintained and the solution is changed often.

Freezing Rate

Depending on the fat content, the water content of various fish species can range from 60 to 90 percent. For the most part this moisture is located within the tissue cells along with dissolved salts and soluble proteins, all of which make up the sarcoplasm. Some water is present in the interstitial spaces between the cells, and some is chemically bound to the muscle proteins. The ability of proteins to bind water is referred to as water holding capacity. When this capacity is impaired in frozen flesh foods, such as through denaturation or damage to the proteins, the product will exude some fluid (drip), and the texture will toughen. When fish muscle is subjected to a subfreezing temperature, the muscle temperature drops at a steady rate until it reaches about 28 to 30°F (–2.2 to –1.8°C), which is the freezing range for fish muscle. At this point ice crystals begin to form within the tissues, and the temperature remains relatively constant. When most of the cellular water has been frozen, the muscle temperature begins to drop rapidly once again, until it eventually equilibrates with the temperature of the environment. With a fast freezing rate, ice crystals that form within the muscles will be numerous but small, resulting in little damage to the tissues. If the freezing rate is slow, a few ice crystals will form, but these will be large and can disrupt tissue cells. The ensuing damage will be evident, upon thawing, as drip. In addition, enzymes, which had been contained in compartments in the intact cell, may now be released to react with suitable substrates to produce undesirable changes in flavor or texture. Other changes besides ice crystallization are also going on within the cells as the cellular water freezes. The naturally present salts are becoming increasingly concentrated in the remaining unfrozen fluid. This concentrated solution damages the proteins and impairs cell permeability as a result of intracellular pH changes and what is referred to as a "salting-out effect." As a consequence, there is a reduced water holding capacity by the proteins, with large amounts of fluid exuded from the frozen fish upon defrosting or cooking.

Loss of a large quantity of cellular water after thawing results in loss of nutrients, flavor, and succulence. The texture will usually be tough, stringy, and fibrous. To help preserve texture during freezing, it is imperative that the fish muscle temperature pass through the critical freezing zone (32 to 23°F/0 to –5°C) as rapidly as possible. This way the formation of large ice crystals within the tissue cells can be avoided. Residence time of concentrated salt solutions with the proteins and effects of intracellular pH changes can be minimized as well. The critical freezing rate is defined as the time required for the internal temperature of a fish product to drop from 32 to 23°F (0 to –5°C) (the critical freezing zone). It is within this temperature region that most of the cellular freezing damage occurs.

There are three general categories of freezing rates: (1) slow or sharp freezing, (2) quick or fast freezing, and (3) ultrarapid freezing. These are discussed in the following section. Figure 13-1 shows the freezing curves for a block of fish fillets frozen by each method.

Slow Freezing

In slow freezing, or sharp freezing, the temperature of the product remains within the critical zone for more than two hours. The term *deep freezing* refers to freezing a food to 0°F (–18°C) and storing it at or below that temperature, without regard to the rate at which the product was frozen. Slow freezing is accomplished by placing the fish, usually on trays or on shelves, in a freezer room or cabinet with little or no air circulation. In this situation the freezing rate is slow because of the poor heat transfer characteristics of still air. If the freezer room temperature is not sufficiently low, the product, if thick, may remain in the critical zone for a relatively long time. Figure 13-1 shows that the 2.25-inch (5.7 cm) thick block of fillets frozen in still air at 0°F (–18°C) (shelf-frozen) remained in the critical zone for about nineteen hours.

Quick or Fast Freezing

A method in which the internal temperature of the product passes through the critical zone in two hours or less is classified as quick freezing or fast freezing. By increasing the flow of cold air over the fish, as in a tunnel blast freezer, the removal

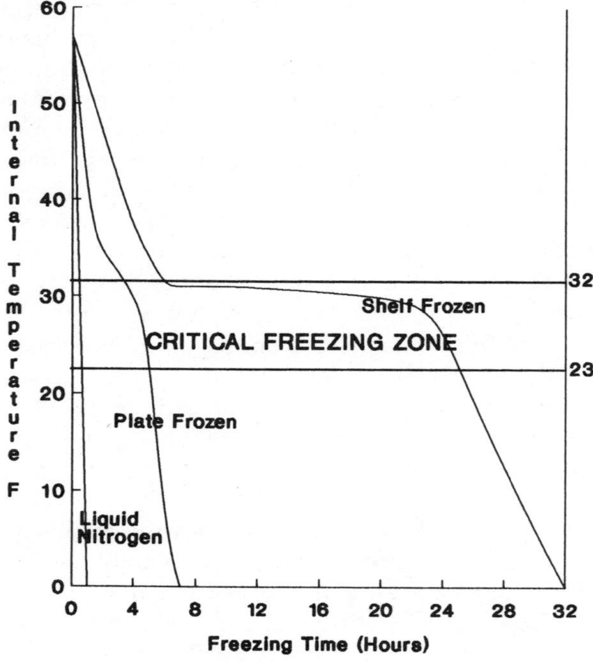

Figure 13-1. Critical Freezing Time.

of heat from the fish is accelerated, and quick freezing can be attained. Placing the product to be frozen in direct or indirect contact with the refrigerant is a still more efficient method for removal of heat. The plate freezer is an example of an indirect contact freezer. Plate freezers can be of the horizontal type, which is preferred for the freezing of blocks or cartons of fish, or the vertical type, developed for freezing whole fish at sea. Fish to be frozen, usually packaged in cartons, are placed in a metal or wooden frame between two parallel movable hollow plates through which a refrigerant is circulated. The product is frozen while under pressure between the plates. The pressurized contact with the plates not only speeds up the rate of freezing, it also produces a smooth flat surface on the faces of the block of fish by preventing the normal expansion that occurs during freezing. It also eliminates voids or air spaces that could be a focal point for oxidation (rancidity) and that could result in irregular shaped fish sticks cut from these blocks.

In direct contact freezing, fish are frozen either by being submerged in or sprayed with a suitable refrigerated liquid, usually a brine solution. A disadvantage of this method is that prolonged contact of the fish flesh with brine will lead to a high salt uptake. Excessive salt absorption not only results in an undesirable salty taste, it may also promote rancidity during frozen storage. Generally, salt uptake is serious only when the fish are kept in the brine (23 percent NaCl) in excess of four hours at a brine temperature below 10°F (–12.2°C). Oily fish do not absorb as much salt in brine freezing as do the lean species; however, rancidity is more of a problem with oily fish. Small fish take up more salt during brine freezing than do large fish because of their greater surface-to-volume ratio.

Immersion brine freezing is generally employed aboard West Coast tuna boats for at-sea freezing. In this application when the temperature of the fish has been lowered close to 0°F (–18°C), the freezing brine is drained and the fish are kept frozen in air maintained at 0°F (–18°C).

Ultrarapid Freezing

Spraying fish fillets or whole fish with or submerging them in either liquid nitrogen (–320°F/–195°C), liquid carbon dioxide (–109°F/–78°C), or Freon 12 (dichlorodifluoromethane) (–22°F/–30°C) results in ultrarapid freezing. Freezing rate is a function of the temperature difference between the surface temperature of the product to be frozen and the temperature at the center of the product. This temperature differential is the driving force in the removal of heat, and with these liquified cryogenic gases it can be very large and thus conducive to very rapid freezing. Another variable associated with freezing rate is the heat transfer coefficient. This parameter is small in the case of cryogenic freezing, which again promotes very rapid freezing. In actual practice, a fish fillet can be hard frozen in liquid nitrogen within several minutes. The disadvantage of this method, disregarding economics, is that the frozen fillet may have a chalky appearance (a physical phenomenon resulting from the light scattering by the numerous small ice crystals formed) and a ragged surface and may be brittle and shatter easily if dropped. The advantage is that the flavor and texture of ultrarapidly frozen fish will more closely resemble that of fresh fish. Freezing time is also a function of the product thickness. Figure 13-2 presents freezing curves which show how long it takes fish fillet slabs of different thickness to reach an internal temperature of 0°F (–18°C). Note the critical freezing time for a 2.5-inch (6.4 cm) thick block compared to a 1-inch (2.5 cm) block. It has been observed that a portion of fish twice as thick as another will require two to four times as long to freeze.

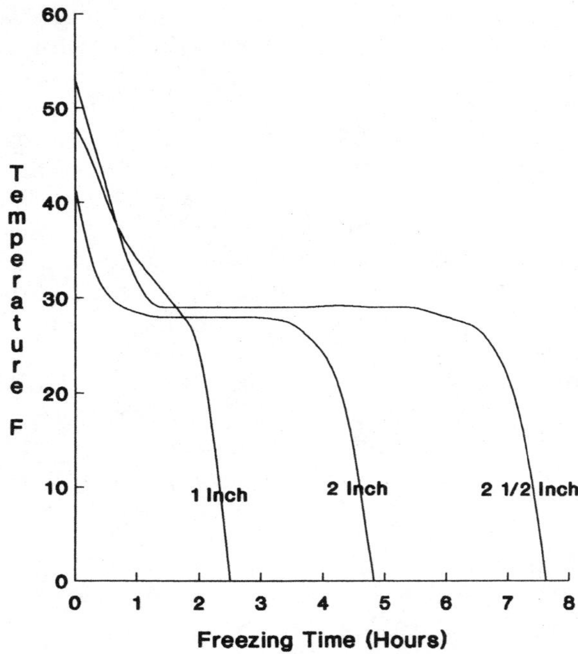

Figure 13-2. Freezing Time/Thickness.

The amount of heat that can be removed from a load of fish per unit of time depends mainly on the horsepower rating of the freezer compressor. Overloading a freezer with product will only serve to lengthen the time required to freeze the entire batch. Overloading a freezer will also restrict air circulation, which can reduce the freezing rate. Unfrozen product packaged in individual retail cartons or in master cartons should not be placed in the freezer storage room to be frozen, because the container material will act as an insulator, slowing the freezing rate.

STORAGE TEMPERATURE

Many variables influence the storage life of frozen fish, but the single most important factor is storage temperature. The rates of quality deterioration for frozen red hake fillets over a wide range of storage temperatures are shown in Figure 13-3. There is a dramatic difference in spoilage rate between fillets stored at +20°F (–6.7°C) and fillets stored at 0°F (–18°C). A further 20° drop in storage temperature produces a significant but much lesser effect. In the temperature region of –20 to –80°F (–29 to –62°C) the difference in spoilage rate appears to be so small as to probably not warrant added cost. It should be pointed out that these data were obtained with a lean fish species and may not apply exactly to a fatty fish. The Association of Food and Drug Officials of the U.S. code of handling practices for frozen foods recommends that frozen foods be stored at a temperature of 0°F (–18°C) or below. For fishery products a storage temperature of 0°F (–18°C) may be adequate for short-term storage where a fast turnover is expected, but for long-term storage this temperature would be inadequate for maintaining quality. In Britain the recommended temperature for long-term storage of frozen fish is –20°F (–29°C).

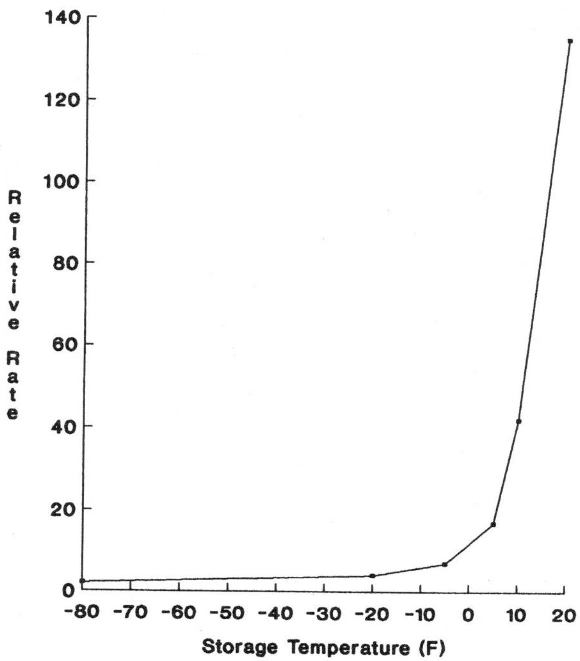

Figure 13-3. Relative Rate/Storage Temperature.

It is a difficult task to assign absolute storage-life values for different fish species at various temperatures because many variables are involved. Some of these variables such as season of year, condition or quality of fish at time of freezing, and freezing rate have already been discussed. Factors not discussed include fishing ground, product style (whole fish, fillets, minced, etc.), and packaging mode. Even the method of preparation or cooking the product can mask subtle storage changes and affect shelf life. For example, a fish fillet fried in oil would have a longer acceptable storage life than the same product baked or steamed. Moreover, the stage of quality at which a frozen fish may be considered unacceptable is highly subjective, varying among individuals, particularly on a regional basis. Nevertheless, based on published scientific data, an attempt has been made in Figure 13-4 to illustrate the effect of storage temperature on shelf life of several common marine fish species. Note the relatively shorter frozen shelf lives of the fatty fish (herring, mackerel) compared to the lean fish (haddock, whiting, pollock). As previously indicated, quality deterioration in frozen stored fatty fish is due to oxidative rancidity, whereas in lean fish protein denaturation initiates textural changes that eventually terminate shelf life. The gadiod fish (cod, haddock, pollock, etc.) are especially prone to protein denaturation during frozen storage because they contain an enzyme whose activity produces compounds that cause the muscle fibers to cross-link, resulting in a tough, fibrous texture. This enzyme activity is greatest in the hakes.

The shelf lives depicted in Figure 13-4 are based on product acceptability. However, it is often of interest to a manufacturer to determine the storage time at a given temperature at which the product retains a high quality. Table 13-4 shows some estimated (by the International Institute of Refrigeration) high quality shelf lives for various seafoods at different storage temperatures.

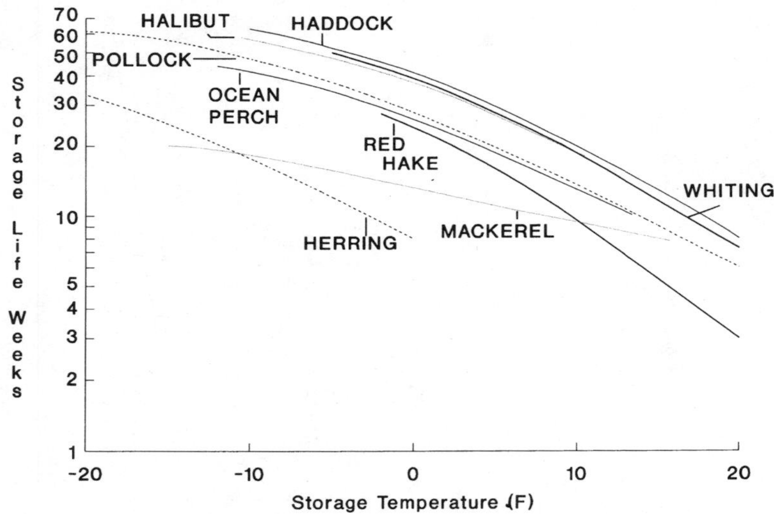

Figure 13-4. Storage Life/Temperature.

PACKAGING

The prime function of frozen seafood packages should be to prevent contact with air and loss of moisture during storage. It also precludes contamination by bacteria or extraneous matter, prevents absorption of refrigerator odors, and facilitates labeling. Migration of moisture from the surface of a frozen fish product to the surrounding air through evaporation, or more precisely sublimation, causes a condition known as freezer burn or desiccation. Evaporation of moisture causes product weight loss, which can lead to legal problems if the product does not comply with the declared net weight. Evaporation also imparts a white, dry wrinkled appearance to the surface, and the affected portion of the fish will be tough and fibrous after cooking. Most freezers do not operate at a constant temperature; instead, they undergo cyclic fluctuations due to defrost cycles and

Table 13-4. *High Quality Shelf Life (Months) of Various Frozen Seafood at Three Different Temperatures*

	Storage Temperatures		
Seafood	0°F (–18°C)	–13°F (–25°C)	–20°F (–28.9°C)
Cod	3–5	6–8	8–10
Haddock	3–5	6–8	8–10
Flatfish	4–6	–10	
Fatty fish	2–3	3–5	6
Lobster, crab	2		
Clams	3–4		
Oysters	2–4		
Scallops	3–4		
Shrimp	6		

opening and closing of the freezer doors. When fish is packaged in a loose fitting plastic bag or oversized container and placed in a freezer, moisture will evaporate from the fish surface until the air within the package becomes saturated or reaches equilibrium relative humidity. If the freezer temperature rises, more moisture will be evaporated until a new equilibrium relative humidity is reached for that temperature. When the freezer temperature decreases, the water vapor in the air space of the package will precipitate as snow inside the package. This continual action of evaporation and precipitation with fluctuating temperature behaves as a water pump and results in dehydration of the fish flesh. A loss in overall product quality generally occurs as a result of cycling freezer temperature. If a fishery product is stored at some fluctuating freezer temperature, such as +10° to –10°F (–12.2 to –23.3°C) the effective mean temperature is not 0°F (–18°C) but a temperature that will be a few degrees above.

Whenever unpackaged fish are stored in a freezer for an appreciable time, the vaporized moisture will condense as frost on the evaporator plates. This will hamper the efficiency of the evaporator in addition to lowering the quality of the fish. This process can be prevented, to an extent, by increasing the surface area and temperature of the evaporator plates. A skintight, moisture-impermeable package and minimal opening of freezer doors will reduce the incidence of freezer burn.

Hydrolytic rancidity is not considered a major cause of quality degradation in frozen fish. On the other hand, oxidative rancidity is charcterized by an objectionable change in flavor producing tastes that are sharp, bitter, or musty, reminiscent of linseed oil, cod liver oil, and paint. Rancidity is often accompanied by a change in appearance (color). The fatty strip along the lateral line or the dark red muscle may change to a yellow or rust color. In pigmented fish, such as salmon and ocean perch, the red color may either fade or become yellow to orange.

How frozen fish is stored affects its susceptibility to becoming rancid. Fish frozen whole are less prone to developing rancidity compared to gutted fish or fillets, because less surface area is exposed. Packing fish tightly in bulk also tends to reduce incidence of rancidity. In fillet blocks, rancidity has been mainly confined to the surface when the blocks were not fully protected from the air. The process of mincing fish creates a large surface area which increases contact of the flesh with air, thus enhancing rancidity. It also disintegrates the integrity of the cell, releasing enzymes and other substances which can promote either oxidative reactions causing flavor changes or textural changes. Thus the frozen shelf life of minced fish is much less compared to that of the intact muscle.

Some practical methods for controlling rancidity are as follows:

1. Store the fish at as low a temperature as is economically feasible. Chemical reaction rates slow down with a decrease in temperature.
2. Avoid contact of the fish flesh with metals such as iron and copper, which act as catalysts in the reaction between oxygen and fat.
3. Treat the fish with an antioxidant, a chemical substance which prevents or retards oxidation. The water-soluble antioxidants such as sodium erythorbate and ascorbic acid (vitamin C), or the fat-soluble phenolic antioxidants such as BHA (butylated hydroxyanisole) and BHT (butylated hydroxytoluene) can delay the onset of rancidity if used properly.
4. Remove the fatty strip or dark muscle along the lateral line and just beneath the skin either manually or with an automatic deep-skinning machine.

5. Wash fish fillets prior to freezing to remove blood, which is known to accelerate rancidity formation.
6. Treat the fish with a chelating agent such as EDTA (ethylenediaminetetra-acetic acid), citric acid, or polyphosphates. These compounds bind metals such as iron and copper which accelerate rancidity.
7. Package fish under vacuum in an oxygen barrier material. Nylon and polyvinylidene dichloride films have excellent oxygen barrier properties. Polyethylene of less than 4 mil thickness would probably not be suitable. Metal foil and metal containers would be highly satisfactory but the cost may be too high.
8. For large fish that are individually frozen or frozen in blocks, a water glaze can form a protective coating. The disadvantage of a water glaze is that during prolonged storage the glaze evaporates if the fish have not been packaged carefully and has to be replenished. A glaze formed from pure water can be brittle. An improvement can be made by adding a small amount of corn syrup to the glazing water. The addition of a water-soluble antioxidant such as ascorbic acid to the glaze water also enhances its protective effect.

THAWING

Frozen fish can be defrosted several ways such as in air, in water, or by cooking directly from the frozen state. With fish and fish products packaged in various ways, some defrost methods may be more applicable than others. Individually frozen fish or fish blocks can be thawed overnight at room temperature in still air. It has been recommended that the air temperature not exceed 65°F (18.3°C). It is also suggested that the defrost time not be too long, otherwise the product may dry out or be at a suitable temperature long enough to favor bacterial growth. Some protein damage also can occur during thawing if the product temperature remains in the critical zone for an excessive time. The frozen product is defrosted by conducting heat from the surface to the center, so product thickness will influence defrost time. A report from the Torry Research Station indicated that a 4-inch (10.2 cm) thick cod block required about twenty hours to thaw in still air at 60°F (15.6°C). The defrost time can be shortened by thawing in moving air. It is recommended that the air be humidified to prevent surface dehydration, at a velocity of not less than 1,200 ft/min. (365.8 m/min.) and not exceed 70°F (21.1°C).

Thawing in water, because of its better heat transfer property, is faster than thawing in air. The water should not be too warm and should be kept moving. Whole fish or packaged fish may be satisfactorily thawed in water, but unpackaged fillets should never be defrosted in this manner because they become waterlogged and lose flavor through leaching.

A vacuum heat thawing system is claimed to reduce thawing time. In this system the frozen food is placed in a vacuum chamber containing a source of warm water. At low pressure the water vaporizes and condenses on the frozen food to provide the heat necessary for thawing. There are some electric/electronic defrosting techniques which are more rapid than those thus far discussed, because the heat generated is produced uniformly throughout the frozen mass. Since frozen fish at low temperatures is a poor conductor of electricity, in practice it is customary to prewarm the frozen fish in water prior to thawing by this method. This pretreatment decreases the electrical resistance of the product, allowing a larger current to pass through and thus producing more internal heat. Microwave heating is another rapid thaw method that employs very high frequency microwaves at 2,450 MHz to generate heat. This operation can be either batch or continuous. Microwave energy can be used to partially thaw a frozen mass of fish, shrimp, and so on, to permit separation of the individual units still in the frozen state. Tempering of fish blocks to be sawed into sticks or portions can also be achieved with microwave heating. In deciding which method to choose, the output of the plant, capital cost, type of operation (batch or continuous), maintenance and operating cost, production rate, and flexibility of the method to accommodate different products must be considered.

In some processing operations double freezing may be necessary. For example, fish may be frozen whole at sea, then defrosted at the processing plant for filleting, and the fillets then refrozen. It must be understood that freezing and frozen storage will cause some damage to the proteins. Upon thawing some drip will be expressed. With repeated freezing and thawing the textural damage will be cumulative. Although an acceptable product can still be attained after double freezing, the quality will be less than with a once-frozen product.

TEMPERATURE INDICATORS

In recent years some regulatory authorities have considered legislation requiring mandatory open date or pull date labeling on frozen and perishable foods to provide quality assurance to the consumer. Opponents argue that the major function affecting quality of frozen food is temperature and not the time elapsed since freezing. If the frozen product were maintained at some known constant temperature from processing plant to consumer, then shelf life would be predictable, and open date labeling would effectively provide quality assurance since time-temperature tolerances could be easily determined for any product. However, in commercial practice once the frozen product leaves the processor's frozen warehouse, it is subjected to fluctuating temperatures during transport, unloading, and in the retail cabinet.

There are some warning devices that reflect the temperature experience of a frozen product. The defrost indicator is a simple device containing a eutectic salts mixture which melts at a given temperature and reacts with indicator paper to produce a color. By sealing one of these devices in each master carton of frozen foods prior to shipping, the receiver can be assured that the product did not warm up in transit to some prescribed temperature for which the indicator was designed to be triggered. The time-temperature indicator provides more information in that it integrates the total time-temperature history the product has experienced and records it in a single reading. As an example of how these devices operate, one indicator contains sealed chemical salts, which are allowed to saturate a yellow paper strip at the time of use. A red color develops at one end of the strip, and during frozen storage this color migrates to the other end at a rate which is dependent on the temperature. By observing the distance which the color has traveled at any given time, we can determine how much of the useful shelf life has expired and how much remains. These devices would more accurately provide quality assurance with frozen seafoods than would a pull date on the package.

REFERENCES

Anon. 1971. "Fishery Products." In *ASHRAE Guide and Data Book,* edited by J. W. Slavin and J. A. Dassow. New York: American Society of Heating, Refrigeration and Air Conditioning Engineers, Inc.

Anon. 1965. *Quick Freezing of Fish.* Torry Advisory Note No. 27. Aberdeen, Scotland: Torry Research Station.

Bramnsaes, F. "Quality and Stability of Frozen Seafood." In *Quality and Stability of Frozen Foods,* edited by W. B. Van Arsdel, M. J. Copley, and R. L. Olson, pp. 217–236. New York: Wiley Interscience.

Dyer, W. J. 1971. "Speed of Freezing and Quality of Frozen Fish." In *Fish Inspection and Quality Control,* edited by R. Kreuzer, pp. 5–81. London: Fishing News (Books) Ltd.

Dyer, W. J., and Peters, J. 1969. "Factors Influencing Quality Changes During Frozen Storage and Distribution of Frozen Products, Including Glazing, Coating and Packaging. In *Freezing and Irradiation of Fish,* edited by R. Kreuzer, pp. 317–322. London: Fishing News (Books) Ltd.

Heen, E., and Karsti, O. 1965. "Fish and Shellfish Freezing." In *Fish as Food* (Vol. 4), edited by G. Borgstrom, pp. 355–418. New York: Academic Press.

Jason, A. C. 1982. "Thawing." In *Fish Handling and Processing,* edited by Aitken, Mackie, Merritt, and Windsor. Aberdeen, Scotland: Torry Research Station.

Khayat, A., and Schwall, D. 1983. "Lipid Oxidation in Seafood." *Food Technol.* 37(7):130–140.

Lane, J. Perry. 1964. "Time-Temperature Tolerance of Frozen Seafoods." *Food Technol.* 18:1100–1106.

Learson, R. J., and Licciardello, J. J. 1986. "Literature Reporting of Shelf-Life Data. What Does It All Mean? *Rev. Int. Froid.* 91:179–181.

Licciardello, J. J., and D'Entremont, D. L. 1987. "Bacterial Growth Rate in Iced Fresh or Frozen-Thawed Atlantic Cod." *J. Food Prot.* 49(4):43–45.

Nicholson, F. J. 1973. *The Freezing Time of Fish.* Torry Advisory Note No. 62. Aberdeen, Scotland: Torry Research Station.

Olavie, E. Nikkila, and Linko, Reino R. 1956. "Freezing, Packaging and Frozen Storage of Fish. *Food Res.* 21(1):42–46.

Pottinger, S. R. 1951. "Effect of Fluctuating Storage Temperatures on Quality of Frozen Fish Fillets." *Comm. Fish. Rev.* 13(2):19–27.

Ronsivalli, L. J., and Baker, D. W. 1981. "Low Temperature Preservation of Seafood: A Review." *Mar. Fish. Rev.* 43(4).

Schoen, H. M., and Bryne, C. H. 1972. "Defrost Indicators." *Food Technol.* 26(10):46–50.

Slavin, J. W. 1963. "Freezing and Cold Storage." In *Industrial Fishery Technology,* edited by M. E. Stansby. Huntington, NY: Krieger.

Stroud, G. D. 1969. *Rigor in Fish, the Effect on Quality.* Torry Advisory Note No. 36. Aberdeen, Scotland: Torry Research Station.

Wells, J. H., and Singh, R. P. 1985. "Performance Evaluation of Time-Temperature Indicators for Frozen Food Transport." *J. Food Sci.* 50:369–378.

CHAPTER

14

Handling of Fresh Fish

Thomas E. Rippen

Fresh seafood's profit potential is substantial because of relatively large margins and increased consumer concern for the nutritional quality of meat. However, this potential can be realized only if consumers are confident about receiving consistently high quality products. Fish lose quality more quickly and by different pathways than red meat and poultry; consequently, they must be handled with special care and with consideration for their unique properties.

Fish begin losing quality the moment they leave the water, so the most we can accomplish is to slow the rate of deterioration. This observation may seem obvious; however, its significance is easy to underestimate. For example, employees may be tempted to dress fish on unsanitary surfaces or to leave a few boxes of fish on the loading dock until after their lunch break. If the fish were prepared immediately such practices would seldom result in a discernible loss of quality. Unfortunately, the damage shows up later by shortening the expected storage life of the product. It is not enough to buy or produce high quality fresh fish. The product must also have a reserve of quality to carry it to the consumer's table. Nearly everything done or not done to fish will eventually impact consumer enjoyment. Consumers are critical judges who ultimately dictate a company's sales, profits, and growth potential.

REVIEW OF FISH SPOILAGE

Bacteria

Bacteria are considered to be a primary cause of spoilage in fresh fish. They exist as a normal condition in the intestinal tract, slime, and gills of fish and contribute the sour and putrid odors characteristic of spoiled fish. Bacterial growth and its effect on quality is detailed in Chapter 17.

Enzymes

Fish are poikilothermic animals: Their body temperature fluctuates with the surrounding water. Many species must tolerate a wide seasonal temperature range. In fish, chemically active proteins known as enzymes function even at low temperatures. These enzymes are essential to life, as they are responsible for digestion and assimilation of food, synthesis of tissues, and regulation of metabolic processes. After death, the enzymes important for body building reactions may reverse and begin to break down muscle while other enzymes "eat" through the digestive tract into surrounding tissues.

Similar processes lead to the desirable ripening (tenderizing) of chilled beef, but the cold tolerant enzymes in fish result in excessive softening of naturally tender flesh. Perhaps even more significant, enzymatic activity releases simple protein building blocks (amino acids and peptide chains) that are readily used as food by bacteria.

Chemical Changes

Seafoods have a large proportion of soft, polyunsaturated fats and oils that are highly vulnerable to attack from oxygen (oxidation). The condition leads to rancidity. Although more commonly associated with frozen fish than fresh, some fish may develop pronounced fishy flavors due to oxidation even when held fresh. The problem is aggravated by exposure to light and by some metals, such as those found in cigarette ashes and the iron present in red flesh.

Other Factors

Like other meat animals, fish enter rigor mortis (stiffening due to muscular contraction) after death with a concomitant drop in pH. Fish have natural defenses against bacteria, which continue to function at a reduced level until after they come out of rigor mortis. Consequently fish that enter rigor late and stay rigid two or three days tend to retain quality longer than those that stiffen quickly and remain in rigor for two to three hours. Fish species, condition, and temperature are all factors that control the time required for rigor mortis to set in and its duration. Rapid cooling to 32°F (0°C) can greatly retard rigor mortis. Uniced fish may suffer severe contractions that tear the flesh and produce an unsightly product. A similar effect occurs when fish are forced into a new position while in rigor. Even when properly iced, fish filleted prior to the onset of rigor mortis may develop an undesirable rough appearance.

Gain or loss of moisture occasionally affects the appearance and flavor of fresh fish. When fish are inadequately iced, dehydration can occur quickly, resulting in discoloration, weight loss, and, in severe cases, a tough, dry texture. When allowed to rest directly in fresh water, fish fillets and shellfish absorb moisture which tends to shorten storage life and to dilute flavoring compounds and pigments.

TEMPERATURE EFFECT

The importance of keeping seafood at low temperatures cannot be overstated. The growth of bacteria and the rates of enzymatic and chemical activity are directly related to temperature. Research shows that refrigerated fish must be maintained near 32°F (0°C) for maximum quality retention. Storage life can be extended several days when temperature is decreased from 35 to 32°F (1.7 to 0°C).

Tray-packed fishery products, shucked shellfish meats, and fillets are sometimes held without ice. In this situation refrigeration units should be adjusted to 28 to 32°F (2.2 to 0°C). Commonly, uniced retail cases are inadequately maintained at 38 to 45°F (3.3 to 7.2°C). This problem and others are alleviated when products are kept in contact with ice. Temperatures should be checked frequently with a reliable thermometer.

Ice—Advantages and Uses

Ice is an ideal cooling medium for fresh fish. When used liberally it has several advantages over standard refrigeration methods. It rapidly removes heat from fish; holds fish at or near 32°F (0°C) throughout distribution; continuously flushes away bacteria, blood, and slime as it melts; and prevents dehydration.

A property of ice that makes it extremely valuable is its high latent heat of fusion. That is, water requires a large amount of energy (as heat drawn from its surroundings) to change from a solid to a liquid at 32°F (0°C). Because melting ice remains constant at near 32°F (0°C), warm fish in contact with it continue to cool until they also reach 32°F (0°C).

The temperature decrease attainable for a given quantity of fish and ice can be calculated from the formula

$$\text{Temperature change, °F} = \frac{(144\ \text{Btu})\ (\text{lbs. ice})}{(\text{lbs. of fish})\ (0.95)}$$

International Equivalent:

$$\text{Temperature change, °C} = \frac{(335\ \text{kJ/kg})\ (\text{kg ice})}{(\text{kg of fish})\ (4.0\ \text{kJ/kg °C})}$$

where 144 Btu = amount of heat (in British thermal units) absorbed by 1 pound of ice during the transition from ice to water, and 0.95 = the specific heat of fish.

For example, if we mix 10 pounds of ice with 100 pounds of fish we can theoretically lower the temperature of the fish by 15°F, from 47°F to 32°F. The calculation required is

$$\frac{144\ \text{Btu} \times 10\ \text{lbs. ice}}{100\ \text{lbs. fish by}\ 0.95} = 15°\text{F}$$

International Equivalent:

$$\frac{335\ \text{kJ} \times 4.54\ \text{kg ice}}{4.54\ \text{kg fish} \times 4.0} = 8.4°\text{C}$$

Perhaps more frequently fish handlers need to estimate the amount of ice required to cool a known quantity of fish at some initial temperature. By rewriting the first equation we get

$$\text{lbs. ice required} = \frac{(\text{fish temp.} - 32°\text{F})\ (\text{lbs. fish})\ (0.95)}{144\ \text{Btu}}$$

International Equivalent:

$$\text{kg ice required} = \frac{(\text{fish temp. } 0°\text{C})\ (\text{kg fish})\ (4.0)}{335\ \text{kJ}}$$

Example situation: Assume a dockside buyer for a seafood processing firm inserts a thermometer into the mouths of several fish selected from a small boatload and finds an average temperature of 62°F (16.7°C). He discovers that the catch was landed only an hour earlier and is still in excellent condition. He decides to buy 1,700 pounds (772 kg) of the fish recognizing from experience that immediate icing is imperative. He determines that 336 pounds (152.5 kg) of ice is the theoretical minimum necessary to do the job. This determination was calculated from 62°F (16.7°C) initial − 32°F (0°C) desired = 30°F (16.7°C) reduction needed and,

$$\frac{30°\text{F} \times 1700\ \text{lbs. fish} \times 0.95}{144\ \text{Btu}} = 336\ \text{lbs. ice}$$

International Equivalent:

$$\frac{16.7°\text{C} \times 771\ \text{kg fish} \times 4.0}{335\ \text{kJ}}\ 153\ \text{kg ice (includes rounding error in conversion)}$$

In practice the buyer probably would double the calculated weight of ice to approximately 670 pounds (304 kg), because ice draws heat not only from the fish but also from the surrounding air and container walls. Also, the formulas used to calculate heat transfer do not allow for the surplus ice required to maintain 32°F (0°C) once the fish are cooled. Obviously after ice melts, the heat of fusion is absorbed and the fish will again warm up to ambient temperature. The amount of ice needed to keep fish at 32°F (0°C) will depend on several factors, including length of time they are held, type of container used, air temperature, and air flow.

The important point is that sufficient quantities of ice be used to completely encompass the fish at all times. To take full advantage of the cooling and flushing functions of ice it must make direct contact with fish and it must melt. The process is facilitated by gutting fish when possible, especially large fish, and packing the body cavity with ice. Simply topping a pile of fish with ice is not sufficient. Place a 2-inch (5 cm) bed of ice in fish-shipping boxes, intersperse some with the fish, and top with 2 to 3 inches (5 to 8 cm) of additional ice. Modern sealed fiberboard shipping boxes are sometimes constructed to allow for adding ice from the bottom as well as the top to replace melt losses. Bins and large containers of fresh fish will require proportionately more ice.

Meltwater must be allowed to drain away from fish because it harbors cold-tolerant bacteria and provides nutrients for their growth. Retail shops with persistent odor problems are frequently a testimonial to this fact. Drip from fish collects in lower layers of ice and produces spoiled fish odors. It also provides a major source of bacterial contamination for products that subsequently come in contact with the ice.

For reasons of health, product quality, and legal compliance, ice must be made of drinkable water. A variety of shapes are available including cubes, cylinders, chunks, crushed, and flaked ice. Maximum cooling is achieved with small ice particles that make intimate contact with the fish. For this reason some seafood handlers prefer flaked ice; however, because of its low density it tends to melt more rapidly than other forms and may be lost in handling channels. Large and irregular pieces may dent or puncture fish and are not recommended. For storage and distribution purposes crushed ice is a reasonable compromise and performs well. Occasionally fancy ices, such as hourglass shapes, find utility in retail displays because they are attractive and appear to sparkle under display lights more than crushed ice.

Adding compounds to ice that kill bacteria or retard their growth has been investigated for many years. Sorbate may extend storage life by hours or even days for some species when well handled. Marginal benefits have also been demonstrated with antibiotic ice, especially tetracyclines. However, many of these chemicals are not permitted for this use, and others come under various legal considerations including product labeling requirements. Even when the end of storage life is delayed with treated ice, loss of freshest quality during the first five to ten days may be just as rapid as with untreated ice.

Ice in Retail Display Cases

Ice used in retail cases should be removed frequently: weekly for refrigerated units, daily for open counters. The cases should be cleaned and sanitized, then refilled. If ice is used liberally, little or no additional refrigeration is required in air-conditioned retail shops. The benefits of melting ice are maximized including a continuous rinsing of the cases. The cases must drain completely and provide discreet disposal of drip so that stagnant pools and odor-causing floor drains are avoided.

Whole or dressed fish should be nestled in ice with some ice on top. Although this arrangement partially obscures fish from view it connotes quality to most customers. Orient dressed fish so that the belly cavity faces down, to avoid collecting meltwater. Recess containers of shellfish in a bed of ice so that only the tops protrude. Fish fillets may become soft if buried directly in ice but are effectively displayed in a single layer on trays or plastic film that possesses drainage holes. Fillets may overlap, but never pile then in multiple layers above the ice because there may be a 30°F (–1.1°C) difference between the bottom and top fillets in such a stack. To prevent dehydration and discoloration occasionally mist with water from a chilled spray bottle, sprinkle a small quantity of additional ice on top, or overlay with plastic wrap. Some display units humidify the air.

Other Cooling Systems

As previously discussed, conventional forced air refrigeration systems are generally less desirable than ice for cooling fresh fish. However they can be used successfully in conjunction with ice when maintained at 35 to 40°F (1.7 to 4.4°C). This method is especially important during summer months and when handling boxed fish, which are time consuming to reice.

A special use for low-temperature cooling systems exists for some overwrapped tray-packaged products. In this instance ice does not contact the fish. Either before or after packaging they are cooled rapidly by exposure to subfreezing temperatures, usually by a blast freezer or by short-term contact with CO_2 snow or other cryogenic media. The superchilled exterior of these products then equilibrates with the interior at an ambient 28 to 32°F (–2.2 to 0°C). Such "chill pack" items offer convenience, economic advantages, minimal contamination, and avoidance of excess fillet leaching.

Weak brine (approximately 4 percent salt) may be chilled with ice or refrigeration coils to cool and hold fish. This method is usually employed on offshore fishing vessels but may prove valuable for bulk storage prior to processing or boxing. Fish are immersed directly in the cooling media, so they are cooled very rapidly and are protected from physical damage. Salt keeps the temperature of a well-iced solution at or below 32°F (0°C) without freezing and reduces water absorption by the fish. Bacterial growth and salt uptake by the flesh will occur with time. Consequently the technique is probably best reserved for short-term holding of whole fish, perhaps in concert with fish washing equipment.

BRUISES AND CUTS

Fish are very delicate and easily damaged. Bruises caused by careless handling produce a nutritious environment for bacteria and frequently form soft, discolored areas. Cuts similarly promote spoilage by introducing bacteria into otherwise sterile tissue. Fish blood coagulates differently than land animals' blood and involves reaction with water. This is one reason that many bruises are not visible in fish muscle until several days after the damage is inflicted. The problem is not limited to handling on fishing vessels but can affect quality when it occurs during any step in the marketing system.

The following list may prove helpful for reducing physical damage.

Avoid overfilling fish boxes because crushing can result if they are stacked. Similarly, never stack fish boxes so that upper boxes or other objects rest directly on the contents of lower boxes.

Hold iced fish in shallow containers. Small, tender fish are especially vulnerable to crushing if piled more than 1½ feet (46 cm) deep.

All surfaces that contact fish should be free of sharp edges, including off-loading equipment, fish washers, conveyor systems, filleting tables, and so on.

Use crushed or flaked ice and keep ice storage bins cold (5 to 10°F/–15 to –12.2°C) to reduce clumping. Large ice chunks promote crushing.

Never use hooks (picks) or pitchforks to handle fish.

Use shovels only with extreme care. File the leading edge blunt and smooth.

Keep knives sharp. Dull blades result in ragged, irregular cuts that promote degradation and damage appearance.

Avoid dropping fish onto hard surfaces. Design product flow patterns so that fish are handled as little as possible and with a minimum of bumps.

BACTERIAL CONTAMINATION

Low initial numbers of bacteria on fish extend storage life compared to high bacteria counts. Fish handlers risk heavy contamination and a corresponding loss of quality each time seafood touches an unsanitary surface. These surfaces need not appear dirty to harbor large numbers of bacteria. Wood notoriously serves as a reservoir for bacteria, particularly those species that spoil fish quickly. Because of its porous nature, wood cannot be adequately cleaned or sanitized. It also holds moisture which is essential for survival of microbes. Therefore, objects that routinely contact fish should be made of appropriate food-grade plastic or corrosion-resistant metal. These include fish storage bins, reusable shipping boxes, cutting boards, and knife handles. The problem is less critical for single-use applications of wood and paper products. Modern plastics are economical, durable, and easily cleaned, and make a sensible alternative to wood and corrodible metals.

A partial list of other contamination sources follows:

1. *Fish washing equipment.* Wash water should be changed frequently. In large tanks use a water intake and overflow system that exchanges the water several times per hour. Stagnant wash water may seed fish with more bacteria than they carry into the washer. Washing works best when fish are agitated with fast-flowing water or, better still, a pressure spray containing 10 to 25 ppm chlorine. Even without chlorine, a high pressure may reduce surface bacteria populations by 90 to 99 percent. Use cold water and transfer fish to ice rapidly to prevent warming.

2. *Ice.* Used ice should be discarded and replaced with clean ice for subsequent batches of fish. Buildup of blood, slime, and feces in ice will significantly contaminate fish with spoilage microorganisms. For similar reasons ice bins should be constructed with an elevated floor and should be cleaned well at least twice per year.

3. *Fish cutting operations.* Most fish maintain quality longer when promptly eviscerated, especially if they were actively feeding prior to capture. Improperly gutted fish may actually spoil faster than whole fish because digestive enzymes and bacteria are exposed to the flesh as internal organs are cut. Remove viscera intact when possible and thoroughly wash the body cavity. Kidney material next to the backbone is enzymatically active and contributes to off-flavors.

4. *Personal hygiene.* Controlling the spread of disease begins with a clean food supply. People are major carriers of disease organisms. All individuals should wash their hands before handling a seafood product and observe sensible health practices. Sanitation dictates the use of clean high quality clothing such as rubber aprons and boots.

5. *Equipment design.* Crevices, pockets, and overlapping joints tend to trap food particles, which permits growth of bacteria. Handling systems and display cases should assure segregation of fresh products from cooked items. Drip from raw fish can contaminate ready-to-eat products.

6. *Construction of seafood handling areas.* Walls, floors, and ceilings should be of hard materials that are impervious and readily cleaned. Slope floors toward drains equipped with traps. Keep window screens, doors, and building foundations in good repair as part of a thorough pest control program. Consult state and local regulatory agencies regarding specific requirements.

7. *Placement of fish.* Avoid placing fish where lubricants, fuels, paints, or other chemicals are found. Storage life may not be affected but unpleasant odors can damage a company's or store's image.

8. *Cleanup practices.* A daily schedule of washing and sanitizing is extremely important to the distribution and sale of high quality seafoods (see following section).

WASHING AND SANITIZING

Cleanup jobs are generally scheduled after processing runs or after busy business periods during the day and before breaks and lunch. As a result, employees are seldom motivated to conduct vigorous washing campaigns. They should understand that thoughtful sanitation can greatly extend the storage life of fish. Modern detergents and cleaning equipment facilitate cleaning of processing plants and retail outlets. However, no system can totally substitute for brooms, brushes, and muscles.

Remember, once quality is lost it cannot be regained. All surfaces that come in contact with fish should be thoroughly washed with detergent and then sanitized. Proper cleaning involves separate applications of detergent, then sanitizer, since combining the two will largely neutralize the sanitizer's bactericidal effect. Detergent alone does little to destroy bacteria but is needed to reduce gross contamination and expose bacteria to the sanitizer.

Follow these steps:

1. Rinse surfaces to remove blood, scales, and other matter.
2. Brush with a warm detergent solution. (A presoak with an alkaline detergent foam may reduce the amount of scrubbing required.)
3. Rinse.
4. Apply an appropriate sanitizer.
5. Rinse off corrosive sanitizers when used on metal.

See Chapter 17 for a detailed discussion of detergents and sanitizers.

Cleaning and sanitizing is not difficult once a routine is established. Benefits realized from consistently high quality products and satisfied customers make the time taken for these activities a very small sacrifice. Thoughtful and careful sanitation is the responsibility of every seafood business from the largest processor to the smallest retailer or restaurant kitchen.

CHAPTER

15

Merchandising and Managing a Fresh Seafood Department

Michael G. Haby and Charles W. Coale, Jr.

Seafood is gaining popularity with large segments of the American population, with this popularity generally felt most strongly in the food service industry. Although Americans still consume most of their seafood outside the home, a growing number are becoming interested in home preparation.

Fresh seafood is here to stay in the supermarket. In major market areas, competitive pressure alone is pushing retail food outlets into some form of a fresh seafood operation. Firms strongly committed to a fresh seafood program have found long-run success; for many, the sheer drawing power is well worth the added expense and effort to operate the department.

Since the mid 1980s the retail sector has steadily increased its commitment to seafoods as an additional component of the meat mix. In 1987, retail seafood sales accounted for 5.7 percent of total store sales. Since 1985, seafood sales through the retail food sector grew at about 17 percent per year. Despite this impressive growth, progressive firms have realized that success in retailing fresh seafood is much more involved than simply investing in equipment and inventory and placing products in the display case.

A seafood merchandising effort may be defined as the process of maximizing consumer satisfaction through buying, pricing, and presenting seafood, related products, and services with the end result being to achieve the seller's financial objectives.

This definition contains two distinct and interconnected goals:

1. To provide customers with satisfaction from their patronage;
2. To achieve the financial target that retailers set for themselves.

Whether these two goals are attained depends on how well retailing efforts (buying, pricing, and presenting seafood, related products, and services) are tailored to the needs of the trade area.

The process of developing and managing a seafood merchandising effort is really commonsensical. To justify the square footage, employee time, and direct costs, the seafood effort must contribute to storewide goals by ultimately providing the customer with desired products and services. Each of the diagrams in Figure 15-1 represents a seafood merchandising system. In the diagram where the circles do not intersect, we can assume the retailing efforts are not contributing to customer satisfaction and therefore departmental and storewide objectives are not being met.

The diagram with the interlocking circles indicates that consumer satisfaction and departmental objectives are being met. In this situation a two-way flow occurs: Products and services flow out of the store in the form of consumer satisfaction while this "satisfaction" is repaid with achievement of departmental objectives. From this diagram, we can assume that the closer we adjust our mix of retailing efforts to meet the needs of our trade area, the easier it will be to obtain departmental objectives.

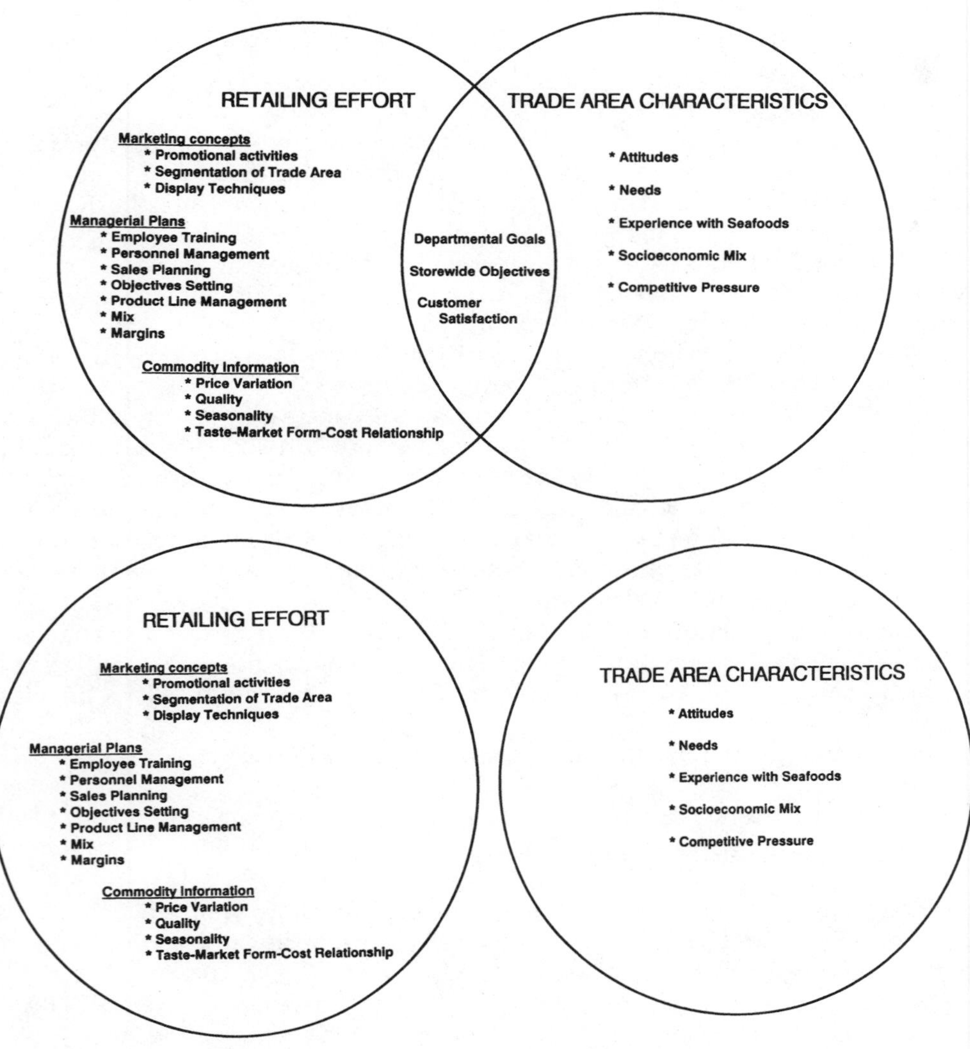

Figure 15.1 Concept of the Seafood Retailing System.

Providing customer satisfaction in purchases and realizing departmental objectives requires the retail food marketing team to have

1. The ability to judge and maintain quality in fresh seafood;
2. Knowledge of the variety of seafood available;
3. The know-how to provide a mix of affordable, acceptable products to the trade area;
4. An understanding of existing consumer attitudes toward shopping for and consuming seafood;
5. An awareness of how to incorporate certain tried and proven marketing techniques to help ensure consumer adoption and acceptance of seafood in the home;
6. The necessary managerial information available to evaluate past experiences and techniques and apply positive experiences to future efforts.

These six merchandising strategy components reflect the normal information needs required to successfully retail most any product. A fresh seafood effort also presents additional challenges because

1. Much of the success in food merchandising is the result of past experience, knowing what is correct in a given situation, and skillful manipulation of events. Seafood is often a completely new product line, and often there is little information available to use in deciding what is correct in a given situation.
2. Retailers generally receive some assistance from manufacturers and middlemen, either in the form of money or such services as promotional allowances and rack jobbers who are responsible for maintaining displays and rotating stock. With a fresh seafood effort, there may be a minimum of assistance from either processors or middlemen. In essence, the retailing firm will generally need to rely on its own motivation, resources, and commitment to ensure success.

The six merchandising strategy components mentioned earlier are discussed here to provide a well-rounded understanding of the activities required to provide an array of affordable, acceptable seafood products and support services. Beyond this understanding, retailers should remember that their enthusiasm and interest is critical to the success of a fresh seafood department.

This chapter was organized by assuming that we should first have some general information about what we are selling: the seafood product. The second informational need, a review of selected attitudinal work on how consumers feel about seafood, provides some basic information useful in developing a communications and display package. The third concern in becoming better equipped to meet seafood department objectives is to tie together the seafood offerings with customer needs through the use of accepted retailing tools.

BUYING FRESH SEAFOOD

Buying for retail establishments is done either by general office personnel or market management in individual outlets. Regardless of who does the buying, procurement of fresh seafood products requires more than simply ordering from a supplier. Follow through is required at the retail level to ensure that incoming products meet your specifications for maximum acceptable product temperatures, correct pack style, and so on.

Besides quality considerations that influence shelf life, shrinkage, and consumer acceptance, product specifications can provide consistency in the products that are bought and sold. Purchasing fresh or frozen seafood is a game of trust between wholesale purveyor and retail buyer. Both parties should understand the other's expectations, so agreeing on a set of guidelines for products will help alleviate the confusion that may surface from time to time. A good set of product standards will earn you the reputation as a marketer of consistent quality and style of products, and ultimately enable you to increase fresh seafood sales.

The third consideration in buying is to provide customers with acceptable products they can afford week in and week out. Given the price variability of fresh seafood, this aspect of buying can only be accomplished with aggressive management of the product line.

These three considerations comprise the buying function, and each component can be expressed as an objective. A hypothetical buying objective may be to maximize customers' value in seafood purchases by:

1. Procuring the highest quality products available;
2. Setting specifications for the types of products ordered; and
3. Procuring a mix of products that is acceptable and affordable to the trade area.

This section on buying seafood discusses the objectives of setting specifications and procuring a mix of acceptable, affordable products.

Setting Specifications for Types of Products Ordered

Seafoods within many product classes have historically been lumped together as agricultural-type commodities. However, all gallons of select oysters, all 5-pound (2.3 kg) boxes of 36–40 count shrimp, all skinless fillets of Gulf red snapper, and all 1-pound (454 g) containers of lump blue crab meat are not the same. Within each product category, there can be significant price variations.

Many variables can influence the price of a particular product. The price for a 50-pound (22.7 kg) bag of crawfish, for example, depends on whether the animals were purged (cleaned) before packing and on the percentage of extraneous material contained in the pack—were bait, mud, and rice stalks included in the 50-pound bag (22.7-kg) or are the 50 pounds 100 percent crawfish? Generally speaking, the price for a particular product is reflected in the species used, the quality of product the processor started with, the quality control of the manufacturing process, the cost of packaging, and the cost of distributing the product.

Marine and aquatic food products are often purchased strictly on the basis of price. Price will always be an important criterion, but it should not be the only one. By coupling price awareness with specifications about quality and style of the pack and using indicators which exist to effectively determine species, a much more comprehensive approach to buying can be used.

Incorporating specifications into the buying and receiving makes these tasks more involved. More time will be required to educate employees about testing incoming products, and additional time will be needed to evaluate incoming goods. The extra time ultimately means more dollars spent. What benefits exist in using product specifications that will offset this additional expense? The most obvious benefit is the retailers' reputation is better protected. Just ask yourself who the consumer will blame for an unpleasant experience with seafood: the fisherman, the processor, the wholesaler, or the retailer? Expressed positively, using specifications helps the seafood department provide the level of satisfaction that customers expect.

Keen price competition is normal in the retail food industry. Establishing specifications will allow retailers to effectively meet the competitive price or compete on the basis of consistency, quality, and value to consumers. For example, many processors would like to know what prices retailers want to charge so they can pack accordingly. Without the use of specifications it is difficult to guess. A hypothetical example may help. Assume a retailer, facing serious seafood competition, would like to sell the 36–40 count shrimp at cost as a sales leader, and he or she wants the price to be competitive. By communicating this information to the wholesaler, the retailer can find the style of pack that will fit the appropriate price range. The pack may have 5 percent pieces, and the grade may average out to be more toward 40-count shrimp than 36 count. Alternatively, an objective may be to have the reputation as the purveyor of the best quality shrimp in town. A set of specifications, in essence a buying guide, enables the retailer or his distributor to seek out shrimp packs which have the fewest pieces, a low average tail count in the grade, and good uniformity in size.

What sort of product specifications need to be established? The simplest answer: Specifications should guard against potential problem areas. Aside from quality, there are essentially three main areas of concern to food retailers:

1. Substituting another product for the requested item;
2. Substituting a different size than what was ordered. This is more critical with shellfish since they are graded and priced by size;
3. Skimming products by adding extra liquid to make up a short weight.

Product Substitution

Accurately identifying the species of skin-off fillets is difficult without a chemical analysis. As an example, skinned cod and haddock fillets almost look as though they were cut from the same fish. The growing practice in New England is to leave the skin on haddock so that a quick recognition can be made. Because haddock has historically been more expensive than cod, the skin provides retailers and consumers alike with proof of what they are purchasing.

The prize finfish in the Gulf of Mexico is the red snapper. Over the years, a variety of less expensive fish have been substituted for red snapper fillets. To be certain, purchase red snapper with the skin on. The distinguishing red iridescent skin is a tip-off that the product is genuine. Frozen snapper fillets are imported from Taiwan and usually sell for much less than genuine fresh red snapper from the Gulf of Mexico. The Taiwanese products are generally sold skin on, but the characteristic red speckled skin is normally faded compared to skin of fresh Gulf snapper.

With the advent of the North Pacific harvesting of "rock fish," which may carry a variety of names including Pacific red snapper, certain purveyors may try to sell these skin-off fillets as Gulf snapper. Although "Pacific rockfish" is a fine seafood product, it should not be confused with the genuine Gulf snapper. Once again, the skin of true Gulf snapper will prove what is being purchased.

Four types of blue crab products are on the market today. Although all grades of blue crab meat have essentially the same flavor, the size of meat segments and meat color determine the relative price. Lump meat, the large chunks found in the back of the crab shell, is from the muscles that drive the swimming legs and is the highest priced meat because of its size. Lump meat is generally used for hors d'oeuvres when eye appeal is as important as taste. Special, body, or flake meat is the muscle removed from the body of the blue crab. This meat is white like the lump, but the individual size of muscle filaments is smaller than in lump meat. Special meat is less expensive than lump and is often used in prepared dishes, such as casseroles, stuffings, and crab cakes where eye appeal is not as critical. Claw meat, the least expensive crabmeat, has some reddish-brown tone to it and is most often used in dishes where color is not important. Blue crab fingers are being marketed in increasing numbers. Prime for appetizers, blue crab fingers are most often sold fresh or pasteurized.

The crabmeat plant is generally responsible for ensuring the integrity of the pack, but it is advisable to check the contents of lump meat containers randomly to be sure there is not any special or claw meat comingled. The reason is not taste difference but the fact that lump meat is more expensive than either special or claw meat.

Size Substitution

Shrimp are sold by count sizes. The green headless shrimp are packed in 5-pound (2.3 kg) boxes. Table 15-1 distinguishes the names and count sizes for tropical shrimp on the market today.

To accurately determine whether the contents of the box corresponds with the specified count size, the following test may be used:

1. Thaw the product in a sieve or a strainer.
2. Remove and weigh the total weight of all pieces. (A piece is defined as any portion of shrimp not possessing at least five segments along with the tail intact. The box should not contain more than 5 percent pieces by weight. In actual practice, a lower percentage of pieces is normally encountered.)

Table 15-1. *Tropical Shrimp Tail Counts Per Pound and the Customary Market Name*

Count	Name
Under 10	Extra colossal
10–15	Colossal
16–20	Extra jumbo
21–25	Jumbo
26–30	Extra large
31–35	Large
36–42	Medium large
43–50	Medium
51–60	Small
61–70	Extra small
Over 70	Tiny

3. Weigh the remaining contents. (The combined weight of thawed pieces and tails should be right at 5 pounds (2.3 kg)).
4. Count the number of remaining whole shrimp.
5. Divide the weight of remaining contents by the number of shrimp.
6. Divide this average weight into 16 ounces (454 g) to determine tail count per pound.
7. If the count per pound falls between the range specified on the box, then the count is acceptable. Ideally the average count should fall along the midpoint of the grade range. For example, the ideal average tail count in a grade size of 36–40 should be 38.

This method quickly determines whether the box is accurately marked. Lower priced shrimp within the same size grade and weight may be indicative of (1) an excessive number of pieces, (2) shrimp which are black-spotted, (3) extraneous material in the box, or (4) a short weight. Most shrimp packers adhere to the guidelines mentioned, and most even perform additional tasks to determine the uniformity of size within a particular grade. However, seafood products are often repacked, so it is a good idea to check the count sizes in brands new to the outlet.

Oysters, like any substance packed in a volume measure, will settle some during the distribution process. Oysters may absorb and release liquid with processing and transportation. Thus, to determine whether oysters have been replaced with liquid, count the meats upon arrival. Oysters are graded by size of meat, with the larger meats commanding a higher price per volume. Table 15-2 indicates the general guidelines for size grades in oysters.

Skimming Products

Like other meats, seafood contains a lot of liquid. Since seafood lacks the connective tissues found in terrestrial animals, it tends to weep liquids once it is harvested. Bulk-packed fresh fillets should normally contain between 1 percent and 1.5 percent liquid in the package. In a 10-pound (4.5 kg) container, you should find 1.6 to 2.4 ounces (0.7 to 1.1 kg) of liquid. Containers with larger amounts of liquid indicate either substitution of liquid for product or a slow freeze, which inevitably ruptures cell walls and releases liquid. An improperly frozen product will have less flavor intensity because most of the flavor elements are water soluble.

This section on specifications is not meant to accuse anyone of deceptive business practices. Rather, the point is that your reputation is at stake with the consuming public. No doubt, honest purveyors realize that in the long run their business depends on retail success. But it is important to understand how certain

Table 15-2. ***Eastern Oyster Meat Counts Per Gallon and the Customary Market Name***

Grade	Meats Per Gallon
Very small	Over 500
Small or standard	301 to 500
Select or medium	211 to 300
Extra select or large	160 to 210
Counts or extra large	Under 160

situations develop in the industry so steps can be taken to ensure credibility with customers.

Incidentally, once buying criteria have been established and accepted by buyers and wholesalers, it is another promotional topic which can be used to differentiate the competition. We all know that anything can be given away, but profitably selling products which customers regularly purchase is a challenge. If customers understand that products which do not provide value are being filtered out, then many of these patrons will become even more loyal.

Procuring Acceptable, Affordable Product Mix

Seafood retailing operations must simultaneously accomplish two objectives. Sales from the seafood marketing effort should generate enough gross margin dollars to meet departmental objectives. In addition, the seafood effort should assemble, price, and present a mix of seafood which consistently provides a selection of affordable, acceptable products.

Assuming that the average retail store's seafood line contains fifteen to forty items, the person responsible for seafood must select the product mix from thousands of fishery products. The seafood line includes an array of finfish, crabs, clams, oysters, shrimps, mussels, and other items. Each species may be sold in a more or less processed state. For example, finfish are sold in many market forms ranging from whole fish to deep-skinned fillets; oysters are sold live or shucked. Many varieties of shucked and picked shellfish meat can be packed to the buyer's specifications with the price based on quality.

Although selecting this mix may seem easy, interruptions in the seafood marketing system may continually plague the seafood merchandiser. These interruptions occur in both the supply of and demand for seafood products. Unless the seafood line is well managed, these interruptions can prevent the seafood retailing effort from attaining its objectives. As logical as this principle may seem, retail management of the seafood product line is one of the most neglected aspects of seafood merchandising. Our objective here is to provide background information about the seafood marketing system and sketch a strategy to assist you in providing a profitable, competitively priced, and acceptable mix of products to your customers.

The requirement for success is first a rethinking of why people buy certain seafood products to the exclusion of others, and second, a slight reorientation in the various functions of merchandising: product procurement, display, and communication with customers.

Seafood Supply

Seafood production can be equated with hunting. Natural fluctuations in climate and water conditions create variations in the presence and abundance of seafood varieties, so one of the most evident supply interruptions is seasonality. This cyclical variation creates fluctuations in prices and in extreme cases may affect the availability of products. Seasonality used to mean that at times of the year certain products were unavailable, while during the "run" these varieties were quite abundant. This idea of feast or famine has changed, however, in part because of a more sophisticated harvesting effort and a more updated communications network among dockside buyers and other seafood marketing intermediaries.

Today, seasonality implies price fluctuations based on the level of production. When certain fish are scarce, the price paid to harvesters goes up, and when fish are plentiful, the ex-vessel price drops. As a rule of thumb, in winter months when the weather is more of a limiting factor, expect prices to be higher for most seafood products.

Seafood Demand

Demand also exerts a strong influence on seafood prices. From an overall industry perspective, demand for seafood has been determined by historic use patterns. Therefore, products such as cod, haddock, flounder, shrimp, salmon, and tuna are traditional favorites and annually are good selling products. These varieties are in great demand almost perpetually, and prices for them are generally high. There is another group of seafood items: the underused, nontraditional, seldom-seen, or unappreciated varieties. This category, which encompasses everything not classified as "traditional," makes up a tremendous resource capable of providing delicious meals. These nontraditional products—including certain species of shark, whiting, cusk, hake, and many others—do not experience the intense nationwide demand as the traditional favorites.

Although production fluctuations create price variations with traditional and underused products alike, prices are generally lower for seldom-used species/products because the demand is not as intense. This issue of traditionally consumed seafoods and seldom-used varieties has come about because of some traditional industry practices and by consumers' reactions to these practices. These industry practices include the historic dependence on just a few species to satisfy fresh market demands of American consumers. For years, the New England groundfish fleet has concentrated on three finfish varieties: cod, haddock, and flounder. In the Gulf states, shrimp production is the most valuable fishery. Alaska, Washington, and Oregon have traditionally produced 90 percent of the salmon. Today, fishermen are faced with higher production costs and are seeking ways to earn more profit. To do this, they are harvesting more varieties of fish and taking better care of landed product. U.S. fishermen are attempting to utilize more fully the abundance of products available off our shores.

This effort, however, is stifled by another traditional industry practice—the retail identification system for seafood. Marketing seafood products is first done by species, then by market form, and in some cases, by size, as in shellfish. Therefore, cod fillets, swordfish steaks, and select oysters typify the retail identification plan for seafood.

Seafood is the only animal protein source that is retailed by species and market form. Retail identification for beef is based solely on the location of the cut; retail poultry identification is based on anatomical features such as legs, thighs, backs, and so on.

The practice of marketing seafood on a species basis may create an artificial sense of exclusiveness among species, which creates barriers for consumers who are somewhat adventurous and willing to try other species. Cod fillets, for example, sound nothing like ocean whitefish, although the meats are very similar. Imagine how difficult red-meat marketing would be if consumers began to request Santa Gertrudis T-bones, Hereford round steaks, or London broil cut from Charolais cattle.

One reason why we find a few highly demanded, traditional species and a host of so-called underused varieties is consumer reaction to typical industry practices. As consumers, we all react to our environment. A variety of attitudinal studies done with consumers consistently indicate that preparation knowledge continues to impede greater retail seafood sales, and that people are not interested in purchasing unfamiliar seafood products. Purchase risk, an outgrowth of consumers wanting to get the most value for their dollar, is a common thread running through these feelings about seafood. Types of seafood are particularly good candidates for purchase risk syndrome because:

1. They are fairly high-priced items, and the degree of purchase risk is proportional to the cost of the item;
2. As edibles, seafoods are experience items which means the product must be purchased to test the claims made;
3. The variety of seafood products may be confusing to the shopper.

Purchase risk translates into low levels of demand and slow retail movement for all but a few tried and proven traditional seafood varieties.

The idea of traditional and underused species has major demand implications for the seafood retailer. Effective demand in a seafood department is influenced by a number of interrelated factors. For example, customers' familiarity with the product influences how intensively they will consume it, but concern for staying within budgets may force patrons to purchase lower-priced items in the meat department. Therefore, seafood departments which incorporate a variety of traditional and seldom-seen products may find profitability enhanced because certain species, although still competitively priced, carry higher gross margins than some more traditional favorites.

From the standpoint of profitability, one of the best reasons for carrying a mix of traditional and underused products is the way that price changes in a seafood variety affect consumption of the product. According to a study conducted at Virginia Tech (Capps and Havlicek, 1981), the factors that most affect consumption of meat and seafood products are changes in product price, changes in income, and changes in family size.[1] Although price changes are only one factor influencing consumer demand, variation in seafood prices is the norm in the seafood industry, and the effect of price changes in certain seafood items generally places the retailer in a no-win situation for that item. As an example of how price changes affect the sales of seafood, researchers at Virginia Tech found that if the price of an item increased by 1 percent, the expected reduction in demand is reduced by more than the 1 percent increase. Thus if we multiply prices times the quantities demanded before and after the price change, total sales would be higher before the price change. For example, if the price of cod fillets increases from $2.89 to $3.49 from one week to the next, it is reasonable to expect reduced sales of cod. Consumption may be increased through an aggressive, intense promotion and advertising effort, but is this a realistic alternative? Or the retailer may decide to maintain the same retail price after the price increase. Here the market manager would be trading off reduced gross margin dollars for constant turnover of product. In essence the department is carrying cod fillets to please customers, not management.

If price variation is a silent partner in the seafood marketing effort, how can a seafood department adjust so it can earn a profit? The only way to achieve the dual objectives of profitably providing competitively priced, acceptable products to customers is to aggressively manage the seafood line.

---

[1]Secondary factors include location of residence, the availability of complementary items, and substitute goods.

Beginning Strategy for Product-Line Management

As stated earlier, the goal in retailing fresh seafood is to provide acceptable, affordable products to the trade area. If this can be accomplished, then enough gross margin dollars should be earned to attain departmental objectives. The key to generating an adequate flow of gross margin dollars is to provide shoppers simultaneously with acceptable products that are also affordable.

Accomplishing this task is difficult because of the idea of traditional and underused products. Although acceptable, many traditionally demanded products are priced beyond many consumers' budget constraints. Conversely, many underused products are well within consumers' budgets, but are unacceptable simply because they are unfamiliar. It appears we are attempting to achieve two mutually exclusive goals simultaneously, because providing an affordable mix of products may force us to handle many of the so-called underused species, and consumers have shown a reluctance to purchase these unfamiliar varieties.

The essence of the strategy is to make affordable products acceptable by relating them to those traditional, and acceptable, products. This is done by understanding why people consume a certain species and not another. As an example, why do people eat haddock? Familiarity is important, but there are other reasons: the flavor, color, texture, and so on. Essentially, people eat haddock because they enjoy its edibility traits. Based on this idea of edibility, a mix of affordable products can be provided by ordering substitutable varieties, which reflect retail prices that contribute to constant demand. In the following, we concentrate on techniques for determining substitute products and presenting this information to the trade area.

Activities Related to Substitutability

Seafood chefs have long known that many finfish varieties are similar in taste. For example, the term *whitefish* is indicative of cooked white flesh with a low fat content and delicate-to-bland flavor. Traditional whitefish products include flounder, halibut, trout, ocean perch, cod, and haddock. Whitefish species which are less familiar include grouper, monkfish, cusk, drum, wolf fish or ocean catfish, pollock, tilefish, shark, and freshwater pond-raised catfish. Many of these whitefish varieties are practically identical in flavor, but the texture can vary from firm with large flakes to soft with a more smooth texture.

The bolder, richer tasting, darker-fleshed varieties also have some similarities in flavor intensity and overall edibility. For example, the Atlantic bluefish and the Atlantic mackerel are quite similar in their edibility.

One technique which has been suggested is to categorize finfish based on similarities in the normal market form, thickness of the form, and flavor. This technique specifies four groupings of finfish:

Group 1: Thin, delicate product
Group 2: Medium dense, light colored
Group 3: Medium dense, darker colored meat
Group 4: Thick and dense-fleshed products

The idea behind this categorization is that cooking techniques should match product characteristics. From a retailers' standpoint, this is a very good technique because consumers can understand it easily.

Products falling into Group 1 include fillets of sole, flounder, some turbot, and Pacific sand dab, all very delicate varieties. They tend to fall apart if handled once cooked. A sauté or a bake are the best cooking techniques for these varieties. When wrapped around a stuffing mixture, these flatfish products make an elegant meal.

The product line in Group 2 is much more extensive. These varieties are firmer than the previous group, and the fillets are generally thicker. Within this category are several species which are generally marketed as headed and gutted, or pan-ready. Small speckled seatrout, scup or porgy, whiting or silver hake, croaker, and catfish are often sold as pan-ready products. Fillets within Group 2 include cod, haddock, pollock, cusk, rockfish, ocean perch, corvina, gray seatrout, sheepshead, catfish, tilefish, sablefish or butterfish, monkfish, red snapper, black drum, Pacific rockfish, and spiny dogfish. Salmon is generally steaked, but demand is growing for salmon fillets. Despite their thickness, most products in this category are flaky. Even the spiny dogfish, a small shark which is not too flaky, can be flaked into a delicious cold salad.

The best cooking techniques for these varieties are baking, poaching, frying, or cooking in foil. Some of these varieties have a higher oil content and will baste themselves while baking. The leaner varieties generally need some adornments to ensure a moist, cooked product.

The medium dense, darker colored fish in Group 3 include tuna, mackerel, mullet, king mackerel, salmon, and bluefish. These are oily and are very good smoked. Poaching and baking are good indoor cooking techniques, but frying these varieties often makes them too rich in oil.

Group 4 consists of the large, meaty, extremely dense fish. Examples include swordfish, shark, grouper, Atlantic and Pacific halibut, and sturgeon. These products are generally sold as steaks, some with the bones removed. Their dense, meaty character makes them ideal for grilling, making kabobs, or barbecuing. Poaching is also a good cooking technique for these varieties.

The strength of this categorization is that each group contains similar tasting but different priced products. This technique provides the shopper with the ability to seek out products that sell for less but bear some similarities to more familiar ones. In Group 1, the most expensive product is fillet of sole; the least expensive is turbot. Haddock, catfish, Pacific rockfish, cusk, and sheepshead represent a group of light, flaky, bland fish which spans a wide price range. As another example, a shark steak generally retails for about one-third the cost of a similar-sized swordfish steak.

The questions retailers need to address are the following: Will the consumer enjoy the seafood purchase? Can the purchase be prepared without a mistake? Does the particular purchase fit into the consumers' overall budget constraints? These questions, and the retailers' efforts to answer them, are the essence of successfully retailing seafood products. Helping the consumer understand the similarities among products is a positive step toward greater home consumption of seafood. Considering that substitutability will require additional time to better understand species' similarities, is it worth the extra time required?

There are several benefits in using this technique. First, some supply-side interruptions can be managed by using substitutability. For instance, in a case when consumers' palates are adjusted to a particular item which goes out of season, a similar tasting product can be substituted.

Silver hake/whiting and seatrout provide a good example of how substitutability can work. For this example, assume that both products are selling for $3.75 per pound and both are typically sold as pan-ready. The silver hake or whiting is a traditional favorite in the Northeast, appearing off the coast of Long Island in late

October and remaining until March. During this fishery season, whiting represents a good value for the consumer and a good product for the retailer. During spring and summer, however, the whiting are gone. For these warmer months, seatrout are available. The whiting and the seatrout have similar taste, are sold in the same market form, and cost roughly the same. Therefore, by using the two species in combination, the retailer can reduce the effects of seasonality.

As another example, red snapper, long the prized food fish of Gulf waters, has many of the same edibility characteristics as sheepshead and shark: light colored meat and bland flavor with a firm texture. In the Texas market, red snapper fillets might retail for $6.00 per pound; shark and sheepshead could sell for approximately $3.00 and $2.25, respectively.

Because so many species have such close similarities, seafood varieties can be substituted without sacrificing the more important edibility traits. Using this tool requires extra skill in managing the seafood product line because a more systematic substitution process exists. If the price of a trade area favorite gets too high, then a similar-tasting, less expensive product of the same market form can be added to the mix. From the consumption standpoint, we know that by handling a mix of items that are similar in taste, we should be able to reduce the impact of weekly demand fluctuations caused by price variation.

Another benefit is that if displayed properly, a fresh seafood program can provide comparison shopping. Studies done in the grocery section of supermarkets found that rearranging the mix so that consumers can actually compare prices among national, private, and generic brands of the same product has increased the sale of private and generic brands, both of which carry higher gross margin percentages than do some national brands.

Other work has shown that repositioning the mix so that national, private, and generic brands of an item can be compared at one location has led to the firm maintaining its image and having the capability to draw from a wider target market. This merchandising strategy can increase total sales volume. For example, assume a trade area comprised of both middle and lower income housholds. By handling both red snapper and sheepshead, each income level can be satisfied with a good tasting product which fits into its budget.

The final benefit depends on how well substitutability is integrated into the personal selling function. If seafood department personnel help consumers better understand the similarities between products, then the department should see greater movement of less-known but greater gross margin items. This type of movement translates into more gross margin dollars to offset direct departmental expenses.

Ensuring Success

Procurement is merely one function in the merchandising process, and simply adopting the concept of substitutability among species is no guarantee of greater sales and profits. This concept must be subjected to the rigorous follow-through that the retail food industry has made so famous. Specifically, sales and margin goals will only by achieved when display techniques, point-of-purchase information, and personal selling/service practices are consistent with procurement strategies.

Managing seafood products to achieve the dual objectives of profit and satisfied customers requires that mechandisers and department managers factor out as many of the artificial differences among finfish species as possible. These "contrived" differences baffle the customer and, in fact, may intensify their sense of purchase risk. Imagine how intimidating a thirty-five-item seafood mix can be when the shopper may be familiar with only five items, or how difficult it is for the infrequent seafood user to make a purchase decision strictly by species name alone.

The first and most difficult "difference" which can be factored out is taste similarities among species. We have already seen that a host of seafood varieties have similar edibility traits. Understanding and using the idea of taste similarities takes time, but it can be an important aspect of managing the product line. Favorite seafood varieties that are either unavailable or priced beyond comparable alternatives represent a lost sale. Systematically selecting similar tasting varieties that are available and competitively priced provides a better opportunity for meeting sales and gross margin goals.

A display technique consistent with the procurement strategy would be to segregate the case based on two variables: market form and taste. Within each market form category, seafood of similar tastes could be arranged. Therefore, when patrons view the "fillet" portion of the case they may see a variety of red snapper, sheepshead, cod, cusk, and so on. Each of these varieties is similar, so by comparing the costs of each item, a purchase decision can be facilitated. This technique helps consumers compare costs of similar tasting market forms.

The last variable cannot be factored out: the cost of the item. Consumers can make intelligent decisions about cost when the differences in taste and market form are alleviated. Returning to the example of red snapper and sheepshead fillets, when customers understand that the two varieties taste basically the same, then their budget helps make the purchase decision. Conversely, if shoppers are not aware of taste similarities, then price does not play as major a role in making the decision as does familiarity with the variety. To return to the original objective, will red snapper move at the retail price needed to generate gross margin dollars? If not, then appropriate substitutes may.

Point-of-purchase information should complement the idea of substitution among species. Generic recipe information makes sense because it provides customers with the idea that a variety of products will work in a recipe. Generic in this sense applies more to finfish than shellfish. For example, a recipe calling for 2 pounds (0.9 kg) of fish fillets provides more flexibility than one calling for a particular variety. With shellfish, varieties of crabmeat or shrimp can often be interchanged if the market forms or sizes are compatible in the recipe.

The training of counter people is extremely important. They should be well versed in the similarities among species and be prepared to assist shoppers. One training technique would be to cook the same recipe using three available products within an edibility grouping, and have seafood personnel try to tell the difference.

Conclusions

Today we find increasing interest in preparing seafood in the home. Although shoppers sense the value of greater seafood consumption, actually comparing and selecting seafood products is a difficult undertaking, in part because the consumer has very little "seafood sense." Customers rely on meat department employees for information to reduce their purchase risk. The idea of substitutability among species is a way for the retail food industry to build customer confidence in the commodity and simultaneously realize the gross margin dollars necessary to keep seafood departments operating.

DISPLAY OBJECTIVES AND TECHNIQUES

Display techniques should effectively communicate all the care and concern put into the seafood effort. A well-planned aggressive consumer package should be reflected in (1) the display case, (2) tie-in sale items, and (3) related services such as knowledgeable counter personnel and supportive point of sale materials such as recipes.

Our intent here is not to define how to arrange products for sale. You are professionals whose job is to create a sales environment which contributes to both routine and impulse buying; your creative skills tell you how to arrange a case. This section discusses the implications of impulse sales on display objectives and provides a framework of merchandising objectives that enable you to create attractive displays of fresh product and ensure that your seafood effort meshes well with trade-area needs.

Eye Appeal

Eye appeal is a critical concern to retailers. One display technique used almost universally is the addition of color through garnishes.

Another display technique which enhances eye appeal is to disperse routinely purchased items throughout the case so that customers are forced to shop the entire display. This practice is successfully used for soft, seasonal produce and generally contributes to a greater volume of impulse sales. This particular technique would also work for firms interested in using the idea of substitutability where similar market forms and classes of finfish are displayed together. To effectively disperse quick movers throughout the department, you have to know what is selling, and the only way to know this is to record which products are moving and which have to be discarded.

Maintaining Quality

Before considering specific handling practices required to maintain quality, it should be noted that nowhere else in the meat department will there be a more diversified product line. A hypothetical seafood product mix may include:

1. Live shellfish: clams, oysters.
2. Jarred shellfish products: oyster meats, clams, and picked crabmeat.
3. Whole cooked shrimp, crabs, and lobsters.
4. Fillets.
5. Whole fish.
6. Smoked fishery products requiring refrigeration.

Each of these product types requires particular handling practices. Additionally, the merchandising of live, cooked, and raw products requires particular attention to minimize the risk of cross contamination.

Service Cases

Maintaining product quality in the display case depends on (1) keeping the display case clean to prevent product contamination and odor development; and (2) making sure the product is kept as close to 32°F (0°C) as possible. Depending on the particular equipment used and the rate of stock turnover, it may be necessary to take precautions to prevent dehydration or "mechanical shrink" of the seafood mix.

Keeping the Display Case Clean

Industry-wide, one week is the standard interval between complete breakdown and cleaning of the case. In cleaning, be sure to wash down all case surfaces completely, including coils that are below the front viewing glass. The mechanical removal of bacteria is quite important, and once this has been done the sanitizer can be applied as directed. One key requirement often overlooked is to allow the case to dry thoroughly overnight.

Keeping the Product as Close to 32°F (0°C) as Possible

Developing tasteful, decorative, eye appealing displays for perishable marine food products is a challenge to the retail food industry. The challenge is to make the display look good—because that is where a sale is made—while maintaining product quality. This is a difficult undertaking because there must be a trade-off between eye appeal and quality maintenance.

If the display environment is clean, maintaining quality revolves around keeping the product cold. A second and closely related quality maintenance factor is ensuring that mechanical refrigeration does not dehydrate products. The amount of dehydration for a particular product is based on how quickly it passes through the case and the type of case used. With slower turning inventory, mechanical dehydration can be a problem because it robs the product mix of some salable weight, an additional shrink factor, and it diminishes the case's eye appeal.

Three types of display equipment are in use today: ice-only cases, refrigerated cases, and refrigerated cases used with ice. Ice-only cases are becoming more popular. Some merchants prefer the simplicity of an ice-only case, but this design requires more scrutiny to ensure that products are held as close to 32°F (0°C) as possible. The procedures recommended for maintaining quality in an ice-only case are as follows:

1. Do not build piles of product because keeping the pile cold can be difficult.
2. If product is stacked, be certain that there is a layer of crushed ice between the layers.
3. A sprinkling of ice on top keeps the product moist and glistening, as well as cold.

Ice-refrigeration cases combine the attributes of temperature control with the effective chilling and washing principles of melting ice. But using an ice-refrigeration combination does not allow you to stock the case and "forget it." As mentioned, there is a trade-off between eye appeal and quality maintenance. Many retailers use ice as a bed for products, but forget that cold flows down and that mechanical refrigeration removes moisture from the product. Therefore, a light top icing will prevent the products from drying out; top icing will not cloud up the viewing windows as misting often does, and the lack of top ice will indicate the need for more.

Keeping the Product Moving

Proper stock rotation through the display case is important. When the case is set, orders should be filled by taking the front products and working back, or by any means that ensures a first-in, first-out rotation. Regardless of the equipment used, closing for the night can be a problem in a service seafood department as a lot of time may be expended removing product, and so on. Seafoods can be effectively held overnight in refrigerated cases. The stepwise procedure is as follows: (a) remove all garnishes, price tags, etc. and (b) liberally top ice the remaining displayed inventory with 3 to 4 inches of crushed ice. Experiments have demonstrated that the "core" temperature of products stored in this manner drops into the low 30s (°F) within one hour of top icing. This approach provides the same product temperature as pulling the product and placing it in walk-in or reach-in storage but without the additional man-hours and handling. The next day, ice can be removed and with minimum rearranging and restocking, the seafood display should be operative. It may take some trial-and-error work to decide how much top ice to use so that the ice just barely shows the following morning.

Self-Service Cases

Two important handling requirements for a self-service program are not stacking the products above the load line and making sure packages are butted up against one another. If tray-packed products are stacked above the load line, the temperature of the product will increase. If products are not butted up against one another, "nosediving" of cold air will occur, a phenomenon that may raise the temperature 2 to 4°F (3.6 to 7.2°C). For cold water varieties, temperature increases of 2 to 4°F (3.6 to 7.2°C) above 32°F (0°C) will significantly reduce the product's shelf life. To close for the evening, a variety of techniques are used, including leaving the products in the case and covering the entire case with cardboard or removing the inventory and placing it in the cold room, held at 29 to 32°F (–1.7 to 0°C).

Use of gondolas (a type of ice-only case) enables consumers to serve themselves. Free-standing gondolas are an effective display technique for use with prepackaged items such as shucked oysters, clams, and crabmeat. The products should be buried in ice up to the lip of the container. Just placing the container on the ice will not provide for effective chilling or a reasonable shelf life. To close down an ice-only, free-standing gondola, all products should be removed, iced, and placed in walk-in or reach-in storage for the night.

Quality Maintenance for Specific Products

Whole or Dressed Fish

Whole or dressed fish should be placed directly on the ice and lightly sprinkled with ice on top. The head area of the fish should be lower than the rest of the body because there are many bacteria on the gills. Therefore, ice melt will run into the gill and head area, which are usually discarded before cooking. Dressed fish should be stored belly cavity down to prevent ice melt from collecting in this space.

Fillets and Steaks

A debate exists about whether to place fillets and steaks directly on bed ice, or place these products in shallow pans which are imbedded on the ice. Experience will help you decide. If pans are used, they should be modified to allow for drainage.

Placing products in shallow pans without drain holes may inoculate fresh product with bacterial ice melt. A top icing is recommended to maintain the "bloom." Many retailers have a tendency to create stacks of product. Stacking products may prevent the continual moistening of fish, but unless the stacking is done in anticipation of a rush, such as on Thursday or Friday afternoon, it is not recommended. If product is stacked, it should be layered with ice to allow for equal chilling.

Shrimp

Shrimp are displayed in various ways, depending on the count sizes. Many retailers hand position large-count shrimp, using a light top icing for chilling. Displaying smaller shrimp is usually done in piles on top of ice. One alternative to this technique is to imbed a stainless or plastic colander in bed ice and subsequently place shrimp in the container. Shrimp displayed in such vessels should be lightly top iced to keep the shrimp cold.

Scallops

Scallops sold by the pound from bulk containers could be displayed similar to small shrimp. As long as the tin is imbedded in ice, the product should stay cold. The liquor naturally present in a gallon of scallops should be retained, because under mechanical refrigeration exposed scallop will dry out.

Oysters, Clams, and Crabmeat in Jars

The processing of jarred products requires hand labor, and therefore the opportunity for contamination is great. To obtain maximum shelf life these products should be kept in slush ice so that the inner temperature hovers around 32°F (0°C).

Live Oysters and Clams

Live oysters and clams are generally displayed on the ice which keeps them cold and extends their longevity. It should be noted that these products cannot be overwrapped, or they will suffocate.

Displaying Raw and Cooked Products Together

Space limitations often make it necessary to merchandise cooked and raw products together. Although this combination introduces the possibility of public health risk through cross contamination, we can minimize this risk. If cooked products are pulled over the raw products, then any bacterial contamination can be diminished when the raw product is cooked. The reverse situation is not recommended since raw product may weep onto cooked items, *which may not be reheated,* thereby contributing to a less than enjoyable meal.

Cross Merchandising

The use of tie-in sales items is a widely used practice in retailing fresh seafood. Tie-ins, both edible and inedible, help the consumer who may be uncertain about seafood by "suggestively" selling. In concert with this idea, there should be the supportive point-of-purchase materials that highlight serving suggestions and function as menu planners for impulse sales.

Although the time taken to develop menu planners, serving suggestions, and cost breakdowns may seem like additional work, remember that the customer's uncertainty is an opportunity. If we can describe preparation and cost per serving, then we have gone one step further in making the shopper a success at the dinner table.

Comparison Shopping

Another display objective underutilized in retailing fresh seafood is providing a comparison shopping experience. As we have seen, substitutable products when supported with generic recipes calling for any number of products can add extra muscle to a retail strategy. Generic recipes are a unique approach. On the demand side, most consumers are generally acquainted with only a few finfish varieties. Most familiar species are traditional products and several carry high prices. In many cases, however, there is a greater difference in the cost of certain similar products than in taste. Therefore, by suggesting that patrons try a variety of products using the same recipe, we may be able to persuade them to try an unfamiliar but lower priced product. Another reason to use a generic recipe program is that the marketing system for seafood is somewhat erratic, with price fluctuations and out-of-stocks a common occurrence. Consumer response to this sort of fluctuation creates problems for retailers because either (1) the price which they must charge to cover these fluctuations leads to reduced demand, or (2) when price increases are absorbed by retailers, the department loses gross margin dollars even though consumer demand may remain constant. Either way, the seafood department may suffer.

Simply stated, a recipe system using generic requests for particular market forms can easily support the idea of substitution among similar species. Retail interest may benefit from greater movement of unfamiliar, less expensive products, which may carry higher gross margins than some traditional varieties.

A generic recipe system also lets customers comparison shop. Many trade areas contain a mix of socioeconomic characteristics, and many retailers dream of being able to appeal simultaneously to a variety of these segments—a goal that is difficult to accomplish when profit performance is considered. By developing cost-per-serving information for a variety of finfish and arranging it in a form that allows for easy comparison, shoppers can choose a product based on their own budgets rather than on product familiarity.

Evaluation of Display Efforts

A final objective is evaluating the display effort. One way of evaluating your entire marketing effort from the customers' perspective is to follow the 3-C rule of convenience, cleanliness, and color.

Is the marketing effort for seafood convenient? This is a broad brush question, but the customer should sense convenience from whatever their vantage point. Thus the departmental "atmosphere," down to the package, should not escape the retailer's scrutiny. Here are some questions that you might want to consider.

1. Is advertising accessible?
2. Can shoppers peruse ads to find specials?
3. Are storefront ads visually accessible?
4. Is the department in a convenient spot?
5. Do customers get snarled up trying to move through the department?
6. Are products visually and physically accessible?

7. Are packages accurately and legibly weighed, labeled, and priced?
8. Is there ample promotion and preparation material?
9. Is point-of-purchase material accessible?
10. Are salespeople helpful?
11. Will actual preparation be helpful?
12. Is the seafood department clean? The manager should be on guard for anything customers may see, smell, or sense which would presuppose an untidy work environment, display case, product, or employee.
13. Do the walls and floors connote cleanliness?
14. Are the walls and floors kept clean through regular maintenance?
15. Is the display case free from any annoying effects, such as a jumbled array, dirty ice, or torn packages?
16. Are the packages themselves odor and leak proof?
17. Do employees intimate the idea of cleanliness in their appearance, their mannerisms, and their handling of a customer's purchase?
18. Colorful is the last C. Is the retailing effort a colorful one?
19. Does the department maintain good color contrast which sets it apart from other perimeter sections?
20. Is the lighting casting the product in a warm, appetizing glow, or washing it out?
21. How well is the promotional material complementing package wrap and other colors in the seafood section?
22. Do labels beckon to the customer and add needed color contrast?
23. Are slogans colorful and vivid in their description of the department and the line it handles?

By using this checklist you can preview your efforts through the consumer's eyes and alter any situations that do not measure up. The 3-C rule also allows a comprehensive assessment of seafood marketing practices, from newspaper ad layout and copy to product labels and point-of-purchase material. Through continual use of these sorts of questions, a seafood department can constantly be evaluated and upgraded.

LONG-RANGE PLANNING

An effective long-range planning program is essential for ensuring success in a retail store's seafood department. As we have noted, research has shown that customers perceive certain risks associated with purchasing and preparing fresh seafood. Further, consumers do not fully understand that seafood, with its many different species and market forms, is highly perishable if not marketed effectively. These two issues require retailers to develop a supportive management program. Long-range planning applied to a retail seafood department by management concerning its policies, procedures, and practices must deal with both customer needs and departmental operations to achieve long-term profitability and growth.

Developing a long-range planning program enables department managers to manage a retail seafood department more effectively. In this section, we create a knowledge base for a seafood department's long-range planning by illustrating principles and case study examples of successful seafood programs.

An effective plan utilizes all the resources available to a seafood department to meet its departmental and retail store objectives. It illustrates customers' needs for products and services demanded from a seafood department. These customer needs represent different demand levels for seafood products. Product information provided for customers in a long-range plan may influence attitudes of shoppers and affect, positively or negatively, the demand for seafood.

The supply side of seafood marketing deals with those activities controlled by retailers and contributing to a profitable department. Topics affecting retailer supply focus on specifying a broad purpose for the department (what customer needs does it serve), the variety of seafood and seafood products merchandised in the department, and the operational practices and employee programs of the seafood department. By working out solutions for the case studies, seafood department managers can improve their management skills.

Food retailers were asked what they saw as the key issues underlying the operation of a successful seafood department. Issues mentioned fell into four categories: (1) long-range planning, (2) personnel, (3) communications, and (4) profitability. Food retailers felt that if a well-planned management program could resolve the four broad issues cited, a seafood department in a retail store would succeed.

Planning

A successful seafood department requires management planning and training just like other in-store departments. Retailers must ask themselves, "How can I allocate my resources most effectively?" Without a long-range plan and a training program, the seafood department will fail to meet the retailers' expectations as they compare the seafood department to other in-store departments.

Personnel

A major concern of food retailers about their personnel was finding ways to motivate key store personnel to recognize the vital role fresh seafood can play in total store sales. Seafood as a food product is unique; therefore, the challenge to store personnel is to determine where seafood fits into consumer needs and how to capitalize on it in a seafood department and relate that to total store sales.

Communications

Management must find ways to communicate its seafood offering of products and services to customers in their trade area. There are many ways—both out-of-store and in-store—of promoting seafood products, including food advertisements in newspapers; maintaining a clean, colorful and conveniently located seafood department; handling a quality-oriented and wide array of seafood products; properly training employees; and maintaining a good reputation with customers.

Profitability

The possibility of limited profitability in a seafood department tends to discourage retailers from committing themselves to seafood sales. Many factors influence profitability in their judgment. Incomplete merchandising programs may cause inactivity in sales of certain species causing product losses through perishability. In some cases, fresh seafood may be underpriced compared to the market, creating lost income on the revenue side. The lack of cost controls could cause total costs to exceed total revenues and create departmental losses.

MANAGEMENT COMMITMENT

A successful fresh seafood marketing program requires a commitment by top management, which incorporates long-range planning, skilled personnel, communications, and a profitable outlook. Management must be willing to support a fresh seafood program through the assignment of trained and qualified personnel, a budget, and facilities. A fresh seafood department should be integrated into the total store format and be viewed the same as other departments for its potential as a sales and profit generator. Management must make a commitment that a fresh seafood department is a vital part of the retail store.

Top management, in both independent and chain retail food stores, have observed consumer trends toward a demand for fresh seafood; however, several barriers must be overcome in order to capitalize on this trend. Typically, fresh seafood sales have been limited because of a lack of supply, fluctuations in price and quality, and higher cost when handled in small volumes. These operational problems were, at times, too much for retailers to easily overcome, so they often devoted their resources to other departments instead of getting involved with fresh seafood sales.

Today, conditions are changing for seafood marketing. U.S. policy regarding fishing rights has changed, which is influencing the supply and availability of seafood. Chain stores have developed an aggressive approach to marketing fresh seafood, and their sophisticated merchandising methods may draw customer traffic from stores not handling fresh seafood.

The second managerial step in supporting a fresh seafood department is assigning qualified and trained personnel to manage the department. The seafood manager implements the long-range plan for the department and is important in its success. Effective fresh seafood marketing does not just happen but is the result of a carefully planned and organized effort on behalf of management. Top management's commitment to a seafood department works hand-in-hand to support the department manager to ensure a positive contribution to store overhead. Seafood managers must accept responsibility for operating the department profitably, be given sufficient authority to accomplish their duties, and be held accountable for the results. The success or failure of a fresh seafood department, assuming top management support, rests with the seafood department manager.

The third step retailers should take in creating a successful seafood department is endorsing a marketing plan, consisting of sales, procurement, merchandising, and inventory unit plans, and then incorporating these plans within an adequate budget. Planning should be flexible enough to meet unexpected situations and be closely tied to the funding available for operating the department. The written plans and the budget must be realistic and fair when compared to other departments.

The final step expected of management in support of a seafood department is providing adequate auxiliary and support facilities. Store management must assign the total space necessary to support the financial and nonfinancial objectives for the seafood department.

UNDERLYING ASSUMPTIONS

Assumptions made by management can influence a seafood department's progress. Two principal assumptions reflect on the overall profitability and growth potential of a seafood department. Without recognizing them, the department may not adequately contribute to its profit potential.

> *Assumption 1:* A seafood department must generate sufficient revenues from the sale of seafood and related products to cover the cost of operating the department.

Positive gross margin dollars result when the selling price of a seafood species exceeds its product cost. Pricing strategies must be set accordingly. Any department in a retail store should, at some time, contribute to store profits. Management may set prices which violate this assumption periodically by featuring a species below its procurement costs. A more desirable strategy may be merchandising seafood products that are in abundant supply. The contribution to overhead from various in-store departments pays for overall operating costs—utilities, management salaries, property and equipment leases, and so on. Overhead costs must be paid; therefore, a contribution to overhead from each store department provides for a profitable store operation.

> *Assumption 2:* A seafood department must provide customers with acceptable, affordable products in the long term.

This assumption focuses on serving customer needs and complements the first assumption. Customers' budget restraints and tastes may limit the sales of certain items. The wrong seafood product or an improperly priced product may cause poor product movement. This increases shrinkage through perishability which in turn reduces gross margin dollars supporting the department.

Several other critical assumptions should be recognized because of their impact on the departments' success.

> *Assumption 3:* Fresh seafood and seafood products are scarce food resources.

Seafood's value tends to increase and decrease with available supplies; however, an abundance is not always available. The implication of this assumption means that pricing strategies must be studied carefully to take full advantage of the intrinsic value of fresh seafood.

> *Assumption 4:* Seafood—you sell it or smell it.

Seafood is a highly perishable product; therefore, management decisions must be made properly to ensure product movement. In the long run, the level of quality of seafood products is vital to the continued success of the seafood department.

PROFILE OF A TRADE AREA

Seafood is gaining popularity with many segments of American society. Americans want to be healthy and slim, and seafood contributes to these objectives. This new-found consumer interest in a variety of seafoods has baffled many seafood managers. The principles and procedures of management discussed here show seafood managers how to think through the consumers' needs and how to serve these needs profitably.

Philosophy and Purpose for Creating a Seafood Department

A profitable retail food store must meet the needs of its customers. To do this the food store reflects the offerings of many departments.

> *Principle:* Customers' needs must be met if a seafood department is to be profitable.

The first step in satisfying this principle is analyzing customer needs of a store trade area. Customer needs can be determined by family income, employment status, and preferences for seafood products and services. Customer needs, when translated through a written purpose statement for the seafood department, can guide management in developing an effective marketing program and result in greater customer satisfaction.

A seafood department *purpose statement* should reflect its overall philosophy by taking into account the needs of its consumers based on their incomes, employment, tastes, and preferences for seafood. For example, if a retail store is located in a trade area where customers have high incomes, a seafood manager may market high-value items such as crabmeat, lobster, and/or traditional finfish. In trade areas with lower income levels, underutilized fish species might be offered to customers. In all cases, customer needs for seafood must be met if the department is to be successful and profitable.

The purpose statement for a seafood department consists of at least five principal categories. An example purpose statement might read as follows:

> *Purpose of the Seafood Department:* To increase store traffic and sales by providing customers with a wide selection of fresh and wholesome seafood products and services at prices that reflect a value while contributing adequate returns to the food store for the resources used and providing employment satisfaction to the personnel involved in the department.

To increase store and sales traffic . . .: This statement creates an agreement among store management that greater emphasis will be given to the sales volume of the seafood department. At the same time, the seafood manager needs adequate resources to make this aspect of the purpose statement a reality.

. . . by providing customers with a wide selection of fresh and wholesome seafood products and services . . .: The product mix statement implies that management expects to provide an array of seafood products, maybe sixteen to thirty different products, for customers' choices. It also may imply that customers with a wide range of incomes shop at the store. In this purpose statement, management has provided many choices to satisfy their customers. It also indicates that management is committed to merchandising a high quality product mix. The word *wholesome* means added care in handling and inventory control will be expected from employees. Adequate "services" in the department will be provided to support the seafood products and their quality until the purchase is completed.

. . . at prices that reflect value . . .: This phrase means that customers will be sold products that represent value for their food dollar. Along with the "wide selection," this will provide customers the opportunity to do comparison shopping and enhance value-seeking shoppers' satisfaction.

. . . while contributing adequate returns to the food store for the resources used . . .: Prices set competitively in a seafood department should provide for adequate gross

margins to cover the costs of department operations and return adequate dollars for store overhead. Management should set sales and overhead objectives expected from the seafood department, and accordingly, departmental prices and gross margin strategies should be set to realize those objectives.

. . . while providing employment satisfaction to the personnel involved . . .: Key personnel in a seafood department help determine its success. These employees must realize the opportunity to work for themselves as well as the company. Seafood marketing is a new venture for many retail stores; consequently, additional employee orientation and training will be necessary to develop and maintain seafood department employees at a competitive edge.

A purpose statement creates a philosophy for a seafood department by causing management to think through the opportunities and problems associated with servicing their customers. In general, the purpose statement sets the standard for department operations. The statement recognizes the key actors in seafood marketing—customers, seafood products and services, the retail department and store, and employees. The purpose statement of a seafood department is the cornerstone for expressing management's philosophy. A well-thought-out purpose statement serves as a guide to a profitable seafood department.

Setting Objectives

Food retailers operate their stores with certain objectives in mind to ensure their competitive position in a trade area. Specific objectives focus on total sales, gross margins, and expenses. These objectives can only be accomplished if each department contributes to the overall results from store operations. For much of the past two decades, many food retailers have not viewed seafood departments as potentially profitable. There were many problems, both external and internal, with a seafood department operation that created a negative image of fresh seafood departments for most retailers, whose simple solution was "Don't sell fish." Today, many of the earlier operational problems associated with seafood have been or are being eliminated, making the profitability of a department more of a reality.

> *Principle:* Successful seafood departments should set objectives for total sales, gross margins, and expenses.

John Troke said, "Objectives are like mile markers on a highway. They keep you on the path and identify your progress toward your destination." By setting goals, the seafood department manager knows the progress being made toward the benchmarks relating to profitability. The department purpose statement sets the broad boundaries, and the objectives further refine the scope of the department.

Departmental objectives generally focus on personnel, preparation, products, and profit (the 4 P's). Written objectives of a seafood department translate tasks into benchmarks (numbers). This information enables a manager to guide a department toward meeting customer needs profitably. The seafood department may have as many as ten specified objectives relating to its operation.

Setting objectives for the seafood department should be a joint venture between store management and the department management. These multiple objectives reflect customer needs in a trade area, the supply conditions of seafood products, and the internal store operations. In supporting the management principle, it is suggested the following objectives be set for a seafood department operation:

dollar sales volume, gross margins (percentage and dollars), shrinkage, direct costs, sales per employee, in-store traffic generator, and contribution to overhead.

Objectives should be written in a format that is easily understood by both those writing them and those using them. The objectives may be written by store management, seafood department manager, and departmental personnel. Objectives should be measurable, have a time limit assigned, and be expressed in either absolute or percentage terms. Suppose a food market sold $2,000 of fresh seafood each week but wanted to increase that sales value. A sales objective might be stated as follows: "To increase sales of fresh seafood by 100 percent by June 30." The implications of the objective means more customer traffic moving through a department, more and varied seafood products merchandised, more support activities, and more facilities space devoted to the seafood department. It may or it may not mean all of the stated changes noted as a result of making one objective statement.

What are some of the implications realized from the sales objectives? Assuming the department has at least one year to work toward the objective, twice as much seafood will be moved through the department annually. New sources of product supply or additional display space may be needed. The seafood department may need relocating within the store, or a new image created. Brainstorming is helpful in determining all the various impacts that will affect the seafood department because of the change in the sales volume objective.

An Action Plan

Develop an action plan to support each stated objective. How will this objective be realized? Information from previous sections will impact the action plan for a sales objective.

Action Plan:

1. Expand seafood products offered by the department.
   a. Factors affecting the trade area impact here.
   b. Availability of supply is a factor.
2. Promote new items.
   a. Attract new customer segment.
   b. Have available recipes.
   c. Conduct cooking demonstrations.
   d. Coordinate newspaper and in-store advertising with available products.

There may be many other parts to the action plans for the sales objective, but the example shows the coordination needed to reach a sales department objective.

The gross margin dollars provide operating dollars for a department to cover the costs of seafood products sold. A gross margin objective will be based on a sales plan and other strategies determined by the store management. An overall gross margin is a product of the retail seafood products sold minus cost of goods. A gross margin on crabmeat, for instance, may be set at 20 percent but a 50 percent margin specified for bluefish, giving an average margin somewhere between 21 and 49 percent, depending on the volume of each product sold during a sales period. If an overall gross margin is specified, the seafood manager may have great latitude in adjusting the gross margin on each of, say, ten to twenty-one different products. Managing the gross margin objective will probably be easiest when seafood supplies are plentiful and most difficult during periods of scarcity.

$$\text{Gross Margin Formula} = \frac{\text{Retail Price} - \text{Cost of Seafood}}{\text{Retail Price of Seafood}}$$

$$30\% = \frac{\$1.00 - \$.70}{\$1.00}$$

Action Plan for Accomplishing Gross Margin Objective

1. Better signage in the department.
   a. Permit customers better comparison shopping.
   b. Show the value of each product in the department.
2. Merchandise more whole fish.
   a. Weigh the fish before filleting.
   b. Buy the species in plentiful supply.
   c. Increase the number of species marketed.

Gross margin dollars cover the department's operating cost plus contributing to overhead costs. Three categories of particular importance to the seafood manager are shrinkage, direct costs, and sales per employee.

Shrinkage is defined as any products not sold because of spoilage or other losses. It has a direct affect on gross margin—a 1 percent increase in shrinkage can reduce the gross margin by 1 percent or more. Management expects some shrinkage in a perishable department such as seafood. Suppose the seafood manager sets an objective of 3 percent for the shrinkage expense. What is the catch?

1. Reduce spoilage of seafood products.
   a. Use ice to cover inventory while on display.
   b. Clean utensils properly to prevent contamination.
   c. Rotate stock to retain shelf life.
2. Account for all incoming products.
   a. Check weight of species against invoice.
   a. Make sure invoice price charged is related to species in the shipment, that is, if invoice price is for haddock, it should be haddock, not turbot.

Direct costs incurred in the seafood department are those costs allocated directly to the operation of the seafood department. A few examples of direct costs are labor, wrapping paper, receipts, and so on. These costs are charged against the gross margin dollars of the department. Efforts to control these expenditures will direct more of the sales dollars into the contribution to overhead column.

Action Plan for Controlling Direct Costs Objective

Reduce labor costs to $5 per hour including fringes.

1. Be more selective in hiring.
2. Devote twenty minutes to employee training per day.
3. Schedule work on a priority basis in the department.
4. Pay on performance.

Reduce packaging costs one-half of 1 percent of sales.

1. Study alternative packaging materials for value and cost.
2. Reduce waste in the wrapping program.

Hold receipt costs to present levels.

1. Focus on receipts that apply to several species.
2. Print recipes in large quantities to realize cost savings.

Productivity standards are important in controlling costs. The most common measure of productivity is the sales per employee value. A reasonable common measure to aim for is the sales per hour in the meat department, because the seafood and the meat departments have similar functions. If the standards are realistic, labor costs should be under control. Sales per employee is measured in dollars and not physical units, yet it should be a figure that valid comparisons can be made from, if used in the same time period. Sales per employee can be affected by an effective labor management program. Tasks in the department should be defined and listed, and these tasks should be classified into duties and assigned on a priority basis.

REFERENCES

Borgstrom, Georg. (ed.). 1965. *Fish as Food.* (Vol. IV.). New York: Academic Press.

Brand Group, Inc. 1978. *A Retail Identification Plan for Seafood Species: A Description of the Product and Recommended Principles of Identification.* Chicago.

Capps, O. and Havlicek, J., Jr. 1981. *Meat and Seafood Demand Patterns: A Comparison of the S_1-Branch Demand System and the Constant Elasticity of Demand System.* Blacksburg, VA: Virginia Agricultural Experiment Station, VPI & SU.

Coale, Charles W., Jr., Ward, D. R., and Haby, M. G. 1982. *A Fresh Seafood Marketing Workshop: Management, Quality Maintenance, Merchandising & Profitability Analysis.* Blacksburg, VA: Virginia Tech Sea Grant Program, VPI & SU.

Krueckeberg, Harry F. and Hamilton, J. R. 1981. "Consumer Perceptives of National, Generic and Private Brand Grocery Products." *J. Food Distribution Res.* 105–113.

Nickelson, Ranzell, II. 1974. *Standard Texas Green Headless Shrimp Pack* (2nd ed.). College Station, TX: Seafood Quality Advisory Laboratory, Texas Agricultural Extension Service.

Winslow, Robert L. 1982. Microbial Control of Meat—A Retailer's Approach. *J. Food Protection.* 45(2):1169–1172.

CHAPTER

16

Nutrition and Preparation

Laurie M. Dean

Foods from the sea have for hundreds of years been a source of high quality protein. In the five basic groups, seafood belongs to the same category as meat, poultry, eggs, dried beans and peas—all major sources of protein. Fish also is a good source of other nutrients. This chapter examines the major nutrients found in seafoods and discusses various preparation methods.

A review of the following will help you understand the measurements referred to in this chapter.

1 pound (lb)	=	16 ounces (oz)
1 ounce	=	Approximately 28 grams (g)
1 gram	=	1000 milligrams (mg)
1 gram	=	1,000,000 micrograms (μg)

MAJOR NUTRIENTS

Protein

Protein is absolutely essential to human diets. It ensures that amino acids are available to build new tissue and maintain old tissue. It forms enzymes, proteins which function to catalyze body reactions. It forms some of the body's hormones, substances which act to regulate some body functions (e.g., regulation of body temperature). Proteins make up the body's antibodies, the body's defense against such things as bacteria, viruses, and toxins. Proteins are also essential for helping to maintain the body's fluid balance, salt balance, and acid-base balance, and they can serve as a source of energy.

The amount of protein in fish varies from species to species and even within species. This variation is caused by differences in feeding habits, age and sex of the fish, and fat and water content of the flesh. Generally speaking, in finfish the muscle contains about 18 to 22 g of protein in each 100 g of edible meat. (A 100-g portion is roughly equivalent to an average-sized serving of 3.5 ounces.) There is an inverse relationship between fat content and water and protein content in fish. High fat content generally means that the moisture and protein contents are lower. Shellfish that are classified as mollusks (oysters, clams, scallops, etc.) generally contain a little less protein than finfish; crustaceans (crabs, shrimp, lobsters, etc.) tend to contain more protein than finfish.

Fish protein is classified as high quality, that is, it contains all the amino acids necessary for growth and maintenance of body tissues. (Amino acids are molecular units that hook together in various formations to form the chains called proteins.) This protein is also highly digestible, due to the short muscle fibers and lack of tough connective tissues.

Fat

Fat performs several essential body functions. It is a major source of energy for the body, making available over twice as much energy per gram as either protein or carbohydrate. (Fat yields 9 calories per gram; protein and carbohydrate both yield 4 calories per gram.) Fat also surrounds and protects the body's organs and helps the body maintain a constant temperature. In addition, fat can be found as an important part of the membranes that surround the body's cells. Finally, many other nutrients are soluble in fat (vitamins A, D, and K), and therefore, fat is a "carrier" for certain fat-soluble nutrients.

Seafood tends to be low in fat content, but what fat it does have differs from that found in many other protein foods. Of greatest interest to most people is that seafood fat contains a great proportion of highly unsaturated fatty acids. (Fatty acids are chains of carbon atoms bonded together; the number of carbons in the chain varies from one fatty acid to another.) The polyunsaturated fatty acids have been shown to help reduce the body's cholesterol level.

The fat content of fish varies with the season, geographical origin, prevailing temperatures of the environment, physiological state of the animal, and the food available to the animal. It is important to realize that the dark flesh of fish has more fat and therefore less protein than the light flesh. Fish are usually categorized as lean, moderately fat, and fat with the percentage of fat being less than 5 percent, from 5 to 10 percent, and greater than 10 percent, respectively. Some examples of each category are given in Table 16-1.

Though the polyunsaturated nature of fats in fish makes it highly desirable in diets, this same characteristic makes it more susceptible to oxidation and rancidity. This is the reason that bluefish, for example, a moderately fat fish, will spoil more rapidly in your freezer than sea trout, a lean fish.

Water

Fish and shellfish are very high in water content, averaging 80 to 85 percent. Generally, mollusks contain more water than either finfish or crustaceans.

Water is essential for body functions—in fact, it makes up about 60 perrcent of body weight. Water performs many functions, among them serving as part of the

Table 16-1. *Fish Categorized by Fat Content*

Lean	Moderately Fat	Fat
Halibut	Bluefish	Mackerel
Flounder	Mullet	Herring
Red snapper	Salmon	Lake trout
Whiting		

source of the chemical structures and compounds that form the cells in the body. It is involved in many chemical reactions and is used as a major medium of transportation in the body. Water is also a very good solvent and therefore dissolves substances and carries them to the cells. Acting as a lubricant and shock absorber, water protects the body's joints in the form of synovial fluid and also serves in such places as the amniotic fluid surrounding a growing fetus. Water helps the body to maintain a constant temperature of 98.6 (37°C).

Minerals

Minerals are inorganic substances that are often referred to as ash when talking about the nutritional composition of a food. To put it simplistically this term refers to the fact that ashes from the body's minerals remain after the carbon atoms comprising carbohydrate, fat, protein, and vitamins in the body form carbon dioxide. The leftover hydrogens and oxygens from these compounds join to form water which, with the rest of the water that comprises the body, evaporates. The only thing left then are ashes from the body's minerals. In humans, the minerals weigh about 5 pounds (2.3 kg). In the edible portion of fish, the percent of ash varies from 0.4 to 1.5 g/100 g. Because there is a large mineral concentration in bones and skin, the percentage of ash is related to the amounts of skin and bone present in the market form consumed.

Seafood includes the following important major minerals (those present in the body in amounts greater than 5 grams): calcium, phosphorus, sodium, potassium, and magnesium. Trace minerals of significance are iodine, iron, copper, fluorine, cobalt, and zinc.

Calcium

In the human body, calcium is largely concentrated in the bones and teeth with a very small percentage (less than 1 percent) found in the fluid surrounding body cells and inside the body's cells. Dietary calcium is essential for the formation of bones and teeth, and helps regulate the transport of ions across cell membranes (Ions are electrically charged particles that function in the body to help regulate water and acid-base balance. Calcium ions carry a +2 charge [Ca^{++}].) It also is important in nerve impulse transmission; is necessary in order for muscles to contract (e.g., maintaining heartbeat); aids blood clotting; and helps to maintain the body's collagen, a substance that functions to hold cells together.

In children, a calcium deficiency can lead to a disease called rickets, usually characterized by a severe bowing of the child's legs. Calcium deficiency leading to bone malformation in adulthood is known as osteomalacia. Both of these diseases also can be attributed to a lack of vitamin D which is necessary in order for calcium to be absorbed across the intestinal cell membranes.

Some types of seafood are excellent sources of dietary calcium with values varying from 5 to 200 mg per 100 g. This variability can be attributed to the amount of calcium in the water and/or food, and the age, size, and sexual maturity of the animal. Whole finfish are a very good source of calcium; crustaceans and mollusks tend to contain more calcium than finfish. Especially good sources are canned fishes with edible bones (sardines, salmon) and oysters.

Phosphorus

About 85 percent of the body's phosphorus is found in the bones and teeth. The remainder is found in small amounts in the body's blood plasma and in larger amounts as phosphoric acid, a constituent of all body cells.

Phosphorus serves many key functions in the body. Along with calcium, it helps give strength to bones and teeth. It is a component of DNA and RNA, both responsible for the cell's genetic code, and as a component of phosphate groups, it is necessary for the activation of some enzymes and the B vitamins. It is a component of ATP, a substance which carries the cell's energy. It is a structural part of some lipids or fats (called phospholipids) that are responsible for transporting other lipids through the blood. It is a component of cell membranes and is essential in helping maintain the body's acid/base balance by acting as a "buffer."

Because it is so abundant in their cells, the muscle tissue from animals is the best source of dietary phosphorus. Deficiencies of phosphorus are unknown. As a matter of fact, since Americans consume so much animal protein and consequently quite a bit of phosphorus along with it, and since any excess phosphorus that the body does not use is excreted carrying along with it some calcium, the Recommended Dietary Allowance (RDA) for calcium is higher here than it is in other countries. Consumption ratios for calcium to phosphorus are recommended to be anywhere from 3:1 to 1:3 with a ratio of 1:1 generally accepted as reasonable.

The phosphorus content of seafood ranges from 100 to 400 mg/100 g of flesh with the variability dependent on the same factor as listed for calcium. Crustaceans and mollusks tend to have less phosphorus than finfish.

Sodium

Of all the minerals, sodium seems to have gained the most attention nationwide. Sodium is the positive ion making up the compound sodium chloride or common table salt. The American public has been advised to reduce sodium intake, and, to this end, manufacturers are introducing new salt substitute products, salt-free and reduced salt products, and are beginning to label sodium contents for various foods.

Some sodium is essential. It is easily absorbed into the body fluids, and the kidneys are thus responsible for filtering excess sodium out of the blood for eventual excretion or, conversely, for conserving sodium when shortages occur in the body. The amount of sodium excreted in a day normally equals the amount consumed. Sodium is the primary positive ion on the outside of the cell helping regulate the total amount of fluid in the body and maintaining a constant ratio of sodium to water. It also permits nerve transmission and muscle contraction.

Deficiencies of sodium are rare. In the United States, the opposite condition, ingestion of too much sodium, usually is the case. In people who are genetically predisposed to developing hypertension (high blood pressure), consumption of a great deal of sodium can lead to problems. Putting it simply, a higher sodium level in the blood increases the fluid level, which puts a strain on the heart by forcing it to work harder to pump the body's fluids. Americans are being urged to reduce their sodium intake by limiting salt consumption to about 5 g (1 teaspoon) per day. As salt is about 40 percent sodium, this would roughly equal about 2,000 mg of sodium per day. Sodium is already present in many foods and is added to some processed foods, so this goal can probably be met by reducing the topical addition of salt to foods and the consumption of high salt foods like potato chips and pretzels.

The sodium content of finfish ranges from 30 to 150 mg with an average of 60 mg/100 grams of muscle. (Variations in sodium content of flesh within species is attributable to size, season, and in some cases time of life cycle). Finfish, therefore, are quite low in sodium content, and, in fact, are recommended for people on low sodium diets. The sodium content of mollusks and crustaceans varies with species, but is higher than that of the same portion of finfish. (For a 100-g cooked portion, hard clams have approximately 205 mg, steamed crabs have 456 mg, fresh lobster has 325 mg, scallops have 265 mg, and shrimp have 140 mg of sodium, respectively.) Canned seafoods, because of the salt added during processing, can be quite high in sodium content.

Potassium

Like sodium, potassium is a positively charged ion; potassium ions are the principal positively charged ions inside the body's cells and, as such, they play a major role in maintaining fluid balance in the body. Potassium is essential for maintenance of heartbeat, nerve transmission, muscle contraction, and plays a catalytic role in carbohydrate and protein metabolism. Because of its role in maintaining fluid balance, if excess water should be lost from the body, with the consequent loss of sodium ions, potassium ions would be drawn from within the cells and excreted. This could, in severe cases, cause sudden death from heart failure because of potassium's role in maintaining the heartbeat. The potassium content of fish varies from 250 to 500 mg/100 g of muscle with an average of 400 mg. The potassium content of shellfish tends to be lower than that of finfish. Though fish and shellfish are not considered to be principal sources of potassium, they are considered reasonable sources considering that the average diet in the United States supplies 1.5 to 2.5 g of potassium daily.

Magnesium

Magnesium, a mineral found in small quantities [about 1.75 ounces (49.5 g) in a 130-pound (59.1 kg) individual] in the human body, is important for several reasons. It serves as a catalyst in activating the enzyme system that aids in the metabolism of carbohydrates, and its major role seems to be related to bonding of phosphate groups to ATP molecules. Other functions of magnesium are as a vital constituent in protein making, as an aid to muscle relaxation after contraction, and as a calcium binder in tooth enamel.

Magnesium deficiencies are not likely but can occur in extreme circumstances (vomiting, diarrhea, protein malnutrition, etc.). It is recommended that adult males consume 350 mg of magnesium/day and females 300 mg/day. Fish is generally considered a good source of magnesium with the amount in the muscle varying with species.

TRACE MINERALS

Iron

Perhaps no other mineral has received as much attention as the trace mineral iron. Television and radio commercials tout the consumption of iron supplements to prevent such maladies as iron deficiency anemia, a disease in which the red blood cells have less than normal hemoglobin and consequently cannot get enough oxygen for the cells to use.

Hemoglobin and myoglobin are proteins that carry oxygen and release it. Hemoglobin is found concentrated in the blood, and myoglobin in the cells. Iron is a part of both compounds and is responsible for the bonding on or release of oxygen by each. Iron performs this crucial function because it can assume a +2 or a +3 charge (Fe^{++}, Fe^{+++}), and as needed, the ionized iron can switch from one charge to the other, with the consequent holding onto or release of oxygen which carries a –2 charge.

It is difficult to say how much of the iron consumed is absorbed by the body, but a rough estimate would be about 10 percent. Iron absorption may be aided by the presence of acid; therefore, it is frequently suggested that citrus fruits or juice (containing ascorbic acid) be taken along with iron-containing food.

Adult males and older females should consume 10 mg of iron/day and females of childbearing age 18 mg/day. Finfish contains about 1 mg of iron/100 g of flesh, with dark meat containing more than white meat. If this iron is absorbed, then fish is a reasonably good source of iron. Oysters are an exceptionally good source of iron. Three-quarters of a cup (177.9 ml) will provide 10 mg of iron. Other shellfish considered good sources of iron are clams (3 ounces/85 g raw have 5.2 mg of iron) and shrimp (which contain about 2.6 mg of iron in 3 ounces/85g of canned product).[1]

Copper

Copper, like iron, is necessary to the formation of hemoglobin. It also plays a role in respiration and in the release of energy, helping iron change from one ionic state to the other (Fe++ to Fe+++), and helps maintain the sheath around the muscle fibers.

The amount of copper estimated to be safe and adequate in the daily diet of adults is 2.0 to 3.0 mg. Shellfish appear to be good dietary sources of copper, generally averaging more than 0.25 mg/100 g given for finfish.

Iodine

Seafoods are the richest natural food source of iodine, a trace mineral that is a component of the hormone thyroxin, which regulates the rate that energy is released. Other good sources of iodine include iodized salt and foods that are grown in soil that has a high iodine content.

It is recommended that the adult intake of iodine be 150 μg per day. This Recommended Dietary Allowance is not difficult to meet if seafoods are included in the diet. The iodine values reported for finfish range from 16 to 318 μg/100 g of flesh with the iodine seemng to concentrate in the oily portions of the fish. Freshwater fish have lower iodine concentration with values ranging from 1.7 to 40 μg/100 g of flesh.

Other Trace Minerals

Fluorine, necessary for healthy, strong teeth and bones; cobalt, an essential component of the vitamin B_{12} molecule; and zinc, a component of many of the body's enzymes, are found in seafood in varying amounts. The elements chromium and vanadium are also found in minute quantities in seafood.

VITAMINS

Vitamins are organic chemical compounds essential for promoting growth, reproduction, and maintenance of normal body health and function. Vitamins are

[1] Nutritional information about seafood is in many cases inadequate and incomplete. This information was taken from the USDA Handbook No. 8.

usually classified into two distinct groups—those that are soluble in water, including the B complex of vitamins and vitamin C (also known as ascorbic acid); and those that are soluble in fat, including vitamins A, D, E, and K. Fat-soluble vitamins, because of their nature, are not quickly excreted from the body; therefore, any quantities of fat-soluble vitamins ingested in excess of the body's needs are stored, mainly in the liver and fatty tissues. Excesses of fat-soluble vitamins can reach toxic levels because of the body's storage capacity.

Unlike fat-soluble vitamins, excesses of the water-soluble vitamins are normally excreted from the body, although extreme excesses provided by vitamin supplements can be toxic. The water-soluble nature of these vitamins makes care in the home preparation of foods containing them essential; they are easily dissolved in the water used in many preparations.

The vitamin content of fish varies with species, age, season, sexual maturity, and geographical area, and specific information about vitamin content is sketchy at best.

Fat-Soluble Vitamins

Vitamin A deficiency is a serious world health problem—lack of vitamin A impairs several crucial bodily functions. Notably, vitamin A is essential to maintaining the health of the outside covering of the eye. Xerophthalmia, an inflammation of the eye that can lead to blindness, can be prevented by proper levels of vitamin A. Other epithelial tissues depend on vitamin A for their health. These epithelial cells normally secrete infection-preventive mucus, but when vitamin A is lacking, they instead secrete a protein called keratin, which causes epithelial cells to become dry and hard and eventually die.

Vitamin A is also known to prevent what is commonly called night blindness, the inability of the eye to quickly adjust from light to darkness. It also plays a role in growth. Lack of vitamin A, causing keratinization of the tongue cells or deterioration of the epithelial tissue of the intestinal tract, can cause a low appetite which results in the cessation of growth.

Vitamin A in fish is found concentrated in the viscera, especially the liver. Fish liver oils like cod liver oil and shark liver oil are excellent seafood sources of vitamin A. As a matter of fact, before vitamin A was synthesized in the laboratory, sharks were caught in large quantities and the oil extracted from the liver to provide vitamin A. Because much of the oil in fish is found in the dark flesh, this flesh has higher concentrations of vitamin A. Among shellfish, oysters appear to be the best source.

Vitamin A is measured in international units (IU) or retinol equivalents (RE) with the average male needing 5,000 IU daily and the average adult female needing about 4,000 IU daily. The vitamin A content of fish flesh ranges from 0 to 18,000 IU with, for example, canned pink salmon (3 ounces/85 g) having 60; and 3 ounces (85 g) of sardines having 190.

As mentioned in the section on calcium, vitamin D is essential for normal bone and tooth development. Proper absorption, movement, deposition, and excretion of calcium and phosphorus is dependent on adequate levels of vitamin D. The estimated safe level of intake for all individuals is approximately 400 IU. Extreme excesses, because it is stored by the body, can lead to toxicity symptoms like diarrhea and nausea. Unique among vitamins, D can be synthesized in the body with the use of the sun's ultraviolet rays. Vitamin D also is found in the lipid portion of food.

The vitamin D content of fish is dependent on the species. Oily fish such as mackerel and herring contain a higher level of vitamin D than leaner fish like flounder and sea trout.

Information on vitamins E and K is sketchy. More work needs to be done in determining nutritional values in seafoods.

Water-Soluble Vitamins

Water-soluble vitamins can be found throughout a fish's body rather than concentrated in the viscera like fat-soluble vitamins. Among the important vitamins in this classification are thiamine, riboflavin, pyridoxine, niacin, folic acid, pantothenic acid, vitamin B_{12}, and vitamin C.

There are a number of vitamins in what is known as the B complex. Generally, they are found in the same groups of foods and their function within the cells has to do with energy release.

Thiamine functions primarily as a coenzyme (a substance that serves to activate an enzyme) to catalyze the breakdown of carbohydrate to glucose and helps store energy in the compound ATP. The lack of thiamine blocks the normal breakdown of carbohydrate and subsequent energy production. The recommended intake for adult males is 12.5 mg/day and for women 1 mg. Fish muscle averages approximately 100 μg/100 g of flesh. Oysters, an especially good source of thiamine, contain about .25 mg in a ¾ ounce (21.3 g) serving.

Fish muscle is a good source of niacin. Like thiamine, niacin forms part of a coenzyme, which is essential in the production of energy. Specifically, niacin is crucial in the body's formation of energy from glucose. Symptoms of niacin deficiency include diarrhea, dementia, and dermatitis in the form of a rash that occurs on parts of the body exposed to the sun. Niacin in fish muscle ranges from 0.9 mg to 3.1 mg/100 g of tissue. Among shellfish, oysters, with .33 mg/cup (236.6 ml), are a reasonably good source of niacin. The RDA for niacin is about 1.0 mg for adult women and 1.4 mg for adult males.

Riboflavin, another of the B-complex vitamins, is essential in the body's energy production, playing an especially important role in breaking down fatty acids and amino acids that are to be used for energy. The RDA for women ranges from 1 to 1.5 mg and for men ranges from 1.5 to 2 mg/day. The concentration of riboflavin in fish is quite variable with the dark meat containing more than the white meat. The amount of riboflavin found in many fish, however, is comparable to that found in terrestrial animals (50 to 980 μg/100 g of muscle).

Vitamin B_6, referred to as pyridoxine, is involved in a number of body functions. It converts one amino acid to another that is needed by the body; aids in the breakdown of amino acids slated for energy production; converts linoleic acid to arachidonic acid (both fatty acids); aids in the synthesis of such substances as hemoglobin; and helps maintain the blood glucose level. Adults need 2 mg/day of pyridoxine. Whole fish is a good source of pyridoxine with values ranging from 100 to 1200 μg/100 g of fish flesh.

Vitamin B_{12}, also known as cobalamin, is found in significant amounts in seafood, especially fatty fish and shellfish. The potency of the vitamin is higher in dark flesh fish like herring than in white flesh fish like flounder. The amount found in fish muscle varies from 0 in shark to 1.9 μg/100 g in Pacific herring. Cobalamin is necessary for maintaining the sheath around nerve fibers, for promoting growth, and especially for the production of red blood cells. Recommended dietary intake of vitamin B_{12} for adults is 3 μg, a very small amount, so seafood can generally be considered a very good source.

Very little is known about the human requirement for pantothenic acid. It is known that, like other B vitamins, it functions in the coenzyme system of the body. Greatest concentration of pantothenic acid in fish appears to be found in the gonads. What concentration is found in the flesh of fish is higher in dark meat than in white meat.

Two other water-soluble vitamins, folic acid and vitamin C, are not found in any significant amounts in the edible portions of fish.

In sum, finfish and shellfish are highly nutritious foods. Additionally, when consumed as a part of a well-balanced diet they can add variety in flavor, texture, and color to meals.

PREPARATION

Fish are delicious—if cooked properly. Cooking fish develops its flavor, softens connective tissue, and makes the protein easier to digest. Cooking fish at too high a temperature or for too long a time toughens them, dries them out, and destroys their flavor.

How can you tell when fish are cooked? Raw fish and shellfish have a translucent, sometimes watery look. During the cooking process the watery juices become milky colored, giving the flesh an opaque, whitish (depending on species) tint. This color change is unmistakable. When the flesh has taken on this opaque whitish tint to the center of the thickest part, fish are completely cooked. At this point the flesh will easily separate into flakes, and if there are bones present, the flesh will come away from them readily. A gereral rule of thumb to go by in baking and broiling finfish is the "ten minutes to the inch" (2.54 cm) rule. Measure the fish in the thickest portion and cook it ten minutes if it is 1 inch thick or whatever corresponding fraction applies if the fish is more or less than 1 inch.

Most cooked fish tend to break up easily, so handle fish as little and as gently as possible during and after cooking to preserve appearance.

Baking is a form of dry heat cooking and one of the easiest ways to cook fish. But "bake fish easy." Fish like a preheated, moderate oven set at 350°F for a relatively short period of time. This temperature keeps the moistness and flavor in the fish, prevents drying, and keeps the fish tender and palatable. Fish not baked in a sauce or with a topping should be basted with melted fat or oil to keep the surface moist. Fish can be baked from the frozen state, if the cooking time is increased to allow for thawing during the baking process and if the recipe does not call for special handling such as stuffing or rolling.

Broiling, like baking, is a dry heat method of cookery but in broiling the heat is direct, intense, and comes from only one source. Thin foods tend to dry out under the broiler, so when planning to use this method, choose pan-dressed fish, fillets, or steaks which are about an inch (2.54 cm) thick in preference to the thinner ones. If frozen, the fish should be thawed. Baste fish well with melted fat or oil or a basting sauce before placing them under the broiler. Baste again while broiling to keep the fish moist. Be sure to adequately grease the broiler pan.

The length of time it takes to broil fish depends on thickness and the distance placed from the heat. As a general guide, have the surface of the fish about 3 to 4 inches (7.6 to 10.2 cm) from the heat source.

Cooking time usually will range from ten to fifteen minutes to reach the "fish flake easily" stage. As a rule, the fish do not need to be turned because the heat of the pan will cook the underside adequately. Turn the thicker pieces, such as pan-dressed fish, when half the allotted cooking time is up. Baste again with fat or sauce. Always serve broiled fish sizzling hot.

Charcoal broiling is a dry heat cooking method over hot coals. Fish, because they cook so quickly, are a natural for this method of cookery. It is quick and, as an extra bonus, adds a delightful flavor. Pan-dressed fish, fillets, and steaks are all suitable for charcoal broiling. If frozen, the fish should be thawed first. Fish are usually cooked about 4 inches (10.2 cm) from moderately hot coals for ten to twenty minutes, depending on the thickness of the fish.

Since charcoal broiling is a dry heat cooking method, thicker cuts of fish are preferable because they tend to dry out less than thin ones. Also, the fish should be basted generously with a sauce containing some fat before and while cooking to keep the fish juicy and flavorful.

SMOKING

Smoking (for flavor only) is a simple technique that requires a minimum of effort and equipment, and the fish smoked in this manner can be used in various recipes from appetizers to salads and casseroles. It is not a method of preserving fish, however. Items needed for smoking are a hooded or covered grill (either gas, electric, or charcoal); briquets (if a charcoal grill is to be used); 1 pound (454 g) of hickory or other hardwood chips; water; salt; oil; and fish. The best smoked fish is produced from "fat" fish like bluefish, mullet, mackerel, herring, and shad to name a few; however, other species can be used.

To smoke fish for flavor,

1. *Soak the chips* in 2 quarts (1.89 l) of water until the fire is ready (or at least as long as the fish marinate).
2. *Marinate the fish* in a brine of 1 cup (236.6 ml) of salt dissolved in 1 gallon (3.79 l) of water for the length of time shown in Table 16-2.
3. *Start the fire* using fewer briquets than for an average broiling fire. Adjust the temperature on gas or electric grills according to the table. When the coals have burned to a red color, spread evenly over the bottom of the grill.
4. *Cover the charcoal* with one-third of the wet chips, which not only produce the smoke but also lower the temperature.

Table 16-2. *Timetable for Smoking Fish*

Size and Shape	How Long to Marinate in Brine	Cook at (°F)	How Long
Fillets or steaks (½ inch thick)	30 min.	150–175	1 hr.
		200	30 min.
		250	20 min.
Fillets or steads (¾ inch thick)	45 min.	150–175	1 hr. + 30 min.
		200	30–45 min.
		250	30 min.
Fillets or steads (1½ inch thick)	1 hr	150–175	2 hr.
		200	1 hr. + 15 min.
		250	45–50 min.

5. *Grease the grill* generously and keep oil handy for basting.
6. *Drain and dry the fish* and place it on the grill skin side down.
7. *Baste the fish* at the start and as needed during cooking to prevent the fish from drying out.
8. *Cover the grill* with the hood.
9. *Smoke the fish* for the amount of time indicated in Table 16-2.
10. *Add the remainder of the chips* as needed to produce smoke.
11. *Fish are done* when they turn to a golden brown and flake easily when tested with a fork.

FRYING

Frying is a method of cooking food in fat. For frying, choose a fat that may be heated to a high temperature without danger of smoking: A smoking fat begins to decompose and will give the food an unpleasant flavor. Vegetable oils and fats are preferable to animal fats. Frozen fish must be thawed before frying. Separate the pieces and cut to uniform size.

The temperature of the fat is extremely important. Too high heat will brown the outside of the fish before the centers are cooked. Too low heat will give a pale, greasy, and fat-soaked product. The most satisfactory frying temperature for fish is 350 to 375°F (194 to 208°C).

After frying, drain the fish immediately on absorbent paper to remove excess fat. Keep the fish warm in a low oven until all pieces are cooked, then serve immediately.

Deep-Fat Frying

Cooking in a deep layer of fat, deep-fat frying is a quick and excellent way to cook tender foods and precooked foods. Use enough fat to float the fish but do not fill the fryer more than half full. You must allow room for the fish and for the bubbling fat.

The fish may be dipped in a liquid and coated with a breading, or dipped in batter. The coating will keep the fish moist during frying and will give them a delicious crispness.

Place only one layer of fish at a time in the fry basket and allow enough room so that the pieces do not touch. This prevents the temperature of the fat from dropping suddenly and assures thorough cooking and even browning. When the fat has heated to the proper temperature, lower the basket into the fryer slowly to prevent excessive bubbling. If the fat is at the right temperature when the fish are added, a crust forms almost immediately, holding in juices and preventing the fat from soaking in. Fry until the fish are golden brown and flake easily, usually about three to five minutes.

Pan Frying

Of all the ways of cooking fish, pan-frying cooking in a small amount of fat in a frying pan is probably the most frequently used—and most frequently abused—method. It is an excellent way of cooking pan-dressed fish, fillets, and steaks.

Generally, the procedure is to heat about ⅛ inch (3.2 mm) of fat in a heavy frying pan to about 350°F (194°C). Place one layer of breaded fish in the hot fat, taking care not to overload the pan and thus cool the fat. Fry until brown on one side, then turn and brown the other side. Cooking time will vary with the thickness of the fish, generally about eight to ten minutes.

POACHING

Poaching is cooking in a simmering liquid. The fish are placed in a single layer in a shallow, wide pan, such as a large frying pan, and covered lightly with liquid. The liquid used in poaching may be lightly salted water, water seasoned with vegetables, spices, and herbs, milk, a mixture of white wine and water, or tomato juice, to name a few. This liquid is often cooked before the fish is added in order to extract the flavors from the spices and aromatic vegetables. This liquid is often referred to as a stock or court bouillon. As with other methods of fish cookery, it is important not to overcook the fish. Simmer the fish in the liquid in a covered pan until the fish flakes easily, usually five to ten minutes. Because the poaching liquid contains flavorful juices, the liquid is often reduced and thickened to make a sauce.

Poaching is a favorite method of cooking fish. As an entrée, poached fish can be served simply with a sauce or used as the main ingredient of a casserole or other combination dish. Chilled and flaked, poached fish makes a delicious salad.

STEAMING

Steaming is a method of cooking by means of the steam generated from boiling water. When cooked over moisture in a tightly covered pan, fish retain their natural juices and flavors. A steam cooker is ideal, but any deep pan with a tight cover is satisfactory. If a steaming rack is not available, anything may be used that prevents the fish from touching the water. The water used for steaming may be plain or seasoned with various spices, herbs, or wine. When the water boils rapidly, the fish are placed on the rack, the pan is covered tightly, and the fish are steamed five to ten minutes or until they flake easily when tested with a fork. Steamed fish may be served in the same way as poached fish.

MICROWAVE COOKING

Seafood can be rapidly cooked with delicious results in microwave ovens. Cooking times are rapid because water content in fish is high and there are no tough connective tissues. The same test for doneness holds true with fish and shellfish cooked in the microwave as with those cooked conventionally: (1) Fish is done when its flesh turns opaque and when it flakes easily, and (2) shellfish are generally done when the flesh turn opaque, and, if cooked in the shell, the shell turns red.

Different brands of microwave ovens vary in power and features, but some general tips are as follows:

1. Follow the recipe instructions carefully because overcooking can result in a dry, tough product.
2. Cook seafood in a covered container to hold in moisture and further reduce

cooking times. Plastic wrap makes a good covering but be sure to either pierce the paper or turn back one edge to allow excess steam to escape.

3. If cooking more than one piece of seafood, remember to spread the pieces out, allowing space between each, and to put the thickest portions to the outside. Do not stack or layer items in the pan.
4. Remember that microwave cooking involves residual cooking, meaning that the food will continue cooking after it is removed from the oven. Therefore, most recipes allow for a "standing" period to complete the cooking process. Leave the dish covered during this time.
5. Seafood cooks so rapidly and is so delicate that, when preparing a whole meal, it is probably best to cook it last. This method tends to eliminate the need for reheating.
6. It is permissible to use the shells of the shellfish as your cooking utensil.
7. Do not try to fry fish in a microwave because it is almost impossible to control the oil temperature.
8. In some cases, recipes may call for certain parts of a whole or pan-dressed fish to be "shielded" with foil. On a whole fish, for instance, you may want to cover the head and tail for part of the cooking period to prevent excessive drying.
9. You can help the appearance of the final product by brushing with melted butter or margarine, a dilute solution of a gravy browning agent, or by sprinkling it with paprika.

CHAPTER 17

Cleaning and Sanitation

Cameron R. Hackney and Jon Porter

Every segment of today's seafood industry is touched by the increased awareness of seafood quality and the need to have a clean and sanitary processing environment. Controlling the environment to assure sanitary conditions is not new, but it is important that processors direct attention toward cleaning and sanitation problems. Sanitation is the responsibility of all people in the plant, not just the sanitation crew; the production crew, management, and staff must also be involved. Cleaning and sanitation are separate processes and are discussed in different sections of this chapter.

Cleaning is a process to remove soil and prevent accumulation of food residues, which may decompose and support the growth of disease or spoilage-causing organisms. There are many reasons to clean:

1. To remove soils that will contaminate the next food process.
2. To remove and prevent bacterial buildup.
3. To meet regulatory agency standards.
4. To prevent insect and rodent infestation and harborage.
5. To improve product shelf life.
6. To reduce chance of off-flavors.
7. To prevent staining and filming of equipment.
8. To increase equipment's thermal efficiency.
9. To lengthen the life of equipment.
10. To improve morale.
11. To increase pride in the processing facility.
12. To remove odor-causing bacteria.
13. To improve safety conditions.

To fully understand principles of cleaning and sanitation, you should have a knowledge and understanding of the following:

1. Microbiology and the factors affecting microbial growth.
2. The principles of a Hazard Analysis Critical Control Point (HACCP) program.

3. Chemistry of water.
4. Fundamentals of cleaning.
5. Fundamentals of detergents.
6. Fundamentals of sanitation.
7. Environmental control in processing and packaging.

MICROBIOLOGY AND FACTORS AFFECTING MICROBIAL GROWTH

All raw foods contain microorganisms; therefore a knowledge of microbiology is essential for food safety, quality control, and food preservation. Microorganisms are controlled by slowing down or stopping their growth and by destroying them. Quality control and sanitation, in a broad sense, are used to control microbial growth. We explore both microbiology and ways to control growth, including control by reducing initial numbers and control by retarding growth. Finally we present a brief discussion of pathogens that may be present in seafood.

Microbiology is the study of living organisms so small that they can only be observed with the aid of a powerful microscope. Food microbiologists usually divide organisms of concern into four categories: bacteria, viruses, molds, and yeasts. With respect to seafood, bacteria and viruses are the most troublesome organisms. Molds are often observed in processing plants, and most workers are aware of problems with mildew and other fungal problems. Yeasts have been found in a number of seafood products. They are usually found in oysters and can be isolated from other seafood products.

Human enteric viruses (viruses shed in the feces) are important from a public health standpoint. Viruses are the smallest of the microorganisms. They are inert in food systems and are only active inside the host. Only a few viruses can be passed on through food. These are usually transmitted by the fecal-oral route, which includes contamination from human sewage. Enterovirus infections are limited mostly to the intestine; however, when the infection goes past the intestine a more serious illness, such as hepatitis, may result. When people become infected they may shed viruses in their feces, which may in turn contaminate seafood through pollution or poor personal hygiene. Viruses have the potential to contaminate seafood during processing as has happened with other food products.

Bacteria are the microorganisms of most concern to the seafood microbiologist, from the standpoint of both quality and safety. All raw seafood contain bacteria, which are the principal agents responsible for spoilage. Bacteria reproduce by fission, where one bacteria divides to form two and those two divide to make four, and so on.

Bacteria are described by their ability to absorb dyes and to form spores, their shape, motility, requirements for oxygen, and temperature range for growth. The Gram-reaction is a differential staining reaction that gives an indication of the makeup of the cell wall. Gram-positive bacteria have a more rigid cell wall with less lipid (fat); Gram-negative bacteria have a more flexible cell wall that contains more lipid.

Bacteria come in a variety of shapes and sizes. To the seafood microbiologist, rod, spherical, and comma-shaped bacteria are of the most concern. Also, many bacteria are motile by means of flagella, which is a whiplike appendage. The flagella's location is important for describing the bacterium.

Some bacteria have the ability to form spores, not as a means of reproduction, but as a way of surviving adverse conditions, which they can do far better than vegetative cells. For example, some spores can survive boiling water for several hours and are resistant to many chemical sanitizers. Spore-forming bacteria are of special concern in canning and pasteurization processes because underprocessing may allow survival that can lead to spoilage or illness.

Microorganisms vary in their growth requirements, including their need for oxygen, temperature, and moisture. Temperature control is perhaps the most widely used method for slowing microbial growth in seafood; however other factors, including atmosphere, also are used to slow growth and prolong shelf life.

Temperature

Four major physiological groups of bacteria may be distinguished by their temperature ranges for growth: thermophiles, mesophiles, psychrophiles, and psychrotrophs. Thermophiles prefer high growth temperatures. They are usually spore-forming bacteria and may be involved in the spoilage of canned foods. Mesophiles, which are often of animal origin, prefer moderate temperatures. Most bacterial pathogens are mesophiles. Psychrophiles prefer cold temperatures and do not grow at temperatures above 68°F (20°C). They are very important to their environments, but not as important in food spoilage or safety. Psychrotrophs are organisms which will grow at 32°F (0°C), but their optimum temperature is higher than 59°F (15°C), usually between 68 and 86°F (20 to 30°C). Psychrotrophs are important in food microbiology because they are responsible for the spoilage of refrigerated foods.

Temperature has a pronounced effect on the growth of bacteria. Bacteria grow fastest at their optimum temperatures, and even small temperature decreases can greatly slow growth. For example, if we assume that if the generation time (time it takes to double numbers) of a psychrotrophic bacteria is 30 minutes at 77°F (25°C), it will be 75 minutes at 68°F (20°C), 120 minutes at 59°F (15°C), 200 minutes at 50°F (10°C), and 1200 minutes at 32°F (0°C). Considering that spoilage is to a large extent a function of bacterial growth and that seafood will be spoiled at somewhere between 10^6 and 10^8 cells per gram, it is obvious that the initial population and generation time are critical factors in determining shelf life and quality.

For example, if 8.3 days shelf life is expected when fillets are held at 32°F (0°C), only 2.6 days of shelf life will be obtained at 41°F (5°C) and at 50°F (10°C) the expected shelf life is only 1.4 days. Of course the shelf life would have been longer if the initial population were lower. The initial population can be controlled by sanitation. Also, if the temperature was 28°F (–2°C) the shelf life would be considerably longer, since the generation time would be much longer.

Fluctuations in temperature also can greatly affect shelf life. For example, if a product with an initial population of 10,000 organisms per gram is held at 77°F (25°C) for just two hours before cooling to 32°F (0°C) the expected shelf life will be reduced nearly 45 percent. The important point is that rapid cooling of seafood products is essential. Seafood should not be left at room temperature during workers' lunch or any other breaks. This practice can greatly reduce the shelf life and affect safety. Also, the seafood should be cooled to its storage temperature within two to four hours of processing.

Oxygen

Bacteria vary in their requirements for oxygen. Those requiring oxygen for growth are called *aerobes;* those requiring a lack of oxygen for growth are *anaerobes.* Organisms that can grow in either the presence of absence of oxygen are referred to as *facultative anaerobic,* and organisms that require some oxygen for growth but are inhibited by atmospheric concentrations are called *microaerophilic.* Vacuum packaging and modified atmosphere packaging have long been used to extend the shelf life of foods including seafood. Many of the spoilage organisms are aerobes; removing oxygen decreases their growth. However, there are safety concerns with *Clostridium botulinum* type E.

Water Activity

Water in food may exist in either the free or bound form. Bound water is chemically bound to the food molecule and is not available for microbial growth. Free water can be exchanged with the atmosphere and is available for microbial growth. Microorganisms require free water to grow. The water activity (Aw) of the food is a measure of the free water. Water activity is measured by placing a food in a closed container, allowing the water in the food and air to reach equilibrium, and measuring the relative humidity above the food. Water activity is the Equilibrium Relative Humidity divided by 100. Pure water has a water activity of 1.0; the addition of solutes reduces the water activity. Salting a food lowers the water activity.

Microorganisms have minimum water activities for growth. In general, molds have the lowest minimum water activities, followed by yeast and bacteria with the highest minimum water activity. Bacteria usually do not grow when the water activity is between 0.90 and 0.93, which is equivalent to a 10 to 12 percent salt concentration. Dried seafood are slow to spoil because the water activity is low. These foods are not sterile and may actually have high microbial numbers that could quickly spoil the food if the product is allowed to rehydrate. Water activity is also important in plant sanitation. If a surface is kept dry, microorganisms cannot grow, even if nutrients are present. After cleanup it is important that water not be allowed to pool on equipment and tables.

Acidity and pH

Acidity and low pH have long been used as methods of food preservation. The pH scale goes from 0 to 14; 7 is neutral. Because pH is measured on a log scale, a pH of 6 is ten times more acid than a pH of 7, and pH of 5 is ten times more acid than a pH of 6 and a hundred times more acid than a pH of 7, and so on. In general, organic acids, such as acetic or citric, are more detrimental to microorganisms than strong acids at the same pH, because organic acids act both internally and externally on the cells. Acidity and pH are important factors in sanitation and cleaning. We discuss the effect of different cleaners and the effect of pH later.

PRINCIPLES OF A HACCP PROGRAM

The responsibility for food safety is shared by processors and regulatory agencies. In a broad sense, food safety considerations must start at harvest and continue through all stages of the seafood processing chain to the consumer.

Historically, regulatory agencies have used inspections to ensure food safety; however, this approach has several shortcomings. The laws that inspectors are charged with upholding often are not clearly written, and there are questions as to what constitutes compliance. Also, it is sometimes difficult to distinguish between factors of critical importance to safety and aesthetics. In addition, the laws are not always specific; for example, the Good Manufacturing Practices (GMPs) contain phrases like "clean as frequently as necessary." Because of their vagueness the umbrella GMPs do not have the force of law. Another problem is that the inspector can only observe conditions when he or she is there and cannot know what is happening between inspections.

The Hazard Analysis Critical Control Point (HACCP) approach is another method to control microbiological hazards in foods. It provides a more rational approach than traditional inspection. The HACCP concept was first developed in 1971 at the Conference on Food Protection. Then in 1973 the Pillsbury company did a lot of work to refine the program, and the same year HACCP was adopted for low acid canned foods. The concept did not truly catch on with other products, but in 1985 the National Academy of Sciences recommended in a report entitled "An Evaluation of the Role of Microbiological Criteria for Food and Food Ingredients" that most food processing operations should use HACCP. A HACCP approach is being developed for seafood products.

The HACCP concept is divided into two parts: the hazard analysis and determination of critical control points. Hazards include unacceptable levels of either food-borne pathogens or spoilage organisms, to the extent that food is potentially hazardous or has a reduced shelf life. A hazard analysis evaluates all procedures concerned with production, distribution, and use of raw materials and food products. It requires a thorough knowledge of food microbiology in order to know what types of microorganisms might potentially be present and the factors that affect their growth and survival. Food safety and quality problems most often are caused by contaminated raw food or ingredients; improper holding temperatures (time-temperature abuse); improper cooling of foods; improper handling of seafood after processing; cross contamination between products or between raw and processed product; infrequent disassembly and cleaning of equipment; plant design inadequate to allow the separation of raw product from cooked product; poor employee hygiene; and poor sanitation practices. Roughly 25 percent of food-borne illnesses can be traced directly to food handlers not washing their hands properly.

A food and its raw materials may be classified into hazard categories by means of a two-step procedure: (1) risk assessment and (2) assignment of hazard categories. Risk assessment is accomplished by examining the food for three possible general hazards, which are then used to develop hazard categories.

Hazard 1: The product contains a sensitive ingredient or ingredients. From a microbiological standpoint, all ingredients have some degree of risk varying from high to essentially zero. In general, products of animal origin and seafood products are considered most sensitive.

Hazard 2: The manufacturing process does not contain a processing step that effectively destroys harmful bacteria. The processing steps referred to here can be cooking, pasteurization, retorting, irradiation, and so on, or the development of a food system that, by its composition, destroys harmful microorganisms. An example of the latter is preparation of a seafood product in an acidic tomato-based product where the equilibrium pH is below 4.6.

Hazard 3: There is substantial potential for microbiological abuse in distribution or consumer handling that could render the product harmful when consumed. The principal judgment criterion for abuse potential is whether the food product—in the state in which it is distributed or as normally prepared by the consumer—is a good medium for microbial growth. Consideration must be given to low levels of microbial contamination which have escaped control screening or processing designed to prevent contamination.

The other step in developing a HACCP program is to determine the Critical Control Points (CCP) within the process, which, if not controlled, could lead to a food safety or quality hazard. A practical approach to determining CCPs consists of utilizing a HACCP worksheet with the following headings:

1. Description of the food product and its intended use.
2. Flow diagram with the following parts:
   - Raw material handling.
   - In-process preparation, processing, and fabrication steps.
   - Finished product packaging and handling steps.
   - Storage and distribution.
   - Point of sale handling.

Each step in the process should be examined and a degree of importance assigned. For example, the steps may be labeled as control points on a scale of 1 to 5 based on their perceived importance. This grading requires a knowledge of factors that can lead to safety and quality problems. Hazard categories of raw materials and ingredients, process foods, and finished product are often assigned to help decide on the degree of importance.

As the flow diagram is made, it is easy to identify CCPs, which can be a location, practice, procedure, or process, and if controlled, can prevent or minimize contamination. CCPs must be monitored to ensure that the steps are under control. Monitoring might include observation, physical measurements [pH, Aw, chlorine concentration (cl)], or microbiological analysis. Monitoring most often includes visual and physicochemical measurement because microbiological testing is often too time-consuming. Exceptions are microbiological analysis of the raw product. When the microbiological status of the raw material is a CCP, then microbiological testing is the only acceptable monitoring procedure. Also, when foods are destined for a high risk population the finished product is tested. In this case the microbiological testing is part of the process. In fact, we want to emphasize that microbiological testing is usually not necessary; however, knowledge of microbiology is required.

If microbial standards are applied within the HACCP program, it should be with careful consideration. Microbial methods can be used directly to determine the presence of hazards in raw materials, during processing, and in the finished product. They can also be used indirectly to monitor effectiveness of control points such as cooking, cooling, cleaning, and employee hygiene. However, this use of microbiology is a check and may not have to be an ongoing process.

The HACCP concept is being used successfully in the low acid canned food industry where it works because

1. Monitoring procedures for CCPs were developed cooperatively by government and industry.
2. Education of processors is required. All operations are under supervision of someone who has completed a "Better Process Control School."

3. FDA inspectors are trained in HACCP.
4. Use of HACCP for low acid canned foods is mandated by law.

If HACCP is to work in the seafood industry, the following problems must be overcome:

1. Plant personnel must become more technically sophisticated.
2. Regulators in the seafood area must be trained.
3. Food processors must be trained.
4. HACCP must be required by law.
5. Trust must be established between regulators and processors, which may be the biggest obstacle.

CHEMISTRY OF WATER

The primary constituent of all food processing plant cleaning is water. Water must be free from disease-producing organisms, toxic metal ions, and objectionable odors and tastes. Pure water presents no problems, but no food processing establishment has an ideal water supply. Therefore, the cleaning compounds must be tailored to the individual water supply and the processing operation. It is important not to assume the water is good. The water should be routinely checked for bacterial levels and for hardness.

An understanding of the chemistry of water is essential for an understanding of the "chemistry of cleaning." Water, the major component in most cleaning solutions, acts as both a solvent and as a carrier for the various ingredients in the cleaning compound. A knowledge of the nature and characteristics of water is valuable in developing an optimum cleaning and sanitizing program.

Pure water is available only in the laboratory. The source of water used for cleaning may contain a variety of dissolved substances that are of concern in developing a cleaning and sanitizing program: calcium, magnesium, iron, chlorides, sulfates, manganese, sulfur, and carbon dioxide. The presence of these substances defines the characteristic of the water and gives rise to terms such as hard, soft, red, black, acid, and so on.

The hardness or softness of water is related to the amount of calcium and magnesium present. The higher the concentration, the "harder" the water. The degree of hardness is measured in parts per million (ppm) or grains per gallon (gpg). One grain per gallon or just one grain hardness is equivalent to 17.1 ppm. There are two types of hardness: temporary and permanent. Hardness is temporary when it can be removed by boiling the water; during boiling, the bicarbonates decompose and react with the calcium and magnesium to form carbonates. Permanent hardness can only be removed by chemical treatment. The sum of the temporary hardness and the permanent hardness is the total hardness of the water.

Using hard water in the cleaning process may result in the formation of a tough adherent scale, which is influenced by the heat of the cleaning solution and the components of the cleaner. If an improper cleaner is selected or if the concentration is not correct, a residue of soil remains and the scale is called a foodstone (milkstone, beerstone, beetstone, etc.). Although most of these scales can be removed, the process is time-consuming and expensive.

Red water is caused by a relatively high concentration of iron. Initially, the iron is present in a soluble, colorless form; however, on exposure to air the colorless form changes to an insoluble form, red in color (rust). Approximately 0.3 ppm iron is required for red color to be evident. The iron will react with chlorine, which is present in many cleaner formulations, to produce ferric chloride, a brown precipitate.

Other problems often encountered in water supplies are the presence of salt and acid. Salt waters, those with a high chloride or sulfate content, are often encountered in coastal areas. Generally, salt waters do not affect cleaner efficiency; however, they do present the danger of corrosion, which can be significant. Water can be quite acidic in some areas. In general, acid waters do not affect cleaner performance; however they may be corrosive. If appreciable amounts of salt are present, the corrosive nature may be increased.

A water supply can have a number of these characteristics in combination. It may be both hard and contain iron or have both temporary and permanent hardness. The character of water may change from day to day or even from hour to hour because of changes in the raw water supply, in municipal treatment, or in plant treatment.

FUNDAMENTALS OF CLEANING

The most important factors in controlling microbial growth are reducing the initial numbers of microorganisms and slowing their rate of growth. Cleaning, defined as removal of soil, can reduce the initial numbers. In addition, the microorganisms that are left after the cleaning step are more susceptible to a sanitizer because of the removal of organic matter. Thus it is important that cleaning and sanitization be a two-step process. The use of sanitizers without proper cleaning is usually a waste of money and time. Cleaning compounds allow water to efficiently penetrate, dislodge, and remove soil.

Four things happen during cleaning. 1) The detergent solutions that come into contact with the soil remove it by means of good wetting and penetrating properties. 2) Solid and liquid soils are displaced from the surface by saponifying the fat, peptizing the proteins, and dissolving the minerals. 3) Dispersion of the soil in the cleaning solution is obtained by deflocculation or emulsification. 4) Soil is prevented from being redeposited on the surface by the good rinsing quality of the cleaning compounds used. The following basic procedures should be used for cleaning under most conditions:

Prerinse: Remove excessive soil with a prerinse either by Clean In Place (CIP) or by a rinse hose designed to provide maximum efficiency and minimal energy loss.

Application of detergent solution: Apply detergent either through a CIP system, high pressure system, or foamer.

Postrinse: Remove the detergent solution with the CIP rinse cycle or moderate high pressure system.

Acid rinse: Under certain conditions, it is necessary to apply acid solution to aid in the removal of soils. Know the soils and conditions.

Sanitize: Sanitizers are either applied through automatic dosing (CIP), fogging, or flooding. Learn which method is the most effective for each given operation. Because of their makeup, some sanitizers should not be used in particular areas of the operation.

Final rinse: A potable water rinse is sometimes required because of potential problems with worker discomfort, off-flavors, and so on. Some are prohibited at particular times by federal regulations. The requirements are specific per sanitizer used. Be safe and read the label!

Nature of the Soil

Soil is defined as out-of-place matter. For example, grease on a gearbox is a lubricant, but that same grease on a food contact surface becomes "soil." Soils vary, depending on the nature of the food and processing conditions. Seafood contain protein, fat, and minerals. In addition, sugar may be used in the formulation of further processed foods. Proteins and fats are not soluble in water but are soluble in alkali, and proteins are slightly soluble in acid. They are hard to remove and heating increases the difficulty. Monovalent salts such as sodium chloride are water soluble and are easy to remove. Heating does not increase the difficulty of their removal. However, polyvalent ions such as calcium phosphate are not soluble in water but are soluble in acid. Heating causes these compounds to interact with other constituents in food which makes removal more difficult. Sugars are water soluble and are easy to remove; however, heating can cause carmelization which increases cleaning difficulty.

Table 17-1 outlines types of soil and their ease of removal under different conditions.

Variables of Cleaning

The variables of time, temperature, concentration, and mechanical action affect cleaning regardless of what is to be cleaned. A specific length of time is required to clean a given surface and a given soil. For example, doctors scrub for a minimum of twenty minutes before surgery simply to remove soil and contaminants. They can take no shortcuts. In the plant situation, time is the most common variable. Production runs are disrupted by mechanical problems, or an important sales order has to be filled now. How do we compensate for the loss of necessary time? The variables of temperature, concentration, and mechanical action can be altered; however, changing other variables can create problems. For example, temperature can be increased, but there is a point where the increased heat is more of a detriment than a help. Increasing temperature often decreases the strength of the

Table 17-1. ***Types of Soil and Ways to Remove Them***

Soil	Solubility	Removal	Heat Change
Fat and oil	Water insoluble, alkali soluble	Difficult	Polymerization: more difficult to clean
Protein	Water insoluble, alkali soluble, acid	Very difficult	Denaturation: much more difficult to clean
Carbohydrates (sugar)	Water soluble	Easy	Carmelization: more difficult to clean
Mineral salts monovalent	Water soluble, acid soluble	Easy	—
Milkstone Foodstone	Water insoluble, acid soluble	Difficult	Interactions with other constituents: more difficult

bond between soil and surface. It can also decrease viscosity while increasing solubility of soluble materials. For every 18°F (10°C) temperature increase, the effectiveness of the solution is doubled; however, for every increase of 4°F (2.2°C) the protein structure is changed. It has been said that for each 4° increase the molecule grows additional suction cups. Residue of burned-on material is very difficult to clean under the best conditions. Concentration can be increased, but if the solution is saturated with cleaning products it cannot clean properly. The correct amount of cleaning solution usually does an excellent job, but too much can greatly decrease effectiveness.

In hand cleaning, mechanical action is applied by "elbow grease"; in CIP systems, fluid flow is used to apply cleaning force. Decreased turbulence provides more effective removal of film from surfaces. However, efficiency is less affected by turbulence as the physical–chemical effectiveness of the detergent increases. CIP cleaning velocities of 5 ft/sec are required to ensure adequate turbulence. In foam cleaning, the mechanical action is provided by the rinse hose. It is important to rinse from the bottom up. Proper procedures are mandatory to ensure a clean surface in any method of cleaning from CIP to hand cleaning. Though the CIP system is automated, it must be observed to assure that the valves actuate, the rinse cycle is the proper length, and the sanitizer is automatically dosed at proper concentration.

In selecting cleaning compounds, many interrelated factors are involved, including quality of water available; temperature; type and amount of soil on the surface; surface to be cleaned; physical nature of cleaning compound (liquid or powder); method of cleaning (foaming, CIP, soaking, manual cleaning); economics; and time available.

FUNDAMENTALS OF DETERGENTS

The term *detergent* is quite broad, referring to any agent that will remove one undesirable substance from another. In the removal of soil, a cleaner works in various ways involving both physical and chemical reactions. These functions do not occur separately or in any particular sequence, but in a complex interrelated manner. All of them are important, and usually all are present in a cleaner to some extent. For cleaning a particular type of soil, certain uses are emphasized more than others to arrive at a balanced product.

Functions of Effective Detergents

An effective detergent must have the following properties:

1. Rapid penetrating and wetting power.
2. Ability to control water hardness.
3. High detergent power to remove soil.
4. Suspending power to keep the removed soil from redepositing on the surface being cleaned.
5. Easy rinsability.
6. Noncorrosiveness to surfaces being cleaned and to cleaning equipment.

In practice these characteristics are not observed independently but all occur together. No simple chemical—alkali, acid, or wetting agent—can supply all the necessary properties. By combining selected chemicals, cleaners can be prepared having the desired characteristics. No one combination will include all the various functions in the right amounts to be effective on a given application; different cleaning compounds are required for different cleaning tasks. One group of detergents that works satisfactorily in one plant may not be effective in a similar plant because of difference in water supply.

An understanding of terms used in detergents will help you understand the proper application and description of the detergents.

Alkalinity of a solution is the actual amount of the alkali present. Because many different alkalies are used in formulating detergents, certain standards of expression have been developed. In the cleaning industry, alkalinity is expressed as the "alkalinity equivalent to sodium hydroxide" or the "alkalinity equivalent to sodium oxide." Sodium oxide is 76 percent that of the alkali expressed as sodium hydroxide. The alkalinity of any product can be expressed in terms of either of these two chemicals regardless of the source of the alkalinity. Thus different alkaline products can be compared to each other. Alkalinity consists of two parts, the active and the inactive, which together comprise the total alkalinity. Active alkalinity is the portion that exists above a pH of 8.4, the point at which a phenolphthalein indicator changes from red to colorless. The term *active* is used because this is the alkalinity responsible for cleaning. Inactive alkalinity is the portion that exists between a pH of 8.4 and 3.4, the point at which a methyl orange indicator changes from yellow to orange. The term *inactive* is used because in this pH range little or no cleaning is obtained.

Acidity of acid detergents is the amount of acid present in the solution. We do not specify an inactive and active form as we do with alkalinity. The importance of acidity is in relation to the amount of mineral salt that can be dissolved in the solution. Above a pH of 3.9 for phosphoric acid products, the mineral dissolving capability of the solution decreases rapidly. A standard of acidity to compare various acid solutions has not been established. Therefore, to compare acid cleaner solutions by titration of the acidity present requires a knowledge of the actual acid present.

Saponification is the chemical conversion by alkali of water insoluble fatty acids soils into more soluble substances—soaps.

Emulsification is the action of breaking up fats and soils and colloidally dispersing them throughout the cleaning solution. The emulsion thus formed must be stable enough to prevent these soils from redepositing on equipment surfaces.

Dispersion is the action of breaking up solid aggregates of soil into smaller particles down to colloidal size. It is accomplished through the action of the chemical media and mechanical agitation.

Peptization, strictly speaking, occurs only by chemical action without agitation and can be considered as spontaneous dispersion of the solid soil throughout the cleaning solution. Peptization is usually associated with the removal of protein soils.

Solubilization occurs in two ways, physically or chemically. Lactose, found in milk solids, is soluble in water and therefore easily removed. Mineral salts found in stone deposits are solubilized by acid cleaning solutions through chemical alteration into soluble substances. Various insoluble oils are easily solubilized by surface active agents by the action of the micellular structure in aqueous media.

Suspension is the act of holding divided particulate matter in the liquid phase. Suspensions can be stabilized by polyelectrolytes in solution which maintains a positive or negative charge on the dispersed phase. A stable suspension of soils is particularly important in preventing redeposition of the soils.

Wetting and penetration are complex phenomena and depend on diffusion rates, surface tension, concentration, and roughness of the surface. Surface active agents are clearly superior in lowering the surface tension of the cleaning solution, allowing the displacement of soils and the penetration into cracks and holes of solid deposits.

Rinsability of detergents cannot be overemphasized. The last step of the cleaning process, it is the result of all the properties previously discussed. An acceptable rinsed surface is one free of all particulate matter and detergent film.

Water softening is the function of rendering the hardness of water unavailable for reaction with certain components of the cleaning solution. For example, caustic soda forms an adherent film of calcium and magnesium carbonates in hard water. Softening can be accomplished by precipitating the hard water elements as insoluble salts. A second method is by sequestration. Certain chemicals, notably the polyphosphates and ethylenediaminetetraacetic acid (EDTA), can form soluble complexes with calcium and magnesium salts. The calcium and magnesium are so firmly held in this complex that they are unaffected by the addition of substances normally reacting with these hardness elements.

Corrosiveness is a property which must be closely controlled to protect equipment both from deterioration due to the aggressiveness of the detergent and from the corrosive nature of accumulated soils.

The ideal detergent, then, would contain all these properties we have described to the maximum extent. This, of course, is not possible. For instance, the most efficient chemical for saponification is caustic soda, which is also the most aggressive toward aluminum and precipitates calcium and magnesium as an adherent film. The addition of glassy silicates will lessen the corrosive effect at a significant loss of alkali available for saponification. Polyphosphates will soften the water and provide other benefits but, again, alkali is decreased. Consequently, each detergent is geared to a specific application or to several very closely related applications. There can be no "all-purpose" cleaner; at best, we can only build in a degree of versatility.

Detergent Ingredients

The components of a detergent exhibiting the properties we have listed can be categorized as follows:

1. Hydroxides
2. Carbonates
3. Silicates
4. Phosphates
5. Chelates
6. Oxidants
7. Acids
8. Surfactants

Sodium hydroxide, commonly called caustic soda, is the strongest alkaline material employed. It is excellent for the saponification of fatty soils such as those found in milk and cooking oils. Caustic soda has some serious limitations, however. It has only fair emulsifying and deflocculating properties, exhibits poor rinsing characteristics, and is corrosive to some of the metals used in food processing equipment. Under the proper conditions—a 1 to 4 percent concentration at 140°F (60°C) to 160°F (72°C) for five to ten minutes—caustic soda has shown bactericidal properties.

Sodium carbonate, commonly called soda ash, is a moderately strong alkali that contributes to the total alkalinity of the composition and is more easily inhibited against attack on soft metals than is sodium or potassium hydroxide. Soda has a relatively high absorption capacity for liquids, thus providing a base for the addition of liquid detergents while maintaining free flowing characteristics. Its major disadvantage in hard water is its property of forming a hard scale of calcium carbonate and similar insoluble salts. Sodium bicarbonate, commonly called baking soda, is used primarily in conjunction with soda ash as a buffering agent in mild, moderately alkaline systems.

The silicates exist in several crystalline forms, providing a range of useful properties. Sodium orthosilicate is next to caustic soda as a saponification agent; however, it also provides much the same undesirable corrosive characteristics as caustic soda. Sodium sequesilicate is lower in alkali content than the orthosilicate and provides good emulsifying and soil suspending properties, and although not as corrosive as the orthosilicate, it is nonetheless aggressive toward soft metals. Sodium metasilicate has much to recommend its use. Its wetting ability is good, emulsification and deflocculation high, and it possesses definite anticorrosive properties. The glassy silicates, those having a silica to sodium oxide ratio greater than 1:1, have excellent corrosion inhibiting properties. Their major disadvantages are a lower solubility rate and greater tendency for moisture absorption which has an adverse effect on the free flowing characteristics of the cleaning composition.

Phosphates, as a group, provide the best means of maximizing all the characteristics of a good detergent with the exception of providing alkali for saponification. Trisodium phosphate was the most outstanding of all basic alkalies in water softening prior to the advent of polyphosphates. Although its softening process occurs by precipitation, the precipitate is very finely divided, nonadherent, and easily rinsed. Its properties of emulsification, dispersion, and wetting are only slightly less than those of sodium metasilicate. A disadvantage is its corrosive effect on aluminum. Polyphosphates have the ability to modify the natural behavior of hard water. As a result, many uses for polyphosphates as water conditioners have been developed. The threshold treatment of hard water involves the addition of a few ppm of polyphosphates, which inhibit the precipitation of hard water salts in many cases. The threshold treatment is limited to additions up to 20 ppm.

Polyphosphate is also a sequestrant. *Sequestration* is the term applied to the mechanism whereby calcium and magnesium are held in a soluble complex which is not affected by the addition of substances normally reacting with and precipitating these hardness elements. The amount of polyphosphate required to function as a sequestering agent in any given specific application depends on several factors, including the polyphosphate used, the water hardness, the nature of the cleaner, and the conditions of the cleaning operation.

Tetrasodium polyphosphate, although a poor calcium sequestrant, is an excellent magnesium sequestrant and is widely used because it is the most stable under conditions of high alkalinity and temperature. Sodium tripolyphosphate has good overall properties, making it perhaps the most widely used of the polyphosphates. It is an excellent sequestrant for both calcium and magnesium and provides good detergency, wetting, deflocculation, and rinsing properties. Sodium hexametaphosphate is used primarily as a calcium sequestrant when hardness alone is considered. It is unstable in hot alkali, reverting to the ortho and pyrophosphate forms. Sodium acid pyrophosphate is an excellent buffering and peptizing agent; however, it is deficient in its sequestering and wetting ability. Note that phosphates are banned in many areas.

The chelates are a class of specialty chemicals of limited versatility but are nonetheless important. They function similarly to the polyphosphates in forming a water soluble complex with the hardness elements, calcium and magnesium. They also chelate iron and other metals that cause staining. The most widely used chelates are ethylenediaminetetraacetic acid (EDTA) and sodium gluconate.

The only oxidants commonly used in detergents are peroxides and those chlorine-bearing compounds capable of forming hypochlorous acid. Their primary functions are as bactericides and bleaches for food stains. Detergent solutions containing available chlorine are particularly effective in the removal of proteinaceous soils.

The majority of detergents today are alkaline-based. However, acid-based detergents are used to perform functions specific to their nature. In general, two types of acid detergents are used on food processing equipment: waterstone/foodstone removers and general purpose acid cleaners.

Waterstone and foodstone are calcareous deposits composed of calcium and magnesium solids reacting with components of alkaline cleaners and food residues. The deposits are for the most part insoluble in alkali and over a period of time will form a hard, tenaciously adherent deposit. Accumulations of these deposits provide harboring areas for bacteria, significantly reduce heat transfer efficiency, and cause corrosion. The use of strong mineral acids such as muriatic acid, although quite effective, have limited applicability due to handling hazards and corrosion problems, even when they contain corrosion inhibitors. The most widely used acids are phosphoric, glycolic, sulfuric, and sodium bisulfite. They are rarely used in concentrated form but rather contain wetting agents and inhibitors to enhance their detersive properties and lessen the corrosive effects.

Surfactants have advanced the technology of detergents immeasurably. Common soap (the saponification product of fatty acids, animal fat, and alkali) was probably the first surfactant. Soaps perform all the desirable functions of a detergent with some serious shortcomings: They are limited to the alkaline pH range, and they are precipitated by hard water, producing the familiar "bathtub ring."

These inherent shortcomings can be overcome only by using an amount in excess to precipitate all the calcium and magnesium, thus softening the water, and by restricting their use to alkaline cleaning. Surfactants have largely supplemented soaps in the detergent industry. Although their chemistry and classification is very complex, they can be labeled quite broadly according to their electrical nature as anionic, nonionic, and cationic.

Synergism of Detergent Ingredients

Blending the inorganic builders and surfactants would appear to dilute the major contribution of each component from the pure form; and this does occur. However, one final concept of detergency comes to light. *Synergism* is defined as the combined or cooperative action of separate agencies which together have greater total effect than the sum of their individual effects. Caustic soda is an excellent saponifying agent, but in hard water we find an adherent film of calcium carbonate. In addition, it is not capable of saponifying all fats and provides poor rinsing properties. The addition of polyphosphates or EDTA softens the water, thus eliminating the calcium film. The addition of a surfactant with good wetting properties carries the detergent solution into the soil, lifting and dispersing the soil for more complete reaction with the alkali. Unreacted soil is emulsified or dispersed and held in solution until final rinsing, which has been greatly enhanced due to the presence of phosphates and surfactants. One final point with regard to the action of a built detergent: The detersive mechanism performs over a period of time at a specific temperature and concentration of detergent. Unless these three factors are carefully controlled, all the time and effort expended in development of detergent will have been wasted.

FUNDAMENTALS OF SANITATION

The most important principle concerning sanitizing/disinfection is that a dirty surface cannot be sanitized. The sanitizer will not be able to reach microorganisms trapped in and under soil. There are many types of sanitizers, and we discuss each separately. See also Table 17-2.

Active Chlorine

For many years, active chlorine has been used because of its broad bactericidal spectrum and economic advantages. The active chlorine carrier has taken several forms, with the liquid types based on inorganic chlorine compounds, such as sodium hypochlorites, and the powder form based on organic chlorine compounds, such as the dichloroisocyanurate group. Most often the bactericidal effect of active chlorine is best in a neutral or weak-acidic condition (pH 5 to pH 7), but the chlorinated alkaline cleaners also have an excellent bactericidal effect against all groups of microbes. Tests have shown that chlorine renders a very fast kill on viruses, bacteria, yeasts, and molds. The activity against spore-forming bacteria is slightly slower. The question of the corrosiveness of hypochlorite solutions on metals such as stainless steel and aluminum is still a matter of intense debate, resulting in certain reservations regarding chlorine-based products.

Advantages

1. Unaffected by hard water scales.
2. Nonfilming.
3. Can be utilized at cool water temperatures without affecting activity.

Disadvantages

1. Precipitation when used in iron-laden water.
2. Short residual effect after sanitizing.

As a general rule of thumb, if chlorine is used as a sanitizer prior to production, the equipment should be used within one hour after the sanitizing procedure.

Iodophor Sanitizers

Acidic iodine-based sanitizers have a universal killing effect on all types of microbes. The amount of active ingredients to achieve the same killing power is lower

Table 17-2. ***Specific Areas or Conditions Where Particular Sanitizers Are Recommended***

Specific Area or Condition	Recommended Sanitizer	Concentration (ppm)
Aluminum equipment	Iodophor	25
	P3-oxonia active®	25
Bacteriostatic film	Quat	200
CIP Cleaning	Acid sanitizer	130
	Active chlorine	
	Iodophor	
	P-3 oxonia active®	100
Film formation, prevention of	Acid sanitizer	130
	Iodophor	
	P3-oxonia active®	150
Fogging atmosphere	Active chlorine	800–1000
Hand dip—production	Iodophor	25
Hand sanitizer—washroom	Iodophor	25
	Phenolic	2–3%
Hard water	Acid sanitizer	130
	Iodophor	25
	P3-oxonia active®	25
High iron water	Iodophor	25
	P3-oxonia active®	25
Long shelf life	Iodophor	
	Quat	
	P3-oxonia active®	
Low cost	Hypochlorite	—
Noncorrosive	Iodophor	—
	Quat	
	P3-oxonia active®	—
Organic matter, stable in presence of	Quat	200
	P3-oxonia active®	200
Plastic crates	Iodophor	25
	P3-oxonia active®	25
Porous surface	Active chlorine	200
	Quat	—
	P3-oxonia active®	200
Processing equipment-stainless steel	Acid sanitizer	130
	Active chlorine	200
	Iodophor	25
	P3-oxonia active®	50
Rubber belts	Iodophor	25
	P3-oxonia active®	25
Tile walls	Iodophor	25
	P3-oxonia active®	25
Visual control	Iodophor	25
	P3-oxonia active®	25
Walls	Active chlorine	200
	Quat	200
	P3-oxonia active®	100
Water treatment	Active chlorine	20
Wood crates	Active chlorine	1000
	P3-oxonia active®	200+

Source: Henkel Corporation, Chemical Services Division, Training Material.

in iodophors than in active chlorine-based products. Usually the killing time is reduced by increasing the temperature of the sanitizing solution, and this holds true for the iodine-type products as well. Iodine will gas off at temperatures of 102°F to 120°F (39°C to 49°C) and the loss of the iodine is high. This characteristic and the possibility of corrosion make it standard practice to use iodophors at room temperature.

Advantages

1. Stable, long shelf life.
2. Active against all microorganisms except bactericidal pores and phages.
3. Unaffected by hard water salts, with the exception of water containing large amounts of chlorides.

Disadvantages

1. Not as effective against spores and phages as chlorine.
2. Expensive.
3. Stain porous metal surfaces and plastics.
4. Severely affected by alkaline conditions above pH 7.

Hypochlorites

The hypochlorites are the most widely used sanitizers in the seafood industry. They are considered more effective against Gram negative than Gram positive bacteria. Six factors influence their effectiveness. They are (1) concentration of chlorine, (2) pH, (3) temperature, (4) amount of organic material (especially protein compounds), (5) time of contact with surface, and (6) types of microorganisms present. Hypochlorites are used in the washing and conveying of raw products, sanitizing equipment, and in cooling water in pasteurization operations.

Advantages

1. As powerful germicides, control a wide range of microorganisms.
2. Deodorizing properties.
3. Nonpoisonous to humans at use concentrations.
4. Free of poisonous residuals.
5. Colorless and nonstaining.
6. Easy to handle.
7. Most economical to use.

Disadvantages

1. Short shelf life.
2. Adverse effect on skin.
3. Corrosive on some metals.

Use Concentrations: 50 to 100 ppm available chlorine should be employed for sanitizing large equipment and utensils and 200 ppm for spraying applications of large equipment. The contact time for effective sanitation should be long enough to produce complete kill of bacteria, usually ten seconds or longer.

Acid Anionic

These are surfactants that are combinations of an organic and inorganic acid (usually phosphoric acid) with a surfactant (usually alkylaryl sulfonate). The combination of pH and surfactant is bactericidal or bacteriostatic.

Advantages

1. Nonstaining, stable, long shelf life.
2. No objectionable odor.
3. Removes and prevents milkstone and waterstone formation.
4. Effective against a wide spectrum of organisms.
5. Stable in concentrated form or use dilutions; action enhanced by high temperatures.
6. Noncorrosive to stainless steel.
7. Provides short duration residual bacteriostatic effect on stainless steel equipment.

Disadvantages

1. Effectiveness at acid pH only.
2. Generation of foam.
3. Low activity against spore-forming organisms.
4. Corrosive to metals other than stainless steel.

Use Concentrations: 100 ppm anionic surfactant.

Quarternary Ammonium Compound (QUAT)

The quats may be bacteriostatic at low concentrations and bacteriocidal at higher ones. Their lethal action has been attributed to their reaction with cell membranes, enzyme inactivation, and protein denaturation. The quats are not as effective as hypochlorites against Gram negative bacteria and viruses, but are very effective against Gram positive bacteria. Quats are not generally allowed on equipment when foods are being processed.

Advantages

1. Stable, long shelf life.
2. Active against many microorganisms.
3. Forms a bacteriostatic film.
4. Noncorrosive and nonirritating to skin.
5. Stable in the presence of organic matter.
6. Stable to temperature changes.
7. Good penetration qualities.
8. Combined with nonionic wetting agents, makes a good detergent sanitizer.

Disadvantages

1. Expensive.
2. Incompatible with common anionic detergent components.

3. Slow to dissipate (residual problem).
4. Germicidal efficiency varied and selective.
5. Foam problem in mechanical application.

Use Concentrations: For sanitizing equipment, a 200 ppm solution is sufficient to reduce bacterial counts with a one-minute exposure.

ENVIRONMENTAL CONTROL IN PROCESSING AND PACKAGING

General Recommendations

1. Make the cleaning and sanitizing of walls, ceilings, floors, and drains part of the daily cleanup program. Use a chlorinated foam product.
2. Eliminate all direct openings from outside into the processing and packaging rooms even though they may contain screens, curtains, and louvers.
3. Use bacterial filtering systems on air handling units and create a positive pressure in the processing and packaging areas. Keep air from blowing onto product or food contact surfaces. This may seem extreme, but it is a positive approach to environmental hygiene.
4. Make sure dehumidifiers or air conditioning units drain away from the processing or packaging room and prevent condensate from reentering the atmosphere. Coils and pans must be cleaned and sanitized routinely. Use a chlorinated foam product.
5. Repair all cracks in walls and floors (especially important for control of *Listeria* in areas around floor drains).
6. Sanitize pallets (wet) before placing them in the process areas.
7. Keep areas under floor conveyors and equipment clean and sanitized, especially in and around coolers. This is critical, because there are numerous instances where *Listeria* have been detected at these points.
8. Allow only employees associated with processing and packaging into these areas. In traffic areas set up properly maintained foot sanitizing baths.
9. Require the use of proper clothing and footwear which must not be worn outside the plant, even at lunchtime.
10. Establish a specific environmental cleaning and sanitizing program for all areas of the plant. Consider using a special crew for this purpose and include the floor drains.

Specific Recommendations

Postprocessing Sanitation Control Program: This program has been designed to cover sanitation in all areas following heat processing (ready-to-eat seafood products)

1. Floor drains
   a. Must be working properly and maintained.
   b. Do not use department hoses to unplug drains. Use a dedicated hose or other appropriate means supplied by mechanical department.
   c. Daily cleaning
      - Remove covers, and clean with detergent and brush.
      - Heavily foam and brush down with at least a 3-foot-long (1-m) brush.
      - Thoroughly spray all sides of drain cover and the drain itself with sanitizer solution.

  - Whenever a stopped-up drain has been fixed, the floor surrounding, drain cover, and drain must be cleaned and sanitized as noted.
2. Standing water: puddles, under equipment, areas of disrepair, or anywhere water collects
   a. Floor maintenance program must be put into effect that repairs broken/depressed areas, seals cracks/crevices, makes sure water will drain from under equipment, and checks to make certain water runs freely to and into drains.
   b. After final cleanup and sanitizing of floors, all free or standing water must be removed by vacuum or squeegee to and into drains.
   c. During production, any standing water on floors must be vacuumed or squeegeed into drains at each break, lunch, and shift change. *Note:* This instruction includes inside and under any equipment.
   d. Vacuum equipment, for example, hose, nozzle, and air filter coming out of tank, must be cleaned and sanitized daily or the vacuum becomes a reservoir for bacteria.
3. Floor cleaning
   a. During production, no high pressure water that produces aerosols can be used to clean floors. Use squeegees and scoops for dry clean only and/or use very low pressure water that will not produce aerosols.
   b. Night Cleanup: After dry cleaning and foaming of equipment, the total floor must be foamed. After rinsing of equipment and floor, all equipment and total floor must be sanitized. *Note:* Pay particular attention that the total floor (under equipment, racks, in corners, around posts and beams, etc.) is thoroughly cleaned and sanitized.
4. Ceilings, cooling units, drip pans, overhead pipes, doors, walls
   a. Fix leaks and remove drip pans when possible.
   b. Clean and sanitize weekly by using the following steps:
      - Thoroughly foam and rinse.
      - After rinse apply a sanitizing solution of quaternary ammonia (10 percent strength) mixed 1 oz/gal of water.
      - After cleaning and sanitizing overheads, all equipment must be cleaned and sanitized.
      - Be sure all product, packaging materials, and so on, are removed from rooms before cleaning and sanitizing.
5. Cleaning aids (mops, brooms, squeegees), floor mats, condensate wipers
   a. Cleaning aids
      - After each usage, cleaning aids must be thoroughly cleaned (including handles) with detergent solution and then stored in an appropriate container filled with a solution of 10 percent quaternary ammonia mixed 1 oz/gal of water. (All handles of cleaning aids must be nonporous material to facilitate cleaning.) The "head" or usage part must be submerged in the sanitizing solution. The sanitizing container must have a drain and be recharged each day. Squeegees used on product contact areas must be stored in a separate sanitizer container.
   b. Floor mats (rubber, soft plastic, or porous material)
      - Must be thoroughly cleaned with detergent, rinsed, and stored until used in a container with sanitizing solution.
   c. Condensate wipers
      - Handles must be nonporous material.

- When not in use, store absorbent head in sanitizer.
- Absorbent heads must be replaced with fresh heads a minimum of once weekly.

6. Hoses (air, water, sanitizer)
   a. Air hoses and air
      - Air must be clean and dry through the use of dryers and water traps.
      - Air hoses should be of the coiled (like a telephone cord) type, suspended so that when in use they cannot contact the floor.
      - Must be cleaned and sanitized each day during normal cleanup.
      - Air filters and traps must be sanitized at least weekly and drained daily.

   b. Water hoses
      - Must not be allowed to lie on the floor other than during cleanup.
      - After each usage, the hose must be hung on wall holder so that it does not contact the floor and must be sprayed with sanitizer as it is hung up.
      - People who handle ready-to-eat product that is not packaged must not be allowed to use hoses.

   c. Sanitizer hoses
      - Must be of a type (coiled or on a retractable drum) that will not allow them to contact the floor when in use.
      - Must be sprayed with sanitizer after each use, paying particular attention to the outlet end that is being handled.

7. Pipes
   a. Any overhead sewer or drain pipes must be checked weekly for any leakage or seepage.
   b. Any insulated pipes must be fully covered with impervious insulation covering. Any exposed insulation should be replaced and properly covered.

8. Air handling systems
   a. Air makeup units
      - All ductwork must be kept clean and dry on a continuing basis.
      - All filters are to be in place and changed regularly.
      - Check to make sure there are no bird nests or birds roosting on or near air intakes.

9. Employee practices/facilities
   a. Employees working on the "raw" side of the plant are prohibited from entering coolers or packaging areas used for ready-to-eat products. Conversely, employees from ready-to-eat side are prohibited from entering the raw side. A different color helmet or apron could be used to distinguish each area.
   b. All ready-to-eat product handlers must
      - Wash and sanitize their hands before going on the line after touching their hair or face, after picking up floor scraps, after adjusting equipment or handling nonproduct contact items.
      - Wear hairnets that cover hair and ears. Snoods must be worn over beards.
      - Put on disposable gloves, aprons, and arm guards after hand washing and sanitizing. After gloves are put on, they must be dipped in sanitizing solution.

- Keep clipboards, and so on, off product contact areas.
- Not put tape, labels, stickers, and the like, on equipment, as they can harbor moisture and be a breeding ground for microbes.
- Wear frocks and shirts.
- Spray and wipe down with clean paper towels all control knobs with sanitizer before start, at breaks, and lunch.
- Not use wooden-handled knives. Use dip stations when knives are not in use. Recharge sanitizer at lunch and shift changes.
- Place knives in a pan of sanitizer at individual work stations.
- Wash, sanitize, and cover hands with fresh disposable gloves when opening reject packages.
- Leave frocks in department when going to break or lunch.
- Use company-furnished knives and at end of shift leave them in the department for daily cleaning and sanitizing.

c. Mechanics
- Before working on ready-to-eat lines, mechanics must wash and sanitize their hands and tools.
- After working on the line, the area or areas touched by mechanics, their clothes, or their tools must be sprayed with sanitizer and wiped down with clean paper towels.

d. Lunchrooms, locker rooms, rest rooms
- Lunchrooms must be kept free of litter, and tabletops and chairs must be wiped down with sanitizer. Floor must be cleaned and sanitized daily.
- Locker room floor should be washed and sanitized daily. Lockers should be wiped down with detergent and sanitized on a periodic basis.
- Rest room floors, commodes (including seats), urinals, and sinks must be washed and sanitized daily. Commodes and urinals must be maintained in working order. If there is any overflow from a clogged commode or urinal, the rest room is to be closed until washed and sanitized.

10. Fork lifts, trash dumpsters
    a. Fork lifts must not be taken from raw area to ready-to-eat or vice versa.
    b. Trash dumpsters must not be taken from raw area to ready-to-eat or vice versa.
    c. Air lock door pull cords and electrical on/off buttons must be sanitized daily (use caution).

APPENDIX
BASIC COMPOUNDS AND CLEANING TERMINOLOGY

Class of Compounds	Major Functions
Acids	Mineral deposit control and water softening.
Basic alkalies	Soil displacement/emulsifying, saponifying, and peptizing.
Chelates	Water softening, mineral deposit control, soil displacement by peptizing and prevention of redeposition.

Class of Compounds	Major Functions
Complex phosphates and water	Soil displacement by emulsifying, peptizing, dispersion of soil, softening, and prevention of soil depositions.
Dispersion or deflocculation	Breaking up solid aggregates of soil into small particles.
Emulsification	Mechanical process where fats are broken into tiny globules and are suspended in the cleaning solution. The alkalies and the complex phosphates are used for emulsification.
Peptizing	Breaking up of solid particles into extremely small particles.
Saponification	Chemical process of breaking down an animal (insoluble) or vegetable fat by alkali into soap (soluble) and glycerol.
Sequestering/Chelating	Ability to prevent deposition of undesirable mineral salts on surfaces being cleaned.
Surfactant	Wetting agent or a compound reducing surface tensions.
Synergism	When a chemical is used as a builder with a soap or detergent, the detergency resulting from the combination is greater than the total detergency of the chemical and the soap when used independently.
Wetting	Ability to lower the surface tension of the water medium so as to increase its ability to penetrate soil.

CHAPTER

18

Aquaculture

George S. Libey and Brian G. Bosworth

Aquaculture is defined as the rearing of aquatic organisms under controlled conditions. The aquaculturist has control over all or a part of the organism's life cycle. This control sets aquaculture apart from traditional fisheries in which organisms are harvested from natural stocks. Aquaculture is similar to terrestrial (land-based) agriculture, except that in aquaculture the crop is reared in water.

This chapter gives a brief overview of aquaculture rather than providing detailed descriptions of culture systems and techniques. Several excellent texts on aquaculture (Hunter and Brown, 1985; Laird and Needham, 1988; Stickney, 1979; Stickney, 1986; and Tucker, 1985) are available if more detailed information is desired.

HISTORY OF AQUACULTURE

Aquaculture probably was first practiced in Asia and has long been a part of the rural economy there (Liao, 1988). Records indicate aquaculture began about 1000 B.C. in China, probably due to the desires of an emperor to have a constant supply of fresh fish. Many aquaculture techniques developed centuries ago are still used in Asian countries. Techniques developed in Asia were later adapted and used by aquaculturists in Europe and Africa.

Compared to Asia, aquaculture in the United States is very young. U.S. fisheries biologists began hatching and stocking fish throughout much of the country during the late 1800s. However, it was not until the late 1950s that large-scale commercial production of aquatic organisms as a food source began (Dupree and Huner, 1984).

Until recently aquaculture has been a subsistence production system in which aquatic species were grown primarily to produce food for personal consumption (Aiken, 1988). Increased demand for seafood products coupled with a leveling off of traditional fisheries harvest have provided the stimulus for rapid growth in aquaculture. Worldwide aquaculture production of fish, crustaceans, and mollusks has increased from approximately 7.3 million tons (6.6 million metric tons) in 1975 to more than 11.0 million tons (10 million metric tons) in 1988, an increase of more than 50 percent in only eight years.

TYPES OF AQUACULTURE

Several criteria are used to describe different types of aquaculture. A common system of classification is based on the taxonomy of the cultured organisms. Included among these are finfish aquaculture (trout, catfish, carp, etc.); crustacean aquaculture (shrimp, crawfish, lobsters, crabs); mollusk aquaculture (clams, mussels, oysters); and plant aquaculture (kelp, algae). Some cultured organisms, such as turtles, frogs, and alligators, do not fit well into these categories and are placed in the "others" category.

The level of management is another criterion used to define the various types of aquaculture. Level of management is usually defined as the quantity of an organism produced per area or volume of water and includes extensive, semi-intensive, intensive, and highly intensive aquaculture.

Extensive aquaculture involves very little if any input of energy (feed, fertilizer, aeration, etc.). The animals are simply placed in a pond, allowed to feed on naturally occurring materials, and harvested when they reach an appropriate size. Production from extensive aquaculture is usually low, less than 500 pounds per acre (566 kg/ha).

Generally, as the level of intensity increases so does production, but so does the amount of energy put into the system. Semi-intensive aquaculture, 2,000 to 4,000 pounds per acre (2,242 to 4,483 kg/ha), involves higher energy inputs, including feeds and perhaps aeration. Intensive aquaculture, 8,000 to 20,000 pounds per acre (8,967 to 22,417 kg/ha), is usually practiced in tanks or raceways and requires very high energy input. High feeding rates, continual aeration, and large water exchanges (old water flushed out and replaced with new) are usually required to maintain animals under intensive culture conditions. Highly intensive systems, up to 3.5 pounds per gallon (400 g/l), are energy costly but allow very high production in a relatively small amount of water. Oxygen injection, water filtration, and continuous water exchange are commonly used in highly intensive systems.

Although the vast majority of aquaculture production is from extensive or semi-intensive systems, the trend is toward intensification. The field of highly intensive aquaculture is fairly new, but is receiving increased interest due to its potential.

Water temperature also is sometimes used to classify the type of aquaculture being practiced. The following arbitrary temperature ranges are often used to describe aquaculture: 32 to 50°F (0 to 10°C) cold water aquaculture—trout, salmon; 50 to 68°F (10 to 20°C) cool water aquaculture—perch, bass; and 68 to 86°F (20 to 30°C) warm water aquaculture—catfish, tilapia.

The salinity of the water is another criterion used to describe aquaculture. Classifications based on water salinity include: fresh water aquaculture (less than 1 o/oo salinity), brackish water aquaculture (1 to 17 o/oo salinity), and mariculture (greater than 17 o/oo salinity).

Some times it is desirable to grow only one species in a given pond or tank; other times it is more efficient to grow several species. The number of species reared is another method for describing the type of aquaculture practiced. *Polyculture* is used to describe systems in which more than one species is cultured in each pond or tank; *monoculture* refers to situations in which only one species in reared.

Obviously there are many ways to describe aquaculture. The criteria and ranges given here are arbitrary and are only intended to give some descriptions of the many types of aquaculture. Other authors may use slightly different ranges or classifications.

ADVANTAGES AND DISADVANTAGES OF AQUACULTURE

The advantages of aquaculture over traditional fisheries include predictability of supply, reduced time from harvest to processing, and control over the organism's environment. Because aquaculturists know approximately how many animals they have and when the animals will be ready for harvest they can guarantee a certain amount of product at a particular time. Aquaculture facilities are usually based on or near land; therefore, the harvested animals can be quickly processed assuring a high quality product. The aquaculturist has at least some control over the animals' environment (water quality, feed quality, etc.) which can also result in improved product quality.

The main disadvantage of aquaculture compared to capture fisheries is the amount of energy (costs) used in aquaculture production. Although a fisherman can have a considerable investment in his boat and harvesting equipment, the aquaculturist has additional costs in facility construction, seed stock, and feeds. Aquaculture will never completely replace traditional fisheries, but it can help meet demands not met by the harvest of natural stocks.

Aquaculture possesses certain advantages and disadvantages when compared to terrestrial agriculture. Among the advantages are (1) water is a three-dimensional culture medium, (2) most aquatic animals are able to maintain neutral buoyancy, and (3) most aquatic animals are poikilothermic (Bardach et al., 1972).

Because water is three-dimensional, several species of fish can be cultured in the same "space." Fish that normally live on the bottom can be cultured in the same volume of water as fish that prefer to reside near the surface. This arrangement allows for efficient utilization of available space.

Most fishes have an air bladder, an organ which allows them to move up or down in the water column while maintaining neutral buoyancy. This feature allows fish to save some of the energy terrestrial animals must expend "fighting" gravity. Other aquatic organisms such as mussels, clams, and oysters live on the bottom and expend little energy moving about. Energy saved can be used for body growth or other physiological activities. The result is that aquatic organisms are often better at converting feed to flesh than terrestrial animals.

Probably more important in producing excellent feed conversion rates is the fact that most aquatic organisms are poikilothermic (cold-blooded). Aquatic animals' internal temperature will be very near that of the surrounding water. Most terrestrial livestock species are homothermic (warm-blooded) and must maintain a constant internal body temperature to maintain physiological functions. Warm-blooded animals expend a great deal of energy maintaining their body temperature when environmental temperature fluctuates. Cold-blooded aquatic animals do not use energy to maintain body temperature and the energy saved can be used for growth, resulting in high feed conversion.

Compared to traditional livestock production aquaculture also has some disadvantages, including (1) physical and chemical contamination of the medium, (2) difficulty in observing the crop, and (3) aquatic animals are poikilothermic. Aquatic organisms are in direct contact with the water they are reared in. High concentrations of metabolic end products (particularly ammonia) produced by the fish can result in reduced growth, poor health, and even death. Aquatic organisms are often sensitive to pollutants or naturally occurring metals found in some water supplies. To provide an adequate environment for the cultured species, these contaminants must be removed or avoided.

Aquaculturists often have difficulty observing their crop because it is under the water's surface. A cattle rancher can quickly assess his animals' environment by simply riding through the field containing the cattle. It is not as easy for aquaculturists, who must instead depend on instruments and chemical tests to evaluate the conditions experienced by their animals. For example, an oxygen meter must be used to determine the dissolved oxygen concentration (a very important parameter) in the water.

Although being cold-blooded has some advantages it also can be a disadvantage because most fish have evolved to grow well only in a fairly small temperature range. Outside this range reduced growth and even death can occur. When environmental temperatures fall outside the preferred range, production rates and thus profits will decline. Unsuitable water temperatures are one of the main constraints to culturing some species in certain parts of the world.

BASIC REQUIREMENTS FOR AQUACULTURE

The prime requirement for a successful aquaculture operation is an adequate supply of suitable quality water. The terms "suitable" and "adequate" vary somewhat with the species being cultured, the type of culture system, and the intensity of production, but water supply is the first thing a potential aquaculturist should check when selecting a site. It is advisable to have an experienced water quality expert evaluate a potential site's water supply before beginning construction of an aquaculture facility.

Along with a good supply of water, the aquaculturist must know which water quality parameters are important and at what levels they can begin adversely affecting the cultured species. Dissolved oxygen, water temperature, hardness, alkalinity, pH, ammonia, and nitrite are important water quality parameters that must be measured regularly. Monitoring of water quality can be performed easily using water test kits and instruments produced by several companies. Boyd (1979) gives a detailed description of important water quality parameters, methods for measurement, and toxic levels.

Another obvious requirement, but one that is often overlooked, is that the organism being cultured has good market demand. Often the culture techniques and biology of an organism are well known, but unless the organism can be reared profitably it is not a good candidate for aquaculture. Aquaculturists need to know the potential markets for their product before producing it. For example, carp are cultured on a large scale in Asia where they are in high demand, but probably could not be cultured profitably in the United States where they are generally considered trash fish. Product value, regional and seasonal trends in demand, availability of processing facilities, and cost of production are areas that should be investigated before beginning to culture an organism.

A certain amount of knowledge is needed to become a successful aquaculturist. An understanding of the organism's biology is very important. Information on optimum water temperatures for growth, nutritional requirements, possible diseases, and their treatments all must be known to successfully culture an organism. In the case of some species (e.g., catfish, trout, crawfish) the biological requirements have been documented (Huner and Barr, 1984; Solbe, 1988; Tucker, 1985). The requirements of organisms which have not been cultured previously or only recently cultured may not be known. Often the general principles of aquaculture (e.g., good water quality, adequate feed) will suffice, but a lack of information on a critical life stage could hinder culture of a particular species. As the science of aquaculture continues to grow, many of the requirements of certain organisms will be determined through research and through trial and error.

An aquaculturist must have some engineering and mechanical skills. Because aquaculture is such a young industry, the equipment needed is often unavailable or requires modification. The abilities to design and build certain equipment can save the aquaculturist time and money. Routine maintenance and repair of equipment are also essential.

Finally, an aquaculturist must possess at least basic business skills if he or she wants to be successful. Knowledge of bookkeeping, accounting, marketing, finance, personnel management, and so on, is necessary in all businesses including aquaculture. Often an aquaculture enterprise will fail not because the aquaculturist was a poor biologist, but because he or she lacked good business skills.

AQUACULTURE PRODUCTION

Worldwide

The most current (1985) estimate of world aquaculture production of finfish, mollusks, crustaceans, and seaweeds is approximately 11.7 million tons (10.6 million metric tons) (Nash, 1988). Aquaculture accounts for approximately 10 percent of world fisheries production from all sources. Of the total aquaculture production in 1985, finfish accounted for 44.5 percent, mollusks for 26.5 percent, crustaceans for 2.5 percent, and seaweeds for 26.2 percent. Of the total production (excluding seaweeds) 53 percent was from freshwater, 40 percent from salt water, and 7 percent from brackish water.

More than 186 aquatic species are under some form of culture. Of these species 102 are finfish, 32 crustaceans, 44 mollusks, and 8 seaweeds (Nash, 1988). Several carp species dominated production; other groups contributing significantly to the total included oysters, mussels, tilapias, salmonids, catfishes, clams, and shrimps (Table 18-1).

The countries of China, Japan, Korea, Philippines, and the United States accounted for approximately 76 percent of 1985 world aquaculture production (Table 18-2). Indonesia showed the greatest increase since 1983 (61 percent) followed by France (31 percent), the Republic of Korea (24 percent), United States (15 percent), and China (14 percent) (Nash, 1988).

Table 18-1. ***Production of Important Aquaculture Species in 1985***

Species	Production (Metric tons)
Carp (25 species)	2,500,000
Oysters (10 species)	1,000,000
Mussels (9 species)	500,000
Tilapias (6 species)	250,000
Salmonids (9 species)	150,000
Catfishes (9 species)	130,000
Clams (15 species)	130,000
Shrimps (20 species)	120,000

Source: FAO, 1987.
Adapted from Nash, 1988.

Table 18-2. *Aquaculture Production from Leading Countries in 1985 (in Metric Tons)*

Country	Total	Finfish	Crustaceans	Mollusk	Seaweed	Other
China	5,202,200	2,392,800	42,700	1,120,000	1,646,700	0
Japan	1,184,300	283,900	2,200	359,800	530,000	8,400
Korea	790,200	3,700	100	369,000	397,800	19,600
Philippines	494,400	243,700	29,900	37,900	182,900	0
U.S.A.	353,200	195,200	29,800	128,000	0	0

Source: FAO, 1987.
Adapted from Nash, 1988.

United States

In 1988 aquaculture production in the United States amounted to 789 million pounds (358 million kg) with a pond-side value (price paid to producer) of $600 million (Dicks and Harvey, 1989). United States aquaculture is dominated (both in terms of quantity and value) by three species: channel catfish *(Ictalurus punctatus),* rainbow trout *(Oncorhynchus mykiss),* and red swamp crawfish *(Procambarus clarkii).* Crawfish and catfish culture are centered in the southeastern United States; the majority of cultured trout are produced in the state of Idaho.

Aquaculture in the United States is not limited to food production. Culture of baitfish (golden shiners, fathead minnows, etc.) and tropical fish are fairly large and growing industries. Production of fish for stocking programs is a major form of aquaculture in the United States. More than 800 million juvenile sport fish are produced in federal, state, and private hatcheries and stocked each year (Sandifer, 1988).

CULTURE SYSTEMS AND TECHNIQUES

The following section briefly describes systems and techniques used to culture some of the more important cultured species. The organisms discussed include catfish, salmon, trout, carp, shrimp, crawfish, oysters, and marine algae.

Catfish

The channel catfish *(Ictalurus punctatus)* is the production and total value "king" of aquaculture in the United States. During 1988 the United States catfish harvest totaled nearly 300 million pounds (136 million kg) with a pond-side value of more than $200 million. Mississippi accounts for 80 percent of U.S. catfish production with more than 84,000 acres (34,000 ha) of ponds devoted to catfish culture (Mississippi Cooperative Extension Service, 1987).

Channel catfish can be grouped into four production categories: brood fish, fry, fingerlings, and marketable fish. Brood fish are adults used to produce offspring for the culture operation. Male and female brood fish are usually placed in a pond together and spawning occurs in the spring when water temperatures reach approximately 80°F (26.7°C). The female lays her egg mass in a container (milk cans are often used) placed in the pond by the culturist. The male fertilizes the eggs and chases the female away. The male will continue to guard and care for the eggs until they hatch; about seven days at 81°F (27°C).

Although eggs can be allowed to hatch in the pond, the farmer usually removes them and incubates them in a hatchery. Use of the hatchery method gives the farmer better control over fry production. The young fry (newly hatched fish) begin to feed five to seven days after hatching and are fed a high protein starter ration several times each day. After a week or two fry are transferred to small ponds (0.5 ha) and are fed larger rations as they grow to fingerling size. After a new months in these ponds the fingerlings are harvested and transferred to larger, 20 to 40 acre (8 to 16 ha) production ponds. In the production ponds the fish are fed a floating, pelleted ration at about 3 percent of body weight per day. A size selective seine is used to harvest the catfish when they have reached a marketable size of 1.0 to 1.5 pounds (0.45 to 0.68 kg). In the southern United States it takes a catfish fry sixteen to eighteen months to grow to harvestable size.

Salmon and Trout

The Atlantic salmon (*Salmo salar)* and the rainbow trout *(Oncorhynchus mykiss)* are the most commonly cultured salmonids. The life cycles of these two species are among the most well understood and controllable of all cultured species, which, along with the high market value, make them ideal candidates for culture.

The majority of Atlantic salmon production is located off the coasts of Norway and Scotland. Norway's exports of farmed salmon were valued at $230 million in 1986 (U.S. Dept. of Commerce, 1988).

A typical salmon production scheme involves fry, smolt, and market fish production. Domesticated broodfish selected for improved production characteristics are usually used to produce seed stock. When broodfish are ready to spawn, the males and females are "stripped" of their gametes. Stripping is accomplished by applying pressure to the fish's abdomen, causing the eggs and sperm to be released. Eggs and sperm are mixed and the fertilized eggs are placed in incubators. The eggs are incubated in cold water, 46 to 54°F (8 to 12°C), and hatch in about thirty days.

When the young fry have absorbed their egg sac they are fed a high protein starter ration. The young salmon are reared in fresh water in large tanks. Later they go through a process called smoltification, a series of physiological changes that prepare them for life in seawater.

Smolts, salmon that have gone through this process, are transferred from fresh water to large net pens or cages in the ocean. The enclosures retain the salmon but allow water to flow through and wash away wastes. Salmon are fed high protein pelleted rations and harvested at a size of 4.5 to 9.0 pounds (2 to 4 kg).

An ideal site for net pen culture is sheltered from the wind, easily accessible, and has a good flow of high quality, and appropriate temperature water. The coasts of Norway and Scotland provide ideal conditions for salmon culture. There has been considerable interest in culturing Atlantic Salmon along the western coasts of the United States and Canada, but development has been slow. Conflicts with commercial and recreational fishermen, interference with boat traffic, and environmental concerns may hinder the development of salmon farming in these areas.

Rainbow trout are cultured primarily in Europe and the United States. Similar techniques are used to culture both trout and salmon although trout remain in fresh water their entire life. Trout are usually cultured in concrete or earthen raceways (long, rectangular tanks) with water continuously flushed through the raceways to carry away wastes.

Trout are stocked at high densities and fed high protein rations. They are graded and harvested when they have reached marketable size. The availability of an adequate quantity of high quality water (appropriate temperature and high dissolved oxygen) are necessary for profitable culture of rainbow trout. Commercial trout production is limited to areas such as Idaho, where free flowing groundwater is available in sufficient quantities.

Carp

Four species of carp: the common carp *(Cyprinus carpio),* grass carp *(Ctenopharyngodon idella),* silver carp (*Hypophthalmichthys molitrix),* and bighead carp *(Aristichtys nobilis)* dominate world aquaculture production. Carp are widely cultured in Europe and Asia but are not grown to a large extent in the United States.

In Europe common carp are cultured extensively in earthen ponds. Manure from other farm animals is often added to the pond to stimulate production of natural food organism. Grains are sometimes added as supplemental feed. Yield from this type of culture is low but the production costs are also low.

In Asia more intensive carp culture is practiced. Often all four of the previously mentioned species of carp are grown together in heavily fertilized ponds in an efficient polyculture scheme. Because each species has a different food preference there is little competition between species for available food, and production is very efficient. The common carp is an omnivore and feeds along the bottom. The silver carp feeds on phytoplankton which it filters out of the water. The bighead carp feeds on zooplankton, and the grass carp feeds on aquatic plants. Polyculture of carp can result in production of up to 7,000 pounds per acre (7,850 kg/ha).

Shrimp

Culture of *Penaeid* shrimp is one of the biggest success stories in aquaculture. Cultured shrimp comprised 16 percent of shrimp harvested from all sources in 1986. China, Equador, and Taiwan are the leading producers of cultured shrimp (Treece, 1985). The shrimp farming industry employs more than 90,000 people in the country of Equador alone.

Typically, postlarval (very young) shrimp are stocked into large earthen ponds, fed a pelleted ration, and harvested when they reach 0.5 to 0.7 ounces (15 to 20 g) each. If the stocking rate is high (intensive culture) the water is periodically exchanged to maintain suitable quality. Shrimp grow to harvestable size fairly quickly, and usually two or three crops can be harvested each year in tropical areas.

Until only a few years ago postlarvae used to stock culture ponds had to be captured from the wild. Recent advances in hatchery techniques have allowed production of hatchery-reared postlarvae. Although wild-caught postlarvae are still used, stockings are now supplemented with hatchery-reared young.

Shrimp culture is practiced only on a very small scale in the United States and may be limited by low winter temperatures and a lack of suitable pond sites. However, recent research on intensive culture of shrimp in South Carolina has shown some potential for development of this industry (Sandifer et al., 1988).

Crawfish

Freshwater crawfish culture is the only large-scale, profitable crustacean culture endeavor in the United States (Avault and Huner, 1985). The majority of crawfish are produced in Louisiana, where area devoted to crawfish culture exceeds 125,000 acres (50,000 ha) and 55 to 66 million pounds (25 to 30 million kg) are harvested annually (Louisiana Cooperative Extension Service, 1986). Red swamp crawfish, *Procambarus clarkii,* account for approximately 90 percent of the pond harvest in

Louisiana. The red swamp crawfish is also cultured in several other southeastern states and several European and Asian countries.

Crawfish are usually grown in shallow earthen ponds with rice as a forage. The production cycles of rice and crawfish complement each other nicely. Ponds are usually drained in the late spring, the crawfish burrow into the pond bottom, and the rice is planted. During the summer crawfish remain in their burrows as the rice grows. In the early fall female crawfish lay eggs and hatch their young. About this time the rice is flooded and the young crawfish emerge from their burrows and feed on the rice as it decays. They reach harvestable size (greater than 3 inches/75 mm total length) by mid to late winter.

Baited wire mesh traps are used to harvest the crawfish. Fifty to one hundred traps are placed per hectare of culture pond. Because the traps must be emptied and baited every day, crawfish farming is a very labor-intensive business. During the late spring the pond is drained, rice planted, and the production cycle begins again. Crawfish are sold live, frozen whole, or are processed and sold as fresh or frozen abdomen meat.

Oysters

Aquaculture accounts for 40 percent of the oysters marketed each year in the United States (Burrell, 1985). Several species are cultured worldwide, but most of them belong to the genus *Ostrea* and *Crassostrea*. Oysters produce a mobile larva that eventually attaches itself to a suitable substrate and becomes sessile (nonmobile) for the remainder of its life. Once attached, shell development begins and the young oyster is called a spat. Oysters feed by filtering phytoplankton and other organic particles out of the water. Spat grow to harvestable size oysters in one to three years.

U.S. oyster growers usually use extensive culture techniques. Wild or hatchery-reared spat are collected and transferred to privately leased oyster beds. The aquaculturist periodically checks his or her "crop" and harvests the oysters when they reach marketable size. Although this system is generally classified as aquaculture it has also been referred to as a highly managed natural fishery.

More intensive, off-bottom culture of oysters is practiced in Europe, Japan, and to a small degree in the United States. Oyster spat, attached to sticks or strings, are suspended in the water column in off-bottom culture, which generally allows higher production per unit volume of water, faster growth, and easier harvest.

Marine Algae

One of the largest, yet often overlooked, segments of the aquaculture industry is the culture of marine algae. World production of marine algae in 1987 was estimated at 100 million tons (91 million metric tons) with a value of $250 million (McCoy, 1987). The majority of cultured algaes are macroalgaes (kelp, red and brown algae).

Macroalgaes, usually referred to as seaweeds, have been cultured for over 300 years (McCoy, 1987). Algal products are used in foods, cosmetics, pharmaceuticals, and for industrial purposes. Seaweeds can be grown extensively in ocean bays or intensively in large tanks. In China, for example, kelp is grown suspended from long bamboo rafts and is fertilized to increase production. Methods of harvesting seaweeds range from labor-intensive hand picking to the use of mechanized harvesters, a kind of underwater hay bailer.

The lack of unused, protected coastal bays necessary for extensive culture of seaweeds limits production in the United States. Intensive tank culture of seaweeds has generated considerable interest and may be a suitable alternative to extensive culture. Recent advances in propagation and genetic manipulation of algae have improved the potential for intensive culture. Although algae culture receives less notice than other types of aquaculture it is a substantial industry in certain parts of the world and has excellent potential for growth.

FUTURE OF AQUACULTURE

Aquaculture is an established industry and appears to have a bright future. The demand for high-value seafood products is growing rapidly, and capture fisheries will be unable to keep pace with the demand. Per capita consumption of seafood is increasing due, at least in part, to the health benefits of eating fish.

Future trends in aquaculture, at least in the United States, will be more toward increasing the intensity of production than increasing area devoted to production. Research on genetic improvement, nutritional requirements, diseases, and marketing of aquatic organisms should result in increased production and profits.

REFERENCES

Aiken, K. E. 1988. "Through the Looking Glass: Yesterday, Today and Tomorrow." *Journal of the World Aquaculture Society*.19(2):58–61.

Avault, J. W., and Huner, J. V. 1985. "Crawfish Culture in the United States." In *Crustacean and Mollusk Aquaculture in the United States,* edited by J. V. Huner and E. E. Brown. Westport, CT: AVI Publishing.

Bardach, J. E., Rythes J. H., and McLarney, W. O., 1972 *Aquaculture*. New York: Wiley-Interscience.

Boyd, C. E. 1979. *Water Quality in Warm Water Fish Ponds*. Auburn, AL: Auburn University Agricultural Experiment Station.

Burrell, V. G., 1985. "Oyster Culture." In *Crustacean and Mollusk Aquaculture in the United States,* edited by J. V. Huner and E. E. Brown. Westport, CT: AVI Publishing.

Dicks, M., and Harvey D., 1989. *Aquaculture, Situation and Outlook Report*. U. S. Department of Agriculture Economic Research Service, Aqua-2, March.

Dupree, H. K., and Huner, J. V., 1984. *Third Report to the Fish Farmers*. Washington, DC: U. S. Fish and Wildlife Service, U. S. Department of the Interior.

Huner, J. V., and Barr, J. E., 1984. *Red Swamp Crawfish: Biology and Exploitation*. Baton Rouge, LA: Louisiana Sea Grant College Program, Center for Wetland Resources, Louisiana State University.

Huner, J. V., and Brown, E. E, 1985. *Crustacean and Mollusk Aquaculture in the United States*. Westport, CT: AVI Publishing.

Laird, L., and Needham, T, 1988. *Salmon and Trout Farming*. New York: Wiley.

Louisiana Cooperative Extension Service 1986. *Agricultural Summary*. Baton Rouge, LA: Louisiana State University.

Liao, I. 1988. "East meets West: An Eastern Perspective of Aquaculture." *Journal of the World Aquaculture Society*. 19(2):62–73.

McCoy, D. H. 1987. "The Commercial Algaes: Prospects for One of the Oldest Industries." *Aquaculture Magazine*. 13(4):46–54.

Mississippi Cooperative Extension Service 1987: *For Fish Farmers.* Jan. 29 newsletter. Starkville, MS: Mississippi State University.

Nash, C. E. 1988. "A Global Overview of Aquaculture Production." *Journal of the World Aquaculture Society* 19(2):51–57.

Sandifer, P. A. 1988. "Aquaculture in the West, a Perspective." *Journal of the World Aquaculture Society.* 19(2):73–84.

Sandifer, P. A., Hopkins, J. S., and Stokes, A. D. 1988. "Intensification of Shrimp Culture in Earthen Ponds in South Carolina: Progress and Prospects." *Journal of the World Aquaculture Society.* 19(4):218–226.

Solbe, J. 1988. "Water Quality." In *Trout and Salmon Farming,* edited by L. Laird and T. Needham, New York: Wiley.

Stickney, R. R. 1979. *Principles of Warmwater Aquaculture.* New York: Wiley.

Stickney, R. R. 1986. *Culture of Nonsalmonid Freshwater Fishes.* Boca Raton, FL: CRC Press.

Treece, G. D. 1985. "Larval Rearing Technology." In *Texas Shrimp Farming Manual,* edited by G. W. Chamberlain, M. G. Haby, and R. J. Miget, College Station, TX: Texas Agriculture Extension Service, Texas A&M University.

Tucker, C. S. 1985. *Channel Catfish Culture.* New York: Elsevier.

U. S. Department of Commerce. 1988. *Aquaculture and Capture Fisheries: Impacts in U. S. Seafood Markets.* Report prepared pursuant to the National Aquaculture Improvement Act of 1985 (P. L. 99-198).

CHAPTER

19

Waste Treatment and Utilization

W. Steven Otwell

Most seafood processing requires a volume of clean water for preparation and preservation of final products. Clean water is used to wash, thaw, transport, cook, formulate, and/or package seafood products. The usual consequence of this water use is the addition of some foreign matter or waste materials which pollute the original water supply. The type and amount of pollutants entering the water will depend on the product forms, processing methods, and amount of product and volume of water used.

Regulations have been developed to encourage industrial wastewater management programs to prevent, control, or remove certain pollutants which could cause adverse environmental problems. These programs can include methods to treat the water and utilize any waste materials. Waste treatment is an additional operating cost, but waste utilization could represent additional profits or a least-cost treatment option. Waste management is not unique to the seafood industry. All industrial users of water must provide some program to prevent water pollution. Fortunately, water pollution from seafood processing is relatively mild compared to hazardous pollution resulting from many other industrial processes. Regardless of the source or amount of pollution, the seafood industry must recognize and support the need for controls to preserve the quality of our nation's waters. The seafood industry depends on production from clean waters.

SEAFOOD WASTEWATER

Materials which can cause water pollution during seafood processing include viscera, offal products, skin, scales, shell, and body parts. Most of these materials are large, visible with the naked eye, and can be removed with simple cleanup procedures, filtering, screens, and settling basins. Smaller, dispersed pollutants, which may be visible only as clouding in the water flow, may be dissolved or suspended in the water when the flow or spray runs along the product surface removing slimes, soluble proteins, body fluids, blood, and small particles of meat. Additions from breadings, batters, and oils also may cause small-size dispersed pollution. If some of these pollutants are not removed, the wastewater could cause adverse environmental consequences.

For example, when the polluting materials in a seafood processing effluent are discharged into the environment (i.e., stream, lake, or bay) they are usually biodegradable, meaning oxygen is required to decompose the materials into their simplest chemical form. The result can be a decreased oxygen level in the environment and an addition of various chemicals as basic nutrients for growth of plants and plankton. Excessive nutrients can cause overfertilization, or eutrophication, which disrupts the ecological balance of the receiving waters' eutrophication may cause a further decrease in the oxygen levels essential for established aquatic life.

These results are a basic explanation of adverse consequences; the actual results are far more complicated. Changes in the existing environmental water chemistry (i.e., altering pH to be more or less acidic) could influence survival of certain animals and plants. Addition of materials which discolor, cloud, or float in the water can be visually degrading and can influence water transparency, thus altering the penetration of essential sunlight. By attracting certain fish or crustaceans looking for food, pollution materials may cause an adverse imbalance in aquatic species competing for the food supply. In general, pollutants in seafood wastewater can disrupt the existing ecology of the receiving waters.

Similarly, seafood processing effluents can affect the operation of local wastewater treatment facilities. Although the facility is designed to treat wastewaters, the concentrations and volume of pollutants flowing from a local seafood processing operation could disrupt or overload the facility's treatment capacity. This outcome is especially true for seafood processing plants operating in a batch-type mode, sending irregular amounts of wastewater for treatment. The irregular surge of wastewater from the seafood processing plant can disrupt the treatment operations, requiring extra time and labor to readjust. The consequence can be increased costs for water use and treatment.

Various analytical methods have been developed to characterize and predict the consequences of wastewaters. These characteristics are commonly called pollutant parameters. The parameters of major significance to seafood processing wastewater are biochemical oxygen demand (BOD), total suspended solids (TSS), and oil and grease (O&G). To establish certain guidelines, pH is included as a parameter that must fall within a specified range. Of occasional importance are temperature, phosphorus, coliform bacteria, chloride, chemical oxygen demand (COD), settleable solids, and nitrogen. All these parameters are considered conventional pollutants.

Fortunately, most seafood processing effluents do not contain toxic pollutants such as heavy metals and pesticides. In high concentrations, both chloride and ammonia could represent a toxic condition for aquatic life, but usually these are not a problem in seafood processing effluents. Discharge of concentrated salt solutions (NaCl brines, etc.) could represent an adverse condition if not diluted and gradually released to prevent sudden impacts.

Pollution Parameters[1]

Biochemical oxygen demand (BOD) is a measure of the amount of oxygen needed to stabilize or biologically decompose (oxidize) the waste in water. The BOD does not cause direct harm to a water system, but it does exert an indirect effect by decreasing the dissolved oxygen content in the receiving waters. Dissolved oxygen (DO) in the water must be maintained at an appropriate level to support biological organisms including certain bacteria, fish, and plants. The BOD analytical method actually simulates the influence waste materials have on the dissolved oxygen. If high BOD is present, the quality of the water is usually visually degraded by the presence of cloudy decomposing materials. Detrimental levels of BOD may be present without visual detection.

Total suspended solids (TSS) includes all suspended matter (undissolved solids) in the wastewater except coarse or floating materials. TSS is measured by laboratory filtration methods which use a specified filter to collect a specified material size. The suspended matter can include organic materials (shell fragments, fats, grease, particle from products, etc.) and inorganic materials such as sand and silt. The level of organic materials can correlate well with the BOD, thus representing a potential decrease in dissolved oxygen. At high concentrations, these materials can be aesthetically displeasing and can increase water turbidity, which reduces light penetration and photosynthetic activity of algae and other aquatic plants. In time, some of these materials can settle on the bottom accumulate, and may cause adverse consequences to organisms dependent on the natural sediments.

Suspended solids which settle under quiescent (calm) conditions are called settleable solids. Measurements for these solids is especially applicable to the analysis of wastewaters being treated by screens, clarifiers, and flotation units. It not only defines the systems, in terms of settleable materials, but provides an estimate of the amount of deposition that might take place under quiescent conditions in the receiving water after discharge from the processing operation.

Oil and grease (O&G) includes substances that can cause surface slicks, scum accumulation, and clogged filters. O&G can contribute to oxygen demand and influence the reaeration of water at the surface. Certain oils can form an oil-water emulsion which could damage aquatic plant and gills of fish. O&G is not a common problem for most seafood processing operations; it is more typical as an adverse consequence of canning and cooking operations which may incorporate oil as an additional ingredient or "cook" oils from the raw materials.

The *pH of water* is a measure of the acidity or alkalinity (reciprocal terms). Values for pH range from 0 to 14. Low pH values indicate acidic conditions, and high pH values indicate alkaline or less acidic conditions. Aquatic life exists at a pH near 7.0. Extremes of pH or rapid changes can exert stress conditions or kill aquatic life outright.

Concentrations for pollutions parameters are usually expressed as pounds of a particular pollutant per 1,000 pounds of product processed. Thus a pollutant concentration in lbs/1,000 lbs or kilograms/1,000 kg (kg/kkg) can be specific for a certain firm, and all processors must meet a specified limit of similar units. This system prevents excessive water use as a possible method to dilute pollutants. The

---

[1]Pollution Parameters with definitions and explanations drawn in part and directly from 1975 *EPA Development Document for Interim Final Effluent Limitation Guidelines and Proposed New Source Performance Standards for the Canned and Preserved Seafood Processing Categories*, and 1973 *EPA Handbook for Monitoring Industrial Wastewaters.*

following formulas are for calculating waste concentrations as lbs/1,000 lbs or kg/kkg, and back-calculation as milligrams/liter (mg/l) or parts per million (ppm). (*Note:* These formulas are taken from Smith, J. O., and Bough, W. A. 1976. *Federal and State Treatment Regulations Affecting Seafood Processors in Georgia.* University of Georgia. Marine Extension Bull. No. 2.)

$$\frac{\text{mg/l}^{a} \times \text{mgd}^{b} \times 8.345^{c}}{\text{tons/day}^{d} \times 2^{e}} = \frac{\text{lb waste pollutant}}{\text{1,000 lb raw material}}$$

$$\frac{\text{mg/l}^{a} \times \text{m}^3\text{/day}^{f} \times 10^{-3\ g}}{\text{kkg/day}^{h}} = \frac{\text{kg}}{\text{kkg}}$$

$$\text{mg/l} \times \frac{10^{-6}\text{kg}}{\text{mg}} \times 10^{3}\ 1/\text{m}^{3} \times \frac{\text{m}^{3}}{\text{day}} = 10^{-3} \times \text{kg/day}$$

$$\text{mg/l} = \frac{\text{lb/1,000 lb}^{i} \times 2^{j} \times \text{tons/day}}{\text{mgd}^{k} \times 8.345^{l}}$$

$$\text{mg/l} = \frac{\text{kg/kkg}^{m} \times \text{kkg/day}^{n} \times 1{,}000^{o}}{\text{m}^3\text{/day}^{p}}$$

[a]The concentration of pollutant (BOD, suspended solids, etc.) determined by chemical analysis; expressed as milligrams per liter.
[b]Flow of wastewater measured in million gallons per day or gal. per day/10^6.
[c]Factor to convert from metric to U.S. measure, mg/l × 8.345 – lb/mil. gal.
[d]Production data for tons raw material processed per day.
[e]Converts tons to 1,000 lb units.
[f]Flow in cubic meters per day.
[g]Composite factor:
[h]Production data in thousand kilogram units per day.
[i]Effluent limitation or production-based waste loading in lb. waste component per 1,000 lb raw product processed.
[j]Converts tons to 1,000 lb units.
[k]Flow of wastewater in million gallons per day.
[l]Converts lb/mil. gal. to mg/l.
[m]Effluent limitation or waste loading in kilogram waste component per thousand kilogram raw product.
[n]Production data in thousand kilogram units per day.
[o]Composite factor, see note g above.
[p]Flow in cubic meters per day.

Some average measurements for the primary pollution parameters for wastewaters from various seafood processing operations are listed in Table 19-1. These measurements represent what can actually occur as a result of seafood processing, thus providing a characterization of the initial wastewater before it enters the environment. Using the first formula, the average pollutant concentrations in Table 19-1 can be expressed as pounds pollutant/1,000 pounds (kg/kkg) raw product processed in a particular seafood plant.

Table 19-1. *Raw Wastewater Characteristics: Canned and Preserved Seafood Processing Industries.*

Subcategory	Flow GPD	BOD mg/l	TSS mg/l	O&G mg/l
Farm-raised catfish	21M–45M	340	400	200
Conventional blue crab	700	4,400	620	220
Mechanized blue crab	20M–73M	600	330	150
Nonremote Alaskan crabmeat and remote Alaskan crabmeat	65M–99M	270	170	22
Nonremote Alaskan whole crab and crab section and remote Alaskan whole crab and crab section	36M–84M	330	210	30
Dungeness and tanner crab	38M–74M	280–1,200*	60–130	28–600
Nonremote Alaskan shrimp and remote Alaskan shrimp	300M–400M	1M*–2M*	1.3M–3M	100–270
West Coast shrimp	90M–160M	2,000*	900	700
Southern nonbreaded shrimp	180M–240M	1,000*	800	250
Breaded shrimp	150M–200M	720*	800	—
Tuna processing	65M–3.6MM	700*	500	250
Fish meal	92M–10M[1]	100–24M[1]*	0–20M[1]	20–5M[1]
All salmon	58M–500M	253–600*	120–1,400	20–5,550
Bottom and finfish (all)	6M–400M	200–100*	100–800	40–300
All sardines	80M	1,300*	921	250
All herring	29M	1,200*–6,000*	600–5,000	600–800
Hand-shucked clam	86M–170M	800*–2,500*	600–6,000	16–50
Mechanized clam	300M–3MM	500–1,200*	200–400	20–25
All oysters	14M–320M	250–800*	200–2,000	10–30
All scallops	1M–115M	200–10,000*	27–4,000	15–25
Abalone	10M–14M	430–580	200–300	22–30

[1] Higher range is for bailwater only
M = 1,000
MM = 1,000,000
*Seafood processing wastewater may contain high concentrations of chlorides from processing water and brine solutions, and organic nitrogen (0–300 mg/l) from processing water.
Table extracted from Carawan, R. E., et al. 1979. *Seafood Water and Wastewater Management Manual*, N.C. State University, Extension Spec. Report No. Am-18F.

WASTEWATER GUIDELINES

Realizing that wastewaters from seafood processing could adversely impact the quality of receiving waters, guidelines were necessary to specify limits for pollution parameters. A brief review of the regulatory history will provide a better understanding of how the guidelines were established and justified. This regulatory process is constant; thus new guidelines are periodically proposed and adopted.

No set of guidelines can suit all situations. The specified guidelines are just general guidance to direct regulatory decisions. Experience is showing regulatory decisions must consider and incorporate some modifications to suit particular situations, industries, and locations.

The prevailing waste management guidelines were originally mandated by the Federal Water Pollution Control Act Amendments of 1972 and 1977, commonly referred to as the Clean Water Act. Basically, these Acts were to "restore and maintain the chemical, physical, and biological integrity of the Nation's waters."[2] The primary administrative authority to plan and enforce these Acts was the U.S. Environmental Protection Agency (EPA). Various state environmental regulatory departments were established and adopted programs patterned on the original federal laws.

The philosophy of the clean water acts is different from previous regulatory schemes. The major difference is that the legislation mandated waste treatment guidelines that would be established relative to technological and economic considerations rather than depending on existing environmental quality. The guidelines would be established if waste treatment was technologically and economically available. Thus extensive field studies were done to review actual operations from various seafood processing categories (Table 19-1), and waste treatment technology was selected that represented the highest level of control which could be practically applied. The review and selection process included an involved cost-benefit assessment which is beyond our scope here, but it will suffice to conclude the economic consequences of various treatment technology options were considered.

The original regulatory plan was to specify a series of interim guidelines or goals which would gradually approach zero pollution discharge into navigable waters by 1985. These guidelines were actual specified concentrations of various pollution parameters which could be permitted for discharge. The pollution parameters for seafood processing plants were the conventional pollutants previously noted (BOD, TSS, O&G, and pH). The schedule for interim guidelines is commonly referred to with acronyms (Table 19-2).

Direct Discharge

Currently, all seafood processing firms which discharge wastewaters directly into the environment have to be in compliance with the Best Practical Technology (BPT) guidelines, which means the concentration of the primary, conventional pollution parameters must not exceed the concentrations specified in the 1977 guidelines (Table 19-3). The regulations include some reference to the BPT which can achieve these guidelines. For most seafood categories the BPT wastewater treatment technology is some form of screening and general in-plant controls.

Table 19-2. *Schedule of Interim Guidelines for Wastewater Regulations*

	Date of Compliance		
Source	July 1, 1977	July 1, 1984	1985
Direct discharge	BPT	BCT (BAT)	ZERO
Municipal discharge	Pretreatment Standards		
New source	Standards (NSPS)		

Note: BPT—Best Practical Technology; BCT—Best Conventional Technology; BAT—Best Available Technology.

[2]Nation's waters includes all navigable waters of the United States, tributaries of these navigable waters; interstate waters; intrastate lakes, rivers, and streams used by interstate travelers for recreational or other purposes; intrastate lakes, rivers, and streams from which fish or shellfish are taken and sold in interstate commerce; and which are utilized for industrial purposes by industries in interstate commerce.

To assure compliance, all firms with direct discharge must obtain NPDES permits (National Pollution Discharge Elimination System). These permits can be issued by the regional EPA office and/or by the respective state environmental regulation office which has been approved for NPDES permitting. Permit applications require a detailed description of the processing operation with specific data on water volumes used, various processing steps, operational schedules, and responsible individuals. After a regulatory review, a permit is issued which specifies the daily average and maximum concentrations of conventional pollutants which can be discharged from the plant.

The sampling point for measuring concentrations is near "the end of the pipe," rather than after discharge into the receiving waters. Monitoring requirements for periodic sampling, tests, and records are stated in the permit.

By July 1, 1984, seafood plants with direct discharge had to comply with the second series of interim guidelines. Initially the 1984 guidelines were established and designated as Best Available Technology (BAT). The pollutant limitations specified by the initial BAT guidelines were far more stringent than the first interim, Best Practical Technology (BPT). After numerous debates and comments, EPA has reconsidered the 1984 BAT guidelines, applied a modified cost-benefit analysis, and proposed the new 1984 guidelines (BCT) in the Federal Register (October 29, 1982). For most seafood categories the proposed 1984 BCT guidelines are equal to the 1977 BPT guidelines (Table 19-3).

Table 19-3. *Existing (1977) and Proposed (1984) EPA Pollutant Guidelines for the Seafood Processing Industries. (Source: Code of Federal Regulations, July 1, 1982)*

	BPT = BCT[1] Pollutant Limitation, lb./1,000 lb. raw material					
	BOD		TSS		O & G	
Seafood Category	d.max[2].	mo.avg.	d.max.	mo.avg.	d.max.	mo.avg.
Catfish, farm raised	—[3]	—	28	9.2	10	3.4
Blue crab, conven.	—	—	2.2	0.74	0.60	0.20
Blue crab, mechan.	—	—	36	12	13	4.2
AK[4] crabmeat, n-r[5]	—	—	19	6.2	1.8	0.61
AK crabmeat, r[5]	—	—	16	5.3	1.6	0.52
AK crab process., n-r[5]	—	—	12	3.9	1.3	0.42
AK crab process., r[5]	—	—	—	—	—	—
Dung./tanner crab	—	—	8.1	2.7	1.8	0.61
AK shrimp, n-r[5]	—	—	320	210	51	17
[a]AK shrimp, r[5]	—	—	—	—	—	—
North. shrimp proc.	—	—	160	54	126	42
South. shrimp proc.,n-b[6]	—	—	110	38	36	12
Shrimp proc., b[6]	—	—	280	93	36	12
Tuna processing	—	—	8.3	3.3	2.1	0.84
b	[b]7.0	3.9	3.7	1.5	1.4	0.6
Fish meal proc.						
c	[c]3.5	2.8	2.6	1.7	3.2	1.4
AK salmon, hand-butch.	—	—	2.6	1.6	0.31	0.19
AK salmon, mechan.	—	—	44	26	29	11
WC[4] salmon, hand-butch.	—	—	2.6	1.6	0.31	0.19
WC salmon, mechan.	—	—	44	26	19	11
AK bottomfish, proc.	—	—	3.1	1.9	4.3	0.56

Table 19-3. *(continued)*

	BPT = BCT[1] Pollutant Limitation, lb./1,000 lb. raw material					
	BOD		TSS		O & G	
Seafood Category	d.max[2].	mo.avg.	d.max.	mo.avg.	d.max.	mo.avg.
NA[4] bottomfish, conven.	—	—	3.6	2.0	1.0	0.55
NA bottomfish, mechan.	—	—	22	12	9.9	3.9
Clam, hand-shucked	—	—	59	18	0.60	0.23
Clam, mechan.	—	—	90	15	4.2	0.97
Oysters, can.& steam.	—	—	270	190	2.3	1.7
Sardine proc.	—	—	36	10	3.5	1.4
AK scallop proc.	—	—	6.6	1.4	7.7	0.24
AK herring fillets	—	—	32	24	27	10
NA herring fillets	—	—	32	24	27	10
PC[4] oysters						
BPT	—	—	47	38	2.4	1.8
BCT	—	—	45	36	2.2	1.7
AC[4] oysters						
BPT	—	—	24	16	1.2	0.81
BCT	—	—	23	16	1.1	0.77
NA[4] scallop proc.						
BPT	—	—	6.0	1.4	7.7	0.24
BCT	—	—	5.7	1.4	7.3	0.23
Abalone						
BPT	—	—	27	15	2.2	1.4
BCT	—	—	26	14	2.1	1.3

[a] No pollutants may be discharged which exceed 1.2 cm (0.5 inch) in any dimension.
[b] Any menhaden or anchovy fish meal reduction facility which utilizes a solubles plant to process stickwater or bailwater.
[c] Any menhaden or anchovy fish meal reduction facility except facilities which utilize a solubles plant to process stickwater or bailwater.
[1] BPT = BCT; BPT, 1977 guidelines equal BCT, 1984 proposed guidelines.
BPT < BCT; BPT, 1977 guidelines less than BCT, 1984 proposed guidelines.
[2] d.max.—daily maximum; mo.avg.—average of daily values for 30 days.
[3] no limitation.
[4] AK—Alaskan; NA—Non-Alaskan; WC—West Coast; PC—Pacific Coast; AG—Atlantic and Gulf Coasts.
[5] n–r—nonremote; r—remote
[6] n–b—nonbreaded; b—breaded

Reviewing the development of the 1984 guidelines is confusing but important to understand and appreciate the special consideration for the seafood industry. In most cases the proposed BCT guidelines were the same as the BPT guidelines. This development is a result of an increased awareness of potential economic damage implied by stringent and certain unreasonable regulations for the seafood industry.

Realizing the seafood industry is not a primary culprit in water pollution, regulatory authorities have adjusted many general cover-all regulations to suit the specific industry situation. The development of proposed BCT guidelines appears more lenient than the original BAT guidelines, but BCT does not compromise the original regulatory scheme. Although a seafood wastewater discharge can comply with BCT, more stringent guidelines can be enforced if site-specific considerations warrant. States are authorized to enforce more stringent discharge regulations considering the water quality in a specific site. Site-specific considerations seem to be the rule of the future and will require more state and local authorization and industry input to establish reasonable, adequate guidelines.

Water quality guidelines are distinct from the direct discharge guidelines specified for BPT and BCT but are similar in purpose. Water quality criteria are used to define a body of water by its physical–chemical properties, most commonly pH, dissolved oxygen, and amounts of suspended material. Founded on these parameters four classes were created on the basis of the designated use of the waters.

Class A or I.	Primarily for water contact recreation (swimming, water skiing, etc.).
Class B or II.	Propagation of desirable species of fish and wildlife.
Class C or III.	Public water supplies (suitable for treatment and use as drinking water).
Class D or IV.	Agricultural and industrial uses.

Each state has to define, designate, and protect water classifications. To provide adequate protection in certain waters or locations, wastewater treatment standards can be more stringent than those outlined by the interim direct discharge guidelines. Likewise, realizing the original intent of zero discharge by 1985, further modifications of the discharge guidelines can be anticipated.

Municipal Discharge

Seafood processors discharging into municipal systems or publicly owned treatment works (POTWs) should not take this service for granted. The demand for municipal treatment is ever increasing, especially in coastal regions where most seafood processing firms locate. The consequence for most seafood processors will be increased pretreatment requirements before discharge, higher use charges, and/or discontinued service. It is not uncommon for industrial and public demand to exceed municipal treatment capability. Additional pressures may come from seafood processors which were originally discharging directly to the environment but were forced to select municipal treatment as their only viable option for compliance.

Pretreatment standards for discharge to municipal facilities can include restrictions on water volume and temperature, BOD, and pH, or simply the timing and duration of flow. The standards were established to ensure that wastewaters would not overload the facility, interfere with the treatment process, or pass untreated. These standards are typically specified in a sewer use ordinance and can be altered to suit changes in demand for treatment. The sewer use ordinance, which governs the use of the public sewer system, may specify pretreatment standards as well as list charges for service. Charges can include cost for water consumption metered into the plant, a computed sewer water cost, a surcharge based on measured wastewater pollution parameters (i.e., BOD, TSS, O&G, pH), and/or an industrial cost recovery established to recover a portion of original construction costs.

Because most seafood processing operations work in a batch-type mode and generate wastewater with relatively high BOD, they are subject to critical review by POTWs that have reached their maximum treatment capacity. A simple solution may be to alert the POTW of your mode of operation, thus avoiding unexpected surges of wastewater. If the problems continue, more expensive pretreatment and a surge tank for temporary wastewater storage and metered release may be required. Regardless of the solution the seafood plant is linked with a waste treatment option which can continue to dictate standards and costs. The best approach to avert problems and unreasonable costs for municipal treatment is to understand and partake in the development of the sewer use ordinance. Legal and engineering counsel is advisable. Maintain and understand records for user charges and compare with similar users. Negotiate reasonable standards and charges, realizing the proper operation of the POTW facility and the economic welfare of the seafood firms are both essential for the welfare of the community.

New Source Discharge

New source dischargers are new seafood processing operations being constructed so that the installation may discharge wastewater directly into the environment or to the local POTW. Pollutant guidelines or pretreatment standards permitted through NPDES or use ordinances are usually intended to be more stringent for new source dischargers than for existing facilities with comparable operations. This form of regulation plans to prevent installation of obsolete technology. Often this consideration is not included in planning new operations. The results can be limiting to the size or success of the new firm. As cautioned, the seafood processor should always check with the NPDES or user ordinance authorities to learn of any specific new source requirements.

TREATMENT

Seafood processors must be prepared to install and practice treatment methods to prevent water pollution. Methods used can include alterations in daily processing which prevent pollutants from entering the processing effluent or specific equipment installed to remove pollutants from the wastewaters. Regardless of which methods are used, every employee should be made aware of the importance of wastewater treatment as an integral part of the entire processing scheme.

In-Plant Controls

The most cost-effective controls to assure wastewater management are basic in-plant changes to prevent the initial polluting of the processing waters. Seafood processors might consider in-plant controls to decrease water usage and minimize water contact with processing materials and products. The suspended solids and BOD loads generally increase as water use and water/material contact increase. Thus the philosophy of in-plant controls is to avert costly waste treatment by decreasing the volume and concentration of wastewater.

Plant surveys to document all water use, flow, and contact with materials is the first step for planning effective in-plant controls. The survey should record all water flowing into the plant, and diagram the flow and amount of water used in all processing operations, including cleanup procedures.

Timing water use can provide some indication of contact time with various materials and products. A comprehensive survey records water leaving the plant and then, realizing a volume differential, attempts to account for water losses during processing. Thus the survey provides an outline of the plant's total water flow. Water analysis for conventional pollutants can provide information indicating the various sources of contamination.

Survey information can be used to direct alterations for in-plant controls. In addition to water conservation, the decision to implement controls should consider consequences for sanitation and efficient processing. Cost comparisons should include assessments for total water use, water treatment requirements, both by the plant and/or contracted facilities, extra piping, control valves and equipment, labor adjustments, and general loss of processing flexibility due to an integrated water system. Thus the decision for in-plant controls should include input from management, engineers, quality maintenance, and production and financial concerns.

Education and training for all plant personnel is essential to assure a successful water management program. Employees must learn the importance and potential adverse consequences of water use. Training seminars and demonstrations are recommended; personnel assigned to monitor water use and/or treatment would be ideal. Employees must realize that water conservation and wastewater management are an integral part of the production process. This attitude must be established and maintained.

Water conservation begins with basic improvements in housekeeping techniques. Uncontrolled water flow for no specific reason should not be tolerated. Leaking and broken water valves and pipes should be continually inspected and repaired. When possible, spring-loaded valves should be installed to restrict water flow; a spring-loaded nozzle is a simple but often overlooked method to control flow from hoses. Check water flow through machines or processing segments which are not currently in operation. Controls should be installed to shut off or redirect water flow from processing operations that are not being used. Likewise, controls should be installed to prevent overflows from cleaning and cooling tanks. In general, controls should be installed to prevent any water use that is not necessary or results from careless practices.

Dry cleanup can be the most effective housekeeping procedure to conserve water and prevent additional water contamination. This can remove potential waste materials, such as viscera, offal products, skin, shell, breading, or batter, without using water to dissolve, transport, or wash down. Dry cleanup can be practiced continually during processing and as the initial step for general cleanup. Continuous use may be made of drip pans to catch breading and batters; trash cans for body parts, shell; and conveyors to transport waste to designated disposal. Cleanup procedures would utilize more brooms, pans, and vacuum systems to remove solid material prior to the initial wash down. The objective is to minimize water contact with potential waste material, thus preventing these materials from becoming an additional substance in the processing effluent.

Experience has shown that it can be more cost effective to prevent water contamination during processing and cleanup than removing contaminates from the processing wastewaters. Similarly, some processing modifications to minimize water use can be more cost effective than wastewater treatment. Excessive use of water fluming to transport products has been a common feature in many seafood processing operations. Where possible dry transport with conveyors, pneumatic systems, and vacuums should be considered. If fluming is essential, then necessary water flow should be controlled as needed for the level of product and processing scheduled. Wash procedures can be more effective and water conservation improved with high-pressure low-volume sprays than with low-pressure open-flow systems. Likewise, thawing procedures should minimize use of cool water and consider processing options for scheduled refrigerated thaw, partial microwave tempering, vibrational shatter packs, and other nonwater methods to assist thawing.

For certain processing applications closed-loop systems, such as a hydrostatic cooker-cooler for canned products, can be installed. The cooker water is reused continuously, and supplemented with necessary water to account for minimal evaporation loss. This system conserves water as well as energy by reclamation of heat between cooks.

The variety of controls to conserve water and minimize water/product contact are numerous, depending on the inventiveness of the operators and on the specific requirements of different seafood processing methods. Each option must be evaluated relative to potential savings versus subsequent treatment costs and production efficiency. In no way should conservation operations compromise product quality, sanitation, or safety.

Reuse and Recycling

Water reuse and recycling are processing concepts which deserve consideration as options for water conservation and treatment. These options involve utilizing water more than once before it leaves the processing plant. This method is accomplished by collecting waters from one or more processes, then directing it for use in another process. The quantity and quality of the collected waters will determine potential reuse. A comprehensive in-plant survey is essential to implement these concepts.

Usually reused water is redirected for successively dirtier application. This scheme is called a countercurrent flow or counterflow reuse. For example, water used in a final product rinse can be redirected for initial product wash or thaw. Between uses a partial water treatment and/or dilution with additional clean water may be necessary. Chlorine could be added to prevent bacteriological conditions which could jeopardize fresh product quality.

Recycling refers to using treated water in the same application(s) for which it was previously used. Water treatment between uses is necessary to remove any microorganisms of public health significance and any substances which could adversely affect product color, flavor, or odor. Thus recycling is reuse with more emphasis on water quality. Neither reuse nor recycling are new concepts; in fact, the entire municipal water treatment concept is reuse and recycling.

In food processing, reuse is employed in fruit and vegetable plants and other canning operations (Fig. 19-1). The distinction for water reuse in most seafood processing is that processing waters are in direct contact with the edible, proteineous portion of the final products. Food processing plants for such products as red meats and poultry must use water that is of potable quality. Federal standards require that potable water must be used for cleaning all equipment which contacts such foods. Additional state health and water quality regulations for food processing can be even more stringent. The regulatory concern is for potential health risk and hazards, and the current regulatory attitude is that renovated wastewater is not suitable when other sources are available.

Regulatory concern for water reuse in seafood processing is justified, but with experience and cooperative demonstrations, reuse and recycling can be developed as a beneficial in-plant method of wastewater management. Recognizing the potential risk for bacteria, suspended materials, and other possible contaminants, the processor should explore options with the advice and assistance of regulatory authorities.

The final decision on whether to initiate such options depends on a careful comparison of cost for reuse and recycling, with necessary treatments, versus the initial costs for water and wastewater treatments.

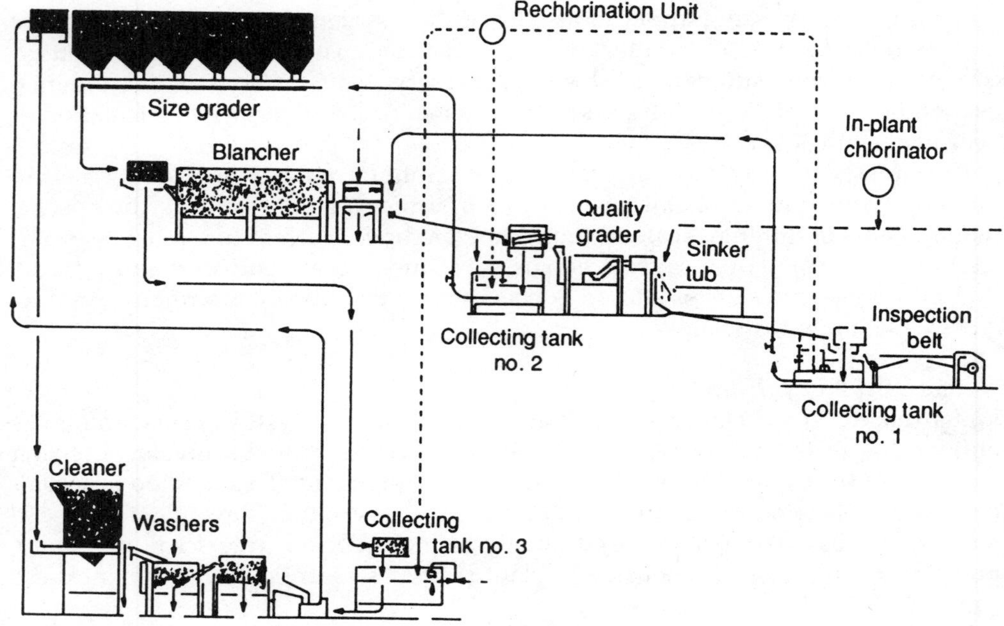

Figure 19-1. Counterflow Reuse System.

Segregation of Waters

Wastewater segregation is the separation of various processing waters according to their waste load or required level of treatment. Just as the sanitary wastewaters are directed separate from the processing flows, a review of the in-plant survey could indicate additional wastewaters for separate treatment.

The benefits are decreased cost for wastewater treatment. For example, noncontaminated waters may require no treatment and can be discharged directly. Contaminated waters may be further segregated according to their levels of BOD, suspended solids, and other pollution parameters. Another segment of the processing waters could be treated by simple on-site methods prior to direct discharge, for example, settling basins and screens, while more contaminated waters would be directed for municipal wastewater treatment. Thus the processing firm does not have to incur municipal cost for treating all processing wastewater volume.

End-of-Pipe Treatment

Assuming the seafood processor has employed all practical and economic methods to conserve water use, to minimize water/material contact, and to segregate wastewaters, additional treatment may be required before the water leaves the plant. The final treatment prior to discharge is called end-of-pipe treatment. If the water is discharged to a municipal facility the final controls are called pretreatments.

Sedimentation, or *settling,* is the separation of solids in water by means of gravity. This treatment requires some form of water retention (for example, grit chamber, catch basin, or clarifier) and a necessary residence time in this position. The design of the retention facility depends on the settling characteristics (velocity) of the solids to be removed.

Grit chambers to catch sand and shell have been useful for certain industries, but finer suspended solids limit their practical application in other industries. Large resettling ponds or tanks provide more retention time to assure effective settling, but land availability around typical seafood coastal locations limits such installations. Likewise, frequent removal of captured solids is essential to avoid putrefaction, and the collected solids may have to be dewatered before final disposal.

Screening implies any device used to actively separate solids from the processing wastewater. The screen can be a crude, coarse series of bars or a fine mesh overlay with agitation. Screens can be classified as

1. Basket screens
2. Bar screens
3. Drilled plates, and so on.
4. Gratings
5. Revolving drums with perforations (inclined, horizontal, and vertical)
6. Vibrating, shaking, or oscillating screens (linear or circular motion)
7. Tangential screens (pressure or gravity fed)
8. Centrifugal screens

Screens typically are installed in combinations to provide a series of progressively finer solids removal. The system should be built large enough to handle the maximum anticipated water and solids loading. This arrangement prevents clogging or restricted water flow and backup.

The best installation utilizes controlled gravity flow to direct water through the screens. If pumps are necessary to lift water across the screens, positive displacement or progressing cavity nonclog pumps are recommended. Centrifugal nonclog pumps can be used, but the pressured flow should not force small particles to clog the screening mesh. Mechanical brushes or sprays can help prevent clogging. The functionality system will have a longer life if the materials used are resistant to saltwater corrosion.

The screened solids must be frequently or continuously removed to prevent clogging or putrefaction. Some method or dewatering, either mechanically with pressure or simply drainage, is usually necessary before final disposal.

Revolving drum screens are basically a cylindrical frame with both ends open. The frame or drum surface is a perforated or sliced mesh of size to suit the particular operation. If the drum is inclined, wastewater can be fed into the raised end and solids are captured as the water seeps through the interior mesh. The revolving action causes the solids to migrate out the lower end of the drum, and the revolving speed can be controlled to provide a variable screening performance. Some revolving drums are used in a horizontal position with the lower side of the drum immersed in the wastewater (Fig. 19-2). Screened solids are held by ribs on the inside of the drum and rotated upward for deposit on a central conveyor belt. Regardless of drum position backwash sprays can be used to prevent clogging.

Vibrating screens are typically employed as unit operations or to handle a segregated water flow rather than as a total wastewater treatment. The vibrating screen is usually more sensitive to variations in water flow and solids content. These screens are mounted on springs to allow either circular or linear vibrations as wastewater flows through the vibrating plate. The solids vibrate to the sides of the plate for removal. Blinding or clogging is a common problem for vibrating screens; therefore, they are better suited for nonfibrous, nonoily wastewater.

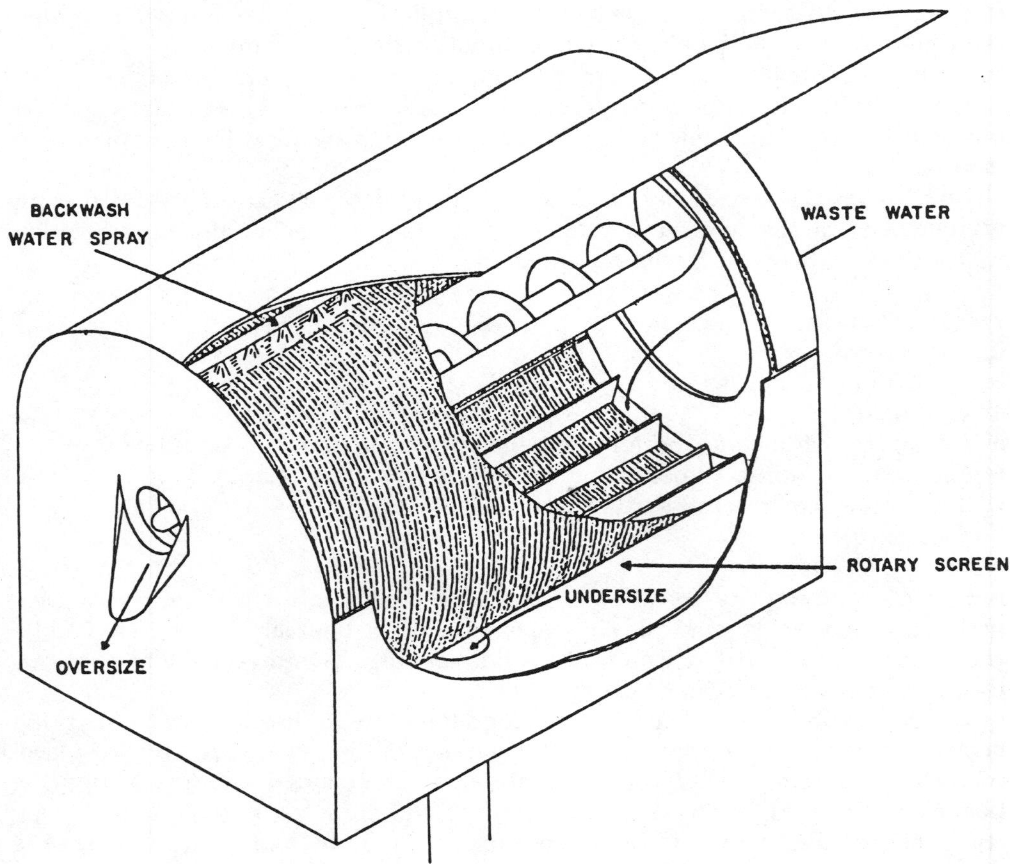

Figure 19-2. Typical Horizontal Drum Rotary Screen.

Tangential screens, the most popular screens for treating seafood processing wastewaters, are effective and generally maintenance free because they require no moving parts. The screen surface is usually inclined and curved about 45° to 60°. The screening feature can be a series of parallel, triangular, or wedge-shaped bars oriented perpendicular to the water flow, or a sheet with fine perforations or slits. Solids are screened as water flows down the surface and through the inclined screen. The solids migrate downward, off the screen for disposal. Gravity-fed tangential screens are common but pressure-fed units can operate with a finer mesh.

Before selecting a particular type and arrangement of screens, the processor should check performance to ensure effective removal of solids. Performance will be determined by the particular characteristics and volume of wastewaters. Likewise, the final installation should be designed to anticipate further treatment requirements. Although screening appears to be the most commonly required treatment technology for seafood processing effluents, it only removes a portion of solids. The screened solids may assure compliance with guidelines for suspended solids, but the remaining BOD could be a problem. The regulatory concern for BOD remaining after screening seafood processing effluents is primarily at the state and local levels and addresses water quality standards.

Biological treatments can be used to decrease wastewater BOD, but most of these methods are unproven and not practiced in the seafood industry. As screening requirements become more common, the potential use of biological systems to remove BOD should be reconsidered. Basically biological treatments are designed to enhance the oxidation processing which would occur naturally in the aquatic environment. By concentrating and directing an aerobic (oxygen-dependent) microbial mass, the level of BOD in the wastewater can be reduced before discharge. In general, biological treatments can be used to reduce BOD so that an effluent is more compatible with the receiving water or municipal facility.

The two basic categories of biological treatment are units with fixed microbial growth (rotating biological contactors, trickle filters, etc.) and systems with suspended microbial growth (activated sludge, lagoons, etc.). These treatments require some initial pretreatment to remove oil and greases which could limit oxygen transfer and to decrease solids which can clog filters. A scheme of flow equalization and continuous flow is necessary to avoid shock loading and to maintain a balanced microbial growth. If salt water or other added chemicals are present in the wastewater, they could be toxic to the microorganisms. After biological treatment, clarification and/or chlorination may be necessary to allow a biomass-liquid separation and prevent adverse bacterial problems.

Rotating biological contactors (RBC), or biodiscs, are fixed growth biological units with a series of cylindrical discs mounted parallel on a shaft placed across a wastewater basin or tank. The discs rotate slowly through the wastewater and air above, thus providing some aeration of the waters. In the presence of oxygen and the organic BOD load, microorganisms begin to grow on the disc surface. Growth of these aerobic organisms reduces the BOD. As growth becomes excessive the biomass will flake from the disc surface and settle while remaining organisms continue the oxidation process. To ensure growth during limited or no-flow situations, the unit can be operated in a closed loop fashion depending on effluent recycling. A series of RBC units could be the most effective design depending on available space. The primary limiting factor is ambient air temperatures. The unit(s) should be housed to insulate the organisms from colder temperatures which reduce or eliminate growth.

Trickling filters are a similar fixed biological system which uses small rocks, fiberglass, plastics, and so on, to provide surface area for microbial growth. The wastewater is passed through the filter for treatment. The size and shape of the filter depend on available space and volume of wastewater. Contact time in the filter must be considered to ensure effective treatment. Also, the biomass will "flake" or slough off as growth continues, and a continuous flow is necessary to promote growth. Insulation is required to control ambient temperatures.

Lagoons or ponds utilize the same aerobic growth concept to remove BOD, but the microbial biomass is suspended in the water rather than fixed on a surface (Fig. 19-3). Supplemental oxygen provided by floating aerators or compressed air diffusers are necessary to support growth for the oxidation process. Pond sizes can be large and cover many square feet or a series of smaller units. Typical depth is 3 to 4 ft. (0.92 to 1.2 m) with natural aeration, or up to 20 ft. (6.1 m) deep with mechanical aeration. Pond design must account for ambient temperatures, winds, run off, and wastewater volume. In addition to the aerobic process, some ponds can incorporate an anaerobic (without oxygen) treatment that decomposes solids which settle in the depths. The primary limiting factor for lagoon or pond treatment, especially for the coastal seafood industries, is land availability and soil conditions.

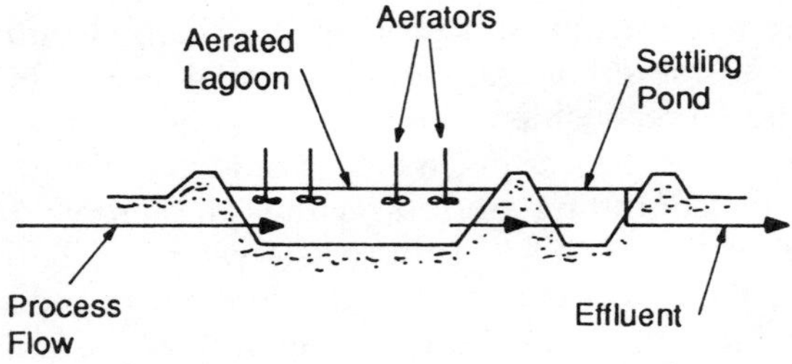

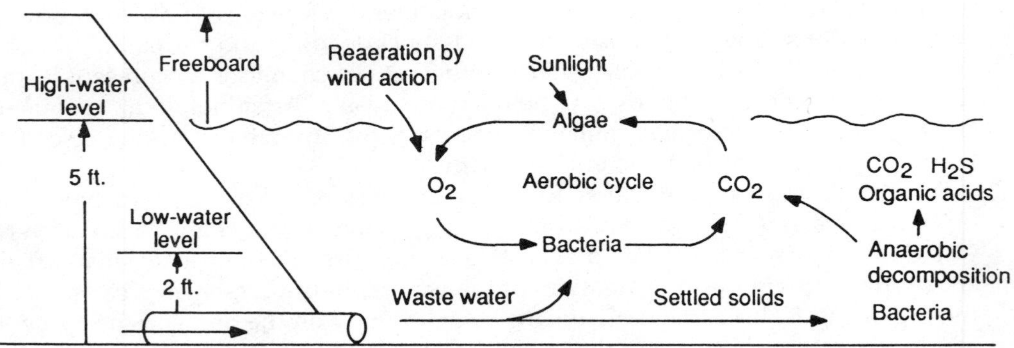

Figure 19-3. Typical Lagoon and Pond System for Biological Treatment of Wastewater.

Activated sludge treatment is similar to the pond concept, but the suspended microbial growth is concentrated and maintained in a specifically built unit (Fig. 19-4). The sludge (growth of microorganisms) is maintained in a controlled mixture of organic material from the wastewater, dissolved oxygen, and some nutrients (nitrogen and phosphorus). Active contact for sludge treatment can be for one to three days. The treated effluent has to be settled to remove biological solids, and a portion of the sludge is recycled to assure a balanced growth media. The primary limiting factor for use of activated sludge to treat seafood wastewater is the necessity for more careful controls versus the batch-type noncontinuous flow typical of many seafood processing operations.

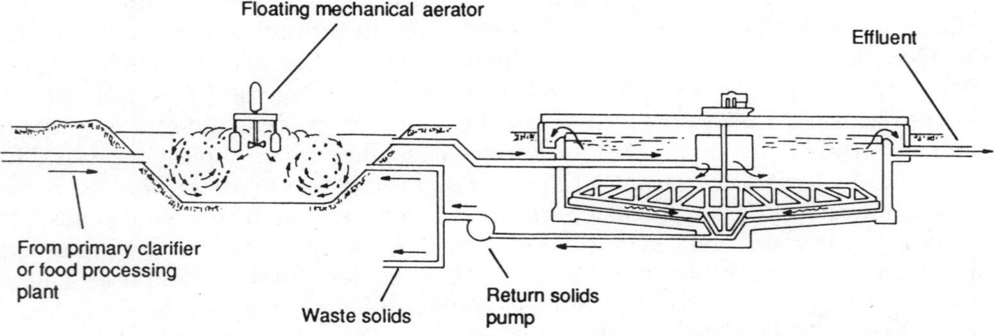

Figure 19-4. Activated Sludge System for Treating Wastewater.

Land applications or land disposal can be a low cost and effective wastewater treatment option if sufficient and suitable land is available. Some seafood wastewater applications have been found to improve certain soils and actually support crops and grasses. The waters are usually pretreated (screening) prior to application. Three basic methods of application are (1) irrigation with sprays or trickle outlets, (2) overland flow with an option to dike or furrow the flow, and (3) infiltration-percolation with natural flow or pressure (septic system, etc.). The concept is to use the filtering and biological features in the soil to eliminate and assimilate the pollutants.

The ability of the soil to perform an effective treatment depends on (1) the soil characteristics and profile, (2) depth of groundwater, (3) terrain and ground cover, (4) ambient temperature and seasons, and (5) wastewater volume and characteristics. Preliminary trial work is recommended to assess soil suitability and estimate maximum loading rates. Adverse concerns include the accumulation of dissolved solids, particularly sodium, and of virus and bacteria production which could present a potential health hazard. Land applications should be mindful of long-term effects and should not compromise land value by disrupting surface vegetation or by polluting groundwaters.

Physical–chemical treatments for seafood wastewater were judged ineffective and financially impractical in the past. Although promoted as options which require less space than biological methods, the installation and operational costs often exceeded benefits. These systems require higher costs for equipment, chemicals, power, and operator training. With more experience, these systems may become better suited for seafood processing applications.

There has been little practical application in the seafood industry of advanced systems such as carbon adsorption, filtration, reverse osmosis, electrodialysis, ion exchange, and chemical oxidation.

Dissolved air flotation (DAF) has been previously recommended as a treatment option for various seafood categories (Fig. 19-5). The DAF processes uses minute air bubbles to attach to and float oil, grease, and suspended matter from the carrying liquid. The separation process can be optimized by using flocculating agents such as ferric chloride, alum, lime (pH 10 to 10.5), anionic polymers, and acid adjustments.

A number of disadvantages have been associated with the dissolved air flotation treatment of seafood processing effluents:

1. *Operational mode* of a DAF unit requires lengthy startup times (one to three hours), continuous flow during operations, and lengthy shutdown and cleanup time (one to three hours). Most seafood processing operations are not a continuous process, varying daily and seasonally.
2. *Trained, experienced labor* is required to operate the DAF systems. This type of labor is generally limited and expensive, and the seasonal schedule of production would be an unattractive feature for such highly trained labor.
3. *High costs* for DAF equipment, chemicals, power (energy), maintenance, and operations may be prohibitive.
4. *Disproportionate costs* are higher for smaller size firms.
5. *Land availability and costs* are not considered in the original cost estimate figures. Coastal real estate is limited and expensive.
6. *Sludge collected* is a highly putrisensible scum (95 percent water) which must be disposed of in an environmentally sound manner.

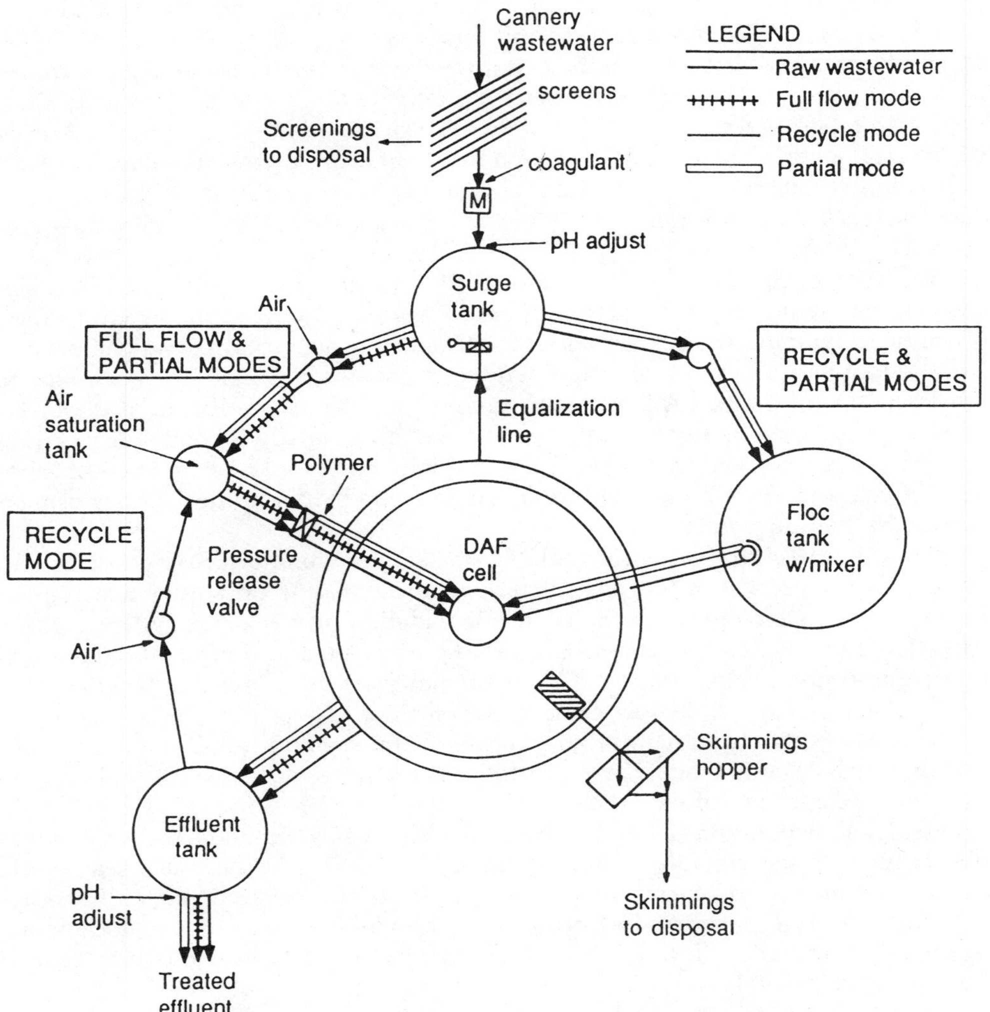

Figure 19-5. Dissolved Air Flotation Wastewater Treatment System.

7. *Sludge odors* can be a problem and will attract flies and rodents, which are unsanitary conditions in conflict with health and food processing regulations.
8. *Sludge disposal* is a major unanswered problem.
   - Fewer landfills will accept sludge (95 percent water), and future environmental regulations could limit sludge disposal in landfills.
   - The chemical additions during DAF treatment limit the use of sludge as a precursor in feeds or fertilizers.
   - Ocean disposal, which has been permitted for raw screened seafood solids, would be restricted for chemically treated seafood sludge.
9. *Energy requirements* for DAF treatment would increase energy use and processing.

SOLIDS DISPOSAL

After wastewater treatment, accumulated solids or waste materials collected by settling, screening, or other methods must be removed from the seafood plant and disposed of in an appropriate manner. These solids usually have a high moisture content which can be evident as drip or actual flow. Dewatering prior to disposal is recommended to minimize problems with handling, transportation, and disposal. Dewatering systems can apply heat to dehydrate the solids and/or use pressure to force moisture from the solids. Cost for dewatering must be compared with reduced costs for transportation and disposal. In some cases dewatering costs are unavoidable in providing solids which are compatible with the available disposal option. Disposal methods must consider odor, insect, and decomposition problems, as well as a general adverse public attitude objecting to the unpleasant aesthetic aspects.

Land disposal in private or municipal sanitary landfills is the most common disposal method. Although most seafood waste solids are suitable for landfills, the availability of sites is decreasing due to (1) increasing public and regulatory concern for potential adverse environmental consequences; (2) state and federal restrictions and operational guidelines to control use of landfills; and (3) decreasing availability of suitable sites due to population growth around certain seafood processing locations and public resistance.

Seafood processors using or considering landfill disposal should not take this option for granted. Regional and local regulations should be studied and future fill capacity determined. A cooperative approach would be to install and emphasize the dewatering systems and controls for temporary storage and transport to the landfill site.

Ocean dumping may be a viable option for seafood waste solids disposal. In the original Marine Protection, Research, and Sanctuaries Act of 1972, commonly called the Ocean Dumping Act, Congress established policy for disposal of materials in the ocean. This policy clearly stated disposal of "fish (and shellfish) wastes" did not require a permit to dump at sea. Seafood waste solids were given this special exclusion because these materials were compatible with the environment whence they came. The EPA retained the right to designate appropriate dump sites. Dumping would not occur in (1) harbors or other protected or enclosed coastal waters; or (2) any other location where EPA finds such dumping may cause adverse results. In general EPA views ocean dumping as a last resort option.

The original EPA criteria for the dump site included (1) geographic location; (2) location relative to reproduction and growth of marine resources; (3) location relative to amenity areas such as swimming beaches; (4) amount and characteristics of waste; (5) ability to observe and monitor; (6) diffusion, dispersion, mixing; (7) interference with shipping, fishing, recreation, and so on; (8) water quality and ecology; (9) previous dumping effects and cumulative effects; (10) attraction of nuisance species; and (11) the cultural and historical aspects of the site.

Although ocean dumping is an alternative for seafood solids disposal, the necessary logistics and cost are usually prohibitive. In addition to costs for operating vessels such as barges, there must be a system to accumulate and store the waste so it does not cause offensive odors or attract insects, with potential health problems. If chemicals are added to stabilize or minimize decomposition of the solids, the chemical addition is a separate solid atypical in raw seafoods; thus an EPA permit would be required to allow disposal of the treated materials. Despite these concerns, seafood processors may consider their option for ocean dumping. A successful system may be integrated with commercial or recreational fisheries, for example, artificial reefs could be considered as sites for solid waste utilization as feed and attractants.

Incineration of seafood waste solids has been suggested, but practical aspects seem unfavorable. Most seafood operations are noncontinuous batch-type operations, and would probably depend on an established incineration system for municipal wastes and sludge. The arrangement would avoid costly startup and shutdown costs, but with increasing fuel costs this option can be expensive and wasteful. By-products generated by combustion could be a problem in populated regions.

UTILIZATION

The average processed yield for whole raw seafoods is approximately 50 percent, so half the nation's seafood production becomes a waste material requiring treatment and disposal to protect the environment. Other muscle food industries incorporate a more total use concept. Seafood waste utilization options are available and should be encouraged as a more attractive waste treatment or disposal alternative. These utilization options typically have not been considered worthwhile because they do not generate a profitable product. Profit, however, should not be the sole determining factor. Utilization could be a least-cost waste treatment option. In addition to recovering an otherwise wasted product, utilization reduces the requirements and costs for further wastewater treatments.

A comprehensive review of all utilization options for seafood waste is beyond the scope of this chapter. Numerous studies have explored the required technology, but seafood processors should carefully review any utilization options with the thought that technological feasibility does not always translate into practical applications. This caution is not negative advice, but an experienced opinion to prevent any reoccurrence of results which sour the waste utilization alternative. In the future, seafood waste utilization will become a more integral part of the successful seafood processing operations. This development will require a progressive commitment from the seafood industry.

Before initiating a seafood waste utilization option the seafood processor should consider the following questions:

1. Is there an identifiable user group for the product?
2. Would distance to and separation of the users cause transportation problems and prohibitive cost? For example, minimum distance to a user group is necessary to consider production of fish silage (high moisture content fermentation or heavy feed).
3. What is the anticipated volume and schedule (monthly, seasonal) production and does this suit demand?
4. Could a more continuous production be established through cooperation with similar and not-too-distant seafood firms?
5. Do similar, cost competitive products exist?
6. What waste and regulatory problems would the seafood waste utilization process cause?
7. If the product is not profitable, is it a least-cost treatment option?

Human Consumption

Edible products for human consumption have received considerable attention with applications for waste protein recovery by screening, filters, concentration, and deboning, and subsequent product fabrication by pressing, extruding, texturizing, pressure heating, and breading. Likewise, recovery of soluble proteins and various body parts has been incorporated in chowders, paste, and various other edible products. Realizing the ever-increasing domestic and foreign demand for seafood, this work is justified. In the United States since 1970 the per capita consumption of fresh and frozen fish and shellfish has increased by more than 20 percent. Current market evaluations indicate this demand trend should continue, but domestic production of many traditional types of seafood is approaching maximum annual sustainable yields. Proper market introduction and quality will be the keys for successful introduction of new by-products. For example, simulated crabmeat and shrimp are finding a niche in the seafood market (for more information on these products and technologies see Chapter 8).

In some cases, edible products also can be recovered without additional processing. Exporting developments for fish roe is a prime example.

Feeds

Edible products for feeds can also be recovered for animal consumption. The most popular seafood by-product for feed is meal or dehydrated protein, for example, poultry ration supplement. The production of meal from fish or shellfish scraps has, at times, become a less favored option due to the costs for heating fuels and cost competition from other vegetable protein meals. An alternative would be to find user groups, such as mink farms, alligator farms, or hog farms that utilize the waste in raw form or after fermentation (silage). If aquaculture develops in the United States, it may represent an impetus for using more seafood waste as feeds.

Industrial Products

Industrial products from seafood waste tend to be less profitable than edible products but can represent alternatives available to specific fisheries. For example, production of chitin/chitosan from crustacean shells has received considerable development work. Studies have shown chitin and its derivative chitosan could be used as coagulants, as emulsifying and thickening agents, and for medical purposes. Attempts to initiate production of chitin/chitosan have failed due to unique handling requirements, expensive capital equipment, and limited demand versus less expensive, competitive products with similar functionality.

Other Uses

Seafood waste as a fertilizer, raw, wet, or dried, could be utilized if directed to specialized markets, such as for houseplants, or for commercial greenhouses. Developing this market would depend on competitive cost and any unique features in seafood fertilizers. Enhanced growth rates and indirect control of soil nematodes have been noted for certain dried seafood waste, for example, shellfish shell. Production of crops and grasses has been demonstrated for certain wet, raw seafood wastes.

Shells from clams and scallops have always been useful for road and landfill construction. Certain mollusk shells can be cleaned and sanitized and then used as attractive containers for dips or deviled items. Likewise, shells from crabs can make attractive containers.

Bait is an often overlooked option for seafood waste utilization. Most fishing operations require some form of bait, either in the whole raw form or ground and packaged. The only processing requirement is packing and freezing. Similarly chum for recreational boats and fishing piers is often overlooked.

EXPECTATIONS

Typically most efforts to prevent waste and pollution are motivated by regulations. Future regulatory schemes will become more regional and localized, thus requiring more site-specific and industry-specific considerations. Seafood processors would be wise to review current waste management methods and prepare to address concerns for local water quality standards. In addition to end-of-pipe guidelines proposed by the EPA, more processors will be faced with water use and effluent limitations and with increasing treatment costs to maintain the quality of waters as designated by the states and localities.

Wastewater treatment options for seafood processing require more development and practice. Requirements for in-plant controls and screening seem reasonable for most situations, but the industry should explore further treatments to lower BOD, decrease operating costs, and recover by-products. Continued dependence on municipal wastewater treatment and solids disposal should not be taken for granted. In most coastal regions these options are vulnerable to expanding populations. More industry self-control may be available with segregation of processing waters, water use and recycling, land and ocean applications, and biological treatments.

Utilization of by-products may prove to be the most cost-effective waste treatment option and should be examined as a least-cost treatment option as well as for profitability.

In general, seafood waste management, including treatment and utilization, should be considered an integral part of all seafood processing and handling operations. The goals should be to comply with existing regulations and prevent pollution, but the motivation is to assure continued seafood productivity from our nation's waters.

REFERENCES

Azad, S. H. (ed.). 1976. *Industrial Wastewater Management Handbook.* New York: McGraw Hill.

Carawan, R. E., Chambers, J. V., Zall, R. R., and Wilkowske, R. H. 1979. *Seafood Water and Wastewater Management.* North Carolina State University Extension Spec. Report No. AM-18F.

Green, J. H., and Kramer, A. 1979. *Food Processing Waste Management.* Westport, CT: AVI Publishing Co.

Katsuyama, A. M. 1979. *A Guide for Waste Management in the Food Processing Industry.* Berkeley, CA: National Food Processors Assoc.

Otwell, W. S. (ed.). 1981. *Seafood Waste Management in the 1980s: Conference Proceedings.* Florida Sea Grant Report No. 40.

Windsor, M., and Barlow, S. 1981. *Introduction to Fishery By-Products.* Surrey, England: Fishing News Books Ltd.

CHAPTER

20

Fish Meal and Oil

Anthony P. Bimbo

The world's catch of fish, crustaceans, and mollusks roughly equals 101 million tons (90 million metric tons) per year, of which 30 percent is processed into fish meal and oil. The preliminary breakdown of catch and fish meal and oil production by country for 1987 is shown in Table 20-1 (Bowman, 1988; Mielke, 1988).

The fish meal and oil industry, which started in northern Europe and North America at the beginning of the 19th century, was based primarily on surplus catches of herring. It consisted mainly of oil production for industrial uses in leather tanning and the production of soap, glycerol, and other nonfood products. The residue was originally used as fertilizer but since the early 1900s it has been dried and ground into fish meal for animal feeding. Its main use is in the diets of poultry, pigs, and fish which need higher quality protein than other farm stock such as sheep and cattle (FAO, 1975).

The U.S. production of fish meal and oil accounts for approximately 10 percent of the world's production of these commodities. Menhaden, *Brevoortia* spp., the principal species of fish landed in the United States, accounts for about 85 percent of the U.S. production of fish meal and oil. Table 20-2 gives the breakdown of fish meal, oil, and solubles produced in the United States by species for 1986 and 1987 together with their relative value.

As mentioned, menhaden on average accounts for approximately 36 percent of the total pounds of fish and shellfish landed in the United States annually, and in 1982 the 2.8 billion pounds (1.3 billion kg) landed set a record and accounted for 44 percent of the commercial fishery landings in the United States, according to U.S. Department of Commerce statistics. Menhaden, cousins of the herring, are characterized by large heads, a slight hump on their backs, and no teeth. Like herring, they are dependent on plankton for their food; unlike herring they are seldom found on menus, yet nearly everyone, at some time, has been indebted to them for something eaten or used (Bimbo, 1970).

Considerable uncertainty exists about the birthplace of the menhaden oil industry, but it was in Rhode Island in 1812 that the first crude process for oil recovery was developed, followed by production facilities in Maine in 1850. From 1865 to 1875, twenty factories were built in Maine and others were erected in Rhode

Table 20-1. ***World Catch of Fish, Crustacean, and Mollusks Compared to Production of Fish Meal and Oil, by Country (1985) (in 1,000 metric tons)***

Country	Catch	Fish Meal Production	Fish Oil Production
E.E.C.	6,819	423	123
Other W. European countries	416	376	198
U.S.S.R.	11,150	729	94
Canada	1,435	60	7
U.S.A.	5,736	490	136
Argentina	460	15	4
Brazil	848	26	—
Chile	4,814	1,081	184
Peru	4,309	821	105
Japan	11,800	950	430
Other	39,159	1,679	195
World Total	90,697	6,650	1,476

(Bowman, 1988; Mielke, 1988).

Island around Narragansett Bay. These early factories were of crude design and were operated entirely by hand. The fish were unloaded from the boats with pitchforks into tanks or directly into small wooden tramcars that were hauled to the plant's upper floor where the fish were dumped into large reservoirs. From there, the fish flowed into cooking tanks, which had perforated pipes in the bottom for the introduction of steam. After cooking, the hot water and oil were drawn off, and

Table 20-2. ***U.S. Production of Fish Meal, Oil, and Solubles, 1986 and 1987***

	1986		1987	
Product	Short Tons	Thousand Dollars	Short Tons	Thousand Dollars
Fish meals				
Menhaden	296,252	73,092	334,442	105,346
Tuna and mackerel	37,120	7,726	42,161	12,892
Unclassified	6,192	1,607	7,917	2,021
Total	339,564	82,425	384,520	120,259
Shellfish meals	11,533	1,051	9,096	952
Grand totals	351,097	83,476	393,616	121,211
Fish solubles				
Menhaden	97,632	11,558	118,765	16,280
Fish oils				
Menhaden	166,009	43,279	147,482	35,086
Unclassified	2,346	452	1,667	433
Total	168,355	43,731	149,149	35,519

Source: National Fisheries Statistics Program.

the mass of fish were drained and cooled. A man then climbed into the tank and pitchforked the fish into *curbs* that confined the fish during the pressing operation.

The first presses received their pressure by weighted rocks or by using a lever to squeeze the oil from the fish. Oil and water, drained from the cooking tanks and presses, ran to a series of settling tanks. The top oil was skimmed off and held in open tanks for one to two weeks to be sun bleached for the best grade of white oil. The lower levels of oil were run off into another tank and yielded progressively poorer grades of oil.

The wet press cake in the curbs was dumped through a trapdoor in the floor to a room or open space beneath the plant. In some plants it accumulated until fall or winter and then sold as fertilizer. Menhaden scrap continued to sell as fertilizer until the late 1920s when it was found that the scrap contained many of the essential nutrients necessary for normal growth. With the discovery of vitamin B_{12} as a source of the animal protein factor in 1949, the use of menhaden scrap in animal feeds was reemphasized. About this time, the water from the pressing operation was also found to be rich in vitamin B_{12} and after concentration to 50 percent solids, this became a new by-product, condensed fish solubles (Frye, 1978; Lee, 1952).

WET RENDERING PROCESS

Raw Material

Fish used for reduction to meal and oil may be divided into three categories:

1. Fish caught for the sole purpose of fish meal production, such as menhaden in the United States, anchovies in Mexico and South America, capelin in Scandinavia, and sardines in Japan and South America.
2. By-catches from another fishery, such as shrimp by-catch.
3. Fish offal and cuttings from filleting plants and canneries.

The three categories all have several things in common: The fish are usually small pelagic species, oily and bony and concentrated in large schools; or the raw material is waste of no edible value; or the fish are classified as industrial and of no economic value when compared with the major fishery in which they are caught (FAO, 1975).

There have been and will be more suggestions for upgrading industrial species of fish to human foods (Ackman, Eaton, and Ratanayoke, 1981; Billy and Dresoti, 1983; FAO and IDRC, 1982; Hansen, 1981). Production and catching costs are making fish meal uneconomical, and worldwide, research is underway to upgrade these fish. We may see more of the traditional fish meal coming from cuttings as opposed to whole fish, but we will not see an end to fish meal production. In general, industrial species are relatively small and oily and are subject to rapid bacterial and enzymatic spoilage, oxidation, and rancidity. These fish must be degutted, or at least have the gut contents removed and the fish deboned. These operations produce waste or offal for the fish meal plant, and it is therefore envisioned that small fish meal plants will be an integral part of any large operation that produces edible fish (Kreuzer, 1974; Lee and Sanford, 1960; Luna, 1981).

Catching

The catching method used depends largely on the fish's habits. For fish that school near the surface—such as menhaden, tuna, mackerel, herring, sardines, and salmon—the easiest and most efficient method is by using encircling nets, such as the purse seine. For fish that live near the floor of the ocean or in the midwater section, trawling is most efficient. The fishing gear used determines, at least in part, the kind of fishing vessel employed. In general, purse seiners and trawlers are large vessels capable of carrying up to 600 tons (535.7 metric tons) and able to range several days in distance from the fishing grounds. Some factory ships are capable of staying on the fishing grounds for many months (Sola, 1978).

Unloading

Many methods have been tested for discharging fish from the vessel to the processing plant. The following are in general use throughout the world and all have advantages and disadvantages:

1. Grabs
2. Elevators
3. Vacuum
4. Air suction (giant vacuum cleaners)
5. Direct pumping

The grab method involves a crane and "grab" to remove fish from the vessel's hold. Although it is an excellent mode of discharge which can be used with a variety of raw materials, it is labor consuming and can result in spills.

The elevator discharge method employs a bucket elevator or chain pump to remove the fish from the vessel. The unit acts like a pump when the fish are soft and as a bucket elevator when the fish are dry. Problems arise when the fish are landed in areas with large tidal differences (Beugelink, 1978).

In the vacuum discharge method, fish and air are sucked from the hold to the separator section where the fish slide down into a tube, which is closed with a rotating valve. When the weight of fish in the tube overcomes the vacuum, the fish will press the valve flap open and slide out. The unit is hydraulically controlled from a control box. It is maneuverable, can be used with different types of boats, and can be moved from hold to hold without moving the vessel.

The air suction method differs from the vacuum discharge in the unit's design. Both remove fish from the hold without the use of water, but the air suction method employs a slide box valve instead of a rotary valve (Konga and Rasmussen, 1978; Tronstad, 1978).

Direct pumping is done by either wet or dry pumping. Dry pumping employs a pump which can be mounted either on board the vessel or lowered by a crane from the dock into the vessel's hold. In either case, the pump operates submerged or partly submerged in the fish mass and delivers the fish through a vertical telescopic tube to the measuring device on the dock. If the fish mass contains no free water, it is necessary to add some water at the beginning of the unloading process. The water is strained off in a rotary strainer and recirculated to the fish hold. The pump mounted on board the vessel is placed in a chute in the center of the hold. The hold is sloped toward the pump to which the pump suction tubes are connected by remote control gate valves. The fish mass is delivered through the rotary strainer and a quick-fit rubber hose to the bin or measuring unit on the dock. The strained-off water is recirculated to the fish hold if necessary to wet the fish mass. This type of direct unloading without water has several advantages.

1. The sealed system causes no air or water pollution and is easy to clean.
2. It requires a very low power consumption.
3. Labor costs are low because the system can be operated with a minimum number of people.
4. Very little additional water is needed.

Direct pumping using water as the transport medium requires a flexible suction pipe and flexible water hoses as connections between vessel and shore. Service water is used to prime the fish mass initially and then provides the carrying medium for the fish during the unloading operation. Water and fish are then separated in rotary strainers and the fish enter the measuring system while the water is recycled and reused until it becomes too thick to pump.

If fresh water was used as the starting water, the used unloading water is added into the process, where valuable protein and vitamins are recovered. If salt water has been used, it must be handled so that the addition of salt to the final product will not cause it to exceed salt limitations. In some areas, the unloading water makes one pass through the fish and is then discharged overboard where it enters into the biological process of the receiving water, adding valuable nutrients (Gibbs and Green, 1978; Nordstrom, 1978).

Cooking

The purpose of cooking is to denature the fish protein, thus making it possible to separate the fat by mechanical means.

Factors influencing the quality of the cooked fish include

1. Heating temperature
2. Heating time
3. pH of the fish
4. Freshness of the fish
5. Particle size of the fish pieces
6. Type of fish

During cooking, the protein coagulates into a firm mass capable of withstanding the pressure required to press out the stickwater and oil. Figure 20-1 shows a typical cooker used in the wet-rendering process. During coagulation, a high proportion of the bound water is liberated and deposits of fat are released from the tissues and thus removed by water and oil separation.

Cooking is an exacting operation in production and, at times, difficult to control. Producing cooked material which can be readily pressed depends on the quality of the raw material and the process conditions. Good cooking results in a mass which can be pressed so that pressliquor can be removed properly and the oil can be recovered efficiently, resulting in a low-fat meal. Overcooking affects pressing also, and causes the formation of fines or suspended particles in the water phase, which makes evaporation difficult (FAO 1975; Ward, Wignal, and Windsor, 1977).

PRODUCTION OF FISH MEAL

Pressing

Deoiling and dewatering are two major processes in manufacturing fish meal and oil. In general, the objective of pressing and screening is to produce a meal with

Figure 20-1. Example of a Typical Cooker Used in the Wet Reduction Process.

the lowest possible oil content. A number of methods can accomplish this, but the major one is the use of presses (Kroken and Utvik, 1978).

Two types of continuous presses are used in the fish meal industry. The single-screw press works on the principle of a helical-screw conveyor rotating in a cylindrical cage, provided with perforations for the drainage of pressliquor. The screw, designed with a taper, exerts an increasing pressure on the mass by reducing the volume as it passes through the cage. When the press is used with poor raw materials, slipping of the soft fish material may occur, and the screw is unable to press the material effectively. This difficulty may be minimized by incorporating special devices in the press or by using twin screw presses.

In the twin screw press, pressing is carried out in a press chamber consisting of two hollow interlocked cylinders. The press consists of a stationary part, the stator; a rotating part, the rotor or the screw; and the gearbox with motor. The free space between the rotor and the stator decreases from inlet to outlet in a taper so that material introduced at the inlet will be compressed and pressure built up as the product travels to the outlet. The built-up pressure causes the liquid to be squeezed through the perforated stator while the solids remain inside (Onarheim and Utvik, 1979).

A variation on pressing involves two-stage pressing or double pressing, which is used with certain types of raw materials that are difficult to press. This variation also is used when a lower fat content is required. The method involves pressing the cooked fish in the normal manner, cooling the presscake to 122°F (50°C) by adding chilled stickwater, and then pressing again. Fat reductions of 2 to 4 percent in the final meal can be achieved this way (T. Onarheim, 1978). Another variation on the pressing technique uses decanters to separate liquid from the cooked fish. This alternative is useful when the fish are old and in poor condition. Apparently, the decanter can deliver a meal product of consistent quality independent of the raw material quality. This meal is not as dry as that produced with a press and thus more energy is required to dry it. However, the decanter lends itself readily to sanitary cleaning and thus fish protein might go into human food products (Rask, 1979).

Drying

The prime reason for drying is to reduce the moisture content of the nonaqueous material to such a level that insufficient water remains to support the growth of microorganisms (Jason, 1980).

There are two types of dryers used in the fish meal industry today: direct and indirect dryers. In direct dryers (Fig. 20-2), heat is transferred by direct contact between the wet solid and hot gases. The vaporized liquid is carried away by the hot gases. Direct dryers also may be called convection dryers. In indirect dryers, heat is transferred to the wet solid through a retaining wall. The vaporized liquid is removed independently of the heating medium. The rate of drying depends on the wet material's contact with hot surfaces. Indirect dryers may also be termed conduction or contact dryers.

Factors to consider in selecting a dryer system are as follows:

1. The dryer must handle all types of fish in all types of conditions.
2. It must be able to handle stickwater concentrate (solubles).
3. It must give a maximum meal yield.
4. It must give a high quality meal.
5. It must have an effective deodorizing system.
6. It must have a reasonable cost and energy consumption (Hetland, 1980).

Figure 20-2. Example of a Direct-Fired Flame Dryer Used throughout the U.S. Fish Meal Industry.

In direct dryers, the quality of the meal is influenced by the inlet temperature, which should be below 1,112°F (600°C). The dryer consists of a large rotary tube in which presscake is tumbled rapidly in a stream of very hot air. Tumbling is provided by the rotating action of the dryer, and a number of flights within the dryer provide a cascading action and good air-to-particle contact. The hot air is provided by a current of flue gases from oil combustion together with diluting secondary air. The meal particles do not reach this high temperature because the rapid evaporation of water from the surface of each particle causes cooling. The temperature of the meal is normally 176°F (80°C). The fish and air move through the dryer in the same direction, and the rapid flow of hot air tends to help carry the particles through the dryer. Air velocity then becomes another important parameter in the direct dryer.

The indirect dryer is also a rotary dryer with a large cylindrical drum in which the presscake is dried. However, the heat is supplied indirectly by contact with heated discs, tubes, coils, or a jacket. A current of air is blown through the dryer to remove water vapor, but the air is not normally heated and travels countercurrently to the meal flow.

The rotary action of the discs, coils, or tubes together with a series of flights within the dryer causes agitation of the meal and enhanced drying. Blades or scrapers are often necessary to prevent the product from sticking to the drying surface, which could reduce drying efficiency. The temperature of the drying surface is decided by the temperature of the heating medium within the discs, coils, or tubes. This medium is normally steam and its temperature is related to its pressure (Windsor and Barlow, 1981). Both types of dryers are utilized in today's fish meal industry, and for all practical purposes, there is very little nutritional difference between meals dried by direct or indirect means. Properly controlled cooking and drying procedures will produce products that are nutritionally sound with no deleterious effect on quality (FAO, 1975).

Antioxidant Addition

Reactive fish meals are stabilized by adding antioxidants immediately after they leave the dryers. In practice, the meal is first cooled to a temperature below the vaporization temperature of the antioxidant and then stabilized. The amount of antioxidant required to prevent this spontaneous heating depends on the type of fish processed and the degree of unsaturation of the lipid (fat) portion of the meal. Northern species of fish with relatively low unsaturation in the fat, such as herring or capelin, require low concentrations of antioxidant and, in some instances, no antioxidant. Southern species such as anchovy, pilchard, and menhaden require higher concentrations of antioxidant. Very careful control is necessary in adding the antioxidant, as the amount is quite small (typically 0.75 to 1.5 pounds per ton/340 to 680 g per 907 kg of fish meal) and dispersion of the chemical in the meal becomes the critical factor.

Normally, the antioxidant is added in a screw conveyor so that there is thorough mixing. Automatic control devices and variable speed pumps assure that changes in the rate of production influence the corresponding changes in antioxidant addition rate. Reportedly some factories add the antioxidant to the presscake prior to drying, but there is little data available on this method.

Antioxidants are free radical acceptors and break the peroxide reaction chains, which is regarded as the best way to stabilize fish meal. Oxidation is checked and lipids in the fish meal remain fully available in the finished feed. The antioxidant's effectiveness is measured by how quickly the product can be stored in bulk or bags with little or no turning of the piles. Ethoxyquin (1,2-dihydro-6-ethoxy-2,2,4-trimethylquinoline) is the antioxidant of choice throughout the fish meal industry. Ethoxyquin has been used safely in animal feeds in the United States when incorporated in accordance with the following prescribed conditions:

1. It is intended for use only
   - As a chemical preservative for retarding oxidation of carotene, xantophylls, and vitamins A and E in animal feed and fish food.
   - As an aid in preventing the development of organic peroxides in canned pet food.
2. The maximum quantity of the additive permitted to be used and to remain in or on the finished feed shall not exceed 150 ppm.
3. To assure safe use of the additive, the label and labeling of the food additive container and that of any intermediate premixes prepared from it shall contain, in addition to other information required by the act,
   - The name of the additive, ethoxyquin.
   - A statement of the concentration or strength contained therein.
   - Adequate use directions to provide for a finished article with the proper concentration of the additive as provided in number 2 of this section, whether or not intermediate premixes are to be used.
   - The label of any animal feed containing the additive shall, in addition to the other information required by the act, bear the statement "Ethoxyquin added to retard the oxidative destruction of carotene, xantophylls, and vitamins A and E (Carter, 1982).

Studies conducted throughout the fish meal industry in the United States and other countries during the 1960s indicated that ethoxyquin was about eight to ten times more effective in stabilizing fish meal than butylated hydroxytoluene, which was then used throughout the industry. Since that date, no other antioxidants have been used for the stabilization of fish meal, although many others have been evaluated (Chahine, 1978; Dreosti, 1980).

Storage and Shipping

Storage methods for fish meal vary, depending on climatic conditions, production capacity, use of antioxidant, and transport and marketing arrangements. Factories usually have a storage capacity for a reasonable quantity of finished product. During times of difficult marketing conditions or glut catches of fish, it may be necessary to use "outside" locations away from the actual processing plant. Fish meal must be stored in weatherproof, well-ventilated spaces with a clear space between walls and the product piles or stacks.

It has been estimated that over half of the world's fish meal is stored in bulk in either sheds or silos. Bulk storage is advantageous because all handling, from production to loading, becomes simpler, cheaper, and results in considerable savings in manpower and maintenance, and because most transport vessels and international receiving centers are geared to the handling of bulk, so factory bulk storage is compatible.

In general, facilities for bulk storage are either open with access of air through doors and windows or are the sealed type such as silos. The open shed or warehouse predominates in the industry today and is equipped with floor and overhead conveyors for turning the fish meal. The sheds may be of single or multiunit construction with concrete walls and floors. Silos offer good protection to stored meal. Specially designed silos keep the meal in motion by continuously extracting the meal from the bottom and returning it to the top by means of automatic conveyor systems. These conveyors keep the meal from compacting and/or bridging.

In addition to bulk storage, fish meal may be bagged and stored on pallets. The bags usually hold about 100 pounds (45 kg), and may be open-ended and stitched, or with valves which are tucked in. Bag material ranges from hessian to multilayer paper, both with and without a plastic liner.

The hessian bag made from woven jute or burlap is frequently used in the tropics or in areas where heat and humidity may be problems. The open texture allows heat and humidity to escape but allows for rapid entry of oxygen, which leads to further oxidation, penetration by insects and rodents, seepage of meal, and under extreme humidity conditions, to the absorption of moisture from the air with resultant moldy conditions. Paper bags, on the other hand, keep insects and rodents out, retard oxidation and absorption of moisture, and do not leak unless broken.

Wooden pallets, often used to facilitate handling and storage of the bagged meal, can hold approximately a ton (0.9 MT) each and can be stacked three high.

PRODUCTION OF FISH OIL

The first part of this chapter followed the solids portion of the production of fish meal from unloading of fish to shipping the final product. In the pressing operation we reach the first step where there is a physical separation of the fish into two fractions, liquids and solid. We now follow the liquid portion of the fish through the process used to produce fish oil. The two intermediate products produced in the pressing operation are called pressliquor and presscake.

Pressliquor contains large particles of fish and bone material which must be removed before the liquor can be separated. Modern presses screen or filter the pressliquor so that the large solid particles remain with the presscake. In plants with old presses, the pressliquor removed from the fish is pumped over vibrating screens to remove the coarse particles. These removed solids are then conveyed into the presscake and become part of the fish meal.

In conventional fish reduction plants, treating the pressed liquid is carried out in three steps: decanting to remove suspended solids; separating to remove oil from water; and purifying or polishing to remove traces of moisture and impurities from the oil. In some plants there also is a fourth step, the deoiling of the fish solubles to produce a high-acid fish oil that is black in color. This fourth step produces low-fat fish solubles which when added to fish meal do not cause unusually high fat in the final wholemeal. Wholemeal is a term applied to fish meal that has had fish solubles dried with it.

The decanter separates suspended solids from the pressliquor. The more deteriorated the raw fish, the higher the content of sludge in the pressliquor and the more important this separation becomes. The decanter consists of a cylindrical bowl and a cylindrical conveyor.

Pressliquor is fed into the rotor where, by centrifugal force, it is thrown toward the bowl periphery where the heavier solids are rapidly precipitated along the inside of the rotor surface. A screw conveyor or scroll, rotating with the bowl but at a different speed, continuously scrapes the precipitated solids off the wall. Before discharge, the solids pass through a dewatering zone which tends to concentrate or thicken the solids before discharge. The separation may be controlled by adjusting the thickness of the liquid layer and the differential speed between the rotor and the screw conveyor (Gloppestad, 1979).

For best results, the pressliquor should be homogenous, which can be accomplished either by recirculation or the use of an agitator in the feed tank. There should be coarse as well as fine particles in the feed because the decanter's efficiency drops as the particle size is reduced. This process can be controlled by using screens with perforations no smaller than 0.012 inches/3 mm (5 to 6 mm/0.020 to 0.024 inches is the preferred size). The finer particles tend to adhere to the coarser particles, facilitating their removal (Christensen, 1978).

Separating

If the raw fish quality is good and the cooking and pressing are done properly, then the efficiency of the separation process depends on temperature, method of feeding the machine, and adjustments or fine tuning of the machines. The temperature of the feed material should be as high as possible but no less than 203°F (95°C). The pressliquor may be heated by direct injection of live steam but indirect heating is preferred. Injection of live steam and violent pumping leads to troublesome emulsions that are difficult to break. Indirect heating can be carried out in spiral exchanges or plate heat exchangers. Waste heat from the cookers, steam driers, or evaporator condensate can be used as the heating medium (Hovad and Lorentzen, 1978).

The separator is a three-phase centrifuge where pressliquor is separated into oil, stickwater, and a solids (sludge) phase. Modern machines remove the oil and water phases on a continuous basis; the solids or sludge is discharged either on a time setting or with a sensor that allows the bowl to discharge the solids when it is full. The efficiency of the separation at a particular feed rate depends on the position of the line separating oil from water. This position is adjusted by a regulating disc, and the further the liquid must pass between intermediate discs, the better the separating effect.

Basically, for maximum oil yield, the stickwater should contain the least amount of oil; therefore, the regulating disc should be chosen so that the radius of the interface is small. As a complement to the regulating disc, it is possible to control the position of the oil/water interface by applying back pressure to the stickwater discharge. By a combination of correct regulating disc, back pressure, high temperature, and correct feed rate, it is possible to remove the maximum amount of oil from the pressliquor.

Polishing

In principle, the purifier or polisher is designed like the separator; however, since its purpose is to polish oil, the interface should be adjusted so that its radius is larger, giving a long distance for the oil to pass the intermediate disc. To get the necessary separation, hot water equal to about 10 percent of the oil volume is added. Temperature is critical, and the water should be the same temperature as the oil. Water and solids removed during polishing are added back to the stickwater (Hovad and Lorentzen, 1978).

Looking at the liquid flow then, the pressliquor from the pressing operation is pumped over vibrating screens where the coarse solids are removed. The screened pressliquor is then pumped to decanters or finer vibrating screens where further suspended solids are removed. These solids also are conveyed to the presscake line for eventual drying. The decanted pressliquor is heated and pumped to the separators where a three-phase separation takes place. The solids portion is pumped to the presscake line for addition to fish meal. The water phase or stickwater is pumped to holding tanks for further processing (which we discuss later). The separated oil phase is pumped to polishers where, with the addition of hot water, the oil is purified. The water phase is pumped to the stickwater tank for further processing. The fish oil phase from the polishing step is the crude fish oil of commerce. It is pumped into holding tanks where it is tested for a variety of parameters and pumped into storage tanks for shipment to customers.

PRODUCTION OF CONDENSED FISH SOLUBLES

Production of fish solubles (stickwater concentrate) begins when the oil and water are separated in the production of fish oil. Water removed from the pressliquor is called stickwater; the concentration of the stickwater to various percentages of dry matter is called evaporation. The concentration of stickwater is carried out in multieffect evaporators with natural or forced circulation. Triple effect evaporators are used extensively throughout the industry but double and quadruple effects are also used.

As the number of effects increase, steam requirements decrease. In conventional operations, dilute stickwater is fed to the first effect where steam heats the stickwater. In the conventional operation, live steam is introduced into the steam jacket in stage 1 through a manually operated regulating valve. The plant's capacity is determined by the quantity of steam and, as the evaporator surfaces become fouled, the pressure in the steam jacket must be increased correspondingly so that capacity is maintained. The condensate is released by a steam trap through a preheater where it preheats the stickwater feed.

The exhaust vapor from stage 1 is led to the jacket of stage 2, and the exhaust vapor from stage 2 is led to stage 3. From here, the exhaust vapor is condensed by a barometric condenser. The condensate from stage 2 is led through an orifice to stage 3 where part of its heat is given off. The impure condensate is drawn off stage 3 by a centrifugal pump. The stickwater flows through a preheater to the liquid side of stage 1.

The flow is regulated by a float switch which opens and closes the control valve. Although regulation is affected by on-off action, the control valve's low speed action is sufficient to ensure even adjustment. Furthermore, there are two other float switches in stage 1 that activate an alarm when the liquid level in the evaporator is either too high or too low. The flow of stickwater from stage 1 to stage 2, and from stage 2 to 3 as it is gradually more concentrated, is regulated by the same type of equipment. In stage 3 the stickwater is finally concentrated to solubles which are drawn off by a positive displacement pump. The pump's speed delivers the amount of dry matter content wanted in the solubles. The dry matter content is determined by use of hand-held refractometers normally used to measure the percentage of solids content of sugar solutions (Onarheim and Utvik, 1978).

As mentioned, the main problems associated with the evaporation process are in the reduced capacity as the tubes become coated and heat transfer is reduced. The evaporator's main disadvantage compared to the other equipment is that during the evaporation process, proteins and calcium phosphate are deposited on the inside walls of the tubes, cresting an insulating effect which increases with time and must be removed periodically.

Most evaporators are designed with a heating surface which ensures six days continuous operation at nominal capacity. If not, the evaporator becomes a bottleneck in production, which may have serious consequences such as loss of stickwater, reduced meal yield, reduced capacity, or even a stop in production. The protein deposits are easily removed by water or a dilute caustic soda solution; the calcium phosphate must be treated with a 15 to 50 percent caustic soda solution.

In the cleaning process the heating body is emptied of stickwater, then filled with water or dilute caustic solution and boiled for fifteen minutes. Then the solutions are discharged and the body filled up with a strong caustic solution and boiled for two hours. The strong caustic solution is then discharged and the body filled up with water, boiled for fifteen minutes, and then discharged. Cleaning time can last as long as eight hours, depending on evaporator size. To reduce the cleaning time, the evaporator may be operated on two effects while one effect is being cleaned. This is accomplished by the use of valves in the system (Onarheim, 1978).

Oil separation from partly concentrated stickwater is practiced by some manufacturers. The stickwater density is higher in the concentrate than in the dilute state. This greater difference between the density of oil and stickwater produces an increase in the centrifugal potential, thus contributing to extra oil removal. Consequently, oil removal from the concentrate leads to a leaner wholemeal and increases the oil yield. The separated oil tends to be rather dark in color, high in free fatty acids, and of less value than oil separated from the pressliquor (FAO, 1975).

A typical flow diagram of a wet reduction fish processing plant is shown in Figure 20-3.

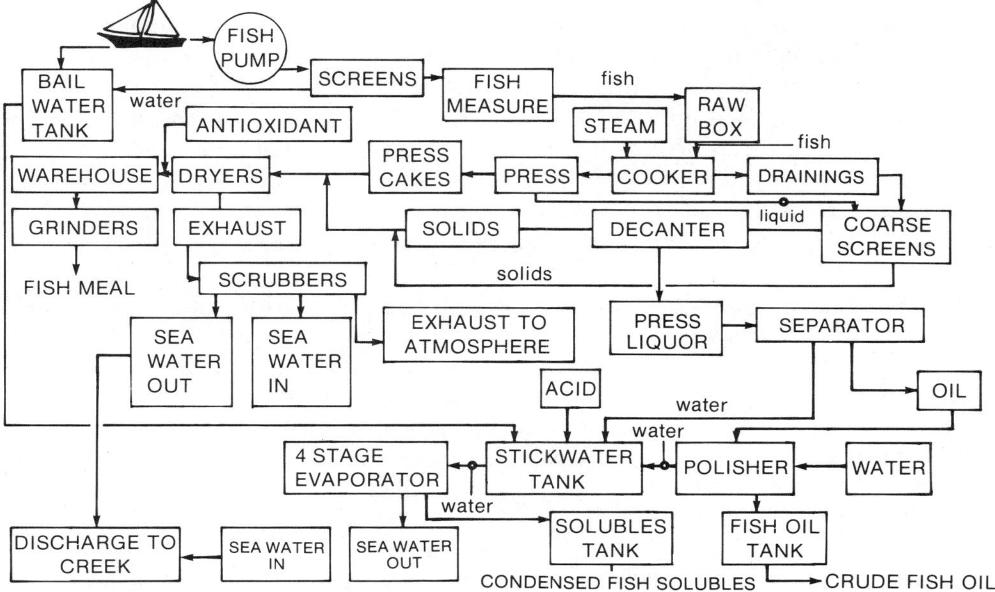

Figure 20-3. Flow Diagram for a Typical Wet Reduction Processing Plant.

POLLUTION CONTROL

Pollution control in the fish meal industry can be divided into water and air pollution categories.

Water Effluent Control

The sources of wastewater produced in the fish meal processing industry can be summarized as follows:

1. Bail water (fish unloading water)
2. Stickwater
3. Equipment wash waters
4. Boiler blowdown water
5. Evaporator condensate water
6. Evaporator cooling water or condenser water
7. Air scrubber water
8. Miscellaneous waters

Whether a plant will have all these discharges depends on the type of process and the degree of plant modernization. Normally, liquid effluent from fish meal plants is contaminated with proteins and fats which exert a biochemical oxygen demand on the body of water into which they are discharged. Control of these effluents therefore usually involves recovery of these valuable commodities. Today, legislation is becoming more restrictive and new methods are being developed to polish further the final liquid effluents being discharged (Cullinane, 1978; Claggett, 1978; FAO, 1975; Nachenius, 1978; Wignall, 1978).

Gaseous Effluent Control

Smells emitted from fish meal plants and other fish processing factories formerly caused less concern than they do today when fish meal plants may be threatened by closure for this reason alone. Public reaction, however, is sometimes tempered by how dependent the local community is on fishing activities. Offensive odors affect the industry's public image and may make construction permits for new plants difficult or even impossible to obtain. It is not that the emissions from the process are harmful to health; the question of toxicity usually does not arise, but the substances responsible are so intensely odorous that they often can be detected a long way from the factory.

Sources of gaseous effluent in a fish meal plant include:

The raw material: unloading, transfer of fish to the factories, and storage conditions at the factory.

Processing-cooking, pressing, deoiling, and evaporation are carried out at elevated temperatures and odorous compounds are produced.

Drying: probably accounts for 60 to 80 percent of the total emissions from a fish meal plant. Direct flame dryers produce more gaseous effluent than indirect steam-heated dryers.

Pneumatic conveying and grinding.

Odor control in fish meal plants can include one or more of the following: condensation of the dryer exhaust to remove water and decrease the air volume;

incineration in the boilers; and chemical oxidation (IAFMM, 1977; Campbell, 1978; FAO, 1975; Hansen, 1978; Onarheim and Utvik, 1978).

QUALITY CONTROL

The quality of fish meal, oil, and solubles in world trade is assessed by standardized methods of analysis which employ physical, chemical, biological, and organoleptic techniques. The American Feed Manufacturers Association publishes buying guides for various feed ingredients including fish meal and solubles. These guides include a product description, typical analysis, factors affecting quality, physical properties, and major feed applications. The first three product descriptions in the appendix at the end of the chapter give typical buying guidelines for Menhaden Fish Meal, Condensed Menhaden Fish Solubles, and Peruvian Anchovy Fish Meal (AFMA, 1973a; AFMA, 1973b; AFMA, 1977).

END USES

Fish Meal and Condensed Fish Solubles

In the past, fish products have contributed importantly in animal feeding by providing various vitamins and minerals that are not adequately supplied by cereal grains or plant protein supplements. Fish products have been used widely in starting rations for pigs and poultry and in breeder rations for poultry because of their "unidentified factor" activity. With the rapid unfolding of nutritional discoveries of recent years, followed by the equally vigorous role of the manufacturing chemist, nearly all of the vitamins and minerals critical for animal feeding are now readily and economically available. This is true for some of the amino acids as well.

Accordingly, the long-term use of fish products for animal feeding must be justified primarily on the basis of their known nutritional contribution in relation to cost and availability from other sources. The value of sources of critically important vitamins and minerals in animal feeds can be determined in terms of the cost of these nutrients from other sources. Of major importance, however, is the ability of fish products to supply those amino acids which are most likely to be critically limited in other available proteins.

Protein is in short supply in many parts of the world, and the proteins of cereal grains and most other plant protein concentrates fail to supply fully the amino acid needs of poultry and swine, particularly the sulfur amino acids (methionine and cystine) and lysine.

Fish protein, on the other hand, is an excellent source of all three of these amino acids, particularly methionine and lysine. Table 20-3 (Bimbo, 1989) gives a comparison of the nutrients present in several fish meals.

Accordingly, the problem of meeting the amino acid needs of poultry and pigs involves more than merely supplying a recommended level of protein in their ration. Intelligent use of the proper combinations of proteins can do much to extend the effectiveness of the presently available protein supplies throughout the world for both animals and humans. Since fish protein contains unusually good levels of methionine and lysine, fish products are especially useful in supplementing plant protein.

The use of fish meal has been greatest in those parts of the United States and in

Table 20-3. *Comparison of the Nutrient Composition of Several Fish Meals*

	Herring Type	White Fish	Anchovy Type	Menhaden
Proximate Composition				
Crude protein, %	71.9	64.5	66.4	61.3
Ether fat	7.5	4.5	9.7	9.91
Ash	10.1	20	15.4	18.9
Protein Characteristics, % of Crude Protein				
Rumen degrad.	48.8	53.3	48.5	50.5
Water soluble	19.8	8.9	18.3	15.5
Pepsin digest.	—	—	95.9	94.4
Energy Content, MJ/kg				
Poultry, M.E.	13.7	11.6	13.5	12.8
Pigs, D.E.	18.1	15.6	16.9	16.5
Ruminant, M.E.	16.4	13.4	13.1	12.8
Amino Acids, % of Protein				
Lysine	7.73	6.9	7.75	7.39
Methionine	2.86	2.6	2.95	2.67
Cystine	0.97	0.93	0.94	0.99
Tryptophan	1.15	0.94	1.2	0.8
Taurine	NA	NA	NA	0.69
Minerals				
Calcium, %	1.95	8	3.95	4.87
Phosphorus	1.5	4.8	2.6	2.93
Selenium, PPM	2.78	1.5	1.39	2.21
Vitamins, PPM				
Choline	4,396	4,396	4,396	4,396
Biotin	0.42	0.08	0.26	0.26
Essential Fatty Acids, % of Fat				
C18:2 N-6	2	1	1	1
C18:3 N-3	1	1	1	2
C20:4 N-6	1	NA	1	1
C20:5 N-3	6	12	16	12
C22:6 N-3	13	19	14	9
TOTAL N-3	22	35	34	26

Source: Bimbo, 1989.

European countries where animal industry is most intensified. Over the years, higher levels of fish products have been used in animal feeds in the European countries than in the United States, largely for economic reasons.

Processed soybean protein has been available in the United States for many years and has become a dominant protein source for pigs and poultry. Soybean protein and supplemental DL-methionine or hydroxy analogue made possible the formulation of satisfactory rations with little or no animal protein supplements. In most starting and breeder feeds for poultry, minimal levels of 2 to 5 percent fish meal or 1 percent condensed fish solubles are still commonly used as a means of supplying "unidentified factors." Small amounts of fish meal have been used in swine rations in the United States, although condensed fish solubles have been used to some extent. Recently, considerably more fish meal is being used for poultry and pigs because of favorable prices in relation to other high protein feedstuffs. In Europe, pig and poultry feeds may contain as much as 10 percent fish meal.

The actual level of fish products used in animal feeds depends on several factors, including the following:

1. Development of intensive animal feeding industries with increased use of nutritionally balanced complete feeds.
2. Realistic and competitive pricing of fish meal in relation to other available supplements.
3. Availability of fish meal in amounts adequate to ensure constant supply.
4. Uniformity and level of quality.
5. Availability and cost of other protein and amino acid supplements.
6. Extent to which nutritional knowledge is applied in animal production (Brody, 1965; Combs, 1961; Sparre, 1965).

There is considerable interest in the use of industrial fish for many other feed purposes, and already such products are being used to feed mink, eels, trout, crustaceans, fish in general, baby pigs, newborn calves, dogs, cats, ruminants, and breeder hens, as well as for the production of penicillin and other antibiotics (Dreosti, 1979).

FISH OIL

For many years, the value of marine oils has been recognized for both edible and industrial purposes, and specific segments of the fishing industry have been developed to provide this product. The supply of marine oils has come from two sources: whales and fish.

Whale oil once accounted for as much as 75 percent of the total aquatic animal oil and fat production, but today it accounts for less than 2 percent of that production. It seems likely that whale oil will continue to decline in commercial significance (Gauglitz et al., 1973).

Fish oils have long been a natural constituent of the human diet because they are a normal part of the edible portion of fish. Although food fish contain substantially less fat than land animals, they do represent a source of a different type of fat from that supplied by animals and plants. Marine fatty acids of the n-3 type have different impacts on our physiology than do the n-6 type of polyunsaturated fatty acids that are present in grains and cereals. These two fatty acids appear to serve different functions in human health and disease. In recent years much research has been conducted to evaluate the possible pharmaceutical uses of fish oils and this work has been reviewed several times (Bimbo, 1983a; Lands and Bimbo, 1983). Table 20-4 gives a comparison of the difference in the fatty acid composition of several fish oils, vegetable oils, and animal fats.

Fish oil is a normal constituent of many animal feeds, which often contain fish meal as a protein source. Fish meal usually contains up to 12 percent fish oil which is metabolized and utilized as an energy source. As a nutritive component of itself, fish oil possesses at least three potentially beneficial properties. It is a concen-

Table 20-4. ***Fatty Acid Composition (percent) of Marine Oils Compared with Several Vegetable Oils and Animal Fats***

	Butter Fat	Corn Oil	Lard	Tallow	Soybean Oil	Herring Oil	Menhaden Oil	Anchovy Oil	Tuna Oil
C4	3.0	—	—	—	—	—	—	—	—
C6	1.0	—	—	—	—	—	—	—	—
C8	1.5	—	—	—	—	—	—	—	—
C10	3.0	—	—	—	—	—	—	—	—
C12	3.5	—	—	—	—	—	—	—	—
C14	12.0	—	1.5	3.5	—	7.0	9.0	7.0	4.5
C16	28.0	12.0	25.0	25.5	11.0	12.0	18.0	15.0	21.0
C16:1	3.0	—	3.0	4.0	—	6.0	9.0	9.0	6.0
C18	13.0	2.0	13.0	19.5	4.0	1.0	3.0	3.0	5.5
C18:1	28.5	25.0	45.5	41.0	21.0	10.0	10.5	10.0	16.5
C18:2	1.0	60.0	10.5	2.5	55.5	2.0	1.0	1.0	1.0
C18:3	—	0.5	1.0	—	8.5	1.0	1.5	0.5	1.0
C20:1	—	—	—	—	—	13.0	1.0	2.0	2.0
C20:5	—	—	—	—	—	9.0	14.5	18.0	6.0
C22:1	—	—	—	—	—	19.0	—	1.0	1.0
C22:6	—	—	—	—	—	8.0	12.0	16.0	23.0

trated source of calories, it contains essential fatty acids, and it provides highly unsaturated fat (Kifer and Miller, 1969). The final three product descriptions in the appendix at the end of the chapter give the typical AFMA buyer's guide for three different fish oils specially selected for use as feeding fats.

As previously noted, the world production of fish oil exceeded 1.12 million tons (1 million metric tons) in 1987. For the most part, the oil is used as an edible fat in all the major countries of the world except the United States. The reason for this exclusion has been discussed many times (Bimbo, 1983b; Gruger, 1963; Stansby, 1973; Stansby, 1978) and we do not pursue it here except to say that the U.S. production of fish oil is exported primarily to Western Europe where it has been used in such products as margarine and shortening for more than fifty years. A GRAS petition for hydrogenated menhaden oil was approved on September 15, 1989.

Fish oil in the United States is utilized as an industrial drying oil and as such competes with linseed and soybean oils. Industrial use of fish oil depends on different chemical modifications of the oil and the resultant physical and chemical properties of the modified products. Fish oils can be chemically altered by reactions of the double bonds or by reactions involving the fatty acid end of the basic molecule in the oil. Each type of modification produces a product with different physical and chemical properties more readily utilized than the original oil (Bimbo, 1989b). Some past and present industrial uses of fish oils are listed here.

1. Linoleum and oilcloth
2. Leather tanning
3. Printing inks
4. Core and foundry oils
5. Lubricants and greases
6. Ore floatation agents
7. Insecticidal compounds
8. Fungicidal derivatives
9. Fire retardants
10. Soap manufacture
11. Protective coatings
12. Pneumatic tool and steam cylinder stock lubricants
13. Rubber compounds
14. Caulking compounds
15. Glazing compounds
16. Automotive gaskets
17. Tin plating oils
18. Rustproofing compounds
19. Refractory compounds
20. Cutting oils
21. Plasticizers
22. Presswood fiberboards
23. Ceramic deflocculants
24. Fermentation substrates
25. Illuminating and fuel oils
26. Mushroom culture
27. Insect and animal attractants
28. Polyurethane foams

ACKNOWLEDGMENTS

The author wishes to thank Zapata Haynie Corporation, Reedville, Virginia; Pesquera Zapata, SA de CV, Ensenada, Mexico; Edw. Renneburg and Sons Co., Baltimore, Maryland; Stord Bartz, s.a. Bergen, Norway; and Alfa Laval Col, Fort Lee, New Jersey, for their assistance in this chapter. He also wishes to thank the American Feed Manufacturers Association, Arlington, Virginia, for permission to use the various buying guides. A special thanks to Mrs. Jane Booth for her general typing, editing, and assistance with this chapter.

APPENDIX
PRODUCT DESCRIPTIONS[1]

Menhaden Fish Meal

Product Description: The product resulting from processing whole menhaden fish.

Typical Analysis:*

Protein	60%
Fat (ether extract)	11%
Fiber	1%
Moisture	7–11%
Pepsin digestible protein	92%
Sand	Content in excess of 1% to be declared
Salt (NaC1)	Content in excess of 3% to be declared

Physical Properties:

Texture 100% to pass U.S. No. 7 Standard Screen
98% to pass U.S. No. 10 Standard Screen

Bulk Density: 32–38 lbs/cubic ft. (512.6–608.7 kg/cubic meter)

Method of Processing: Whole fish are cooked, pressed to remove water and oil, and then dried.

Factors Affecting Quality: Treatment with an antioxidant and holding under conditions permitting detection and avoiding of excessive temperature that could reduce protein quality is desirable.

A self-monitoring salmonella control program is recommended for all fish meal plants.

Major Feed Application: Fish meal is used in chick, broiler, layer, and breeder rations, in turkey and swine feeds, and for commercial fish farming feeds. Fish meal should be incorporated into feed formulas on the basis of its content of essential amino acids, its energy value, available phosphorus, source of unknown growth factor, and trace elements such as selenium.

Trading: All sales are made on the basis of a contractual agreement between buyer and seller.

*Methods of analysis according to Association of Official Analytical Chemists, Current Edition

Adopted: May 1973

AAFCO (1979) page 112 #51.14
NRC Ref. No. 5-01-977

[1]Reprinted with permission of the American Feed Manufacturers Association.

Condensed Menhaden Fish Solubles

Product Description: Condensed Menhaden Fish Solubles are obtained by concentrating via evaporation, the aqueous phase resulting from the wet reduction of menhaden fish.

Typical Analysis:

Crude protein	30.0%
Crude fat	11.0%
Crude fiber	0.0%
Moisture	50.0%
Ash	8.0%
pH	4.8%
Salt (NaCl)	3.0%
Phosphorus	0.6%
Calcium	0.1%

Factors Influencing Quality: A pH value greater than 5.5 may cause fermentation of condensed menhaden fish solubles.

Physical Properties:

Color: Brown
Odor: Fishy
Weight per gallon: 9.5 lbs/gal (1.1 kg/l)
Appearance: Viscous brown liquid

Availability:

Available throughout the year.

Feed Application:

May be used in a wide range of animal feeds, or as a pelleting aid and flavor agent.

Adopted: May 1977

AAFCO (1979) page 112 #51.6
NRC Ref. No. 5-01-969

Peruvian Anchovy Fish Meal

Product Description:

Peruvian Anchovy Fish Meal *(Engraulis ringens J.)* is obtained by cooking, pressing, drying, and grinding of the whole fish. Moisture and fat content are reduced in the process. The solubles removed during cooking and processing are normally added back to the meal.

Typical Analysis:

	Buying Guide	
Crude protein (min.)	65%	63–66%
Crude fat (min.)	7%	7–11%
Crude fiber (max.)	1%	0–1%
Moisture (max.)	10%	8–10%
Calcium (max.)	6%	4–6%
Salt (max.)	3%	0–5%
Sand (max.)	2%	0–3%
Pepsin digestibility (min.)	92%	90–96%

Factors Affecting Quality:

* Meal treated with ethoxyquin (600–800 ppm) will test higher in ether extracted fat than meal not treated.

* Color is not necessarily a measure of quality, but meals dark in color from burning (charring) should be avoided.

* A Salmonella-free meal is desirable. A continuous Salmonella control monitoring system is recommended for all fish meal processing plants.

* Excess moisture will reduce protein content. Excess heat during processing will destroy essential amino acids.

Physical Properties:

Screen Analysis: 95% to 100% through No. 12 screen (1.63 mm). 0% to 5% through No. 200 screen (0.74 mm).

Bulk Density: 40 pounds per cubic foot (approximate). 650 kg/cubic meter (approximate).

Color: Color shall be characteristic of fresh fish meal and free of rancidity and free of evidence of scorching and overheating.

(Detailed information can be obtained from Empressa Publica De Commercializacion, de Harina Y Aceite De Pescado (EPCHAP), Av. 28 De Julio, 715-10 Piso, Apartado 1373, Lima, Peru)

Trading:

As a rule, Peruvian anchovy fish meal is sold on a contract basis between buyer and seller stating certain guarantees.

Adopted: May 1973

AAFCO (1979) page 112 #51.14 / NRC Ref. No. 5-01-977

Anchovy Feed Fat

Product Description:

Anchovy Feed Fat is the fat from processing whole anchovy selected for use as a feed ingredient.

Typical Analysis:

Free fatty acid [FFA (as oleic)]	15.00%
Moisture	2.00%
Impurities	0.75%
Unsaponifiables	1.50%
Fatty acid ratio (% unsaturated/% saturated)	1.90%

Factors Influencing Quality:

Improper storage conditions, and exposure to excessive moisture and impurities should be avoided.

Physical Properties:

Odor: Fishy

Consistency: Fatty, semisolid to liquid at room temperature

Density: 7.7 lbs/gal. (3.5 kg/l) (varies with temperature and fatty acid composition)

Availability:

Year round availability

Major Feed Applications:

Energy source, dust control, pelleting aid, an attractant (aquaculture), and essential fatty acid source.

NOTE: Excessive levels may result in fishy flavor in meat, milk, and eggs.

Additional Information:

NRS 7-08-049

Menhaden Feed Fat

Product Description:

Menhaden Feed Fat is the fat from processing whole menhaden selected for use as a feed ingredient.

Typical Analysis:

Free fatty acid [FFA (as oleic)]	15.00%
Moisture	2.00%
Impurities	0.75%
Unsaponifiables	1.50%
Fatty acid ratio (% unsaturated/% saturated)	1.60

Factors Influencing Quality:

Improper storage conditions, and exposure to excessive moisture and impurities should be avoided.

Physical Properties:

Odor: Fishy

Consistency: Fatty, semisolid to liquid at room temperature

Density: 7.75 lbs/gal (3.5 kg/l) (varies with temperature and fatty acid composition).

Availability:

Year round availability

Major Feed Applications:

Energy source, dust control, pelleting aid, an attractant (aquaculture), and essential fatty acid source.

NOTE: Excessive levels may result in fishy flavor in meat, milk, and eggs.

Additional Information:

NRC 7-08-049

Tuna Feed Fat

Product Description:

Tuna Feed Fat is the fat from processing cannery waste selected for use as feed ingredient.

Typical Analysis:

Free fatty acid [FFA (as oleic)]	15.00%
Moisture	2.00%
Impurities	0.75%
Unsaponifiables	1.50%
Fatty acid ratio (% unsaturated/% saturated)	1.94

Factors Influencing Quality:

Improper storage conditions, and exposure to excessive moisture and impurities should be avoided.

Physical Properties:

Odor: Fishy

Consistency: Fatty, semisolid to liquid at room temperature.

Density: 7.7 lbs/gal. (3.5 kg/l) (varies with temperature and fatty acid composition).

Availability:

Year round availability

Major Feed Applications:

Energy source, dust control, pelleting aid, an attractant (aquaculture), and essential fatty acid source.

NOTE: Excessive levels may result in fishy flavor in meat, milk, and eggs.

Additional Information:

NRC 7-08-049

REFERENCES

Ackman, R. G., Eaton, D. A., and Ratnayake, W. M. N. 1981. "Considerations of Fatty Acids in Menhaden from the Northern Limits of the Species." *Proc. N.S. Inst. Sci.* 31:207–215.

American Feed Manufacturers Association. 1973a. "Menhaden Fish Meal." *AFMA Ingredient Guide,* p. 39.

American Feed Manufacturers Association. 1973b. "Peruvian Anchovy Fish Meal." *AFMA Ingredient Guide,* p. 37.

American Feed Manufacturers Association. 1977. "Condensed Menhaden Fish Solubles." *AFMA Ingredient Guide,* p. 35.

American Feed Manufacturers Association. 1981. Proceedings of the 41st Annual Meeting of AFMA, May 20, St. Louis, MO.

Beugelink, F. 1978. "Dry Off-loading of Fish." *IAFMM News Summary*. 42:143.

Billy, T. J., and Dreosti, G. M. 1983. "Potential Food Products from Industrial Fish." *IAFMM Technical Report,* No. 1.

Bimbo, A. P. 1970. *The Menhaden Industry: Yesterday, Today, and Tomorrow*. Paper presented Oct. 8 to the Dept. of Chemical Engineering, Univ. of Rhode Island.

Bimbo, A. P. 1983a. *Pharmaceutical Uses of Fish Oil.* Paper presented at the 23rd Annual Conference of the IAFMM, Nov., Boca Raton, FL.

Bimbo, A. P. 1983b. *Fish Oils Then and Now*. Paper presented at the NFMOA Congressional Breakfast, Sept. 28, Washington, DC

Bimbo, A. P. 1989a. "Recent Advances in Upgrading Industrial Fish to Value-Added Products." Proceedings of AOCS symposium *Value-added Feed Products from Protein and Co-products: Changing Resources and Needs*. May 3–6, Cincinnati, OH.

Bimbo, A. P. 1986b. "Technology of Production and Industrial Utilization of Marine Oils." In *Marine Biogenic Lipids, Fats, and Oils,* edited by R. G. Ackman. Boca Raton, FL: CRC Press.

Bowman, S. J. 1988. "Digest of Selected Statistics." Compiled for the 28th Annual IAFMM Conference. Nov. 1988, Lima, Peru.

Brody, J. 1965. *Fishery By-Products Technology*. Westport, CT: AVI Publishing Co.

Campbell, M. 1978. "Boiler Incineration of Odourous Gases." *IAFMM News Summary #43:* 122.

Carter, B. R. (ed.). 1982. Food and Drug Administration, Department of Health and Human Services, Code of Federal Regulations, Subpart B, Section 573380, p. 581. Washington, DC: U.S. Government Printing Office.

Chahine, M. H. 1978. (May 1). "Antioxidants to Stabilize Fish Meal." *Feedstuffs,* p. 28.

Christensen, S. 1978. "Control of Decanters and Separators." *IAFMM News Summary #44:* 104.

Claggett, F. G., and Eng, P. 1978. "Practical Measures of Liquid Effluent Control." *IAFMM News Summary #44:*12.

Combs, G. E. 1961. "Role of Fish in Animal Feeding." In *Fish in Nutrition,* edited by E. Heen and R. Kreuzer. London: Fishing News Books, Ltd.

Cullinane, M. J., Jr. 1978. "Water Pollution Control in the Fish Meal Processing Industry—A Rational Approach." *IAFMM News Summary #44:* 22.

Dreosti, G. M. 1980. "Spontaneous Heating." *IAFMM News Summary #49:*154.

FAO. 1975. "The Production of Fish Meal and Oil." *FAO Fisheries Technical Paper* 142.

FAO and IDRC. 1982. *Fish By-Catch . . . Bonus from the Sea.* Ottawa, Ontario, Canada: IDRC-198e.

Frye, John. 1978. *The Men All Singing.* Norfolk, VA: Donning.

Gauglitz, E. et al. 1973. *Application of Fish Oils in the Food Industry.* Paper presented at the technical conference on fishery products, Apr. 11–12, Tokyo.

Gibbs, C. R., and Green, C. F. A. 1978. "Offloading and Transportation of Fish—the Hidrostal System." *IAFMM News Summary #42:*137.

Gloppestad, E. 1979. "Techniques for the Use of Decanters in Separating Liquid from Solids in the Fish Meal Industry." *IAFMM News Summary #44:* 71.

Gruger, E. H., Jr. 1963. "Uses of Industrial Fish Oil." In *Industrial Fishery Technology,* edited by M. Stansby. New York: Reinhold.

Hansen, Knud, W. 1978. "Ventilation Systems of Chemical Treatment of Odour." *IAFMM News Summary #44:*66.

Hansen, P. 1981. *Alternative Uses of Industrial Fish.* Lyngby, Denmark: Technological Laboratory.

Hetland, J. D. Y. 1980. "Techniques and Economics of Direct (Flame) and Indirect Drying." *IAFMM News Sumary #49:*35.

Hovad, H., and Lorentzen, J. 1978. Automatic Control of Stickwater Evaporators." *IAFMM News Summary #44:* 120.

IAFMM. 1977. "Reducing Odour in Fish Meal Production." Torry Advisory Note No. 72. *IAFMM News Summary #41:* 52.

Jason, A. C. 1980. "General Theory of Drying Fish." *IAFMM News Summary #49:* 5.

Kifer, R. R., and Miller, D. 1969. "Fish Oils—Fatty Acid Composition, Energy Values, Metabolism and Vitamin Content." *Fisheries Indus. Res.* 1, 5.

Konge, J., and Rasmussen, I. 1978. "Pneumatic Off-loading of Fish—The IRAS System." *IAFMM News Summary #42:*155.

Kreuzer, R. (ed.). 1974. *Fishery Products.* Surrey, England: Fishing News Ltd.

Kroken, E., and Utvik, A. Ø. 1978. "Two-Stage Pressing to Reduce Oil Content in Fish Meal." *IAFMM News Summary #43:*65.

Lands, W. E., and Bimbo, A. P. 1983. "Possible Beneficial Effects of Polyunsaturated Fatty Acids in Maritime Foods." Special report for IAFMM, Sept.

Lee, C. F. 1952. "Menhaden Industry Past and Present." U.S. Dept. of Interior, Wildlife Service, Fishery Leaflet No. 412.

Lee, C. F., and Sanford, F. B. 1960. *U.S. Fish-Reduction Industry.* Washington, DC: U.S. Department of the Interior, Commercial Fisheries TL14, 8.

Luna, J. (ed.). 1981. *Non-Traditional Fish Products for Massive Human Consumption* (Vol. 1 and 2). Washington, DC: IADB.

Mielke, S. (ed.). 1988. *Oil World.* Hamburg: ISTA.

Nachenius, R. J. 1978. "Water Pollution in the Fish Meal and Oil Industry." *IAFMM News Summary #44:*1.

Nordstrom, R. 1978. "Offloading and Transportation of Fish by Mono Pumps." *IAFMM News Summary #24:*175.

Onarheim, R. 1978. "Stickwater Evaporator Designed for Cleaning During Operation. *IAFMM News Summary #43:*140.

Onarheim, R. 1978. "Two-stage Pressing." *Stord Bartz Review.* 78(4):30.

Onarheim, R., and Utvik, A. Ø. 1978. "A System of Complete Effluent Control." *IAFFM News Summary #44:*75.

Onarheim, R., and Utvik, A. Ø. 1979. "The Design and Operation of Screens and Presses." *IAFFM News Summary #46:*105.

Rask, R. 1979. "Techniques for the Use of Decanters in Separating Liquid from Solids in the Fish Meal Industry." *IAFFM News Summary #46:*87.

Sola, E. 1978. "Discharge of Fish for Meal and Oil Production." *IAFFM News Summary #42:*117.

Sparre, T. 1965. "Fish Meal: Manufacture, Properties, and Utilization." In *Fish as Food* (Vol. 3), edited by G. Borgstrom. New York: Academic Press.

Stansby, M. 1973. "Problems Discouraging Use of Fish Oil in American Manufacturing Shortening and Margarine." *JAOCS.* (6)50:220–225.

Stansby, M. 1978. "Development of Fish Oil Industry in the United States." *JAOCS.* (2)55:238–243.

Tronstad, I. M. 1978. "Myrens Raw Material Pump—BRP 1." *IAFMM News Summary #42:*161.

Ward, A., Wignal, J., and Windsor, M. L. 1977. "The Effect of Cooking Temperature and Applied Pressure on the Release of Liquor from Fish." *IAFMM News Summary #41:*24.

Wignall, J. 1978. "Odour Pollution in the Fish Meal and Oil Industry." *IAFMM News Summary #44:*44.

Windsor, M., and Barlow, S. 1981. *Fish Meal Production, Introduction to Fishery By-Products* (1st ed.). Surrey, England: Fishing News Books Ltd.

CHAPTER

21

Regulations

Roy E. Martin

This chapter explains how the industry is regulated and by whom. The reason for a special chapter will become obvious as you move through the tangled web of federal, state, and local regulations that have been imposed on the seafood industry over the years.

FOOD AND DRUG ADMINISTRATION

The Food and Drug Administration (FDA) regulates the production and marketing of most food products, including fish, under the Federal Food, Drug, and Cosmetic Act of 1938, as amended (FDC Act). FDA's authority is limited to food in, intended for, or having passed through interstate commerce, but interstate commerce has been very broadly construed. FDA jurisdiction may even extend to products that are intended for intrastate use or trade if they are produced, transported, or stored by a person or company engaged in interstate commerce. It is important to understand that the U.S. Department of Agriculture (USDA) plays no direct role in the seafood industry, a situation unlike that of the USDA with other fresh food industries.

With FDA's broad authority there are few aspects of the seafood industry that it cannot regulate, should it choose to do so. To be more specific: FDA has issued regulations covering every aspect of food production and marketing, including food name and ingredients, food quality, manufacturing practices, packaging, and labeling. Depending on the regulation involved, noncompliance constitutes misbranding or adulteration and subjects the food to possible seizure and condemnation.

Adulteration refers to unacceptable food quality and results from such things as contamination with filth or toxic substances, preparation under unsanitary conditions, the use of unsafe ingredients, the presence of concealed defects, the omission of a valuable ingredient, or the like.

A food is *misbranded* when it is the subject of a deceptive representation, such as false or misleading packaging or labeling; when it is not accompanied by a required disclosure, such as name, ingredients, quantity, and so on; or when it is misrepresented.

The FDC Act authorized the FDA to establish "a reasonable definition and *standard of identity*" for a food where it will "promote honesty and fair dealing in the interest of consumers." A standard of food identity is, in essence, a recipe designed to avoid confusion among consumers by assuring that a food designated by a specific name contains certain ingredients in certain proportions and only a limited number of other ingredients. Any product which purports to be or is represented as a food for which a definition and standard of identity has been prescribed is subject to and must comply with that standard.

There are standards of identity for various fish products, including

1. Oysters—there is a separate standard of identity for each of twelve different varieties and sizes
2. Canned Pacific salmon
3. Canned wet pack shrimp in transparent or nontransparent containers
4. Frozen raw breaded shrimp (regular or lightly breaded)
5. Canned tuna

A food which fails to conform to an applicable definition and standard of identity is considered to be misbranded. A product generally will be considered nonconforming if it fails to contain an ingredient that is required by the definition and standard, or if it contains any unspecified ingredients.

Many food standards allow for the use of specific optional ingredients, particularly seasonings. Some standards include provisions for the substitution or addition of any "safe and suitable" *optional ingredients* of a certain type, such as any safe and suitable flavorings. To be safe and suitable, an ingredient must (1) perform an appropriate function in the food; (2) be present at a level no higher than necessary to achieve its intended purpose in that food; and (3) qualify as an approved food or color additive or as a nonadditive. Any ingredient that would significantly change or degrade the basic characteristics of the food (e.g., nutritional value, taste, smell, appearance, stability, etc.) would not be considered suitable.

Temporary Marketing Permits is an administrative mechanism developed by FDA to permit the test marketing of nonconforming products for a limited time, sometimes in limited amounts, and for the limited purpose of obtaining marketing data for use as evidence in support of a petition to amend an applicable standard. Permits are available only where the interests of consumers are adequately safeguarded, and generally only for a period not to exceed fifteen months.

Common or Usual Names

Foods not subject to standards of identity are nonetheless subject to certain requirements concerning names and identifying terms. Under FDA regulations, the identity of such "nonstandardized" foods must be stated as "the common or usual name of the food" which is one that accurately identifies or describes the basic nature or characteristics of the food in terms as simple and direct as possible.

> If the food contains any characterizing ingredient(s) or component(s) which have a material bearing on the price or consumer acceptance of the product, the name must include a statement of their presence and amount. The name must also state the absence of such a characterizing component if that fact would have a material bearing on price or consumer acceptance.

FDA has issued numerous rulings and guides on these issues as well as regulations that specify common or usual names or other required designations for certain nonstandardized foods, including a variety of fish and fish products.

1. Fish sticks or portions *(made from minced)* fish
2. Pacific whiting *(previously known as hake)*
3. Bonito *(cannot be called tuna)*
4. Fried clams *(made from minced)* clams
5. Crabmeat *(identifies species)* to be designated as King, anasaki, Korean variety, kegani, or Snow crabmeat
6. Seafood cocktails *(percentage labeled)*
7. Nonstandardized breaded *(composite shrimp units)*
8. Greenland turbot *(cannot be labeled halibut)*
9. Crustaceans *(quantity of contents)*
10. Caviar *(names given only to sturgeon roe)*
11. Crabmeat products with added fish *(cannot be labeled only as "crabmeat")*
12. Kipper and kipper unsplit *(defines both forms)*
13. Canned shrimp *(size and count labeling)*
14. Snapper *(designates certain species)*
15. Capelin and smelt *(smelt cannot be called capelin)*

A common or usual name may also be established by consumer use and understanding, rather than by regulation, for example, the court case *Mrs. Paul's Kitchens, Inc. v. Califano* (Civ. No. 77-592) (E.D.Pa. 1978) (fish fillets).

If a food has no established common or usual name, it may be identified by "an appropriately descriptive term," or where the nature of the food is obvious, "a fanciful name commonly used by the public for such food." It must always, however, be truthful, nonmisleading, and provide an accurate description of the basic nature of the product.

Imitations

A food that resembles and is intended to substitute for another food and that is nutritionally inferior to that food is an imitation and must be clearly labeled as such.

1. A product may be an imitation of any food (standardized or nonstandardized). However, a nontraditional food (i.e., one that is manufactured with the use of modern food technology) may be marketed without being designated imitation so long as it is clearly identified as a product different from the traditional food.
2. *Nutritional inferiority* is defined as any reduction in the content of an essential nutrient that is present in a measurable amount (i.e., 2 percent or more of the U.S. RDA).
3. *Substitution:* A question of fact based on the promotion and suggested use of the product, consumer understanding, and whether the form of the product indicates that it is intended to substitute for something else.

The act specifies numerous *defects in the quality and composition* of food, from missing ingredients to the presence of toxic chemicals, that constitute adulteration.

1. *Economic Adulteration.* The FDC act condemns any deception as to the quality

or value of a food or its ingredients as economic adulteration. For example, a food is deemed adulterated if any valuable constituent has been omitted or any substance has been substituted in whole or in part therefore. In addition, a food is declared to be adulterated if it has been treated in a manner that conceals damage, inferiority, or dilution, or if anything has been added to it that makes it appear bigger, better, or of greater value than it is.

2. *Filthy, Putrid, or Decomposed Substances.* Any food product that includes any "filthy, putrid or decomposed substances," or any food product that is "otherwise unfit for food" is adulterated. These terms subsume such things as dirt; wood splinters; insect, worm, and rodent parts; mold; and damage from water and freezing temperatures. Although the statutory prohibition is absolute and condemns even the smallest quantity of such substances in food, FDA generally will not take any enforcement action unless the contamination rises to a certain level, or violations of other requirements are also present. The FDA has informally established "Defect Action Levels" which specify the amount of foreign substance in any particular food that will trigger legal action by the FDA to remove the product from the market (see Table 21-1).

Any food that contains an unsafe *food additive* is adulterated, and every food additive is deemed unsafe unless there is in effect a food additive regulation that prescribes the conditions for its use or it is used for investigational purposes only.

1. The definition of food additive is cast broadly to comprehend any substance whose intended use "results or may reasonably be expected to result, directly or indirectly, in its becoming a component or otherwise affecting the characteristics of any food."

a. Includes substances used not only in the production and manufacture, but also in the packaging, transportation, and storage of food.
b. Substances such as cleaning solutions or paint, which are used in conjunction with food handling operations in a manner not ordinarily expected to result in food contamination but that inadvertently or accidentally do so, are not considered to be food additives. However, such accidental contaminants are subject to provisions regarding poisonous and deleterious substances.

2. *Generally Recognized as Safe (GRAS).* By definition, the term food additive does not apply to any substance that qualified experts in food safety generally recognize as having been proven safe for its intended use. FDA has published lists of GRAS substances. Although a substance may be GRAS without specifically being recognized as such by FDA, food manufacturers often avoid the risk of challenge to their use of a substance by petitioning the FDA for a GRAS determination. A GRAS proceeding will result either in an affirmation of GRAS or a finding that the substance is a food additive. In the latter event, FDA will issue a food additive regulation prescribing conditions of use, or an interim food additive regulation providing for use of the substance pending further study, or a ban on use of the additive.

3. The definition of food additive also expressly excludes color additives, new animal drugs, pesticide chemicals used on or in connection with raw agricultural commodities, and prior sanctioned substances—substances used in accordance with sanctions or approvals granted by FDA prior to September 6, 1958, when the Food Additives Amendment was enacted. However, these substances are all subject to a prior approval process of one sort or another.

Table 21-1. *FDA Defect Action Levels*

Product	Defect Action Level
Fish, fresh or frozen (applies only to fish fillets weighing 3 pounds or less.)	Decomposition in 5% or more of the fish or fillets in the sample (but not less than 5 fish) show Class III decomposition over at least 25% of their areas; or 20% or more of the fish or fillets in the sample (but not less than 5 fish) show Class II decomposition over at least 25% of their areas; or the percentage of fish or fillets showing Class II decomposition as above, plus 4 times the percentage of those showing Class III decomposition as above equals at least 20% and there are at least 5 decomposed fish or fillets in the sample. Classes of Decomposition I. No odor of decomposition II. Slight odor of decomposition III. Definite odor of decomposition
Tullibees, ciscoes, inconnus, chub, whitefish	50 parasitic cysts per 100 pounds (whole or fillets) and provided that 20% of the fish examined are infested.
Blue fin and other freshwater herring	60 cysts per 100 fish (fish 1 pound or less) or 100 pounds of fish (fish over 1 pound) provided that 20% of the fish examined are infested.
Red fish and ocean perch	3% of the fillets examined contain 1 or more copepods accompanied by pus pockets.
Shrimp, fresh or raw, headless, peeled or breaded	Decomposed as determined by organoleptic frozen, examination. 5% Class III, or 20% Class II. (See above, or, if percentage of Class II shrimp plus 4 times percent of Class III, equals 20%.)
Salmon, canned	Decomposition: A defective can is defined as one that contains Class II or Class III decomposition. (See above.) Two Class III defective cans, regardless of lot and container size; or 2 to 30 Class II and/or Class III defective cans as required by sampling plan based on lot size and container size.
Calico scallops	If 20% or more of calico scallops are contaminated with nematodes, the scallops should be recommended for seizure. All samples should consist of ten 1-pound subsamples. Samples should not be frozen because the scallop meat will become opaque.

4. Approval of a food additive requires a finding by FDA that use of the additive will be safe and will not promote consumer deception.

a. Safety, for purposes of food regulation under the act, is always determined by reference to the effects of a substance on the health of humans or animals.
b. If necessary to assure its safety, FDA may restrict use of an additive to certain foods or certain amounts or in other respects. In such cases, the

maximum allowance is set by statute as the quantity of additive reasonably required to accomplish its intended effect. FDA's current practice is to set limitations or *tolerances* at 1/100 of the amount that has been used without harm to experimental animals.

c. In addition, there is an effectiveness requirement; tolerances may not be issued at all if the additive cannot be shown to achieve its intended purpose.

d. *Color Additives.* A food that contains an unsafe color additive is also adulterated, and as with food additives, color additives are automatically deemed unsafe unless they have been approved for use and listed in a regulation by FDA in accordance with procedures outlined in the act, or they are used under an investigational use exemption. In addition, unless excepted by the FDA, color additives must be tested on a batch-by-batch basis to ensure compliance with the applicable listing regulation.

   Color additives include any dye, pigment, or other substance that is capable of imparting color (including white, black, and grays) to food. Other substances that are used solely for purposes other than coloring may be exempted by regulation from application of the color additive provisions where the color imparted "is clearly unimportant insofar as the appearance, value, marketability, or consumer acceptability is concerned."

e. *Pesticides.* The FDC Act specifically addresses the safe use of pesticides in connection with raw agricultural commodities, such as fresh fruits and vegetables, grains, nut, eggs, raw milk, meat, and seafood. It declares adulterated any food commodity that bears or contains an unsafe pesticide chemical. The status of pesticide residues in processed food is not clearly defined in the act. The statute does specify, however, that the presence of pesticide residues will not be considered to adulterate a processed food so long as the chemical has been removed to the extent possible using good manufacturing practices, and the chemical concentration does not exceed the tolerance prescribed for the raw product. The FDA considers a processed food to be adulterated if it contains pesticide residues for which no tolerance has been established, or if it contains residues in excess of an established food additive tolerance or pesticide chemical tolerance.

Although we would not generally think of pesticides in connection with fish, fish are often exposed to and have a tendency to retain varying levels of pesticides and industrial wastes that are deposited directly and indirectly into the water where they live. It is important to note that products containing a pesticide above a specific tolerance level are considered adulterated, as they contain an unapproved food additive notwithstanding that the substances are present in raw product and are not themselves added or changed by processing of the fish.

Poisonous and Deleterious Substances

A naturally occurring poison is one that exists as an inherent natural constituent of the food rather than as a result of environmental, agricultural, industrial, or other contamination. A food that may be harmful to human health because it contains such a substance is adulterated, unless the quantity of such substance in the food "does not ordinarily render it injurious to health." Although the FDA is not authorized to establish tolerances for natural contaminants, an informal tolerance system exists in FDA's Defect Action Levels (Table 21-2) which specify the levels of contamination that FDA considers to warrant enforcement action.

An added poisonous or deleterious substance is any contaminant other than a naturally occurring one that may render food injurious to health. It includes substances introduced into natural foods and any substance intentionally included in a processed food product. It also includes any extraordinary amount of a natural contaminant that is caused by the mishandling or improper treatment of food.

The FDA is authorized to establish tolerances for added poisonous and deleterious substances that either are required for production or cannot be avoided by good manufacturing practice. The presence in food of an added poisonous or deleterious substance in excess of, or in the absence of, an applicable tolerance is unsafe and constitutes adulteration.

Good Manufacturing Practices (GMPs)

Under the FDC Act, any food that has been prepared, packed, or held under unsanitary conditions whereby it *may* have become contaminated with filth or rendered injurious to health is deemed adulterated, whether or not the food actually was made harmful or unsafe.

FDA's initial efforts to enforce this provision consisted primarily of case-by-case adjudications based on ad hoc product surveillance and plant inspections. In the early 1960s, FDA developed standardized forms, inspection checklists, and formal industry guidelines in order to make its enforcement more uniform and more efficient. Ultimately, FDA invoked its general rule-making authority to promulgate regulations that include detailed requirements for food production and handling facilities and that specify what the FDA considers to be "good manufacturing practice to assure that food for human consumption is safe and has been prepared, packed, and held under sanitary conditions."

Table 21-2. *FDA Action Levels for Poisonous or Deleterious Substances in Seafood*

Substance	Possible Sources	Action Levels
Aldrin	Fish and shellfish	0.3 ppm
Dieldrin	Fish and shellfish	0.3 ppm
Benzene hexachloride	Frog legs	0.5 ppm
Chlordane	Fish	0.3 ppm
DDT, DDE, TDE	Fish	5.0 ppm
Endrin	Fish and shellfish	0.3 ppm
Heptachlor	Fish and shellfish	0.3 ppm
Heptachlor epoxide	Fish and shellfish	0.3 ppm
Kepone	Crabmeat	0.4 ppm
Kepone	Fish and shellfish	0.3 ppm
Mercury (measured as methyl mercury)	Fish, shellfish, and crustaceans	1.0 ppm
Mirex	Fish	0.1 ppm
PCB	Fish	2.0 ppm
Toxaphene	Fish	5.0 ppm
Paralytic shellfish toxin	Clams	80 μg/100 g meat
Paralytic shellfish toxin	Mussels	80 μg/100 g meat
Paralytic shellfish toxin	Oysters	80 μg/100 g meat

These GMP regulations represented a clear shift in focus at FDA from unsafe products to deficient production systems and from random post hoc detection and apprehension of defective products to a system of preventive maintenance. Certainly from FDA's point of view, this approach is advantageous, since primary responsibility for enforcement actually rests with a firm's quality assurance staff, and FDA can monitor compliance simply by conducting a paperwork audit.

FDA issued its food GMP regulations as a two-tier system: "umbrella" GMPs that apply to all food handling operations and "categorical" GMPs that contain additional requirements specifically applicable to certain types of food.

The umbrella GMPs, promulgated in 1969, consist of generally applicable specifications for personnel practices, buildings and grounds, sanitary facilities, design and care of equipment, and production and process controls—all aimed at maintaining adequate sanitary conditions in all food handling facilities and during all food handling operations. It is difficult to provide a useful summary of the regulations, in part because they range from mandatory to precatory and from very general to very specific. We discuss the issue of categorical GMPs later.

A major issue regarding GMPs is the tension between specificity and flexibility. Although the FDA's specification of operating requirements provides industry with a clear statement of what is expected, it also limits industry's ability to adopt alternative or innovative procedures that could work better in a particular plant or that may be necessitated by a change in technology. The further problem encountered is that there is no provision for exemption from the food GMPs, although it may be possible to petition for an exemption notwithstanding the absence of any specific statutory or regulatory authority for same. FDA generally takes the position that its GMP regulations constitute mandatory requirements for food handling, a violation of which automatically establishes a violation of the FDC Act. In at least one case, however, defendants in a criminal action were acquitted where their operations clearly violated GMP regulations for smoked fish but "were generally consistent with those observed at the time by other smoked fish processors," and the government failed to prove that their products "may have been rendered injurious to health."

Revision of Umbrella GMPs

FDA published a revision of its umbrella food GMPs in 1986. Although reasserting its position that the GMPs are intended to have the force and effect of law, FDA has made some effort to incorporate a more flexible approach. Thus, in certain sections, FDA has stated a general objective in mandatory terms, and has listed acceptable, but not exclusive, means of meeting that objective.

The revision retains many original GMP provisions but also includes some new requirements and procedures. One significant change requires product coding and record keeping. The product codes would identify at least the processing plant and packaging lot for each food product. The record-keeping provision requires the retention of three categories of records, including distribution records, for a period equivalent to the shelf life of the product, not to exceed two years. The coding and record-keeping provisions are intended to facilitate recalls.

In light of the revised GMPs, FDA has revoked categorical GMPs for smoked and smoke-flavored fish and frozen raw breaded shrimp.

Emergency Permit Control

In limited circumstances, FDA may require that certain products get formal clearance before being marketed, but this requirement can be invoked only when necessary to prevent an epidemic or other health emergency. The emergency permit control system is designed to give FDA the wherewithal to prevent the outbreak of disease from food that is contaminated during processing, where that contamination is not readily detectable before the food is likely to be consumed.

FDA has issued regulations for producers and packagers of *acidified foods* and *low acid canned foods*. The regulations require that manufacturers of these products register with FDA, submit processing information, comply with the processes described, maintain records, and comply with all applicable GMPs.

Compliance with these requirements operates, in effect, to exempt the manufacturer from the need to obtain premarketing clearance for its product on a lot by lot basis. This exemption may be revoked, however, and a permit for shipping or selling the food may be required if FDA finds a violation of these rules.

Labeling

A label is defined as any printed or graphic display on a food container, and labeling includes package labels as well as any written, printed, or graphic matter that accompanies a food product.

FDA administers a set of very detailed and intricate regulations that dictate not just the content of product label information, but also its layout, including location and type size. The general rule for all required product information is that it must appear on the labeling with such prominence and in such terms that it is likely to be read and understood by the ordinary consumer. Required information that appears on a product label must be visible to the consumer through any outer packaging that is used.

General Information

Every packaged food product must bear the product name and a statement of net contents by weight, count, and so on, on the principal display panel of the package (that part of the label most likely to be displayed by the retailer). Where a food is marketed in various forms (e.g., whole, slices), the particular form is considered a necessary part of the statement of identity, and must appear on the label unless the form of the food is clearly visible through the package.

The statement of quantity is subject to very detailed regulations concerning location (within the lower 30 percent of principal display panel and separate from other printed matter), print size (depends on package size), and type of measure (fluid measure—gallon, quart, pint, and fluid ounce—for liquid foods; standard weight—pounds and ounces—for solid, semisolid, and viscous foods). A statement of the number of servings contained in the package is not required. However, if serving information is provided, it must include the serving size, expressed in common measurement or cooking terms, such as cups, tablespoons, or ounces.

The label also must state the name and place of business of the manufacturer, packager, or distributor. If the designated company is not the manufacturer, its connection with the food must be demonstrated by a qualifying phrase such as "Manufactured for ______," or "Distributed by ______." This information may appear anywhere on the label so long as it is conspicuous.

Ingredient Information

As a general rule, a food product made from two or more ingredients must list those ingredients on the product label in descending order of predominance by weight. Foods that are subject to standards of identity are encouraged, but not required, to bear full ingredient listing, and in any event must list any optional ingredients. Ingredients must be listed by their common and usual names, subject to a number of specific rules.

Spices, colorings, and flavorings need only be listed by those general terms. Artificial flavoring or coloring, however, must always be designated as such. Where a mixture of natural and artificial flavorings is used, a designation like "natural and artificial crab flavoring" is appropriate. A preservative must be designated both as "preservative" and by its common or usual name.

If an ingredient has two or more components, it must be followed immediately by a parenthetical listing of those components, for example, "onion paste (dehydrated onion, spices, and water)," unless the ingredient is a sauce of standard composition (e.g., chili sauce, tomato sauce). Water is considered an ingredient and must be listed in its proper order (judged by the water content remaining in the product following any evaporation in the preparation process).

Nutrition Labeling

Current regulations do not require nutrition labeling on all foods, but whenever nutrition information is disclosed, whether voluntarily or otherwise, it must be presented in FDA's standard format.

Mandatory nutrition labeling in accordance with these regulations is triggered by any kind of claim in labeling or in advertising about the nutritional value of the food, by including in the food any added vitamin, mineral, or protein, or by providing information on the label concerning cholesterol or fatty-acid content.

The mere statement that a food is nutritious is sufficient to trigger the regulations. However, an offer to provide nutrition information upon request (e.g., label statements such as, "For nutrition information write to . . .") or providing nutrition information in response to a direct request does not subject the food to nutrition labeling requirements.

The standard format requires disclosure of serving size, servings per container, and, for each serving the calories, protein, carbohydrates, fats in grams; sodium in milligrams, followed by protein and a list of seven specified vitamins and minerals in terms of their percentage of the U.S. Recommended Daily Allowances (U.S. RDA). Quantitative information on the content of other vitamins and minerals, potassium, cholesterol, and polyunsaturated and saturated fatty acids also may be included in a specified format.

Special Dietary Uses

As with general statements of nutritional value, certain special purpose claims for food also trigger special labeling requirements. Current regulations cover hypoallergenic foods, low-salt/no-salt foods (food represented for use in regulating sodium or salt intake), diet foods (food represented as useful in maintaining or reducing caloric intake or body weight, including but not limited to low calorie/reduced calorie claims), and foods represented as useful in the diet of diabetics.

Regulations governing caloric- and weight-control foods not only establish labeling information requirements, but also place restrictions on the use of terms such as "diet," "low calorie," "sugar free," and so on. The designation "low calorie" or "low in calories," or "a low calorie food" may be used only with foods that contain 40 calories/serving or fewer and that have a caloric density of 0.4 calorie/gram or less. A low calorie designation for a food that is naturally low in calories must be in the form of "a low calorie food" (for example, "celery, a low calorie food"). A food may be called "reduced calorie" or may be accompanied by "lower in calories" claim only if it has at least one-third fewer calories than, and is not nutritionally inferior to, the compared food. In addition, its label must list the compared food, the calorie differences per serving, and any other differences between the foods in taste, texture, composition, and so on (e.g., "packed in water").

Exemptions

Some exemptions from these requirements may apply depending on how the products are marketed. If fish is repackaged in a retail establishment (e.g., sold in bulk to fish or specialty stores, then weighed and packaged for each customer), it will be exempt from many of the labeling rules as long as it is plainly labeled with either the bulk container labeling or a card containing a list of ingredients (if made from two or more ingredients). Wrapped fish fillets of nonuniform weight intended to be unpacked and marked with the correct weight at the point of retail sale are specifically exempt from weight labeling requirements while in transit.

Advertising

As a general rule, advertising is the province of the FTC rather than the FDA. Certain advertising or promotional claims, however, have a direct bearing on the nature and amount of data required to appear on product labels. For example, any food that is advertised on the basis of its nutritional value must include certain specified nutrition information on its label. Also, particular label information is required for food promoted for certain special uses (e.g., weight control, low sodium, etc.). In addition, promotional materials (labeling) that accompany food products are regulated directly by FDA, and in certain areas, FDA has restricted the kinds of claims that can be made about particular foods, for example,

Standardized designations for special dietary use claims. Standards for promoting a food as a "significant source" of a nutrient or as "nutritionally superior" to another food.

Any promotional claim that goes beyond the mere statement of nutritional benefit to an assertion of therapeutic value (e.g., "cures . . ., prevents . . .") is not only prohibited for food, but might even subject the product to regulation as a drug.

Enforcement

1. Inspections. All food processing establishments are subject to FDA compliance inspections. Any such inspections are limited to the plant and "all pertinent equipment, finished and unfinished materials, containers, and labeling."
2. Regulatory action letters
3. Seizure
4. Criminal actions

5. Injunctions
6. Recall policies. The recall of a defective or possibly harmful consumer product often is highly publicized in newspapers and on news broadcasts. This is especially true when a recall involves foods, drugs, cosmetics, medical devices, and other products regulated by FDA. Despite this publicity, FDA's role in conducting a recall often is misunderstood, not only by consumers, but also by the news media, and occasionally even by the regulated industry. The following headlines, which appeared in two major daily newspapers, are good examples of that misunderstanding: "FDA Orders Peanut Butter Recall," "FDA Orders 6,500 Cases of Red-Dyed Mints Recalled." The headlines are wrong in indicating that the agency can "order" a recall. FDA has no authority under the Federal Food, Drug, and Cosmetic Act to order a recall, although it can request a firm to recall a product.

Most recalls of products regulated by FDA are carried out voluntarily by the manufacturers or distributors of the product. In some instances, a company discovers that one of its products is defective and recalls it entirely on its own. In others, FDA informs a company of findings that one of its products is defective and suggests or requests a recall. Usually, the company will comply; if it does not, FDA can seek a court order authorizing the federal government to seize the product. This cooperation between FDA and its regulated industries has proven over the years to be the quickest and most reliable method to remove potentially dangerous products from the market. This method has been successful because it is in the interest of FDA, as well as industry, to get unsafe and defective products out of consumer hands as soon as possible.

FDA has guidelines for companies to follow in recalling defective products that fall under the agency's jurisdiction. These guidelines make clear that FDA expects companies to take full responsibility for product recalls, including follow-up checks to assure the recall is successful. Under the guidelines, companies are expected to notify FDA when they start a recall, to report to FDA on a recall's progress, and to undertake recalls when asked to do so by the agency.

The guidelines also call on manufacturers and distributors to develop contingency plans for product recalls that can be put into effect if and when needed. FDA's role is to monitor company recalls and assess the adequacy of a firm's action. Once the recall is completed, FDA assures that the product is destroyed or suitably reconditioned and also investigates why the product was defective. The guidelines categorize all recalls into one of three classes based on the level of hazard involved.

Class I recalls are for dangerous or defective products that predictably could cause serious health problems or death. Food found to contain botulinal toxin, a label mix-up on a lifesaving drug, or a defective artificial heart valve are examples of products that could fall into this category.

Class II recalls are for products that might cause a temporary health problem, or pose only a slight threat of a serious nature. Examples might be a drug that is understrength and that is not used to treat life-threatening situations.

Class III recalls are for products that are unlikely to cause any adverse health reaction, but that are in violation of FDA regulations. An example might be a bottle of aspirin that contains ninety tablets instead of the one hundred stated on the label.

FDA's strategy for each individual recall sets forth how extensively it will check on a company's performance in recalling the product in question. For a Class I recall, for example, FDA would check to make sure that each defective product has been recalled or reconditioned; for a Class III recall the agency may decide that it only needs to spot-check to make sure the product is off the market.

FDA seeks publicity about a recall only when it believes the public needs to be alerted about a serious hazard. For example, if a canned food product, purchased by a consumer at a retail store, is found by FDA to contain botulinal toxin, an effort would be made to retrieve all the cans in circulation, including those in the hands of consumers. As part of this effort the agency also would issue a public warning via the news media to alert consumers to the potential hazard.

Imports

FDA reviews entry notice or other documents to determine whether to take samples for examination. Sampling may be required depending on the nature of the product, history of problems presented by such commodity, and FDA priorities. After sampling, imports may be released or detained. In the latter event, the importer is given an opportunity for a hearing to present evidence of compliance with the FDC Act. If FDA issues refusal of admission, the importer may apply for permission to recondition the shipment to bring it into compliance by relabeling or other appropriate action. FDA has a Memorandum of Understanding with the Customs Service that authorizes FDA employees to take samples and issue notices, including refusals of admission, regarding imported products subject to the FDC Act.

Import Alerts are directives to FDA field offices regarding specific imported products or product hazards and an appropriate enforcement program, from specific sampling requirements to automatic detention ("Blocklisting"). Following are some examples: sampling swordfish from several countries for excessive mercury content; examination at the wharf and sampling as indicated for canned baby clams; upholding detention of shrimp from India containing salmonella based in part on FDA's broad discretion to regulate imports differently than domestic products in the absence of an opportunity to inspect foreign food processing facilities; and detaining samples of imported fresh or frozen raw shrimp when analysis of six 2 to 3 pound subsamples shows filth at or above the specified levels, as shown below.

Flies (whole or equivalent)
1. Filth flies—2 in a sample.
2. Incidental flies—10 in a sample.

Filth Fly Fragments
1. Three fragments (excluding setae) in 5 of 6 subsamples (these fragments are clearly identified as parts of a filth fly).
2. Large body parts (i.e., thorax, abdomen)—1 in 3 of 6 subsamples

Cockroaches
1. One whole or equivalent in the sample.
2. Excreta—1 in 2 of 6 subsamples

Hairs
1. Rat or mouse—3 of any size in a sample.
2. Striated but not rat or mouse—4 of any size in a sample.

Filth Flies Definition:
Houseflies (Muscidae), humpbacked flies (Phoridae), moth flies

(Psychodidae), black scavenger flies (Sepsidae), small dung flies (Sphaeroceridae), Chloropoid flies (Chloropidae), Anthoymiid flies (Anthoymiidae), blow flies (Calliphoridae), and flower flies (Syrphidae). This is not necessarily a complete list of filth flies which might be found in shrimp.

Incidental Flies Definition:

Dance flies (Empidiidae), beach flies (Canaccidae), shore flies (Ephydridae), bachinid flies (Tachinidae). This is not necessarily a complete list of incidental flies which might be found in shrimp.

Note: These quidelines do not include all types of filth or different combinations of filth which may be found in shrimp. Therefore, samples containing filth elements not covered by these guidelines will still have to be submitted to the Division of Regulatory Guidance for evaluation.

Exports

Food that does not comply with FDC Act requirements may be produced and sold for export without being deemed adulterated or misbranded if it complies with the laws of the importing country, meets specifications of the foreign purchaser, is labeled for export, and is not offered for sale in the United States. Export exemption cannot be used to save adulterated or misbranded products in domestic commerce; it applies only to products originally intended for export.

Fines

Misdemeanor fines under the Food, Drug, and Cosmetic Act have been increased so that they may now reach a maximum of $500,000 under some circumstances.

The Criminal Fine Enforcement Act of 1984 (Public Law 98-596) set new fines for federal law violations perpetrated on or after January 1, 1985. Although the act is an amendment to Title 18 of the U.S. Code, not the Food, Drug, and Cosmetic Act, the Justice Department has advised FDA that it applies to the fines of the FDC Act, other statutes which contain provisions enforced by the FDA and, indeed, to all federal crimes in federal law.

The Criminal Fine Enforcement Act provides these fines applicable to the FDC Act for each offense:

1. A fine of up to $100,000 for a misdemeanor by a corporation or individual not resulting in death.
2. A fine of up to $250,000 for a misdemeanor perpetrated by an individual that results in death, or for a felony.
3. A fine of up to $500,000 for a misdemeanor perpetrated by a corporation that results in death, or for a felony.

The maximum imprisonment for a misdemeanor under the FDC Act remains a year for each offense.

NATIONAL MARINE FISHERIES SERVICE

The Department of Commerce carries out a variety of activities relating to fish and the fishing industry, including operation of research and inspection programs through the National Marine Fisheries Service (NMFS). NMFS has the dual role of administering grade and quality standards for fish and fish products (see Table 21-3), and also of promoting the fish industry.

Inspections

NMFS operates an inspection and certification service that is entirely voluntary and is supported primarily by industry fees (see the appendix at the end of the

Table 21-3. ***Minimum Flesh Content Requirements for USDC Inspected Standardized and Nonstandardized Breaded and Battered Products. (All Species of Fish and Shellfish).***

Products	USDC Grade Marks[a]	PUFI Mark
Fish Fillets		
Raw breaded fillets	—	50%
Precooked breaded fillets	—	50%
Precooked crispy/crunch fillets	—	50%
Precooked battered fish fillets	—	40%
Fish Portions		
Raw breaded fish portions	75%	50%
Precooked breaded fish portions	65%	50%
Precooked battered fish portions	—	40%
Fish Sticks		
Raw breaded fish sticks	72%	50%
Precooked breaded fish sticks	60%	50%
Precooked battered fish sticks	—	40%
Scallops		
Raw breaded scallops	50%	50%
Precooked breaded scallops	50%	50%
Precooked crispy/crunchy scallops	—	50%
Precooked battered scallops	—	40%
Shrimp		
Light breaded shrimp[b]	65%	65%
Raw breaded shrimp[b]	50%	50%
Precooked crispy/crunch shrimp	—	50%
Precooked battered shrimp	—	40%
Imitation breaded shrimp[c]	—	No minimum. Encouraged to put % on label.
Oysters		
Raw breaded oysters[d]	—	50%
Precooked breaded oysters[d]	—	50%
Precooked crispy/crunch oysters[d]	—	50%
Precooked battered oysters[d]	—	40%
Miscellaneous		
Fish and seafood cakes	—	35%
Extruded and breaded products	—	35%

[a]No USDC grading standard currently exists.

[b]FDA standards of identity require that any products USDC minimum of 50% shrimp flesh by weight and if labeled "lightly breaded" must contain not less than 65% shrimp flesh.

[c]Any product with a standard of identity which contains less flesh than the standard calls for must be labeled imitation.

[d]Flesh content on oyster products can only be determined on an input weight basis during production.

chapter). About 11 percent of the approximately 400 million pounds (1.8×10^8 kg) of fish consumed annually in the United States, and approximately 6 percent of fish processors undergo NMFS inspection. The cost varies depending on a number of factors, but on average is about $.09/lb ($.02/kg) of fish.

Anyone may apply for NMFS inspection and certification, but NMFS services may be refused for nonpayment of fees, abuse of or interference with the program, consistent refusal to respond to NMFS findings and recommendations, illegal practices, and so on. Inspection service may include evaluation of

1. Fish identity, type, style, size, etc.
2. Class, quality, condition or wholesomeness of product, including
   a. Compliance with various aspects of FDA regulations, i.e., standards of identity, adulteration, etc.
   b. NMFS grade standards.
   c. Compliance with company's own specifications.
3. Sanitation standards during fish handling, processing, packing and storage operations (Sanitary Inspected Food Establishment, SIFE)
   a. Measures compliance with GMPs and NMFS fish plant sanitation standards.
   b. Required for participation in government procurement programs.

NMFS Grade Standards

1. Whole or Dressed Fish
   a. General
   b. Frozen headless dressed whiting
2. Fish Steaks
   a. Frozen halibut steaks
   b. Frozen salmon steaks
3. Fish Fillets
   a. General
   b. Cod fillets
   c. Flounder sole fillets
   d. Haddock fillets
   e. Ocean perch fillets
4. Frozen Fish Blocks and Products Made Therefrom
   a. Frozen fish blocks
   b. Frozen minced fish blocks
   c. Frozen raw fish portions
   d. Frozen raw breaded fish sticks
   e. Frozen raw breaded fish portions
   f. Frozen fried fish sticks
   g. Frozen fried fish portions
5. Crustacean Shellfish Products
   a. Shrimp
   b. Frozen raw breaded shrimp
6. Molluscan Shellfish
   a. Frozen raw scallops
   b. Frozen raw breaded scallops and frozen fried scallops
7. Proposed Standard for Minced Fish Meat (Surimi)

Enforcement

Limited authority for dealing with violations of health, safety or other standards. Actions to be taken include:

a. Notify FDA
b. Notify states
c. Quarantine contaminated molluscan shellfish under Lacey Act
d. Detain products in facilities receiving inspection services on contract basis

Memorandum of Understanding Between FDA and NMFS

NMFS takes the lead in inspection activities under voluntary inspection programs. NMFS inspections include verifying compliance with FDA rules regarding GMPs, additives, standards of identity, and labeling and packaging requirements, although FDA retains authority to conduct its own inspections and make its own determinations regarding violations of the FDC Act. At a minimum, FDA keeps NMFS apprised of regulatory standards and criteria, as well as notifies NMFS of seizure actions. NMFS gives FDA a list of plants inspected by NFS; specific information, upon request, regarding products or product lots against which FDA has taken or is considering taking enforcement action; and information regarding products placed under official retention by NMFS.

LACEY ACT

We draw the Lacey Act to your attention specifically because it has been seen, in some circumstances, as a disadvantage to the seafood industry. The National Fisheries Institute has worked for years to have the act better defined but to no avail. The purpose of the Lacey Act amendments of 1981 (commonly referred to as the Lacey Act) is to defer illegal trade in fish by improving civil and criminal penalties for violations of federal, state, and foreign laws. Because of the severity of these penalties, seafood dealers, importers, distributors, processors, and retailers should be familiar with the act.

It is unlawful under the Lacey Act for any person

1. To "import, export, transport, sell, receive, acquire, or purchase any fish . . . taken or possessed in violation of any law, treaty, or regulation of the United States, or in violation of any Indian tribal law."
2. To "import, export, transport, sell, receive, acquire, or purchase in interstate or foreign commerce any fish . . . taken, possessed, transported, or sold in violation of any law or regulation of any state or in violation of any foreign law."
3. Within the maritime and territorial jurisdiction of the United States to "possess any fish . . . taken, possessed, transported, or sold in violation of any law or regulation of any State or in violation of any foreign law or Indian tribal law."
4. Having imported, exported, transported, sold, purchased, or received any fish imported from any foreign country or transported in interstate or foreign commerce, to "make or submit any false record, account, label, or identification thereof."

5. To attempt to commit any prohibited act described in paragraphs 1 through 4.
6. To "import, export, or transport in interstate or foreign commerce any container or package containing any fish unless the container or package has previously been plainly marked, labeled, or tagged in accordance with regulations issued jointly by the Secretaries of the Interior and Commerce."

Penalties

The Lacey Act imposes both civil and criminal penalties depending on the knowledge of the defendant, the type of violation, and the value of fish involved.

Civil

For any violation of the act, except marking violations, a maximum civil penalty of $10,000 may be assessed when there is evidence that the violator *in the exercise of due care* should have known that the fish was taken, possessed, transported, or sold in violation of any underlying law. If the violation involves the transportation, acquisition, or receipt of fish with a market value of less than $350 that were taken or possessed in violation of any underlying law, the maximum civil penalty that may be assessed is the maximum penalty provided by the underlying law or $10,000, whichever is less. For marking violations there is a maximum strict liability civil penalty of $250.

Criminal

There is a maximum $20,000 fine and/or five years of imprisonment for each violation of the act, except marking violations, where the violator *knew* that the fish had been taken, possessed, transported, or sold in violation of any underlying law and *knowingly* committed a violation of the act involving (1) importation or exportation or (2) the sale or purchase, the offer of sale or purchase, or the intent to sell or purchase fish, wildlife, or plants with a market value of more than $350. A maximum $10,000 fine and/or one year imprisonment is imposed for any violation of the act *knowingly* committed, except marking violations, where the violator *in the exercise of due care* should have known that the fish was taken, possessed, transported, or sold in violation of any underlying law.

Forfeitures

All fish involved in any violation of the act, other than marking violations, are subject to strict liability forfeiture to the United States. All vessels, vehicles, aircraft, and other equipment used to aid in the criminal violation of the act for which a felony conviction has been obtained are subject to forfeiture to the United States if (1) the owner of the vessel, vehicle, aircraft, or equipment was at the time of the alleged illegal act a consenting party or privy thereto or in the exercise of due care should have known that the property would be put to an illegal use, and (2) the violation involved the sale or purchase of, the offer of sale or purchase of, or the intent to sell or purchase fish.

Culpability Standards

For the most part, there are two standards of fault under the Lacey Act: "knowingly" and "due care."

Due Care

To be assessed a civil penalty under the act, a person must have failed to exercise due care. This standard of due care means that degree of care which a reasonably prudent person would exercise under the same or similar circumstances. The due care standard is applied differently to different categories of persons who have varying degrees of knowledge and responsibility. Persons such as fish dealers, aquaculturists, and others who are involved in commercial fish transactions are held to a higher degree of responsibility and knowledge than the average citizen. They are assumed to know that they are dealing with a highly regulated product at both the state and federal levels. The Departments of the Interior and Commerce take the view that in the exercise of due care commercial fish dealers are expected to take some affirmative action to ensure that their dealings are in accordance with all applicable federal and state laws. Due care requires them, when facing a particular set of circumstances, to undertake steps which a reasonable person in their business would take to ensure that the law is not being violated.

Knowingly Violates

To commit an act "knowingly" is to do it with knowledge or awareness of the true facts or situation, and not because of mistake, accident, inadvertence, or some other innocent reason. Knowledge of the Lacey Act itself, however, is not required to be shown.

Questions and Answers Concerning the Lacey Act

1. Can I be held liable under the Lacey Act if I ship fish into a state that prohibits their entry?

Yes, if it can be shown by the government that you failed to exercise "due care" in finding out what the laws of that state are, or if you knew those laws and shipped the fish anyway. This provision of the law was supported by a number of states that believed a remedy was needed to deter shipment of fish products to the receiving state which are not prohibited by the law of the shipper's state. The specific example cited was of farmed white amur (grass carp) shipped from Arkansas to California in violation of California laws.

2. Does an interstate shipper of fish have to know the laws of all fifty states regarding fish shipments to avoid a felony prosecution under the Lacey Act?

No, you can only be convicted of a felony if it can be shown that you had actual knowledge of a violation of the underlying law and chose to ignore it. To satisfy the "due care" standard of the lesser penalties, however, you should make a reasonable effort to determine the laws of those states to which you ship fish.

3. Why does the definition of "wildlife" include fish that are bred, born, and raised in captivity or on a fish farm?

Congressional intent in passing the Lacey Act was to conserve wildlife. As there are not reliable ways to distinguish between captive-bred specimens and those specimens taken from the wild, effective implementation of the Lacey Act requires a comprehensive definition of wildlife.

4. Are intrastate shipments that violate an underlying state law subject to the Lacey Act?

No.

U.S. CUSTOMS

The U.S. Customs Service enforces country-of-origin labeling requirements under the Tariff Act. Seafood importers should ensure that packaging labels comply with present regulatory standards. The general rule is that the marking of the country of origin on a seafood package must be "legible, indelible, and permanent." Markings must include the English name of the country of origin, unless another marking is specifically authorized by the Commissioner of Customs. The degree of permanence should be at least sufficient to ensure that in any reasonably foreseeable circumstance, the marking shall remain on the container until it reaches the ultimate purchaser unless it is deliberately removed. The marking must survive normal distribution and store handling. The ultimate purchaser in the United States must be able to find the marking easily and read it without strain.

A *special rule* applies if the words "United States," or "American," the letters "U.S.A." or any variation of such words or letters or the name of any city or locality in the United States, or the name of any foreign country or locality other than the country or locality in which the article was manufactured or produced, appear on an imported article or container. In this instance, the name of the country of origin preceded by "made in," "product of," or other words of similar meaning must appear, legibly and permanently, in close proximity to such words, and in at least a comparable size. The FDA administers a set of very detailed regulations regarding the content, layout, location, and size of product label information. One of these regulations requires that the label state the name and place of business of the manufacturer, packager, or distributor. Special care should be taken to ensure that package labels required by FDA under this regulation also comply with the special country-of-origin rule administered by the U.S. Customs Service.

Bulk Containers

When an article is imported in the container in which it will reach the ultimate purchaser it is relatively simple to determine the sufficiency of the country of origin marking. However, special rules apply to so-called J-list articles (including fish and shellfish) which are imported in bulk and then repacked in the United States by the importer or a subsequent purchaser. In these cases, although the container in which the article is imported is usually marked, the container in which the article is repacked for sale to an "ultimate purchaser" is frequently not.

The *ultimate purchaser*, as defined in Customs Regulations, is generally the last person in the United States who will receive the article in the form in which it was imported. It is not feasible to state who will be the ultimate purchaser in every circumstance. However, the following examples may be helpful:

1. If an imported article will be used in manufacture, the manufacturer may be the ultimate purchaser if he or she subjects the imported article to a process which results in a substantial transformation of the article, even though the process may not result in a new or different article.
2. If the manufacturing process is merely a minor one which leaves the identity of the imported article intact, the consumer or user of the article who obtains it after the processing will be regarded as the ultimate purchaser.
3. If an article is to be sold at retail in its imported form, the purchaser at retail is the ultimate purchaser.

To minimize the practice of not disclosing country of origin information on the new containers, customs has adopted a procedure requiring importers of repacked J-list articles, articles incapable of being marked, and articles intended to be repacked in retail containers (e.g., blister packs) to certify to the district director having custody of the articles that (1) if the importer repacks the article, he or she shall do so in accordance with the marking requirements, or (2) if the article is sold or transferred, the importer shall notify the subsequent purchaser or repacker, in writing, at the time of sale or transfer, that any repacking must conform to these requirements.

OTHER LEGISLATION

Magnuson Fishery Conservation and Management Act

The Magnuson Act (MFCMA) provides a national program for the conservation and management of all fishery resources, except tuna, within the U.S. Exclusive Economic Zone (EEZ). The EEZ extends from the seaward boundary of the coastal states to 200 nautical miles (370 km) from the shore.

The MFCMA authorizes eight Regional Fishery Management Councils made up of federal and state fishing administrators and knowledgeable citizens to prepare fishery management plans (FMPs) for their regions. Citizens are appointed by the Secretary of Commerce from a list of individuals nominated by state governors. Each council has a scientific and statistical committee consisting of fishery scientists and an advisory panel made up of people knowledgeable in each fishery under the council's jurisdiction.

Optimum Yield

All fishery management plans must be developed in accordance with seven national standards. These standards deal with conservation of stocks, use of the best available scientific information, scope of the management units, fair and equitable allocation of fishery resources, flexibility of management, and minimizing costs of management. For each fishery management plan, the councils determine the maximum level of harvest that can be taken without endangering the stock's ability to sustain itself. This level, commonly referred to as the maximum sustainable yield (MSY), is adjusted for relevant economic, social, or ecological reasons to obtain the optimum yield (OY). The regional councils use optimum yield as the maximum amount of fish which may be harvested each year.

Management plans govern both foreign and domestic fishing. Each plan must contain a description of optimum yield, a determination of that portion of the optimum yield that will be harvested by U.S. fishermen, a determination of that portion of the OY that can be made available to foreign fishermen, and an assessment of the extent to which U.S. processors will utilize the U.S. harvest. Discretionary provisions, which may be written into a management plan, include requirements for domestic permits and fees, data collection programs, designation of fishing zones and periods, limits on size of catch, limits on the number of fishermen permitted in each fishery, or assessments of the plan's impact on naturally spawning stocks of anadromous fish.

Plan Review

After allowing for public comment and input, regional councils submit the management plan to the National Marine Fisheries Service (NMFS) for approval. NMFS has 110 days to allow for additional public comment and review the plans on behalf of the Secretary of Commerce to ensure that they are consistent with the national standards, the provisions of the Magnuson Act, and other applicable law. If a management plan is needed but has not been prepared by the appropriate council, the secretary may prepare a plan.

Regulations

Once a management plan is approved, the Secretary of Commerce issues regulations implementing the plan. The secretary also may promulgate regulations to address emergencies involving any fishery either on his or her own initiative or under the direction of a council by a unanimous vote. Emergency regulations remain in effect for no longer than ninety days and may be repromulgated for one additional ninety-day period. All regulations are enforced with the help of the U.S. Coast Guard and state officials. Civil and criminal penalties for violations include forfeiture of vessels, gear, or catch.

Foreign Agreements

The Magnuson Act allows foreign vessels to fish in the fishery conservation zone only for that portion of the optimum yield which will not be harvested by U.S. vessels. Foreign fishing for "surplus" fish is allowed only if (1) the nation has an existing international fishing agreement or has signed a governing international fishery agreement (GIFA) with the United States; (2) the nation extends reciprocal fishing privileges to U.S. vessels; and (3) foreign vessels have valid permits issued by the Secretary of Commerce. By signing a GIFA, a foreign nation recognizes the sovereign rights of the United States in the EEZ and agrees that its citizens will obey all applicable rules and regulations. GIFAs are not required for foreigners to participate in recreational fishing in U.S. fisheries.

Foreign Fishing

The total amount of "surplus" fish which is available to foreign vessels is called the total allowable level of foreign fishing (TALFF) and is determined by the appropriate council. The Secretary of State, in cooperation with the Secretary of Commerce, determines how the TALFF is divided among each eligible nation. Under the so-called fish and chips policy, foreign nations which assist the U.S. fishing industry receive a greater allocation. In making the allocations, the Secretary of State considers the nation's tariff and other import barriers, fisheries trade cooperation, fisheries enforcement cooperation, their domestic consumption needs, their contribution to the growth of the U.S. fishing industry, cooperation in resolution of gear conflicts, cooperation in transferring technology, traditional fishing activities in the EEZ, cooperation in fisheries research, and other appropriate matters. Half of the allocations are withheld in the beginning of each year and released later, provided the foreign nations are complying with the fish and chips policy.

Foreign Permits

Permits are required for each foreign vessel that will catch, process, or otherwise support fishing operations in the EEZ. Foreign fishing activity is regulated through area and season closures, gear restrictions, and catch quotas as specified in each permit. The Magnuson Act requires 100 percent observer coverage of foreign fishing to monitor compliance with all U.S. regulations.

Foreign Fees

Foreign vessels fishing in the EEZ pay permit registration fees, poundage fees, surcharges for vessel and gear damage claims filed by U.S. fishermen, and surcharges for observers. Permit registration fees cover the administrative cost of processing foreign permit applications. The poundage fee is based on the number of metric tons of fish caught, and varies with each fishery. Foreign fishing vessels are also assessed a surcharge based on their total vessel fees that is deposited into the Fishing Vessel Gear Damage Compensation Fund. The observer surcharge goes into the Foreign Fishing Observer Fund to cover all costs of providing U.S. observers on the foreign vessels concerned. The vessel registration fee and poundage fees are required to be at least equal to the total cost of carrying out all management, research, administrative, and enforcement activities required under the Magnuson Act.

Foreign Fishing Vessels

Permits are also required for foreign vessels to receive fish from U.S. vessels in the FCZ. These over-the-side transfers or "joint ventures" may only be approved if fish processors do not have the capacity, and will not use such capacity, to process all U.S. harvested fish. If a joint venture permit is approved, the amount of U.S. harvested fish received by a foreign vessel is limited to the portion of the optimum yield that will not be used by U.S. processors.

Foreign Harvesting and Processing

The Magnuson Act does provide a mechanism to phase out foreign fishing activities in the FCZ. In general, as the domestic harvest increases, foreign fishing allocations may be decreased. The act also addresses U.S. fishing rights in foreign waters. Specifically, foreign nations that do not extend reciprocal fishing privileges to U.S. fishing vessels may be subject to import prohibitions on its fish and fish products normally imported by the United States.

States

Individual state's authority to regulate fishing in their waters [generally within 3 miles (4.8 km) of the shoreline] is unchanged by the Magnuson Act. However, if state action or inaction adversely affects the implementation of a fishery management plan for a fishery primarily within the FCZ, the Secretary of Commerce may preempt state authority and regulate the fishery within that state's water pursuant to the management plan. The Magnuson Act also allows foreign processing vessels to operate in the internal waters of a state (waters within the baseline used to measure the territorial sea). If a nation has a governing international fishery agreement or international fishing treaty, the governor may grant permission to a foreign vessel to process fish within a state's internal waters unless he or she determines that fish processors within the state have adequate capacity, and will utilize such capacity, to process all of the U.S. harvested fish from the fishery concerned that are landed in the state.

Anadromous Fish Conservation Act

The Anadromous Fish Conservation Act authorizes the secretaries of Interior and Commerce to enter into cooperative agreements with states and other nonfederal agencies for the conservation and development of anadromous fish (including salmon, shad, steelhead trout, and striped bass). It authorizes investigations, engineering and biological surveys, research, stream clearance, construction, maintenance, and operations of hatcheries and devices and structures for improving movement, feeding, and spawning conditions.

Capital Construction Fund Act (Merchant Marine Act of 1970)

The Capital Construction Fund Act provides that any citizen of the United States owning or leasing one or more "eligible vessels" (including eligible fishing vessels) may enter into an agreement with the Secretary of Commerce to establish a capital construction fund that will be used for the eventual replacement or reconstruction of the vessel or gear and equipment.

Eligible vessel is defined as any vessel constructed in the United States, or if reconstructed, reconstructed in the United States, documented under the laws of the United States, and operated in the foreign or domestic commerce of the United States with the grandfather provision that any ship built abroad but documented under U.S. flag on April 15, 1970, or built abroad before that date for use in foreign trade pursuant to a contract entered into before that date shall be considered as though built in the United States.

Section 607 provides for a deferral of federal income taxes on deposits into the fund from the following sources:

1. Earnings from shipping operations of agreement vessels.
2. Net proceeds from the sale or of the disposition of, or from insurance on, agreement vessels.
3. Earnings from investment or reinvestment of amounts held in the fund. This has the effect of deferring tax on ordinary income or capital gains on these deposits so long as they remain in the fund.

Endangered Species Act

The Endangered Species Act protects endangered and threatened species and their critical habitats. It prohibits taking, importing, exporting, and interstate commerce of any endangered species with exceptions for scientific research, enhancement, economic hardship, and subsistence taking by Alaska natives.

Federal Aid in Fish Restoration Act (The Dingell-Johnson Act)

Dingell-Johnson provides federal aid to states for management and restoration of fish having "material value in connection with sport or recreation in the marine and/or fresh waters of the United States." Funds are derived from a federal excise tax on certain sportfishing equipment and apportioned to states by a formula based on each state's area and number of sportfishing licenses issued. To participate, states must have fishery conservation laws, including a prohibition against the use of license fees paid by fishermen for any purpose other than the administration of that state's fish and game department.

Federal Ship Financing Act of 1972

The Federal Ship Financing Act amends Title XI of the Merchant Marine Act (1936) by replacing authority to insure vessel mortgages and loans with authority to guarantee loans. Fishing vessels of 5 net tons or over are one of several classes of eligible vessels. Generally, loans (owed to private lenders) eligible for guarantee must have aided in financing or refinancing the cost of constructing, reconstructing, or reconditioning vessels, facilities, or equipment pertaining to marine operations.

Federal Water Pollution Control Act

The Federal Water Pollution Control Act requires permits from the EPA for the discharge of any pollutant into navigable waters. It provides for the Army Corps of Engineers to issue permits for the discharge of dredged or fill materials into the navigable waters, with oversight by the EPA. Permit applications are reviewed by the U.S. Fish and Wildlife Service for impacts on fish and wildlife.

Fish and Wildlife Act of 1956

The Fish and Wildlife Act establishes a comprehensive fish and wildlife policy. It authorizes the Secretary of the Interior to develop measures for "maximum sustainable production of fish," make economic studies, and recommend measures to ensure the stability of domestic fisheries. It also undertakes promotional and informational activities to stimulate consumption of fishery products and takes steps required "for the development, management, advancement, conservation, and protection of fishery resources." Functions are related to marine commercial fisheries and sport fisheries. Great Lakes fishery research and certain other fishery related activities are assigned to the National Oceanic and Atmospheric Administration, under the Department of Commerce Act, to provide for cooperation between the secretaries of State and Interior and to provide representation at international meetings relating to fish and wildlife. The 1974 amendment stipulates that the Small Business Administration may make loans to fishermen, under certain situations, while the Fisheries Loan Fund moratorium exists.

Fish and Wildlife Coordination Act

The Fish and Wildlife Coordination Act authorizes the Secretary of the Interior to assist federal, state, and other agencies in developing, protecting, rearing, and stocking fish and wildlife on federal lands. It also authorizes studies on the effects of pollution on fish and wildlife.

Fishermen's Protective Act of 1967

The Fishermen's Protective Act authorizes the Secretary of State to reimburse damages to the owner or charter of a U.S. fishing vessel that has been seized by a foreign country while operating on the high seas or while fishing between 3 and 200 miles (4.8 to 370 km) offshore of a foreign nation for highly migratory fish such as tuna. Payments may be paid for the cost of having the vessel released, replacement of confiscated gear, spoiled fish, and loss of income to commercial fishermen.

It also authorizes the withholding of financial aid to any country that seizes a U.S. fishing vessel illegally. It gives the president discretionary authority to prohibit the importation of fishery products from nations which conduct fishing operations in a manner that diminishes the effectiveness of multilateral international fishery conservation programs in which the United States participates.

Fishery Cooperative Act of 1934

The formation of fishery marketing cooperatives and their administration are provided for in the Fishery Cooperative Act. Responsibility for administering it lies with the Secretary of the Interior.

Marine Mammal Protection Act of 1972

The Marine Mammal Protection Act establishes federal responsibility for the conservation of marine mammals with management under the Department of the Interior for sea otter, walrus, polar bear, dugong, and manatee, and under the Department of Commerce for all whales, porpoises, seals, and sea lions. It establishes (with certain exceptions) a moratorium on the taking and importation of marine mammals and products made from them, and it provides for the establishment of a three-member Marine Mammal Commission, supported by a nine-member Committee of Scientific Advisors.

Marine Protection, Research, and Sanctuaries Act of 1972

A program administered by the EPA to regulate dumping of materials into ocean waters was established under the Marine Protection, Research, and Sanctuaries Act. The Secretary of Commerce, in coordination with the Coast Guard and the EPA and in consultation with the Secretary of Interior, is directed to determine long-range effects of pollution over fishing and other activities on ocean ecosystems. The Secretary of Commerce is authorized to designate and protect marine sanctuaries after consultation with the secretaries of the Interior, State, Defense, and Transportation and the administrator of the EPA. If waters within the territorial limits of any state are involved, state officials must also be consulted.

Merchant Marine and Shipping Act of 1916

The Merchant Marine and Shipping Act comprises a vast body of legislation amended and supplemented many times. The Jones Act is the generic term used for various sections regulating U.S. commercial shipping, including the fisheries. As it pertains to fishing boats, it does not allow any vessel of 5 net tons or over to participate in coastal fisheries if it was not built in the United States. Vessels over 5 net tons and engaged in commercial fishing are required to be documented. Under 5 net tons a vessel cannot be documented, but must be registered according to state regulations.

Other provisions under the Merchant Marine law concern licensing of fishing vessels, fines for trading without license, load lines for vessels, and regulation of fishing voyages. Another provision gives seamen a right of action against their employer for negligence, or for injury caused by the unseaworthiness of a vessel or its tackle.

Rivers and Harbors Act of 1899

The Rivers and Harbors Act makes it unlawful for anyone to conduct any work or activity in navigable waters of the United States without a federal permit. The Secretary of the Army is authorized to issue permits to construct piers, jetties, and similar structures, or to dredge and fill. The Corps of Engineers issues permits for the discharge of refuse affecting navigable waters. The Fish and Wildlife Coordination Act provides authority for the U.S. Fish and Wildlife Service to review and comment as to the effects proposed activities would have on fish and wildlife.

Saltonstall–Kennedy Act of 1954

The Saltonstall–Kennedy Act directs the Secretary of Agriculture to transfer annually to the Secretary of the Interior funds equal to 30 percent of receipts from customs duties on fisheries products. These funds are used for fishery research and development.

STATE REGULATIONS

The states all have "little FDC" Acts that follow the federal law to a greater or lesser degree. In addition, state and local governments generally play an active and primary role in regulating the handling and processing of fresh fish and shellfish within their borders. They may specify what, where, when, and how fish may be caught and processed and may conduct related inspection programs. In contrast, FDA activity with respect to fresh fish and shellfish is generally concentrated on identity and labeling issues and on the surveillance of imports.

Some states also have laws applicable to fish imported into the state from other states or countries (e.g., minimum length required for salmon brought into California or country or state of origin labeling required for fish sold in Arkansas.).

INTERSTATE SHELLFISH SANITATION CONFERENCE (ISSC)

The ISSC is a voluntary cooperative framework for establishing and implementing uniform standards for the safe and sanitary harvesting, processing, and distribution of molluscan shellfish (oysters, clams, and mussels). The ISSC, a successor to the National Shellfish Sanitation Program, was formed in 1982.

Members include representatives from shellfish producing and consuming states and FDA, NMFS, and industry representatives, but only the state representatives have voting rights. In addition, several foreign governments participate as observers in ISSC activities.

The ISSC is intended to provide a forum for developing uniform and up-to-date guidelines, standards, and procedures for the states to use in conducting their sanitary control activities. The primary role in ISSC is played by the states which undertake to adopt the necessary laws and regulations for ensuring the safe and sanitary production of shellfish and to take the necessary steps to implement those laws, by, for example, identifying pollution sources; testing waters for possible bacteriological or other contamination; patrolling growing areas to detect and deter illegal harvesting; and inspecting processing plants for sanitary practices. In addition, the ISSC is managed and controlled by the states, unlike the NSSP which originally was run by the Public Health Service and later by FDA.

FDA's role in the ISSC is purely advisory. Under its Memorandum of Understanding with the ISSC, FDA agrees to evaluate state sanitary control programs and offer suggestions; provide technical support and training; coordinate federal activities pertaining to ISSC issues; publish a monthly list of all state-certified shellfish producers and shippers; and establish agreements with foreign governments to provide for the adoption and use of sanitary controls equivalent to those used by the states. The foreign agreements currently approved are with Canada, Japan, Korea, Iceland, Mexico, England, and New Zealand.

ISSC builds on the work of the NSSP (i.e., NSSP Manual of Operations, Parts I and II, as amended has been formally adopted by ISSC and redesignated as the ISSP) and is structured to avoid some of NSSP's problems (e.g., ISSC includes a voting mechanism to avoid the NSSP problem of being unable to resolve issues on which there was no consensus). Nonetheless, some issues persist from the voluntary nature of the organization and its activities, the absence of any legal sanctions for noncompliance, and the always delicate nature of federal/state relations.

FEDERAL TRADE COMMISSION (FTC)

FTC has primary jurisdiction over advertising of foods under a Memorandum of Understanding with FDA. The FTC Act prohibits "unfair or deceptive acts or practices in or affecting commerce."

False or Misleading

An advertisement violates the law if it is false or misleading in any respect. An advertisement may be considered false or misleading if it has the capacity or tendency to deceive, regardless of advertiser's intent and regardless of whether anyone was actually fooled. Currently FTC may require a showing of actual and material deception, however, before taking enforcement action. Advertisements are viewed as a whole and may be considered deceptive if the "net impression" is false or misleading, even though each sentence, taken individually, may be literally true. Meanings of advertisements are determined with reference to the "ordinary purchaser," including "the ignorant, the unthinking, and the credulous." Currently, FTC may apply a "reasonable consumer" standard. The advertiser is responsible for every claim perceived by consumers, expressed and implied, intended and unintended.

Substantiation

An advertisement violates the law if the advertiser lacks substantiation for its claims. Advertiser must have proof, in the form of a "reasonable basis," for its claims *before* including them in an advertisement. What constitutes a reasonable basis is a question of fact depending on specificity of the claim; type of product; consequences of false claim; degree of reliance by consumers; and type and accessibility of supporting evidence.

(*Note:* The laws and regulations described in this chapter are not intended to be all inclusive. Other federal and local agencies that deal with discharges, for example, EPA, or with the workplace (OSHA) also have regulations that impact the industry. In addition, governmental agencies at all levels are constantly modifying existing regulations and/or writing new ones.)

APPENDIX

NMFS Inspection Services

Inspection services available from the National Marine Fisheries Service (U.S. Department of Commerce) on fee basis:

Technical Assistance and Sanitary Inspected Fish Establishment (SIFE) Services

These services provide for the inspection of plants for sanitation only. No product inspection, certification, or grading is conducted. The services consist of two phases, as follows:

Phase I—Sanitary Consultative Services. This service includes inspecting the facility to identify the strengths and weaknesses of the plant's sanitation to determine if it meets minumum Commerce Department (USDC) and Food and Drug Administration (FDA) sanitary requirements and consulting with the firm on correction of any deficiencies. The inspector conducts inspections and provides technical advice to the plant to assist in upgrading sanitation practices. When a plant meets USDC requirements, it is eligible to contract for regular sanitation inspections under

Phase II described below. Plants with sanitation deficiencies can remain in Phase I if they agree to a minimum of 4 hours of consultative services monthly at prevailing inspection rates. If there are several plants in the same area interested in inspection, mileage and inspection travel time costs can be prorated among them.

Phase II—Sanitarily Inspected Fish Establishment Service (SIFE). Plants meeting all sanitary requirements receive inspection for sanitation for a minimum of 12 hours per month at the same hourly rate as Phase I. These plants are recognized as official establishments, operate under the FDA/NMFS Memorandum of Understanding, are awarded a certificate attesting to their sanitation compliance, and are listed in a NMFS biannual publication available to potential seafood buyers, such as schools, food chains, government purchasing agencies, and consumers.

Packed Under Federal Inspection Service (PUFI)

The "Packed Under Federal Inspection" mark or statement on a federally approved label signifies that the product is safe, wholesome, has good flavor or odor, and was produced under Federal inspection in an officially acceptable establishment. The product is not graded for a quality level but must meet acceptable commercial quality criteria in accordance with approved Federal standards of USDC approved processor specifications. If the company's own in-plant quality control system meets the approval of, and is certified by, the NMFS Inspection Service, the number of hours necessary for the inspector to be on-site during the processing of produce bearing the PUFI mark can be reduced, thus reducing the overall cost.

Product Grading Service

This service is available to processors participating in the PUFI program who pack products for which there are U.S. Grade Standards. Participation in the program permits the use of U.S. Grade marks on products meeting these standards. This service requires that a USDC inspector perform the grading. There is no additional cost for this service beyond the fee per hour for the PUFI service.

Lot Inspection Service

Inspections are performed on specific lots of products of domestic or foreign origin. Generally, inspections are conducted to determine a product's compliance with criteria or specifications furnished by the requester. Since the USDC inspection net is nationwide these lots can be located in processing plants, warehouses, cold storage plants, or terminal markets anywhere in the United States. This service can be contracted for by a broker, buyer, or processor with a financial interest in the product. The contract can be on an individual request or continuing basis. An official certificate documenting the quality and condition of the lot is supplied the client upon completion of the inspection (usually within 2 days). These certificates have proven valuable in lawsuits concerning product quality and in-transit damage because they are accepted as "prima facie" evidence in U.S. courts. Master cartons of products lot inspected can be marked by the inspector as officially sampled or accepted per specification.

REFERENCES

Federal Food, Drug & Cosmetic Act of 1938 as amended "Code of Federal Regulations," 21 U.S.C. sec. 321.

Agricultural Marketing Act of 1946 "Code of Federal Regulations," 7 U.S.C. sec. 1621–1627.
Codex Alimentarius Standards "Federal Register" 1984 Vol. 49, pp. 7584–9749.
FDA Compliance Guides, section 7108.
FDA Fair Packaging & Labeling Act "Code of Federal Regulations," 21 U.S.C. sec. 343, part 101.
U.S. Customs Regulations "Code of Federal Regulations," 44 U.S.C.
National Marine Fisheries Service "Grade Standards, Code of Federal Regulations," 50 U.S.C. part 260.
The Lacey Act, Fish & Wildlife Service, Dept. of Interior "Code of Federal Regulations", U.S.C. sec. 16.
National Shellfish Sanitation Program—Manual of Operations, Part I & II, 1988 Revision, Food & Drug Administration, Washington, DC.

CHAPTER

22

Smoked, Cured, and Dried Fish

Michael W. Moody and George J. Flick

Before refrigeration and canning techniques, humans preserved food caught in times of plenty to use in times of scarcity by taking advantage of environmental conditions, both induced and natural. In addition, they used naturally occurring preservatives such as salt and smoke. Undoubtedly one of the first foods cooked on an open wood fire was some form of fish.

Although the origin of fish smoking is obscured by antiquity, aboriginal men and women must have developed this method of preserving their catch shortly after they discovered how to make fire (Crance, 1955; Paparella, 1979). Experience soon told them that the barbecuing process made food keep longer and added a distinctive flavor. As time continued, these prehistoric cooks noticed that the flavor varied with the kind of wood burned, and other improvements gradually followed.

Proper timing and correct temperature, which to primitive peoples meant the correct position of the fish over the fire, were determined. Becoming more familiar with using salt, they found that a preliminary salting or brining further improved the flavor and the keeping qualities. Present methods of hot-smoking or barbecuing, as it is sometimes called, surely evolved from these crude beginnings.

About the time humans were learning how to barbecue fish, they discovered the possibilities of drying fish in the open air. And they also found that a wood smudge burning under their hanging fish not only preserved the fish but also imparted a smoky flavor. With certain types of fish the smoke flavor was preferred, thus a smudge fire under the drying fish became an essential part of the process. Use of proper wood, regulation of the fire's heat, and the density of smoke, together with a preliminary salting or brining, completed the evolution of what is known as fish smoking.

It was not until the development of controlled smokehouses that any significant advances were made over those early preservation methods. Controlled processes for both cold- and hot-smoking based on scientific principles have just begun to come into use in fish smoking; today, smoking is being changed from an art to a science.

The primary curing ingredient is still salt, but additional curing ingredients may be used such as sugar, spices and, in some products, sodium nitrite. The cured products may or may not be subsequently smoked, smoke-flavored, and/or partially dried. In this discussion, our emphasis is on fresh- and saltwater species of fish that are both cured and smoked or smoke-flavored. Preparation of these food products has long been a tradesman's art. Applying scientific principles to this ancient art can produce a safer and more consistent, appetizing, and wholesome product.

Development of modern refrigeration has meant that there is no longer the need for the high salt content previously required. Although less salt is now used in curing smoked fish, it still contributes to the finished product's shelf life, safety, and flavor. The modern mild-cured products, which may be cold- or hot-smoked, are made possible by adherence to good sanitation practices and proper refrigeration during processing, distribution, and storage. *These products require proper refrigeration for preservation.*

The smoked fish industry has achieved an excellent reputation for producing high quality, wholesome products. However, the industry has experienced some problems that have resulted in serious economic loss and, to a degree, an erosion of consumer confidence. There have been periodic food poisoning outbreaks associated with cured and cured-and-smoked fish products, some of which have resulted in fatalities. Case studies of these relatively infrequent outbreaks, which often involved *Clostridium botulinum* toxin, consistently appear related to improper processing procedures applied by inexperienced or unknowledgeable processors, inadequate sanitation, abusive product storage conditions (primarily by the consumer), and sometimes to consumers' erroneous belief that smoking negates the need for refrigeration or that the product has an unlimited shelf life.

It is the processor's responsibility to adhere to manufacturing procedures that result in products that are not only appealing in appearance and flavor, but are wholesome, prepared under sanitary conditions, and are safe to eat.

ECONOMIC IMPORTANCE

Today, people continue to smoke, cure, and dry seafood, not so much for preservation—modern preservation techniques give a superior product more closely associated to fresh—but for the delightful tase and texture and because of cultural preferences. The selection of smoked fish products is extensive, and regional preferences exist for both the type of fish and the style of preparation. In some countries salted and dried fish remain an important commercial product.

In 1986 the United States commercially salted and pickled approximately 14 million lbs. (6.4×10^6 kg) of fish worth $25 million. Also in that year, a total of 19 million lbs. (8.6×10^6 kg) of fish worth more than $82 million were smoked (Figs. 22-1 and 22-2). When we consider that more than $5.3 billion worth of seafood was processed that same year, the amount salted, pickled, or smoked seems quite small (Processed Fishery Products, 1986).

PRINCIPLES OF SMOKING, DRYING, AND CURING

The two most common sources of spoilage in foods come from the actions of bacteria and autolytic enzymes. Although both are extremely important, the major emphasis here is on controlling the adverse effects of spoilage organisms in smoked, cured, and dried fish.

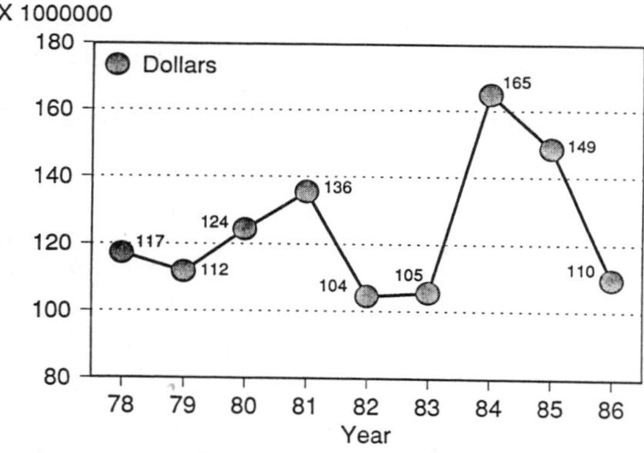

Figure 22-1. Annual Production of Cured Fishery Products.

Water is the basic ingredient of all foods. Every food contains water even though the amounts may vary, and for the most part, the amount of available water in a food determines how rapidly that food will spoil. Foods with a high available water content (such as meats, seafood, milk, etc.) spoil quickly; foods with a low available water content (such as flour, honey, cereal grains, etc.) may last for years even at room temperature (Troller and Christian, 1978).

Bacteria and other spoilage microorganisms must have a minimum level of available water before they can carry out essential metabolic functions. If there is not sufficient available water, the bacteria die or become inactive. The amount of available water in a food is measured by the water activity (abbreviated a_w). Do not confuse this measurement with the percentage of water in a food. Water activity is a measurement of the water available for microorganisms to use for metabolism. Salt and sugar can "tie up" water so that it is not available for microorganisms to use. Consequently, by adding enough salt to fish, the growth and destructive action of bacteria can be minimized. In addition, salt draws moisture from the tissue of the fish by osmotic pressure to make less water available.

Pure water has a water activity (a_w) measure of 1.0. As the amount of available water decreases, so does the water activity value. Most bacteria must have a water activity of 0.95 or higher to grow. Table 22-1 lists some common foods and their water activity values.

Note that fresh fish has a water activity close to 1.0 but after heavily salting and drying, the water activity is between 0.80 and 0.70, a level far below the threshold

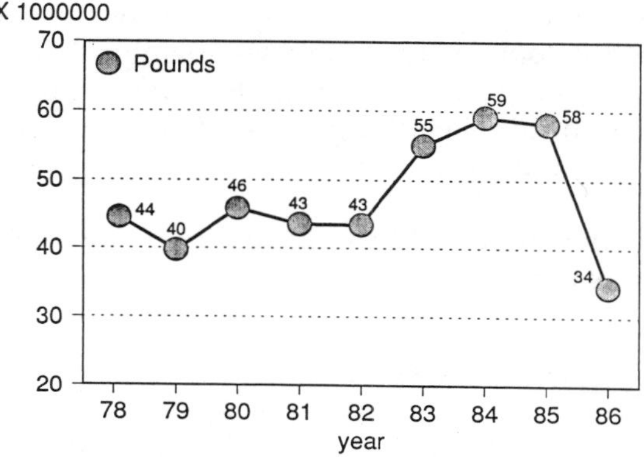

Figure 22-2. Value of Cured Fishery Products.

Table 22-1. ***Approximate a_w Values of Some Foods and of Sodium Chloride and Sucrose Solutions***

a_w	NaCl (%)	Sucrose (%)	Foods
1.00–0.95	0–8	0–44	Fresh meat, fruit, vegetables, canned fruit in syrup, canned vegetables in brine, frankfurters, liver, sausage, margarine, butter, low-salt bacon
0.95–0.90	8–14	44–59	Processed cheese, bakery goods, high-moisture prunes, raw ham, dry sausage, high-salt bacon, orange juice concentrate
0.90–0.80	14–19	59–saturation	Aged cheddar cheese, sweetened condensed milk, Hungarian salami, jams, candied peel, margarine
0.80–0.70	19–saturation	—	Molasses, soft dried figs, heavily salted fish
0.70–0.60	—	—	Parmesan cheese, dried fruit, corn syrup, licorice
0.60–0.50	—	—	Chocolate, confectionery, honey, noodles
0.40	—	—	Dried egg, cocoa
0.30	—	—	Dried potato flakes, potato crisps, crackers, cake mixes, pecan halves
0.20	—	—	Dried milk, dried vegetables, chopped walnuts

Source: Troller and Christian, 1978

Table 22-2. ***Lowest a_w Values Permitting Spoilage-Organism Growth***

Group of Microorganisms	Minimal a_w Value
Bacteria	0.91
Yeasts	0.88
Molds	0.80
Halophilic bacteria	0.75

at which normal bacteria can grow. We must point out, however, that there are some bacteria, called halophiles (meaning salt-loving), that can grow at a water activity value as low as 0.75 (see Table 22.2). Occasionally, these bacteria can cause considerable spoilage during the salting of fish. Some contain a red pigment, and fish contaminated with them are referred to as "pink" spoiled (Troller and Christian, 1978).

The preservation effects of dried and salt cured fish are obtained by removing or displacing available water to prevent bacterial growth.

SMOKED FISH PROCESSING

Although the general operations in all smoked fish processing plants are similar, the specific processing procedures can vary considerably. This variability relates to differences in equipment, regional and ethnic consumer preferences, raw materials, and tradition.

We discuss the basic operations involved in the processing of smoked fish and the manufacturing practices necessary to minimize the hazard of Type E botulism and the risks of food-borne infections in the consumption of smoked fish. Effective sanitation considerations, including plant design, construction, water, and personal hygiene are areas that must be carefully evaluated to minimize bacterial contamination (Crance, 1955; Dougherty and Seagran, 1967).

The unit operations involved in the processing of smoked fish can be categorized as follows:

1. Purchasing and receiving
2. Raw material storage (refrigerator and freezer)
3. Raw material preparation
4. Salting: dry and brining
5. Drying
6. Smoking
7. Cooling
8. Packaging
9. Finished product storage
10. Distribution and sale

We discuss each category briefly.

Purchasing and Receiving

A processor should be aware that various state and federal statutes exist concerning the purchase and possession of various fish species and size. It is important that a purchaser's plan incorporate these aspects into the program.

Selecting and Initial Preparation

It is imperative that only fresh, properly prepared fish be used for smoking. Smoking will not mask or otherwise make a poor quality or spoiled fish acceptable. Smoking enhances the flavor and texture of fish; fish with a high oil or fat content are generally more suitable for smoking than lean fish. Some examples of high-fat fish are salmon, eels, whitefish, catfish, sturgeon, chubs, mackerel, mullet, and bluefish. Examples of low-fat fish, which do not smoke as well, are flounder and snapper.

When selecting fish for smoking, choose only those that are of high quality and free from bruises, torn skin, or other physical damage. Fish may be smoked whole, gutted, filleted, steaked, or chunked depending on the species and desired style. Large fish obviously should be filleted or cut into smaller pieces so that proper cooking temperatures can be achieved without overcooking the outside of the fish.

Receiving

Production of a quality finished product starts at the Receiving Department. This operation not only involves physical control of incoming raw materials and supplies but is usually the first inspection point.

It is essential that all processing begin with a high quality product. Containers and fish should be inspected on arrival at the plant. All fish must have been shipped at suitably low temperatures, and they should be free from adulteration and not have detectable off-odors or flavors. Special attention should also be given to firmness of flesh, eye condition, and gill color.

It is highly recommended that all incoming fish be divided into lots and given an identification tag which will accompany the product throughout the entire process and become part of the process records. Information on the tag would include point of product origin; date received; condition of fish (physical state as well as appropriate quality attributes); lot number (if desired); and size and type of fish.

Freshwater and saltwater finfish species represent the major tonnage of incoming materials. Depending on the species and ultimate use, fish may be received whole, gutted, or headed-and-gutted and may be fresh and iced or frozen.

Inspections at the receiving department should include other edible raw materials used in the processing of smoked or smoke-flavored fish, including salt, sugar, spices, and, in some products, smoke flavoring, artificial color, sodium nitrite, vegetable oil, and other ingredients. Wood smoking materials such as chips and excelsior, packaging materials, and cleaners and sanitizers also should be examined.

Raw Material Storage

All reasonable precautions should be taken to ensure that all products and raw materials are handled in a manner that will not contribute to their contamination or deterioration. Lots should be appropriately identified to assure their timely use on a first-in first-out basis whenever possible.

Fish that are not smoked immediately can be iced and/or refrigerated for a short period. Fresh fish which are not to be processed immediately should be refrigerated at a temperature near 32°F (0°C). Frozen fish should be either thawed promptly and processed or stored at a temperature that will maintain them in a frozen state. Fish that are to be kept for an extended period prior to cooking and smoking should be properly frozen and stored to maintain desired quality. Usually a temperature no higher than 0°F (–18°C) should be used, with –20°F (–29°C) preferred. Proper chilling and/or freezing retards bacteria growth and enzyme activity, the major causes of spoilage in fishery products.

Dry and nonperishable food ingredients and package materials should be stored in a dry area in a manner that protects against contamination and deterioration. Cleaning and sanitation chemicals should be stored in a separate area.

Sodium nitrite requires special handling and should be stored in a locked area restricted to those few who will use this ingredient and who have been properly instructed regarding its use and potential hazard. Only quantities needed in a given brine should be permitted out of the room.

Raw Material Preparation

Proper cleaning and preparation prior to smoking improves product quality. Immediately before processing begins, both fresh and thawed fish should be thoroughly washed by a vigorous water spray or a continuous water flow system with chlorinated water (25–50 ppm). This process helps increase shelf life and also removes blood and reduces bacterial populations that cause spoilage and food poisoning. Washing fish after brining is not as effective as a prewash because once the product has been brined, a water-soluble protein layer covers the fish surface, making it more difficult to remove entrapped bacteria.

Whole fish should be thoroughly washed prior to gutting and dressing to remove external debris and blood and the natural slime that encases most fish.

Generally slime can be easily removed by washing the fish in cool water and rubbing the slime off. At times, slime can be difficult to remove, especially from heavily slimed fish like eels. To make removal easier, one of the four following methods can be used:

1. Soak the fish in a heavy brine solution for a few minutes. Often, this will quickly separate the slime from the fish.
2. Wash the fish in a chlorine solution (one tablespoon of liquid hydrochlorite bleach in four gallons of water). (Dudley et al. 1973). Make sure that fish washed in chlorine solution are thoroughly rinsed in fresh clean water.
3. Quickly dip the fish in hot water (about 180°F/82°C) to coagulate the slime (Dudley et al. 1973).
4. Freeze the fish. When fish are thawed in preparation for smoking, the slime often is loosened and can be easily washed off.

The thawing or defrosting of frozen fish should be carried out in a sanitary manner and by methods that will not adversely affect the wholesomeness of the fish. Whole fish should not be mixed with gutted fish during thawing. Different species of fish should be thawed separately.

To maintain quality thaw fish in air at a temperature of 45°F (7°C) or below so that no part of the fish exceeds 45°F (7°C). If the fish are thawed in water, then a continuous chilled water-overflow tank, a spray system, or other process which provides frequent water exchange should be used. The fish should not remain in the tank longer than is needed to sufficiently thaw them for further processing, preferably no more than a half hour after the fish are completely defrosted. Care should be taken to ensure that fish entering the thaw tank are completely free of packaging liner material. Cleaning and sanitizing the tank is essential to maintain sanitary conditions and should be conducted as often as necessary.

Fish should be eviscerated before salt curing and smoking. Whole fish should be eviscerated with a minimum disturbance of intestinal tract contents; all viscera should be completely removed. Cut the fish and thoroughly wash the cavity in fresh clean water. Be sure to remove all organs without puncturing or cutting them. The kidneys are usually lodged along the backbone and require extra effort to remove sufficiently. After evisceration, the fish (including the body cavity) are given a second thorough wash with a vigorous chlorinated water spray or a continuous waterflow system. All offal should be placed in suitable covered containers and removed at least once a day or more frequently if necessary. Depending on offal refuse pickup, the offal containers may require refrigeration.

Consider the cut of fish to be smoked. Style and form depends on the size of fish, desired product, and personal preference. Small fish such as chubs, white fish, and eels are usually smoked whole, eviscerated and gills removed. Larger fish such as salmon, sturgeon, sable, and bluefish are cut into steaks, fillets, split, or butterflied. The cuts may be skinless. Always keep fish or cuts of fish packed in ice or properly refrigerated to retard decomposition.

Rinsing

Both fresh and thawed fish that have been eviscerated should be rinsed thoroughly before brining. All rinsing operations should be carried out with chlorinated water, either as a vigorous spray or in a continuous water flow system. The concentration of chlorine in the rinse water should be maintained between 25 and 50 ppm.

Salting

One of the most difficult, but most important, steps in preparing smoked fish is obtaining the desired concentration of salt or other preservatives in all parts of the product. Uniform salt concentrations are important. Depending on the concentration, salt can slow the growth of spoilage microorganisms and some food poisoning bacteria. However, the main purpose of adding salt is to impart flavor, because the amount used in modern smoked products has little effect on keeping quality. Again, we stress that the smoked fish available today are perishable and require refrigeration.

Factors contributing to salt variation in smoked fish include fish size; species; fat content; condition (fresh or frozen, skin on or skin off, state of rigor); method of salt application; brine concentration; brine temperature; brining time; brine-to-fish ratio; circulation of brine; and section of fish, to name the variables. (Several of these factors are discussed in more detail later in this chapter.)

In recent years there has been a trend toward lowering the salt content in processed foods as a means of reducing dietary sodium. Smoked fish processors have been very sensitive to this issue, because they are interested in adjusting to consumer tastes without sacrificing product safety or market share.

The salt used should be of food-grade quality, low in calcium and magnesium and essentially free of iron and copper. The application of salt to fresh or thawed fish is carried out prior to either hot- or cold-smoking by exposing the fish, or portion thereof, to dry salt or, more commonly, to salt brine. Some processors use a combination of the two procedures. Although there is no hard and fast rule that dictates the use of one procedure over the other, salt brines are most widely used because they are easier to handle and offer better control.

With dry salting, the amount of salt, the time, and the temperature should be carefully controlled to attain desired product. The amount of salt-to-fish by weight may vary from 1:8 for light salting, 1:3 for split fish, or 1:1 for heavy salting. Dry salting should be carried out at a temperature not exceeding 38°F (3°C). (In the preparation of some Nova Scotia salmon by the dry-salting procedure, brown sugar is also sprinkled in with salt.) Because of the variations possible, only through experimentation and experience can the proper curing be ascertained.

Brining or Curing

Brining serves three purposes: it firms the texture of the fish, provides seasoning or flavor, and acts as a preservative in some types and styles of smoked fish. But brining must be carried out under the most careful conditions to prevent making an unpalatable salty product.

Liquid salt solutions, or brines, are an important step in processing smoked fish and require some precision and vigilance on the part of the preparer. A saturated brine is made from good quality bulk or bagged salt in equipment available from the major salt companies. Salt storage and brine making can be confined to one location and the brine pumped to the points of use. A brief explanation of the arithmetic of salt solutions is appropriate. Quantity of salt is usually stated in pounds. One gallon of fully saturated brine at 60°F (15°C) contains exactly 2.987 pounds of salt and tests 100°S (100° Salometer). In making brine, the concentration of the solution must be measured reasonably accurately (within 5°S) to predict the proper amount of time to soak the fish. The best and most common way to measure brine concentration is with a salometer, which is a floating scale that measures the density of the brine according to its buoyancy when placed in the brine. The denser the solution, the more buoyant the salometer will be. The scale gives readings in salometer degrees from 0° to 100°S (corresponding to 0 to 100 percent saturation—0°S for pure water and 100°S in fully saturated brine. For example, 40°S is 40 percent saturated). When using a salometer, it is important that the brine temperature be considered. Ordinarily, salometers are scaled for reading at a temperature of 60°F (15°C). Table 22-3 gives an accurate conversion of salometer degrees to salt concentration when the brine is 60°F (15°C). However, if the temperature is below or above 60°F (15°C), the reading will not be correct and adjustments must be made. Adjustments are made by adding or subtracting *one* salometer degree for each 10°F (each 5.6°C) that the brine temperature deviates from 60°F (15°C). For example, if the temperature of the brine is 80°F (27°C), you would *add* 2°S to the reading on the chart. If the temperature of the brine is 45°F (7°C), you would *subtract* 1.5°S (Bankston, 1973; Hilderbrand, 1973).

The typical brine used to soak fish for smoking varies from 30 to 50°S although higher concentrations can be used. Refer to Table 22-3 to determine the pounds of salt/gallons of water to be dissolved for a particular salometer degree brine. For example, if you need an 80°S mixture, this would be a 21.116 percent sodium chloride solution requiring 2.229 pounds (1.012 kg) of salt to 1 gallon (3.785 l) of water. Obviously, if you are making up 100 gallons of solution, you would add 222.9 pounds (2.229 × 100) of salt to 100 gallons of water. The resulting solutions would give a total volume of more than 100 gallons because water would be displaced by the dissolved salt.

Diluted brine solutions are commonly made in the smoked fish industry by volumetric dilution of fully saturated brine (100°S). To make 100 gallons of a 40°S brine requires 40 gallons of fully saturated brine and 60 gallons of water. Adjustments for temperature may be required. Diluted brines should be checked for salometer reading.

If a diluted brine is to be prepared from dry salt and water, use a brine table to establish the amounts of salt and water necessary to make the volume of diluted brine required. The salt should be completely dissolved before using the brine.

When making brine, several principles should be kept in mind.

1. To achieve a rapid and predictable salt penetration, use as pure a salt (NaC1) as possible. For example, calcium and magnesium, which are common salt impurities, hinder the proper penetration of salt into the fish tissues. Improper or delayed salt penetration can cause spoilage. In addition, these impurities may cause a chalky, bleached-out, unappetizing, or unnatural color that will detract from the product's appearance. Consequently, avoid using sea salts or other salts with known impurities.

2. Salt used for brining should be fine textured so it will dissolve quickly. Table salt has a suitable texture, but rock salt may take an inordinate amount of time to dissolve. For consistency, it is important that an accurate measurement of salt be added to the water and that it be completely dissolved prior to use as a brine. When salt is initially added to water, it begins to dissolve quickly but the rate may slow considerably as the brine strength increases.

3. Stirring or agitating the brine will increase the rate at which the salt dissolves. Mechanical agitation by a pump, sparge, or propeller is highly recommended, but manual agitation with a paddle or stirrer could be employed. Agitation helps dissolve the salt and also is useful during the brining process to maintain consistent absorption. We discuss this process in more detail later.

Table 22-3. ***Brine Conversion Tables (60°F)***

Salometer Degrees	Percentage Sodium Chloride by Wt.	Pounds Salt Per Gallon of Water
0	0.000	0.000
2	0.528	0.044
4	1.056	0.089
6	1.586	0.134
8	2.112	0.179
10	2.640	0.226
12	3.16	0.273
14	3.695	0.320
16	4.223	0.367
18	4.751	0.415
20	5.279	0.464
22	5.807	0.512
24	6.335	0.563
26	6.863	0.614
28	7.391	0.665
30	7.919	0.716
32	8.446	0.768
34	8.974	0.821
36	9.502	0.875
38	10.030	0.928
40	10.558	0.983
42	11.086	1.039
44	11.614	1.094
46	12.142	1.151
48	12.670	1.208
50	12.198	1.266
52	12.725	1.325
54	14.253	1.385
56	14.781	1.444
58	15.309	1.505
60	15.837	1.568
62	16.365	1.629
64	16.893	1.692
66	17.421	1.756
68	17.949	1.822
70	18.477	1.888
72	19.004	1.954
74	19.532	2.022
76	20.060	2.091
78	20.588	2.159
80	21.116	2.229
82	21.644	2.300
84	22.172	2.372
86	22.700	2.446
88	23.338	2.520
90	23.755	2.594
92	24.283	2.670
94	24.811	2.745
96	25.339	2.827
98	25.86	2.906
100	26.395	2.98

Note: Special salometers are available scaled for reading at 38°F. And special brine tables at 38°F are available to extrapolate salometer degree at 38°F to the percent sodium chloride by weight, weight per gallon of brine freezing point, and other information.

4. As the water's temperature is increased, so is the rate at which the salt dissolves. Dissolving all the salt in nonchilled water and then chilling the solution to the proper brining temperature may save some effort. Prior to adding fish, it is important that the brine solution be chilled to at least 40°F (4.5°C), which maintains the quality of the fish during the procedure. Although the rate of salt penetration is retarded by chilled brine, fish quality should never be sacrificed in order to speed the process.

During the brining procedure several phenomena occur.

1. Water migrates from the fish tissues because of osmotic pressure. This water loss causes some weight loss but will favorably affect the texture of the fish.
2. The salt concentration in the tissue increases with soaking time. Consequently, if the fish are brined for longer than the recommended time, the final product may be unpalatable because of the high salt content.
3. Salt from the brine is absorbed by the fish, and water from the fish is expelled into the brine. The end result is diluted brine. Since brine is generally changed between batches of fish, this probably has little impact on brine quality.

As mentioned earlier, numerous factors influence the rate that fish absorb salt (Burgess et al., 1967). Among the most significant are

1. *Exposed flesh.* Salt penetrates skinless and/or filleted areas much more rapidly than areas protected by skin.

2. *Fat content.* As the percentage of fat increases, the rate at which the salt penetrates the fish flesh decreases. Consequently, fat content and the species of fish brined have a significant impact on brine concentration and brining time.

3. *Size and shape of fish or pieces of fish.* All other factors being equal, the thinner the fish portions, the faster the salt penetration. Fish of reasonably uniform size should be brined together. Fish of different species should not be mixed in the same tank.

4. *Agitation.* Stirring the brine should give more even penetration of salt. Pockets of diluted or concentrated brine are blended to give an overall even concentration.

5. *Strength of brine.* Brine strength is important to ensure a uniform and standard product from batch to batch. For example, if one vat of brine has a 80°S value and another vat for the same product has a 45°S value because of a careless worker, then the final products will not be the same. As a general rule, the stronger the brine, the shorter the brining time. Typically brine concentrations of between 30°S and 50°S are used (Bannerman, 1980).

6. *Submerge.* For a fish to brine properly and uniformly, it must be completely submerged in the brine. Floating fish or too many fish (which prevents complete coverage) causes uneven salt penetration and a substandard product.

7. *Weight ratio.* As the brine-to-fish ratios increase, the amount of salt per unit weight of fish increases. A longer refrigerated brining time (eighteen to thirty-six hours) with a more dilute brine (20° to 45°S) often results in a more uniform salt concentration than a short brining time (two to six hours) in a more concentrated brine (over 45°S). However, either brining procedure is acceptable.

8. *Temperature control.* The brining process should be performed so that the temperature of the fish and brine does not exceed 60°F (15°C) at the start of brining. If the fish are between 38°F (3°C) and 50°F (10°C) at the start of brining, the temperature should be continuously lowered to 38°F (3°C) or below within twelve hours. If the temperature is between 50° and 60°F (10° and 15°C) at the start of the

brining process, the temperature should be continuously lowered to 50°F (10°C) or below within two hours and to 38°F (3°C) or below within the following ten hours. Once the brining process reaches 38°F, the temperature should be constantly maintained during the entire operation.

Water-Phase Salt Content

Salt content in the finished smoked fish product is typically determined on the loin muscle of the fish and is expressed as percentage of salt in the water phase. To determine the salt content in the water phase of the muscle, it is necessary to remove and analyze the loin muscle for both moisture content and salt content.

$$\%\text{ Salt in Water Phase} = \frac{\%\text{Salt}}{\%\text{ Moisture} + \%\text{ Salt}} \times 100$$

A dry salting or brining process is established to attain no less than a minimum water-phase salt content appropriate for the product. There has been considerable debate over what constitutes an appropriate minimum water-phase salt content. The minimum water-phase salt content considered appropriate for smoked fish products can vary, based on use of sodium nitrite, heat processing, type of packaging, intended shelf life, and expected storage conditions.

Typically the rate or amount of salt uptake increases with increased brine concentration, higher brine temperature, greater brine-to-fish ratio, smaller fish, longer brining period, a soft (postrigor) condition, aged fish, and prefrozen fish. Although some factors increase the salt uptake, this should not be construed as optimum brining conditions. Brining conditions are selected to produce a uniform and high quality product within a reasonable production schedule.

Brine tanks should be cleaned and made sanitary before each use. Brine should be prepared fresh for use from food-grade salt. Brines should not be reused unless there is a suitable procedure such as ultrafiltration to return the brine to an acceptable microbiological level.

Although some organisms grow in salt water, most spoilage organisms are severely restricted by brine concentrations above 7 percent salt (approximately 27°S).

Before the fish are removed from the brining process they are generally evaluated by a chemical and sensory analysis. If the fish do not have an acceptable salt level, brining time is extended. If too salty, the product is rinsed in water to remove some of the salt. Both of these processes must be carefully monitored to ensure that the fish are removed at the correct time. The actual required brining time can vary depending on the factors mentioned but it may be quite rapid (Childs et al., 1976). It is common practice to rinse fish after brining to remove surface salt. This operation must be done cautiously to avoid leaching excessive salt from the product.

Ingredients

Other ingredients, such as sugar, other flavor ingredients, coloring agents, and sodium nitrite can be added during the brining process. Special brining formulas are proprietary to each smoked fish processor. All ingredients must be generally recognized as safe and approved. The use of sweeteners, liquid smoke, and coloring agents is at the discretion of the processor and should be used in accordance with good commercial practice by procedures determined appropriate for the product in preparation. Finished products should be labeled in accordance with regulatory requirements to reflect the presence of all ingredients.

Some fish are placed into a tank or tub of coloring agent to achieve a desired color or the dye may be added to the brine, combining the two operations in one. The concentration of dye used in dipping is greater than when it is incorporated into the brining solution. In some cases, dye may be injected into the fish. For coloring consistency, some types of smoked fish are dipped after preslicing. FDA permitted list may also be used. Dye solution, approved by FDA, is made up in strengths dictated by the experience of the individual curer, and it is not possible to establish exact rules which will apply universally. Processors must determine requirements by experimentation and according to the desires of their customers. The use of dyes in smoked fish and the labeling required for such processes are subject to specific state and federal regulations.

Sodium nitrite is a curing agent currently permitted only in smoked chub; smoked, cured salmon; smoked, cured sablefish; smoked, cured shad; and smoked, cured hena as a preservative and color fixative. Sodium nitrite enhances the inhibitory effectiveness of salt against the outgrowth of *Clostridium botulinum* Type E spores. The use level in brines, either in the premix or pure form, is adjusted to attain in the finished smoked chub not less than 100 ppm and not greater than 200 ppm in the loin muscle. In finished smoked sablefish, salmon, or shad, the level should not exceed 200 ppm. A rule of thumb is to add twice as much sodium nitrite to the brine as desired in the final product. For example, to obtain 200 ppm in the final product, add 400 ppm to the brine. In a 35°S brine at 60°F (15°C), the amount of sodium nitrite (400 ppm) per 50 gals (189.3 l) of brine would be approximately 2 3/4 ounces (78 g). The actual amount required should be established by controlled experimentation. In practice, it should be thoroughly dissolved in the brine before the fish are added.

Sodium nitrite can be broken down by bacteria present on smoked fish, and its inhibitory effect is diminished. To retain its maximum effectiveness, good sanitation procedure must prevail, and the product should be stored at 32° to 34°F (0° to 2°C). It is strongly recommended that a processor obtain the services of a reputable supplier or qualified consultant for the development of safe and effective brining mixtures and their applications.

Drying Fish

After brining, fish are hung or laid on racks for drying, smoking, and heat processing. If these processes cannot be conducted within two hours after removal from the brine, fish should be stored in a refrigerator at 38°F (3°C) or below. Drying allows for good color formation, forms a "skin" that holds in juices, and gives the strength needed to keep fish from falling from hooks, rods, or other holding devices.

Positioning Fish for Drying and Smoking

Fish are usually dried in the same position in which they will be smoked, and obviously fish should be smoked with as much surface area exposed as possible. For example, a split fish should be hung or presented in such a way that split halves are open. Depending on the size and cut of fish, there are three common methods for hanging or holding fish for drying and smoking.

1. Rods may be used to thread fish through the head, gills, or mouth. This method is good for smaller fish and for some fish that have been headed and split. Fish normally hang tails down when placed on a rod.

2. Hooks or nails allow the fish to be hung in any position, although usually they are hooked through the head. If they are hooked through the fleshy part of the body, the hooks leave an undesirable mark. In hanging fish, sufficient space should be between the fish to prevent faulty processing. Overcrowding or overloading the smokehouse could result in an inferior product and should be avoided.

3. Racks are useful for pieces of large fish such as chunks, steaks, blocks, sides, or fillets that do not have skin or skeletal structure to support hanging. Racks should be made of large mesh screens or other materials that allow good exposure to smoke and air circulation (Dudley et al., 1973).

Mesh bottom trays, made of half-inch mesh, may be used for some products, such as fillets and steaks. The trays are sometimes coated with edible oil to prevent pieces of fish from sticking. Pieces in the tray should be close to the same size and should not touch each other. Remove as much free liquid as possible because pools of brine lying in depressions in the fish will be slow to dry, and these damp areas may spoil rapidly during subsequent refrigerated storage. The trays may be placed directly on fixed racks in the smokehouse, or they may be conveyed into a cage which is placed into the smokehouse after it has been filled.

During hanging, dissolved proteins in the brine solution dry on the fish surface and produce the familiar glossy skin which is one of the commercial criteria for quality. When properly dried, this "pellicle" will form and the outer surface will be smooth, dry, and glossy (Crance, 1955). Without proper brining and drying, a glossy pellicle will not form. A properly formed pellicle helps give the finished product an attractive appearance because smoke readily adheres to it. A poorly formed pellicle allows the outer surface of the fish to burst or erupt, emitting coagulated body fluids, resulting in an unattractive appearance.

After hanging, the product is dried. Drying is an important step that must be controlled to produce a high quality product. In almost all instances, fish must first be dried by removing surface moisture to a certain degree, prior to heating or smoking. When properly done, drying will make the flesh firmer and prepare it for further cooking and smoking.

Forced drying—raising the temperature and drawing a current of air through the smokehouse—reduces the time required for the smoking process. Drying time depends on such factors as air circulation, temperature, and the relative humidity of the air. Normally, it takes several hours. Generally it is recommended that fish be dried in a cool place with circulating air created by a blower or fan, especially when home smoking fish. Some commercial processors dry fish in the smoking chamber at an elevated temperature. The processor must be sure, however, that all air vents and doors are open to provide a good circulation of air and that the temperatures are carefully controlled so that the fish are not cooked.

If too much humidity builds up during this step, or if processing takes too long and the meat and bone are exposed to heat before drying, the product will fall apart. To prevent this, the protein must be set or denatured with low temperature drying *before* applying higher temperatures. If the air is too hot and moving too quickly, the surface of the fish will be damaged and will not dry properly. Fish flesh, like that of other animals, is primarily composed of protein. When proteins are dried too fast, they harden, or "denature" and the skin forms a hard case. When this happens, water cannot escape from the core of the fish and the outside forms a crust. Consequently, the oven must dry the fish slowly enough to prevent this process, called *case hardening*, but fast enough to avoid deterioration caused by bacterial and enzymatic activities. If the surface of the fish is overdried, it will crumble later and smoke color formation will be poor because of inadequate smoke absorption.

If the fish are not properly dried and the fish smoked while too moist, the smoke will not be evenly absorbed, resulting in a "streaky" product. Time is also an important factor in drying. The longer the drying process, the greater the protein degradation.

Smokehouses vary in design and many variables must be taken into consideration. Some of the important factors are as follows:

1. *Air circulation*. The air inside a processing chamber must have a certain velocity and volume to achieve efficient, even processing. The volume of air can determine the distribution of heat and moisture. If the air velocity is too much or too little, the resultant product may be defective. In addition, the air must flow evenly through the product zone. Driving the air for too great a distance will result in uneven processing.

2. *Heating and cooling*. An efficient way to heat chamber air must be designed into the system. Optimum design places the heating element directly into the chamber, eliminating heat loss during transfer and using all the heat for processing. The shorter the air flow distance from heating element to processing area, the more efficient the system. Air used in processing must be clean and its heat and moisture content controllable. This can be assured only if the air begins free of impurities and the by-products of fish cooking are not allowed into the processing area.

3. *Humidity*. Humidity control is an important but often misunderstood factor in producing smoked fish. Humidity is the water content of air. Relative humidity is expressed as a percentage and measures the water content of air at a particular temperature compared with the maximum amount of water air could hold at that temperature.

The higher the temperature, the more water the air can hold. To have meaning, relative humidity must be expressed as a percentage at a given temperature. To determine wet bulb temperature, take the air temperature with a wet sock placed over the bulb end of the thermometer. The water evaporates off the sock, cools the thermometer, and results in a temperature reading lower than actual air temperature. The drier the air, the faster the evaporation, the quicker the thermometer cools, and the lower the reading. Comparing the difference between the air temperature (dry bulb) and the evaporation temperature (wet bulb) on a prepared scale gives relative humidity. Air must blow at and around the wet bulb at a specific rate [approximately 800 ft. (244 m) per minute] to give a correct reading. Also, the wetted wick should be kept free of contamination (cleaning chemicals, smoke particles, tar, creosote, or organic vapors) which may retard water evaporation. If the velocity is too low, there is not enough evaporation and the wet bulb temperature will be too high. If the air velocity is too great, the evaporation will be too fast and the temperature reading too low. Either way, the moisture reading is incorrect.

This discussion brings us back to the importance of air velocity. The product is saturated with water and acts much like the wet bulb thermometer at a specific temperature and air velocity. The location of the wet bulb thermometer during the reading is crucial. If the reading is taken near the supply ducts, it will measure the humidity of the air before it picks up or gives off moisture to the product. If a reading is taken at the exhaust duct, it will measure the humidity of the air after processing has taken place. Every point in the chambers will have a different reading because of evaporation or condensation. Depending on circumstances however, readings eventually equalize.

Because fish products contain a high percentage of water, the effect of the product on the air is as important as the effect of the air on the product. The product gives off or absorbs moisture at a rate dependent on its own temperature and pressure differential. As the product absorbs or gives off heat or dries, that rate changes, even if processing air values stay the same. Thus the relative humidity, or web bulb reading, becomes only a guide to the type of air to use. There may be times when it is desirable to reach or even exceed the saturation point of air, called *steaming*. Moisture condenses on the product, passing its energy content to the product.

Sometimes dehumidification at a specific point is more important than humidification. It is also possible that a slowly rising or falling humidity over a certain time interval is more important than maintaining a constant humidity. To get this effect, humidity must be removed or added on a time interval rather than at a constant rate. When excess humidity occurs, a dehumidification cycle is automatically initiated to reduce the moisture content of the air in the processing chamber. This dehumidification can be accomplished in a number of ways. The simplest, fastest, and most economical method is to introduce fresh, ambient air into the oven while removing some of the moist air, until the humidity drops to the desired set point. It is important that your system be properly engineered because smoke air pollution may occur. If the community has stringent air pollution requirements, a small afterburner, electric precipitator, or water scrubber can be used to further reduce the pollution in the exhaust air.

Another way to dehumidify is with a semiclosed system with water spray dehumidification. A fine spray of water is introduced into a chamber through which the air is recirculated during the dehumidification cycle. The water cools the air, forcing out moisture. There are numerous disadvantages in this system, however. First, the water must be colder than the air at all times, resulting in high water use even if recirculating pumps are used. Second, the smoke is removed by the water spray, causing a reduction in smoke concentration and an increase in water pollution. Third, maintenance requirements are greatly increased because of its costs and limitations.

When temperatures exceed 212°F (100°C), relative humidity readings are not possible. However, air moisture content can still be controlled by adding moisture to the air, and the easiest way to add moisture is steam. Using water droplets or fog can cause water droplets to form on the product. Even when using steam, care must be taken. If the steam is too hot (at pressures over 7 psi) the air will be overheated and unwanted excess condensation will occur, causing spotting, burning, and separation. The air must have time to absorb the moisture introduced. Thus injections of moisture that are small and fast are preferred over one continuous injection.

Smoking

Smoking fish, like salting, dates back to early times. Probably smoking was an ancillary benefit in the drying of salt-cured fish over open fires. The smoke contributed a pleasing flavor as well as facilitating preservation. Although many refinements have been made in smoking fish, the overall process retains many of the original attributes. Methods for smoking fish vary greatly, depending on such factors as the type of fish, desired flavor, desired texture, cooking method employed, cultural preferences, and so on.

Today we make distinctions between smoked and smoke-flavored fish, between hot- and cold-smoked fish, and between the various methods of applying the smoke constituents.

Traditionally, smoke applied to fish came from burning hardwoods such as maple, oak, alder, hickory, birch, and fruitwoods. Liquid smoke was prepared as early as the late 1800s, but only within the last ten to fifteen years has it been commercially used in the smoked fish industry. Even today, smoke-flavored fish represents a small percentage of the total industry output.

The three kinds of smoke-flavor additives are natural smoke extracts, synthetic smoke flavors, and substances unconnected with smoke, such as yeast derivatives, that have a smoky flavor and smell. Smoke-flavored fish, processed using liquid smoke, can be prepared by including liquid smoke in the brine, or applying it as a dip after brining, or as an atomized spray within a modern automatic smokehouse. There is no single recommended method of application; its use depends on the processor's objectives, ingenuity, and facilities. However, recent research suggests that spraying is preferable to dipping as a means of accurately controlling flavor and acceptability. It may be necessary to dry some products after the flavor has been added in order to obtain a texture comparable with traditional products. During spray application, there are several positive results if air is circulated at a low velocity, if air temperature is raised by 10° to 15°F (5.6 to 7.2°C), and if the liquid is injected in short bursts as a fine fog. This method provides improved flavor; a better, more even color throughout the load; faster processing; and less liquid smoke is used, lowering costs.

In general, smoking of fish is carried out as a cold-smoking process or as a hot-smoking process, and the equipment used in either process can be a traditional gravity oven or a modern electric oven.

Cold-smoking is exactly that. The fish are not cooked because the temperature during smoking generally does not exceed 110°F (43°C). If the temperature is allowed to rise, the muscle texture could be adversely affected. To maintain the proper temperature during smoking and to ensure uniform drying and desired color, it is necessary to use an indirect source of heat and smoke. Proper cold-smoking often takes less than 24 hours. The cold-smoking process is primarily used for salmon. Other traditional cold-smoked items include black cod (sablefish) and herring.

The curing process may differ slightly since both liquid and dry cures are used. Sugar and salt may be added to the cure mixture. Achieving quality results in cold-smoking is somewhat more difficult than in hot-smoking. Drying, an important part of the process, must be slow and the humidity carefully controlled to attain the desired surface hardening. The drying and cold-smoking process typically requires eighteen to twenty-four hours.

With traditional gravity ovens it is particularly difficult, if not impossible, to carry out cold-smoking on warm and humid days unless the system is specially modified to cool and dehumidify. Often heat and smoke are produced separately and then carried to the fish by fan or pipe. Careful temperature controls with thermometers, ventilators, dampers, and fire controls are necessary to achieve a good finished product. Because of the flexibility of control in modern automatic ovens, they are adaptable to cold-smoking. Again, equipment installation is a factor. In most processing plants a number of ovens are required to simultaneously process different items, and equipment cost must be considered.

The temperatures and times used in processing cold-smoked fish are very favorable for the proliferation of food spoilage and food poisoning types of microorganisms. Therefore particular attention to sanitation, proper brining, limitation of the process to specific product types, careful handling, process control, and prompt refrigeration after smoking are essential. Although the finished product has not been cooked, it has excellent keeping properties because it has been dehydrated sufficiently to retard most bacterial growth.

Hot-smoking is the process used in the majority of smoked fish products. A hot-smoked product has been fully cooked and may reach temperatures as high as 180°F (82°C). Because of the higher temperature, hot-smoking takes only a short time, depending on the internal temperature of the product. Different species of fish tolerate heat differently; consequently, the hot-smoke process is not the same for all products. The process must be tailored to the species, the processing equipment used, market demand, distribution considerations, and regulatory requirements. Hot-smoked fish are moist and juicy when properly finished. Because of this, they have a relatively short shelf life and must be refrigerated.

In processing, the intention is to cook the fish as well as smoke it. Processing temperatures used in the industry vary significantly, but like for cold-smoked fish, it is necessary to maintain careful temperature controls and always to use a thermometer to monitor the coldest part of the fish (Dudley et al., 1973; Hilderbrand, 1980). Because elevated temperatures are used in hot-smoking, fish are generally close to the heat source.

The minimum internal temperature for adequate processing of hot-smoked fish has been a major issue of concern for years. Generally, the main considerations when determining process times and temperature are water-phase salt content, use of sodium nitrite, and the use of vacuum packaging. Proper heating helps to eliminate food poisoning bacteria and to extend the fresh shelf-life. Both state and federal regulations that are currently in effect will dictate actual hot-smoked process minimum temperatures. Processors should always consult appropriate regulatory and health sources before the establishment of process times and temperatures.

In traditional gravity ovens, heat may be produced by charcoal briquets supplemented with gas burners. The rate of heat application, the type of fuel, and the sequence of its use are variables adjusted by the skilled smoker. Experienced smokers can usually produce acceptable results with these ovens.

Modern smoke ovens, available in many designs and sizes, can be equipped with as much automation as a processor is willing to pay for. Heat is generated by electricity, gas, or oil. The choice is dictated largely by convenience and cost. Heat transferred to the oven is usually in the form of steam and controlled air flow. The ovens can be automatically programmed to conduct a series of sequenced operations to accomplish the necessary drying, smoking, heating, and cooling. Humidity control and air flow rates during the sequenced operations also can be programmed.

The basic processing cycle includes drying, smoking, and heating. If the fish is dried a little more in the beginning and the humidity is raised a bit in the smoking step, the need for smoke venting to reduce the humidity within the smoke can be eliminated. During cooking, the moisture in the air can be increased to raise the temperature inside the fish. At the end of the cycle, smoke can be vented up the chimney slowly to minimize air pollution problems. You should have the ability to program these functions into your unit.

Electronic advances in modern smokehouses permit exact control of the operation. It requires a skilled smoker and assistance from the equipment manufacturer to carry out the controlled testing necessary to attain the desired program for processing various products. The processing still requires judgment from the smoker because other factors such as brining and fish size must be considered. Because of the control advantages of this equipment, the industry trend is certainly toward greater use of this processing method. Wood is no longer used as a heat source because it is too expensive and makes the moisture content of the air too difficult to control. Most modern machines use steam generated by electricity, oil, or gas, but selecting a heat source is largely a matter of convenience.

Smoke Generation

Today's smoke generators are often separate from the processing unit.

The primary function of smoke components is to provide the desirable color, aroma, and flavor of smoked products and to contribute to product preservation by acting as an effective bactericide and antioxidant agent. The kinds and quantities of chemicals present in smoke depend on the type of wood, its water content, the temperature to which it is heated, and the precise manner in which it is heated. For example, there is a difference between smoke produced from slowly smouldering sawdust and from the same sawdust heated to a high temperature by blowing a strong current of air over it.

The different volatile chemical compounds in wood smoke are known to have varying levels of bacteriostatic and bactericidal effects. Smoke's effect on microorganisms is heightened by increasing its concentration and temperature. It also varies with the kind of wood used. It has been reported that the residual effect of smoke is greater against bacteria than against molds. However, the preservative properties are not nearly as important as strict hygienic requirements, modern packaging, and continuous refrigeration.

Aroma and flavor are a blend of smoke components. The influence of wood variety on smoke flavor is caused by the basic pattern of smoke compounds formed during thermal degradation of the wood. Each type of wood gives a different quality or taste and some even make the product unedible. Softwoods may cause flavor problems and are not generally used. Hardwoods are usually used and many times are legally required. Hardwoods result in both good color and good flavor but the process takes longer than when softwoods are used, all other processing factors being equal. The type of wood chosen depends on the product desired and market preference.

The amount and chemical composition of curing smoke is strongly influenced by the temperature of smoke generation and by smoking technology. The composition of liquid smoke shows an extremely wide variation. During the normal smoking process, the smoke compounds penetrate into the product only a fraction of an inch (a few millimeters), but if liquid smoke preparations or other smoked ingredients are added to the curing mixture, these compounds are found in the center of the product.

Keeping the product at the proper temperature and moisture and carefully controlling the smoke addition are critical points and usually are best controlled by an automatic system which consistently monitors and records these factors. Smoke is acidic and will dry the product and if added at a certain temperature, it will denature the product. A high smoke temperature can impart a burned odor and flavor to the product. The concentration of smoke per cubic foot of air has a direct effect on the process: the higher the concentration, the quicker the deposition.

Composition of Smoke

The deposit of smoke on fish is responsible for the golden color and delightful flavor of the finished product; however, there has been much discussion and much written about the composition of smoke and the possible side effects on consumers of smoked food products. The composition of smoke is complex, with hundreds of chemical compounds. The physical state of smoke, however, is composed of gases and droplets. Two chemical compounds of special concern are polycyclic aromatic hydrocarbons and nitrosamines. Both are considered carcinogenic (cancer causing) by scientists. By using certain techniques (lower temperatures during smoking, the use of an electrostatic filter, or the use of liquid smoke in place of actual smoking), it has been shown that the polycyclic aromatic hydrocarbons can be reduced.

Cooling

After the smoking operation, whether cold-smoking or hot-smoking, the product must be promptly cooled. Proper cooling is essential in hot-smoked fish (Eklund, 1982). Hot-smoked products require more cooling, so it is expected that the cold-smoked product will be cooled at least as efficiently.

The finished product should be cooled to a temperature of 50°F (10°C) or below within three hours after cooking and further cooled to a temperature of 38°F (3°C) or below within twelve hours. This temperature should be maintained during all subsequent storage and distribution. Smoked fish should never be packaged hot because excessive condensation may form inside the package.

Packaging

Shipping containers, retail packages, and shipping records should indicate by appropriate labeling the perishable nature of the product and should specify that the product be shipped, stored, and held for sale at 38°F (3°C) or below until consumed. Permanently legible code marks should be placed on both the outer layer of every finished product package and on the master carton. Such marks should identify, at least, the plant where packed, the date of packing, and the oven load. Records must be maintained as to positive identification of the process, procedures used, and of the finished product's distribution.

It cannot be overemphasized that most smoked fish products, unless canned and sterilized by retorting, have about the same or just slightly longer shelf life than fresh fish. Consequently, smoked fish should be handled, packaged, and stored much like fresh fish. It should be kept frozen or under refrigeration just above freezing temperatures. Vacuum-packed smoked fish makes a beautiful package, but potentially it can be hazardous because the organisms that normally provide visual and odor indications of spoilage are retarded in growth, and certain food poisoning organisms, if present, are favored in outgrowth

Currently scientists recommend that vacuum packaging be restricted to cured salmon (lox), cold-smoked salmon (nova), hot-smoked salmon (kippered salmon), and sablefish. These products should be processed with nitrate, have the required water-phase salt content, and meet all prevailing regulations pertaining to heating and cooling. Products should be cooled to 38°F (3°C) before packaging, and packaged products stored at 38°F (3°C) or below, or frozen. The immediate package should be prominently marked with a use-by date.

Noncommercial smoked fish products are popular and are commonly made at home (Crance, 1955; Berg, 1965; Bradley, 1977; Richards and Price, 1979; Waters and Bond, 1960), however, the same requirements and safety precautions taken by commercial producers should be observed by home producers.

Low Temperature Smoking (LTS)

Variations in smoked fish products and processing have made it possible to offer smoked-flavored fish that have many of the characteristics of hot-smoked fish with less smoking time and lower processing temperatures (Otwell et al., 1980). LTS products require additional cooking before consumption.

Storage, Distribution, and Sale

The need for proper refrigeration cannot be overemphasized. The finished product should not be distributed until it has been properly cooled to 38°F (3°C)or below. Furthermore, because of smoked fish's perishable nature, it is imperative that the finished product be maintained in a refrigerated condition at 38°F (3°C) or below until consumed. Most food poisoning outbreaks related to smoked fish have been related to abusive storage temperature conditions.

SPOILAGE AND CONTAMINATION OF SMOKED FISH

Smoked fish is a perishable food, so to maintain its good quality and to prevent food-borne illness, it must be preserved after smoking by processing techniques. *Clostridium botulinum* is a spore-forming bacterium. Because it forms heat-resistant spores, it is not destroyed by heat as easily as other nonspore-forming bacteria. In addition, *C. botulinum*, Type E, has been shown to grow and produce toxin at temperatures as low as 38°F (3°C). Consequently, it is important that proper processing techniques are strictly followed to prevent the rare but potentially dangerous growth of *C. botulinum* in smoked fish.

Equipment

The smoked fish industry has realized the need for modernization of its physical facilities. Although this industry has been, and continues to be, quite labor intensive, improvements have been made in materials handling, processing, and packaging. Among the most evident changes are the expansion and improvements in refrigeration and the transition to sophisticated, programmed, and environmentally controlled smoking ovens. However, gravity ovens are still the traditional means of processing smoked fish in the industry today.

With refrigeration, each freezer and cold storage compartment used to store food should be fitted with an indicating thermometer and should have a temperature-recording device installed to show the temperature accurately within the compartment. It also should be fitted with automatic controls for regulating temperature or with an automatic alarm system to indicate a significant temperature change in a manual operation. Thermometers and other temperature measuring devices must have an accuracy of ± 2°F (1.1°C).

Generally, smoked fish have been processed in a traditional smokehouse or in the more consistent mechanical smoking chamber. Many disadvantages are associated with the traditional smokehouse, which is basically a room with a large chimney to vent the smoke and heat, making uniform temperature and smoke control a problem. Cold spots or hot spots occur, making it difficult to produce a consistent batch. In fact, fish sometimes must be shifted to get an even cook and smoke. In addition, traditional smokehouses depend heavily on climatic conditions, so that a product smoked on a cool dry day will not be the same as a product smoked on a warm humid day. Significant adjustments in cooking time and temperature must be made to compensate for weather changes. These gravity smoke ovens, a tradition for more than a century, are being replaced by progressively more sophisticated systems.

Modern smoke ovens vary in size, design, sophistication, and, accordingly, cost. They can be used for both cold- and hot-smoking and can be programmed to control temperature, time, humidity, air circulation, cooking rates, cooling rates, and smoke density in an infinite number of combinations and sequences and can clean themselves when they are emptied. In addition, mechanical smoking usually has a separate smoke generator and, consequently, can introduce the correct amount of smoke evenly over the fish. Many times mechanical smoking can take advantage of electrostatic filters to remove unwanted components in the smoke.

All equipment and utensils used in smoked fish processing plants should be constructed of suitable materials and be designed for adequate cleaning and proper maintenance.

DRIED SALTED FISH

Although not a common commercial seafood product in this country, the process has been described as follows (Burgess et al., 1967): Lean fish, such as cod, are normally used for dry salting. The first step involves splitting the deheaded fish, usually from head to tail along the backbone, and removing the backbone. By splitting the fish, salt penetration is more easily controlled. Salting is done by stacking the fish in layers, alternating each layer with a layer of salt. The pile should be restacked and resalted periodically, to assure a consistent cure. After the fish have cured this way, the fish are in the "green cure" state, at which point the water content has been reduced to two-thirds of its original amount and the salt has penetrated throughout the fish and has saturated the remaining fluids. These green cured fish must now be dried to get the final water content down to 25 to 38 percent. The fish are hung to dry either by using the sun and breeze, or more likely, by artificial means such as warm air circulating within an indoor drying chamber. The final salt content may be as much as one-third the weight of the finished product.

Burgess et al. (1967) give the following description of cured fish. Fatty fish such as herring, mackerel, or anchovies are best suited for brining or curing. First the guts and gills are removed, then the remaining whole fish is packed into barrels or casks, again alternating a layer of fish with a layer of salt. The salt removes water from the fish by osmotic pressure and forms a brine. Removing water from the fish causes the fish to shrink considerably. Consequently, after about ten days of curing, the barrel must be repacked by first draining off excess brine and then adding additional cured fish to make up for the shrinkage. Additional brine may have to be added to displace air introduced as a result of disturbing the barrel. The barrel is tightly capped and sealed. At this point, the fish have been stabilized and are suitable for storage.

Pickled Fish

Pickled fish relt on salt and the action of acetic acid in vinegar for preserving. Prior to shipping to a packing plant, herring, the most popular pickled fish, are normally cured several days in a 80 to 90° S brine with 2.5 percent 120-grain distilled vinegar. They are shipped to the packing plant in barrels with a 70° S brine. The herring may be cut into the desired shape and freshened overnight in water. Prior to packing, the pieces are generally cured three days in a solution containing 3 percent white distilled vinegar and 6 percent salt. The last step is the final cutting and packing into jars with the desired curing solution.

GOVERNMENT REGULATIONS

Obviously, commercially smoking fish requires that a processor meet all state and federal regulations applicable to the general food processing industry. The manufacturing of smoked fish products in the United States is subject to the same general governmental regulations as other foods. If the processor's operation is solely intrastate (within a state), then that state's laws apply; if, on the other hand, the enterprise involves interstate (between states) commerce, compliance with both state and federal law is required.

A brief introduction to the regulatory aspects of manufacturing food, and smoked fish in particular, is considered a prerequisite. It is the manufacturer's responsibility to be familiar with the regulations. The laws and regulations governing the seafood industry are discussed in detail in Title 21, Code of Federal Regulations.

In 1969 the FDA promulgated regulations to establish criteria for current good manufacturing practice (sanitation) in manufacture, processing, packing, or holding human foods (21 CFR 128). This regulation soon became known as the Food GMP. Later that same year, the FDA promulgated a food additive regulation entitled "Sodium nitrite used in processing smoked chub." The regulation not only specifies the limits of use of sodium nitrite in smoked chub (100 to 200 ppm in the loin muscle) but specifies other processing requirements for brining, cooking, and cooling that must be followed if sodium nitrite is used in the product.

In June 1986 the "Food GMP," or "Umbrella GMP," as it was known, was revised. This regulation should be familiar to all those currently in the industry or contemplating being in the smoked fish industry. (*Note:* The FDA has revoked the smoked-fish GMP based on a U.S. Court of Appeals decision.)

Personnel

Compliance with good manufacturing procedures in any food establishment is only as good as that demanded by plant management and supervisory personnel. Food handlers and supervisors should receive appropriate training in proper handling techniques and food protection principles and should be informed of the danger of poor personal hygiene and unsanitary practices. Any person who is ill or has open sores, such as boils or infected wounds, or who might reasonably contaminate food, food-contact surfaces, or food packaging should be excluded from such operations until the condition is corrected.

All persons working in direct contact with food, food-contact surfaces, and food packaging are expected to conform with hygienic practices necessary to protect the food from contamination. Some of these guidelines are as follows:

1. Wear outer garments suitable to the operation.
2. Maintain personal cleanliness.
3. Wash and sanitize hands before starting work and after each absence from the work station.
4. Remove all insecure jewelry and other objects that might fall into the food during preparation.
5. Wear impermeable gloves as appropriate and maintain them in an intact, clean, and sanitary condition.
6. Do not store clothing or other personal belongings in areas where food is exposed or where equipment or utensils are washed.
7. Refrain from eating food, chewing gum, drinking beverages, or using tobacco where food may be exposed or where equipment and utensils are washed.
8. Take any other precautions to avoid contamination of foods, food-contact surfaces, and food packaging.

The National Fisheries Institute has produced a videotape on personal hygiene that should be used for training plant workers.

Building and Facilities

Although no two smoked fish processing plants are the same, they share a number of characteristics. The buildings and facilities of smoked fish processing plants, like all food processing plants, should meet GMP regulations. In the GMP, consideration is given to outside grounds, plant construction and design, general maintenance, substances used in cleaning and sanitizing, storage of toxic materials, pest control, sanitation of food-contact surfaces, and the storage and handling of cleaned equipment and utensils. These regulations also extend to sanitary facilities and controls which include the water supply, plumbing, sewage disposal, toilet facilities, hand-washing facilities, and rubbish and offal disposal.

Plants and Ground

Unloading platforms should be made of readily cleanable materials and equipped with drainage facilities to accommodate all seepage and wash water. In order to prevent cross contamination between raw and finished products, the following processes should be carried out in separate rooms or facilities:

1. Receiving or shipping
2. Storage of raw fish
3. Presmoking operations, including such processes as thawing, dressing, and brining
4. Drying and smoking

Cooling and packaging processes must be carried out in a separate room or facility from the storage of the final product. The product should be processed to prevent contamination by exposure to areas, equipment, or utensils involved in earlier processing, or to refuse or other objectionable areas.

Sanitary Facilities

Adequate hand-washing and sanitizing facilities should be located in the processing room(s) or in one area easily accessible from the processing room(s). Readily understandable signs directing employees to wash and sanitize their hands must be posted conspicuously in the processing room(s) and other appropriate areas. Debris or refuse should not be allowed to accumulate and should be placed in suitable covered containers for removal at least once a day or more frequently if necessary.

Sanitary Operations

Before beginning the day's operation, all utensils and product-contact surfaces of equipment must be rinsed and sanitized. Containers used to convey or store fish should not be nested while they contain fish or otherwise handled during processing or storage whereby their contents may become contaminated. Cleaning and sanitizing utensils and equipment should be conducted in an area designated for these purposes and performed in a manner to prevent contamination of the fish or fish products.

QUALITY CONTROL

A meaningful quality control program should be in effect in every smoked fish processing operation. The program should be under the supervision of knowledgeable management personnel and should encompass all phases of operation from receiving inspection to finished product quality. Appropriate records should be maintained to document incoming raw material, brining procedures, cold-smoking and hot-smoking procedures used with each fish lot, storage temperature monitoring, and quality control or quality assurance testing. Testing should include both microbiological and chemical examination.

Microbial examination of in-line and finished product samples should be conducted with sufficient frequency to assure that processing steps and sanitary procedures are adequate. Microbial evaluation should include total aerobic plate count, *Salmonella* count, and coliform count. The finished product should be chemically analyzed often enough to assure that the fish has the proper salinity content and that sodium nitrite, if used, is present at authorized levels.

As the seafood processing industry embraces the Hazard Analyses Critical Control Point (HACCP) concept as the primary method of achieving processing, sanitation and quality standards, it is evident that this concept will play a major role in the smoked fish industry. HACCP offers a means of assuring consistently produced product that will minimize the microbiological hazards associated with smoked fish.

ACKNOWLEDGMENT

The authors acknowledge and express appreciation for the contributions and suggestions by Dr. George W. Bierman, Herbert V. Shuster, Inc.

REFERENCES

Bankston, D. *Brine Freezers*. Marine Advisory Leaflet, Louisiana Cooperative Extension Service, Louisiana State University.

Bannerman, A. McK. 1980. *Hot Smoking of Fish.* Torry Advisory Note No. 82. Ministry of Agriculture, Fisheries and Food. Torry Research Station, Aberdeen, Scotland.

Berg, I. I. 1965. *Smokehouses and the Smoke Curing of Fish.* Olympia, WA: Washington State Department of Fisheries.

Bradley, R. L., Dunn, C. M., Mennes, M. E., and Stuiber, D. A. 1977. *Home Smoking and Pickling of Fish.* Pub. No. 2000-318A009-77. The University of Wisconsin Sea Grant Program.

Burgess, G. H. O., Cutting, C. L., Lovern, J. A., and Waterman, J. J. 1967. *Fish Handling & Processing.* New York: Chermical Publishing Company.

Childs, E. A., Al-Dabbagh, F., Sanders, O. G., and Sheddan, T. L. 1976 (July, August, September). "Techniques for Smoking Rough Fish." *Tennessee Farm and Home Science.*

Crance, J. H. 1955. *Smoked Fish.* Texas A&M University. Fact Sheet #L-1043.

Dougherty, J. B., and Seagran, H. L. 1967. *Steps to Effective Sanitation in Smoked-Fish Plants.* Washington, DC: Bureau of Commercial Fisheries.

Dudley, S., Graikoski, J. T., Seagran, H. L., and Earl, P. M., 1973. *Sportsman's Guide to Handling, Smoking and Preserving Coho Salmon.* Fishery Facts—5. National Marine Fisheries Service Extension Publication.

Eklund, M. W. 1982. "Significance of *Clostridium botulinum* in Fishery Products Preserved Short of Sterilization." *Food Technology.* 12:107.

Hilderbrand, K. S. 1980. *Smoking Fish at Home—Safely.* SG 66. Oregon State University, Extension Marine Advisory Program.

Otwell, W. S., Koburger, J. A., and Degner, R. L. 1980. *Low Temperature Smoked Fish Fillets: A Potential New Product Form for Florida Fish.* Tech. paper No. 19. Florida Sea Grant.

Paparella, M. 1979 (January). *Information Tips.* University of Maryland Sea Grant.

Price, R. J., and York, G. K. 1980. *Smoking Fish at Home.* Leaflet 2669. Division of Agricultural Sciences, University of California.

Processed Fishery Products—Annual Summaries. 1986. U. S. Department of Commerce, National Oceanic and Atmospheric Administration, National Marine Fisheries Service. Washington, DC.

Richards, J. B., and Price, R. J. 1979. *Smoked Shark and Shark Jerky.* Leaflet 21121. Division of Agricultural Sciences, University of California.

Troller, J. A., and Christian, J. H. B. 1978. *Water Activity and Food.* New York: Academic Press.

Waters, M. E., and Bond, D. J. 1960. "Construction and Operation of an Inexpensive Fish Smokehouse." *Commercial Fisheries Review.* 22(8):8.

CHAPTER

23

Transportation, Distribution, and Warehousing

Roy E. Martin

Through the efforts of everyone associated with it, the American food supply has become the best, safest, and cleanest in the world. The public has come to expect such high standards. It thus becomes the everyday responsibility of people in many diverse industries to see that our food is produced, processed, and packed under clean conditions and that it is kept that way throughout the distribution chain. The public health ramifications of handling shipments of food and related products demand that each and every employee accept these as very special categories of commodities and learn to handle them as such.

TRANSPORTATION

As shippers and receivers the industry uses truck, rail, and air to move shipments of seafood. The FDA states under its Good Transportation Practices Model Code that establishments engaged in the processing, packing, and storage of human food are subject to comprehensive government regulations which require that the food be prepared, packed, and held under sanitary conditions. With few exceptions, persons engaged in transporting food are only indirectly subject to these controls. Compliance with the regulations described here should assist those of you in the transportation industry in assuring that foods for human consumption are handled and shipped under conditions that (1) prevent contamination; (2) protect against product deterioration and container damage, and (3) assure that conveyances intended, offered, or used for transporting food are suitable for that purpose.

The criteria in these regulations apply in determining whether conveyances, appurtenances, storage facilities, methods, practices, and controls used in transporting food are in conformance with, or are operated or administered in conformity with, good transportation practices. These regulations apply to all persons engaged in the transportation of human foods, including manufacturers, processors, distributors, common carriers, contract haulers, and private individuals. Conveyances when used solely for the purpose of transporting raw agricultural commodities from the field to a point of initial storage and/or processing are excluded from the requirements of these regulations, provided that special regulations covering these exclusions may be adopted whenever necessary to protect the public health.

FDA defines the following transportable classes of food: (1) "Perishable food" is food which includes, but is not limited to, fresh fruits, fresh fish, fresh vegetables, and other products which need protection from extremes of temperatures in order to avoid decomposition by microbial growth or otherwise; (2) "Readily perishable food" is food or a food ingredient consisting in whole or part of milk, milk products, eggs, meat, fish, poultry, or other food or food ingredient which is capable of supporting rapid and progressive growth of infectious or toxigenic microorganisms; and (3) "Frozen food" is food which is processed and preserved by freezing in accordance with good commercial practices and which is intended to be sold in the frozen state.

Other definitions used in the code include the following:

"Delivery equipment" means any truck, railcar, ship, barge, aircraft, or other conveyance together with its appurtenances, used or offered for the transportation of food.

"Special purpose delivery equipment" means those conveyances that are not designed for general purpose transportation but are built specifically for the handling of foodstuffs and which in themselves may be immediate containers.

"Storage facility" means any warehouse, freight terminal, or other storage facility, including all loading docks and other appurtenances associated with and used in the storage of food during transportation.

"Carrier" is any person who owns, operates, or controls delivery equipment or storage facilities.

"Shipper" is any person of record who initiates the transportation of food from one place to another.

"Carrier controlled equipment" means any delivery equipment, the movement of which is controlled exclusively by a common carrier or contract hauler.

"Shipper controlled equipment" means any delivery equipment which the carrier has assigned to a shipper for his exclusive use.

"Sanitize" means adequate treatment of surfaces by a process that effectively destroys cells of pathogenic microorganisms and substantially reduces other microorganisms. Such treatment shall not adversely affect the product and shall be safe for the consumer.

"Adequate" means that which is needed to accomplish the intended purpose in keeping with good public health practice.

Delivery Equipment Design and Construction

All delivery equipment shall be constructed of material that will withstand repeated cleaning and shall be designed to be easily cleaned and to protect the food being handled from dust, dirt, and other contaminating materials. In addition, delivery equipment used or intended for handling perishable food shall be constructed to protect such food from temperatures which may cause or permit damage.

Special purpose delivery equipment used for transportation of processed or partially processed bulk food shall be constructed of smooth, corrosion-resistant, nontoxic materials, and shall be so designed and constructed as to be easily cleanable.

Delivery equipment used to handle readily perishable food requiring refrigeration, in addition to the requirements just outlined, shall be provided with mechanical aeration equipment or other methods or facilities capable of maintaining a product temperature of 45°F (7°C) or below. Delivery equipment used for handling frozen food shall be capable of maintaining the product temperature at 0°F (–18°C) or lower.

Delivery equipment used for delivery of readily perishable or of frozen foods shall be equipped with a thermometer or other appropriate means for measuring and indicating the air temperature in the shipping compartment. The dial or reading element of the temperature measuring device must be located where it can be easily read from the outside of the conveyance.

Preloading Controls

All conveyances which are under the carrier's control and are offered to shippers for the purpose of transporting food shall, at time of delivery, be in a clean and sanitary condition, be in good repair, and be of adequate design and construction for the intended purpose. The carrier shall take all reasonable precautions, including the following, to assure that such conveyances will not contribute to contamination or deterioration of food products.

1. Effective measures shall be taken to remove and exclude all vermin (including, but not limited to birds, rodents, and insects). The use of pesticides for this purpose shall include precautions to prevent contamination of food or packaging material with illegal chemical residues.
2. The interior of each conveyance shall be cleaned as needed to ensure removal of all debris, filth, mold, toxic chemicals, undesirable odors, or any other objectionable condition that may result in the contamination of food. When appropriate to control microbiological contamination, food-contact surfaces shall be sanitized with a safe and effective sanitizing agent.
3. All doors and hatches shall be kept in good repair, be tight fitting, and when closed and sealed shall be capable of excluding rodents, birds, and other pests.
4. All refrigeration equipment shall be in proper working condition, and capable of holding transported food products at temperatures specified by the shipper.
5. Except in the case of assigned equipment, the carrier at time of delivery shall certify to the shipper that the equipment has been inspected in accordance with and conforms to these regulations. Such inspection records shall be retained by the carrier for one year from the date of issuance.

The shipper shall inspect all equipment offered or intended for food loading to determine if said equipment is in acceptable physical condition or whether it contains any potential food contaminant. The shipper shall refrain from loading food into any equipment deemed unacceptable until such time as all noted defects are corrected. When defects noted in carrier-controlled equipment cannot be corrected at the shipper's plant, the shipper shall reject such defective equipment to the carrier, stating the reasons for said rejection. The shipper shall maintain inspection records of all defects that cause equipment to be rejected and shall maintain such records for one year.

Loading Controls

Food products to be loaded shall be free from contaminants which may contribute to adulteration during transit of other products in the load or which may result in the contamination of the conveyance.

All packaged food products shall be loaded in such a manner as to minimize physical damage while in transit.

All containers used for transporting food shall be of such design and construction to protect the contents from damage and/or contamination under usual conditions of loading, shipment, and transshipment.

In the loading of food products, adequate precautions shall be taken to minimize contamination of the vehicle through hatches, pipes, hoses, vents, conveyors, or other potential routes of contamination. Food products shall not be loaded into the same vehicle or shipped with fungicides, insecticides, rodenticides, or any other poisonous, toxic, or deleterious industrial chemicals.

Before and after closing doors or hatches of the loaded conveyance, persons responsible for the loading operation shall take all other precautions as may be appropriate to protect the integrity of both the vehicle and its contents.

The transshipment and en route storage of food products should be under such conditions as will prevent contamination and will protect against undesirable deterioration of the product or containers.

Unloading Controls

All incoming conveyances shall be carefully examined upon arrival at the delivery point to determine if doors or hatches are intact and untampered. Where appropriate, the seal numbers of the doors and hatches shall be recorded prior to their removal. Any broken or damaged seals shall be noted and reported to the carrier.

Upon opening and prior to unloading of the food, the interior of the conveyance shall be examined for evidence of any detectable signs of potential contaminants and adulterants including but not limited to insects, rodents, mold, or undesirable odors. This examination shall continue during the entire unloading operation.

Before unloading refrigerated products, the internal temperature of the food products shall be taken and recorded.

A record shall be kept indicating the type and disposition of damaged, adulterated, and deteriorated products or conveyance. Such record shall indicate the disposition of the defective products and/or conveyance.

All food products, dunnage, debris, and other materials connected with the inbound shipment shall be completely removed from the conveyance before returning or releasing such conveyance to the carrier.

Special Handling and Protection of Perishable, Readily Perishable, and Frozen Foods

All perishable foods shall be protected at all times from extremes of temperature that may cause or permit damage or deterioration of the food.

All readily perishable food shall be transported and handled in transit at a product temperature of 45°F (7°C) or lower, except that during loading and unloading the product temperature shall not exceed 60°F (17°C).

All frozen food shall be transported and handled in transit at a product temperature of 0°F (–18°C) or lower, except that during defrost cycles, loading and unloading such product temperature shall not exceed 10°F (–10°C).

Any variation from these temperature limits due to failure or faulty operation of temperature control equipment during transportation should be reported by the carrier to the nearest office charged with enforcing these regulations.

Special Concerns: Railcars

Because of the special nature of food, there are now evolving special categories of railcars for use with food shipments. Of particular interest, in relation to these guidelines, is the XF boxcar. This car, specially prepared with an easily cleaned, FDA-approved interior white coating, can be effective in protecting food shipments if it is maintained in good condition. All users of these specialized railcars should realize that extra care in maintaining the condition and cleanliness of this equipment is an investment in protecting the food supply.

Three types of railcars are used to transport food: the free-running car; the car dedicated to food or related-product service; and the car assigned to the use of a particular shipper. Although there are some differences in the specific responsibilities of shippers, carriers, and receivers when different cars are considered, the basic principles remain the same. A car must be clean and in good repair in order to protect the food.

A *clean car* is free from evidence of vermin infestation (including but not limited to birds, rodents, and insects); and free from debris, filth, visible mold, undesirable odors, and evidence of residues of toxic chemicals. A car in *good repair* should have structurally sound interiors and exteriors, including doors and hatches that are tight-fitting and, when closed and sealed, are capable of excluding rodents, birds, and other pests.

For many new users of railcar service, and for some experienced users, questions arise over who takes responsibility for certain activities involved in transporting food by rail. The following information is intended to provide guidance as to what the shipper, carrier, and receiver is responsible for.

Ordering a car(s) is the shipper's responsibility, of course. The shipper should place car orders with the appropriate railroad personnel, specifying in each order

1. type and size car required (e.g., Class A—50′ boxcar, airslide car, etc.);
2. The commodity to be loaded;
3. Whether commodity is bulk or packaged;
4. Date required;
5. Location (track and door number if applicable) where car is to be spotted; and
6. Load destination and route (if known).

Furnishing Car

Where cars are required for transportation of food or related items, the carrier is responsible for furnishing cars suitable for the intended purpose and for providing cars that are in a clean condition, in good repair, and of adequate design and construction for the intended purpose.

In furnishing free-running cars, the carrier must take necessary precautions to ensure that the car is suitable for the intended purpose. Where cars are dedicated to food or related product category use, the carrier is to furnish cars with doors and hatches closed and sealed.

Although most responsibilities in furnishing cars falls on the carrier, the shipper does assume one responsibility: Where a car is assigned to a shipper's exclusive use, the shipper must inspect and maintain the car in a clean and sanitary condition.

Car Loading

It is the shipper's responsibility to inspect all railcars offered or intended for loading to determine if they are clean and in good repair. Shippers should refrain from loading any railcar deemed unsuitable until such time as all noted defects that may contribute to contamination are corrected. Such defects may include

1. Damage to floors, walls, ceilings, doors, and hatches;
2. Protruding nails or bolts;
3. Dunnage, trash, or other debris;
4. Residue of prior loading;
5. Evidence of contamination by prior toxic material loading;
6. Vermin infestation or visible mold; and
7. Objectionable odors.

Whenever defects noted in a railcar are not corrected at the shipper's plant, the shipper should reject the defective railcar to the rail carrier, stating the reasons for rejection, and maintain inspection records of all defects causing railcars to be rejected.

The shipper should load only products which are themselves uncontaminated and are free from substances or components which are likely to contribute to contamination of other products in the load during transit or are likely to result in contamination of the railcar. All packaged food products are to be appropriately packaged and loaded in order to minimize physical damage or contamination under reasonable transportation conditions and procedures.

In the loading of products, shippers should take adequate precautions to minimize contamination of the railcar through hatches, pipes, hoses, vents, conveyors, or other potential routes of contamination. They also must see that persons responsible for the loading operation take all other precautions, as may be appropriate, to protect the integrity of both the transportation equipment and its contents. Once the car is loaded, the shipper is responsible for closing and sealing all doors and hatches and then tendering the billing instructions to the carrier.

Car Transporting and Delivery

The carrier should remove the car(s) from shipper's siding and transport cars to destination with all due care for the integrity of the lading. The carrier also must use reasonable diligence to prevent unauthorized entry into cars and maintain all seals intact and all doors and/or hatches secured.

In the event of derailment or other type of major accident or damage, natural catastrophe (such as a flood), or detection of unauthorized entry into car, it is the carrier's responsibility to notify shipper and receiver promptly.

Once the car has reached its destination, the carrier will notify the receiver that the car has arrived and will spot the car according to receiver's instructions. The carrier also will notify the receiver if a car is in shipper's assigned service or is dedicated to food or related product category use.

Car Unloading

The receiver is responsible for examining all incoming railcars carefully to determine if doors, hatches, and seals are intact and untampered with. Whoever is inspecting the cars should record the seal numbers of the doors and hatches prior to their removal, and the receiver should note any broken or damaged seals and report such findings to the rail carrier and shipper.

Once these steps are completed, but before unloading begins, the receiver should examine the railcar's exposed interior for any evidence of potential contaminants and adulterants including but not limited to insects, rodents, mold, or undesirable odors. Continue this examination during the entire unloading operation. In the event contaminants and/or adulterants are noted,

1. Notify rail carrier to make an inspection and provide an inspection report.
2. Notify shipper for disposition.
3. Where the shipment contains contamination or damage which could lead to contamination of the receiver's establishment, do not permit the product to enter the building; in other cases, separate damaged or contaminated product from the remainder of the load.
4. Keep a record indicating the type and disposition of damaged, adulterated, and deteriorated product, and of railcar.

Before releasing a car to the carrier as an "empty," the receiver must completely remove all products, including damaged or refused product, dunnage, debris, and other materials connected with the inbound shipment from the railcar. Two additional steps that should be completed before the car is released to the carrier are (1) reporting all contamination, physical damage, or other conditions incompatible with further use of the car for food and related products to the carrier, and (2) replacing and/or securing all bulkheads and other appurtenances that are a part of the railcar.

Once these prerelease conditions are met, the receiver should close all doors and hatches. If a car is in a shipper's assigned service or is dedicated to food or related product service, the receiver should seal the car after complete unloading.

Removing Empty Car and Subsequent Handling

It is the carrier's responsibility to determine that the car has been completely unloaded and emptied as required. A car sealed by the receiver is considered to have been completely unloaded and emptied. The carrier should not remove a car if it is not completely unloaded and free from product, dunnage, or other debris.

If the carrier is notified by the receiver that a car contains contamination or physical damage, it must take necessary action for cleaning and/or upgrading the car before returning it to food or related product category use.

Special Concerns: Air Shipping

With approximately 6 billion pounds (2.72×10^9 kg) of seafood currently shipped by air, the air cargo industry is responsible for transporting about 4 percent of the world's annual catch of approximately 154 billion pounds (69.9×10^9 kg) of seafood. Forecasts suggest that in the coming decades the air cargo industry can expect a growing demand for air shipment of fish and seafood.

Air transport provides the essential link between landlocked communities and the world's great fishing ports. However, successful air transport of fishery products requires special care in preparation and handling of the shipments, and excellent communication among the shipper, carrier, and consignee. This section contains voluntary guidelines—developed through the cooperation of the Air Transport Association of America (ATA) and the National Fisheries Institute (NFI)—for the handling, packaging, and acceptance of fresh fish and seafood.

Prospective shippers need to keep a number of issues in mind. Narrow-body aircraft are common in U.S. fleets, as are hub airports that may necessitate cargo transfers under tight schedules. In addition, the reliance on combination passenger-cargo aircraft in many markets, as well as volatility in pricing, entry, and exit in all markets can influence the transport of fishery products. Finally, and most importantly, the air shipment of improperly packaged fishery products is a safety hazard because of potential damage to the interiors and control mechanisms of aircraft. In one recorded case, for example, a major U.S. carrier removed an aircraft from service for an entire week, spending $750,000 to repair damage that resulted from leaking seafood packages.

For prospective seafood shippers, these factors mean that air carriers must seek to eliminate leakage from seafood shipments. In addition, airlines are likely to require shipments packed in lighter-weight units that can be transferred easily and handled manually within the confines of the smaller aircraft in a carrier's fleet. Many airlines will prefer gross weight limits of 60 to 80 pounds (27 to 36 kg), although individual carriers will accept units of 100 to 150 pounds (45 to 68 kg) or perhaps more.

The air shipping environment is the sum of all conditions affecting a shipment: scheduling, weather, shock variables, handling techniques and equipment, and vulnerability to theft and pilferage. A prospective shipper must follow an approach to packaging, handling, and tendering seafood for air transport that accounts for all aspects of this environment. These ATA/NFI voluntary guidelines seek to assist prospective shippers by guiding them in the selection of packaging materials and development of practices to preserve their perishable but highly valuable cargo in prime condition through air shipment to final destination, and to prevent leakage and damage to expensive aircraft interiors, other cargo, or passenger baggage that may result.

ATA and NFI recognize that many suitable packaging systems have been developed for air transport of fishery products. These guidelines are not intended to exclude the use of proven shipping containers or those that may be developed in the future. Therefore, if a shipping container that lies outside the scope of these guidelines is being considered, the shipper must communicate with the carrier to establish whether the packaging is acceptable for its intended use.

General Considerations for Packing

Whole or dressed fish should be cooled to 32°F (0°C) before packing. Several practices are used to reduce temperatures, including icing, brine chilling, and other chilling methods. Time is a major factor when reducing product temperature because cooling is a gradual process; therefore, random temperature checks are recommended regardless of the cooling method used. By cooling fish, a shipper can slow spoilage and reduce the melting of the refrigerant used in shipping containers.

Prechilling of shipping containers before packing will prevent fish from absorbing heat from the packaging. Take care to avoid overfilling the package, which increases the risk of damaging product, the package itself, and the aircraft during shipment. When packed in shipping containers, all fish should be near 32°F (0°C).

The temperature of packed fish can be effectively maintained but not easily reduced; therefore, packing procedures should be quick and efficient to minimize temperature rise. Coolants, such as gel refrigerants, dry ice, and wet ice sealed in polyethylene bags, should be placed along the bottom and at the top of the container to absorb heat from the outside. Poor placement of coolant will reduce its effectiveness (see Fig. 23-1). An absorbent pad should be placed in the package to absorb possible leakage, unless packaging design ensures that liquids cannot escape.

Fish packed for shipment should be placed on vehicles as soon as possible for

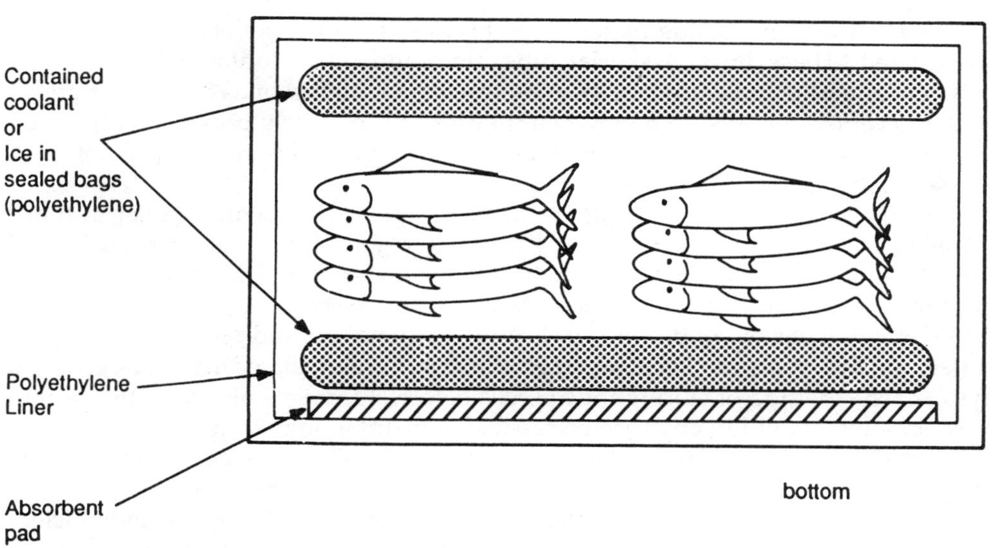

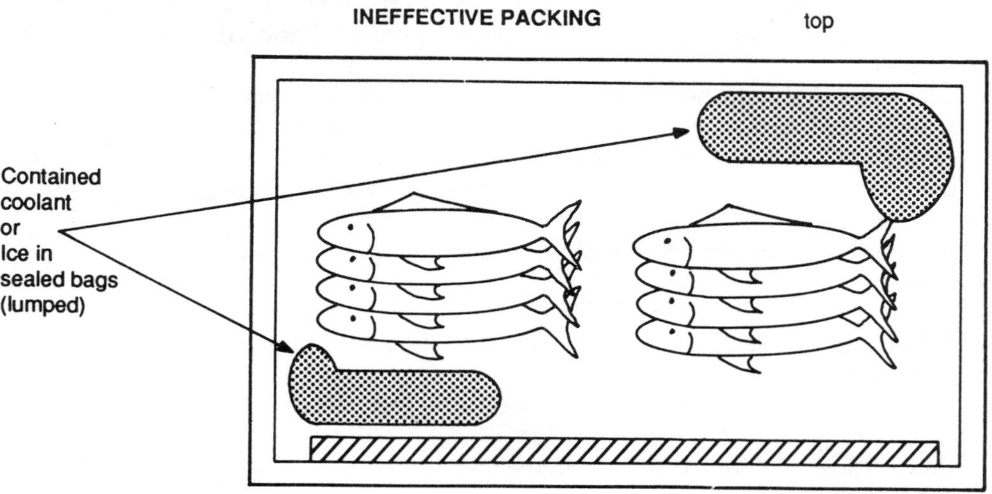

Figure 23-1. Example of Proper Packaging.

transport to the airport. If a delay is anticipated, it is recommended that packages be placed in refrigerated storage. However, even when held in refrigeration, the time between packing and shipment should be minimized.

As with whole and dressed fish, handling procedures for fillets should be rapid and well organized. Fillets cut from small and medium-sized fish are not very thick and although this means that they chill very quickly, it also means that they warm up rapidly as well. The need to precool fillets to 32°F (0°C) before packing is equally important as with whole and dressed fish. In some cases, fillets may be chilled by brief immersion in ice water. Chilling by short exposure to subfreezing temperatures is another satisfactory cooling method, but care should be taken to avoid freezing the fillets.

A wide variety of packing materials and styles of packing fillets for distribution are utilized. These include special tubs, tins, and other containers, as well as polyethylene bags, polyethylene sleeves, tray packs, and so on. These styles are all widely accepted for air shipment when they are subsequently packed and handled by methods and in shipping containers similar to those described for whole and dressed fish.

The successful air shipment of live seafood depends on factors similar to those involved in whole/dressed fish and fillets. However, there are some additional considerations because the product is live. For instance, adequate air for live product is essential. *Do not seal bags containing live seafood.*

One general set of conditions applies to the handling and shipping of a wide variety of live seafood, such as crabs, lobsters, crawfish, clams, mussels, and oysters. The method of storing the animals before shipments may vary by shipper or species but should in any case be capable of maintaining temperatures between 34 and 45°F (2 and 7°C). The cool temperature beneficially slows body metabolisms. Only the healthiest of animals should be selected for shipment.

As with other fishery products, packing procedures should be quick and efficient to minimize handling time and temperature rise. Refrigerants should be placed at the bottom of containers, and a layer of moist packing material (burlap, seaweed, and synthetic products are common) placed over the refrigerant to protect the animals from direct contact with refrigerant and provide the high relative humidity needed to prevent mortality. Both the packing material and container should be prechilled.

Live seafood should be carefully packed in successive layers. The final layer of animals should be topped with a layer of moist packing material. Generally, it is recommended that an additional layer of refrigerant be added before closing the container. Once packed, the same considerations for shipment of whole/dressed fish and fillets apply.

A summary of important handling and packing considerations for all seafood follows:

1. Select appropriate packing materials according to durability, watertightness, and insulation.
2. Prechill product before packing to preserve low temperatures for as long as possible.
3. Prechill live seafood to reduce body metabolism. Adequate air for live product is essential. *Do not seal bags containing live seafood.*
4. Choose proper cooling media, for example, gel refrigerant, wet ice in sealed bags, or dry ice (check regulatory compliance for dry ice).

5. Place cooling media to absorb heat entering package from top and bottom.
6. Minimize time between packing and shipment.

Fish and Seafood Acceptance by Air Carriers

Acceptable Weights per Box or Carton

Differences in the kinds of aircraft and ground support equipment used by the various air carriers require that each airline have its own limitations on weight and dimensions of acceptable shipments. The most common maximum acceptable weight per box for carriage on passenger aircraft is 150 pounds (68 kg); however, many airlines have the capability to accept heavier weights per box or container and some have lower acceptable weights. A shipper's ability to pack in 60- to 80-pound (27 to 36 kg) increments facilitates handling in aircraft. In designing containers for heavier weights, provision should be made for a pallet base to accommodate a forklift. Shippers should verify each carrier's limitations on size and weight of containers.

Acceptable Refrigerants and Insulation

Most air carriers prefer that shippers use chemical coolants or dry ice; however, many air carriers will also accept wet ice if it is contained in sealed polyethylene bags. Information on acceptable refrigerants may be obtained from each carrier. (*Note:* Under normal conditions, wet ice by itself will melt five times faster than chemical/gel type refrigerants.)

The refrigerant used, in combination with insulation, should protect product for the length of exposure to ambient temperatures, taking into consideration the time required for consignee pickup. Additional protection should be provided for shipments requiring transfer to connecting carriers because of longer transit times, possible exposure to higher temperatures, more frequent handling, weather delays, and so on. Every attempt is made to keep seafood shipments refrigerated at airport facilities; however, because of differences in available facilities, refrigeration cannot be guaranteed without specific arrangements, thus making proper insulation essential.

With regard to insulation, the following selected materials are listed in descending order of their ability to insulate:

1. Urethane foam
2. Polystyrene foam
3. Shredded paper
4. Double-wall corrugated cardboard
5. Excelsior

(*Note:* The insulating abilities of materials are additive, so that a packaging system assembled of various components, e.g., a fiberboard box with expanded polystyrene inserts, would have insulation properties from the EPS (expanded polystyrene) and a small amount from the fiberboard.)

Dry Ice

Because it transforms from solid to gaseous carbon dioxide, dry ice has the ability to displace oxygen in enclosed spaces such as aircraft interiors and cargo holds.

Dry ice is therefore considered dangerous goods for air transport, even when used as a refrigerant, and is subject to parts of the governmental regulations controlling dangerous goods. Among these controls are restrictions on placing packages containing dry ice in compartments with live animals, such as pets accompanying passengers.

A shipper who uses dry ice must comply with specific governmental regulations, which specify that packages containing dry ice be designed to permit carbon dioxide gas to escape without rupturing the package. In addition, shippers using dry ice must supply specific information on the air waybill (these special requirements are discussed in detail later) and mark the net quantity of dry ice on each package (see the next section on Markings and Labelings). It is strongly suggested that a shipper make advance arrangements with the carrier when the net quantity of dry ice exceeds 5 pounds (2.3 kg) per package. This information is essential, as carriers must notify pilots of the presence of dangerous goods and must obey federal regulations restricting the total amount of dry ice to 440 pounds (200 kg) per inaccessible cargo compartment. By stating this information on the air waybill and marking it on the outside of each package, shippers enable carriers to determine the total amount of dry ice present in all shipments aboard an aircraft.

External Markings and Labeling

Seafood transported as air cargo should be identified on the outside of the carton by markings or labels which state, PERISHABLE SEAFOOD or PERISHABLE FISH.

Arrows, such as the ISO standard arrows or THIS SIDE UP markings, should be used to indicate the upright position. Also, packages containing live product should carry special LIVE SEAFOOD warnings for extra care in handling.

It is essential that complete contact information be displayed on the outside of the carton. Contact information should include a twenty-four-hour telephone number for the shipper, which should also be included on the air waybill. Labels should be designed to adhere to the external surface material. Indicate on the outside of the package whether the contents are LIVE, FRESH, or FROZEN.

In addition to the preceding guidelines, there are special dry ice marking requirements. According to governmental regulations, the net weight of dry ice (carbon dioxide, solid) must be marked on the outside of each package in which it is used as a refrigerant, so that carriers may monitor the quantity of dry ice loaded aboard their aircraft. For example, a package containing 5 pounds of dry ice should be marked DRY ICE, UN 1845, NET WEIGHT 5 LBS. (*Note:* Some states require that the name of the species and total weight of each species be stated on the shipping unit.)

Additional marking requirements may be imposed in the United States under the Federal Lacey Act Amendments of 1981 [16 USC 3376(a) (2)]. Rules have been proposed (51 FR 24559) which would require containers of fish to be marked with the term FISH or the common name of the species, and be accompanied with a "readily accessible" document containing the following information:

1. Name and address of the shipper and consignee;
2. Total number of packages in the shipment;
3. Common name of each species in the shipment;
4. Number or weight of each species in the shipment.

The term *fish* as defined in the Lacey Act encompasses shellfish as well as other types of fish. The marking/labeling guidelines described in these guidelines are subject to change in accordance with the issuance of final federal regulations.

Banding

Banding and other types of external sealing materials should be designed not to cut or damage the container or other packages with which it may come into contact. Cartons should have a minimum of two bands around the width of each box.

Factors Involved in Packaging Design

Inside Packaging

Inside the box, the product should be completely enclosed in a sealed polyethylene bag of sufficient thickness to resist puncture and retain liquids. A polyethylene bag of at least 3 mil, or two bags of 2 mil should be sufficient. In special cases, polyethylene bags may be omitted if container design ensures against leakage (i.e., combinations of paper/fiberboard, and molded EPS). In appropriate cases, protective padding, absorbent materials, or wrapping such as seaweed or EPS inserts should be used to assure a puncture-proof inner package. Exposed fins, claws, or other sharp objects should never be in direct contact with an inner bag.

Adequate absorbent material or padding should be used between the sealed polyethylene product bag and the inner wall of the outer packaging, unless packaging design ensures that liquids cannot escape.

Polyethylene bags containing product (excluding live shellfish) should be large enough to overlap and fold closed. Polyethylene bags used for live seafood must not be sealed.

Outside Packaging

Outer boxes should be constructed of corrugated paper board or solid fiberboard. In some cases, the various plies of paperboard should be wax-saturated, impregnated, wax-coated, or treated by other water-resistant processes. Treatments or coatings to the paperboard are necessary to provide wet-strength in case of exposure to moisture. A gussetted style is recommended whenever container design permits.

Containers of molded expanded polystyrene are virtually leakproof. However, the combination of a corrugated box and a molded foam box is recommended. Of course, other methods of combining insulation, leakproofness, and external strength are acceptable.

Box and container design should take account of the density of the product to be transported. The ability to withstand the strain of dense inside weight is as important as the ability to withstand external compression and strains. External puncture-resistance is critical to assuring that the shipping container will remain leakproof in transportation. The complete package (i.e., the assembly of all package components) should be designed to withstand shock, handling, and stacking to at least five units high without damage to the package. [*Note:* Governmental regulations require that packages containing dry ice be designed to release carbon dioxide gas. In general, this is not a problem with seafood shipments, since leakproof container designs are not normally airtight. A possible exception is when "barrier" (gas-impermeable) bags are used inside containers of vacuum or modified atmosphere stored shipments; for these packages, dry ice is not recommended.]

Shipments in Unit Load Devices (ULDs)

Shippers should contact individual carriers for specific policy on accepting and loading shipments packed in ULDs (large shipping containers).

Transportation from Packing House to Airport

Complete package design should provide conditions suitable for maintaining the product temperature as near as possible to 32°F (0°C). It is essential that the packaged fish reach the airport quickly. Transporting shipments in refrigerated or insulated vehicles is useful when packages may be exposed to elevated temperatures and/or when long trips to the airport are expected. Packages should be loaded in transport vehicles so as to minimize movement and susceptibility to dropping. In addition, any stacks of seafood packages should be planned to avoid tilted or overhanging boxes that would place undue stress on any package structure. Methods and equipment used to load and unload shipments must protect package integrity.

Although advance arrangements are not essential for all seafood shipments, they are advisable for large loads. The carrier will be better able to accommodate such a shipment if advance arrangements have been made.

Air Waybill

Inclusion of a twenty-four-hour telephone number of the shipper is essential on the air waybill, as well as on the container.

Information about the contents of shipments, such as whether the seafood is live, fresh, or frozen should be noted in the "Handling Information" box of the air waybill. Other details, such as in the following examples for use of coolers, should also be stated in the Handling Information box:

"In case of delay, please refrigerate if available."
"Hold in cooler for pickup, if available."

Limits of liability are shown in the carrier's "Contract for Carriage" on the air waybill. Such limits vary among carriers, and shippers may wish to declare the value of a shipment for insurance above the carrier's limits. There is an additional charge for such declarations.

Air Waybill Requirements for Dry Ice

Dry ice, when shipped by air, is considered a dangerous good. (See comments on dry ice and special marking requirements for dry ice.)

No "Shipper's Declaration for Dangerous Goods" form (a special dangerous goods air waybill) is required when dry ice is used as a refrigerant. Instead, the normal air waybill must be filled out so that the entry for handling information shows the words "Dangerous Goods—Shipper's Declaration Not Required." The entry for the "Nature and Quantity of Goods" box should describe the seafood and present the following dangerous goods information (in this sequence):

1. Proper shipping name for the dangerous goods, which in this case is either "carbon dioxide, solid (dry ice)" or "dry ice"
2. Hazard class or division number for the dry ice, which is "9";
3. UN identification number for the dry ice, which is "UN1845";
4. The number of packages containing dry ice;
5. Net quantity of dry ice per package;
6. UN Packing Group for the dry ice, which is "III."

For example, the entry in the "Nature and Quantity of Goods" box for a shipment of four packages of fresh fish, each containing 5 pounds of dry ice, would read: "FRESH FISH, DRY ICE 9 UN 1845, 4 × 5 lbs III."

Seafood Claims

Every effort is made by the air carrier to meet delivery needs and arrival notification within operational constraints. However, if an unforeseen delay or other problem results in a delayed shipment a consignee should nevertheless be prepared to take delivery and remember that settlement procedures exist for resolution of any claims following final delivery of the cargo. Where there is a potential for a loss, all relevant records should be kept.

Final Delivery

As with tendering to the air carrier from the packing house, timely delivery of the seafood shipment from the air carrier to the consignee is vital to assuring freshness of the seafood and ultimately to assuring customer satisfaction.

Conclusions

ATA and NFI believe that use of the guidelines described will promote customer satisfaction in the seafood shipping, packaging manufacture, and air transport industries. With packaging that meets the needs of the air transport environment and with shipments prepared to stay in prime condition through the journey, air carriers can provide the key link to delivering quality products to distant markets.

DISTRIBUTORS THAT TAKE OWNERSHIP OF PRODUCT

To ensure product wholesomeness and proper sanitation, the food distributor must have the commitment of top management, and that commitment must be implemented by operating supervision and supported by the entire food distribution staff. Preventive sanitation—the performance of inspection, sanitation, building maintenance, and pest control functions designed to prevent insanitation in preference to correcting it—should be an important goal of food distribution management and of food distribution operations.

Organization and Programs

A program to ensure continued success in safeguarding the wholesomeness of food and in providing good sanitation will ordinarily include

1. An organizational chart showing chain of authority and responsibility.
2. A flow diagram of receiving, storage, and shipping operations.
3. Regular maintenance schedules.

4. Regular sanitation programs.
5. Regular pest control programs.
6. An effective program of follow-up and control including reports to responsible executive officer(s).

Checkpoints and Additional Guides

Grounds

1. Keep nearby grounds free of liquid or solid emissions that could be sources of contamination.
2. Prevent grounds from providing conditions for insect or rodent harborage.
3. Check paving, drainage, weed, and litter control regularly.
4. Stack materials which are stored in the open neatly and away from buildings and on racks above ground level where feasible.
5. No-vegetation strips around exterior building walls and at property lines adjacent to properties containing potential harborages are helpful for discovering and discouraging travel by rodents.

Buildings

1. Provide separate and sufficient space for placement of equipment and storage of materials necessary for proper operations.
2. Separate activities that might cause contamination of stored foods by chemicals, filth, or other harmful material.
3. Check structural conditions, pest barriers, repair of windows, screens, and doors continuously.
4. Seal and clean floor-and-wall junctions and fill holes and cracks; a painted inspection strip is also recommended.
5. Keep offices, including overhead offices, clean and do not permit them to become attractants or harborages for insects or vermin. Include them in the pest control program.
6. Check false ceilings for harborage of insects and possibly rodents.
7. Give basements, attics, elevators, and rail sidings special attention.

Sanitary Operations

1. Keep walls, ceilings, and rafters free of soil, insect webbing, mold, and similar materials.
2. Do not leave unscreened doors and windows open unnecessarily.
3. Do not permit dust to accumulate.
4. Keep floors free of product spillage, oil drippage, and buildup in all areas.
5. Provide proper trash and refuse storage and removal.
6. Store tools and equipment properly.
7. Clean and flush floor drains regularly.
8. Maintain railroad and truck courts free of debris, and properly patrol them for pest control.
9. Keep eating and break areas, locker rooms, and so on, clean and orderly. Vending machines are often overlooked; keep them and adjacent areas clean and sanitary. Maintain equipment in a properly functioning condition and do not permit it to serve as a source of sanitation or harborage problems.

Receiving and Inspection

1. Inspect the materials which are being received for evidence of damage; insect, bird, rodent, or other vermin infestation; and moisture, odor, or chemical contamination.
2. Exclude contaminated materials, including product, pallets, and slip sheets from the building.
3. If damaged merchandise is accepted, segregate it for special handling.
4. Make sure that incoming and outgoing vehicles are free of conditions that could contaminate product—no birds, rodents, insects, spillage, or objectionable odor should be evident.
5. At the receiving point, code or mark food received to ensure proper stock rotation.
6. To facilitate handling of rejected and suspect product, it is a good idea to develop procedures with individual shippers, carriers, and/or manufacturers for reinspections, returns, and so on.

Storage

1. Store products in an orderly manner and so that date codes are visible for proper rotation.
2. Generally, it is desirable to stack foods on pallets or racks (or on slip sheets, where a clamp truck operation is utilized), and away from walls to allow for inspection aisles between stacks and walls. Painting inspection aisles in a light color is often helpful in maintaining their effectiveness. Where full inspection aisles are not provided, take special care (such as more frequent inspection, rotation, and removal of product for cleaning) to ensure sanitary, pest-free conditions.
3. Separate bagged foods to provide visibility between stacks.
4. Dispose of contaminated or infested merchandise, or otherwise promptly remove it from the premises.
5. Promptly remove damaged merchandise and broken containers from general food storage areas. Handle and process salvageable merchandise separately in an area isolated from general food storage; this area probably will require extra sanitation and pest control attention.
6. If salvage operations include the repackaging or other manipulation of exposed foods, conduct such operations in compliance with good food sanitation practices, guidelines, or regulations.
7. Do not intermingle chemicals, including pesticides, with food or food products. Such products are best separated by an aisleway.

Pest Control

1. Maintain written schedules, log activity, and monitor traps and bait stations regularly.
2. Use covered bait stations which are of such types and so located as to reduce the danger of spillage; and where appropriate, use moisture-proof bait stations.
3. Keep pesticides used in the facility secure and separate from foods. Permit their use only by properly trained personnel. Use only types registered and approved by an appropriate government agency for the intended use.

4. Check especially for rodent burrows in nearby grounds, activity at floor-wall junctions and doorways, and insect crawl marks in dust accumulation, especially on overhead pipes, beams, windowsills, around flour, sugar, and pet food storage.
5. Where feasible, seal load levelers at docks to prevent trash accumulations and rodent harborage and entry, and clean them frequently.
6. Look for insect activity in folds of bagged ingredients.
7. Use black light, supplemented with means for distinguishing other chemicals that fluoresce, to check for rodent urine stains; use flashlights to check for other evidence of contamination.

Shipping

1. Make sure that transportation equipment into which food is loaded is maintained in a sanitary condition comparable to that of a food warehouse.
2. Make sure that railcars, trailers, and trucks are free of birds, rodents, and insects or contamination from them; are free of odors, nails, splinters, oil, and grease; are free of accumulations of dirt or dunnage; and are in good repair and have no holes, cracks, or crevices that could provide entrances or harborages for pests.

Follow-Up: Exercise programs of follow-up and control to ensure that your employees, consultants, and outside services are doing their jobs effectively.

WAREHOUSING

As mentioned earlier, if proper care is not given to good handling and warehousing practices all the effort put into harvesting and processing will have been for naught. This aspect of the food handling system is just as important as any other. We begin our study of this subject with the following principles.
Ten Rules for Food Warehousemen

1. Promote personal cleanliness among employees.
2. Provide proper toilet and hand-washing facilities.
3. Adopt good housekeeping practices.
4. Keep food handling equipment clean.
5. Reject all incoming contaminated foods.
6. Maintain proper storage temperature.
7. Store foods away from walls.
8. Rotate stock and destroy spoiled foods.
9. Do not use or store poisonous chemicals near foods.
10. Maintain an effective pest control program:
    - assign inspection and reporting duties to a dependable employee.
    - keep buildings insect-, bird-, and rodent-proof.
    - keep doors closed when not in use.
    - follow label directions exactly when applying insecticides or rodenticides.
    - use highly toxic rodenticides only in locked bait boxes.
    - remove and prevent litter around buildings.
    - be alert for signs of rodents and insects.

The goal is to protect the public health and avoid economic loss for both warehousemen and customer.

The Federal Food, Drug, and Cosmetic Act requires that foods be clean, free from insect, bird, rodent or other animal filth, and chemicals which may render the food harmful to health. Warehousemen have the burden for compliance if they receive, ship, or store foods in interstate commerce.

Failure to comply may result in seizure of adulterated foods and prosecution of responsible individuals. FDA inspectors leave a written report of objectionable conditions.

Buildings and Grounds

Maintain Grounds Around Food Warehouses in a Sanitary Manner

1. Maintain the grounds around food warehouse building under the control of the operator in a well-drained condition, and free from conditions that are likely to lead to contamination of foods in the food warehouse, leaving the warehouse, or being delivered to the warehouse.
2. Keep grounds including wharf areas clean and free of discarded equipment, lumber, litter, waste, refuse, and uncut weeds or grasses within the immediate vicinity of the food warehouse which may provide breeding places or harborages for rodents, insects, and other pests.
3. Locate outside waste disposal containers on properly drained areas, clean them as needed, and keep them covered between use.
4. Maintain and surface driveways, truck aprons, and rail sidings at receiving and shipping areas and parking areas to facilitate good drainage and to minimize dust and dirt being blown or tracked into the food warehouse. Maintain them in a clean, well-drained condition.
5. If the food warehouse buildings are closely bordered by grounds not under the operator's control, exercise special care in the food warehouse, by inspection, extermination, or other means, to exclude and control pests, dirt, and other potential contaminants originating from such noncontrolled grounds.

Maintain and Operate Food Warehouse Buildings and Structures in a Sanitary Manner

1. Provide floors and interior walls which are adequately cleanable and keep them clean and in good repair.
2. Suspend fixtures, ducts, and pipes which are over working areas so as to prevent drip or condensate from contaminating food or food packages.
3. Maintain adequate separation by location or other effective means for those operations which may cause contamination of foods with undesirable chemicals, filth, or other extraneous material.
4. Provide adequate lighting to areas where food is received, stored, held, or assembled for delivery, in order to facilitate handling, processing, and examination of merchandise and to permit adequate inspection, cleanup, and repair of the buildings and their structures.
5. Provide adequate lighting in hand-washing areas, dressing and locker rooms (if present), and toilet rooms.
6. Employ appropriate special efforts to maintain sanitation whenever necessitated by unique features of structure or design.

7. In a food warehouse utilizing light bulbs, light fixtures, skylights, or other glass over exposed food, use safety type bulbs or shielded fixtures to prevent food contamination in case of breakage.

Fixtures and Equipment

Provide food warehouse equipment that is suitable as used and maintained and is of design, material, and workmanship which permits it to be adequately cleaned and properly maintained by the methods used at the establishment. Use and maintain the equipment so as to prevent the adulteration of foods with lubricants, fuel, metal fragments, contaminated water, or any other contaminants. Install and maintain equipment in a manner which will facilitate its cleaning and the cleaning of adjacent spaces.

Sanitary Facilities

Provide the food warehouse with adequate sanitary facilities and accommodations.

Water Supply

From an adequate source, provide a water supply which is sufficient for the food warehouse operations.

Sewage

Dispose of sewage into an adequate sewerage system or through other appropriate means.

Plumbing

Install and maintain plumbing of adequate capacity and design and in accordance with applicable governmental sanitation requirements, if any, so as to provide sufficient quantities of water to required locations through the food warehouse, and to properly convey sewage and liquid disposable waste from the food warehouse.

Toilet Facilities

Provide toilet facilities which are adequate, kept in good repair, conveniently located, well ventilated, and are in compliance with applicable governmental sanitation requirements, if any. They should have self-closing doors and walls, ceilings, and floors which are tight fitting and of a material which can be easily cleaned and kept in good repair. Maintain them in a clean condition, furnish with toilet tissue, and post signs instructing employees to wash their hands with soap or detergent before returning to work.

If toilet rooms are located near areas where exposed foods might be subjected to airborne contamination, provide them with self-closing doors which do not open directly into such areas.

Hand-Washing Facilities

Provide adequate hand-washing facilities in the toilet rooms or in places convenient to the toilet rooms for hand washing after use of the toilets. Furnish such facilities with hot and cold running water, hand-cleansing soaps or detergents, sanitary towels, or other suitable drying devices.

Provide adequate receptacles, with covers, for disposal of hand-drying articles or waste material. Maintain the washing facilities and the surrounding areas in a clean condition.

Dressing and Locker Areas

If dressing and locker areas are present, provide them with adequate ventilation and lighting, and maintain them in a clean and orderly condition.

Provide lockers with sufficient ventilation to keep them dry for the retardation of mold and odors, and maintain them in a clean condition, free from trash, food scraps, or litter which serve as insect or rodent attractants. Keep the tops of lockers clean and do not use them as surfaces for the storage of materials.

Eating Areas

If there are eating areas in the food warehouse, enclose them adequately or locate them in areas away from operations. Provide adequate space, light, and ventilation. Clean eating areas regularly, and provide a sufficient number of covered receptacles for disposal of meal trash. Clean such trash receptacles regularly and do not permit them to become insect or rodent attractants.

Clean and inspect vending machines and surrounding areas at regular and frequent intervals to detect and correct unsanitary conditions which may exist. If drinking fountains are provided, locate them conveniently and clean them regularly.

Sanitary Operations

Keep buildings and equipment sanitary.

1. Maintain buildings, fixtures, equipment, and other physical facilities of the food warehouse in good repair and in a sanitary condition.
2. Conduct cleaning operations in such a manner as to minimize the danger of contamination. For cleaning and sanitizing procedures, utilize detergents, sanitizers, and other supplies which are safe and effective for their intended uses.
3. Exclusive of packaged products held for distribution, store and use only such toxic materials as are required for necessary activities, such as for maintaining sanitary and pest free conditions; for use in laboratory testing procedures; or for food warehouse and equipment maintenance and operation. Identify and use such products only in such manner and under such conditions as will be safe.
4. Use pesticides only under such precautions and restrictions as will prevent the contamination of food and food packaging materials.

Convey, store, and dispose of rubbish in a manner which will minimize the development of odor, prevent waste from becoming an attractant and harborage or breeding place for vermin, and prevent contamination of warehoused food, food containers, ground surfaces, and water supplies.

Another important factor in sanitary operations is pest control programs. It is necessary to

1. Establish and maintain positive control programs designed to exclude and eliminate pests from the food warehouse and to deny them harborage, in

order to protect against the contamination of food in or on the premises by animals, birds, and vermin (including, but not limited to, rodents and insects).

2. Keep trained security dogs out of actual storage areas to avoid excreta contamination of food stored at floor level. Keep cats out of the food warehouse.
3. Implement these programs as an integral part of the construction, maintenance, operational, and personnel programs.

Procedures and Controls

Conduct operations in the receiving, inspection, transporting, handling, segregating, recouping, and storing of foods in accordance with appropriate sanitation principles. Implement overall sanitation under the supervision of an individual assigned responsibility for this function. Take reasonable precautions, including the following, to assure that warehouse procedures do not contribute to contamination of foods by harmful chemicals, objectionable odors, or other objectionable materials.

1. *Incoming product shipments.* The integrity of the sanitation program requires that the materials, including foods and their packaging, do not expose the food warehouse to contamination by reason of infestation by insects, birds, rodents, or other vermin, or by introduction of filth or other contaminants. It is often useful to work with suppliers and shippers in advance to establish guidelines for acceptance, rejection, and where appropriate, reconditioning of particular product, taking into consideration factors such as the nature, method of shipment, and ownership of the product, in order to effectively implement these programs.

a. Within a reasonable time after arrival of a car or truck and before unloading, the product should be inspected to the extent permitted by the loading of the vehicle for evidence of damage or of insect or rodent infestation, objectionable odor, or other forms of contamination. Where an adequate inspection has not been possible prior to unloading, further inspect such product during and immediately after unloading.

b. If damaged product has been accepted, keep it separate and recondition or otherwise handle it as necessary in a manner which will not expose foods or the food warehouse to contamination or infestation.

c. If the inspection reveals evidence of infestation or contamination, determine whether the condition is only "suspect," or is superficial (such as surface infestation of flying insects which may be on, but have not penetrated, soiled, or compromised the integrity of the packaging) and might be fully correctable by fumigation or other means. In each such case, remove the product from the food warehouse area, utilizing the vehicle in which it arrived, if feasible, after closing and sealing it. In case of contamination, if rejection is appropriate (based on the origin and ownership of the product), promptly notify the carrier and shipper of the time, place, and circumstances of the rejection. After removal from the food warehouse because of suspect and/or superficial conditions, concentrated efforts can be made to evaluate further the actual condition of the product, and to recondition it when possible.

d. Give special attention to product which has previously been rejected, or has otherwise been removed from the food warehouse because of suspect and/or superficial conditions, when it is subsequently received again, to assure that the product and packaging are fully acceptable on reinspection.

e. In the event of serious question, or of a failure to agree with the shipper or carrier as to condition or reconditioning, consider requesting evaluation of the suspect or rejected product by appropriate federal, state, or local authorities.

2. *Store product properly.* Place foods received into the food warehouse for handling or storage in a manner which will facilitate cleaning and the implementation of insect, rodent, and other sanitary controls and will maintain product wholesomeness.

3. *Proper stock rotation.* Adopt and implement effective procedures to provide stock rotation appropriate to the particular food.

4. *Contaminated or damaged foods.* Unless promptly and adequately repaired or corrected at or near the point of detection, promptly separate foods which are identified as being damaged or are otherwise suspect from other foods for further inspection, sorting, and disposition. Promptly destroy or remove from the food warehouse any product determined to present a hazard of contamination to foods already in the warehouse.

5. *Hazardous nonfood products.* Nonfood products which present hazards of contamination—undesirable odors, toxicity, or otherwise—to foods in the warehouse should be handled and stored in a manner which will keep them from contaminating the foods. Take special measures to safeguard from damage and infestation those foods which are particularly susceptible to such risks.

6. *Avoid damage to packaging.* Exercise care in moving, handling, and storing product to avoid damage to packaging which would affect the contents of food packages, cause spillage, or otherwise contribute to the creation of unsanitary conditions.

7. *Shipping.* Prior to loading with foods, inspect railcar and truck and trailer interiors for general cleanliness and for freedom from moisture; from foreign materials which would cause product contamination (such as broken glass, oil, toxic chemicals, etc.) or damage to packaging and contents (such as boards, nails, harmful protrusions, etc.); and from wall, floor, or ceiling defects that could contribute to unsanitary conditions.

Clean, repair, or reject them as necessary to protect foods before loading. Exercise care in loading foods to avoid spillage or damage to packaging and contents. Maintain docks, rail sidings, truck bays, and driveways free from accumulations of debris and spillage.

8. *Warehouse temperatures.* Maintain warehouse temperatures (particularly for refrigerated and frozen food storage areas) in compliance with applicable governmental temperature requirements, if any, for maintaining the wholesomeness of the particular foods received and held in such areas.

9. *Housekeeping, sanitation, and inspection.* Establish a regularly scheduled program of general housekeeping, sanitation, and inspection to maintain floors, walls, fixtures, equipment, and other physical facilities in a state of sanitation sufficient to protect foods from contamination or adulteration, and to prevent waste from becoming an attractant and harborage or breeding place for vermin.

In addition, develop and implement an effective program and procedure for timely cleanup of any debris and spillage resulting from accidents or other unscheduled occurrences.

10. *Pest control measures.* Implement pest control measures designed to prevent

the entrance of pests, to deny them harborage, and to detect and eliminate them, with such scheduled instructions and procedures, and by such trained and qualified personnel or professional representatives as may be necessary, based on the nature of the foods and other products handled, the structure and condition of the building and equipment, and the surroundings and environment of the warehouse.

Monitor traps and bait stations, whether inside or outside of buildings, on a regular basis. Use covered interior bait stations designed, located, or protected to prevent spillage. Where appropriate, use bait stations constructed of moisture-proof material.

11. *Pesticides.* Use only pesticides with labels showing USDA or EPA registration numbers, and only for the uses specified in the labeling. Have them applied only by responsible personnel in accordance with manufacturer's labeling instructions and in a manner which prevents contamination of foods. While not in use, clearly mark and store pesticides in a secure place apart from foods.

12. *Audit food warehouse sanitation programs.* Establish programs internally and/or through outside consultants for effectively auditing the food warehouse sanitation program.

Personnel

Employee Practices

1. Prohibit employees affected by communicable disease while carriers of such disease, or while afflicted with boils, sores, infected wounds, or other abnormal sources of bacterial infection, from working in the food warehouse in capacities in which there is a likelihood of food becoming contaminated or of disease being transmitted to other persons.
2. Prohibit clothing or other personal belongings from being stored, food and beverages from being consumed, and tobacco from being used in areas where foods are handled or stored.
3. Instruct employees who are working in direct contact with exposed or partially exposed foods to maintain personal cleanliness and to conform to hygienic practices to avoid contamination of such foods with microorganisms or foreign substances such as human hair, perspiration, cosmetics, tobacco, chemicals, and medicants. If gloves are used in handling such foods, use only gloves which are of an impermeable material and maintain them in a clean and sanitary condition.

Management Responsibilities

1. Assign responsibility for the overall food warehouse sanitation program and authority commensurate with this responsibility to persons who, by education, training, and/or experience are able to identify sanitation risks and failures and food contamination hazards.
2. Instruct employees in the sanitation and hygienic practices appropriate to their duties and the locations of their work assignments. Instruct employees to report observations of infestations (such as evidence of rodents, insects, or harborages) or construction defects permitting entry or harborage of pests, or other developments of unsanitary conditions.
3. Exercise programs of follow-up and control to ensure that employees, consultants, and outside services are doing their jobs effectively.

Temperature Control and Handling Practices

Foods for Freezing

1. Quick freezing seldom changes original quality; hence, only sound and wholesome raw materials at an optimum level of freshness should be frozen.
2. Freezing should be performed with appropriate equipment in such a way as to minimize physical, biochemical, and microbiological changes. With most products this goal is best achieved by ensuring that the product passes through the temperature range of maximum crystallization (for most products +30 to +23°F/–1 to –5°C) in an appropriate time.
3. On leaving the freezing apparatus, the product should be minimally exposed to humidity and warm temperatures and moved into a cold warehouse as quickly as practical and then allowed an adequate dwell time for temperature equilibration.
4. Where a processor has his own freezer and warehouse, product should leave the warehouse at 0°F (–18°C) or lower.

Packaging and Identification of Frozen Foods

1. Packaging and outer cases for frozen foods should be of good quality in order to prevent contamination, ensure the integrity of the product during normal transit and storage, and minimize dehydration.
2. Package coding should be adequate for effective identification.
3. Outer case coding is useful to enable proper stock rotation of individual cases. It can be preprinted on shipping cases, leaving the number to be applied at the moment of packaging, if necessary. It may also be printed on an adhesive label or applied to the case at the moment of packing. Ideally, it should appear on two or three sides of the shipping case.
4. Lot, pallet, or unit load identity is useful in enabling loads to be properly rotated while the identity of the load is maintained.

Warehouse Equipment

1. Each warehouse should have adequate capacity and should be equipped with suitable mechanical refrigeration to maintain, under anticipated conditions of outside temperature and peak loading, a reasonably steady air temperature of 0°F (–18°C) or colder, in all cold storage areas where frozen foods are stored.
2. Each storage area should have an accurate temperature measuring device installed to reflect correctly the average air temperature. Every day the warehouse is open, temperatures of each area should be recorded and dated, and a file of such temperatures should be maintained for a period of at least two years.

Warehouse Handling Practices

1. The warehouse operator should record the product temperature of each lot of frozen food received and should accept custody only in accordance with

good commercial practice. He should retain lot arrival temperature records for a period of at least one year.

2. Whenever frozen food is received with product temperatures of 15°F (–9°C) or warmer, the warehousemen should immediately notify the owner or consignee and request instructions for special handling. These procedures may consist of any available method for effectively lowering temperatures such as blast freezing, low temperature areas with air circulation, and proper use of dunnage or separators in stacking.
3. Before a shipment of frozen food is placed in storage, it should be code marked for effective identification.
4. Frozen food should be moved promptly over loading and unloading areas to minimize exposure to humidity, elevated temperatures, or other adverse conditions.
5. During defrosting, product should be effectively covered or removed from beneath areas of accumulated frost.
6. Frozen food going into a separate breakup room for order assembly should be moved out promptly unless the breakup room is maintained at a reasonably uniform temperature of 0°F (–18°C) or colder.
7. As many operations as practicable (casing, palletizing, etc.) should be carried out in the cold storage area to reduce the heat gain and concomitant quality deterioration, energy, and dollar loss resulting from the exposure of frozen product to ambient temperatures.
8. If slip sheets are employed, the bottom unit load should be spaced from the floor of the cold warehouse by pallet or other means. To permit air circulation, sufficient space must be allowed between stacks and walls.

Transportation

1. All vehicles used to transport frozen foods, for example, trucks, trailers, or containers, railcars, ships, and aircraft should be
   - so constructed, properly insulated, and equipped with appropriate refrigeration continuously to maintain product temperature of 0°F (–18°C) or colder;
   - equipped with an appropriate temperature recording device to measure accurately the air temperature inside the vehicle. The dial or reading element of the device should be mounted in a readily visible position;
   - equipped with tight-fitting doors and suitable closure for drain holes to prevent air leakage;
   - clear and free from dirt, debris, offensive odors, or any substances that could, with reasonable possibility, contaminate the food;
   - precooled prior to loading. The object of precooling is to establish a gradient across the insulation from 0°F (–18°C) on the inner surface to the prevailing temperature on the outer skin. If the interior of the truck is exposed to warm, humid air during loading, precooling is not recommended, since it leads to condensation on internal surfaces.
2. Product temperatures should be measured and be at 0°F (–18°C) or colder when tendered to the carrier for loading. The carrier should not accept product tendered at a temperature warmer than 0°F (–18°C).
3. The shipper, consignor, or warehouseman should not tender to a carrier

any container which has been damaged or defaced to the extent that it is in unsalable condition.

4. Free air circulation all around the load is essential during transport. Slip sheets should be supported on a pallet (not loaded directly onto the floor of the vehicles) to allow for adequate air circulation under the load.
5. The thermostat on the vehicle's refrigeration unit should be set to maintain an air temperature of 0°F (–18°C).

Storage on Retail Premises

1. Frozen food storage facilities should be capable of maintaining a reasonably steady product temperature of 0°F (–18°C) or colder. In addition, they should be of sufficient size to provide for proper stock control.
2. Frozen food storage facilities should have sufficient circulation of refrigerated air. Cases of frozen food should be on a pallet or other means of providing adequate air circulation between the bottom case and the floor. To permit air circulation, sufficient space should be allowed between stacks and walls.
3. Frozen food storage facilities should be equipped with a thermometer (accurate to ±2°F/1.1°C) which is easily read and sited to measure representative air temperatures.
4. Frozen food storage facilities should be defrosted, as necessary, to maintain refrigeration efficiency.

Temperature Measurement

1. *Measuring temperature without opening packages:* Select seven cases of frozen foods. Stack any three of the seven on the floor area of the natural cold environment for the lot being sampled. Cut sidewall of top case (number 3 of stack) at either end with a sharp knife. Bend the cut tab outward. Insert probe of temperature measurement device at about the center of the first stack of packages and between the first and second layers of packages so that all of the sensing element is in firm contact with package walls. Stack the other four cases on top of the case containing the probe.
   Read and record the temperature observed when the needle gives a steady reading. This is generally five minutes or less for a dial thermometer. Close and tape the cut sidewall areas of the case.
   For solid pack products, cut sidewall of case at either end and insert probe at approximate center of first stack and between first and second layers of packages so that all of the sensing element is in firm contact with package walls. For poly bags, insert probe in the same direction as the length of the bag and deep enough for firm contact between bags.
   For products in paperboard packages with metal ends, turn case on side to give end view, cut sidewall of case, and follow the same procedure as above.
   For products with an air space between edge of wall of individual carton, cut any side of case and then follow the above procedure.
2. *Measuring temperature by opening packages:* Whenever there is doubt about product temperatures measured without opening packages, the following

procedure should be used. (It is also recommended for product packed in cans, because the bead rim of cans does not allow for firm contact of the probe and sidewall surfaces.)

Cut the cover of case to expose a package or can that is surrounded by other packages. Using a sharp instrument such as an ice pick, punch hole through cut portion of case wall and into central area of the exposed package or can. Insert probe so that all of the sensing element is in central portion of package and record steady temperature. Replace the punctured container with a good container from a case reserved for this purpose. Close and tape case cover.

3. *Another approach:* Choose a reliable, accurate (±1°F) thermometer with a short response time (time required to reach a steady reading) which must be calibrated frequently. Calibration can most easily be carried out by immersing in melting ice (32°F/0°C). Mercury-in-glass or alcohol-in-glass thermometers are available with either flat blade or needle probes. Bimetal dial thermometers, which can be easily calibrated, are also suitable. Highly satisfactory digital thermometers are available with either flat blade or needle probes.

Before recording a temperature, precool the probe by inserting it between two packets of frozen food and waiting until a steady reading is reached. If the product is a large bulk and an internal temperature is required, precool the drill before boring the hole for the thermometer probe. To obtain a reading insert the precooled probe either into a hole bored in the product or between packets, ensuring that good contact is made with the packages. The temperature of individually quick frozen product exiting from a freezing tunnel is best measured by filling a previously precooled vacuum flask with the product closely surrounding the probe and reading the thermometer when a steady reading is reached.

REFERENCES

Guidelines for the Air Shipment of Fresh Fish & Seafood (2nd ed.). 1988. Washington, DC: National Fisheries Institute & Air Transport Association of America.

Proceedings of First National Conference on Seafood Packaging and Shipping. 1982. Washington, DC: National Fisheries Institute.

Voluntary Industry Sanitation Guidelines for Food Distribution Centers and Warehouse. 1974. Washington, DC: Grocery Manufacturers of America.

Warehouse Sanitation Handbook. Washington, DC: FDA Publication No. 81-2138.

A Manual of Recommended Practices for the Warehousing of Frozen Foods. 1978. Washington, DC: American Frozen Food Institute.

Voluntary Transportation Guidelines. 1976. Washington, DC: Cooperative Food Distributors of America.

Index